간접의문문 CHAPTER 1 PSS 1-3, 4

종류	형식	예문
의문사가 있는 경우	의문사+주어+동사	• I don't know **how old your sister is**.
의문사가 없는 경우	if[whether]+주어+동사	• I wonder **if[whether] I can** finish it by this Sunday.
생각, 추측을 나타내는 동사 (think/believe/ suppose/guess)	간접 의문문의 의문사가 문장 맨 앞에 위치	• **What** do you **think** we should do to win the game? • **Who** do you **suppose** can do that?

문장의 5형식 CHAPTER 1 PSS 2-1~7

종류	형식	예문
1형식	주어+동사	I ran.
2형식	주어+동사+주격보어	She became a teacher.
3형식	주어+동사+목적어	I bought a piece of cake for her.
4형식	주어+동사+간접목적어(사람)+직접목적어(사물)	I gave him a piece of advice.
5형식	주어+동사+목적어+목적격 보어	He asked me to wait in line.

3형식 vs 4형식 CHAPTER 1 PSS 2-5

give, lend, send, show, teach, tell, write, pay, sell　+직접목적어+to+간접목적어

• He showed me his old pictures. = He showed his old pictures to me.

buy, do, find, get, make, cook　+직접목적어+for+간접목적어

• John bought his mother a dishwasher. = John bought a dishwasher for his mother.

ask　+직접목적어+of+간접목적어

• Can I ask you a favor? = Can I ask a favor of you?

I wish+가정법 과거	I wish+주어+동사의 과거형	**I wish** (that) I **had** an opportunity to travel around the world.
as if[though] +가정법 과거	동사의 현재형/과거형+as if [though]+주어+동사의 과거형	**I feel as if[though]** I **were** a real astronaut. 
without +가정법 과거	without+명사, 주어+would/ could/should/might+동사원형	**Without air pollution,** we **could have** fresh air.
if+가정법 과거완료	if+주어+had+과거분사, 주어+would/could/should/ might+have+과거분사	**If** Akiko **had written** the letter in Japanese, I **couldn't have read** it.

관계사 CHAPTER 14 **PSS 1, 2-1, 1-7**

Ⅰ. 관계대명사

선행사＼격	주격	소유격	목적격
사람	who	whose	whom
사물, 동물	which	whose	which
사물, 동물, 사람	that	–	that
사물(선행사 포함)	what	–	what

Ⅱ. 관계부사

구분	선행사	관계부사	전치사+ 관계대명사
장소	the place, the country, the city, the house…	where	at/in/to which
시간	the time, the year, the month, the day…	when	at/in/on which
이유	the reason	why	for which
방법	(the way)	how	in which

Ⅲ. 관계대명사의 생략

목적격 관계대명사 who(m), which, that 생략	주격 관계대명사+be동사+현재분사/과거분사가 올 때 「주격 관계대명사+be동사」를 함께 생략
I couldn't trust some people (who(m)) I worked with.	Those kids (who are) standing in front of that building are waiting for the famous singer.
You can't cancel the meeting (which) you arranged.	The teapot (which was) put on the stove was handmade.

「It is/was ~ that」 강조구문 CHAPTER 18 **PSS 2-2**

예문 : I saw Nancy in front of the hospital an hour ago.	
주어 강조	It was **I** that saw Nancy in front of the hospital an hour ago.
목적어 강조	It was **Nancy** that I saw in front of the hospital an hour ago.
장소를 나타내는 부사구 강조	It was **in front of the hospital** that I saw Nancy an hour ago.
때를 나타내는 부사구 강조	It was **an hour ago** that I saw Nancy in front of the hospital.

동명사의 관용 표현 CHAPTER 8 PSS 3, 4

관용표현	뜻	예문
feel like＋-ing	～하고 싶다	I **feel like** work**ing** out today.
succeed in＋-ing	～하는 데 성공하다	Jason is going to **succeed in** find**ing** a new job.
prevent…from＋-ing	…가 ～하는 것을 막다	This alarm system will **prevent** a thief **from** break**ing** into the house.
be capable of＋-ing	～할 능력이 있다	This **is capable of** measur**ing** the length.
apologize for＋-ing	～에 대해 사과하다	I **apologize for** be**ing** late again.
be used to＋-ing	～에 익숙하다	I **am used to** walk**ing** to school.
cannot help＋-ing	～하지 않을 수 없다	I **cannot help** think**ing** that I was really stupid.
need＋-ing	～되어야 할 필요가 있다	I think your computer **needs** formatt**ing**.
be busy＋-ing	～하느라고 바쁘다	Mina **is busy** prepar**ing** for the party.
have trouble[difficulty, a hard time]＋-ing	～하는 데 어려움을 겪다	Tom **had trouble** mak**ing** new friends.
It is no use＋-ing	～해도 소용없다	**It is no use** cry**ing** over spilt milk.
be worth＋-ing	～할 가치가 있다	This book **is worth** read**ing**.
look forward to＋-ing	～을 고대하다	I'm **looking forward to** hear**ing** from you soon.

분사구문 만드는 법 CHAPTER 9 PSS 4-1

~~When~~ I knew the truth, I could be relieved. ① 접속사 제거

⇩

✗ knew the truth, I could be relieved. ② 주절과 같은 주어 제거

⇩

Knowing the truth, I could be relieved. ③ 주절의 동사와 같은 시제일 때 동사를 -ing형태로

cf. 분사구문에서 접속사의 의미를 분명히 하기 위해 분사 앞에 접속사를 쓰기도 한다.

가정법 CHAPTER 12 PSS 2-1~4, 3-1

가정법 종류	형식	예문
if＋가정법 과거	if＋주어＋동사의 과거형, 주어＋would/could/should /might＋동사원형	**If** I **could** fly, I **would follow** the bird.

조동사+have+과거분사 CHAPTER 3 **PSS 10**

should have + 과거분사	~했어야 했다	You **should have defended** yourself in the first place. 너는 처음부터 네 자신을 방어했어야 했다.
must have + 과거분사	~였음에 틀림없다	He looks tired. 그는 피곤해 보인다. He **must have stayed** up all night. 그는 밤을 꼬박 새운 것이 틀림없다.
may have + 과거분사	~했을지도 모른다	At least 5,000 people **may have been killed** during the war. 최소한 5,000명의 사람들이 그 전쟁 중에 죽었을지도 모른다.
cannot have + 과거분사	~했을 리가 없다	She **can't have been** more than 15 years old at that time. 그녀가 그 당시에 15살이 넘었을 리가 없다.

부정사 CHAPTER 7 **PSS 1-1, 3-1, 3-3**

Ⅰ. to부정사 - 가주어 It 구문

to부정사(주어) + 동사 + 형용사

It + 동사 + 형용사 + to부정사
가주어   진주어

Ⅱ. to부정사의 부사적 용법과 다양한 표현

1) 「in order to/so as to+동사원형」 = 「so that+주어+can/could+동사원형」 (~하기 위해서)

I ran toward him **to get** his autograph.
= I ran toward him **in order to / so as to get** his autograph.
= I ran toward him **so that I could get** his autograph.

2) 「too+형용사/부사+to부정사」 = 「so+형용사/부사+that+주어+can't/couldn't」 (~하기에는 너무 …한)

The young girl was **too** nervous **to** sit still.
= The young girl was **so** nervous **that** she **couldn't** sit still.

3) 「형용사/부사+enough+to부정사」 = 「so+형용사/부사+that+주어+can/could」 (~할 정도로 충분히 …한)

This cellphone is small **enough to fit** in my pocket.
= This cellphone is **so** small **that** it **can** fit in my pocket.

중학영문법 3800제 열공 학습진도표 3학년

CHAPTER 1 문장의 기초

PSS		체크	학습날짜
PSS 1	1-1	☐	/
	1-2	☐	/
	1-3	☐	/
	1-4	☐	/
PSS 2	2-1	☐	/
	2-2	☐	/
	2-3	☐	/
	2-4	☐	/
	2-5	☐	/
	2-6	☐	/
	2-7	☐	/
중간·기말 대비		☐	/

CHAPTER 2 시제

PSS		체크	학습날짜
PSS 1	1-1	☐	/
	1-2	☐	/
	1-3	☐	/
PSS 2	2-1	☐	/
	2-2	☐	/
	2-3	☐	/
	2-4	☐	/
	2-5	☐	/
	2-6	☐	/
	2-7	☐	/
PSS 3		☐	/
중간·기말 대비		☐	/

CHAPTER 3 조동사

PSS	체크	학습날짜
PSS 1	☐	/
PSS 2	☐	/
PSS 3	☐	/
PSS 4	☐	/
PSS 5	☐	/
PSS 6	☐	/
PSS 7	☐	/
PSS 8	☐	/
PSS 9	☐	/
PSS 10	☐	/
중간·기말 대비	☐	/

CHAPTER 4 수동태

PSS	체크	학습날짜
PSS 1	☐	/
PSS 2	☐	/
PSS 3	☐	/
PSS 4	☐	/
PSS 5	☐	/
PSS 6	☐	/
PSS 7	☐	/
PSS 8	☐	/
PSS 9	☐	/
중간·기말 대비	☐	/

CHAPTER 5 명사와 관사

PSS		체크	학습날짜
PSS 1	1-1	☐	/
	1-2	☐	/
	1-3	☐	/
PSS 2	2-1	☐	/
	2-2	☐	/
	2-3	☐	/
	2-4	☐	/
PSS 3	3-1	☐	/
	3-2	☐	/
PSS 4	4-1	☐	/
	4-2	☐	/
PSS 5	5-1	☐	/
	5-2	☐	/
PSS 6		☐	/
중간·기말 대비		☐	/

CHAPTER 6 대명사

PSS		체크	학습날짜
PSS 1		☐	/
PSS 2	2-1	☐	/
	2-2	☐	/
PSS 3	3-1	☐	/
	3-2	☐	/
	3-3	☐	/
	3-4	☐	/
	3-5	☐	/
	3-6	☐	/
	3-7	☐	/
	3-8	☐	/
중간·기말 대비		☐	/

CHAPTER 7 부정사

PSS		체크	학습날짜
PSS 1	1-1	☐	/
	1-2	☐	/
	1-3	☐	/
	1-4	☐	/
PSS 2	2-1	☐	/
	2-2	☐	/
PSS 3	3-1	☐	/
	3-2	☐	/
	3-3	☐	/
PSS 4		☐	/
PSS 5		☐	/
PSS 6		☐	/
PSS 7		☐	/
중간·기말 대비		☐	/

CHAPTER 8 동명사

PSS		체크	학습날짜
PSS 1		☐	
PSS 2	2-1	☐	/
	2-2	☐	/
	2-3	☐	/
PSS 3		☐	/
PSS 4		☐	/
PSS 5		☐	/
PSS 6		☐	/
중간·기말 대비		☐	/

CHAPTER 9 분사

PSS		체크	학습날짜
PSS 1	1-1	☐	/
	1-2	☐	/
PSS 2		☐	/
PSS 3		☐	/
PSS 4	4-1	☐	/
	4-2	☐	/
	4-3	☐	/
	4-4	☐	/
중간·기말 대비		☐	/

CHAPTER 10 형용사

PSS		체크	학습날짜
PSS 1		☐	/
PSS 2		☐	/
PSS 3		☐	/
PSS 4		☐	/
PSS 5	5-1	☐	/
	5-2	☐	/
	5-3	☐	/
PSS 6	6-1	☐	/
	6-2	☐	/
	6-3	☐	/
	6-4	☐	/
	6-5	☐	/
	6-6	☐	/
중간·기말 대비		☐	/

CHAPTER 11 부사

PSS		체크	학습날짜
PSS 1	1-1	☐	/
	1-2	☐	/
	1-3	☐	/
	1-4	☐	/
PSS 2	2-1	☐	/
	2-2	☐	/
	2-3	☐	/
	2-4	☐	/
	2-5	☐	/
	2-6	☐	/
	2-7	☐	/
중간·기말 대비		☐	/

CHAPTER 12 가정법

PSS		체크	학습날짜
PSS 1		☐	/
PSS 2	2-1	☐	/
	2-2	☐	/
	2-3	☐	/
	2-4	☐	/
PSS 3	3-1	☐	/
	3-2	☐	/
	3-3	☐	/
	3-4	☐	/
PSS 4		☐	/
PSS 5		☐	/
PSS 6		☐	/
중간·기말 대비		☐	/

CHAPTER 13 비교구문

PSS		체크	학습날짜
PSS 1	1-1	☐	/
	1-2	☐	/
	1-3	☐	/
	1-4	☐	/
PSS 2	2-1	☐	/
	2-2	☐	/
PSS 3	3-1	☐	/
	3-2	☐	/
	3-3	☐	/
	3-4	☐	/
	3-5	☐	/
	3-6	☐	/
PSS 4	4-1	☐	/
	4-2	☐	/
	4-3	☐	/
	4-4	☐	/
중간·기말 대비		☐	/

CHAPTER 14 관계사

PSS		체크	학습날짜
PSS 1	1-1	☐	/
	1-2	☐	/
	1-3	☐	/
	1-4	☐	/
	1-5	☐	/
	1-6	☐	/
	1-7	☐	/
	1-8	☐	/
PSS 2	2-1	☐	/
	2-2	☐	/
	2-3	☐	/
중간·기말 대비		☐	/

CHAPTER 15 접속사

PSS		체크	학습날짜
PSS 1		☐	/
PSS 2		☐	/
PSS 3		☐	/
PSS 4		☐	/
PSS 5		☐	/
PSS 6		☐	/
PSS 7		☐	/
PSS 8		☐	/
PSS 9	9-1	☐	/
	9-2	☐	/
PSS 10		☐	/
PSS 11		☐	/
PSS 12		☐	/
PSS 13		☐	/
PSS 14		☐	/
중간·기말 대비		☐	/

CHAPTER 16 전치사

PSS		체크	학습날짜
PSS 1	1-1	☐	/
	1-2	☐	/
	1-3	☐	/
	1-4	☐	/
	1-5	☐	/
	1-6	☐	/
PSS 2	2-1	☐	/
	2-2	☐	/
	2-3	☐	/
	2-4	☐	/
	2-5	☐	/
	2-6	☐	/
	2-7	☐	/
	2-8	☐	/
PSS 3	3-1	☐	/
	3-2	☐	/
	3-3	☐	/
	3-4	☐	/
	3-5	☐	/
	3-6	☐	/
	3-7	☐	/
중간·기말 대비		☐	/

CHAPTER 17 일치와 화법

PSS		체크	학습날짜
PSS 1	1-1	☐	/
	1-2	☐	/
	1-3	☐	/
	1-4	☐	/
	1-5	☐	/
PSS 2	2-1	☐	/
	2-2	☐	/
PSS 3	3-1	☐	/
	3-2	☐	/
	3-3	☐	/
중간·기말 대비		☐	/

CHAPTER 18 특수구문&속담

PSS		체크	학습날짜
PSS 1		☐	/
PSS 2	2-1	☐	/
	2-2	☐	/
PSS 3	3-1	☐	/
	3-2	☐	/
PSS 4		☐	/
중간·기말 대비		☐	/

2026 새 교과서에 맞춘 16차 개정판

중학영문법 3800제 3학년

발행 16차 개정판 3쇄 (2026년 1월 31일)

교재 개발 책임 서은숙　**교재 개발 진행** 박상우, 이혜빈, 최민정, 최은조, 김현수, 도예원, 이윤정, 성은혜

문제편 집필 김미경(서울 서초) 선생님, 문명기(서울 강동) 선생님, 소피아(김규은 경기 분당) 선생님, 남현정, 서연서, 이윤정, 이옥현, 양진희, 고미라(서울 상경중) 선생님, 김현, 김석화(수원 수원여고) 선생님, 김다영, 박혜미

교재 검토 김석화(수원 수원여고) 선생님, 윤미선(서울 가양) 선생님, 김미경(서울 동작) 선생님, 김경미(강남 대치) 선생님, 문명기(서울 강동) 선생님, 양원석(서울 서초) 선생님

교정 김경미(강남 대치) 선생님, 김현수, 최은조, 박상우, 신소미, 이혜빈, 최민정, 신준기, 정은주, 유지원, 김다영, 황희진, 홍지민, 신진실, 임미진, 박혜미, 도예원, 조수성, 서연서, 이윤정, 윤수경, 양진희, 성은혜, 홍성경, 오정훈, 하은옥, 이은영

감수 김유경(서울 목동) 선생님, 최주영(강남 대치) 선생님, 김태욱(서울 신촌) 선생님, 이태규(서울 대치) 선생님

영문 감수 Kathryn O' Handley　**디자인** 김연실, 양은선　**삽화** 박주혜, 정제욱, 이혜승, 백승현, 이유진, 이순웅, 정재환

단어장 녹음 손정은, Janet Lee, 최석환　**녹음 편집** 와이알 미디어　**인디자인 편집** 박경아

제작 이주영　**발행인** 문숙영　**발행처** 마더텅(Mother Tongue Co., Ltd.)

주소 서울시 금천구 가마산로 96, 708호(가산동, 대륭테크노타운 8차)

팩스 02-3142-9126 **홈페이지** www.toptutor.co.kr **등록번호** 제 1-2423호

* 이 책에 실린 모든 내용에 대한 저작권은 (주)마더텅에 있으므로
  적법한 허락 없이는 어떠한 형태나 수단으로도 전재, 복사할 수 없습니다.
* 잘못 만들어진 책은 바꾸어 드립니다.

마더텅 교재를 풀면서 궁금한 점이 생기셨나요?

교재 관련 내용 문의나 오류신고 사항이 있으면 아래 문의처로 보내 주세요!
문의하신 내용에 대해 성심성의껏 답변해 드리겠습니다.
또한 교재의 **내용 오류** 또는 **오·탈자**, **그 외 수정이 필요한 사항**에 대해
가장 먼저 신고해 주신 분께는 감사의 마음을 담아
네이버페이 포인트 1천 원 을 보내 드립니다!

＊기한: 2026년 10월 31일
＊오류신고 이벤트는 당사 사정에 따라 조기 종료될 수 있습니다.
＊홈페이지에 게시된 정오표 기준으로 최초 신고된 오류에 한하여
　상품권을 보내 드립니다.

● 카카오톡 mothertongue　◎ 이메일 mothert1004@toptutor.co.kr
⌂ 홈페이지 www.toptutor.co.kr　▯ 교재Q&A게시판　♋ 고객센터 전화 1661-1064(07:00~22:00)
✉ 문자 010-6640-1064(문자수신전용)

구성

1 PSS(Problem Solving Skill) - 문제해결능력

한꺼번에 여러 가지 개념을 다루고 있는 기존 문법서의 단점을 보완하기 위해 문법 단위를 보다 세분화하였습니다. 한 번에 한 가지 문제해결능력을 완전히 익히고 다음 단계로 넘어가도록 구성되어 있어서 학생들은 더욱 체계적으로 문법을 습득할 수 있습니다. 어렵고 긴 설명보다는 풍부한 예문으로 문법을 익힐 수 있기 때문에 재미있게 공부할 수 있습니다.

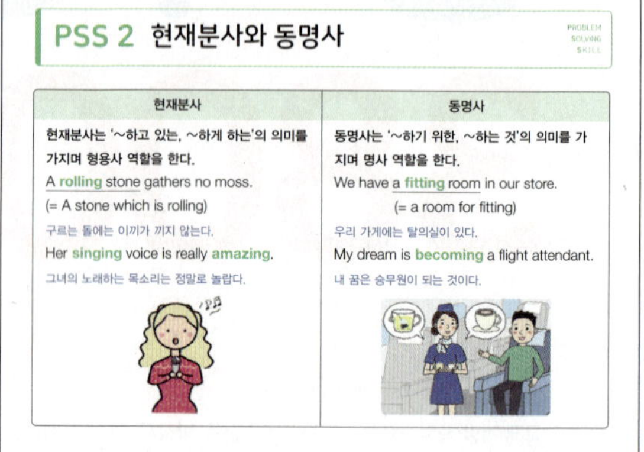

2 PRACTICE

앞에서 공부한 PSS 내용을 잘 이해했는지 확인하는 주관식 문제입니다. 단답형 · 선택형 · 문장완성형 · 서술형 형태의 다양하고 풍부한 문제를 통해서 공부한 내용을 바로 문제로 적용할 수 있기 때문에 더욱 확실히 이해하고 오랫동안 기억할 수 있습니다.

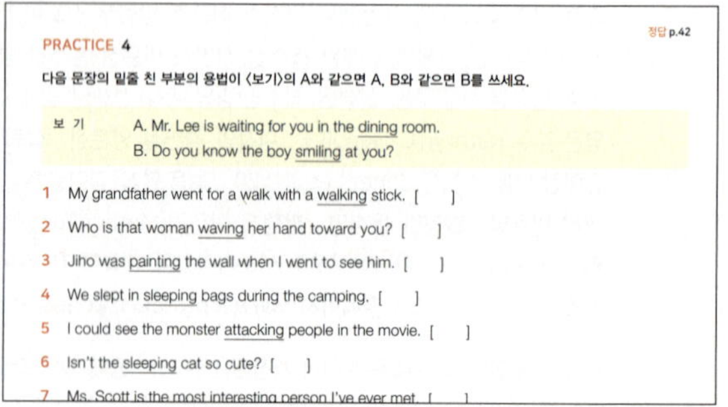

3 중간·기말고사대비문제

각 챕터에서 공부한 내용을 총정리하는 동시에 중간 · 기말고사를 대비하기 위한 문제입니다. 쉬운 문제에서 어려운 문제까지 학교시험에 출제될 가능성이 있는 다양한 문제를 수록하였기 때문에 학교시험에 완벽히 대비할 수 있는 실력을 길러줍니다.

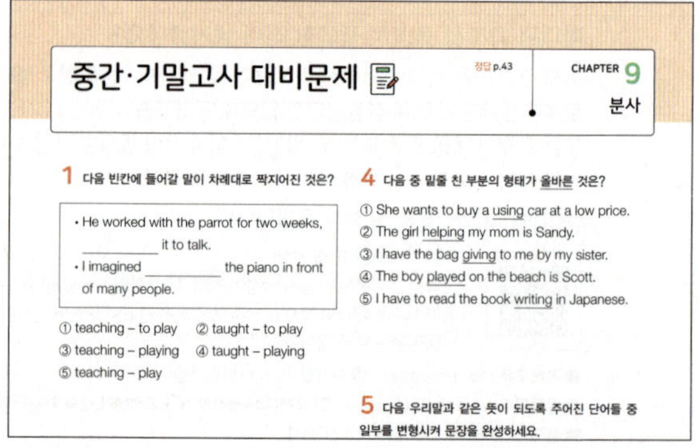

차례

CHAPTER 1 | 문장의 기초 Introduction to Sentences

PSS 1 의문문
PSS 1-1 부가의문문 I ······ 8
PSS 1-2 부가의문문 II ······ 9
PSS 1-3 간접의문문 I ······ 10
PSS 1-4 간접의문문 II ······ 11

PSS 2 문장의 5형식
PSS 2-1 목적어 유무에 따른 동사 구분 ······ 12
PSS 2-2 주격 보어를 필요로 하는 불완전자동사 I ······ 13
PSS 2-3 주격 보어를 필요로 하는 불완전자동사 II ······ 14
PSS 2-4 주의해야 할 완전타동사 ······ 15
PSS 2-5 두 개의 목적어를 필요로 하는 동사 ······ 17
PSS 2-6 목적격 보어를 필요로 하는 동사 I ······ 18
PSS 2-7 목적격 보어를 필요로 하는 동사 II ······ 19

중간·기말고사 대비문제 ······ 21

CHAPTER 2 | 시제 Tense

PSS 1 과거시제
PSS 1-1 동사의 과거형 만들기 ······ 28
PSS 1-2 규칙 변화 과거형 동사의 발음 ······ 30
PSS 1-3 불규칙 동사의 과거형과 과거분사형 ······ 31

PSS 2 완료시제
PSS 2-1 현재완료시제 ······ 34
PSS 2-2 for와 since ······ 36
PSS 2-3 현재완료시제와 과거시제 ······ 37
PSS 2-4 현재완료 진행시제 ······ 39
PSS 2-5 진행형을 쓰지 않는 동사 ······ 40
PSS 2-6 과거완료시제 ······ 42
PSS 2-7 과거완료 진행시제 ······ 43

PSS 3 미래시제 ······ 45

중간·기말고사 대비문제 ······ 46

CHAPTER 3 | 조동사 Modals

PSS 1 do ······ 52

PSS 2 can, could I ······ 53
PSS 3 can, could II ······ 54
PSS 4 must I ······ 56
PSS 5 must II ······ 57
PSS 6 may, might ······ 59
PSS 7 will, would ······ 61
PSS 8 should, ought to, had better ······ 62
PSS 9 used to, would ······ 64
PSS 10 조동사+have+과거분사 ······ 65

중간·기말고사 대비문제 ······ 67

CHAPTER 4 | 수동태 Passive Voice

PSS 1 조동사가 있는 수동태 ······ 74
PSS 2 진행형의 수동태 ······ 75
PSS 3 완료형의 수동태 ······ 76
PSS 4 4형식 문장의 수동태 ······ 77
PSS 5 5형식 문장의 수동태 I ······ 79
PSS 6 5형식 문장의 수동태 II ······ 80
PSS 7 동사구의 수동태 ······ 81
PSS 8 It is ~ that … ······ 82
PSS 9 수동태의 관용 표현 ······ 84

중간·기말고사 대비문제 ······ 86

CHAPTER 5 | 명사와 관사 Nouns and Articles

PSS 1 명사의 복수형
PSS 1-1 명사의 복수형 I ······ 92
PSS 1-2 명사의 복수형 II ······ 94
PSS 1-3 복합명사의 복수형 ······ 96

PSS 2 명사의 쓰임
PSS 2-1 셀 수 있는 명사 ······ 97
PSS 2-2 셀 수 없는 명사 ······ 98
PSS 2-3 물질명사의 수량 표현 ······ 99
PSS 2-4 추상명사의 관용적 용법 ······ 101

PSS 3 소유격 만들기
PSS 3-1 명사의 소유격 ······ 102
PSS 3-2 이중소유격 ······ 104

PSS 4 부정관사 a, an
PSS 4-1 a, an의 쓰임 ······ 105

PSS 4-2 a, an의 의미 ··········· 106

PSS 5 정관사 the

PSS 5-1 the의 쓰임 Ⅰ ··········· 107

PSS 5-2 the의 쓰임 Ⅱ ··········· 108

PSS 6 관사를 쓰지 않는 경우 ··········· 109

중간·기말고사 대비문제 ··········· 111

CHAPTER 6 │ 대명사 Pronouns

PSS 1 재귀대명사 ··········· 118

PSS 2 it

PSS 2-1 it의 용법 Ⅰ ··········· 119

PSS 2-2 it의 용법 Ⅱ ··········· 121

PSS 3 부정대명사

PSS 3-1 one ··········· 123

PSS 3-2 other, another ··········· 124

PSS 3-3 관용 표현 ··········· 126

PSS 3-4 all, both ··········· 128

PSS 3-5 each, every ··········· 129

PSS 3-6 some-, any- ··········· 131

PSS 3-7 no- ··········· 132

PSS 3-8 부분부정 ··········· 133

중간·기말고사 대비문제 ··········· 134

CHAPTER 7 │ 부정사 Infinitives

PSS 1 명사적 용법

PSS 1-1 주어와 주격 보어로 쓰이는 to부정사 ··········· 142

PSS 1-2 목적어로 쓰이는 to부정사 ··········· 144

PSS 1-3 목적격 보어로 쓰이는 to부정사 ··········· 145

PSS 1-4 의문사+to부정사 ··········· 146

PSS 2 형용사적 용법

PSS 2-1 명사를 꾸미는 to부정사 ··········· 147

PSS 2-2 be to 용법 ··········· 149

PSS 3 부사적 용법

PSS 3-1 목적을 나타내는 to부정사 ··········· 150

PSS 3-2 형용사 수식, 결과, 판단의 근거를 나타내는 to부정사 ··········· 152

PSS 3-3 too ~ to, enough to ··········· 153

PSS 4 원형부정사 ··········· 154

PSS 5 부정사의 부정형 ··········· 155

PSS 6 대부정사 ··········· 156

PSS 7 부정사의 의미상의 주어 ··········· 157

중간·기말고사 대비문제 ··········· 159

CHAPTER 8 │ 동명사 Gerunds

PSS 1 주어와 보어로 쓰이는 동명사 ··········· 168

PSS 2 동사의 목적어로 쓰이는 동명사

PSS 2-1 동사+동명사 ··········· 169

PSS 2-2 동사+동명사/to부정사 Ⅰ ··········· 170

PSS 2-3 동사+동명사/to부정사 Ⅱ ··········· 171

PSS 3 전치사의 목적어로 쓰이는 동명사 ··········· 173

PSS 4 동명사의 관용 표현 ··········· 175

PSS 5 동명사의 부정형 ··········· 176

PSS 6 동명사의 의미상의 주어 ··········· 177

중간·기말고사 대비문제 ··········· 179

CHAPTER 9 │ 분사 Participles

PSS 1 분사의 역할

PSS 1-1 한정적 용법 ··········· 186

PSS 1-2 서술적 용법 ··········· 188

PSS 2 현재분사와 동명사 ··········· 189

PSS 3 감정을 나타내는 분사 ··········· 190

PSS 4 분사구문

PSS 4-1 분사구문 만드는 법 ··········· 192

PSS 4-2 완료형 분사구문 ··········· 194

PSS 4-3 with+명사+분사 ··········· 195

PSS 4-4 분사구문의 관용적 표현 ··········· 197

중간·기말고사 대비문제 ··········· 198

CHAPTER 10 │ 형용사 Adjectives

PSS 1 형용사의 쓰임 ··········· 206

PSS 2 -thing, -one, -body, -where+형용사 ··········· 208

PSS 3 the+형용사 ··········· 209

PSS 4 형용사의 어순 ··········· 210

PSS 5 부정수량형용사

PSS 5-1 many, much ··········· 211

PSS 5-2 few, a few, little, a little ··········· 213

PSS 5-3 some, any ··········· 215

PSS 6 수사

PSS 6-1 기수와 서수 ····· 217
PSS 6-2 정수 ····· 218
PSS 6-3 분수와 소수 ····· 219
PSS 6-4 연도와 날짜 ····· 220
PSS 6-5 배수사 ····· 221
PSS 6-6 시각 ····· 222

중간·기말고사 대비문제 ····· 223

CHAPTER 11 | 부사 Adverbs

PSS 1 부사의 형태

PSS 1-1 형용사를 부사로 만드는 법 I ····· 230
PSS 1-2 형용사를 부사로 만드는 법 II ····· 231
PSS 1-3 형용사와 형태가 같은 부사 ····· 232
PSS 1-4 형용사 형태의 부사에 '-ly'를 붙이면 다른 뜻이
　　　　 되는 부사 ····· 235

PSS 2 여러 가지 부사의 용법

PSS 2-1 빈도부사 ····· 237
PSS 2-2 already, yet, still ····· 239
PSS 2-3 too, either, neither ····· 241
PSS 2-4 very, much ····· 242
PSS 2-5 else, even ····· 243
PSS 2-6 ago, before ····· 245
PSS 2-7 「타동사+부사」의 어순 ····· 246

중간·기말고사 대비문제 ····· 248

CHAPTER 12 | 가정법 Conditionals

PSS 1 조건을 나타내는 if ····· 254

PSS 2 가정법 과거

PSS 2-1 if+가정법 과거 ····· 256
PSS 2-2 I wish+가정법 과거 ····· 258
PSS 2-3 as if[though]+가정법 과거 ····· 260
PSS 2-4 without ····· 261

PSS 3 가정법 과거완료

PSS 3-1 if+가정법 과거완료 ····· 262
PSS 3-2 I wish+가정법 과거완료 ····· 263
PSS 3-3 as if[though]+가정법 과거완료 ····· 265
PSS 3-4 without ····· 266

PSS 4 혼합가정법 ····· 267

PSS 5 가정법 현재 명사절 ····· 268

PSS 6 if의 생략 ····· 269

중간·기말고사 대비문제 ····· 271

CHAPTER 13 | 비교구문 Comparisons

PSS 1 비교급과 최상급 만드는 법

PSS 1-1 규칙 변화 I ····· 276
PSS 1-2 규칙 변화 II ····· 277
PSS 1-3 규칙 변화 III ····· 278
PSS 1-4 불규칙 변화 ····· 282

PSS 2 원급을 이용한 비교

PSS 2-1 as+원급+as ····· 283
PSS 2-2 as+원급+as+주어+can[could] ····· 286

PSS 3 비교급을 이용한 비교

PSS 3-1 비교급+than I ····· 288
PSS 3-2 비교급+than II ····· 289
PSS 3-3 비교급 강조 ····· 291
PSS 3-4 less+원급+than ····· 292
PSS 3-5 the+비교급, the+비교급 ····· 293
PSS 3-6 비교급+and+비교급 ····· 294

PSS 4 최상급을 이용한 비교

PSS 4-1 the+최상급 ····· 295
PSS 4-2 one of+the+최상급+복수 명사 ····· 296
PSS 4-3 There is nothing ～ 비교급+than … ····· 297
PSS 4-4 최상급의 다른 표현 ····· 299

중간·기말고사 대비문제 ····· 301

CHAPTER 14 | 관계사 Relatives

PSS 1 관계대명사

PSS 1-1 who ····· 308
PSS 1-2 which ····· 310
PSS 1-3 that ····· 312
PSS 1-4 what ····· 314
PSS 1-5 계속적 용법 ····· 315
PSS 1-6 전치사+관계대명사 ····· 317
PSS 1-7 관계대명사의 생략 ····· 318
PSS 1-8 복합관계대명사 ····· 319

PSS 2 관계부사

PSS 2-1 관계부사의 종류 ····· 321
PSS 2-2 관계부사의 주의해야 할 용법 ····· 323
PSS 2-3 복합관계부사 ····· 326

중간·기말고사 대비문제 ──────── 328

CHAPTER 15 | 접속사 Conjunctions

PSS 1 and, but, or ──────── 336
PSS 2 명령문+and/or ──────── 337
PSS 3 not only A but also B ──────── 338
PSS 4 both A and B, either A or B, neither A nor B ──────── 340
PSS 5 because, so ──────── 342
PSS 6 as ──────── 344
PSS 7 조건을 나타내는 접속사 ──────── 345
PSS 8 so that ~, so ~ that … ──────── 347
PSS 9 명사절을 이끄는 접속사
PSS 9-1 that ──────── 349
PSS 9-2 whether ──────── 351
PSS 10 시간을 나타내는 접속사 Ⅰ ──────── 353
PSS 11 시간을 나타내는 접속사 Ⅱ ──────── 355
PSS 12 even though, even if ──────── 356
PSS 13 접속부사 Ⅰ ──────── 357
PSS 14 접속부사 Ⅱ ──────── 359
중간·기말고사 대비문제 ──────── 361

CHAPTER 16 | 전치사 Prepositions

PSS 1 시간을 나타내는 전치사
PSS 1-1 at, on, in Ⅰ ──────── 370
PSS 1-2 at, on, in Ⅱ ──────── 371
PSS 1-3 from, since ──────── 374
PSS 1-4 by, until ──────── 375
PSS 1-5 before, after ──────── 377
PSS 1-6 for, during ──────── 379
PSS 2 장소, 방향을 나타내는 전치사
PSS 2-1 at, in, on Ⅰ ──────── 381
PSS 2-2 at, in, on Ⅱ ──────── 384
PSS 2-3 above, below, over, under ──────── 385
PSS 2-4 up, down, into, out of, onto, off ──────── 386
PSS 2-5 across, along, through, around ──────── 390
PSS 2-6 by, in front of, behind, near ──────── 391
PSS 2-7 between, among ──────── 392
PSS 2-8 to, for, toward(s) ──────── 393

PSS 3 그 밖의 전치사
PSS 3-1 with, without, for, against ──────── 395
PSS 3-2 like, by, in, as ──────── 396
PSS 3-3 except, due to, according to, instead of ──────── 398
PSS 3-4 형용사와 함께 쓰이는 전치사 Ⅰ ──────── 399
PSS 3-5 형용사와 함께 쓰이는 전치사 Ⅱ ──────── 401
PSS 3-6 동사와 함께 쓰이는 전치사 Ⅰ ──────── 402
PSS 3-7 동사와 함께 쓰이는 전치사 Ⅱ ──────── 404
중간·기말고사 대비문제 ──────── 409

CHAPTER 17 | 일치와 화법 Agreement and Narration

PSS 1 주어와 동사의 일치
PSS 1-1 A and B ──────── 420
PSS 1-2 either A or B, neither A nor B, not only A but also B, not A but B ──────── 421
PSS 1-3 every, each+단수 동사 ──────── 422
PSS 1-4 some, most, none, half+of ──────── 423
PSS 1-5 복수 주어+단수 동사 ──────── 424
PSS 2 시제의 일치
PSS 2-1 시제 일치의 원칙 ──────── 425
PSS 2-2 시제 일치의 예외 ──────── 427
PSS 3 화법
PSS 3-1 평서문의 화법 전환 ──────── 428
PSS 3-2 의문문의 화법 전환 ──────── 430
PSS 3-3 명령문의 화법 전환 ──────── 432
중간·기말고사 대비문제 ──────── 434

CHAPTER 18 | 특수구문 & 속담 Inversion, Emphasis, Ellipsis & Proverbs

PSS 1 도치 ──────── 440
PSS 2 강조
PSS 2-1 강조 어구 ──────── 441
PSS 2-2 「It ~ that …」 강조구문 ──────── 443
PSS 3 생략
PSS 3-1 공통되는 부분의 생략 ──────── 445
PSS 3-2 「주어+be동사」의 생략 ──────── 447
PSS 4 속담 ──────── 448
중간·기말고사 대비문제 ──────── 452

CHAPTER 1
문장의 기초

PSS 1 의문문	페이지	성취도				
		100%	99~75%	74~50%	49~25%	24~0%
PSS 1-1 부가의문문 Ⅰ	8					
PSS 1-2 부가의문문 Ⅱ	9					
PSS 1-3 간접의문문 Ⅰ	10					
PSS 1-4 간접의문문 Ⅱ	11					

PSS 2 문장의 5형식	페이지	성취도				
		100%	99~75%	74~50%	49~25%	24~0%
PSS 2-1 목적어 유무에 따른 동사 구분	12					
PSS 2-2 주격 보어를 필요로 하는 불완전자동사 Ⅰ	13					
PSS 2-3 주격 보어를 필요로 하는 불완전자동사 Ⅱ	14					
PSS 2-4 주의해야 할 완전타동사	15					
PSS 2-5 두 개의 목적어를 필요로 하는 동사	17					
PSS 2-6 목적격 보어를 필요로 하는 동사 Ⅰ	18					
PSS 2-7 목적격 보어를 필요로 하는 동사 Ⅱ	19					
중간·기말고사 대비문제	21					

PSS 1 의문문

PSS 1-1 부가의문문 I

1. 주어+동사의 긍정형 ~, be / do / 조동사의 부정 축약형+인칭대명사?

The boys **are** watching a baseball game, **aren't they?**
그 소년들은 야구 경기를 보고 있어, 그렇지 않니?
She **finished** her homework, **didn't she?** 그녀는 그녀의 숙제를 끝냈어, 그렇지 않니?
Peter **has** been to Paris, **hasn't he?** Peter는 파리에 간 적이 있어, 그렇지 않니?

> ***cf.*** 주어가 this나 that이거나, 또는 이를 포함하여 단수 사물을 가리킬 때, 부가의문문의 인칭대명사
> 는 항상 it으로 쓴다. 마찬가지로 these나 those 또는 복수 사물에 관해서는 항상 they로 쓴다.
> That room **is** for visitors, **isn't it?** 저 방은 손님들을 위한 것이야, 그렇지 않니?
> These apples **are** fresh, **aren't they?** 이 사과들은 신선해, 그렇지 않니?

2. 주어+동사의 부정형 ~, be / do / 조동사의 긍정형+인칭대명사?

He **wasn't** late for the meeting, **was he?** 그는 회의에 늦지 않았어, 그렇지?
You **don't** want to lose weight, **do you?** 너는 체중 감량을 원하지 않아, 그렇지?
It **won't** rain tomorrow, **will it?** 내일은 비가 오지 않을 거야, 그렇지?

정답 p.2

PRACTICE 1

다음 문장의 빈칸에 알맞은 부가의문문을 쓰세요.

1 Junho is preparing for the test, _______________?

2 You haven't watched this movie yet, _______________?

3 We should wear uniforms on that day, _______________?

4 Those motorcycles aren't cheap in Vietnam, _______________?

5 Ms. Lee couldn't use her earphones because of earache, _______________?

6 They had a chance to go abroad as a prize, _______________?

7 The customers in the restaurants were very understanding, _______________?

8 You and I don't have to hand in this report right now, _______________?

9 This is Beethoven's Symphony No. 9, _______________?

10 Your father doesn't allow you to come home late, _______________?

PSS 1-2 부가의문문 Ⅱ

1. **Let's ~, shall we?**

   Let's hurry to the hospital, **shall we?** 병원에 서둘러 가자, 어때?
   Let's not go there by train, **shall we?** 그곳에 기차를 타고 가지 말자, 어때?

2. **명령문, will you?**

   Take your umbrella with you, **will you?** 우산을 가져가라, 알겠니?
   Don't make a noise in the classroom, **will you?** 교실에서는 시끄럽게 하지 마라, 알겠니?
   cf. 긍정명령문 뒤에는 어조에 따라 'will you?' 또는 'won't you?'를 쓸 수 있다.
   　　　명령조로 말할 때는 'will you?', 정중하게 권할 때는 'won't you?'를 쓴다.

3. **I am ~, am I not[aren't I]?**

   I'm doing okay, **am I not?** 나는 잘 하고 있어, 그렇지 않니?
   = **I'm** doing okay, **aren't I?**
   cf. 구어체에서는 aren't I?가 더 많이 쓰인다.

4. **There is ~, isn't there? / There are ~, aren't there?**

   There is a bus every ten minutes, **isn't there?** 10분마다 버스가 한 대씩 있어, 그렇지 않니?
   There weren't dogs in the park, **were there?** 그 공원에는 개들이 없었어, 그렇지?

정답 p.2

PRACTICE 2

다음 문장의 빈칸에 알맞은 부가의문문을 쓰세요.

1　Be polite when you speak to the elderly, _______________?

2　That's your favorite book, _______________?

3　Let's ask the principal what to do next, _______________?

4　I'm your true friend, _______________?

5　You can make a decision about the matter yourself, _______________?

6　Let's not waste time on Web surfing any more, _______________?

7　There weren't any tall buildings in the town, _______________?

8　Don't look at your phone while walking, _______________?

9　They don't know what is important in life, _______________?

10　There are several serious environmental problems, _______________?

한 문장 안에서 의문문이 문장의 일부로 쓰이는 경우 어순이 평서문처럼 바뀌는 데, 이것을 간접의문문이라고 한다.

1. 의문사가 있는 경우 – 의문사+주어+동사

   This app shows. + How can I go to the train station?

   ➡ This app shows **how I can go to the train station**.

   이 앱은 내가 어떻게 기차역에 가야 할지 보여준다.

   I don't know. + What is his name?

   ➡ I don't know **what his name is**. 나는 그의 이름이 무엇인지 모른다.

   cf. 간접의문문에서 의문사가 주어로 쓰인 경우에는 직접의문문의 어순을 그대로 쓴다.

   Please tell me. + Who can solve the problem?

   ➡ Please tell me **who can solve the problem**. 누가 그 문제를 풀 수 있는지 나에게 말해 줘.

2. 의문사가 없는 경우 – if[whether]+주어+동사

   I wonder. + Can I finish it by this Sunday?

   ➡ I wonder **if[whether] I can finish it by this Sunday**.

   나는 내가 그것을 이번 주 일요일까지 끝낼 수 있을지 궁금하다.

정답 p.2

PRACTICE 3

다음 주어진 문장을 간접의문문으로 바꾸어 문장을 완성하세요.

1 Where are the dairy products?
   ➡ Could you tell me ______________________________?

2 How did the food taste?
   ➡ She explained ______________________________.

3 What made her so happy?
   ➡ Can you tell me ______________________________?

4 When did the tragic accident happen?
   ➡ Nobody knows ______________________________.

5 Did he get married to the English girl?
   ➡ Can you tell me ______________________________?

6 Who will look after her while her parents are working?
   ➡ I wonder ______________________________.

7 Why didn't you agree with him?
   ➡ Please tell me ______________________________.

8 How far is it from here to the airport?
   ➡ Do you know ______________________________?

9 Will my dream come true?

➡ I'd like to know ____ .

10 Does he have any brothers or sisters?

➡ I don't remember ____ .

PSS 1-4 간접의문문 Ⅱ

주절의 동사가 think, believe, suppose, guess, imagine과 같이 생각이나 추측을 나타
낼 때는 간접의문문의 의문사가 문장 맨 앞에 위치한다.

Do you **think**? + **What** should we do to win the game?

➡ **What** do you **think** we should do to win the game?

너는 우리가 경기를 이기기 위해 무엇을 해야 한다고 생각하니?

Do you **suppose**? + **Who** can do that?

➡ **Who** do you **suppose** can do that? 너는 누가 그것을 할 수 있다고 추측하니?

cf. 'Can you guess?'의 경우는 의문사가 문장 앞으로 나가지 않는다.

Can you guess? + **What** did I buy? ➡ Can you guess **what** I bought?

정답 p.2

PRACTICE 4

다음 주어진 두 문장을 연결하여 한 문장으로 바꾸어 쓰세요.

1 Do you think? + Why did she quit school?

➡ ____

2 Do you guess? + How can you discover your hidden talents?

➡ ____

3 Please tell me. + Are you an FBI agent?

➡ ____

4 Do you suppose? + Where does he come from?

➡ ____

5 I know. + What did you do after school yesterday?

➡ ____

6 Do you believe? + When can you afford to buy the house?

➡ ____

7 Do you think? + Which is the faster way to go there?

➡ ____

8 Do you guess? + Where did you lose your passport?

➡ ____

PSS 2 문장의 5형식

동사의 분류

1. **자동사**: 목적어가 필요 없는 동사. 자동사 뒤에 (대)명사를 쓸 경우에는 전치사(to, for, with…)와 함께 쓴다. 자동사가 쓰인 문장에 보어가 없으면 1형식, 보어가 있으면 2형식 문장이 된다.

2. **타동사**: 목적어가 필요한 동사. 1개의 목적어를 가지면 3형식, 2개의 목적어(간접목적어, 직접목적어)를 가지면 4형식, 목적어와 목적격 보어를 가지면 5형식 문장이 된다.

PSS 2-1 목적어 유무에 따른 동사 구분

1. 목적어를 필요로 하지 않는 동사

① 1형식 - 주어 + 동사 [S+V]

I **ran**. 나는 달렸다.

cf. 「주어+동사」 뒤에는 부사(구)와 같은 수식어를 수반하는 경우가 많다.

He **lay** on the sofa. 그는 소파에 누웠다.

cf. '~가 있다'의 뜻을 나타내기 위해 there가 문장의 맨 앞에 올 때는 「There+be동사+주어 ~」의 어순으로 쓴다.

There **is a book** on the desk. 책상 위에 한 권의 책이 있다.

② 2형식 - 주어 + 동사 + 주격 보어 [S+V+S.C.]

She **became a teacher**. 그녀는 선생님이 되었다.

cf. 주격 보어로는 명사나 형용사가 온다.

2. 목적어를 필요로 하는 동사

① 3형식 - 주어 + 동사 + 목적어 [S+V+O]

I **saw the cartoon** on the Internet. 나는 인터넷에서 그 만화를 보았다.

② 4형식 - 주어 + 동사 + 간접목적어 + 직접목적어 [S+V+I.O.+D.O.]

I **bought my mother some flowers**. 나는 엄마에게 약간의 꽃을 사 드렸다.

③ 5형식 - 주어 + 동사 + 목적어 + 목적격 보어 [S+V+O+O.C.]

They **call her an angel**. 그들은 그녀를 천사라고 부른다.

People **recognize water essential for life**. 사람들은 물이 생명에 필수적이라고 인식한다.

The touching speech **made the crowd emotional**.

그 감동적인 연설은 군중들을 감동시켰다.

PRACTICE 5

〈보기〉에서 밑줄 친 부분에 해당하는 문장 성분을 찾아 번호를 쓰세요. 그 다음, 괄호 안에 그 문장의 형식을 쓰세요.

보 기	① 주어 ② 동사 ③ 목적어 ④ 간접목적어 ⑤ 직접목적어 ⑥ 주격 보어 ⑦ 목적격 보어

1 The Sun rises in the east. [   ]

2 Mr. Kim teaches English to us every Thursday and Friday. [   ]

3 At first, I thought him honest. [   ]

4 It was getting colder and colder. [   ]

5 There is an old castle on the hill. [   ]

6 The audience gave the lead male and female actors a big hand. [   ]

7 He remained calm and patient unlike others. [   ]

8 He wanted her to do it instead of himself. [   ]

PSS 2-2 주격 보어를 필요로 하는 불완전자동사 I

다음의 불완전자동사는 주격 보어로 명사나 형용사를 취한다.

be	~이다	+ 명사 / 형용사
keep	(~인 상태로) 있다	+ 형용사
remain, stay	(~인 상태로) 있다	+ 명사 / 형용사
become	~가 되다	+ 명사 / 형용사
get, grow, go, turn, run	~하게 되다	+ 형용사

London **is the capital** of the U.K. 런던은 영국의 수도이다.

They **kept quiet** about the surprise party. 그들은 깜짝 파티에 관해 조용히 있었다. (비밀을 지켰다.)

The weather **remained warm** for three days. 날씨가 3일 동안 따뜻했다.

She **became sick** after eating the seafood. 그녀는 해산물을 먹은 후에 아프게 되었다.

Since we **aren't fit**, we will **get tired** very soon.

우리는 건강하지 않기 때문에, 매우 빨리 지치게 될 것이다.

They have **run short** of money. 그들은 돈에 쪼들리고 있다.

PRACTICE 6

괄호 안에 들어갈 알맞은 말을 골라 동그라미 하세요.

1   The boy was absolutely (brilliant, brilliantly).

2   The weather remained (cloud, cloudy).

3   You can get (tiring, tired) easily after a long walk.

4   We kept (silent, silently) while Peter was talking with Sally.

5   Luckily, he became (popular, popularly) after his first performance.

6   She can speak four foreign languages quite (fluent, fluently).

7   The weather turned very (cold, coldly) after the rain.

8   I was (late, lately) for an important meeting this morning.

9   His wound on his left thigh got (serious, seriously).

10   The pilot (calm, calmly) landed the plane during the storm.

11   The food will go (bad, badly) if you don't put it in the refrigerator.

12   His face grew (pale, palely) and began to tremble.

13   James (quick, quickly) shut the door.

14   The river ran (dry, dryly) after months without rain.

15   Despite his apology, she continued to treat him (cold, coldly).

PSS 2-3 주격 보어를 필요로 하는 불완전자동사 Ⅱ

다음의 동사들은 주격 보어로 형용사를 취한다.

1.   감각을 나타내는 동사 – sound '~하게 들리다', smell '~한 냄새가 나다',
taste '~한 맛이 나다', feel '~한 느낌이 들다'

That **sounds great**. 그 말은 아주 좋게 들린다.
Roses **smell sweet**. 장미에서는 달콤한 향이 난다.
This cake **tastes good**. 이 케이크는 맛이 좋다.
This cloth **feels smooth**. 이 천은 부드럽게 느껴진다.

2.   '~로 보이다' – look, seem, appear

You **look interested** in African-American music. 너는 미국 흑인 음악에 관심이 있어 보인다.
They **seem** very **puzzled** about the question. 그들은 그 질문에 매우 당혹스러워하는 것 같아 보인다.
He **appeared depressed** last night. 그는 지난밤에 우울해 보였다.

cf. 「감각동사 like+명사」 '~처럼 …하다'

She doesn't **look like a Japanese**. 그녀는 일본 사람처럼 보이지 않는다.

It **sounds like a wonderful idea**. 그것은 멋진 생각처럼 들린다.

This candy **tastes like apples**. 이 사탕은 사과처럼 맛이 난다.

정답 p.3

PRACTICE 7

괄호 안에 들어갈 알맞은 말을 골라 동그라미 하세요.

1 Those apples in the basket taste (good, well).

2 His speech sounded (strange, strangely) to me.

3 She (looks, looks like) her sister.

4 The cats were moving (dull, dully) along the fence.

5 The cold soft drink made me feel (freshly, fresh) and (energetic, energetically).

6 You look (youth, young) for your age.

7 The man doesn't feel (guilty, guiltily) about the accident.

8 The book in your hands seemed very (heavy, heavily).

9 The Coke doesn't sell well because it tastes too (sweetly, sweet).

10 The Kims appear (rich, richly) but very (stingy, stingily).

11 The students worked (good, well) together as a team to complete the project.

12 That (sounds, sounds like) an excellent movie!

13 Due to the traffic jam, the commute to work was (great, greatly) delayed.

PSS 2-4 주의해야 할 완전타동사

다음의 동사들은 목적어 다음에 특정한 전치사를 수반한다.

1. provide[supply]+A+with+B 'A에게 B를 제공[공급]하다'
    I can **provide** you **with** what you want. 나는 너에게 네가 원하는 것을 제공할 수 있다.
    cf. 「provide+사물+for[to]+사람」으로도 쓸 수 있다.
    The hotel **provides** a laundry service **for[to]** guests.
    그 호텔은 고객들에게 세탁 서비스를 제공한다.

2. name ~ after … '…의 이름을 따서 ~의 이름을 짓다'
    His parents **named** him **after** his grandfather.
    그의 부모님은 할아버지의 이름을 따서 그의 이름을 지었다.

3. help ~ with … '~가 …하는 것을 돕다'
What can I **help** you **with**? 무엇을 도와 드릴까요?

4. prevent ~ from … '~가 …하는 것을 방해하다[막다]'
Stress **prevented** me **from** taking a rest. 스트레스 때문에 나는 휴식을 취할 수 없었다.

5. pay ~ for … '…에 대해 ~를 지불하다'
I **paid** $200 **for** this bicycle. 나는 이 자전거를 사는 데 200달러를 지불했다.

6. prefer A to B 'B보다 A를 더 좋아하다'
He **prefers** reading books **to** watching TV.
그는 TV를 보는 것보다 책 읽는 것을 더 좋아한다.

정답 p.3

PRACTICE 8

〈보기〉에서 알맞은 전치사를 골라 빈칸에 쓰세요.

보 기	after for from to with

1 Cows provide us _______________ milk.

2 The newborn baby was named _______________ a famous TV star.

3 They supplied the tsunami victims _______________ clothing and food.

4 I prefer pop music _______________ classical music.

5 I paid $500 _______________ the mask and costume for Halloween.

6 Her ankle injury may prevent her _______________ playing in today's game.

7 I'll help you _______________ your homework.

8 They named the statue _______________ the angel "Gabriel."

9 Could you help me _______________ this suitcase?

10 My sister prefers winter _______________ summer because she can't stand hot weather.

11 I prefer being an early bird _______________ being a night owl.

12 Did you pay a lot of money _______________ that dress?

PSS 2-5 두 개의 목적어를 필요로 하는 동사

다음은 두 개의 목적어를 필요로 하는 4형식 문장에 해당하는 동사로서, to, for, of의 전치사를 이용하여 3형식으로 바꿀 수 있다.

1.

give lend send show teach tell write pay sell	+직접목적어+to+간접목적어

I **gave** him a piece of advice. 〈4형식〉 ➡ I **gave** a piece of advice **to** him. 〈3형식〉
나는 그에게 충고 한 마디를 해 주었다.

He **showed** me his old pictures. 〈4형식〉 ➡ He **showed** his old pictures **to** me. 〈3형식〉
그는 내게 그의 오래된 사진들을 보여주었다.

He **told** the children a story. 〈4형식〉 ➡ He **told** a story **to** the children. 〈3형식〉
그는 아이들에게 이야기를 말해 주었다.

2.

make buy cook get find do	+직접목적어+for+간접목적어

I **found** her a four-leaf clover. 〈4형식〉 ➡ I **found** a four-leaf clover **for** her. 〈3형식〉
나는 그녀에게 네 잎 클로버를 찾아주었다.

John **bought** his mother a dishwasher. 〈4형식〉
John은 그의 어머니께 식기세척기를 사 드렸다.
➡ John **bought** a dishwasher **for** his mother. 〈3형식〉

Get the customers some complimentary samples. 〈4형식〉
그 고객들에게 무료 샘플들을 좀 갖다 드려라.
➡ **Get** some complimentary samples **for** the customers. 〈3형식〉

3.

ask	+직접목적어+of+간접목적어

Can I **ask** you a favor? 〈4형식〉 ➡ Can I **ask** a favor **of** you? 〈3형식〉
너에게 부탁을 해도 되겠니?

정답 p.3

PRACTICE 9 [1-10]

다음 4형식 문장을 3형식 문장으로 바꾸어 쓰세요.

1 My wife's full support gave me strength.

➡ ______________________________________

2 He teaches the children English speaking and writing.

➡ ______________________________________

3 They didn't ask me anything.

➡ ____

4 I bought my friend an ice cream cone and a soft drink.

➡ ____

5 Can you tell us the reason for your decision?

➡ ____

6 The machine will make you different types of cookies.

➡ ____

7 Would you do me a favor?

➡ ____

8 The instructor showed me how to snowboard.

➡ ____

9 The gentleman found me my diamond necklace.

➡ ____

10 A customer wrote the manager a thank-you email.

➡ ____

PSS 2-6 목적격 보어를 필요로 하는 동사 I

1. keep, find, call, make, turn, elect – 목적격 보어로 명사나 형용사가 온다.

   We **found** the story **true**. 우리는 그 이야기가 사실이라는 것을 알았다.
   I **made** him very **upset** in the car. 나는 차에서 그를 매우 화나게 만들었다.
   They **elected** him their new **leader**. 그들은 그를 그들의 새로운 지도자로 선출했다.

2. want, tell, ask, cause, force, allow, encourage, order, advise, enable, teach, expect, need, persuade – 목적격 보어로 to부정사가 온다.

   I **want** you **to rest** for a while. 나는 네가 잠깐 동안 쉬기를 원한다.
   He **asked** me **to wait** in line. 그는 내게 줄을 서서 기다리기를 요구했다.
   My teacher **encouraged** me **to participate** in the race.
   나의 선생님께서 내가 경주에 참가하도록 격려해 주셨다.
   They **ordered** him **to leave**. 그들은 그에게 떠나라고 명령했다.

정답 p.3

PRACTICE 10

괄호 안에 들어갈 알맞은 말을 골라 동그라미 하세요.

1 Did you find the novel (interest, interesting)?

2 She asked us (come, to come) over to her house the other day.

3 I will persuade him (go, to go) camping tomorrow.

4 Jason made me (angry, angrily) because he didn't keep his promise again.

5 Why didn't you keep the children (quiet, quietly)?

6 The police want him (to confess, confessing) everything about the crime.

7 My teacher encouraged me (having, to have) an interest in paintings.

8 Hot temperatures turned the milk (sour, sourly) and (smelly, smell).

9 The man allowed the students (go, to go) to the haunted house.

10 Mom told me (get, to get) rid of stains on the wall.

PSS 2-7 목적격 보어를 필요로 하는 동사 Ⅱ

1. 사역동사 let, make, have는 목적어와 목적격 보어의 관계가 능동일 때 목적격 보어로 동사원형을 취한다. 단, 준사역동사인 help는 목적격 보어로 to부정사를 취하기도 한다.

   My mom won't **let** me **have** a sleepover. 나의 엄마는 내가 친구 집에서 자지 못하게 하실 것이다.
   I can't **make** the baby **stop** crying. 나는 그 아기가 우는 것을 멈추게 할 수 없다.
   I **helped** her **(to) choose** her dress. 나는 그녀가 그녀의 드레스를 고르는 것을 도왔다.

   cf. get은 let, make, have와 비슷한 의미로 쓸 수 있지만 목적격 보어로 to부정사 또는 현재분사를 취한다. 어떤 행동을 하도록 설득, 유도할 때는 to부정사를, 그 행동이 시작됨을 강조할 때는 현재분사를 쓴다.
   I **got** my sisters **to repeat** what I had said. 나는 내 여동생들에게 내가 말한 것을 따라하게 했다.
   Our conversation **got** me **thinking**. 우리의 대화는 나를 생각하게 만들었다.

2. 지각동사 feel, see, hear, watch는 목적어와 목적격 보어의 관계가 능동일 때 목적격 보어로 동사원형을 취한다.

   My brother **felt** something **touch** his head. 내 동생은 무엇인가가 그의 머리를 건드리는 것을 느꼈다.
   I often **watch** her **play** the piano. 나는 종종 그녀가 피아노를 연주하는 것을 본다.

   cf. 지각동사는 동작이 진행 중임을 강조할 때, 목적격 보어로 현재분사를 취한다.
   I **heard** the rain **falling**. 나는 비가 내리는 소리를 들었다.

3. 목적어와 목적격 보어의 관계가 능동일 때는 목적격 보어로 동사원형이나 현재분사를, 수동일 때는 목적격 보어로 과거분사를 취한다.

   He **found** an old man **living** alone in the cabin.
   그는 한 노인이 오두막집에 혼자 사는 것을 발견했다.
   You have to **get** it **finished** by seven in the evening.
   너는 그것을 저녁 7시까지 끝내도록 해야 한다.
   I **had** my car **washed**. 나는 내 차가 세차되게 했다.

PRACTICE 11

괄호 안에 들어갈 알맞은 말을 골라 동그라미 하세요.

1 Let me (help, to help) you fix the computer.

2 You have to get her (wake, to wake) up early.

3 Sujin had her daughter (decorate, decorated) the living room for the holidays.

4 You may find yourself (enjoyed, enjoying) the music.

5 The man helped his guests (carry, carrying) their bags.

6 What makes you (think, to think) so?

7 I will get the wedding invitations (printed, to print) next month.

8 Where will you have your shoes (repair, repaired)?

9 She tried to do everything to make her husband (succeed, to succeed).

10 Did you see the people (to cross, crossing) the street at the red light?

11 I had all the household chores (do, done) by Liz.

12 The boss got me (attend, to attend) the meeting on Friday.

13 Ms. Smith let her son (buy, bought) all that he wanted.

14 We watched the full moon (to rise, rising) yesterday evening.

15 He had his hair (cut, to cut) by his sister.

16 Let's have the car (washed, wash) on the way.

17 Team sports help children (develop, developing) their social skills.

18 I felt the chair (to move, moving) back little by little.

19 I'll have you (know, to know) that I'm a black belt in taekwondo.

20 Nothing will make me (change, to change) my mind.

21 Did you hear the teenagers (fighting, fought) each other last night?

22 You should see our baby (walk, to walk) by himself.

23 She had her watch (steal, stolen) a few weeks ago.

24 Those rules helped the town (to be, being) kept clean.

25 I find myself (thinking, thought) about Nick.

중간·기말고사 대비문제 📝

1 다음 밑줄 친 단어의 형태가 옳은 것은?

① He wants to <u>success</u> in his new business.
② The <u>explain</u> of the experiment was confusing.
③ He gave me a <u>recommend</u> for a good restaurant.
④ She made a quick <u>decision</u> before leaving the office.
⑤ She has been working as a medical <u>translation</u> for over 10 years.

2 다음 우리말을 영어로 바르게 옮긴 것은?

> • 패스트푸드를 먹을 때 당신의 건강을 위해 큰 사이즈를 주문하지 마세요, 알겠죠?

① When you eat fast food, don't order large portions for the sake of your health, don't you?
② When you eat fast food, don't order large portions for the sake of your health, do you?
③ When you eat fast food, don't order large portions for the sake of your health, will you?
④ When you ate fast food, don't order large portions for the sake of your health, did you?
⑤ When you will eat fast food, don't order large portions for the sake of your health, will you?

3 주어진 두 문장을 한 문장으로 바꿔 쓰세요. (단, 간접의문문을 포함할 것.)

> She wants to know. + How long does it take to get to the airport?

➡ ________________________________
____

4 다음 밑줄 친 부분 중 어법상 틀린 것은?

① He was very scared, but he <u>remained calm</u>.
② You can <u>get healthy</u> through this training.
③ I think your symptom is part of <u>growing older</u>.
④ As the company <u>became richly</u>, they felt proud of their company.
⑤ While studying, you can't <u>stay focused</u> with the TV on.

5 다음 중 네모 안의 밑줄 친 단어의 의미와 다른 것은?

> <u>Lies</u> run sprints, but the truth runs marathons.

① His strength <u>lies</u> in his determination.
② They tried to cover up the truth with <u>lies</u>.
③ Trust is fragile and easily shattered by <u>lies</u>.
④ His <u>lies</u> made it hard for people to believe him.
⑤ She learned that <u>lies</u> always have consequences.

6 주어진 우리말과 같은 뜻이 되도록 빈칸을 채울 때 알맞은 것은?

> • Brown 선생님은 내가 곤경에 처할 때 도망갈 친구를 사귀지 말라고 항상 말씀하신다.
> = Mr. Brown always tells me __________ friends with someone who will run away when I am in trouble.

① not to make　　② making not
③ not make　　④ not making
⑤ to not make

7 주어진 우리말과 같은 뜻이 되도록 빈칸을 채우세요.

> • 그녀는 회의에 참석해 달라고 나에게 요청했다.
> = She has _______________ me
> _______________ _______________ the
> meeting.

8 다음의 우리말을 영어로 바르게 옮긴 것을 <u>모두</u> 고르세요.

> • 매일 운동하는 것은 우리가 병에 걸리는 것을 막아준다.

① Working out every day stops us of getting sick.

② Working out every day prevent us from getting sick.

③ Working out every day prevents us from getting sick.

④ Working out every day prevents us to get sick.

⑤ Working out every day keeps us from getting sick.

9 〈보기〉의 문장 중, 어법상 <u>틀린</u> 것끼리 짝지어진 것은?

> 보 기
> ⓐ I think you look a lot like your father.
> ⓑ She stayed calm at her mother's death.
> ⓒ His singing sounded beautifully to everyone.
> ⓓ Your new perfume smells well.
> ⓔ His face grew palely and began to tremble.

① ⓐ, ⓑ, ⓒ ② ⓐ, ⓑ, ⓔ ③ ⓑ, ⓒ, ⓓ
④ ⓑ, ⓓ, ⓔ ⑤ ⓒ, ⓓ, ⓔ

10 주어진 문장과 문장의 형식이 같은 것을 <u>모두</u> 고르세요.

> The doctors in the hospital just called it a miracle.

① He saw an old friend of his on the street.

② She heard a baby cat crying for food.

③ Minsu gave us a big hand on our new project.

④ She taught me a lot of things about the history of Canada.

⑤ The lava from the volcanoes made the land smooth.

11 다음 두 문장을 연결하여 한 문장으로 쓰세요.

> Do you know? + Do the birds cry like human beings?

➡ _______________________________________
____

12 [A]~[C]에 들어갈 표현이 바르게 짝지어진 것은?

> • My daughter always helps me _____[A]_____ care of our pets when I'm away.
> • I felt something _____[B]_____ my leg.
> • Let our dreams _____[C]_____ high.

	[A]	[B]	[C]
①	to take	crawl up	soaring
②	take	crawled up	soar
③	take	crawl up	soaring
④	taking	crawling up	soar
⑤	to take	crawling up	soar

13 다음 두 문장을 한 문장으로 바꿔 쓰세요. (단, 간접의문문을 포함할 것.)

> Do you think? + What should we do to get out of here?

➡ ____

____

14 다음 밑줄 친 부분이 **틀리게** 해석된 것을 **모두** 고르세요.

① I <u>used to watch</u> airplanes take off or land.
나는 비행기들이 이륙하거나 착륙하는 것을 보는 데 익숙하다.

② I want my situation <u>to be understood</u> better.
나는 내 상황을 더 잘 이해하기로 했다.

③ Finally, she felt the train <u>start to move</u>.
마침내 그녀는 기차가 움직이기 시작한 것을 느꼈다.

④ I didn't want anyone <u>to see my diary</u> when I was a student.
나는 내가 학생이었을 때 나의 일기를 어느 누구도 보는 것을 원하지 않았다.

⑤ A woman saw a large rock <u>blocking the main road</u>.
한 여성은 큰 바위 하나가 대로를 가로막고 있는 것을 보았다.

15 괄호 안에 주어진 단어를 활용했을 때 〈보기〉의 밑줄 친 부분과 활용된 형태가 같은 것은?

보 기	Yoonju had her hair <u>cut</u> last week.

① He saw a woman (stand) on the hill.
② What makes you (think) that it's true?
③ I had to have my dog (wash) after a walk.
④ I suddenly found myself (enjoy) the concert.
⑤ Kelly asked them (be) quiet during the class.

16 다음 문장 중 어법상 **옳은** 문장의 개수는?

> ⓐ The children were exciting about the picnic.
> ⓑ I don't remember where she went yesterday.
> ⓒ Could you tell me how can I get to the library?
> ⓓ We need to find out what caused the problem.
> ⓔ People have been shocked by the news since it was announced.

① 0개　② 1개　③ 2개　④ 3개　⑤ 4개

17 빈칸에 들어갈 전치사로 알맞은 것은?

> I couldn't do anything when she asked a favor _________ me. I feel really sorry for her.

① to　② in　③ of　④ for　⑤ from

18 빈칸에 들어갈 말로 알맞은 것을 **모두** 고르세요.

> You may also be able to read many books, which will help you _________ more about other cultures.

① learn　　② learning　　③ learned
④ be learned　⑤ to learn

19 다음 대화의 빈칸에 알맞은 부가의문문을 쓰세요.

> *A*: Let's find out the best way to improve our English speaking skills in a short period of time, _________________?
> *B*: That's a good idea.

20 괄호 안에 주어진 단어를 올바르게 배열하여 문장을 완성하세요.

> • 여유 시간이 있을 때 그는 외출하는 것보다는 집에서 책을 읽는 것을 더 좋아한다.
> = When he has free time, ___________
> ___________________________
> ___________________________ .
> (prefers, going out, to, he, reading books, at home)

21 다음 문장의 빈칸 중 어떤 위치에도 들어갈 수 <u>없는</u> 단어는?

> a. What part of the book did you like the ___________ ?
> b. Some kinds of drinks are ___________ hot only.
> c. I was so ___________ by my mistake during the presentation.
> d. People sometimes forget how ___________ rest is.
> e. He made ___________ of his language skills during his trip to Spain.

① important   ② most
③ embarrassing   ④ use
⑤ served

22 다음 대화의 빈칸에 들어갈 말로 알맞은 것은?

> *A*: There are so many things for us to know in this alarming world, ___________ ?
> *B*: You're absolutely right.

① don't you   ② do you
③ are there   ④ aren't there
⑤ aren't you

23 빈칸에 들어갈 전치사가 차례대로 짝지어진 것은?

> • Her father named the girl ___________ her grandmother.
> • Thank you for helping me ___________ this matter.

① from – on   ② on – with   ③ after – with
④ after – to   ⑤ from – to

24 다음 대화 중 어법상 <u>틀린</u> 것은?

① A: He has gone back to Germany, hasn't he?
   B: No, he hasn't. He is still in Seoul.
② A: They were on vacation last week, weren't they?
   B: Yes, they were. They went to Tokyo.
③ A: Let's go on a short trip tomorrow, shall we?
   B: I'm sorry. I'm going to visit my aunt.
④ A: You had a long conversation with Jina last night, hadn't you?
   B: Yes, we talked for about three hours.
⑤ A: Jihoon didn't do his homework yesterday, did he?
   B: No, he didn't.

25 ①~④ 중 <u>잘못된</u> 것을 <u>두 개</u> 찾아서 바르게 고치세요.

> Minsu is a new student. I would like to know ① where he comes from. I wonder ② he thinks what about our school. I want to know ③ what he usually does in his free time. After class, I will ④ help him finding his locker.

틀린 번호	고쳐 쓴 답

26 다음 중 어법상 틀린 것은?

① His story appears very likely, but I can't believe it.
② The baby plays all the time but never seems tired.
③ Everything in the ads sounds truly but the fact is different.
④ The cookies that my dad had bought in Belgium tasted good.
⑤ Whenever I visit the country, I feel friendly without any reason.

27 다음 중 밑줄 친 부분을 어법상 옳게 고친 것은?

① I wanted you to give(→ give) some money to the poor beggar.
② You have to get it to finish(→ finished) by the day after tomorrow.
③ It will help them to conduct(→ conducting) research to find good sources of food.
④ She asked her parents to let(→ let) her go to the concert with her friends.
⑤ This prize will encourage people with big dreams to work(→ working) harder.

28 ⓐ와 ⓑ를 각각 어법에 맞게 고치세요.

After finishing the science project, I told my teacher ⓐ how challenging was the experiment and ⓑ what a great result did we achieve. She praised our effort.

ⓐ ______________________________

ⓑ ______________________________

29 그림을 보고 주어진 〈조건〉에 맞게 빈칸에 알맞은 말을 쓰세요.

조 건	간접의문문을 활용하여 그림 상황에 맞는 문장을 완성할 것
예 시	The girl wants to know who he is.

(1) The man is asking the park guard

______________ ______________

______________ ______________.

(2) The boy doesn't know ______________

______________ ______________ ______________.

30 다음 중 어법상 올바른 문장끼리 짝지어진 것은?

(a) We watched the players practicing on the field.
(b) He heard his name mention in the conversation.
(c) The shoes made in Italy look nice.
(d) After five laps of swimming, he was breathing heavy.
(e) Drinking more water helped me feel more energetic.
(f) Don't let shyness keeps you from making new friends.

① (a), (b), (d)　　② (a), (c), (e)　　③ (b), (c), (f)
④ (a), (e), (f)　　⑤ (c), (d), (e)

31 다음 중 어법상 알맞은 문장을 <u>모두</u> 고르면?

① I wonder whether the rumor is true.
② Do you think who needs the most help?
③ Let's consider how can we solve the problem.
④ What language do you know he wants to learn?
⑤ I'd like to know how long you will stay at my place.

32 다음 두 문장을 연결하여 한 문장으로 쓰세요.

• I wonder.
• Why did they wear uncomfortable high heels?

➡ ________________________________

____

33 다음 중 어법상 올바른 대화는?

① A: Where can you tell me I can find more information on the event?
　 B: You can visit our website www. seoulvillage.com.
② A: Who encouraged you becoming a scientist?
　 B: My science teacher in high school did.
③ A: What do you like about your partner James?
　 B: His jokes always make me to laugh.
④ A: Did you feel the earth to move?
　 B: No, I didn't. Did you?
⑤ A: What's wrong? You look really upset.
　 B: I had my wallet stolen on the bus. All my credit cards were in it.

34 밑줄 친 @~@ 중, 어법상 <u>틀린</u> 것의 개수는?

　Mrs. Park, my homeroom teacher, told us @ <u>to prepare</u> for the talent show at the end of the semester. She asked each of us ⓑ <u>to decide</u> what to do. My classmates began to talk about their plans, but I had ⓒ <u>to stay silently</u> because I had no ideas. I wanted someone ⓓ <u>help</u> me make a decision. After school, I asked Mom to give me some advice. She encouraged me ⓔ <u>choosing</u> what I would enjoy performing, and not to worry too much about how well I would do.

① 1개　　　　② 2개　　　　③ 3개
④ 4개　　　　⑤ 5개

35 다음 중 어법상 옳은 문장을 <u>모두</u> 고른 것은?

ⓐ Sujin doesn't even make an effort to get it done on time.
ⓑ Regular reading helps us to expand our vocabulary.
ⓒ Lauren lets her kids to do whatever they like.
ⓓ The railway workers' strike made me waited for an hour.
ⓔ Mom tells me where to shop for the best bargains.
ⓕ I just had new tires putting on the car.
ⓖ I couldn't get Tommy signing the agreement.

① ⓐ, ⓑ, ⓔ　　　　　② ⓑ, ⓓ, ⓕ
③ ⓒ, ⓔ, ⓖ　　　　　④ ⓐ, ⓑ, ⓓ, ⓖ
⑤ ⓓ, ⓔ, ⓕ

CHAPTER 2
시제

PSS 1 과거시제	페이지	성취도				
		100%	99~75%	74~50%	49~25%	24~0%
PSS 1-1 동사의 과거형 만들기	28					
PSS 1-2 규칙 변화 과거형 동사의 발음	30					
PSS 1-3 불규칙 동사의 과거형과 과거분사형	31					

PSS 2 완료시제	페이지	성취도				
		100%	99~75%	74~50%	49~25%	24~0%
PSS 2-1 현재완료시제	34					
PSS 2-2 for와 since	36					
PSS 2-3 현재완료시제와 과거시제	37					
PSS 2-4 현재완료 진행시제	39					
PSS 2-5 진행형을 쓰지 않는 동사	40					
PSS 2-6 과거완료시제	42					
PSS 2-7 과거완료 진행시제	43					
PSS 3 미래시제	45					
중간·기말고사 대비문제	46					

PSS 1 과거시제

PSS 1-1 동사의 과거형 만들기

일반적인 경우	동사원형+ed	mix – mix**ed** guess – guess**ed** lock – lock**ed** maintain – maintain**ed**
-e로 끝나는 경우	동사원형+d	agree – agree**d** animate – animat**ed** arrange – arrang**ed** breathe – breath**ed**
자음+y로 끝나는 경우	자음+i+ed	apply – appl**ied** bury – bur**ied** classify – classif**ied** cry – cr**ied**
모음+y로 끝나는 경우	동사원형+ed	enjoy – enjoy**ed** stay – stay**ed** spray – spray**ed** survey – survey**ed**

단모음+단자음으로
끝나는 경우
	동사원형+마지막
	자음+ed
		chat – chat**ted** grab – grab**bed**
		clap – clap**ped** stop – stop**ped**
		commit – commit**ted** refer – refer**red**
		
		cf. 강세가 앞에 있는 2음절 동사
		➡ 동사원형+ed
		  visit – visit**ed** offer – offer**ed**
		  enter – enter**ed**

정답 p.7

PRACTICE 1

다음 동사의 과거형을 쓰세요.

1 bow　　　– ______________________　　**2** accomplish – ______________________

3 affect　　– ______________________　　**4** declare　　– ______________________

5 chat　　　– ______________________　　**6** grab　　　– ______________________

7 aim　　　– ______________________　　**8** scratch　　– ______________________

9 tie　　　– ______________________　　**10** destroy　　– ______________________

11 soak　　– ______________________　　**12** envy　　　– ______________________

13 appoint – ______________________　　**14** design　　– ______________________

15 tap　　　– ______________________　　**16** attempt　　– ______________________

17 classify – ______________________　　**18** avoid　　　– ______________________

19 try	– __________		**20** dispatch	– __________
21 beg	– __________		**22** carry	– __________
23 download	– __________		**24** board	– __________
25 boil	– __________		**26** display	– __________
27 disturb	– __________		**28** dry	– __________
29 accept	– __________		**30** dye	– __________
31 bury	– __________		**32** buzz	– __________
33 challenge	– __________		**34** amount	– __________
35 defeat	– __________		**36** cherish	– __________
37 demand	– __________		**38** apply	– __________
39 assign	– __________		**40** clap	– __________
41 reunify	– __________		**42** snap	– __________
43 focus	– __________		**44** enroll	– __________
45 reply	– __________		**46** complain	– __________
47 perform	– __________		**48** attract	– __________
49 connect	– __________		**50** hum	– __________
51 establish	– __________		**52** inherit	– __________
53 gasp	– __________		**54** curl	– __________
55 succeed	– __________		**56** export	– __________
57 cough	– __________		**58** count	– __________
59 crawl	– __________		**60** regard	– __________
61 fry	– __________		**62** review	– __________
63 chew	– __________		**64** stir	– __________
65 hug	– __________		**66** conquer	– __________
67 control	– __________		**68** jog	– __________
69 weigh	– __________		**70** pardon	– __________
71 rip	– __________		**72** limit	– __________
73 mix	– __________		**74** occur	– __________
75 perch	– __________		**76** refund	– __________
77 permit	– __________		**78** sniff	– __________
79 copy	– __________		**80** publish	– __________

PSS 1-2 규칙 변화 과거형 동사의 발음

발음	용법
[t]	[t]음을 제외한 무성음으로 끝나면 [t]로 발음한다. ➡ establish**ed**, fix**ed**, ripp**ed**, guess**ed**, lock**ed**, touch**ed**
[d]	[d]음을 제외한 유성음으로 끝나면 [d]로 발음한다. ➡ bother**ed**, fulfill**ed**, maintain**ed**, refill**ed**, believ**ed**, hurri**ed**
[id]	[t], [d]음으로 끝나면 [id]로 발음한다. ➡ object**ed**, project**ed**, provid**ed**, want**ed**, need**ed**, nodd**ed**, add**ed**

정답 p.7

PRACTICE 2

〈보기〉와 같이 주어진 단어의 밑줄 친 부분의 발음으로 알맞은 것을 [t], [d], [id] 중에서 골라 쓰세요.

> 보 기   relax**ed** [t]   aim**ed** [d]   object**ed** [id]

1 bother**ed**	[	]	**2** scratch**ed**	[	]	**3** fulfill**ed**	[	]
4 maintain**ed**	[	]	**5** tapp**ed**	[	]	**6** nodd**ed**	[	]
7 dispatch**ed**	[	]	**8** connect**ed**	[	]	**9** believ**ed**	[	]
10 cherish**ed**	[	]	**11** review**ed**	[	]	**12** succeed**ed**	[	]
13 guess**ed**	[	]	**14** attempt**ed**	[	]	**15** copi**ed**	[	]
16 push**ed**	[	]	**17** count**ed**	[	]	**18** design**ed**	[	]
19 scrap**ed**	[	]	**20** project**ed**	[	]	**21** ripp**ed**	[	]
22 perch**ed**	[	]	**23** chatt**ed**	[	]	**24** lock**ed**	[	]
25 establish**ed**	[	]	**26** board**ed**	[	]	**27** gasp**ed**	[	]
28 dy**ed**	[	]	**29** classifi**ed**	[	]	**30** provid**ed**	[	]
31 furnish**ed**	[	]	**32** hurri**ed**	[	]	**33** committ**ed**	[	]
34 focus**ed**	[	]	**35** ti**ed**	[	]	**36** export**ed**	[	]
37 clapp**ed**	[	]	**38** refill**ed**	[	]	**39** mix**ed**	[	]
40 add**ed**	[	]	**41** print**ed**	[	]	**42** enroll**ed**	[	]
43 need**ed**	[	]	**44** soak**ed**	[	]	**45** want**ed**	[	]

PSS 1-3 불규칙 동사의 과거형과 과거분사형

원형	과거형	과거분사형	원형	과거형	과거분사형
arise	arose	arisen	bear	bore	born/borne
beat	beat	beaten	become	became	become
begin	began	begun	bend	bent	bent
bet	bet	bet	bite	bit	bitten
blow	blew	blown	break	broke	broken
bring	brought	brought	build	built	built
burst	burst	burst	buy	bought	bought
catch	caught	caught	choose	chose	chosen
come	came	come	cost	cost	cost
creep	crept	crept	cut	cut	cut
deal	dealt	dealt	dig	dug	dug
draw	drew	drawn	dream	dreamed/dreamt	dreamed/dreamt
drink	drank	drunk	drive	drove	driven
eat	ate	eaten	fall	fell	fallen
feed	fed	fed	feel	felt	felt
fight	fought	fought	find	found	found
fly	flew	flown	forget	forgot	forgotten
forgive	forgave	forgiven	freeze	froze	frozen
get	got	got(ten)	give	gave	given
grind	ground	ground	grow	grew	grown
hang	hung	hung	hide	hid	hidden
hit	hit	hit	hold	held	held
hurt	hurt	hurt	keep	kept	kept
kneel	knelt	knelt	know	knew	known
lay	laid	laid	lead	led	led
leave	left	left	lend	lent	lent
let	let	let	lie	lay	lain

원형	과거형	과거분사형	원형	과거형	과거분사형
lose	lost	lost	mean	meant	meant
meet	met	met	overcome	overcame	overcome
pay	paid	paid	put	put	put
quit	quit	quit	read	read	read
ride	rode	ridden	ring	rang	rung
rise	rose	risen	run	ran	run
sell	sold	sold	send	sent	sent
set	set	set	sew	sewed	sewn/sewed
shake	shook	shaken	shine	shone/shined	shone/shined
shoot	shot	shot	shrink	shrank	shrunk
sing	sang	sung	sink	sank	sunk
sit	sat	sat	sleep	slept	slept
sow	sowed	sown/sowed	speak	spoke	spoken
spend	spent	spent	spread	spread	spread
stand	stood	stood	steal	stole	stolen
stick	stuck	stuck	strike	struck	struck
sweep	swept	swept	swim	swam	swum
swing	swung	swung	take	took	taken
teach	taught	taught	tear	tore	torn
think	thought	thought	throw	threw	thrown
understand	understood	understood	wake	woke	woken
wear	wore	worn	weave	wove	wove(n)
weep	wept	wept	win	won	won
wind	wound	wound	write	wrote	written

PRACTICE 3

다음 불규칙 동사의 과거형과 과거분사형을 쓰세요.

원어민 발음 들어보기 ▶ 

CH 2 시제

1 begin	– ___ – ___		2 drink	– ___ – ___	
3 meet	– ___ – ___		4 deal	– ___ – ___	
5 creep	– ___ – ___		6 arise	– ___ – ___	
7 pay	– ___ – ___		8 bite	– ___ – ___	
9 lay	– ___ – ___		10 beat	– ___ – ___	
11 wear	– ___ – ___		12 dig	– ___ – ___	
13 build	– ___ – ___		14 cut	– ___ – ___	
15 send	– ___ – ___		16 bring	– ___ – ___	
17 fall	– ___ – ___		18 sell	– ___ – ___	
19 fly	– ___ – ___		20 sit	– ___ – ___	
21 buy	– ___ – ___		22 forget	– ___ – ___	
23 come	– ___ – ___		24 burst	– ___ – ___	
25 fight	– ___ – ___		26 bend	– ___ – ___	
27 shine	– ___ – ___		28 eat	– ___ – ___	
29 feed	– ___ – ___		30 drive	– ___ – ___	
31 kneel	– ___ – ___		32 sleep	– ___ – ___	
33 get	– ___ – ___		34 find	– ___ – ___	
35 cost	– ___ – ___		36 freeze	– ___ – ___	
37 grind	– ___ – ___		38 keep	– ___ – ___	
39 hurt	– ___ – ___		40 weave	– ___ – ___	
41 choose	– ___ – ___		42 forgive	– ___ – ___	
43 spread	– ___ – ___		44 hit	– ___ – ___	
45 hang	– ___ – ___		46 set	– ___ – ___	
47 ring	– ___ – ___		48 know	– ___ – ___	
49 lead	– ___ – ___		50 mean	– ___ – ___	

PSS 2 완료시제

PSS 2-1 현재완료시제

현재완료시제는 과거에 일어난 사건이 현재와 관련이 있음을 나타낼 때 쓴다. 과거의 한 시점에 발생하여 과거에 종료된 일로서 현재와의 관련성이 적을 때는 현재완료시제를 사용하지 않는다.

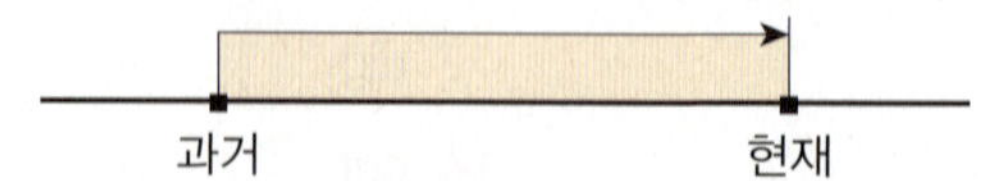

과거 ——————→ 현재

I / We / You / They	have	과거분사
He / She / It	has	

용법	예문	주로 함께 쓰이는 단어
완료	I **have finished** my homework **now**. 나는 지금 숙제를 끝마쳤다. He **has already eaten** breakfast. 그는 이미 아침을 먹었다.	already, yet, just, now
경험	I **have been** to the amusement park **twice**. 나는 놀이공원에 두 번 가 본 적이 있다. She **has never ridden** a horse. 그녀는 결코 말을 타본 적이 없다.	ever, never, before, often, sometimes, once, ~ times
결과	He **has left** for Hawaii. 그는 하와이로 떠났다. I **have lost** my keys again. 나는 내 열쇠를 또 잃어버렸다.	go, come, leave, lose, buy
계속	She **has lived** in Jejudo **for** 5 years. 그녀는 5년 동안 제주도에서 살아왔다. We **have been** friends **since** elementary school. 우리는 초등학교 이래로 (계속) 친구 사이이다.	for, since

PRACTICE 4

괄호 안에 주어진 단어를 이용하여 현재완료시제 문장을 완성하세요.

1 I ___________________________ them invitation cards for the violin concert. (send, already)

2 They ___________________ to Europe for their summer holidays. (go)

3 He ___________________ attending music festivals since 2021. (enjoy)

4 I ___________________________ the zoo in the city yet. (visit, not)

5 The boy ___________________ to the National Assembly Library. (be, never)

6 Jessica ___________________ some international chess contests. (win)

7 It ___________________ quite hard in the city for three days. (rain)

8 Susan and I ___________________________ at the park. (arrive, just)

9 ___________________ you ___________________ about the Mona Lisa before? (hear)

10 My parents ___________________ English at the middle school for 5 years. (teach)

PRACTICE 5

그림을 보고, 괄호 안에 주어진 단어를 이용하여 현재완료시제 문장을 완성하고, 각 문장의 용법을 쓰세요.

1 ___________________________ writing my science report yet. (I, not, finish) [   ]

2 ___________________________ in Tokyo, Japan for 3 years. (Ms. Kim, live) [   ]

3 ___________________________ pearl earrings at the department store for Jane. (he, buy) [   ]

4 ___________________________ since Monday. (My brother, sick) [   ]

5 ___________________________ lunch, so she doesn't want anything to eat. (Sally, already, have)

[   ]

6 ___________________________ each other before? (you, meet) [   ]

PSS 2-2 for와 since

1. **for** – '~ 동안'의 뜻으로 사건이 일어나 지속된 시간의 길이를 나타낸다.

   She started to study psychology two years ago. She still studies psychology.
   ➡ She **has studied** psychology **for** two years. 그녀는 2년 동안 심리학을 공부해 왔다.

2. **since** – '~ 이후로'의 뜻으로 사건이 시작된 시점을 나타낸다.

   I started to raise the pine trees in 2020. I still raise the pine trees.
   ➡ I **have raised** the pine trees **since** 2020. 나는 2020년 이후로 소나무를 길러 왔다.

   cf. 주절이 현재완료 시제이며 since가 접속사로 쓰일 경우, since가 이끄는 절은 과거시제를 쓴다.
   I have raised the pine trees **since** I **moved** to this town.
   나는 이 도시로 이사 온 이후로 소나무를 길러 왔다.

정답 p.8

PRACTICE 6

괄호 안에 주어진 단어를 이용하여 두 문장을 현재완료시제 문장으로 바꾸세요.

1 Jack checked in the hotel two weeks ago. He still stays at the hotel.

   ➡ ____ (for)

2 I began to compose songs seven years ago. I still compose songs.

   ➡ ____ (for)

3 Liz started to visit the nursing home three months ago. She still visits there.

   ➡ ____ (for)

4 My brother bought the laptop computer in 2021. He still has it.

   ➡ ____ (since)

5 We became friends when we were kids. We are still friends.

   ➡ ____ (since)

6 Mark started to play tennis in 2022. He still enjoys playing tennis.

   ➡ ____ (since)

7 She started painting landscapes five years ago. She still paints landscapes.

   ➡ ____ (for)

8 He started gardening last year. He still enjoys gardening.

   ➡ ____ (since)

현재완료	과거
1. 과거에 시작된 동작이나 상태가 현재와도 연관이 있음을 나타낸다. Mr. Brown **has worked** as a firefighter for fifteen years. (He still works as a firefighter.) Brown 씨는 15년간 소방관으로 일해 왔다. (그는 여전히 소방관으로서 일한다.)	1. 과거에 시작되어 과거에 종료된 동작이나 상태를 나타낸다. Mr. Brown **worked** as a firefighter for fifteen years. (He doesn't work as a firefighter anymore.) Brown 씨는 15년간 소방관으로 일했다. (그는 더 이상 소방관으로서 일하지 않는다.)

2. 과거의 불특정한 시점에 일어난 동작이나 상태를 나타낸다. 따라서 과거의 특정한 때를 나타내는 부사와는 함께 쓰지 않는다. She **has** already **gone** back to England. 그녀는 이미 영국으로 돌아갔다. **Have** you **visited** the temple in my town? 너는 나의 도시에 있는 사원을 방문한 적이 있니?	2. last ~, yesterday, ~ ago, When ~? 과 같이 과거의 특정한 때를 나타내는 부사와 함께 쓸 수 있다. She **went** back to England **yesterday**. 그녀는 어제 영국으로 돌아갔다. **When did** you **visit** the temple in my town? 너는 언제 나의 도시에 있는 사원을 방문했니?

PRACTICE 7

괄호 안에 들어갈 알맞은 말을 골라 동그라미 하세요.

1 Where (did you go, have you been) with your family last Sunday?

2 What time (did you meet, have you met) Mr. Jones the day before yesterday?

3 The weather (was, has been) very hot and humid lately.

4 When I (came, has come) back home last night, she (was, has been) sick in bed.

5 There (weren't, haven't been) any accidents on the new highway yet.

6 Susan (wasn't, hasn't been) in Paris in the summer of 2021.

7 You (helped, have helped) us a lot since you (joined, have joined) the club last month.

8 I (didn't speak, haven't spoken) to Patrick since last week, so I don't know what happened to him.

9 I (didn't drive, haven't driven) a truck before. This is my first time to drive a truck.

10 We (fell, have fallen) in love with each other when we first (met, have met) at the party.

PRACTICE 8

다음 밑줄 친 부분이 맞으면 ○, 틀리면 어법에 맞게 고쳐 쓰세요.

1 They <u>didn't find</u> a suitable apartment in the city yet.

➡ ______________________________

2 You <u>have grown</u> so much since last year that none of your old clothes fit anymore.

➡ ______________________________

3 He <u>felt</u> much healthier since he started exercising regularly last month.

➡ ______________________________

4 I <u>have baked</u> cookies at home last Sunday.

➡ ______________________________

5 She <u>improved</u> her English since she began taking online English classes last month.

➡ ______________________________

6 I <u>ate</u> breakfast an hour ago at the new café on the corner.

➡ ______________________________

7 Lana <u>played</u> the piano since she was six years old.

➡ ______________________________

8 The boy <u>has broken</u> his leg last weekend while playing soccer with his friends.

➡ ______________________________

PSS 2-4 현재완료 진행시제

현재완료 진행시제는 과거에 시작한 동작이 현재까지 계속되고 있다는 의미를 강조할 때 쓴다.

> **have/has+been+-ing**

It started raining three hours ago. It is still raining now.

3시간 전에 비가 오기 시작했다. 지금도 여전히 비가 내리고 있다.

➡ It **has been raining** for three hours.

3시간 동안 비가 내리고 있다.

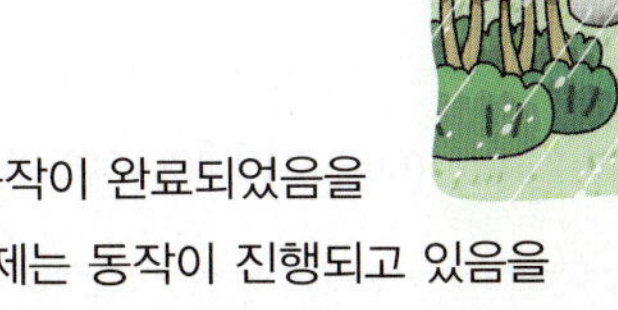

cf. 동작을 나타내는 동사의 현재완료시제는 동작이 완료되었음을
나타내기도 한다. 반면에, 현재완료 진행시제는 동작이 진행되고 있음을
강조한다.

James **has talked** to my son on the phone a few times.

James는 내 아들과 몇 번 전화로 이야기한 적이 있다.

(→ 그는 지금은 통화를 하고 있지 않다.)

James **has been talking** to my son on the phone
for twenty minutes.

James는 20분 동안 내 아들과 전화로 이야기하고 있다.

(→ 그는 지금도 통화를 하고 있다.)

정답 p.8

PRACTICE 9

괄호 안에 주어진 동사를 이용하여 현재완료 진행시제 문장을 완성하세요.

1 I ___________________ for tomorrow's English quiz since 11 o'clock. (study)

2 The boys ___________________ outside until now. (play)

3 I ___________________ forward to meeting you since last year. (look)

4 I ___________________ a sweater for her birthday present for an hour. (knit)

5 How long ___________ your friend ___________ your computer in your room? (fix)

6 Korean scientists ___________________ on spacecraft for many years. (work)

7 The environmental group ___________________ the government to ban the use of plastic
straws for a long time. (urge)

8 For centuries, Koreans ___________________ pots to store gimchi. (use)

9 More and more people ___________________ bills online. (receive)

10 She ___________________ from cancer since 2020. (suffer)

PRACTICE 10

주어진 두 문장을 for나 since 중 알맞은 것을 사용하여 현재완료 진행시제 문장으로 바꿔 쓰세요. (단, 밑줄 친 단어를 주어로 사용하세요.)

1 It began to snow 30 minutes ago. It is still snowing.
   ➡ ____

2 Mr. Harmon moved to Korea six months ago. He is still living in Korea.
   ➡ ____

3 Mom began writing novels when she was 28 years old. She is still writing them.
   ➡ ____

4 The boys started to plant trees and flowers at noon. They are still planting them.
   ➡ ____

5 My dad started to build a model plane three hours ago. He is still building it.
   ➡ ____

6 Jina began teaching Korean in China two years ago. She is still teaching Korean there.
   ➡ ____

7 Stuart and I started to play soccer at 2 o'clock. We are still playing soccer.
   ➡ ____

PSS 2-5 진행형을 쓰지 않는 동사

상태를 나타내는 동사는 진행형으로 쓰지 않는다.

소유	have, own, belong
감정	admire, like, love, prefer, hate, respect, want, wish, need
인식	appreciate, believe, forget, know, remember, think, understand, realize
감각	see, smell, taste, hear, feel
기타	seem, appear, consist, contain, keep, continue

This house **belongs** to Mr. Lee. 이 집은 Lee 씨의 소유이다.
She **wants** to buy a diamond necklace. 그녀는 다이아몬드 목걸이를 사기를 원한다.
I don't **know** how to use this machine. 나는 이 기계를 어떻게 쓰는지 알지 못한다.
The food **smells** very delicious. 그 음식은 매우 맛있는 냄새가 난다.
This book **consists** of 18 chapters. 이 책은 18장으로 이루어져 있다.

> **cf.** 위의 동사들이 동작을 나타내는 의미로 쓰일 경우에는 진행형을 쓸 수 있다.
>
> She **was having** lunch with him. (○) 그녀는 그와 함께 점심을 먹고 있었다.
>
> He is having a car. (×) He **has** a car. (○) 그는 차를 갖고 있다.
>
> The judges **are tasting** Jack's dishes. (○) 심사위원들이 Jack의 요리를 맛보고 있다.
>
> The cake is tasting sweet. (×) The cake **tastes** sweet. (○) 그 케이크는 달콤한 맛이 난다.
>
> I **am thinking** about emigrating to Singapore. (○)
>
> 나는 싱가포르로 이민을 가는 것에 대해 생각하고 있다.
>
> He is thinking math is boring. (×) He **thinks** math is boring. (○)
>
> 그는 수학이 지루하다고 생각한다.

정답 p.9

PRACTICE 11

괄호 안에 들어갈 알맞은 말을 골라 동그라미 하세요.

1   Mark (respects, is respecting) his homeroom teacher the most.

2   He (plays, is playing) basketball with his two friends in the backyard now.

3   Junho (has read, was reading) a magazine when I visited him.

4   I (know, am knowing) your cellphone number. It is 010-555-7777, right?

5   I (admire, am admiring) all her efforts to help poor people.

6   She (has slept, was sleeping) when I called her last night.

7   That (sounds, is sounding) good. Let's go to the stadium as fast as possible.

8   Did you finish the movie? What (do you think, are you thinking) about it?

9   I (prefer, am preferring) to sit at the back of the car.

10   (Do you have, Are you having) an umbrella with you?

11   I (don't understand, am not understanding) the reason why he suddenly left the party.

12   Jason (smelled, was smelling) some flowers in the flower shop when I saw him.

13   I'm really bored with my job. I (think, am thinking) about getting a new job right now.

14   My new classmate Sandy always (appears, is appearing) very quiet and shy.

15   This school (consists, is consisting) of three buildings and a playground.

16   This book (belongs, is belonging) to Martha.

17   I (was believing, believed) his lies for years.

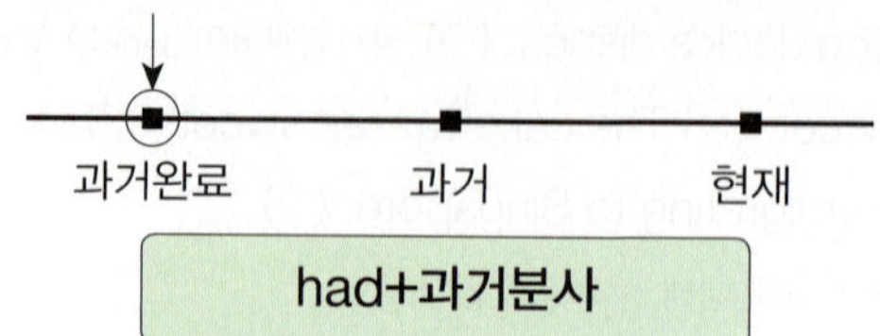

PSS 2-6 과거완료시제

과거의 어느 시점을 기준으로 그 이전에 일어난 동작이나 상태를 나타낸다.

Our team **had** already **left** when I got to the terminal.
내가 터미널에 도착했을 때 우리 팀은 (그 전에) 벌써 떠났다.
He cherished the watch that his grandfather **had given** him.
그는 그의 할아버지가 주신 시계를 소중히 여겼다.

cf. before, after와 같이 시간의 앞뒤 순서를 분명하게 알 수 있는 접속사가 있을 때는 과거시제
를 써서 과거완료시제를 대신할 수 있다.
Cathy **had** often **gone** fishing **before** she moved to Seoul.
Cathy는 서울로 이사 가기 전에는 종종 낚시하러 가곤 했었다.
➡ Cathy often **went** fishing **before** she moved to Seoul.

정답 p.9

PRACTICE 12

괄호 안에 주어진 동사를 이용하여 빈칸을 과거시제 또는 과거완료시제 중 알맞은 것으로 채우세요.

1 The package arrived after my parents ________________ out for work. (go)

2 She lost the ring I ________________ to her on her birthday. (give)

3 I remember the person who I ________________ at last week's dance party. (meet)

4 I couldn't date the girl because I ________________ all my money last Saturday. (spend)

5 They ________________ the restaurant before I got there. (already, leave)

6 He ________________ a chef of the restaurant two years after he started to work. (become)

7 Mr. Park ________________ English for 30 years when I met him again. (teach)

8 My younger brother had an upset stomach after he ________________ too much. (eat)

9 Lisa couldn't work because she ________________ her contact lenses. (lose)

10 The driver tried to stop the car when he ________________ a strange object in the middle of the road. (see)

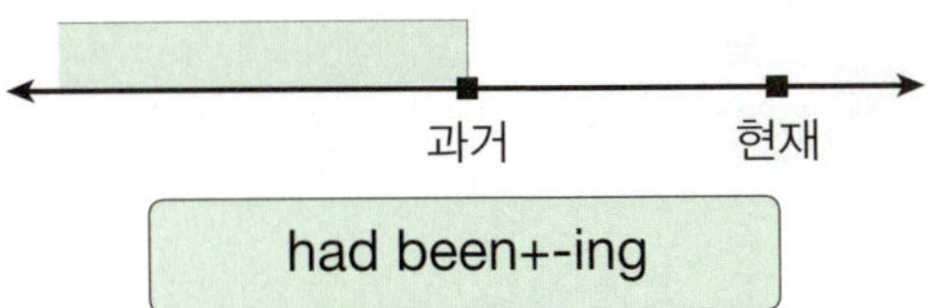

PSS 2-7 과거완료 진행시제

과거의 어느 시점을 기준으로 그 이전에 진행 중이었던 동작을 강조할 때 쓴다.

과거　　현재

had been+-ing

Mary didn't show up until 2 o'clock. I **had been waiting** for thirty minutes by then.

Mary는 2시가 되어서야 나타났다. 나는 그때까지 30분 동안 기다리고 있었다.

He **had been writing** fairy tales for 5 years when his wife had her first book published.

그의 아내가 그녀의 첫 번째 책을 출간했을 때, 그는 5년간 동화를 계속 써 온 상태였다.

I **had been standing** for over an hour before the meeting started.

그 회의가 시작되기 전에 나는 한 시간 넘게 서 있었다.

정답 p.9

PRACTICE 13 [1-4]

그림을 보고, 괄호 안에 주어진 동사를 이용하여 과거완료 진행시제 문장을 완성하세요.

1 
I _________________ for hours when my parents came home. (read)

2 
We _________________ soccer for two hours when Hana came to us. (play)

3 
She _________________ a letter from him for a long time. Finally she got it. (expect)

4

It _________________________ before the snow was piled up. (snow)

정답 p.9

PRACTICE 14

괄호 안에 들어갈 알맞은 말을 골라 동그라미 하세요.

1   Sam (has played, played) baseball since he was an elementary school student.

2   The girl (has been watching, had been watching) TV since her parents went out.

3   After they (have been walking, had been walking) for a day, they finally found an oasis.

4   I don't know which of them is Mike. I (haven't met, didn't meet) either of them before.

5   The two teams (have already finished, had already finished) the match before I got to the stadium.

6   I (have been trying, had been trying) to solve the problem for an hour, but I can't get the answer yet.

7   Mrs. Dillan went to the school to pick up her son, but he wasn't there. He (has left, had left) for home.

8   My son got back home at 11 o'clock in the evening. I (have been waiting, had been waiting) for him for over two hours.

9   What time (have you handed, did you hand) in the report to the math teacher yesterday?

10 Mr. Park's line (has been, was) busy when the customer tried to talk with him several times.

11 Julia (hasn't got, hadn't been getting) along with her classmates before she moved to London.

12 I (have locked, had locked) the door after hearing a noise before I went to bed.

13 I (have stayed, had stayed) in this apartment since Jimmy moved out.

14 Mom (has been cooking, had been cooking) since you called her.

15 By the time the concert began, many of the people (has been standing, had been standing) in line for hours.

16 The baby had a high fever last night. She (hasn't eaten, hadn't eaten) anything until now.

17 The police (have been looking, had been looking) for the thief for a week before they caught him.

PSS 3 미래시제

---

1. will – 강한 의지나 계획되지 않은 단순한 미래에 대해 말할 때

   I **will** come to see you more often. 나는 너를 보러 더 자주 올 것이다.

2. be going to – 미래의 계획이나 예정

   I **am going to** see a movie with Jane this Sunday.
   나는 이번 주 일요일에 Jane과 영화를 볼 것이다.

3. 현재진행형 – 미래를 나타내는 부사(tomorrow, tonight, this weekend)와 함께 쓰여 가까운 미래의 계획

   Mike **is leaving** for America tomorrow. Mike는 내일 미국으로 떠날 것이다.

   cf. 시간, 조건의 부사절에서는 현재시제가 미래시제를 대신한다.
   When I **see** him tomorrow, I **will give** him your message.
   내가 내일 그를 보면, 그에게 너의 메시지를 전해 줄게.

정답 p.9

PRACTICE 15

괄호 안의 말을 이용하여 B의 대답을 완성하세요.

1 A: What will you buy for Susan's birthday?
   B: I ________________________ for her. (buy, a necklace)

2 A: What is Susan doing this weekend?
   B: She ________________________ with her friends this weekend. (throw, a party)

3 A: What are you going to do next Monday?
   B: I ________________________ . (have, a piano lesson)

4 A: What will he do to improve his English?
   B: He ________________________ . (keep, a diary, in English)

5 A: What are you doing next Saturday?
   B: I ________________________ . (eat out, with my family)

6 A: What are you going to do during the winter vacation?
   B: I ________________________ at a nursing home. (do, volunteer work)

7 A: What are we going to do this Wednesday?
   B: We ________________________ . (have, a picnic)

1 두 문장의 뜻이 같도록 빈칸을 채울 때 가장 알맞은 것은?

> • He left for London, so he is not here now.
>   = He ＿＿＿＿＿＿＿ for London.

① leaves　　② is leaving　　③ has left
④ had left　　⑤ has been leaving

2 Which is correct for the blank?

> I am a freshman in college, and I am majoring in piano. Since I was a six-year-old child, I ＿＿＿＿＿ in playing the piano. My dream is to become a world-famous pianist.

① had been interested
② had been interesting
③ have been interested
④ have been interesting
⑤ am interested

3 다음 중 어법이 바른 문장의 개수는?

> • The class had already started before we got there.
> • I have seen a shooting star just a minute ago.
> • After a long conversation, I realized that my brother had disappeared.
> • Ms. Jackson has been teaching English for almost ten years.

① 없음　　② 1개　　③ 2개
④ 3개　　⑤ 4개

4 괄호 안의 단어를 이용하여, 주어진 〈조건〉에 맞도록 다음 문장을 완성하세요.

> | 조 건 | 1. 반드시 현재완료 진행형을 사용할 것 |
> | | 2. 빈칸에 맞게 다섯 단어로 쓸 것 |

> • 그는 5년 동안 거기서 일을 해오고 있다. (work)
>   ➡ ＿＿＿＿ ＿＿＿＿
>   ＿＿＿＿ ＿＿＿＿ for five years.

5 〈보기〉를 참고하여 주어진 두 문장을 한 문장으로 영작하세요.

> | 보 기 |
> • It started to rain three hours ago.
> • It is still raining.
> → It has been raining for three hours.

> • We started to discuss the issue an hour ago.
> • We're still discussing it.

➡ ＿＿＿＿＿＿＿＿＿＿

6 〈보기〉의 밑줄 친 부분과 그 용법이 같은 것은?

> | 보 기 | John has lost his guitar case.

① I have never driven a car before.
② Have you heard about his bicycle accident?
③ They have already finished cleaning the classroom.
④ He has gone to Mexico on a business trip.
⑤ It has been two years since she sent me the last email.

7 우리말에 맞게 주어진 단어를 바르게 배열하세요.

> Tom은 그곳에 가는 도중에 그의 차가 고장 났었기 때문에 수업에 늦었다.
> (had, was, his, class, late, down, broken, car, because, for)

➡ Tom ______________________________________
______________________________ on the way there.

8 다음 문장에 대한 설명으로 **틀린** 것은?

> By the time they reached the beach, the sun had set.

① The sun had already set before they reached the beach.
② They must have enjoyed the sunset since they got to the beach.
③ After the sun had set, they reached the beach.
④ They couldn't enjoy the sunset when they reached the beach.
⑤ As they got to the beach, the sun had set some time earlier.

9 〈보기〉의 밑줄 친 부분과 용법이 같은 것은?

> 보 기 | I <u>have been</u> to Hawaii twice with my family.

① I <u>have lost</u> my necklace during my trip.
② She <u>has</u> just <u>called</u> you to make an appointment.
③ She <u>has been</u> absent from school for five days.
④ I <u>have</u> never <u>tasted</u> such delicious kimchi.
⑤ I <u>have</u> already <u>finished</u> my homework.

10 ⓐ~ⓔ 중 틀린 것을 찾아 <u>바르게</u> 고친 사람은?

> ⓐ She has waited for him for an hour when he called her.
> ⓑ I have had this dog since it was born.
> ⓒ All the artworks in the gallery are belonging to his family.
> ⓓ They concluded which method was better after the experiment was over.
> ⓔ They are leaving for Busan tomorrow morning.

① 정원: ⓐ는 그가 전화를 걸었을 때까지 그녀가 계속 기다리고 있었다는 의미이기 때문에 현재완료 진행 시제를 써서 has been waiting이라고 수정해야 해.
② 서윤: ⓑ는 시제 일치를 위해 since it was born을 since it has been born으로 고쳐야 해.
③ 세현: ⓒ에서 '소유'를 의미하는 belong은 진행형으로 쓸 수 없기 때문에 are belonging을 belong으로 써야 해.
④ 하은: ⓓ에서 결론을 내린 것보다 실험이 끝난 것이 더 먼저 일어난 일이기 때문에 after the experiment was over를 after the experiment had been over로 고치는 것이 문법적으로 맞아.
⑤ 동민: ⓔ는 내일 아침에 일어날 일이기 때문에 They are leaving을 They will leave로 쓰는 것이 맞아.

11 빈칸에 들어갈 말이 차례대로 짝지어진 것은?

> I ______________ my sister the book this morning, which I ______________ three weeks before.

① give – have bought
② give – was buying
③ gave – had bought
④ gave – have bought
⑤ have given – had bought

12 ⓐ~ⓔ 중 어색한 표현을 모두 고르세요.

> *A*: Jenny, ⓐ <u>you look gorgeous today!</u>
> *B*: Thanks! ⓑ <u>I had my hair cutting yesterday.</u>
> *A*: Oh, which hair salon did you go to?
> *B*: Kelly's Hair. ⓒ <u>I have been there three times, including yesterday.</u>
> *A*: ⓓ <u>I will go there next week, then.</u> ⓔ <u>It's really difficult to find a good hair stylist, hasn't it?</u>

① ⓐ   ② ⓑ   ③ ⓒ
④ ⓓ   ⑤ ⓔ

13 다음 중 밑줄 친 부분의 쓰임이 잘못된 것은?

① She <u>was having</u> dinner when I visited her yesterday.
② The rotten tomato in the refrigerator <u>smells</u> bad.
③ I <u>have been respecting</u> him since my school days.
④ They <u>admired</u> him for his courageous challenge.
⑤ The farmers <u>were tasting</u> the first wine of the year.

14 다음 중 어법상 어색한 문장은?

① He had read that book once before the teacher assigned it in class.
② I have never seen a film that moved me as deeply as this one.
③ They had been studying for hours when the power went out.
④ He has saved the document before the computer crashed.
⑤ She has been writing fantasy novels for over ten years.

15 두 문장의 뜻이 같도록 빈칸을 채울 때 가장 알맞은 것은?

> • She is going to take him to the airport tonight.
> = She _______________ him to the airport tonight.

① took   ② is taking   ③ has taken
④ had taken   ⑤ will be taken

16 다음 중 옳은 문장은?

① When have you left for America?
② He has eaten three bananas five minutes ago.
③ They have started studying English in 2022.
④ I have found the treasure yesterday.
⑤ She has been working for IBM since 2020.

17 다음 중 어법상 올바른 문장을 모두 고른 것은?

> ⓐ Kevin has just completed his leg workout for the day.
> ⓑ For our project, we have succeeded in researching what kinds of dinosaurs lived in the Jurassic period.
> ⓒ I haven't already made up my mind.
> ⓓ He has seen every one of director Claire's movies.
> ⓔ Tim has played for that soccer team since three years.
> ⓕ A group of tourists have finished the museum tour.
> ⓖ My mother has been using her phone since over 10 years.

① ⓐ, ⓑ, ⓖ   ② ⓐ, ⓑ, ⓓ
③ ⓑ, ⓔ, ⓖ   ④ ⓐ, ⓒ, ⓓ, ⓕ
⑤ ⓑ, ⓓ, ⓔ, ⓕ

18 다음 빈칸 (A), (B)에 들어갈 말로 알맞게 짝지어진 것은?

> I _______(A)_______ on a business trip last week. I was worried about my pets at home. Fortunately, my sister _______(B)_______ them when I was out of town.

	(A)	(B)
①	have gone	has taken care of
②	went	have taken care of
③	have been	was taking care of
④	have gone	took care of
⑤	went	took care of

19 다음 중 밑줄 친 부분의 쓰임이 올바른 것은?

① I <u>have never been</u> to foreign countries when I was a child.

② She <u>has already finished</u> the homework 5 minutes ago.

③ The price <u>has been</u> going up by 10% lately.

④ He <u>has often visited</u> the bookstore until last month, when it shut down.

⑤ He <u>has stayed</u> at his uncle's house last night.

20 다음 우리말을 참고하여 괄호 안에 주어진 동사를 알맞은 형태로 바꾸어 빈칸에 쓰세요.

> • 그 소년은 드디어 그의 할머니가 그에게 특별한 약초에 대해 말씀하셨던 것을 기억했다.
> = The boy finally remembered that his grandmother _______________ him about a special herb. (tell)

21 밑줄 친 ⓐ~ⓔ 중 어법에 맞게 고친 것은?

> A large ship began pulling away from the dock, ⓐ <u>head</u> out toward the open ocean. The ship had only been sailing for a short time when there was a loud bang. Some of the ⓑ <u>startle</u> passengers rushed to the deck. Flames burst from one side of the vessel. Operators at the harbor heard the captain ⓒ <u>said</u>, "I'm turning back!" Then one more explosion followed. Soon after, the ship ⓓ <u>is disappeared</u> from the port's tracking systems. By the time the police reached the scene, half of the ship ⓔ <u>has already sunk</u> beneath the waves.

① ⓐ head → headed

② ⓑ startle → startling

③ ⓒ said → to say

④ ⓓ is disappeared → was disappeared

⑤ ⓔ has already sunk → had already sunk

22 다음 주어진 두 문장의 시간 순서에 유의하여 빈칸에 알맞은 말을 넣어 한 문장으로 완성하세요.

> • Jenny left her pencil case at school.
> • Later, she realized it.

➡ Jenny realized that _______ _______ _______ _______ _______ _______ at school.

23 다음 중 밑줄 친 부분의 쓰임이 잘못된 것은?

① We <u>have been stuck</u> in a traffic jam.

② The dog <u>has been ill</u> since last night.

③ The pond <u>has frozen</u> for a week.

④ It <u>has been taking</u> me five hours to get here.

⑤ I'm glad that your dream <u>has come</u> true.

24 괄호 안에 주어진 동사를 알맞은 형태로 바꾸어 빈칸에 쓰세요.

> I came to know that my classmates misunderstood that Mary ___________ ___________ the money. (steal)

25 다음 글의 ⓐ～ⓒ에 들어갈 표현이 바르게 짝지어진 것은?

> In 1901, the American inventor Willis H. Carrier _____ⓐ_____ what can be called the first modern air conditioner. He built it to control the temperature and humidity of a printing plant. Thanks to the device, the paper and ink _____ⓑ_____ maintained in good condition. His invention was very successful. So later, he _____ⓒ_____ the Carrier Air Conditioning Company of America, a company that specialized in heating, ventilating, and air conditioning.

	ⓐ	ⓑ	ⓒ
①	has invented	were	founded
②	invented	were	found
③	has invented	was	found
④	invented	were	founded
⑤	invented	was	was founded

26 다음 중 어법상 맞는 문장을 <u>모두</u> 고르세요.

① This bag is belonging to my mother.
② They were having dinner in a nice restaurant.
③ I am wanting to know the truth.
④ The committee is consisting of 10 members.
⑤ She was thinking about her next plan.

27 다음 빈칸 ⓐ,ⓑ에 들어갈 말로 알맞게 짝지어진 것은?

> _____ⓐ_____ the company manufactured its first car in 1955, Korea _____ⓑ_____ to be one of the largest automobile producers in the world.

	ⓐ	ⓑ
①	For	grew
②	For	has grown
③	Since	grew
④	Since	will grow
⑤	Since	has grown

28 다음 괄호 ⓐ～ⓒ에 들어갈 말을 알맞게 짝지은 것은?

> The patient ⓐ(suffered / has suffered) from diabetes ⓑ(since / for) several years and is ⓒ(considered / considering) an early retirement.

	ⓐ	ⓑ	ⓒ
①	has suffered	for	considering
②	has suffered	for	considered
③	has suffered	since	considering
④	suffered	for	considered
⑤	suffered	since	considered

29 다음 중 어법상 <u>어색한</u> 문장은?

① I've decided to learn Spanish.
② She has never seen such a cute dog.
③ How have you been?
④ Everybody said they have failed.
⑤ I didn't know that he had asked me a question.

CHAPTER 3
조동사

조동사: **be**동사와 일반동사를 도와주며 의미(능력, 허가, 요청, 추측, 제안, 의무, 충고 등)를 더해 준다.

① 뒤에 항상 동사원형이 온다.　　　　　You **must wear** a helmet.

② 주어의 수나 인칭의 영향을 받지 않아 형태가 변하지 않는다.

He cans speak English. (X)　　　　He **can** speak English. (O)

③ 한번에 하나만 사용되며, 두 개 이상을 연속해서 쓸 수 없다.

I will can ride a bike. (X)　　　　I **will be able to** ride a bike. (O)

④ 부정문: 조동사 바로 뒤에 not을 붙인다.　　　I **will not** give up.

　　의문문: 문장 맨 앞에 조동사가 나온다.　　**May** I ask a question?

Problem Solving Skill	페이지	성취도				
		100%	99~75%	74~50%	49~25%	24~0%
PSS 1 do	52					
PSS 2 can, could Ⅰ	53					
PSS 3 can, could Ⅱ	54					
PSS 4 must Ⅰ	56					
PSS 5 must Ⅱ	57					
PSS 6 may, might	59					
PSS 7 will, would	61					
PSS 8 should, ought to, had better	62					
PSS 9 used to, would	64					
PSS 10 조동사+have+과거분사	65					
중간·기말고사 대비문제	67					

PSS 1 do

1. 일반동사의 의문문과 부정문에 쓰인다.

    Do you think that our team will win this time? 너는 우리 팀이 이번에 이길 것이라고 생각하니?
    I **do** not know which I should choose. 나는 어떤 것을 선택해야 할지 모른다.

2. 앞에 있는 문장이나 절에 나온 동사 또는 동사구의 반복을 피하기 위해 쓰이는 대동사의 역할을 한다. 단, 일반동사에 한해서만 대신할 수 있다.

    I think you should go to see a doctor. – I already **did**. (did = went to see a doctor)
    너는 의사를 만나러 가야 할 것 같아.   벌써 만나 봤어.

    cf. So do I. (I do, too.) 나도 그래. / Neither do I. (I don't, either.) 나도 그렇지 않아.
    I like soccer very much. – **So do I.**
    나는 축구를 매우 좋아해.   나도 그래.
    I don't think he's a good leader. – **Neither do I.**
    나는 그가 좋은 지도자라고 생각하지 않아.   나도 그렇게 생각하지 않아.

3. 동사의 의미를 강조하기 위해 쓰인다.

    Honesty **does pay**. 정직함은 정말로 제값을 한다.
    You **do have** a warm-hearted mind. 너는 정말로 따뜻한 마음을 가졌어.
    My mom **did live** in the city a few years ago. 우리 엄마는 몇 년 전에 정말로 그 도시에 사셨다.

정답 p.12

PRACTICE 1

do를 알맞은 형태로 바꾸어 빈칸을 채우세요.

1 ___________ that mean something to you?

2 I saw Miyoung in the library. – So ___________ I.

3 James runs faster than Mark ___________ .

4 I think you should visit Mr. Kim. – I already ___________ .

5 I ___________ not want to meet him again.

6 They climbed the mountain just as we ___________ before.

7 I speak English as fluently as he ___________ .

8 Jihoon doesn't work hard. – Neither ___________ Giho.

9 We thought they were going to visit Vietnam, but they ___________ .

PRACTICE 2

주어진 문장의 밑줄 친 부분을 do를 이용한 강조 용법으로 바꾸어 빈칸에 쓰세요.

1 I <u>met</u> him in the stadium. ➡ I ________________ him in the stadium.

2 I <u>think</u> he is right. ➡ I ________________ he is right.

3 Matthew <u>looks</u> like a real prince. ➡ Matthew ________________ like a real prince.

4 I <u>hope</u> he can come home soon. ➡ I ________________ he can come home soon.

5 <u>Tell</u> me the truth. ➡ ________________ me the truth.

6 He <u>taught</u> English. ➡ He ________________ English.

7 My father <u>loves</u> me very much. ➡ My father ________________ me very much.

8 She <u>goes</u> abroad once or twice a year. ➡ She ________________ abroad once or twice a year.

PSS 2 can, could I

PROBLEM SOLVING SKILL

능력 (~할 수 있다)	과거	We **could** finish these cartoons 6 months later. 우리는 6개월 후에 이 만화를 끝낼 수 있었다. = We **were able to** finish these cartoons 6 months later.
	현재	My sister **can** speak English and Chinese. 나의 누이는 영어와 중국어를 말할 수 있다. = My sister **is able to** speak English and Chinese.
	미래	Jenny **can** get the license next month. Jenny는 다음 달에 자격증을 딸 수 있다. = Jenny **will be able to** get the license next month. *cf.* 조동사끼리는 나란히 쓸 수 없다. Jenny **will can** get the license next month. (×)

PRACTICE 3

be able to를 이용하여 짝지어진 두 문장의 의미가 같도록 빈칸을 채우세요.

1 Mike can speak four languages now.

= Mike ________________________ four languages now.

2 He could ride a horse when he was young.

= He ________________________ a horse when he was young.

3 The twins couldn't play the violin then.

= The twins ________________________ the violin then.

4 You can drive a car when you grow up.

= You ________________________ a car when you grow up.

5 He couldn't solve any problems at all.

= He ________________________ any problems at all.

6 I can't see him from next month.

= I ________________________ him from next month.

7 Susan couldn't join the club.

= Susan ________________________ the club.

8 I can manage the situation by myself for now.

= I ________________________ the situation by myself for now.

9 I can't find out the difference.

= I ________________________ out the difference.

10 They can't change their decision next week.

= They ________________________ their decision next week.

PSS 3 can, could Ⅱ

| 허락 | ~해도 된다 | You **can** leave now if you want.
원한다면 너는 지금 떠나도 된다. |
| | ~해도 되겠습니까? | **Can I** ask you a favor? 부탁을 드려도 될까요?
Could I borrow your handkerchief?
제가 당신의 손수건을 빌려도 될까요?

cf. Could I ~?가 Can I ~?보다 더 공손한 표현이다. |

요청	~해 주시겠습니까?	**Can you** water the flowers for me? 나 대신 그 꽃들에 물을 주겠니? **Could you** remove it before he comes? 그가 오기 전에 그것을 제거해 주시겠습니까? *cf.* Could you ~?가 Can you ~?보다 더 공손한 표현이다.
추측	과연 ~일까?	**Can** it be possible? 과연 그것이 가능할까?
	~일 리가 없다	She **can't** be a doctor. 그녀가 의사일 리가 없다.
가능성	~할 가능성이 있다	This problem **can[could]** happen again. 이 문제는 다시 발생할 가능성이 있다. *cf.* could는 can보다 불확실한 가능성을 나타낸다.

정답 p.12

PRACTICE 4

〈보기〉에서 알맞은 단어를 고른 다음, can이나 could 또는 can't와 함께 사용하여 문장을 완성하세요.

보 기	drink be work carry affect know see help be tell

1 _____________ this _____________ real?

2 I'm so thirsty. _____________ I _____________ this juice?

3 Her performance was terrible. She _____________ _____________ a pianist.

4 You _____________ _____________ this story to anyone. I don't care.

5 _____________ this machine _____________ again?

6 This bag is too heavy. _____________ you _____________ it for me?

7 _____________ I _____________ your report for a while?

8 He _____________ _____________ about the surprise party tomorrow. Nobody told him about it.

9 This _____________ _____________ you succeed in losing weight.

10 Lack of sleep _____________ _____________ the quality of your daily life.

PSS 4 must I

의무 · 필요 (~해야 한다, ~해야 할 필요가 있다)	과거	They **had to** find evidence to prove it. 그들은 그것을 증명하기 위해 증거를 찾아야 했다. *cf.* 조동사끼리는 나란히 쓸 수 없다. They **did must** find evidence to prove it. (×)
	현재	You **must** cancel the meeting by tomorrow. 너는 내일까지 그 회의를 취소해야 한다. = You **have to** cancel the meeting by tomorrow.
	미래	I **must** wear a mask when I go out tomorrow. 내일 밖에 나갈 때 나는 마스크를 써야 할 것이다. = I **will have to** wear a mask when I go out tomorrow. = I **have to** wear a mask when I go out tomorrow. *cf.* 조동사끼리는 나란히 쓸 수 없다. I **will must** wear a mask when I go out tomorrow. (×)

정답 p.12

PRACTICE 5

괄호 안에 들어갈 알맞은 말을 골라 동그라미 하세요.

1 You (must, have, had) to eat more fresh vegetables and fruit from now on.

2 I will (must, have, had) to read the book until I totally understand it.

3 Jisu (must, has, had) to get home before her dad arrived.

4 He (must, has, had) register his motorcycle to take part in the race.

5 They will (must, have, had) to prepare for the presentation by the end of the day.

6 The mayor (must, has, had) to apologize in public last night.

7 You (must, have, had) get on the plane by 9:30.

8 We (must, have, had) tell him what everyone thinks about his new plan.

9 He will (must, have, has) to take care of everything by himself.

10 The Johnsons (must, has, had) to help Sujin look for her purse.

PRACTICE 6

괄호 안의 단어와 have to를 이용하여 빈칸을 채우세요.(단, have to는 알맞은 형태로 변형해야 합니다.)

1 We found that it was already 2 o'clock. We ___________________ to the office. (return)

2 The alarm clock ___________________ to the correct time before you sleep. Then you can wake up on time. (be set)

3 You ___________________ the fact that they always take care of you and help you. (appreciate)

4 Mr. and Mrs. White ___________________ back to their country in a month. (go)

5 The lawyer will come here to ask you several questions. You ___________________ that you're innocent then. (prove)

6 Yesterday, the class finished earlier than expected. Amy and Liz ___________________ until their mom came to pick them up. (wait)

PSS 5 must Ⅱ

추측	(~임에 틀림없다)	He **must** be warm-hearted like his father. 그는 그의 아버지처럼 마음이 따뜻함이 틀림없다. ⟺ He **can't** be warm-hearted like his father. 그는 그의 아버지처럼 마음이 따뜻할 리가 없다. ***cf.*** 「can't + 동사원형」은 '~일 리가 없다'의 뜻으로 강한 부정의 추측을 나타낸다.
부정	금지 (~해서는 안 된다)	You **must not** cheat in exams. 너는 시험에서 부정 행위를 해서는 안 된다. We **must not** miss this great opportunity. 우리는 이 좋은 기회를 놓쳐서는 안 된다.
	불필요 (~할 필요가 없다)	He **doesn't have to** take off his shoes here. 그는 여기에서 그의 신발을 벗을 필요가 없다. = He **need not** take off his shoes here. (O) He needs not take off his shoes here. (X) ***cf.*** need not은 조동사이므로 주어가 3인칭 단수일 때 needs not으로 쓰지 않음에 유의한다.

PRACTICE 7

그림을 보고, must 또는 can't 중 알맞은 것을 괄호 안의 단어와 함께 써서 문장을 완성하세요.

1 
2 
3 

4 
5 
6 

1 My father is bald just like my grandfather. It ________________ genetic. (be)

2 He doesn't seem to understand what the woman is talking about. He ______________ Chinese. (speak)

3 I just saw David eating at a restaurant with his friends. He _______________ sick in bed now. (be)

4 Every time Jiyoung sees Minho, her face turns red. She _______________ him a lot. (like)

5 Mr. Jung stayed up all night talking with his foreign clients on the phone. He _______________ exhausted. (feel)

6 If I grow my mustache and wear sunglasses, she _______________ me. (recognize)

PRACTICE 8

〈보기〉에서 알맞은 단어를 골라 must not 또는 don't / doesn't have to를 이용하여 빈칸을 채우세요.

보 기	climb	happen	make	be	speak	pretend
	drive	tell	take	eat	go	

1 You ___________________________ without a license. It's illegal.

2 I ___________________________ there early. He's going to be about an hour late.

3 This kind of accident ___________________________ again.

4 You ___________________________ a lie to your parents. You should always be honest with them.

5 Bill will be given three days to think about it. He ___________________________ a decision now.

6 The cold was finally gone. I ___________________________ these pills anymore.

7 You ___________________________ a word about this to anybody. It's a secret.

8 You ___________________________ that you like the food. I understand because it's my first time
   to make it.

9 Yesterday, I promised I would be on time, so I ___________________________ late today.

10 There is an elevator in the building, so Susan ___________________________ the stairs.

11 I ___________________________ too much. I'm supposed to be on a diet.

PSS 6 may, might

추측	~일지도 모른다, 아마 ~일 것이다	This method **may** help you save some money. 이 방법은 아마 당신이 돈을 절약하는 것을 도와줄 것이다. She **may** not be at school now. 그녀는 지금 학교에 없을지도 모른다. You **might** not totally understand his lecture. 너는 그의 강의를 완전히 이해하지 못할지도 모른다. *cf.* might는 may보다 불확실한 추측을 나타낸다. He **might** be able to help you make the cake. 그는 아마 네가 케이크를 만드는 것을 도와줄 수 있을 것이다.
허가	~해도 좋다	You **may** do as you wish. 너는 네가 바라는 대로 해도 좋다. **May** I borrow your cellphone? 네 휴대폰 좀 빌려도 될까? – Yes, you **may**. 응, 그래. – No, you **may not**. 아니, 그럴 수 없어. – No, you **must not**. 아니, 안 돼. *cf.* must not이 may not보다 더 강한 금지의 표현이다.

PRACTICE 9

〈보기〉에서 알맞은 단어를 골라 may 또는 might를 이용하여 대화를 완성하세요.

보 기	visit not, come ask have not, be break

1 A: Where are you going to stay during the vacation?

B: I don't know. I ___________________ my cousin's in Thailand.

2 A: Can you finish it by yourself in time?

B: I'm not sure. I ___________________ Mina for help tonight.

3 A: Did you hear the rumor about Sam? I can't believe it.

B: I can't, either. It ___________________ true.

4 A: I'm worried that we left the kids alone at home.

B: Me, too. They ___________________ something while we're away.

5 A: I heard that Bill got a bad cold.

B: I heard that, too. He ___________________ to our party tomorrow.

6 A: I don't have a hat to wear to the beach for our field trip.

B: Ask Minji. She ___________________ an extra one.

PRACTICE 10

괄호 안에 들어갈 알맞은 조동사를 골라 동그라미 하세요.

1 May I go to the bathroom? – Yes, you (may, will).

2 Good morning, sir. (May, Must) I see your passport and ticket?

3 Where did she go? – I'm not sure, but she (does, might) be at her dad's office.

4 Jason might (be able to, can) play the guitar better than I do.

5 May I have the last piece of pie? – No, you (may, must not). We need to leave it for Dad.

6 I don't believe what he said. It (can't, must) be true.

7 Christine doesn't always show up on time. We might (can, have to) wait for another thirty minutes.

8 (Do, Could) I watch the soccer match on TV with some of my friends?

9 He (could, would) manage it instead of me, but he didn't want to.

10 Don't worry. You (must not, don't have to) do it right away.

PSS 7 will, would

Will[Would] you ~?	~해 주시겠습니까?	Will you ~?보다 Would you ~?가 더 공손한 표현이다. **Will you** taste this soup? 이 수프 맛 좀 봐 주시겠어요? **Would you** mind repeating that part? 그 부분을 반복해 주시겠습니까?
would like+명사	~을 원하다	**I'd like a cheeseburger**. 저는 치즈버거를 원해요. = I **want** a cheeseburger. **Would** you **like something** to drink? 마실 것을 원하니? = Do you **want** something to drink?
would like to +동사원형	~을 하고 싶다	**I'd like to thank** you for helping us. 우리를 도와준 것에 대해 당신에게 감사하고 싶어요. = I **want to** thank you for helping us. **Would** you **like to leave** a message? 메시지를 남기고 싶으세요? = Do you **want to** leave a message?
would rather +동사원형	차라리 ~하는 편이 낫다	**I'd rather wait** and **see** him. 나는 차라리 기다렸다가 그를 만나 보는 편이 낫겠다. 부정형은 would rather not이다. **I'd rather not go** out tonight. 나는 오늘 밤에 나가지 않는 편이 낫겠다. ***cf.*** would rather A than B 'B 하느니 차라리 A 하겠다' **I'd rather stay** at home **than go** out in this cold weather. 나는 이런 추운 날씨에 나가느니 차라리 집에 있겠다.

정답 p.13

PRACTICE 11 [1-18]

괄호 안에 들어갈 알맞은 조동사를 골라 동그라미 하세요.

1 I (will, would) rather look for ways to get out of here than just be sitting here.

2 (Will, Would) you like some biscuits before dinner?

3 Will you (can, be able to) go to the movies with me?

4 (Will, May) you wrap each of the boxes separately?

5 He didn't make even a single goal. He (must, can't) be a professional player.

6 I (will, would) like to exchange this skirt for a smaller one.

7 James (do, does) work at the British Embassy.

8 You (must not, don't have to) turn left here. You can only go straight or turn right.

9 I (will, would) like a cup of coffee with a piece of chocolate cake.

10 A: My daughter doesn't eat breakfast. – B: Neither (do, does) my daughter.

11 I'm sorry, but (would, do) you help me finish this report?

12 What (could, would) you like to be in the future?

13 You will (have to, must) remain silent until the teacher comes back.

14 I (will, would) rather bake cookies by myself than buy them at the store.

15 Mike (did, does) cry when he saw you walk out of the gate at the airport.

16 Tell Jane about your problem. She might (can, be able to) help you.

17 You (must not, don't have to) be a good player to enjoy soccer.

18 I left before the end of class. I (had to, would) get home early.

PSS 8 should, ought to, had better

should / ought to	의무 (~해야 한다)	should와 ought to는 도덕적인 책임이나 의무에 대한 충고를 나타낸다. You **should[ought to]** take good care of your dog until he gets better. 너는 네 강아지가 나아질 때까지 잘 돌보아야 한다. You **should not[ought not to]** ignore people who need help. 너는 도움을 필요로 하는 사람들을 외면하지 말아야 한다.
	가능성 (~일 것이다)	My son **should[ought to]** come back home in a few minutes. 내 아들은 몇 분 후에 집에 돌아올 것이다.
had better	충고 · 권유 (~하는 게 낫다)	had better는 should나 ought to와 비슷하지만 더 강한 어조의 표현으로, 주로 'd better로 줄여서 쓴다. Your health is getting worse. You**'d better** cut down on fatty food. 네 건강이 점점 더 악화되고 있다. 너는 기름진 음식을 줄이는 게 좋겠다. You**'d better not** take the medicine. 너는 그 약을 먹지 않는 게 낫다.

PRACTICE 12

〈보기〉에서 알맞은 말을 고른 다음, should 또는 ought to와 함께 사용하여 빈칸을 채우세요. (단, 필요한 경우 부정문으로 쓰세요.)

보 기	reply watch warn be tell listen apply apologize cross go

1 You missed the question again. You ___________________ carefully to what the teacher says.

2 I sent Mark an email yesterday. He ___________________ to it by Monday.

3 Minji always has difficulty getting up early. She ___________________ to bed late.

4 Traffic signals must be observed. You ___________________ the road when the traffic light is green.

5 Bob still often breaks our rule. We ___________________ him one more time.

6 Why don't you check out the kitchen? There ___________________ scissors somewhere.

7 Do you remember that you ___________________ for the job by April 2nd?

8 You watch TV all the time. You ___________________ TV so much.

9 Cathy is very angry at me. I ___________________ to her right away.

10 You ___________________ this secret to anybody.

PRACTICE 13

〈보기〉에서 알맞은 말을 고른 다음, 'd better 또는 'd better not과 함께 사용하여 빈칸을 채우세요.

보 기	overeat stay lose renew be think go sit

1 You ___________________ your driver's license before it gets expired.

2 The manager has been watching you these days. You ___________________ late for this conference.

3 A lot of rich companies will support our team. We ___________________ this great chance.

4 The bench has just been painted. You ___________________ on it.

5 Since a snowstorm has been forecasted, you ___________________ at home.

6 I had a stomachache after I went to the buffet restaurant. I ___________________ anymore.

7 She ___________________ about looking for another job if she's not satisfied with it.

8 The film starts in 20 minutes. You ___________________ now or you'll be late.

PSS 9　used to, would

1. used to와 would는 '～하곤 했다'의 뜻으로 과거에 반복적으로 일어났던 행위를 나타낸다.

   I went to play golf every weekend before, but I don't anymore.
   나는 전에는 주말마다 골프를 치러 갔었지만, 더 이상은 아니다.
   ➡ I **used to** go to play golf every weekend. 나는 주말마다 골프를 치러 가곤 했다.
   ➡ I **would** go to play golf every weekend. 나는 주말마다 골프를 치러 가곤 했다.

   Tom fought with his brother over food before, but he doesn't anymore.
   Tom은 전에는 그의 남동생과 음식을 가지고 싸웠지만, 더 이상은 아니다.
   ➡ Tom **used to** fight with his brother over food. Tom은 그의 남동생과 음식을 가지고 싸우곤 했다.
   ➡ Tom **would** fight with his brother over food. Tom은 그의 남동생과 음식을 가지고 싸우곤 했다.

2. 행위가 아닌 과거의 상태를 나타낼 때는 used to를 사용한다.

   I lived in Thailand when I was young, but I live in Korea now.
   나는 어렸을 때 태국에 살았지만 지금은 한국에 산다.
   ➡ I **used to** live in Thailand when I was young. 나는 어렸을 때 태국에 살았었다.
   ➡ I **would** live in Thailand when I was young. (×)

   cf. used to의 부정형은 didn't use to 또는 used not to이다.
   I **didn't use to[used not to] like** eggplant when I was younger, but now I love it. 나는 어렸을 때 가지를 좋아하지 않았지만, 지금은 그것을 아주 좋아한다.

정답 p.14

PRACTICE 14

괄호 안의 단어와 used to 또는 would를 이용하여 문장을 완성하세요.

1　I _________________ rope in the front yard when I was a little boy. (jump)

2　My sister _________________ afraid of pigeons flying over her head. (be)

3　I _________________ up early to deliver newspapers. (wake)

4　There _________________ a stream flowing by my house. (be)

5　She _________________ looking out the window when it rained. (like)

6　I _________________ my entire weekend experimenting in the lab. (spend)

7　Jina _________________ long straight hair when she was a middle school student. (have)

8　We _________________ on the rooftop to see the stars at night. (gather)

9 My brother _____________________ behind the curtain when he played hide-and-seek. (hide)

10 Mr. Jackson _____________________ happy while he was painting. (feel)

PSS 10 조동사＋have＋과거분사

should have +과거분사	～했어야 했다	You **should have defended** yourself in the first place. 너는 처음부터 네 자신을 방어했어야 했다. You **should not have scolded** him so severely. 너는 그를 그렇게 심하게 꾸짖지 말았어야 했다.
must have +과거분사	～였음에 틀림없다	He looks tired. He **must have stayed** up all night. 그는 피곤해 보인다. 그는 밤을 꼬박 새운 것이 틀림없다. You **must have been** so happy to see the actor. 넌 그 배우를 봐서 정말 행복했음에 틀림없다.
may have +과거분사	～했을지도 모른다	At least 5,000 people **may have been killed** during the war. 최소한 5,000명의 사람들이 그 전쟁 중에 죽었을지도 모른다. John **may have forgotten** the appointment with the doctor. John은 의사와의 약속을 잊었을지도 모른다.
cannot have +과거분사	～했을 리가 없다	She **can't have been** more than 15 years old at that time. 그녀가 그 당시에 15살이 넘었을 리 없다. My puppy **cannot have eaten** all the food on the table. 내 강아지가 테이블 위에 있던 모든 음식을 먹었을 리가 없다.

정답 p.14

PRACTICE 15 [1-6]

우리말에 맞게 주어진 단어를 이용하여 문장을 완성하세요.

1 지난밤에 비가 많이 왔음에 틀림없다.

➡ It _____________________ a lot last night. (rain)

2 너는 Jenny에 대해 많은 것을 들었을지도 모른다.

➡ You ________________________ many things about Jenny. (hear)

3 너는 그런 말을 하기 전에 두 번 생각했어야 했다.

➡ You ________________________ twice before you said such a thing. (think)

4 너는 그런 상황에서 즐거웠을 리가 없다.

➡ You ________________________ fun in that situation. (have)

5 그는 수업 중에 휴대폰을 사용하지 말았어야 했다.

➡ He ________________________ his cell phone in class. (use)

6 그녀는 그곳에 비행기를 타고 가지 않았을지도 모른다.

➡ She ________________________ there by plane. (go)

정답 p.14

PRACTICE 16

괄호 안에 들어갈 알맞은 조동사를 골라 동그라미 하세요.

1 The mother and the daughter haven't met for a year. They (must, should) have missed each other so much.

2 The broken computer is now working all right. Namsu (must, should) have fixed it without telling you.

3 Sean is such a calm and cautious person. He (cannot, may) have made such a big mistake.

4 They were supposed to get here an hour ago, but they didn't. They (should, must) have missed the first train for this town.

5 The kids were at home all day long with me. They (cannot, must) have gone there.

6 Dad was so excited to hear that Minji would come back today. He (may, can't) have already left for the airport to pick her up.

7 It was so dry and there was no light in this room. The flowers (can, should) not have survived in this environment.

8 Bob looked very sad and unhappy when I saw him. You (can, should) not have made a fool of him.

9 The manager wasn't at his desk all afternoon. He (may, can't) have left work early.

10 I've worn this just once so far. I (shouldn't, must) have bought such an expensive dress.

11 Susan didn't know that Tom would also come to the meeting. She (cannot, must) have been embarrassed by his sudden appearance.

12 I saw that Bill was cheating during the test. Mr. Kim (cannot, should) have seen that and warned him.

13 I wonder why you are so late. You (must, should) have been here two hours ago.

중간·기말고사 대비문제 📝

1 다음 중 밑줄 친 do 동사의 쓰임이 나머지 넷과 다른 것은?

① She <u>does</u> need a change right now.
② I <u>did</u> go to the English camp last winter.
③ I <u>did</u> taste the same food that astronauts eat.
④ Last summer in New York, I <u>did</u> meet the actor.
⑤ You would look silly if you <u>did</u> this again.

2 문장의 해석이 옳지 <u>않은</u> 것은?

① Do I have to finish this report today?
(제가 오늘 이 보고서를 끝내야 하나요?)
② She should visit her grandparents more often.
(그녀는 그녀의 조부모님을 더 자주 방문해야 한다.)
③ You must not enter this building without permission.
(당신은 허락 없이 이 건물에 들어가면 안 된다.)
④ They need not prepare any food for the picnic.
(그들은 소풍을 위해 어떤 음식도 준비하지 말아야 한다.)
⑤ You don't have to work on Sundays.
(당신은 일요일에 일할 필요가 없다.)

3 다음 밑줄 친 부분을 바르게 고치세요.

Misa won first prize in the singing contest. She <u>must have not practice</u> hard.

➡ ______________________________

4 다음 우리말과 같은 뜻이 되도록 괄호 안에 주어진 말을 바르게 배열하세요.

• 나는 혼자 요리를 하느니 차라리 외식을 하겠다.
= I ______________________________
______________________________ cook
for myself. (would rather, eat, than, out)

5 주어진 문장의 밑줄 친 부분과 쓰임이 같은 것을 있는 대로 고른 것은?

They climbed the mountain just as we <u>did</u> before.

ⓐ <u>Does</u> Tom have a good idea to share?
ⓑ We <u>did</u> not expect to succeed in business.
ⓒ I <u>do</u> believe you can make it.
ⓓ Amy runs better than her sister <u>does</u>.
ⓔ My son sings well as I <u>did</u> when I was young.

① ⓐ, ⓑ   ② ⓓ, ⓔ   ③ ⓐ, ⓑ, ⓒ
④ ⓐ, ⓓ, ⓔ   ⑤ ⓑ, ⓒ, ⓓ, ⓔ

6 주어진 우리말과 같은 뜻이 되도록 빈칸에 알맞은 말을 쓰세요.

• 당신은 당신의 불확실한 미래에 대해 걱정할 필요가 없다.
= You __________ __________ __________
worry about your uncertain future.

7 다음 문장의 밑줄 친 <u>must</u>를 보고, 표의 알맞은 칸에 해당하는 기호를 쓰세요.

ⓐ You <u>must</u> do what I told you to do right now.
ⓑ Every student <u>must</u> learn to play at least two musical instruments.
ⓒ Look at that basketball player. He <u>must</u> be 2 meters tall.
ⓓ We <u>must</u> look for food, clothes, and a shelter to survive here.
ⓔ The fans <u>must</u> be excited when they see the superstar.
ⓕ To protect the crops from the hurricane, the farmers <u>must</u> do their best.

추측	(1)
의무	(2)

8 빈칸에 들어갈 말로 알맞은 것은?

A lot of foreigners come to Korea to work these days. So you ___________ meet them at any moment, especially in Seoul.

① must
② may
③ can't
④ need to
⑤ had better

9 밑줄 친 단어의 쓰임이 나머지 넷과 <u>다른</u> 것은?

① It <u>can't</u> be true that he did survive in the end.
② They <u>couldn't</u> find the secret of the temple.
③ I <u>can</u> help you learn to deal with this hard situation.
④ The young girl <u>could</u> get to the destination by herself.
⑤ I wonder if animals <u>can</u> think.

10 다음 우리말과 같은 뜻이 되도록 괄호 안에 주어진 단어를 변형하여 알맞게 영작하세요. (단, 6단어여야 함.)

A: It's getting cold. Do you have a jacket?
B: No, I don't. ___________

____

(나는 재킷을 가져왔어야 했어.)
(bring)

11 다음 중 어법상 <u>어색한</u> 문장은?

① You will have to go to Korea in the near future.
② They will not just do what they are told to do.
③ Will you can go to the concert next Saturday with me?
④ That will be my third experience to an unknown world.
⑤ The customers will be able to buy the new product next month.

12 주어진 우리말과 같은 뜻이 되도록 빈칸을 채울 때 알맞은 말은?

• 우리는 10년 동안 이 마을에서 함께 살아왔기 때문에 나는 너를 돕고 싶다.
= I ___________ you since we have been living together in this village for 10 years.

① would to help
② would like help
③ would like helping
④ would like to help
⑤ would like to helping

13 다음 주어진 상황에서 영주가 할 질문으로 적절한 것은?

> Young-ju is out at the park, taking a walk, when she sees a cute dog passing by. Immediately, she feels like taking pictures with the dog. So, she wants to ask the dog owner if she may do that or not.

① Are you interested in taking pictures with me?
② May I take pictures with your dog?
③ Do you enjoy walking your dog?
④ How often do you go for walks?
⑤ Do you mind if I pet your dog?

14 다음 중 어법상 <u>어색한</u> 문장은?

① I don't know how long I will have to stay in this room.
② You had better go there more than once a month.
③ You don't have to bringing that many books for a three-day trip.
④ We are going to make some friends on the Web.
⑤ You should not be afraid of starting something new.

15 주어진 우리말과 같은 뜻이 되도록 빈칸을 채울 때 알맞은 말은?

> • 너는 그 낯선 사람의 조언에 따르지 않는 것이 낫다.
> = You ___________ follow the stranger's advice.

① had not better
② not had better
③ had better not
④ don't had better
⑤ don't have better

16 다음 중 어법상 <u>틀린</u> 문장의 개수는?

> ⓐ He needs not pack thick clothes for the trip.
> ⓑ You had not better ignore what he said about the deadline.
> ⓒ Jake did contributed a lot of time and energy to organizing the event.
> ⓓ She must have changed the recipe for the dish since it tasted different.
> ⓔ He used to fear speaking in public, but now he's confident.
> ⓕ They should have considered the potential risks, but they didn't.

① 1개　② 2개　③ 3개　④ 4개　⑤ 5개

17 다음 밑줄 친 부분과 그 쓰임이 같은 것은?

> This physical training <u>does</u> help increase the students' concentration.

① Where <u>do</u> you think they sell the products?
② He plays the computer game better than I <u>do</u>.
③ When you go jogging, you <u>do</u> run fast.
④ Never put off until tomorrow what you can <u>do</u> today.
⑤ Those who <u>do</u> not take enough nutrition are not likely to be healthy.

18 빈칸에 들어갈 말로 알맞은 것은?

> • 나의 부모님이 집을 비우실 때면, 조부모님께서 나를 돌봐주시곤 했다.
> = When my parents were away, my grandparents ________ take care of me.

① had
② could
③ would
④ might
⑤ should

19 대화를 읽고, 그림을 참고하여 빈칸에 들어갈 충고의 말을 완성하세요.

조 건 | 'had better'를 포함할 것

Jane: Oh, my bus is leaving!

Insu : You should wait another twenty minutes.

Jane: No, the movie will start soon.
What should I do?

Insu : You __________ __________

__________ __________ __________ .

20 우리말을 참고하여 주어진 〈조건〉에 맞도록 문장을 완성하세요.

조 건 | 1. used to와 like를 포함할 것.
(필요시 형태를 변형시킬 것.)
2. 5단어로 쓸 것.

• 우리가 학교에 다닐 때는 내가 그를 별로 좋아하지 않았다.

= I __________

__________ much when we

were at school.

21 괄호 안에 주어진 단어를 바르게 배열하여 문장을 만드세요.

I think __________

__________ to be happy.

(don't, be, we, rich, have, to)

22 다음 우리말과 같은 뜻이 되도록 괄호 안에 주어진 말을 바르게 배열하세요.

• 그 와인과 함께 치즈를 드시겠습니까?

= __________

____

(you, like, with that wine, would, some cheese)

23 다음 밑줄 친 may의 의미가 <u>다른</u> 하나는?

① She <u>may</u> join us for dinner tonight.

② This book <u>may</u> help you understand the topic better.

③ He hasn't answered my calls, so he <u>may</u> be busy.

④ You <u>may</u> not use your phone during the exam.

⑤ The weather <u>may</u> get warmer next week.

24 다음 빈칸에 들어갈 말로 가장 알맞은 것은?

Steve: Look at that! A man rescued a child from the water.

Mina: Wow, it is not easy to do that.

____

① He should be a good swimmer.

② He must be a good swimmer.

③ He had better be a good swimmer.

④ He needs to be a good swimmer.

⑤ He would rather be a good swimmer.

25 주어진 우리말과 같은 뜻이 되도록 빈칸을 채울 때 알맞은 말은?

- 그는 회의에 참석하지 않았다. 그는 바빴음에 틀림없다.

  = He didn't take part in the meeting. He _____________ busy.

① could have been
② should have been
③ must have been
④ cannot have been
⑤ would have been

26 주어진 문장에 대한 추측 또는 설명이 <u>틀린</u> 것은?

He should have brought an umbrella to stay dry.

① He experienced problems due to getting wet in the rain.
② He didn't get wet because he had remembered to bring his umbrella.
③ A different action in the past could have resulted in a more positive outcome.
④ It suggests a sense of regret that bringing an umbrella would have kept him dry.
⑤ Bringing an umbrella would have been a better course of action, as it would have kept him from getting wet.

27 빈칸에 들어갈 말로 알맞은 것은?

A: What was this place like about twenty years ago?
B: Well, there _____________ be only factories and empty fields.

① could
② would
③ might
④ should
⑤ used to

28 주어진 우리말과 같은 뜻이 되도록 빈칸을 채울 때 알맞은 말은?

- 어떤 사람은 건강한 유전자를 물려받았을지도 모르나 나쁜 습관은 그 또는 그녀의 건강을 나쁘게 할 수도 있다.

  = A person _____________ inherited healthy genes, but a bad habit may ruin his or her health.

① have
② must have
③ should have
④ may have
⑤ will have

29 주어진 우리말과 같은 뜻이 되도록 빈칸에 알맞은 말을 쓰세요.

- 당신이 가수가 되고 싶어 한다고 들었어요. 우선, 가수가 되기 위해서는 노래를 잘할 수 있어야 해요.

  = I heard that you want to be a singer. First of all, you should _____________ _____________ _____________ sing well in order to become a singer.

30 주어진 대화의 밑줄 친 (A)와 그 쓰임이 같은 것은?

Luke : There are a lot of fancy shoes in that store.
Jenny: But they (A) <u>must</u> be quite expensive.

① We <u>must</u> see the movie.
② You <u>must</u> keep quiet in the library.
③ You <u>must</u> practice the piano every day.
④ He <u>must</u> be very popular all over the world.
⑤ They <u>must</u> arrive early in order to find a seat.

31 두 문장이 같은 뜻이 되도록 빈칸을 채울 때 가장 알맞은 것은?

> It is possible that Brian told her the truth.
> = Brian _________ told her the truth.

① may
② may have
③ cannot have
④ should have
⑤ may not have

32 주어진 우리말과 같은 뜻이 되도록 빈칸에 알맞은 말을 쓰세요. (단, 3단어로 쓸 것.)

> A: He couldn't stand the noise any longer.
> B: ______________________________
>   (나도 그럴 수 없었어.)

33 짝지어진 대화 중 자연스러운 것은?

① A: I'm so tired. I spent five hours in the gym exercising.
　 B: Well, you should have exercised so much.
② A: I hope I can do well on my piano contest tomorrow.
　 B: You must not have practiced after school.
③ A: Sally is trying to lose weight these days.
　 B: She should eat snacks late at night.
④ A: I cannot believe that Jason talked behind my back.
　 B: Jason is honest and kind. He cannot have done such a thing.
⑤ A: The ground is so dry that it has deep cracks in it.
　 B: It must have rained for a long time.

34 주어진 문장에 대한 추측 또는 설명이 <u>틀린</u> 것은?

> He should have arrived at the airport earlier to avoid long lines.

① It expresses regret for what had already happened to him.
② As he didn't arrive early enough at the airport, he waited in long lines.
③ If he had arrived at the airport earlier, he could have avoided long lines.
④ Arriving early at the airport would have been a better way to help him avoid long lines.
⑤ Even if he had come to the airport early, he couldn't have avoided long lines.

35 빈칸 (a)～(d) 중 어느 곳에도 들어갈 수 <u>없는</u> 것은?

> W: Did you hear that Kate Jane, the teenage pop star will take part __(a)__ this year's pop concert? I'm so excited that I __(b)__ see her perform live!
> M: Yeah, I __(c)__ hear that. I love her voice and her songs! But I'm more excited about Ethan Murray. He's my favorite pop singer.
> W: We __(d)__ get tickets for the show and watch it live.
> M: I'll look it up on the Internet right now.

① did
② should
③ can
④ in
⑤ does

CHAPTER 4
수동태

Problem Solving Skill	페이지	성취도				
		100%	99~75%	74~50%	49~25%	24~0%
PSS 1 조동사가 있는 수동태	74					
PSS 2 진행형의 수동태	75					
PSS 3 완료형의 수동태	76					
PSS 4 4형식 문장의 수동태	77					
PSS 5 5형식 문장의 수동태 I	79					
PSS 6 5형식 문장의 수동태 II	80					
PSS 7 동사구의 수동태	81					
PSS 8 It is ~ that …	82					
PSS 9 수동태의 관용 표현	84					
중간·기말고사 대비문제	86					

PSS 1 조동사가 있는 수동태

조동사가 있는 수동태는 다음과 같은 어순으로 쓴다.

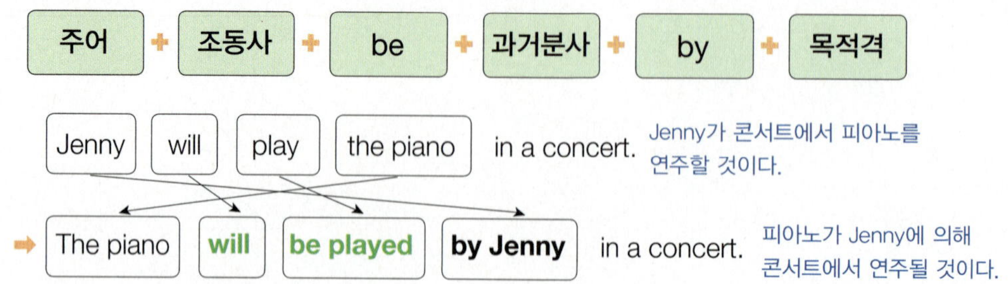

cf. 행위의 주체가 일반인이거나 말하지 않아도 알 수 있는 경우, 또는 굳이 언급할 필요가 없을 때는 「by+목적격」을 생략할 수 있다.

We can plant these flowers next to the spring. 우리는 이 꽃들을 옹달샘 옆에 심을 수 있다.

➡ These flowers **can be planted** next to the spring **(by us)**.

이 꽃들은 옹달샘 옆에 심어질 수 있다.

정답 p.17

PRACTICE 1

다음 능동태 문장을 수동태 문장으로 바꾸어 쓰세요.

1 The manager may accept my proposal.

➡ ____

2 Brian must send an e-mail in advance.

➡ ____

3 Her natural beauty might attract them.

➡ ____

4 You should not forget the deadline for reports.

➡ ____

5 The women ought to clean all the hotel rooms.

➡ ____

6 You can't copy other people's design concepts.

➡ ____

7 They will remember him as a good leader.

➡ ____

8 His words could break her heart.

➡ ____

9 She will perform a piece of music.

➡ ____

10 The two boys must keep this secret forever.

➡ ____

PSS 2 진행형의 수동태

진행형의 수동태는 다음과 같은 어순으로 쓴다.

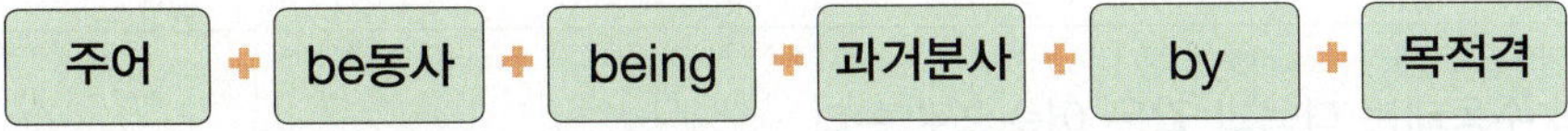

My friends are making a model of the house. 내 친구들이 그 집의 모형을 만들고 있다.

➡ A model of the house **is being made** by my friends.

그 집의 모형이 내 친구들에 의해 만들어지고 있다.

They were building a small cottage. 그들은 작은 오두막집을 짓고 있었다.

➡ A small cottage **was being built**. 작은 오두막집이 지어지고 있었다.

정답 p.17

PRACTICE 2 [1-10]

다음 능동태 문장을 수동태 문장으로 바꾸어 쓰세요.

1 James was catching a lot of fish in the lake.

➡ ____

2 My daughter was cleaning the refrigerator.

➡ ____

3 People are polluting the air and water.

➡ ____

4 The kids were painting the walls of the doghouse.

➡ ____

5 Mr. Jones is developing a new business.

➡ ____

6 Dad is repairing the car in the garage.

➡ ____

7 Kate is washing the dirty plates and bowls.

➡ ____

8 Bob and Paul were selling used books at the flea market.

➡ ____

9 He was preparing dinner for his wife and children.

➡ ____

10 The police are investigating the shooting incident.

➡ ____

PSS 3 완료형의 수동태

완료형의 수동태는 다음과 같은 어순으로 쓴다.

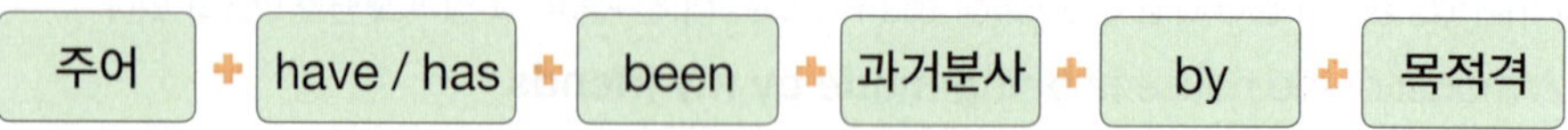

The young man has created the games. 그 젊은 남자가 그 게임들을 만들어왔다.

➡ The games **have been created** by the young man.

그 게임들은 그 젊은 남자에 의해 만들어져 왔다.

Politicians have used the information from the lawyer.

정치인들은 그 변호사에게서 얻은 정보를 써 왔다.

➡ The information from the lawyer **has been used** by politicians.

그 변호사에게서 얻은 정보가 정치인들에 의해 쓰여져 왔다.

정답 p.17

PRACTICE 3

다음 문장이 능동태이면 수동태로, 수동태이면 능동태로 바꾸어 쓰세요.

1 A famous artist has painted her family portrait.

➡ ____

2 Cheating has never been accepted by the school.

➡ ____

3 Paul has composed songs for five years.

➡ ____

4 The school has held a graduation party in December.

➡ ____

5 A free lunch for senior citizens has been provided by the government.

➡ ____

6 I have used this app since last month.

➡ ____

7 The park has preserved a lot of endangered animals for several years.

➡ ____

8 The director has postponed the performance several times.

➡ ____

9 The kindergarten teachers have been helped by the volunteers.

➡ ____

10 The servants have been treated cruelly by the master.

➡ ____

PSS 4 4형식 문장의 수동태

4형식은 간접목적어와 직접목적어 둘 다를 수동태의 주어로 쓸 수 있지만, 주로 사람을 나타내는 간접목적어를 주어로 하는 경우가 많다. 직접목적어가 수동태의 주어가 되는 경우에는 간접목적어 앞에 to, for, of와 같은 전치사를 써 주어야 한다.

to＋간접목적어	give, lend, send, show, teach, tell, write, pay, sell, offer
for＋간접목적어	buy, do, find, get, make, cook, choose
of＋간접목적어	ask

Julie gave me some exciting work. Julie는 내게 어떤 재미있는 일을 주었다.

➡ **I was given** some exciting work by Julie. 나는 Julie에게 어떤 재미있는 일을 받았다.

➡ **Some exciting work was given to me** by Julie.

어떤 재미있는 일이 Julie에 의해 내게 주어졌다.

The boy asked them the direction to the station. 그 소년은 그들에게 역으로 가는 방향을 물었다.

➡ **They were asked** the direction to the station by the boy.

그들은 그 소년에 의해 역으로 가는 방향을 질문받았다.

➡ **The direction to the station was asked of them** by the boy.

역으로 가는 방향이 그 소년에 의해 그들에게 물어졌다.

cf. 직접목적어만을 수동태의 주어로 쓰는 동사 – buy, write, get, cook, make, choose, find

I bought my brother an expensive shirt. 나는 내 남동생에게 비싼 셔츠를 사 주었다.

➡ **An expensive shirt was bought for my brother** by me. (O)

비싼 셔츠가 나에 의해 내 남동생에게 사서 주어졌다.

My brother was bought an expensive shirt by me. (X)

PRACTICE 4

다음 능동태 문장을 두 가지의 수동태 문장으로 바꾸어 쓰세요. (단, 한 가지만 되는 경우도 있습니다.)

1 They showed me the sales result of their department.

➡ _I was shown the sales result of their department by them._

➡ _The sales result of their department was shown to me by them._

2 My brother taught me English grammar.

➡ ____

➡ ____

3 Dad bought my sister a new laptop.

➡ ____

➡ ____

4 I didn't ask him such stupid questions.

➡ ____

➡ ____

5 She told her students surprising news about black holes.

➡ ____

➡ ____

6 She found me a nice hotel.

➡ ____

➡ ____

7 The villa owner lent those visitors the rooms.

➡ ____

➡ ____

8 She gave me an honest opinion.

➡ ____

➡ ____

9 His professor offered him a good internship program.

➡ ____

➡ ____

10 My grandfather will make me a wooden boat.

➡ ____

➡ ____

PSS 5 5형식 문장의 수동태 Ⅰ

5형식 능동태 문장을 수동태 문장으로 전환할 때 목적격 보어인 형용사, 분사, 명사, to부정사는 「be동사+과거분사」 뒤에 그대로 이어서 쓴다.

His announcement made all of us happy. 그의 발표는 우리 모두를 행복하게 만들었다.

➡ All of us **were made happy** by his announcement.

Sally and I saw some boys swimming in the river.

Sally와 나는 몇몇 소년들이 강에서 수영하고 있는 것을 보았다.

➡ Some boys **were seen swimming** in the river by Sally and me.

They elected him chairman. 그들은 그를 의장으로 선출했다.

➡ He **was elected chairman**.

Her mom didn't allow her to go out late at night.

그녀의 엄마는 그녀가 밤 늦게 밖에 나가는 것을 허락하지 않았다.

➡ She **wasn't allowed to go** out late at night by her mom.

정답 p.18

PRACTICE 5 [1-10]

다음 능동태 문장을 수동태 문장으로 바꾸어 쓰세요.

1 They named the hamster Steve.

➡ ____

2 The coach always encourages them to do their best.

➡ ____

3 The prosecutor found the suspect guilty of fraud.

➡ ____

4 My friends call me Ice Princess.

➡ ____

5 The cat helped the kitty to get out of the box.

➡ ____

6 He heard her speaking some foreign language on the phone.

➡ ____

7 The team elected Jina chief editor.

➡ ____

8 We saw an airplane flying under the cloud.

➡ ____

9 The talk show made the singer popular.

➡ ____

10 Everyone expected him to arrive in time.

➡ ____

PSS 6 5형식 문장의 수동태 Ⅱ

지각동사나 사역동사가 목적격 보어로 동사원형을 취하는 능동태 문장을 수동태 문장으로 전환할 때 동사원형은 to부정사로 바뀐다.

I heard someone knock on the door. 나는 누군가가 문을 두드리는 것을 들었다.

➡ Someone **was heard to knock** on the door by me.

The teacher made Nari finish the work. 그 선생님은 나리가 그 일을 끝내도록 만들었다.

➡ Nari **was made to finish** the work by the teacher.

cf. 사역동사 let은 수동태 문장으로 전환될 때 「be allowed+to부정사」로 표현된다.

The guard didn't let us enter with a drink.

그 경비원은 우리가 음료를 가지고 들어갈 수 없게 했다.

➡ We **weren't allowed to enter** with a drink by the guard.

정답 p.18

PRACTICE 6

다음 능동태 문장을 수동태 문장으로 바꾸어 쓰세요.

1 He heard his daughter play the flute in her room.

➡ ____

2 Jim made me water the flowers.

➡ ____

3 Some people saw Adam hang around the house at midnight.

➡ ____

4 He let his sister take a walk with his dog last night.

➡ ____

5 I heard him make a strange sound.

➡ ____

6 He made her run faster for a good record.

➡ ____

7 Susan watched Minho carry the bag for the elderly.

➡ ____

8 I felt the tea table shake slightly.

➡ ____

9 He doesn't let his daughter leave for New York.

➡ ____

10 John watched a lot of people walk across the street.

➡ ____

11 I didn't let her borrow anything.

➡ ____

PSS 7 동사구의 수동태

동사에 부사나 전치사가 이어져 두 개 이상의 단어가 하나의 동사 역할을 하는 동사구가 있는 문장을 수동태로 전환할 때는 동사구를 하나의 단어처럼 취급하여 항상 함께 붙여 쓴다.

① laugh at '비웃다'

Most of the students **laughed at** the boy. 대부분의 학생들이 그 소년을 비웃었다.

➡ The boy **was laughed at** by most of the students.

그 소년은 학생들 대부분에 의해 비웃음을 당했다.

② take care of '돌보다'

The nurse **took care of** the wounded soldiers. 그 간호사는 부상병들을 돌보았다.

➡ The wounded soldiers **were taken care of** by the nurse.

부상병들은 그 간호사에 의해 돌보아졌다.

③ put off '연기하다'

The company has **put off** the payment. 그 회사는 지불을 연기해 왔다.

➡ The payment has **been put off** by the company. 지불은 그 회사에 의해 연기되어 왔다.

PRACTICE 7

다음 능동태 문장을 수동태 문장으로 바꾸어 쓰세요.

1 The police couldn't catch up with him.

➡ _______________________________________

2 The volunteer workers looked after the old people.

➡ _______________________________________

3 Many magicians make use of this trick.

➡ _______________________________________

4 My sister took care of my little son in the daytime.

➡ _______________________________________

5 Brian laughed at my brother so hard.

➡ _______________________________________

6 Jihye turned off the TV at midnight.

➡ _______________________________________

7 He looks down on weak and poor people.

➡ _______________________________________

8 We can't put off the meeting with that company anymore.

➡ _______________________________________

PSS 8 It is ~ that …

다음 동사들의 목적어가 that이 이끄는 절일 때는 「It is ~ that …」이나 that절의 주어를 문장 전체의 주어로 하여 주어가 단수이면 「is[was]+과거분사+to부정사」, 주어가 복수이면 「are[were]+과거분사+to부정사」의 형태로 수동태를 만들 수 있다.

> say   think   believe   report   know   expect   consider   suppose

They say that Busan is famous for its beaches.

그들은 부산이 해변으로 유명하다고 말한다.

➡ **It is said that** Busan is famous for its beaches.

➡ Busan **is said to be** famous for its beaches.

People believed that Mr. Jackson owned the largest house in the town.

사람들은 Jackson 씨가 그 도시에서 가장 큰 집을 소유하고 있다고 믿었다.

➡ **It was believed that** Mr. Jackson owned the largest house in the town.

➡ Mr. Jackson **was believed to** own the largest house in the town.

> *cf.* that절의 시제가 주절의 시제보다 더 과거일 때 「~ is/was/are/were+과거분사+ to have p.p.」의 형태로 나타낸다.
>
> They say that he had a car accident. 그들은 그가 자동차 사고를 당했다고 말한다.
> ➡ He **is said to have had** a car accident.
> They said that he had had a car accident. 그들은 그가 자동차 사고를 당했었다고 말했다.
> ➡ He **was said to have had** a car accident.

정답 p.18

PRACTICE 8

다음 능동태 문장을 두 가지 형태의 수동태 문장으로 바꾸어 쓰세요.

1 They said that she was the best actress in the film festival.
➡ It was said that she was the best actress in the film festival.
➡ She was said to be the best actress in the film festival.

2 We think that Daniel sang better than anyone else.
➡ ____
➡ ____

3 They reported that the man had been lost in the mountain.
➡ ____
➡ ____

4 They expect that the book will be published soon.
➡ ____
➡ ____

5 We know that a friend in need is a friend indeed.
➡ ____
➡ ____

6 They say that English examinations are always difficult.
➡ ____
➡ ____

7 Everyone believed that the man had won the lottery.
➡ ____
➡ ____

8 We suppose that the movie is awesome.
➡ ____
➡ ____

PSS 9 수동태의 관용 표현

1. **be excited at[about]** '~에 흥분하다'
   They **were excited at** the game. 그들은 그 경기에 흥분했다.

2. **be bored with** '~에 지겨워지다'
   The students **were bored with** eating the same food.
   학생들은 같은 음식을 먹는 것에 지겨워졌다.

3. **be disappointed with[in]** '~에 실망하다'
   I **am disappointed with[in]** your poor service. 나는 당신의 엉성한 서비스에 실망했다.

4. **be interested in** '~에 관심이 있다'
   What **are** you **interested in**? 넌 무엇에 관심이 있니?

5. **be pleased with** '~에 대해 기뻐하다'
   The baby **was pleased with** the new toy. 아기는 새 장난감에 대해 기뻐했다.

6. **be satisfied with** '~에 대해 만족하다'
   I **am** not **satisfied with** his short answer. 나는 그의 짧은 대답에 만족하지 않는다.

7. **be surprised at[by]** '~에 놀라다'
   My brother **was surprised at[by]** the news. 내 동생은 그 소식에 놀랐다.

8. **be tired of** '~에 싫증나다'
   I **am tired of** my daily routines. 나는 내 일상에 싫증났다.

9. **be worried about** '~에 대해 걱정하다'
   She **was worried about** her wounded son. 그녀는 부상당한 아들에 대해 걱정했다.

10. **be based on** '~에 근거를 두다'
    The movie **is based on** a true story. 그 영화는 실화에 근거를 둔다.

11. **be covered with** '~로 덮여 있다'
    His new car **was covered with** dust. 그의 새 차는 먼지로 덮여 있었다.

12. **be dressed in** '~을 입고 있다'
    She **was dressed in** white. 그녀는 흰 옷을 입고 있었다.

13. **be filled with** '~로 가득 차다'
    When I saw her again, my heart **was filled with** joy.
    내가 그녀를 다시 보았을 때, 내 마음은 기쁨으로 가득 찼다.

14. **be known as** '~로 알려져 있다'
    He **is known as** a famous poet in Korea. 그는 한국에서 유명한 시인으로 알려져 있다.

15. **be known to** '~에게 알려지다'
    Your name **isn't known to** any of us. 네 이름은 우리 중 누구에게도 알려져 있지 않다.

16. be made of '~로 만들어지다' – 재료의 성질이 변하지 않은 경우

This ring **is made of** gold. 이 반지는 금으로 만들어져 있다.

17. be made from '~로 만들어지다' – 일련의 과정을 거쳐 재료의 성질이 변한 경우

Paper **is made from** trees. 종이는 나무로 만들어진다.

18. be made with '~로 만들어지다' – 식음료의 재료를 나타내는 경우

This dish **is made with** beef, mushrooms and garlic.

이 요리는 소고기, 버섯, 그리고 마늘로 만들어진다.

19. be supposed to+동사원형 '~을 하기로 되어 있다[~을 해야 한다]'

You **are supposed to** hand in your report by Friday.

너는 금요일까지 보고서를 제출해야 한다.

정답 p.19

PRACTICE 9

괄호 안의 단어와 〈보기〉의 단어를 이용하여 문장을 완성하세요.

보 기	about as at in of on to with by from

1 Is your sister _______________ travel? (interested)

2 She is _______________ the result of her final test. (excited)

3 The teacher was _______________ his students' exam results. (satisfied)

4 They were _______________ the lengthy talk of the salesman. (bored)

5 Ann was _______________ their children's good manners. (pleased)

6 Most countries in Europe are _______________ the low birth rate. (worried)

7 Korean chopsticks are usually _______________ metal. (made)

8 I am _______________ your complaining about everything. (tired)

9 His painful life was _______________ tears and sighs. (filled)

10 The movie was _______________ a true story about a soldier. (based)

11 The mountain is _______________ snow throughout the year. (covered)

12 Professor Kim was _______________ the Schweitzer from Korea. (known)

13 They were _______________ the team's defeat in the game. (disappointed)

14 He is _______________ all students in his school. (known)

15 Everyone in the ceremony was _______________ a black suit. (dressed)

16 They were _______________ the total expense of the package trip. (surprised)

17 Chocolate is _______________ cocoa beans. (made)

18 The plane was _______________ arrive at 9:00. (supposed)

중간·기말고사 대비문제

1 다음 중 밑줄 친 부분의 쓰임이 잘못된 것은?

① Icebergs are melting in the polar regions.
② The young are taught to be respectful of the old.
③ To be honest, I was watching TV last night.
④ Someone was seen standing near the window.
⑤ Non-recyclable plastics are not considering environmentally friendly.

2 다음 중 어법상 틀린 문장을 모두 고르세요.

① The subway is being held because of signal delays.
② He was called "the miracle man" after he survived a lightning strike.
③ Smartphones have been improved a lot since they were first released.
④ When she was asked of a sudden question, her mind went blank.
⑤ The computer will be fix in a minute, so don't worry too much.

3 다음 질문에 대한 답으로 가장 적절한 것은?

> When do we have to send the invitation letters?

① They must send until this Thursday.
② They must be sent by this Thursday.
③ They must be sending by this Thursday.
④ We must send them until this Thursday.
⑤ We must be sent until this Thursday.

4 다음 주어진 단어들을 반드시 모두 사용하여 우리말을 영작하세요. (총 9단어로 쓸 것.)

> 그 과학자는 그의 동료들에 의해 매우 똑똑하다고 여겨졌다. (consider, intelligent, colleague)

➡ ___________________________

____

5 다음 글의 밑줄 친 부분 중 쓰임이 올바른 것을 모두 고르세요.

> Mosquitoes are small insects that fly around and bite people. They ① found all over the world. Mosquitoes are annoying because they can bite you and make you ② itchy. Not only are mosquitoes annoying, but they can also be dangerous to your health. They ③ are known for their ability to carry diseases, such as malaria. Many people ④ are worried from engaging in outdoor activities because of mosquitoes. You can protect yourself from mosquitoes by wearing long sleeves and pants when you're outside and ⑤ use mosquito repellent.

6 다음 문장을 능동태 문장으로 바꿀 때 밑줄 친 부분을 어법에 맞도록 고쳐 문장을 완성하세요.

> Her birthday party was being prepared for by us when she came home.

➡ We ___________________ her birthday party when she came home.

7 ⓐ~ⓔ 중 어법상 <u>틀린</u> 것을 <u>있는 대로</u> 고른 것은?

> ⓐ The equipment had been used since this morning.
> ⓑ I was being punished when my mom visited my school.
> ⓒ The stories have been told for 1,000 days.
> ⓓ The players will trained by the coach.
> ⓔ The party will hold on December 5th.

① ⓐ, ⓑ   ② ⓑ, ⓒ   ③ ⓐ, ⓑ, ⓒ
④ ⓐ, ⓓ, ⓔ   ⑤ ⓑ, ⓒ, ⓓ, ⓔ

8 다음 글의 ⓐ, ⓑ에 주어진 말을 문맥과 어법에 맞도록 고쳐 쓰세요. (단, 필요시 다른 단어를 추가하거나 어형을 바꿀 수 있음.)

> After winning the important battle, the general ⓐ (award) a medal by the president. The president was very ⓑ (please) the good news because they had lost the previous battle.

➡ ⓐ ＿＿＿＿＿＿   ⓑ ＿＿＿＿＿＿

9 밑줄 친 단어의 쓰임이 <u>어색한</u> 것은?

① Are these seats <u>taken</u>?
② Who will be <u>catering</u> the wedding?
③ Dad was <u>carried</u> a number of files under his arm.
④ Why does the actor seem to be <u>getting</u> younger?
⑤ Advice was <u>given</u> to help her make the right decision.

10 다음을 두 가지 형태의 수동태 문장으로 바꿀 때 빈칸에 알맞은 말을 쓰세요.

> The company paid the employees a lot of money as a reward.

➡ The employees ＿＿＿＿＿ ＿＿＿＿＿ a lot of money as a reward by the company.
➡ A lot of money ＿＿＿＿＿ ＿＿＿＿＿ ＿＿＿＿＿ the employees as a reward by the company.

11 ⓐ~ⓔ 중 어법이 올바른 것의 개수는?

> The school has updated the rules regarding the usage of the school gym. As always, it ⓐ <u>can only be used</u> by school students on weekdays. However, on weekends, outsiders may use it if ⓑ <u>approved</u> by the school. For those who wish to use the school gym, they ⓒ <u>may be reserved</u> a specific date and time on our school's website. Please be aware that the purpose of using the gym ⓓ <u>must be stated</u> in order to book the gym. Finally, if any damage is done, those who are using the gym ⓔ <u>must take responsibility</u> for it.

① 1개   ② 2개   ③ 3개
④ 4개   ⑤ 5개

12 다음 중 밑줄 친 전치사의 쓰임이 올바른 것은?

① The brand new laptop was bought <u>to</u> him by his uncle.
② Spaghetti was cooked <u>to</u> the kids by their mom.
③ Directions were asked <u>of</u> the old man.
④ A new room was made <u>to</u> me by my dad.
⑤ A love letter was written <u>for</u> her by the poet.

13 다음을 수동태 문장으로 바꿀 때 빈칸에 알맞은 말을 쓰세요.

> The people elected him mayor of Seoul.

➡ He ___________ ___________ ___________
___________ ___________ by the people.

14 다음 중 어법상 옳은 것은?

① He was chosen nice pants by his girlfriend.
② The movie star was written enormous letters by his fans.
③ The girl was bought a computer by her parents.
④ The part-timers are paid their wages weekly.
⑤ The guests were cooked a special meal by her.

15 다음을 수동태 문장으로 바꾸어 쓰세요.

> They called the soccer player a free kick artist.

➡ ___________________________________
____

16 다음 중 어법상 어색한 것은?

① The victim was heard cry by the policemen.
② He was allowed to leave work earlier than usual.
③ The students were made to clean their classroom.
④ She wasn't allowed to sleep all day long.
⑤ The suspect was seen by a witness.

17 다음을 수동태 문장으로 바꿀 때 빈칸에 알맞은 말을 쓰세요.

> The police do not let the demonstrators cross the police line.

➡ The demonstrators ___________
___________ ___________ ___________
___________ the police line by the police.

18 주어진 우리말을 참고하여 빈칸에 알맞은 말을 쓰세요.

(1) She ___________ ___________ ___________
red.
(그녀는 붉은색 옷을 입고 있었다.)
(2) His generosity ___________ ___________
___________ everyone in the town.
(그의 너그러움은 그 도시의 모든 사람에게 알려져 있다.)

19 다음을 수동태 문장으로 바꾸세요.

> She always speaks ill of her neighbors.

➡ ___________________________________
____

20 다음을 수동태 문장으로 바꿀 때 빈칸에 알맞은 말을 쓰세요.

> The nurse looked after the patient who didn't have a family.

➡ The patient who didn't have a family
___________ ___________ ___________ by
the nurse.

21 다음을 두 가지 형태의 수동태 문장으로 바꿀 때 빈칸에 알맞은 말을 쓰세요.

> We believe that freedom is an essential human right.

➡ It _____________ _____________ _____________ freedom is an essential human right.
➡ Freedom is _____________ _____________ _____________ an essential human right.

22 다음 능동태 문장을 수동태 문장으로 바꾼 것 중 잘못된 것은?

① You must keep your words.
  ➡ Your words must be kept by you.
② I saw him standing there.
  ➡ He was seen standing there by me.
③ They laughed at Judy.
  ➡ Judy was laughed at by them.
④ I heard her sigh with relief.
  ➡ She was heard to sigh with relief.
⑤ My father is making a doghouse.
  ➡ A doghouse is being made for my father.

23 다음을 두 가지 형태의 수동태 문장으로 바꿀 때 빈칸에 알맞은 말을 쓰세요.

> People believed that he had become a millionaire.

➡ It _____________ that he _____________ _____________ a millionaire.
➡ He _____________ _____________ to _____________ _____________ a millionaire.

24 다음 문장의 빈칸에 들어갈 말이 차례대로 알맞게 짝지어진 것은?

> - In autumn, the park is covered _____________ red and yellow leaves.
> - As her song was on the Billboard chart, her name was known _____________ many people.
> - They will hold a dinner party and serve wine made _____________ green grapes.

① with – to – of
② with – for – from
③ with – to – from
④ to – for – of
⑤ to – to – from

25 다음 중 밑줄 친 부분의 쓰임이 잘못된 것은?

① I was surprised at the news.
② The room was filled of so many books.
③ My teacher was satisfied with the result.
④ Billy is interested in playing the guitar.
⑤ The movie is based on a novel.

26 다음을 수동태 문장으로 바꿀 때 빈칸에 알맞은 말을 쓰세요.

> The newspaper reports that the oil price is rising.

➡ The oil price _____________ _____________ _____________ _____________ _____________ by the newspaper.

27 다음을 수동태 문장으로 바꿔 쓰세요.

> The committee has put off the decision.

➡ _____________________________________

28 Which sentence is NOT correct in grammar?

① The kids were excited about the upcoming field trip to the zoo.
② My country is filled with wonderful sightseeing places.
③ She was disappointed with her score in math.
④ He was satisfied with her present.
⑤ Haydn, who is known to "the Father of the Symphony", was born in 1732.

29 어법상 옳은 문장을 2개 고르세요.

① Do you know why Rachel is mad for me?
② This clothing is made from recycled materials.
③ His dad was proud with his son's successful debut.
④ The lyrics of the song are known to fans worldwide.
⑤ Human body consists with cells, tissues, and organs.

30 다음 중 빈칸에 들어갈 단어가 나머지 넷과 <u>다른</u> 것은?

① The jazz singer was dressed ___________ a blue rain coat.
② The building is located ___________ the center of the city.
③ The meeting was interrupted ___________ the call.
④ She is interested ___________ Chinese history.
⑤ I was disappointed ___________ the movie's ending as it left many unanswered questions.

31 다음을 수동태 문장으로 바꿀 때 빈칸에 알맞은 말을 쓰세요.

> They called off the baseball game because of the rain.

➡ The baseball game ___________ ___________ ___________ because of the rain.

32 다음 문장을 능동태로 바꾸어 쓰세요.

> A lot of studies on genes have been done since the 18th century by the scientists.

➡ ___________
____

33 다음 중 어법상 <u>틀린</u> 문장끼리 짝지어진 것은?

① • This meeting has been one of the most useful we have had so far.
  • Tom called me three days ago, and I haven't spoken to him since.
② • People generally see which they look for, and hear which they listen for.
  • The one place where a man should receive a fair deal is in a courtroom.
③ • The moon was appeared over the mountain just after sunset.
  • Before the book publishes, it is reviewed by several editors for accuracy.
④ • Don't let yourself drawn into an unnecessary argument.
  • If the event is cancelled due to the weather conditions, notice will be given via text message.
⑤ • I was made waiting four hours before I was examined by a doctor.
  • The government must be seen to be doing something about the rise in violent crime.

CHAPTER 5
명사와 관사

PSS 1 명사의 복수형	페이지	성취도				
		100%	99~75%	74~50%	49~25%	24~0%
PSS 1-1 명사의 복수형 Ⅰ	92					
PSS 1-2 명사의 복수형 Ⅱ	94					
PSS 1-3 복합명사의 복수형	96					

PSS 2 명사의 쓰임	페이지	성취도				
		100%	99~75%	74~50%	49~25%	24~0%
PSS 2-1 셀 수 있는 명사	97					
PSS 2-2 셀 수 없는 명사	98					
PSS 2-3 물질명사의 수량 표현	99					
PSS 2-4 추상명사의 관용적 용법	101					

PSS 3 소유격 만들기	페이지	성취도				
		100%	99~75%	74~50%	49~25%	24~0%
PSS 3-1 명사의 소유격	102					
PSS 3-2 이중소유격	104					

PSS 4 부정관사 a, an	페이지	성취도				
		100%	99~75%	74~50%	49~25%	24~0%
PSS 4-1 a, an의 쓰임	105					
PSS 4-2 a, an의 의미	106					

PSS 5 정관사 the	페이지	성취도				
		100%	99~75%	74~50%	49~25%	24~0%
PSS 5-1 the의 쓰임 Ⅰ	107					
PSS 5-2 the의 쓰임 Ⅱ	108					

PSS 6 관사를 쓰지 않는 경우	109

중간·기말고사 대비문제	111

PSS 1 명사의 복수형

PSS 1-1 명사의 복수형 Ⅰ

일반적인 경우	명사+s	festival – festival**s**　　peak – peak**s** citizen – citizen**s**　　souvenir – souvenir**s** dinosaur – dinosaur**s**　astronaut – astronaut**s** crab – crab**s**　　zebra – zebra**s**
-s, -x, -ch, -sh로 끝나는 경우	명사+es	bus – bus**es**　　address – address**es** box – box**es**　　fox – fox**es** branch – branch**es**　match – match**es** wish – wish**es**　　toothbrush – toothbrush**es** *cf.* stomach – stomach**s**
자음+y로 끝나는 경우	자음+i+es	fairy – fair**ies**　　dynasty – dynast**ies** therapy – therap**ies**　diary – diar**ies** *cf.* 모음+y로 끝나는 경우 → 명사+s 　journey – journey**s**　essay – essay**s** 　monkey – monkey**s**　way – way**s**

정답 p.22

PRACTICE 1

다음 명사의 복수형을 쓰세요.

1	citizen	– __________	2	witness	– __________
3	dictionary	– __________	4	journey	– __________
5	address	– __________	6	straw	– __________
7	nail	– __________	8	calendar	– __________
9	therapy	– __________	10	astronaut	– __________
11	maze	– __________	12	fox	– __________
13	tomb	– __________	14	bottle	– __________
15	guy	– __________	16	employee	– __________
17	bunch	– __________	18	dinosaur	– __________
19	peak	– __________	20	copy	– __________
21	match	– __________	22	language	– __________

23 award – __________
24 dynasty – __________
25 radish – __________
26 photocopier – __________
27 troop – __________
28 toothbrush – __________
29 fairy – __________
30 wish – __________
31 foreigner – __________
32 stomach – __________
33 gas – __________
34 monkey – __________
35 way – __________
36 prize – __________
37 souvenir – __________
38 principle – __________
39 cobra – __________
40 bush – __________
41 program – __________
42 essay – __________
43 crab – __________
44 scratch – __________
45 branch – __________
46 baby – __________
47 festival – __________
48 activity – __________
49 eyebrow – __________
50 opinion – __________
51 accident – __________
52 professor – __________
53 battery – __________
54 client – __________
55 factor – __________
56 helmet – __________
57 janitor – __________
58 memory – __________
59 symptom – __________
60 consumer – __________
61 history – __________
62 magazine – __________
63 penny – __________
64 agent – __________
65 brick – __________
66 chapter – __________
67 sandwich – __________
68 column – __________
69 portrait – __________
70 sketch – __________

PSS 1-2 명사의 복수형 Ⅱ

-o로 끝나는 경우	명사+es	hero – hero**es** potato – potato**es** mosquito – mosquito**(e)s**	echo – echo**es** tomato – tomato**es** volcano – volcano**(e)s**
	명사+s	studio – studio**s** kangaroo – kangaroo**s**	piano – piano**s** radio – radio**s**
-f, -fe로 끝나는 경우	f, fe → v+es	thief – thie**ves** calf – cal**ves** scarf – scar**ves**/scarf**s**	leaf – lea**ves** life – li**ves**
	명사+s	chief – chief**s** cliff – cliff**s**	belief – belief**s** roof – roof**s**
불규칙 변화		tooth – **teeth** goose – **geese** ox – **oxen** basis – **bases** deer – **deer** Swiss – **Swiss**	woman – **women** mouse – **mice** child – **children** sheep – **sheep** Chinese – **Chinese** Japanese – **Japanese**

정답 p.22

PRACTICE 2

다음 명사의 복수형을 쓰세요.

1	roof	– __________	2	potato	– __________
3	hero	– __________	4	fish	– __________
5	radio	– __________	6	Swiss	– __________
7	man	– __________	8	weed	– __________
9	studio	– __________	10	cliff	– __________
11	scarf	– __________	12	kangaroo	– __________
13	thief	– __________	14	sheep	– __________
15	basis	– __________	16	promise	– __________
17	tooth	– __________	18	leaf	– __________
19	volcano	– __________	20	mouse	– __________
21	safe	– __________	22	Japanese	– __________
23	piano	– __________	24	reporter	– __________

25 child – _____________

26 factory – _____________

27 goose – _____________

28 foot – _____________

29 deer – _____________

30 chief – _____________

31 belief – _____________

32 key – _____________

33 tomato – _____________

34 flash – _____________

35 medicine – _____________

36 mix – _____________

37 life – _____________

38 calf – _____________

39 ox – _____________

40 couch – _____________

41 apron – _____________

42 canary – _____________

43 character – _____________

44 receipt – _____________

45 housewife – _____________

46 cherry – _____________

47 assistant – _____________

48 enemy – _____________

49 guest – _____________

50 instructor – _____________

51 grocery – _____________

52 proof – _____________

53 witch – _____________

54 hobby – _____________

55 market – _____________

56 railway – _____________

57 architect – _____________

58 handle – _____________

59 shampoo – _____________

60 wolf – _____________

61 rumor – _____________

62 donkey – _____________

63 ghost – _____________

64 watch – _____________

65 method – _____________

66 puppy – _____________

67 donut – _____________

68 article – _____________

69 harbor – _____________

70 zoo – _____________

71 symbol – _____________

72 designer – _____________

73 palace – _____________

74 chimney – _____________

75 fisherman – _____________

76 reef – _____________

77 tailor – _____________

78 skill – _____________

79 satellite – _____________

80 instrument – _____________

가장 중요한 의미를 가진 단어에 '-s'나 '-es'를 붙여 복수형으로 만든다.

girlfriend – girlfriend**s** 여자친구

boyfriend – boyfriend**s** 남자친구

mother-in-law – mother**s**-in-law
시어머니, 장모

brother-in-law – brother**s**-in-law
시동생, 시아주버니; 처남; 매부, 자형

passer-by – passer**s**-by
통행인

mother-to-be – mother**s**-to-be
임신한 여자

commander in chief – commander**s** in chief
최고 사령관

bystander – bystander**s**
구경꾼, 행인

fountain pen – fountain pen**s**
만년필

application form – application form**s**
신청서

cf. 명사가 포함되지 않거나 또는 가장 중요한 의미를 가진 단어를 결정할 수 없는 복합어는 맨 끝에 '-s'나 '-es'를 붙인다.

merry-go-round – merry-go-round**s**
회전목마

forget-me-not – forget-me-not**s**
물망초

정답 p.22

PRACTICE 3

괄호 안에 주어진 말을 이용하여 빈칸을 채우세요.

1 I'm going to attend the ceremony with some of my ________________. (girlfriend)

2 Do you mind if we go there with your two ________________? (brother-in-law)

3 I asked three ________________ for help, but all of them refused. (passer-by)

4 There are five ________________ from other countries in this area. (commander in chief)

5 We need to buy seven ________________ for the teachers. (fountain pen)

6 I'm sure that she has many ________________ that would do anything for her. (boyfriend)

7 Some married women have a lot of trouble with their ________________. (mother-in-law)

8 A lot of ________________ were waiting for the doctor in the waiting room. (mother-to-be)

9 Hundreds of ________________ have already arrived before the deadline. (application form)

10 There are two ________________ near the lake in the amusement park. (merry-go-round)

PSS 2 명사의 쓰임

PSS 2-1 셀 수 있는 명사

셀 수 있는 명사는 a(n)을 붙이거나 복수형으로 쓸 수 있고, many, few, some, any, no 와 같은 수량형용사와 함께 쓸 수 있다.

1. 보통명사 – 사람, 사물, 동물을 가리키는 명사이다.

   There is **a horse** in the **stable**. 마구간에 말 한 마리가 있다.
   I met **two doctors** for the **research**.
   나는 그 조사를 위해 두 명의 의사를 만났다.

2. 집합명사 – family, class, audience, team과 같이 사람이나 사물이 모여 이루어진 집합체를 나타내는 명사이다. 이때는 집합체를 하나의 단위로 보아 단수 취급한다. 단, 영국식 영어에서는 구성 요소를 강조하고자 할 경우 단수 형태라도 복수 취급한다.

   My **family is** more important to me than anything. 나의 가족은 내게 어떤 것보다도 더 중요하다.
   I hope that your **family are[is]** fine. 나는 네 가족이 건강하기를 바란다.
   Fifty **families live** in this apartment building. 50가구가 이 아파트에 산다.

   My **class is** the largest in my school. 나의 반은 나의 학교에서 가장 크다.
   My **class are[is]** very friendly. 나의 반은 매우 다정하다.
   There **are ten classes** in each grade. 각 학년에는 10개의 학급이 있다.

   cf. police, people과 같은 집합명사는 형태는 단수형이지만 복수 취급한다.
   The **police are** coming close to the criminal. 경찰이 범인에게 가까이 다가가고 있다.
   The **people** at the square **are** waving their hands to the mayor.
   광장에 있는 사람들이 시장에게 손을 흔들고 있다.

정답 p.23

PRACTICE 4 [1-15]

괄호 안에 들어갈 알맞은 말을 골라 동그라미 하세요. (복수 정답 가능)

1   The girl with a green (apron, aprons) is my sister.

2   The class (is, are) excited about the upcoming science fair.

3   The police (has, have) arrested the bank robbers.

4   His family (is, are) quite small. There are only three people in his family.

5   There are four baseball (team, teams) in my town.

6   The audience (was, were) waiting for the singer to show up.

7   The project faced a serious money (problem, problems).

8 A lot of people in Africa (has, have) difficulty in making a living.

9 Many (family, families) are moving to bigger cities.

10 He showed me several magic (trick, tricks).

11 Our team (has, have) always won in the championship since 2020.

12 There (isn't, aren't) either any window seats or any aisle seats left on Flight 919.

13 Five (team, teams) will compete to enter the contest.

14 Mina registered for a bowling class, but the class (was, were) canceled.

15 The (activity, activities) provide students with intercultural experiences.

PSS 2-2 셀 수 없는 명사

셀 수 없는 명사는 a(n)을 붙이거나 복수형으로 쓸 수 없다.

1. **고유명사** – 사람, 장소, 요일과 같은 고유한 이름을 나타내는 명사로 첫 글자는 항상 대문자로 쓴다.

> John   Youngjoo   Busan   Mexico   Sunday

I ran into **Linda** in **London** last month. 나는 지난달에 런던에서 Linda를 우연히 만났다.
I'm going to attend the graduation ceremony next **Friday**.
나는 다음 주 금요일에 졸업식에 참석할 것이다.

2. **물질명사** – 일정한 형태가 없는 물질을 나타내는 명사로 much, (a) little, some, any, no와 같은 수량형용사와 함께 쓸 수 있다.

> water   money   luggage   bread   salt   paper   furniture

I'd like to have some cold **water**. 나는 찬물을 마시고 싶다.
I have no more **money** left. 나는 더 이상 남은 돈이 없다.

cf. furniture는 의미상으로는 집합명사에 가깝지만, 셀 수 없는 명사이므로 수량 표현 시 물질명사처럼 취급한다.

3. **추상명사** – 눈에 보이지 않는 개념을 나타내는 명사로 much, (a) little, some, any, no와 같은 수량형용사와 함께 쓸 수 있다.

> information   travel   knowledge   truth   love   kindness   advice

The book doesn't have any **information** about **travel**.
그 책에는 여행에 대한 어떠한 정보도 없다.
You need to have some background **knowledge** to understand it.
너는 그것을 이해하려면 약간의 배경 지식을 가지고 있어야 한다.

PRACTICE 5

다음 문장의 밑줄 친 부분을 바르게 고치세요.

1 We arrived in <u>a Japan</u> late yesterday afternoon. _______________

2 Did you get <u>a packages</u> from Mr. Smith? _______________

3 Jack wants some <u>furnitures</u> such as a bed and a table. _______________

4 How much <u>moneys</u> do you need to start the project? _______________

5 A lot of <u>leaf</u> are floating on the lake after the rain. _______________

6 I've got a lot of <u>homeworks</u> to do for this week. _______________

7 My brother often gives me good <u>advices</u> on studying. _______________

8 I'll hand in the biology report on <u>a Thursday</u>. _______________

9 Ms. Park teaches <u>a math</u> at the middle school. _______________

10 Her hobby is listening to <u>a music</u> and playing musical pieces. _______________

11 I have worked for several <u>restaurant</u> for two years. _______________

12 A lot of people believed that <u>an honesty</u> is the best policy. _______________

13 I have been to many <u>country</u> in Europe and in Asia. _______________

PSS 2-3 물질명사의 수량 표현

셀 수 없는 물질명사는 단위명사를 이용하여 「수사+단위명사+of+물질명사」로 표현하여 수량을 나타낸다.

a piece of cake

a glass of juice

a bar of soap

a sheet of paper

a loaf of bread

a bowl of rice

> a glass[bottle] of milk/water/juice/wine/beer
> a cup of tea/coffee/juice
> a spoonful[teaspoonful] of sugar/salt
> a pound of meat/beef/pork/gold
> a bowl of rice/soup/water
> a slice of cheese/bread/pizza   a loaf of bread
> a bar of soap/chocolate   a sheet of paper
> a piece of paper/cheese/cake/bread/cloth/advice/furniture

cf. 물질명사는 아니지만 advice(추상명사), furniture(의미상으로는 집합명사)도 수량 표현 시
piece를 사용한다.

I had **two pieces of cake** for dessert. 나는 디저트로 케이크 두 조각을 먹었다.
He drinks **a glass of milk** every morning. 그는 아침마다 우유를 한 잔씩 마신다.
She bought **three pounds of beef** for the party. 그녀는 파티에 쓸 쇠고기 3파운드를 샀다.

정답 p.23

PRACTICE 6

괄호 안에 주어진 단어와 알맞은 단위명사를 이용하여 빈칸을 채우세요.

1 I ate two _______________________ for breakfast. (bread)

2 Every student has to prepare a pen and a _______________________. (paper)

3 Please bring me three _______________________. (orange juice)

4 We need to buy two _______________________ for the bathroom. (soap)

5 There's only one _______________________ left. (cheese)

6 I ordered 100 _______________________ for the party. (beer)

7 Why don't we have a _______________________ after dinner? (green tea)

8 She prepared several _______________________ to make curtains. (cloth)

9 I want to put two _______________________ in my coffee. (sugar)

10 To make this food, you need a _______________________, some salt, flour and eggs. (meat)

11 Can I have one more _______________________? (onion soup)

12 Let me give you a few _______________________ on choosing good books. (advice)

13 We ate up four _______________________ in a moment. (fried rice)

14 I'm looking for some _______________________ for my new apartment. (furniture)

15 He always drinks a _______________________ before going to bed. (wine)

1. of+추상명사 = 형용사

of use = useful 유용한	of no use = useless 쓸모 없는
of importance = important 중요한	of courage = courageous 용기 있는
of value = valuable 가치 있는	of wisdom = wise 현명한

This information is **of no use**. = This information is **useless**. 이 정보는 쓸모 없다.

Mr. Smith is a man **of courage**. = Mr. Smith is **courageous**. Smith 씨는 용기 있는 남자이다.

2. 전치사+추상명사 = 부사

with ease = easily 쉽게	in haste = hastily 서둘러서
on purpose = purposely 고의로	with care = carefully 조심스럽게

I feel tired **with ease** after getting the surgery.

나는 그 수술을 받고 나서 쉽게 피곤함을 느낀다.

= I feel tired **easily** after getting the surgery.

You seemed to have broken the bowl **on purpose**.

넌 일부러 그 그릇을 깨뜨린 것 같았다.

= You seemed to have broken the bowl **purposely**.

cf. 추상명사의 본래 형태와는 다르게 변화하는 경우도 있다.

on time = punctually 제시간에   by degrees = gradually 점차로

정답 p.23

PRACTICE 7 [1-10]

다음 두 문장이 같은 뜻이 되도록 빈칸에 알맞은 말을 써 넣으세요.

1 It was of value for us to help poor people all over the world.

= It was ___________________ for us to help poor people all over the world.

2 It's useless to talk about the seriousness of this situation.

= It's ________________ to talk about the seriousness of this situation.

3 Mr. Brown looks like a man of wisdom.

= Mr. Brown looks like a ________________ man.

4 Tom studied hard and he could solve these math problems easily.

= Tom studied hard and he could solve these math problems ________________.

5 He will arrive at the airport on time, so don't worry.

= He will arrive at the airport ________________, so don't worry.

6 It is important to review your notes after class.

= It is ________________ to review your notes after class.

7 My aunt is one of the women of courage in my town.

= My aunt is one of the ________________ women in my town.

8 Sumi is loved because she always treats others kindly.

= Sumi is loved because she always treats others ________________.

9 This book will be useful for your history test next week.

= This book will be ________________ for your history test next week.

10 Bob lied to his sick mother on purpose.

= Bob lied to his sick mother ________________.

PSS 3 소유격 만들기

PSS 3-1 명사의 소유격

1. **사람이나 동물을 나타내는 명사의 소유격**

   ① 「단수 명사+'s」

   Bob's bicycle Bob의 자전거

   a **cat's** eyes 고양이의 눈

   my **brother's** dictionary 내 남동생의 사전

   Mr. Johnson's business card Johnson 씨의 명함

Bob's bicycle

   ② 「복수 명사+'」

   Daehan **Girls'** High School 대한 여자 고등학교

   those **birds'** nest 저 새들의 둥지

   a **teachers'** room 교무실

   my **parents'** car 나의 부모님의 차

those birds' nest

   cf. 명사의 복수형이 -s로 끝나지 않는 경우에는 「복수 명사+'s」로 쓴다.

   women's clothes 여성복

   children's storybooks 어린이들의 이야기책

③ 명사의 반복을 피하기 위해서나 가리키는 대상이 명백할 때는 소유격 뒤의 명사를 생략할 수도 있다.

Look at the house on the hill. That's **my grandfather's**.
언덕 위의 집을 봐. 저것은 나의 할아버지 댁이야. (= my grandfather's house)
This is a new bicycle. Is it **Minsu's**? 이것은 새 자전거네. 민수의 것이니?
(= Minsu's bicycle)

2. 무생물의 소유격 – 「of+명사」

the roof **of my house** 나의 집의 지붕   the legs **of the table** 탁자의 다리

cf. 시간, 거리, 장소, 금액을 나타내는 명사의 소유격은 무생물이지만 's 또는 '로 나타낸다.
today's newspaper 오늘의 신문   **ten miles'** distance 10마일의 거리
Korea's biggest industry 한국의 가장 큰 산업   **twenty dollars'** worth 20달러의 가치

PRACTICE 8 [1-16]

괄호 안에 주어진 단어를 소유격 형태로 바꾸어 문장을 완성하세요.

1 He expected ___________________________, but she didn't even look at him. (his sister, smile)

2 One of ___________________________ broke while we were moving it. (the legs, the sofa)

3 ___________________________ is on the fourth floor of the building. (the manager, office)

4 She always tries to sit on ___________________________. (the car, the front seat)

5 ___________________________ are really big and beautiful. (the twins, eyes)

6 It was ___________________________ from my house to the museum. (thirty minutes, walk)

7 Luckily, I might meet Mr. Davis at the ___________________________. (next week, meeting)

8 ___________________________ is next to my house. (Mr. and Mrs. Wilson, house)

9 Please write your name and the phone number at ___________________________.
(the page, the top)

10 He is so proud of himself, and he doesn't consider ___________________________.
(other people, opinions)

11 I drop by the ___________________________ first every time I go to the shopping
mall. (women, clothing department)

12 I could see a lot of coins at ___________________________. (the fountain, the bottom)

13 I want to know ___________________________. (the air conditioner, the cost)

14 There are three ___________________________ in the town. (girls, high schools)

15 I saw your article in ___________________________. (yesterday, newspaper)

16 ___________________________ is going to be snowy. (tomorrow, weather)

PSS 3-2 이중소유격

소유격은 관사, 지시형용사, 수량형용사 등과 나란히 쓸 수 없으므로 「of+소유대명사」 또는 「of+'s」의 형태로 명사 뒤에 이어서 쓴다.

| a an the
this that
some any no | +명사+of+소유대명사 / 's |

some my friends (×) ➡ **some** friends **of mine** (○) 내 친구들 중 몇 명

that your shirt (×) ➡ **that** shirt **of yours** (○) 네 저 셔츠

Mr. Smith's the house (×) ➡ **the** house **of Mr. Smith's** (○) Smith 씨의 그 집

Mina's this camera (×) ➡ **this** camera **of Mina's** (○) 미나의 이 카메라

정답 p.24

PRACTICE 9

다음 문장의 밑줄 친 부분을 바르게 고치세요.

1 I came across <u>my a friend</u> from elementary school at the mall.

➡ I came across ___________________________ from elementary school at the mall.

2 Never mind. It's <u>no your business</u>.

➡ Never mind. It's ___________________________.

3 <u>This my brother's cell phone</u> is the company's latest model.

➡ ___________________________ is the company's latest model.

4 Suji introduced me to <u>a relative of her</u> at the social party.

➡ Suji introduced me to ___________________________ at the social party.

5 It was <u>a good idea of your</u> to make a guest list.

➡ It was ___________________________ to make a guest list.

6 I took a trip with <u>my brother's some friends</u> last year.

➡ I took a trip with ___________________________ last year.

PSS 4 부정관사 a, an

PSS 4-1 a, an의 쓰임

1. 첫소리가 자음으로 발음되는 단수 명사 앞에는 a를, 모음으로 발음되는 단수 명사 앞에는 an을 붙인다.

> **a** girl   **a** movie   **a** tree   **a** hero   **a** computer
> **an** artist   **an** elephant   **an** idea   **an** officer   **an** umbrella

2. 명사 앞의 형용사의 첫소리가 자음으로 발음되면 a를, 모음으로 발음되면 an을 붙인다.

> **a** great time   **a** big apple   **a** science teacher
> **an** old woman   **an** interesting question   **an** English version

3. 모음으로 시작되지만 자음으로 발음되는 명사 앞에는 a를, 자음으로 시작되지만 모음으로 소리 나는 명사 앞에는 an을 붙인다. 명사 앞에 형용사가 있을 경우에는 그 형용사의 발음에 따라 a와 an을 구별하여 쓴다.

> **a** university   **a** uniform   **an** hour   **an** MVP
> **a** European family   **a** useful tool   **an** honest person   **an** ambitious man

cf. MVP나 FBI 같은 약어를 Most Valuable Player나 Federal Bureau of Investigation과 같이 풀어 말하면 첫소리가 자음으로 발음되므로 이때는 an이 아니라 a를 쓴다.
He was chosen as **a most valuable player** by newspaper sports reporters.
그는 스포츠 담당 신문 기자들에 의해 최우수 선수로 선정되었다.

정답 p.24

PRACTICE 10 [1-11]

다음 문장의 빈칸에 a 또는 an을 알맞게 써 넣으세요.

1 My family went to ___________ American cultural heritage museum.

2 That was ___________ perfect example of animals' aggressive behavior.

3 I saw ___________ young boy playing alone with a model plane.

4 I'm planning to send my son to ___________ international school.

5 She couldn't say ___________ word for a while when her daughter showed up.

6 She has ___________ eight-year-old son and a five-year-old daughter.

7 Uncle Jack has worked at ___________ grocery store since last year.

8 Volunteer service in the area was ___________ useful experience to me.

9 I think he is ___________ honest and sincere man.

10 Father bought ___________ air fryer for mother and gave it to her.

11 She has worked for this company for about ___________ year.

PSS 4-2 a, an의 의미

one '하나의'	Rome was not built in **a** day. 로마는 하루에 지어지지 않았다.
a certain '어떤'	**A** strange man was waiting for you. 어떤 낯선 남자가 너를 기다리고 있었다. ***cf.*** a가 사람의 이름 앞에 쓰여 '~라는 사람'의 의미로 쓰일 수 있다. There's **a** Mrs. Green to see you. Green 부인이라는 분이 당신을 만나고 싶어 해요.
some '약간의, 어느 정도'	I couldn't say a word for **a** while. 나는 잠시 동안 한 마디도 할 수가 없었다.
the same '같은, 동일한'	Bill and Sumi are of **an** age. Bill과 Sumi는 동갑이다.
per '~당, ~마다'	I brush my teeth three times **a** day. 나는 하루에 세 번 이를 닦는다.
대표 단수	**A** dog is a faithful animal. 개는 충성스러운 동물이다.

정답 p.24

PRACTICE 11

밑줄 친 a(n)의 올바른 의미를 〈보기〉에서 찾아 해당 번호를 쓰세요.

보 기	① one ② a certain ③ some ④ the same ⑤ per ⑥ 대표 단수

1 We might stay at his house for a day or two. [   ]

2 Kate takes an aerobics lesson in the health center once a week. [   ]

3 Birds of a feather flock together. [   ]

4 A Ms. Miller called you this morning. [   ]

5 A dolphin is a smart animal. [   ]

6 The captain continued to sail for the island after a while. [   ]

7 The children in the playground are all of an age. [   ]

8 In a way, the new rule of the school is not fair. [   ]

9 My granddaughter sends a card to me twice a year. [   ]

10 We have a son and two daughters. [   ]

PSS 5 정관사 the

PSS 5-1 the의 쓰임 Ⅰ

1. **앞에 나온 명사가 다시 반복될 때**

   There is a garage in the backyard. I hid money in **the garage**.
   뒷마당에 차고가 있다. 나는 차고에 돈을 숨겨놓았다.

2. **문맥이나 상황으로 보아 말하는 이가 무엇을 가리키는지 알 수 있을 때**

   Will you pass me **the salt** over there? 그쪽에 있는 소금 좀 건네주시겠어요?

3. **유일한 것을 말할 때**

   The Earth goes around **the Sun**. 지구는 태양 주위를 돈다.

4. **서수, 최상급, only, very, same 앞**

   March is **the third** month of the year. 3월은 한 해의 세 번째 달이다.
   It was **the only** thing that I could do in that situation.
   그것이 내가 그 상황에서 할 수 있었던 유일한 것이었다.

5. **대표 단수 앞**

   The cat is a clever animal. 고양이는 영리한 동물이다. = **A cat** is a clever animal.
   　　　　　　　　　　　　　　　　　　　　　　　　= **Cats** are clever animals.

   cf. 종족을 대표하는 명사는 「the+단수명사」, 「a/an+단수명사」, 또는 복수명사로 나타낼 수 있다.

정답 p.24

PRACTICE 12

괄호 안에 들어갈 알맞은 말을 골라 동그라미 하세요.

1　He has (a, the) big bag. (A, The) bag is brown and light.

2　I go to my uncle's house and stay one night once (a, the) month.

3　Human beings have explored (a, the) Moon since the 20th century.

4　The speed limit on this road is 80 kilometers (an, the) hour.

5　Everybody looked at her at (a, the) same time when she shouted.

6　Tim is (a, the) tallest boy of my son's friends.

7　This will explain the origin of (a, the) universe.

8　She arrived here (a, the) while ago and she waited for you.

9　Do you mind if I open (a, the) back door?

10　We missed (a, the) first train, so we had to wait until the next one arrived.

PSS 5-2 the의 쓰임 Ⅱ

1. **악기명을 나타낼 때**

   He used to play **the guitar** and **the piano**. 그는 기타와 피아노를 치곤 했다.

2. **특정한 고유명사 앞**

   the White House 백악관   **the Pacific** 태평양   **the Himalayas** 히말라야 산맥

   the United States of America 미국   **the Netherlands** 네덜란드

3. **the+형용사 / 분사 '~한 사람들'**

   She wanted to help **the poor** for the rest of her life.

   그녀는 남은 일생 동안 불쌍한 사람들을 돕기를 원했다.

   cf. 「the+형용사」가 추상명사의 의미로 쓰여 '~한 것'으로 해석되기도 한다.

   It's no use wishing for **the impossible**. 불가능한 것을 기원해 봐야 소용없다.

4. **구나 절이 뒤에서 명사를 꾸며줄 때**

   There are **the jeans** that I wanted in the show window of the store.

   저 가게의 진열창 안에 내가 원했던 청바지가 있다.

   cf. 대상을 특정하지 않으면 부정관사를 쓴다.

   There is **a** man who is waiting for you. 당신을 기다리고 있는 한 사람이 있다.

5. **동작의 대상이 되는 신체의 일부를 나타낼 때**

   Someone caught me by **the hand**. 누군가가 내 손을 잡았다.

정답 p.24

PRACTICE 13

빈칸에 a(n) 또는 the를 넣어 문장을 완성하세요.

1 There are seats for ___________ elderly and ___________ pregnant in the subway in Korea.

2 He hit me on ___________ head behind me.

3 It'll take ___________ hour to go up and down the hill.

4 Jenny started to play ___________ flute when she was 6 years old.

5 I spent two months at an English camp in ___________ Philippines.

6 Can I drink ___________ glass of water, please? I'm very thirsty.

7 When I lied to Dad, I couldn't look him in ___________ eye.

8 ___________ Mr. Green came to meet you a few minutes ago.

9 Mom usually calls me three times ___________ day to check if I had a meal.

10 ___________ skirt that Ms. Scott designed for this season sells well.

PSS 6 관사를 쓰지 않는 경우

1. **식사를 나타내는 명사 앞**

   My family had **breakfast** a bit earlier than usual this morning.
   우리 가족은 오늘 아침 평소보다 좀 더 일찍 아침식사를 했다.

   cf. 식사를 나타내는 명사 앞에 형용사가 있으면 관사를 쓸 수 있다.
   I had a **light** breakfast. 나는 간단한 아침을 먹었다.

2. **운동 경기를 나타내는 명사 앞**

   We're going to work on **tennis** for the next match.
   우리는 다음 경기를 위해 테니스를 연습할 것이다.

3. **「by+교통수단」으로 쓰일 때(by 이외의 전치사를 쓸 때는 관사가 필요함)**

   Traveling **by ship** was a wonderful experience. 배를 타고 여행한 것은 굉장한 경험이었다.

4. **장소를 나타내는 명사가 본래의 목적으로 쓰일 때**

   I go to **school** every day. 나는 매일 학교에 간다. (공부하러 학교에 간다는 의미)
   He will go to the school to pick up his kid. 그는 그의 아이를 데리러 학교에 갈 것이다.
   (학교의 본래 목적인 공부하러 가는 것이 아니라 다른 이유로 가는 경우 관사를 씀)

5. **가족 구성원을 나타내는 명사 앞**

   Father is going to build a cottage on the hill. 아버지는 언덕 위에 오두막을 지을 것이다.

6. **관직, 신분, 호칭을 나타내는 명사 앞**

   Professor Kim is known for his influential contributions to the field of economics.
   김 교수님은 경제학 분야에서 그의 영향력 있는 공헌으로 알려져 있다.

7. **과목을 나타내는 명사 앞**

   I like **chemistry** more than any other subject.
   나는 다른 어떤 과목보다도 화학을 더 좋아한다.

8. **그 외의 경우 – listen to music과 watch TV는 관용적으로 관사 없이 쓴다.**

   Nancy **listens to music** when she walks on the street.
   Nancy는 길을 걸을 때 음악을 듣는다.
   My brother **watches TV** from morning to night. 내 남동생은 아침부터 밤까지 TV를 본다.

PRACTICE 14

다음 문장의 밑줄 친 부분이 바르면 ○, 틀리면 ×를 쓰세요.

1 We didn't want to go sightseeing by <u>a taxi</u> because it was too expensive. (   )

2 'B' is <u>second letter</u> of the alphabet. (   )

3 I called Mark because he didn't come to <u>school</u>. (   )

4 Since I'm on a diet, I'm not going to have <u>dinner</u>. (   )

5 <u>Mom</u> cooked many kinds of food for my birthday party. (   )

6 Would you like to play <u>the soccer</u> with us after school? (   )

7 The shadows lengthened as <u>the sun</u> went down. (   )

8 <u>Professor</u> Philips is very popular at my university. (   )

9 I'm so tired. I will go to <u>bed</u> earlier tonight. (   )

10 Jimin was watching <u>a TV</u> when I called him. (   )

11 I found that <u>the biology</u> is a very interesting but difficult subject. (   )

12 I bought <u>same car</u> as yours. (   )

PRACTICE 15

다음 문장의 빈칸에 a(n)이나 the 중 알맞은 것을 쓰고, 필요 없는 곳에는 ×표 하세요.

1 I had a sandwich and fruit for __________ lunch.

2 Can you change __________ channel? I don't like rock music.

3 I water my indoor plants once __________ week to keep them healthy.

4 It takes about ten minutes to go there by __________ bus.

5 She is __________ only girl who doesn't wear glasses in my class.

6 They go to __________ church on Sunday morning.

7 I'm sorry, but can you hold __________ minute? I'll be back soon.

8 I was happy that __________ grandmother made us some sweet apple pies.

9 They're going to play __________ basketball in the stadium.

10 __________ friend of mine loves swimming.

11 I think it's __________ very place where I lost my laptop.

12 They don't tend to respect __________ old.

중간·기말고사 대비문제

1 다음 문장의 빈칸에 들어갈 말로 알맞은 것은?

> I was sitting by his hospital bed watching several ___________.

① passer-by
② passers-by
③ passer-byes
④ passer-bys
⑤ passer-bies

2 ⓐ~ⓔ의 밑줄 친 부분 중 어법상 틀린 것을 있는 대로 찾아 옳게 고쳐 쓰세요.

> ⓐ A chair and a table were the only furniture in the room.
> ⓑ Jaesuk found that it had many information.
> ⓒ We should have a little knowledge in order to enjoy the paintings.
> ⓓ It made people in the village earn few money.
> ⓔ If teachers gave many homeworks, would students do better?

➡ _______________________________________

____

3 주어진 우리말과 같은 뜻이 되도록 빈칸에 알맞은 말을 쓰세요.

> • 옛 치료제들 중 일부는 현대 의학에 유용한 물질들을 가지고 있다.
> = Some of the old cures have materials that are ___________ ___________ in modern medicine.

4 Choose the grammatically correct sentence.

① The matchs are on your left hand.
② It can also be cooked and eaten in different way.
③ We can save water by using a cup when we brush our tooth.
④ She had saved enough money to buy a car.
⑤ Green was chosen for grass and leafs.

5 다음 대화에서 어법상 틀린 부분을 찾아 바르게 고치세요.

> *Father*: I'd like to eat chicken. But I'm the one who needs to lose weight. I'll just have fruit and vegetables.
> *Sumi* : I'll have a steak and fried potato. Let's call the waitress.

___________________ ➡ ___________________

6 다음 중 어법상 틀린 것을 모두 고르세요.

① You are supposed to write two essays by tomorrow.
② It is important to have various hobbies to live a healthy life.
③ Make sure you bring photoes of you and your best friends.
④ Susie bought souvenirs at a store in Canada while traveling.
⑤ I wonder how thiefs can get into one's house without being caught.

> • People who aren't physically healthy get tired easily.
> = People who aren't physically healthy get tired ___________ ___________.

8 다음 중 어법상 어색한 것은?

① Busan is Korea's most beautiful seaport.
② I read the story about cloning in the newspaper of today.
③ The land near the lake is not the government's.
④ Doing physical activities should be a part of your daily routine.
⑤ I used to stay at my friend's house while my parents were away.

9 주어진 우리말과 같은 뜻이 되도록 다음 대화의 빈칸에 알맞은 말을 쓰세요.

> David : Hi. What are you doing?
> Jenny : Hi. I'm writing emails to some friends ___________ ___________ in Canada. (내 친구들 중 몇 명)

10 다음 중 어색한 표현은?

① a cup of tea　　② a slice of cheese
③ a piece of advice　　④ a loaf of beer
⑤ a pound of gold

11 밑줄 친 a(n)의 의미가 나머지 넷과 다른 것은?

① Can you give me <u>an</u> example?
② May I ask <u>a</u> question of you?
③ At the end of the sentence, type <u>a</u> period.
④ <u>A</u> month later, he invited his friends to lunch.
⑤ She allowed me to play games for an hour <u>a</u> day.

12 다음 중 어법상 어색한 것은?

① His family is large.
② My family members are all diligent.
③ The police is chasing after a thief.
④ Cattle are grazing on the field.
⑤ The audience is crazy about the singer.

13 다음 대화에서 (A)와 (B)가 주어진 우리말과 같도록 괄호 안에 주어진 단어를 바르게 배열하세요.

> A: What are you doing on Thanksgiving Day?
> B: I have to study at the library.
> A: You're kidding. How can you study on a holiday?
> B: Well, (A) <u>우리 반 친구들 몇 명도 연휴에 공부해.</u> (classmates, too, holidays, on, some, of, study, mine)
> A: That's too bad. Do you want me to bring some food to the library?
> B: No, thanks. (B) <u>나는 내 친구 한 명과 함께 저녁을 먹을 거야.</u> (dinner, mine, going, with, of, I'm, to, have, friend, a)

(A) ____

____

(B) ____

____

14 다음 중 어법상 옳은 것은?

① He still trains for a hour a day.
② One day a old woman asked me for directions.
③ Many people loved her because she was an honest person.
④ He studied at an university to become an architect.
⑤ Moldova is an European country, which is between Romania and the Ukraine.

15 두 문장이 같은 뜻이 되도록 빈칸에 알맞은 전치사를 쓰세요.

- When you travel in a bus, let your mind think of what you have read.
  = When you travel ___________ bus, let your mind think of what you have read.

16 다음 중 어법상 옳은 것은?

① The first scene is my favorite part in the movie.
② She pointed to second man and asked a question.
③ He had the dinner and then went to bed.
④ He plays drums in a boy band.
⑤ Will you teach me how to play the baseball?

17 다음 문장에서 틀린 부분을 찾아 바르게 고치세요.

Dad went to school to visit my teacher.

___________________ ➡ ___________________

18 다음 중 어법상 어색한 것은?

① Mother doesn't understand why I spend so much money on clothes.
② She expressed feeling guilty for homeless.
③ I'm going to study math, history, and English.
④ They had to cross the field in order to reach the church.
⑤ The man who is carrying two blue boxes has brown eyes.

19 두 문장이 같은 뜻이 되도록 빈칸에 알맞은 말을 쓰세요.

- She patted my shoulder.
  = She patted _______ on _______ shoulder.

20 밑줄 친 (A), (B)를 〈조건〉에 맞게 바꾸세요.

My dad bought a beautiful necklace for my mom's birthday. It was so beautiful that I wanted to try it on before Mom came home. As soon as I held up the necklace, (A) my dad told me to handle it [carefully]. I was afraid that I might ruin the necklace. Since (B) my mom said that she would arrive home [punctually], I decided not to try on her necklace.

조 건	[ ] 안의 단어를 다음의 전치사를 활용해 바꿔 쓰세요. (A): with　　　(B): on

(A) ___________________________________

(B) ___________________________________

21 두 문장이 같은 뜻이 되도록 빈칸에 알맞은 말을 쓰세요.

- There are so many good books that young people should read.
= There are so many good books that __________ __________ should read.

22 다음 중 어법상 옳은 것은?

① I experienced the same feelings as Michael.
② I'll tell you a most interesting story among them.
③ The math is the most difficult subject to me.
④ I would like to thank a father for his help.
⑤ Only thing that I could do was prevent him from watching TV.

23 두 문장이 같은 뜻이 되도록 빈칸에 알맞은 말을 쓰세요.

- She always pronounces the actor's name wrong. Do you think she does it purposely?
= She always pronounces the actor's name wrong. Do you think she does it __________ __________?

24 다음 중 밑줄 친 부분의 쓰임이 잘못된 것은?

If you find any ① difficulty in ② opening these ③ applications forms, please ④ download this ⑤ program.

25 다음 중 어법상 옳은 것은?

① A man saved an woman from the deep river.
② Are you sure the metal dish you saw is an UFO?
③ He appeared in the stadium in an wheelchair.
④ I bought an umbrella made with UV protective material.
⑤ I want to be a nurse, but my parents want me to become a artist.

26 밑줄 친 (a)~(e) 중 어법상 옳은 것은?

In our science club experiment, we tried using lemons as tiny batteries. We connected wires to the lemons (a) to make a small clock to run. First, the lemons were cut in half by the teacher. Then we pushed copper and zinc nails into the fruit (b) so that electricity could flow. The teacher told us afterwards that (c) the experiment is a success. Only after the clock started (d) we realized how amazing simple science can be. Finally, we (e) cleaned up a equipment before leaving the lab.

① (a)　　② (b)　　③ (c)　　④ (d)　　⑤ (e)

27 다음 중 어법상 어색한 것은?

① We had few snow this year.
② I have little interest in politics.
③ Could I try a little of your wine?
④ His ideas are difficult, and few people understand them.
⑤ Few of us can say that we always tell the truth.

28 다음 중 명사의 단수형과 복수형이 바르게 연결되지 <u>않은</u> 것은?

① thief – thieves ② cliff – cliffs
③ chief – chiefs ④ life – lives
⑤ belief – believes

29 다음 중 빈칸에 the가 들어가야 하는 것은?

① She always listens to __________ music when she studies.
② I didn't have much interest in __________ basketball.
③ I think he was __________ first boy to win the contest.
④ If you don't eat __________ lunch, you'll be very hungry.
⑤ I want to watch __________ TV and do some silly things.

30 다음 우리말을 영어로 바르게 옮긴 것은?

> 수학이 모든 과목 중에서 가장 어려운 것 같다.

① Mathematics seem to be the hardest subject of all.
② It seems that mathematics are the hardest subject of all.
③ It seems that mathematics is the hardest subject of all.
④ Mathematic seems to be the hardest subject of all.
⑤ It seems that the mathematics is the hardest subject of all.

31 다음 중 어법상 <u>어색한</u> 것은?

① I will never forget the five days' journey.
② She was going to spend her vacation at her uncle's.
③ Taekwondo became Korea's national sport in 1971.
④ The grass is always greener on the other side of the fence.
⑤ You should remember that you can't live without others's help.

32 다음 대화에서 <u>틀린</u> 부분을 찾아 바르게 고치세요.

> A: Can I borrow your sister's some books?
> B: Let me ask her first.

➡ __________________________________

33 다음 중 어법상 <u>어색한</u> 것은?

① I heard many times that a dog is a faithful animal.
② The earth is the only place we can live on.
③ A proverb says that an apple the day keeps the doctor away.
④ Are you sending the same kind of message back?
⑤ The book is the oldest record of Korean history.

34 다음 빈칸 ⓐ, ⓑ에 들어갈 표현이 알맞게 짝지어진 것은?

> Today is my dad's birthday. I'm going to make a chocolate cake. I found out how to make it. I need a cup of flour, two ____ⓐ____, five spoonfuls of sugar, and four ____ⓑ____.

      ⓐ   ⓑ

① cups of milk   – bar of chocolates
② cup of milks   – bars of chocolate
③ cups of milks – bars of chocolates
④ cup of milks   – bars of chocolates
⑤ cups of milk   – bars of chocolate

35 밑줄 친 단어의 쓰임이 어색한 것은?

① She was one of the <u>witnesses</u> at our wedding.
② The recipe is of no <u>use</u> if we don't have the ingredients.
③ Oil spills are having a devastating effect on coral <u>reefs</u> in the ocean.
④ The country has suffered from <u>persistence</u> economic problems.
⑤ Packing in <u>haste</u>, I left behind my favorite book.

CHAPTER 6
대명사

Problem Solving Skill	페이지	성취도				
		100%	99~75%	74~50%	49~25%	24~0%
PSS 1 재귀대명사	118					

PSS 2 it	페이지	성취도				
		100%	99~75%	74~50%	49~25%	24~0%
PSS 2-1 it의 용법 Ⅰ	119					
PSS 2-2 it의 용법 Ⅱ	121					

PSS 3 부정대명사	페이지	성취도				
		100%	99~75%	74~50%	49~25%	24~0%
PSS 3-1 one	123					
PSS 3-2 other, another	124					
PSS 3-3 관용 표현	126					
PSS 3-4 all, both	128					
PSS 3-5 each, every	129					
PSS 3-6 some-, any-	131					
PSS 3-7 no-	132					
PSS 3-8 부분부정	133					
중간·기말고사 대비문제	134					

PSS 1 재귀대명사

1. 재귀 용법 – 문장의 주어와 목적어의 대상이 같을 때는 목적어 자리에 인칭대명사의 목적격 대신 재귀대명사를 쓴다. 이 경우 재귀대명사는 생략할 수 없다.

   Above all, you should know **yourself** first. 무엇보다도 네 자신을 먼저 알아야 한다.
   Above all, you should know **you** first. (×)

   I'll take care of **myself** from now on. 나는 지금부터 내 자신을 돌볼 것이다.
   I'll take care of **me** from now on. (×)

2. 강조 용법 – 명사나 대명사를 강조하기 위해 쓰이는 재귀대명사는 강조하고자 하는 (대)명사 바로 뒤에 오거나 문장의 끝에 올 수 있고, 생략할 수도 있다. 강조 용법의 재귀대명사를 생략하면 강조의 의미도 사라진다.

   I **(myself)** had the same experience when I was a kid.
   내가 어린아이였을 때, 나 (자신)도 똑같은 경험을 했다.
   Have you seen the famous director **(yourself)**? 너는 그 유명한 감독을 (직접) 본 적이 있니?

3. 전치사+재귀대명사

   ① by oneself '혼자, 다른 사람 없이'
   I couldn't control the situation **by myself**. 나는 혼자서 그 상황을 통제할 수 없었다.

   ② for oneself '혼자 힘으로, 스스로'
   He tried to solve the problems **for himself**. 그는 혼자 힘으로 문제를 해결하려고 했다.

정답 p.27

PRACTICE 1

괄호 안에 들어갈 알맞은 말을 골라 동그라미 하세요.

1 I can't finish the assignment by (me, myself).

2 She needed space to be (her, herself).

3 He managed to fix the car for (him, himself).

4 I'll lend (you, yourself) some of the money you need.

5 The foreigner asked (me, myself) how to get to the community center.

6 Socrates said, "Know (you, yourself)."

7 She didn't seem quite (her, herself) this morning.

8 Mr. Cohen introduced both of (us, ourselves) to his family.

9 Help (you, yourself) to those cookies.

10 I saw your sister packing the suitcase by (her, herself).

11 Ben is not going to tell this to (them, themselves).

12 She is very gorgeous. I can't even look at (her, herself).

13 They had the whole campsite to (them, themselves).

14 Most nights she would cry (her, herself) to sleep.

15 Brian is not going to talk to (me, myself) anymore.

정답 p.27

PRACTICE 2

다음 문장에 쓰인 재귀대명사 중 생략할 수 있는 것에 괄호 표시 하세요.

1   I kept saying to myself, "I can do it."

2   The boy found the office building himself.

3   My sisters themselves are going to pick up the kids at the port.

4   They are going to cook dinner for themselves.

5   You deserve to give yourself a prize.

6   I myself witnessed the bomb attack last night.

7   Cathy took these amazing photos in Africa herself.

8   I can't make myself understood in Chinese.

9   The little boy was waiting for his mom by himself.

10   Sara doesn't think that Jason came up with the idea himself.

PSS 2 it

PROBLEM
SOLVING
SKILL

PSS 2-1 it의 용법 I

1. 가주어 it

   ① to부정사(구)를 진주어로 하는 경우
   It is impossible **to swim across this river**. 이 강을 수영을 해서 건너는 것은 불가능하다.

② 동명사(구)를 진주어로 하는 경우

It is no use **blaming the doctors for his death**.

그의 죽음에 대해 의사들 탓을 해 봐야 소용 없다.

③ 명사절을 진주어로 하는 경우

It is surprising **that you are disappointed**. 네가 실망했다는 것은 놀랍다.

2. 가목적어 it

① to부정사(구)를 진목적어로 하는 경우

I found **it** refreshing **to take a walk every morning**.

나는 매일 아침 산책을 하는 것이 기분을 상쾌하게 한다는 것을 알았다.

② 동명사(구)를 진목적어로 하는 경우

I thought **it** dangerous **climbing the mountain alone**.

나는 혼자 등산하는 것은 위험하다고 생각했다.

③ 명사절을 진목적어로 하는 경우

I made **it** clear **that I would go abroad**. 나는 해외로 가겠다는 것을 분명히 했다.

정답 p.27

PRACTICE 3

우리말과 같은 뜻이 되도록 괄호 안에 주어진 말을 바르게 배열하세요.

1 그 토론에 참여하는 것은 꼭 필요하다.

= ______________________________

(it, to, in the debate, is, necessary, participate)

2 나는 두 그림 사이의 차이점을 구별하는 것이 어렵다는 것을 알았다.

= ______________________________

(it, to, I, found, hard, the two paintings, between, tell the difference)

3 친구들과 보드게임을 하는 것은 아주 재미있었다.

= ______________________________

(it, friends, playing, board games, with, fun, a lot of, was)

4 나는 여기 있는 것이 이상하다고 느낀다.

= ______________________________

(it, here, I, being, strange, find)

5 Garcia 씨가 빨리 승진할 것은 확실하다.

= ______________________________

(it, will, that, is, Mr. Garcia, get promoted, certain, quickly)

6 외국어를 배우는 것은 흥미롭다.

= ____

　　(it, is, to, interesting, learn, foreign languages)

7 그 새로운 식당에서 당신과 함께 식사하는 것은 기쁜 일이었다.

= ____

　　(it, with, was, dining, a pleasure, you, the new restaurant, at)

8 Tony가 일부러 창문을 깨뜨렸다는 것은 충격적이다.

= ____

　　(it, shocking, that, Tony, on purpose, is, the window, broke)

9 그녀는 공상과학소설을 읽는 것이 매우 재미있다는 것을 알았다.

= ____

　　(it, she, science fiction, reading, found, a lot of, fun)

10 나는 다른 사람들의 의견을 구하는 것이 좋은 생각이라고 생각했다.

= ____

　　(it, I, a good idea, thought, others' opinions, to seek)

CH
6
대명사

PSS 2-2 it의 용법 Ⅱ

1. It seems[appears] that ~ / It happens that ~ '~인 것 같다, ~처럼 보인다'

   It seems[appears] that you are a little tired. 너 약간 피곤한 것 같다.
   = You **seem[appear] to** be a little tired.

   It happened that I met her in front of your office. 나는 우연히 네 사무실 앞에서 그녀를 만났다.
   = I **happened to** meet her in front of your office.

2. (관용적 표현에서 사용하는) 상황을 나타내는 it

   How's **it** going with your new friend, Mark? 새 친구 Mark랑은 어떻게 되어 가고 있니?
   Take **it** easy. 마음 편히 가져.

3. 「It ~ that …」 강조구문 – 강조하고자 하는 말을 It is/was와 that 사이에 쓴다. 단, 동사와 형용사는 It is/was와 that 사이에 쓸 수 없다.

   It is a new photocopier **that** we need to buy right now.
   지금 당장 우리가 사야 할 것은 새 복사기이다.
   It was you **that** helped me at that time. 그때 나를 도왔던 것은 너였다.
   It was not until this morning **that** I realized that I had lost it. 내가 그것을 잃어버렸다는
   것을 오늘 아침까지 알아차리지 못했다. (오늘 아침이 되어서야 그것을 잃어버렸다는 것을 알아차렸다.)

PRACTICE 4

〈보기〉와 같이 주어진 문장을 같은 뜻의 다른 문장으로 바꾸어 쓰세요.

> **보 기** It seems that she is surprised to see the magician again.
> = She seems to be surprised to see the magician again.

1 It appeared that they knew the truth about my family.

= ____

2 There happened to be no one at home.

= ____

3 My brother seems to have a plan to stay at my uncle's for a while.

= ____

4 She appears to feel quite satisfied with the result.

= ____

5 It happened that the teacher showed up very late.

= ____

PRACTICE 5

밑줄 친 it의 쓰임이 같은 것끼리 연결하세요.

1 It would be helpful to join the club.

2 It seems that you and I have a lot in common.

3 I'm sorry but I can't make it to your party.

4 I thought it impossible to spend my holiday with Chris.

5 It was my cat that ate my cheese cake.

① I found it pretty safe going there by myself.

② It is always exciting going on a field trip.

③ It is already over with me.

④ It isn't the money that I asked you for.

⑤ It appears that Hana is the most active student in the class.

PRACTICE 6

다음 밑줄 친 it의 용법을 〈보기〉에서 골라 그 번호를 쓰세요.

> **보 기** ① 가주어   ② 가목적어   ③ It seems that ~
> ④ 상황을 나타내는 it   ⑤ 「It is ~ that …」 강조구문

1 It is no use crying over spilt milk. [   ]

2 It seems that it is his first time to be on a plane. [   ]

3 I found it exciting having a variety of foreign friends. [   ]

4 It was Ms. Lopez that came here to pick you up. [   ]

5 Take it easy. [   ]

6 It is unbelievable that he failed the driver's license test again. [   ]

7 How's it going with you? [   ]

8 It appears that most of the students will cancel the class. [   ]

9 It was a personal question that I was going to ask you. [   ]

10 I made it a rule to read the newspaper every morning. [   ]

PSS 3 부정대명사

PSS 3-1 one

1. 앞에 나온 명사와 종류는 같지만 대상이 다른 경우에는 명사의 반복을 피하기 위해 one 을 쓴다.

I have lost my **watch**, so I must buy **one**. 나는 시계를 잃어버려서 하나 사야 한다.
(내가 사야 하는 시계는 앞에서 언급한 my watch가 아닌 막연한 시계들 가운데 하나를 가리키므로 one을 쓴다.)

cf. I've downloaded **a cool app**. You should check **it** out as well.
나는 멋진 앱을 다운받았어. 너도 확인해 봐.
(앞에서 언급한 멋진 앱을 가리키므로 one이 아닌 it을 쓴다.)

2. 복수일 때는 one 대신 ones를 쓴다.

I want to buy a pair of **shoes**. How much are those black **ones**?
나는 신발 한 켤레를 사고 싶어요. 저 검정색 신발은 얼마인가요?

cf. 명사가 복수형이고 앞에서 언급한 명사와 동일한 대상을 지칭할 때는 they[them]를 쓴다.
Did you order **the books**? - Yes, **they** will arrive tomorrow.
너는 그 책들을 주문했니?   응, 그것들은 내일 도착할 거야.

3. 일반적인 사람들을 나타낸다.

One should eat and exercise regularly. 사람은 규칙적으로 먹고 운동해야 한다.

PRACTICE 7

다음 빈칸에 it, them, one, ones 중 어법상 알맞은 것을 써 넣으세요.

1   Is this science magazine yours? Can I borrow ___________ after you finish it?

2   I lost my student ID card, so I need to request a new ___________.

3   I'd like a watermelon. Give me a good ___________ among them.

4   These pants are too small for me. Can you give me bigger ___________?

5   I was looking for the key for an hour, and I found ___________ in the closet.

6   There were a lot of weeds. I pulled ___________ out for 2 hours.

7   I don't need blue pens now. Can I have two black ___________ instead?

8   The first chapter was much more interesting than the second ___________.

9   Which dress do you like? – I like that ___________ with a ribbon on the waistline.

10   These bananas are much better than the ___________ we bought there.

11   You already have lots of hats. Are you sure you need another ___________?

12   Here's the sweater that I made myself. I'll show ___________ to everybody I know.

13   Have you read Mr. Park's new poem? – No, I haven't read ___________ yet.

14   This computer is as good as my new ___________.

15   The apples in that box were rotten, so we didn't eat ___________.

16   ___________ usually finds that friendship is very important.

17   The purpose of education is to replace an empty mind with an open ___________.

18   I took the papers and threw ___________ away.

PSS 3-2 other, another

1.   others '(불특정한) 다른 사람[것]들'

   You shouldn't talk like that to **others**.
   너는 다른 사람들에게 그렇게 얘기해서는 안 된다.

2.   the other '(둘 중) 나머지 하나'

   I have two pets. One is a dog and **the other** is a cat.
   나는 반려동물이 두 마리 있다. 하나는 개이고 나머지 하나는 고양이다.

---

3. the others '나머지 사람[것]들'

She told me to take **the others** to the school safely.

그녀는 내게 나머지 사람들을 안전하게 학교로 데리고 가라고 말했다.

4. another '또 하나, 또 다른 사람[것]'

This is my favorite cookie. Can I have **another**?

이것은 내가 가장 좋아하는 쿠키야. 하나 더 먹어도 될까?

To know is one thing, and to teach is **another**. 아는 것과 가르치는 것은 별개이다.

cf. other+복수 명사 '다른, 그 밖의' / another+단수 명사 '또 하나의, 또 다른'

There are **other reasons** that I want to study psychology.

내가 심리학을 공부하기를 원하는 다른 이유들이 있다.

There is **another reason** that I want to study psychology.

내가 심리학을 공부하기를 원하는 또 다른 이유가 있다.

정답 p.28

PRACTICE 8

괄호 안에 들어갈 알맞은 말을 골라 동그라미 하세요.

1 Between the two, I'd rather choose (the other, the others) than this one.

2 When you don't feel good, it's hard to be nice to (others, the other).

3 Only Ben, Julie, and I know the truth in my class. (Another, The others) have no idea about this.

4 I'm sorry, but (other, another) nurse will take care of you from today.

5 Do you have (other, another) opinions to share with us?

6 Don't care about (another, others). It's time to think about yourself.

7 There are two places that I'd like to recommend to you. One is an old castle and (the other, another) is a museum.

8 Have you ever thought about why (others, the others) try to make more money?

9 I have four cats. Two of them have gray hair and (others, the others) have yellow hair.

10 The boy isn't going to lose (other, another) chance to enter the class.

11 I think we should make (other, another) plans just in case.

12 Painting is just (other, another) way of keeping a diary.

13 Look at your fingers. Two of them are short, and (others, the others) are long.

14 I've read the books you gave me. Do you have any (other, another) books?

one ~ the other …
(둘 중에) 하나는 ~, 다른 하나는 …

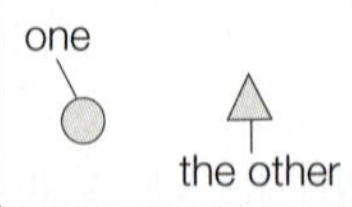

There are two girls in the bus. **One** has straight hair and **the other** has curly hair.

버스 안에 두 명의 소녀가 있다. 한 명은 직모이고, 다른 한 명은 곱슬머리이다.

one ~ another … the other −
(셋 중에) 하나는 ~, 다른 하나는 …, 나머지 하나는 −

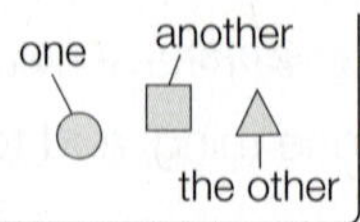

There are three dogs on the street. **One** is white, **another** is brown, and **the other** is black.

거리에 세 마리의 개가 있다. 하나는 흰색이고, 다른 하나는 갈색이고, 나머지 하나는 검정색이다.

one ~ the others …
(셋 이상에서) 하나는 ~, 나머지는 …

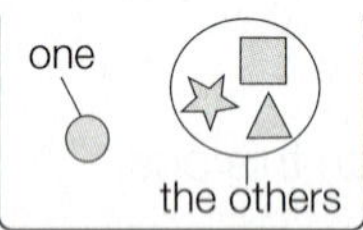

I bought four oranges at the market. **One** was sweet, and **the others** were not ripe yet.

나는 시장에서 오렌지 4개를 샀다. 하나는 달았고, 나머지는 아직 익지 않았다.

one ~ another …
(셋 이상에서) 하나는 ~, 다른 하나는 …

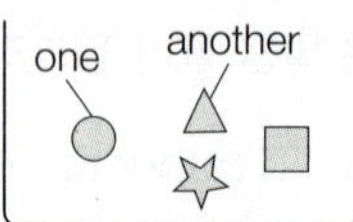

I bought **one** souvenir for my mother at the store. Then, I bought **another** for my girlfriend.

나는 그 가게에서 엄마를 위해 기념품 하나를 샀다. 그리고 나서 나는 여자친구를 위해 또 하나를 샀다.

some ~ others …
(불특정한 수의 사람[것]들 중에서) 몇몇은 ~, 다른 사람[것]들은 …

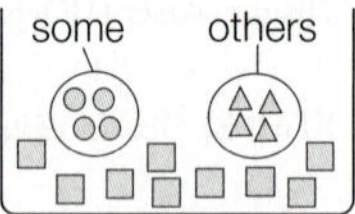

There were a lot of balls on the floor. **Some** were tennis balls and **others** were baseballs.

바닥에 많은 공들이 있었다. 몇 개는 테니스공이었고, 다른 것들은 야구공이었다.

some ~ the others …
(특정한 수의 사람[것]들 중에서) 몇몇은 ~, 나머지는 …

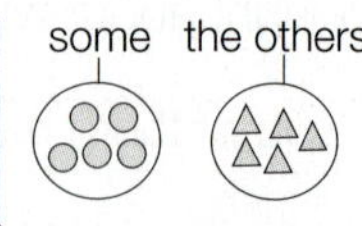

There were ten clocks on the wall of the clock shop. **Some** were grandfather clocks and **the others** were cuckoo clocks.

그 시계 가게의 벽에는 열 개의 시계가 있었다. 몇 개는 괘종 시계였고, 나머지는 뻐꾸기 시계였다.

PRACTICE 9

다음 빈칸에 들어갈 알맞은 말을 〈보기〉에서 골라 써 넣으세요.

> 보 기   one   some   the other   the others   others   another

1   Only one of the twenty students was for the proposal. _______________ were against it.

2   You don't need to listen to him. Let it go in one ear and out _______________ .

3   I got three shirts for my birthday presents. One is red, another is white, and _______________ is green.

4   I bought ten flowers yesterday. Some are tulips, and _______________ are carnations.

5   There are several ways to keep in touch with her. Making a phone call is one. Sending an e-mail is _______________ .

6   Of the 30 people, some say it is true, but _______________ say it is not.

7   Some parents send their kids to kindergarten, while _______________ don't.

8   Three boys are cleaning the house. _______________ is dusting, _______________ is vacuuming and _______________ is washing the dishes.

9   I have two sisters. _______________ is Susan and _______________ is Jane.

10   There were six kids in the room. _______________ were watching TV, and _______________ were playing games.

11   Mr. Jackson recommended two books to me. _______________ was about ancient history, and _______________ was about modern art.

12   There are three people. One is a doctor, another is a teacher, and _______________ is a lawyer.

13   Some animals have a backbone, while _______________ don't.

14   I met five foreigners at church. One is from Germany, and _______________ are from Switzerland.

15   Jina picked a few balls from the bag. Among them, one was blue, and _______________ was red.

16   I have two computers. _______________ is in my office and _______________ is in my room.

17   Some are resting under the trees and _______________ are having lunch.

18   Only five of the 20 passengers were rescued. _______________ are still missing.

1. all – '모든, ~ 모두'의 뜻으로, all 뒤에 of가 올 때는 명사 앞에 관사나 소유격 등의 수식어가 붙는다.

   ① all+셀 수 있는 명사의 복수형+복수 동사

   All students were present at the school festival. 모든 학생들이 학교 축제에 참석했다.

   ② all (of)+관사/소유격+셀 수 있는 명사의 복수형+복수 동사

   All (of) the books are supposed to be delivered by tomorrow.

   그 책들은 전부 내일까지 배달되기로 되어 있다.

   ③ all (of)+관사/소유격+셀 수 없는 명사+단수 동사

   All (of) the furniture there **was** made in Japan.

   거기에 있던 모든 가구는 일본에서 만들어졌다.

   ④ 동격 용법

   They all have to wait in line to get an autograph from the author.

   그 저자의 사인을 받기 위해 그들은 모두 줄을 서서 기다려야 한다.

   cf. all은 all과 동격을 나타내는 단어 뒤에 위치한다.

   All they have to wait in line to get an autograph from the author. (×)

2. both – '양쪽, ~ 둘 다'의 뜻으로 both 뒤에 of가 올 때는 명사 앞에 관사나 소유격 등의 수식어가 붙는다.

   ① both+셀 수 있는 명사의 복수형+복수 동사

   Both teachers are upset about the students' misbehavior.

   두 명의 선생님들 모두 그 학생들의 잘못된 행실에 화가 났다.

   ② both (of)+관사/소유격+셀 수 있는 명사의 복수형+복수 동사

   Both (of) his daughters leave for England next Friday.

   그의 딸 둘 다 다음 주 금요일에 영국으로 떠난다.

   ③ 동격 용법

   They both did their best throughout the game. 그들 둘 다 경기 내내 최선을 다했다.

   cf. both는 both와 동격을 나타내는 단어 뒤에 위치한다.

   Both they did their best throughout the game. (×)

PRACTICE 10

괄호 안에 들어갈 알맞은 말을 골라 동그라미 하세요.

1 I wanted to express all of (emotions, the emotions) that I felt.

2 Kelly found that all her money (was, were) stolen while she was away from home.

3 Both of you guys (have, has) done a great job on this project.

4 Both of (countries, the countries) have a good reputation as a tourist spot.

5 (All they, They all) had to wait for the bus to arrive.

6 All the members of the club (is, are) under age 30.

7 Both (hotel, hotels) have a variety of facilities for customers.

8 All the claims (have, has) been made by the same person.

9 Tony planned to introduce both of (his friends, friends) from Africa to me.

10 (Both they, They both) are going to stay at the resort during the vacation.

PSS 3-5 each, every

1. each – '각자, 각기, 각각의'의 뜻으로 명사를 수식하고 단수 취급한다.

    ① each+단수 명사+단수 동사 (형용사 역할)
    Each person has different goals to achieve. 각각의 사람은 이루어야 할 다른 목표들이 있다.

    ② each+of+관사/소유격+복수 명사+단수 동사 – each 뒤에 of가 올 때는 명사 앞에 관사나 소유격 등의 수식어가 붙는다. (대명사 역할)
    Each of the students has to select a topic to write about.
    각각의 학생은 작문할 주제를 골라야 한다.

    ③ 부사적 용법 (부사 역할)
    The guests paid 20 dollars **each** for the extra meals.
    손님들은 추가 식사에 대해 각각 20달러를 지불했다.

2. every – '모든'의 뜻으로 명사를 수식하고 단수 취급한다.

    ① every+단수 명사+단수 동사
    Every building in Singapore **was** very modern and beautiful.
    싱가포르에 있는 모든 건물은 매우 현대적이고 아름다웠다.

    ② '~마다, 매 ~'
    Our club members get together **every Saturday**.
    우리 클럽 회원들은 토요일마다 모인다.

cf. every+기수사+복수 명사 = every+서수사+단수 명사 '~간격으로, ~마다'

My father goes on a business trip **every two months**.

우리 아버지는 두 달에 한 번씩 출장을 가신다.

= My father goes on a business trip **every second month**.

정답 p.29

PRACTICE 11

우리말과 같은 뜻이 되도록 괄호 안에 주어진 말을 바르게 배열하세요. (필요시 어형변화 가능)

1 모든 아이들은 그들의 뒷마당에 나무집을 갖는 것을 꿈꾼다.

(their backyard, dream of, kid, have, every, in, a treehouse)

➡ ____

2 북클럽 회원들은 2주일에 한 번씩 만난다.

(the book club, week, members, every two, meet)

➡ ____

3 이들 시스템 각각은 장단점을 가지고 있다.

(have, its advantages, each of, and disadvantages, this system)

➡ ____

4 회의가 끝난 후에 각각의 회원들은 저녁을 제공받았다.

(the meeting, dinner, each member, after, be offered)

➡ ____

5 모든 도로가 교통사고 때문에 막혀 있다.

(the traffic accident, every road, because, be blocked, of)

➡ ____

6 각각의 선수들이 오른손에 국기를 들고 있었다.

(be holding, his national flag, each of, his right hand, the player, in)

➡ ____

정답 p.29

PRACTICE 12

괄호 안의 단어를 알맞은 형태로 바꾸어 빈칸에 써 넣으세요.

1 I listened carefully to every ___________ the teacher said. (word)

2 Each restaurant ___________ its own special menu and service. (have)

3 Each of the ___________ of the game can have two options. (participant)

4 My friend Suji stops by my house every ___________ day. (two)

5 The shuttle bus that goes to the city hall runs every three ___________. (hour)

6 Each student ___________ going to be awarded by the principal this Friday. (be)

1. **somebody[someone], something**

   ① 긍정문에 쓰인다.

   I'd like to show you **someone** very famous in Korea.

   나는 한국에서 매우 유명한 누군가를 네게 소개해 주고 싶다.

   ② 권유나 요구를 나타내는 의문문에 쓰인다.

   Would you like to have **something** to drink? 마실 것 좀 드릴까요?

   ③ 긍정의 대답을 예상하는 의문문에 쓰인다.

   You look gorgeous today. Are you meeting **somebody**?

   너 오늘 정말 예뻐 보인다. 누구 만날 거니?

2. **anybody[anyone], anything**

   ① 부정문에 쓰인다.

   He didn't receive **anything** from his sister on his birthday.

   그는 생일에 누나로부터 아무것도 받지 못했다.

   ② 의문문에 쓰인다.

   Do you have **anyone** to help you move out? 네가 이사 가는 것을 도와 줄 누가 있니?

   ③ '어떠한 ~라도'의 뜻일 때는 긍정문에도 쓸 수 있다.

   Anybody can enter the exhibition after the security check.

   보안 검사 후에는 누구라도 전시회에 입장할 수 있다.

   ④ 조건을 나타내는 if절에 쓸 수 있다.

   If you have **anything** to ask, feel free to contact me.

   물어볼 것이 있으시면 부담 갖지 말고 제게 연락 주세요.

정답 p.29

PRACTICE 13 [1-10]

다음 빈칸에 들어갈 알맞은 말을 〈보기〉에서 골라 써 넣으세요.

보 기	somebody something anybody anything

1 There isn't _________________ serious that you have to worry about.

2 _________________ threw away a lot of garbage in the river.

3 I am eager to find out _________________ new from the person.

4 Don't let _________________ leave this room without my permission.

5 You have a ketchup stain on your face. Did you eat _________________ before you came here?

6 Did _________________ call while I was in the meeting room? I'm just wondering.

7 Can I say _________________ about what you just said?

8 Everyone knows about it. Did you tell _________________ about it?

9 If _________________ goes wrong, I'll take care of it.

10 Isn't there _________________ who can get me an ambulance?

PSS 3-7 no-

nobody[no one]는 「not+anybody[anyone]」로, nothing은 「not+anything」으로 바꾸어 쓸 수 있다.

I told **nobody** that it was my fault. 나는 그것이 내 잘못이라고 아무에게도 말하지 않았다.
= I did **not** tell **anybody** that it was my fault.

I saw **no one** in the playground that night. 나는 그날 밤 놀이터에서 아무도 보지 못했다.
= I did**n't** see **anyone** in the playground that night.

There is **nothing** I like more than snowboarding.
스노우보드를 타는 것보다 내가 더 좋아하는 것은 아무것도 없다.
= There is**n't anything** I like more than snowboarding.

정답 p.29

PRACTICE 14

짝지어진 두 문장의 의미가 같도록 빈칸에 알맞은 말을 써 넣으세요.

1 The police found out nothing about the accident.
= The police _________________ find out _________________ about the accident.

2 She doesn't know anyone who speaks more than five languages.
= She knows _________________ who speaks more than five languages.

3 She has nothing to talk to you about.
= She _________________ have _________________ to talk to you about.

4 There isn't anybody here by that name.
= There is _________________ here by that name.

5 I didn't say anything about the result.
= I said _________________ about the result.

6 Mr. Lee told no one why he rejected my request.
= Mr. Lee _________________ tell _________________ why he rejected my request.

every, all 등 전체를 나타내는 말이 부정어와 함께 쓰이면 일부분을 부정하는 부분부정이 된다.

1. 「not+every」 '누구나[어느 것이나] ~한 것은 아니다'

   Not every boy likes playing soccer.
   모든 소년들이 축구 하기를 좋아하는 것은 아니다.
   Not every rabbit is white. 모든 토끼가 하얀 것은 아니다.

Not every rabbit is white.

2. 「not+all」 '모두가 ~한 것은 아니다'

   Not all birds can fly. 모든 새가 날 수 있는 것은 아니다.
   Not all of the invitations for the party were sent out.
   파티의 초대장이 모두 발송된 것은 아니다.

3. 「not+always」 '언제나 ~한 것은 아니다'

   Rich people are **not always** happier than poor people.
   부유한 사람들이 언제나 가난한 사람들보다 더 행복한 것은 아니다.

Not all birds can fly.

cf. 전체 부정: 대상 전체에 대해 부정하는 경우에는 no, none, never, nothing과 같은 부정어를 사용한다.

   전체 부정 He **never** eats meat. 그는 고기를 전혀 먹지 않는다. (100% 부정)
   부분 부정 He **doesn't always** eat meat. 그는 항상 고기를 먹는 것은 아니다. (가끔 먹지 않음)

정답 p.29

PRACTICE 15

다음 두 문장의 뜻이 같도록 괄호 안에 주어진 말을 이용하여 문장을 완성하세요.

1 Some of my friends have arrived, but others haven't.
= _________________________________ have arrived. (all)

2 Some fruit is sweet, but other fruit isn't.
= _________________________________ is sweet. (every)

3 Some pieces of clothing are comfortable, but other pieces aren't.
= _________________________________ is comfortable. (every)

4 Meeting new people is interesting sometimes, but at other times, it isn't.
= Meeting new people is _________________________________ . (always)

5 Some TV programs are harmful, but others are not harmful.
= _________________________________ are harmful. (all)

6 Doing group projects is helpful most of the time, but at other times, it isn't.
= Doing group projects is _________________________________ . (always)

1 〈보기〉의 단어 중 적절한 것을 골라 조건에 맞게 영작하세요.

보 기	what, how, clear, problem, really mean, solve, important

조 건
(1) 알맞은 의문사를 이용하여 가주어, 진주어 구문을 만들 것
(2) 〈보기〉의 단어를 한 번씩만 사용하되 필요하면 형태를 바꿀 것

1) 우리가 그 문제를 어떻게 해결하느냐가 중요하다.

➡ ______________________________________

2) 그가 진정 무엇을 의미한 것인지 명확하지 않았다.

➡ ______________________________________

2 다음 중 밑줄 친 It의 용법이 나머지 넷과 <u>다른</u> 것은?

① It is her laughter and her friendship that brighten my day.
② It was in L.A. that I earned the money.
③ It is the Ivy League that she is aiming at now.
④ It was raining so much that I had to stay at home.
⑤ It is in the morning that I am supposed to meet her.

3 다음 밑줄 친 itself 중 생략할 수 <u>없는</u> 것은?

① She is kindness itself.
② Even the well itself was dried up.
③ Nothing is evil in itself.
④ In summer the mountain is a green forest itself.
⑤ You will be impressed with the building itself.

4 주어진 우리말과 같은 뜻이 되도록 괄호 안의 단어를 사용하여 빈칸을 채우세요.

• 암벽을 오르기 위해, Charlie는 밧줄을 움켜잡고 자기 자신을 끌어올렸다.
= To climb up the rock, Charlie grabbed the rope and ______________ ______________ ______________. (pull)

5 다음 중 어법상 옳은 문장끼리 모인 것은?

a. After the singer finished the rehearsal, the fans asked herself for autographs.
b. During the exam, each of the students was concentrating hard.
c. They themselves prepared the meal without any help.
d. I was happy because both of my cousin had arrived safely.
e. The problem lies in the software itself, not in the hardware.

① a, b, c　　② a, b, d　　③ b, c, d
④ b, c, e　　⑤ b, d, e

6 다음 우리말 해석을 참고하여 빈칸에 알맞은 말을 쓰세요.

몇몇 사람들은 피자를 좋아하지만, 다른 사람들은 그것을 싫어한다.
= ______________ people love pizza, while ______________ hate it.

7 다음 중 밑줄 친 It이 가주어로 쓰인 것은?

① It is not my car but my father's.
② It was I that broke the window yesterday.
③ It is hard to speak English like a native speaker.
④ It is hot and humid today.
⑤ It seems that she has the key.

8 두 문장이 같은 뜻이 되도록 빈칸에 알맞은 말을 쓰세요.

- Wild horses are hard to tame.
  = It ________ ________ ________
  ________ ________ ________ .

9 주어진 우리말과 같은 뜻이 되도록 괄호 안 단어를 사용해서 빈칸을 채우세요.

- 우리 둘 다 네가 거짓말을 하고 있다고 생각한다.
  = ________ ________ ________ ________
    that you are telling a lie. (think)

10 다음 중 밑줄 친 someone의 쓰임이 잘못된 것은?

① Are you waiting for someone now?
② I'm sure that he's not going to invite someone.
③ Open the window and shout for someone to call the fire department.
④ Maybe we can find someone who can help your brothers.
⑤ Everyone assumes that someone must have stolen it.

11 다음 글의 빈칸에 들어갈 표현과 같은 표현이 들어가는 것은?

I bought two hair bands for my little sister's birthday. One is yellow with a flower pattern and ____________ has black and white stripes. I hope she will like both of them.

① I can't come up with ________ ideas.
② When he was a kid, he didn't get along with ________ kids.
③ One of the two options is to leave now. ________ is to stay here.
④ According to the store manager, this coupon is good for ________ month.
⑤ Only three of the 10 passengers were rescued. ________ are still missing.

12 다음 중 어법상 어색한 것은?

① Every student in this class studies hard.
② All of the planes were delayed due to the weather.
③ Both of the countries agree to quit the struggle.
④ I don't like this baseball cap. Show me another.
⑤ Each of the girls are interested in plastic surgery.

13 두 문장이 같은 뜻이 되도록 빈칸에 알맞은 말을 쓰세요.

- The kids seem to be interested in physics.
  = ________ ________ that the kids ________ interested in physics.

14 다음 중 빈칸에 it[It]이 들어갈 수 <u>없는</u> 것은?

① I make ___________ a rule to work out every evening.

② ___________ was by accident that he met his teacher.

③ ___________ seems that somebody else knows the secret.

④ I thought ___________ she had a brilliant idea.

⑤ How long does ___________ take you to go to school?

15 우리말과 같은 뜻이 되도록 괄호 안에 주어진 말을 바르게 배열하세요.

> • 대기오염이 그 나라에 사는 것을 어렵게 만든다.
> = ___________________________________
>
> ___________________________________
>
> (it, makes, live, to, air pollution, the country, in, difficult)

16 우리말 해석에 맞게 빈칸에 알맞은 표현을 쓰세요.

> • 만약 생태계의 한 부분이 피해를 입는다면, 그것은 생태계의 다른 부분들에도 영향을 미친다.
> = If ___________ part of an ecosystem is damaged, it affects ___________ parts of the ecosystem.

17 다음 문장의 밑줄 친 <u>one</u>과 같은 용법으로 쓰인 것은?

> Some people say that <u>one</u> should never judge a person by his or her appearance.

① <u>One</u> cannot reach the sky by climbing a ladder.

② This machine was the first <u>one</u> to be called a bicycle.

③ Try to finish your homework in <u>one</u> sitting.

④ As an old thing dies, a new <u>one</u> is born to take its place.

⑤ I saw <u>one</u> of your friends on the street.

18 다음 문장을 It was ~ that 구문으로 바꾸어 쓸 때 어법상 <u>잘못된</u> 것은?

> He won the gold medal for the first time in the 1976 Olympics.

① It was he that won the gold medal for the first time in the 1976 Olympics.

② It was won that he did the gold medal for the first time in the 1976 Olympics.

③ It was the gold medal that he won for the first time in the 1976 Olympics.

④ It was for the first time that he won the gold medal in the 1976 Olympics.

⑤ It was in the 1976 Olympics that he won the gold medal for the first time.

19 빈칸에 들어갈 말로 알맞은 것은?

> There are two official languages in Hong Kong. One is English and ___________ is Chinese.

① the other ② another
③ other ④ a second
⑤ one

20 다음 문장의 밑줄 친 it과 같은 용법으로 쓰인 것은?

> It was her that both of us wanted to marry.

① It was in the closet that I found my lost watch.
② People take it for granted that man is mortal.
③ It is disappointing that he cheated in the exam.
④ The clerk called it a day and left the office.
⑤ It is believed that human beings are born equal.

21 다음 글의 빈칸에 들어갈 말이 차례대로 짝지어진 것은?

> Three girls went to a coffee shop. ___________ of the girls ordered a glass of juice; ___________ a cup of coffee; ___________ a glass of lemonade.

① Some – another – the other
② One – another – the other
③ One – another – the latter
④ One – the other – a third
⑤ Some – the other – the third

22 빈칸에 들어갈 말로 알맞은 것은?

> Read your choices again. Then, think about which are good habits and which are bad ___________.

① one ② ones ③ it
④ them ⑤ others

[23~24] 다음 대화를 읽고, 물음에 답하세요.

> *John*: Will you tell me how to get to the nearest post office? I need to mail ___(A)___ packages.
>
> *Jane*: Sure. There's ___(B)___ very near here. Go to that tall building and turn right. You'll see a post office on your left, across from the police station. You can't miss ___(C)___.

23 빈칸 (A)에 알맞은 말을 고르세요.

(any / some)

24 빈칸 (B)와 (C)에 들어갈 말이 차례대로 짝지어진 것은?

① it – one ② one – another
③ it – other ④ some – others
⑤ one – it

25 빈칸에 들어갈 말로 알맞은 것은?

> To understand the theory is one thing; to apply it effectively is ___________.

① one ② other ③ others
④ another ⑤ the others

26 다음 글의 빈칸 (A)~(E)에 들어갈 말이 차례대로 짝지어진 것은?

> Mike has five homing pigeons. Tom is his favorite ___(A)___ . ___(B)___ calls ___(C)___ Tom and it was named after his grandfather. ___(D)___ flies home faster than his ___(E)___ birds.

(A)　(B)　(C)　(D)　(E)
① one – He – one – It – other
② ones – It – one – One – another
③ one – It – one – It – other
④ ones – It – it – One – another
⑤ one – He – it – It – other

27 다음 우리말과 같은 뜻이 되도록 괄호 안에 주어진 말 중 알맞은 것을 고르면?

> 그녀는 너무나 아름다워서 그 누구도 다른 소녀들에게 관심을 주지 않는다.

➡ She is so beautiful that (no / any) one gives (other / another) thought to (other / another) girls.

28 다음 두 문장의 의미가 같도록 빈칸에 알맞은 말을 쓰세요.

> • The train passes this station every two days.
> = The train passes this station every ___________ day.

29 다음 중 주어진 문장의 밑줄 친 It과 쓰임이 같은 것은?

> It will be hard for you to see him again.

① It was too expensive to buy within my budget.
② It was 20 kilometers to the island.
③ It is believed that the woman has left the country.
④ It rained so heavily that we canceled the game.
⑤ It was not until last night that I checked my email.

30 다음 중 밑줄 친 anyone의 쓰임이 잘못된 것은?

① Don't forget that anyone can guess about you by the clothes you wear.
② He will offer a great reward to anyone who can cure his eyes.
③ I don't want anyone else to succeed at this.
④ Anyone stole my purse that had 60 dollars in it.
⑤ We welcome anyone with a passion for music to join our choir.

31 가주어 구문을 사용하여 밑줄 친 (A)와 같은 뜻의 문장을 영작하세요. (단, 의미상 주어 him을 넣을 것.)

> Mr. Park is planning to donate a million dollars to his college. (A)To make such a big donation is very generous.

➡ _______________________________

____

32 밑줄 친 (a)~(e)를 바르게 고치지 <u>못한</u> 사람을 고르세요.

Recently, there have been reports of record-breaking rainfall across several cities. (a) <u>How the authorities have responded</u> to the flooding so far? It took several hours (b) <u>rescue</u> people trapped in their homes. Many streets were (c) <u>flood</u> after the river overflowed. About a (d) <u>three</u> of local businesses had to close temporarily. This is bad for the economy, but it's (e) <u>very</u> worse for low-income families.

① 지훈: (a)는 의문문의 어순을 맞추기 위해 How have the authorities responded로 고쳐야 해.
② 소연: 문장에서 It은 가주어이고, 진주어를 표현하려면 (b)를 to부정사인 to rescue로 바꿔야 해.
③ 민재: (c)는 홍수가 나고 있는 진행 상황을 나타내므로 flooding으로 고쳐야 해.
④ 수빈: (d)는 '3분의 1'을 나타내므로 third로 고쳐야 해.
⑤ 현우: (e)는 비교급 worse를 강조하고 있으므로 much로 수정해야 해.

33 다음 중 부분부정 문장이 <u>아닌</u> 것은?

① She didn't invite any of them.
② Not everyone can get the prize.
③ I don't always follow his advice.
④ He didn't understand all of her speech.
⑤ Expensive restaurants aren't necessarily the best.

34 다음 중 어법상 <u>어색한</u> 것은?

① All we had to run away from the fierce dog.
② Both of the conditions were too good to be true.
③ All of them are learning English at school.
④ They both wanted to take part in the election.
⑤ All the furniture in the castle is now for sale.

[35–38] 다음 글을 읽고, 물음에 답하세요.

To me, you are still only a little boy who is just like a hundred thousand ____(A)____ little boys. And (B) <u>I have no need of you.</u> And you, on your part, have no need of me. To you, I am just a fox like a hundred thousand ____(C)____ foxes. But if you tame me, then we shall need ____(D)____ other. To me, you will be unique in ____(E)____ the world. To you, I shall be unique in ____(F)____ the world.

35 (A)와 (C)에 공통으로 들어갈 말로 알맞은 것은?

① another　　② of　　③ the other
④ many　　⑤ other

36 밑줄 친 (B)를 아래와 같이 바꿀 때 빈칸에 알맞은 말을 쓰세요.

➡ I ____________ have __________ need of you.

37 (D)에 들어갈 알맞은 단어를 쓰세요.

➡ ________________________

38 (E)와 (F)에 공통으로 들어갈 말로 알맞은 것은?

① every　　② all　　③ both
④ any　　⑤ each

39 밑줄 친 곳에 들어갈 단어를 옳게 배열한 것은?

> • I lost my wallet but I found ⓐ __________ in my locker.
> • I lost my wallet, so Mom bought me a new ⓑ __________ .
> • I don't like this wallet. Could you show me ⓒ __________ ?

	ⓐ		ⓑ		ⓒ
①	it	–	another	–	it
②	it	–	one	–	another
③	one	–	one	–	one
④	one	–	one	–	it
⑤	one	–	another	–	another

40 다음 중 바르게 영작된 것은?

① 그 대학교는 외국어에 특화된 것으로 유명하다.
→ The university is known as its specialization in foreign languages.

② Karl이 깨뜨린 것은 바로 이 꽃병이다.
→ It is Karl that broke this vase.

③ 모두가 눈을 싫어하지는 않는다.
→ Not everyone hates the snow.

④ 그녀는 정말 사랑스럽다!
→ How lovely is she!

⑤ 모든 가구는 그 장인에 의해 만들어졌다.
→ All of the furniture were made by the craftsman.

41 대화의 ⓐ~ⓒ에 들어갈 알맞은 말을 순서대로 연결한 것은?

> G: Are you ready for our school project presentation today, Matt?
> B: Natalie, didn't you check your email?
> G: __________ⓐ . What did it say?
> B: The presentation has been postponed until next week.
> G: Oh, no. I was all prepared for today.
> B: Yeah, but this gives us more time to improve our slides.
> G: True. We can add __________ⓑ example to make it better.
> B: You're right. I'll inform __________ⓒ group members about the new date.

	ⓐ		ⓑ		ⓒ
①	Yes, I did.	–	another	–	the other
②	Yes, I didn't.	–	the other	–	another
③	No, I did.	–	another	–	the other
④	No, I didn't.	–	the other	–	another
⑤	No, I didn't.	–	another	–	the other

42 우리말 해석과 같은 뜻이 되도록 빈칸에 알맞은 말을 쓰세요. (단, 재귀대명사를 반드시 포함시킬 것)

(1) 그 로봇은 스스로 바닥을 청소한다.
= The robot __________ the floor __________ __________ .

(2) 나는 마음속으로 '이럴 리가 없어.'라고 생각했다.
= __________ __________ __________ __________ , "This can't be happening."

CHAPTER 7
부정사

PSS 1 명사적 용법	페이지	성취도				
		100%	99~75%	74~50%	49~25%	24~0%
PSS 1-1 주어와 주격 보어로 쓰이는 to부정사	142					
PSS 1-2 목적어로 쓰이는 to부정사	144					
PSS 1-3 목적격 보어로 쓰이는 to부정사	145					
PSS 1-4 의문사+to부정사	146					

PSS 2 형용사적 용법	페이지	성취도				
		100%	99~75%	74~50%	49~25%	24~0%
PSS 2-1 명사를 꾸미는 to부정사	147					
PSS 2-2 be to 용법	149					

PSS 3 부사적 용법	페이지	성취도				
		100%	99~75%	74~50%	49~25%	24~0%
PSS 3-1 목적을 나타내는 to부정사	150					
PSS 3-2 형용사 수식, 결과, 판단의 근거를 나타내는 to부정사	152					
PSS 3-3 too ~ to, enough to	153					

PSS 4 원형부정사	154					
PSS 5 부정사의 부정형	155					
PSS 6 대부정사	156					
PSS 7 부정사의 의미상의 주어	157					
중간·기말고사 대비문제	159					

PSS 1 명사적 용법

PSS 1-1 주어와 주격 보어로 쓰이는 to부정사

「to+동사원형」의 형태로 문장에서 명사, 형용사, 부사의 역할을 하는 것을 to부정사라고 한다.

A: It's interesting **to learn** about other countries.
다른 나라에 대해 배우는 것은 흥미로워.
B: I agree with you. I hope **to travel** around the world someday.
네 말에 동의해. 난 언젠가 세계 여행을 하고 싶어.

1. 주어 – to부정사가 문장의 맨 앞에서 주어의 역할을 할 때는 it을 주어의 자리에 두고, to부정사는 문장의 뒤로 보낸 형태를 주로 쓴다. 이때의 it을 가주어, to부정사가 이끄는 구를 진주어라고 한다.

   To prepare for the school festival was hard. 학교 축제를 준비하는 것은 어려웠다.
   = **It** was hard **to prepare** for the school festival.
   가주어 / 진주어

2. 주격 보어 – to부정사는 주어에 대해 보충 설명하는 역할을 한다.

   The final step is **to make** a program for himself.
   마지막 단계는 그 자신의 힘으로 프로그램을 만드는 것이다.
   The best thing you can do is **to keep** an open mind to your friends.
   네가 할 수 있는 최선의 것은 네 친구들에게 열린 마음을 갖는 것이다.

   cf. 주격 보어로 to를 생략하고 원형부정사를 쓰는 경우: 일상체에서 All you have to do나 이와 비슷한 구문(What I have to do)이 주어로 쓰인 문장의 보어가 되는 경우 대부분 원형부정사를 씀에 유의할 것.
   All you have to do is **apologize**. 당신은 사과하기만 하면 돼요.

정답 p.32

PRACTICE 1

주어진 문장을 「It ~ to …」 구문으로 바꾸어 쓰세요.

1 To pronounce the word correctly is very difficult.

   = ____

2 To arrive there in time was almost impossible.

   = ____

3 To play volleyball at the beach is always exciting.

= ____

4 To visit such a good place will be nice.

= ____

5 To know what you can do the best is important.

= ____

6 To study for a short time just before the test was not helpful.

= ____

정답 p.32

PRACTICE 2

그림을 보고, 괄호 안에 주어진 말을 바르게 배열하여 문장을 완성하세요.

1 My job was ____ .

(on the street, to hand out, free samples)

2 My wish is ____ .

(photographer, to become, a world-famous)

3 The only way to get there is ______________________ . (a subway, to take)

4 His advice was ______________________ . (to send, to the teacher, an e-mail)

5 The aim of the game was ____ .

(each other, to get to know, better)

6 What I want is ____ .

(to pass, my parents, the exam, and, happy, make)

다음 동사들 뒤에 다른 동사가 목적어로 올 때, 목적어는 「to+동사원형」의 형태로 쓴다.

> want   agree   choose   decide   expect   fail   hope   learn   plan   wish
> pretend   manage   would like   would love   promise   refuse   aim

They **agreed to stop** their quarrel for a while.
그들은 잠시 동안 그들의 싸움을 멈추는 것에 동의했다.
The fielder **failed to catch** the ball again.
그 외야수는 또 다시 공을 잡는 것을 실패했다.
You must **learn to think** differently for our work.
너는 우리 일을 위해서 다르게 생각하는 것을 배워야 한다.
The airplane **managed to land** on time.
비행기는 가까스로 제시간에 착륙했다.
Kevin **refused to confess** why he was there.
Kevin은 왜 그곳에 있었는지 자백하기를 거부했다.

정답 p.32

PRACTICE 3

〈보기〉에서 알맞은 단어를 골라 to부정사의 형태로 바꾸어 빈칸에 써 넣으세요.

> 보 기   come   forgive   see   hurt   study   major   solve   join   live   preserve

1   I hope _______________ snow at Christmas.

2   Jack chose _______________ in mathematics in college.

3   He agreed _______________ our club from next semester.

4   Many foreigners wanted _______________ to the U.S. in the 20th century.

5   He failed _______________ the problem by himself.

6   The victim's family decided _______________ the criminal.

7   Sally expected _______________ with her grandparents this year.

8   The new project aimed _______________ the area.

9   She didn't mean _______________ the boy so badly, but she did.

10   I pretended _______________ when Mom knocked on the door.

다음은 「동사+목적어+to부정사」의 형태로 자주 쓰이는 동사들이다.

> tell ask want allow would like expect enable invite advise force
> cause teach encourage order persuade need request warn

I will not **ask you to help** me before I try.

나는 내가 해 보기 전에 네게 나를 도와 달라고 요청하지 않을 것이다.

The security guard didn't **allow me to swim** across the river.

그 안전요원은 내가 수영을 해서 강을 건너가는 것을 허락하지 않았다.

Would you **like me to order** Thai food?

내가 태국 음식을 주문하기를 원하니?

It will **enable you to understand** the culture easily.

그것은 네가 그 문화를 쉽게 이해할 수 있도록 할 것이다.

정답 p.32

PRACTICE 4 [1-8]

Brian과 Cathy의 대화를 참고하여 문장을 완성하세요.

1. B: Would you take care of the cat while I go on a trip?	C: No problem. Don't worry about the cat.
2. B: Can you fix my broken computer now?	C: I'm sorry. I have to go out now. I'll do it when I get back.
3. B: The question is too difficult to solve.	C: Why don't you review the lesson?
4. B: Can I share your science book? I didn't bring mine.	C: Of course. Go ahead.
5. B: Why don't you act more responsibly?	C: You're right. I need to be more responsible.
6. B: If you're interested in drama, join my club.	C: Thanks. I really want to join your club.
7. B: I don't know what to do to raise my grades.	C: Well, I think you'd better talk to Mr. Kim.
8. B: Will you make ten copies of the report? I don't have time to do that now.	C: OK. Just leave the original on the table.

1 Brian asked <u>Cathy to take care of the cat while he went on a trip</u>.

2 Brian expects _______________________________________.

3 Cathy told _______________________________________.

4 Cathy allowed _______________________________________.

5 Brian wants _______________________________________.

6 Brian invited _______________________________________.

7 Cathy advised _______________________________________.

8 Brian asked _______________________________________.

PSS 1-4 의문사 + to부정사

「의문사(how, what, where, when)+to부정사」는 「의문사+주어+should+동사원형」과 같은 의미이다. 「의문사+to부정사」 앞에는 주로 다음과 같은 동사가 온다.

> know   show   tell   talk about   think about   learn   decide   teach   explain

1. how to+동사원형 '어떻게 ～할지'

   He wanted to **learn how to make** kimchi.
   그는 김치를 어떻게 만드는지를 배우고 싶어 했다.
   = He wanted to **learn how he should make** kimchi.

2. what to+동사원형 '무엇을 ～할지'

   I don't **know what to do** for my parents on Parents' Day.
   나는 어버이날에 부모님을 위해 무엇을 해야 할지 모르겠다.
   = I don't **know what I should do** for my parents on Parents' Day.

3. where to+동사원형 '어디에서 ～할지'

   He hasn't **decided where to stay** during his trip.
   그는 여행하는 동안 어디에서 머물지 결정하지 않았다.
   = He hasn't **decided where he should stay** during his trip.

4. when to+동사원형 '언제 ～할지'

   Mom didn't **tell** me **when to turn** off the oven.
   엄마는 내게 언제 오븐을 꺼야 할지 말씀하지 않으셨다.
   = Mom didn't **tell** me **when I should turn** off the oven.

PRACTICE 5

〈보기〉에서 알맞은 단어를 골라 빈칸에 「how/what+to부정사」 형태를 쓰세요.

보 기	cooperate use play wear eat save prepare do say get

1 Does Jenny know ______________________ golf?

2 I can't decide ______________________ for the party. I don't have any fancy dresses.

3 You should learn ______________________ with each other.

4 He will explain to you ______________________ for the event.

5 I was thinking about ______________________ when I grow up.

6 Mark showed me ______________________ the new washing machine.

7 I don't know ______________________ to her to make her feel better.

8 Ms. Park is going to teach us ______________________ much money.

9 Could you tell me ______________________ to the fire station?

10 Sam and I were talking about ______________________ at the Chinese restaurant.

PSS 2 형용사적 용법

PSS 2-1 명사를 꾸미는 to부정사

1. to부정사는 '~할'의 뜻으로 명사 뒤에서 명사를 꾸미는 형용사의 역할을 한다.

   I have **some questions to ask** you. 네게 물어볼 질문들이 좀 있다.

   cf. to부정사가 수식하는 명사가 전치사의 목적어일 경우 꼭 전치사를 써야 함에 유의한다.

   (학교 내신 빈출 문법 사항!)

   Could you lend me **a pen to write with**? (O)

   Could you lend me **a pen to write**? (X)

2. -thing, -one, -body로 끝나는 대명사 뒤에 이들을 수식하는 형용사가 나오면 to부정사는 형용사 뒤에 위치한다.

   I need to buy **something cold to drink**. 시원한 마실 것 좀 사야 한다.

3. 「It's (about) time ~」은 '~할 시간이다'의 뜻으로 time 뒤에 동사가 올 때는 to부정사의 형태로 쓴다.

> **It's time to start** a new semester. 새 학기를 시작할 시간이다.
> = **It's time** I **started** a new semester.
> **cf.** 「It's time ~」 뒤에 절이 나올 때는 현재의 일을 나타내더라도 과거형으로 쓴다.

정답 p.32

PRACTICE 6

괄호 안에 주어진 말을 바르게 배열하여 문장을 완성하세요.

1 I know a lot of ______________________________________ . (to tell, fun stories, the kids)

2 There's ______________________________________ on TV. (to watch, nothing, interesting)

3 I want to have ______________________________ when I'm in trouble. (to talk, true friends, with)

4 There were ______________________________ in Europe. (so many, to visit, places)

5 They are looking for ______________________________________ . (to live, a house, in)

6 The city has to make ____ .
(to keep, clean, the streets, rules)

7 Is there ______________________________ ? (to help, anybody, me, carry, the stones)

8 He brought ______________________________ . (to look, his babies, after)

9 Why don't you join our table and have ______________________________________ ?
(to eat, something)

10 We're looking for ______________________________ during the holiday. (to go, a method, there)

정답 p.32

PRACTICE 7

다음은 Mina의 하루 일과입니다. 각각의 시간에 해야 할 일이 무엇인지 쓰세요.

have breakfast	clean the living room	read books	walk the dog	go swimming
8:00	10:00	13:00	16:00	19:00

1 8 A.M. – *It's time to have breakfast. [It's time I had breakfast.]*

2 10 A.M. – ______________________________________

3 1 P.M. – ______________________________________

4 4 P.M. – ______________________________________

5 7 P.M. – ______________________________________

PSS 2-2 be to 용법

「be+to부정사」는 다음과 같은 의미를 갖는다.

운명	'~할 운명이다'	Ulysses **was to come** back home in 20 years. Ulysses는 20년 후에 집에 돌아올 운명이었다.
명령 · 의무	'~해야 한다'	You **are to submit** the term paper by this Friday. 당신은 이번 주 금요일까지 기말 보고서를 제출해야 합니다.
예정	'~할 예정이다'	We **are to meet** at 9 a.m. in front of the subway station. 우리는 지하철역 앞에서 오전 9시에 만날 예정이다.
의도 · 의지	'~할 작정이다'	If you **are to get** pearls, you must dive deep in the sea. 진주를 캐려면, 당신은 바다 속 깊이 잠수해야 한다.
가능	'~할 수 있다'	The knife **was** not **to be** found. 그 칼은 찾을 수 없었다. *cf.* 가능의 의미로 쓰일 때는 수동태로 쓰이는 경우가 많다.

정답 p.33

PRACTICE 8 [1-12]

짝지어진 두 문장이 같은 뜻이 되도록 「be+to부정사」 구문을 이용하여 빈칸을 채우세요.

1 Mary and I are going to go to a movie this evening.

= Mary and I ________________ to a movie this evening.

2 If you intend to succeed in anything, you must work hard.

= If you ________________ in anything, you must work hard.

3 Not a star could be seen in the sky.

= Not a star ________________ in the sky.

4 Achilles was destined to die in the Trojan War.

= Achilles ________________ in the Trojan War.

5 You have to hand in the lab report by tomorrow.

= You ________________ in the lab report by tomorrow.

6 The food on the table couldn't be eaten.

= The food on the table ________________.

7 The clerk is going to come back to work tomorrow.

= The clerk ________________ back to work tomorrow.

8 If you want to be good at English, you should make a strong effort.

= If you ___________________ good at English, you should make a strong effort.

9 The princess was destined to sleep for one hundred years.

= The princess ___________________ for one hundred years.

10 You must not make a noise in the library.

= You ___________________ a noise in the library.

11 My English textbook couldn't be found in my backpack.

= My English textbook ___________________ in my backpack.

12 The concert will be held at Seoul Olympic Park.

= The concert ___________________ at Seoul Olympic Park.

PSS 3 부사적 용법

PSS 3-1 목적을 나타내는 to부정사

1. to부정사가 '~하기 위해서'의 뜻으로 목적이나 의도를 나타낼 때는 「in order to(so as to)+동사원형」이나 「so that+주어+can[could]+동사원형」으로 바꾸어 쓸 수 있다.

   I ran toward him **to get** his autograph. 나는 그의 사인을 받기 위해 그를 향해 달려갔다.

   = I ran toward him **in order to get** his autograph.

   = I ran toward him **so as to get** his autograph.

   = I ran toward him **so that I could get** his autograph.

   She came early **to take** a good seat. 그녀는 좋은 자리를 잡기 위해 일찍 왔다.

   = She came early **in order to take** a good seat.

   = She came early **so as to take** a good seat.

   = She came early **so that she could take** a good seat.

   cf. 「in order to+동사원형」이 「to+동사원형」보다 좀 더 격식을 차린 표현이다.

2. to부정사 대신 「for+명사」를 써서 목적과 의도를 나타낼 수 있다.

   James visited the hospital **to take care of** the patients.

   James는 환자들을 돌보기 위해 그 병원을 방문했다.

   = James visited the hospital **for** the patients.

PRACTICE 9

짝지어진 세 문장이 같은 뜻이 되도록 빈칸을 채우세요.

1 Dan and I met the counselor to talk about our son.

   = Dan and I met the counselor _____*in order to[so as to] talk about our son*_____.

   = Dan and I met the counselor _____*so that we could talk about our son*_____.

2 I dropped by his house to give him the invitation card.

   = I dropped by his house _______________________________.

   = I dropped by his house _______________________________.

3 Cathy is thinking of going to the nursing home to take part in volunteer work.

   = Cathy is thinking of going to the nursing home _______________________.

   = Cathy is thinking of going to the nursing home _______________________.

4 I will call Mark to let him know the truth about the rumor.

   = I will call Mark _______________________________.

   = I will call Mark _______________________________.

5 He sent me an e-mail to remind me of the plans.

   = He sent me an e-mail _______________________________.

   = He sent me an e-mail _______________________________.

6 I pressed the button to roll down the window.

   = I pressed the button _______________________________.

   = I pressed the button _______________________________.

PRACTICE 10

빈칸에 to나 for 중 알맞은 것을 쓰세요.

1 ① I'm going to the market ___________ some cheese and milk.

   ② I'm going to the market ___________ buy some cheese and milk.

2 ① You should be ready by 7:00 ___________ the party.

   ② You should be ready by 7:00 ___________ go to the party.

3 ① We need to stop by the dry cleaner's ___________ pick up the sweater.

   ② We need to stop by the dry cleaner's ___________ the sweater.

4 ① I checked out some books from the library ___________ my homework.

   ② I checked out some books from the library ___________ do my homework.

5 ① My friends and I went to the community center ___________ do some volunteer work.

   ② My friends and I went to the community center ___________ some volunteer work.

1. to부정사가 형용사를 뒤에서 수식할 때는 '～하기에'의 의미를 가진다.

   This book is **hard to understand**. 이 책은 이해하기 힘들다.

2. to부정사가 다음과 같은 감정을 나타내는 형용사를 수식할 때는 '～해서, ～하게 되어'의 뜻으로 감정의 원인을 나타낸다.

   > happy pleased delighted excited glad
   > surprised sorry sad disappointed

   I'm **pleased to hear** that she won the gold medal again.
   나는 그녀가 또 다시 금메달을 땄다고 들어 기쁘다.
   Dad was **disappointed to find** that I lied to him.
   아버지는 내가 그에게 거짓말을 했다는 것을 알고 실망하셨다.
   cf. 「to+have+과거분사」는 본동사보다 과거의 일을 나타낸다.
   I'm sorry **to have kept** you waiting. 나는 너를 기다리게 해서 미안하다.
   = I'm sorry that I **kept** you waiting.

3. '～해서 (결국) …되다'의 뜻으로 결과를 나타낸다.

   My daughter grew up **to be** a movie director. 내 딸은 자라서 영화 감독이 되었다.
   He worked hard only **to fail**. 그는 열심히 일했으나 (결국) 실패했다.

4. '～하다니'의 뜻으로 판단의 근거를 나타낸다.

   He must be a genius **to solve** it within 10 minutes. 그는 그것을 10분 안에 풀다니 천재임이 틀림없다.

정답 p.33

PRACTICE 11

괄호 안에 주어진 말을 바르게 배열하여 문장을 완성하세요.

1 I was ___________________________. (the frog, alive, to find, delighted)

2 I'd be ___________________________. (glad, with you, to go there)

3 He ___________________________. (a great artist, to be, grew up)

4 He cannot be ___________________________. (to sing, an opera singer, like that)

5 His lecture was ___________________________. (to understand, so hard)

6 She must be ___________________________. (a word, disappointed, not to say)

7 I was ___________________________.
   (to have a chance, excited, to talk with him)

8 George ___________________________. (himself, to find, famous, woke up)

PSS 3-3 too ~ to, enough to

1. 「too+형용사/부사+to부정사」는 '〜하기에는 너무 …한'의 의미를 가지고, 「so+형용사/부사+that+주어+can't/couldn't」로 바꾸어 쓸 수 있다.

   The young girl was **too nervous to** sit still. 그 어린 소녀는 가만히 앉아 있기에는 너무 긴장했다.

   = The young girl was **so nervous that she couldn't** sit still.

   cf. to부정사의 행동의 주체가 주어가 아닌 경우 「for+의미상 주어」를 사용한다.

   The table is too heavy **for me** to carry. 그 테이블은 내가 나르기에는 너무 무겁다.

   = **The table** is so heavy that **I** can't carry it.

2. 「형용사/부사+enough+to부정사」는 '〜할 정도로 충분히 …한'의 의미를 가지고, 「so+형용사/부사+that+주어+can/could」로 바꾸어 쓸 수 있다.

   This book is **small enough to** fit in my pocket.

   이 책은 내 주머니에 들어갈 정도로 충분히 작다.

   = This book is **so small that it can** fit in my pocket.

   My brother is **strong enough to** reach the summit.

   내 남동생은 정상에 이를 정도로 충분히 강하다.

   = My brother is **so strong that he can** reach the summit.

정답 p.33

PRACTICE 12 [1-10]

짝지어진 두 문장의 의미가 같도록 빈칸에 알맞은 말을 쓰세요.

1 Kate is smart enough to answer all of the questions.

= Kate is __________ smart __________ she __________ answer all of the questions.

2 He was too tired to clean the room.

= He was __________ tired __________ he __________ clean the room.

3 The man was so ambitious that he couldn't be satisfied with the prize.

= The man was __________ ambitious __________ be satisfied with the prize.

4 Her grades were high enough for her to get the license.

= Her grades were __________ high __________ she __________ get the license.

5 Adam is too young to travel long distances.

= Adam is __________ young __________ he __________ travel long distances.

CHAPTER 7 _ 부정사　**153**

6 He is so skillful that he can manage the project by himself.

= He is skillful _____________ _____________ manage the project by himself.

7 It was too dark to follow the bear's tracks.

= It was _____________ dark _____________ we _____________ follow the bear's tracks.

8 The boy is so strong that he can carry all those bricks at a time.

= The boy is strong _____________ _____________ carry all those bricks at a time.

9 The car was small enough to enter the narrow road.

= The car was _____________ small _____________ it _____________ enter the narrow road.

10 The pants that Jordan gave me are so small that I can't wear them.

= The pants that Jordan gave me are _____________ small _____________ me _____________ wear.

PSS 4 원형부정사

to가 없이 동사원형의 형태로만 쓰이는 원형부정사는 사역동사나 지각동사의 목적격 보어로 쓰인다.

1. 사역동사(let, make, have)+목적어+원형부정사

   Let me **check** if that's what he wanted to have.

   그것이 그가 가지고 싶어 했던 것인지 내가 확인할게.

   I **made** my daughters **visit** their grandparents more often.

   나는 내 딸들이 그들의 조부모님을 더 자주 방문하게 했다.

   cf. help는 준사역동사로 목적격 보어 자리에 원형부정사 대신 to부정사를 쓰기도 한다.

   My husband kept **helping** me **(to) do** gardening.

   내 남편은 내가 정원을 가꾸는 것을 계속해서 도왔다.

2. 지각동사(see, watch, hear, feel, listen to, look at, notice)+목적어+원형부정사

   We **watched** the full moon **rise** yesterday. 우리는 어제 보름달이 뜨는 것을 보았다.

   Chris **heard** some strange sound **come** out of the bathroom.

   Chris는 화장실 밖으로 이상한 소리가 나는 것을 들었다.

   cf. 동작이 진행 중임을 강조할 때는 지각동사의 목적격 보어로 원형부정사 대신 현재분사를 쓰기도 한다.

   I **noticed** the man with glasses **following** me.

   나는 안경을 쓴 그 남자가 나를 따라오고 있는 것을 알아차렸다.

PRACTICE 13

괄호 안에 주어진 단어를 빈칸에 알맞은 형태로 쓰세요.

1 Let me ________________ some salt in the soup. (add)

2 I heard someone ________________ over there. (shout)

3 I made them ________________ their own ideas. (use)

4 Didn't you listen to your brother ________________ the flute? (play)

5 Look at the two snails ________________ on the grass. (crawl)

6 He helped my mother ________________ the dishes. (wash)

7 The teacher had students ________________ together in the playground. (get)

8 She watched something ________________ behind the curtain. (move)

9 They didn't notice the cat ________________ into the kitchen. (sneak)

10 Jimin felt someone ________________ his shoulder. (rub)

11 I saw the children ________________ a walk around the lake with their parents. (take)

12 She lets her daughters ________________ as late as they like. (stay up)

PSS 5 부정사의 부정형

PROBLEM SOLVING SKILL

---

to부정사의 부정형을 만들 때는 「to+동사원형」 앞에 not이나 never를 쓴다.

My teacher told me **not to worry** about that.

나의 선생님은 내게 그것에 대해 걱정하지 말라고 말씀하셨다.

cf. My teacher **didn't** tell me **to worry** about that.

나의 선생님은 내게 그것에 대해 걱정하라고 말씀하지 않으셨다.

She did her best **(in order/so as) not to lose** the race.

그녀는 경주에서 지지 않으려고 최선을 다했다.

cf. She **didn't** do her best **(in order/so as) to lose** the race.

그녀는 경주에서 지려고 최선을 다하지 않았다.

I decided **never to take** the money to the police station.

나는 그 돈을 경찰서에 절대로 가져다주지 않기로 결정했다.

cf. I **never** decided to take the money to the police station.

나는 절대로 그 돈을 경찰서에 가져다주기로 결정하지 않았다.

PRACTICE 14

우리말과 같은 뜻이 되도록 괄호 안에 주어진 말을 바르게 배열하세요. (단, to부정사구를 반드시 사용할 것)

1   우리는 물을 오염시키지 않기 위해 노력해야 한다. (pollute, should, the water, try, we, not)
    ➡ ____

2   그녀는 그 소문에 대해서 아무것도 모르는 척했다.
    (about, she, not, the rumor, pretended, anything, know)
    ➡ ____

3   우리는 마지막 기차를 놓치지 않기 위해서 서둘러야 한다.
    (hurry up, the last train, miss, have to, not, we)
    ➡ ____

4   그녀는 너무 피곤했어서, 운전해서 집으로 돌아가지 않기로 선택했다.
    (too tired, so, was, not, she, chose, she, drive home)
    ➡ ____

5   넌 연습 동안 네 자신을 절대 다치게 하지 않도록 더 조심하는 게 낫다.
    (during, never, yourself, you'd, practice, be, hurt, more careful, better)
    ➡ ____

6   Bob은 과학 시험에 낙제하지 않기 위해서 매우 열심히 공부했다.
    (fail, Bob, hard, the science test, very, studied, not)
    ➡ ____

7   그 결과에 대해 너무 속상해하지 않도록 해. (upset, the result, try, about, not, so, be)
    ➡ ____

8   그는 수업을 절대 빠지지 않기로 약속했지만, 또다시 그것을 빠졌다.
    (again, he, it, skip, never, class, skipped, promised, but)
    ➡ ____

PSS 6 대부정사

앞에 나온 말의 반복을 피하기 위해 to부정사에서 동사원형을 생략하고 to만 쓰는 것을 대부정사라고 한다.

You may use my computer if you want **to** (use my computer).
너는 원한다면 내 컴퓨터를 써도 된다.

Will you come to the party? – Sure, I'd love **to** (come to the party).
파티에 올래? – 물론이지, 그러고 싶어.

She didn't open the present until I arrived, because I told her not **to** (open the present). 내가 그러지 말라고 했기 때문에 그녀는 내가 도착할 때까지 선물을 열어 보지 않았다.

PRACTICE 15

우리말과 같은 뜻이 되도록 괄호 안에 주어진 말을 바르게 배열하세요.

1 너는 원한다면 이것을 네 엄마에게 말해도 된다.

= ____

(you, your mom, to, if, can, tell, to, this, you, want)

2 나도 너희와 함께하고 싶지만 그럴 수 없을 거야.

= ____

(I, join, but, to, 'd like to, you, won't, able, I, be)

3 네가 원할 때면 언제든지 도와줄게.

= ____

(I, whenever, you, will help, you, to, me, want)

4 Jason은 그의 강아지를 할머니께 보내고 싶지 않았지만, 그렇게 하기로 결정했다.

= ____

(Jason, his puppy, to, his grandmother, he, decided, but, send, didn't, to, want, to)

5 나는 그와 함께 등산하러 가고 싶지 않지만, 해야 한다.

= ____

(I, go climbing, to, don't, to, have, I, but, want, with him)

6 내가 그녀에게 기다리지 말라고 이야기했음에도 불구하고 미라는 자정까지 나를 기다렸다.

= ____

(Mira, I, until midnight, told, to, waited for, me, not, although, her)

CH
7
부
정
사

PSS 7 부정사의 의미상의 주어

to부정사의 의미상의 주어는 to부정사가 나타내는 동작의 주체를 의미한다.

1. 의미상의 주어를 쓰지 않는 경우

① 일반 사람이거나 문맥상 주어가 뚜렷한 경우

It is not easy **to speak** English fluently. 영어를 유창하게 말하는 것은 쉽지 않다.

My dream is **to travel** around the world. 내 꿈은 세계를 여행하는 것이다.

② 문장의 주어와 같은 경우

I wish **to major** in literature. 나는 문학을 전공하고 싶다.

③ 문장의 목적어와 같은 경우

They want you **to know** more about their products.

그들은 네가 그들의 제품에 대해 더 많이 알기를 원한다.

2. 의미상의 주어를 나타내야 하는 경우

① 부정사의 의미상의 주어가 문장의 주어와 일치하지 않을 때는 부정사 앞에 「for+목적격」의 형태로 의미상의 주어를 밝혀 준다.

It is very important **for you** **to take** the new class.

네가 그 새로운 수업을 듣는 것은 매우 중요하다.

I opened the door **for the fly** **to get** out of the room.

나는 파리가 방에서 나가도록 문을 열었다.

② 부정사 앞에 사람의 성질이나 특징을 나타내는 형용사(kind, bad, nice, foolish, wise, silly, generous, careless, clever, cruel, honest, polite, rude, thoughtful)가 있으면 의미상의 주어는 「of+목적격」으로 쓴다.

It is **generous** **of you** **to invite** them for dinner.

그들을 저녁 식사에 초대하다니 당신은 관대하다.

It is **kind** **of him** **to help** the old lady to get on the bus.

그 나이 든 부인이 버스에 타는 것을 도와 주다니 그는 친절하다.

정답 p.34

PRACTICE 16

괄호 안에 들어갈 알맞은 말을 골라 동그라미 하세요.

1 It's impossible (to, for, of) me to stay up until late at night.

2 It is dangerous (to, for, of) you to swim in this river.

3 I asked him (to, for, of) come over to my house.

4 It was good (to, for, of) me to see the children feel happy.

5 It is nice (to, for, of) you to say hello to all of my family.

6 It is such a pleasure (to, for, of) me to meet you.

7 Those black pants in the drawer are too big for me (to, for, of) wear.

8 It is cruel (to, for, of) him to make me kill the frogs.

9 My parents don't allow me (to, for, of) watch TV later than 10 o'clock at night.

10 His questions were too confusing (to, for, of) me to answer.

11 It is foolish (to, for, of) you to make the same mistake.

12 It is hard (to, for, of) believe that Jinho is the youngest boy of the three brothers.

13 It is very thoughtful (to, for, of) them to prepare the present for him.

14 There are some ways (to, for, of) her to become an actor.

15 It was wise (to, for, of) her not to spend much money on that.

1 괄호 안에 주어진 단어들을 어법에 맞게 배열한 것은?

> Thanks to the development of transportation, the world is ______________ anywhere in a day. (to, go, enough, small)

① small enough to go
② go to small enough
③ to go small enough
④ small enough go to
⑤ enough small to go

2 두 문장이 같은 뜻이 되도록 빈칸에 알맞은 말을 쓰세요.

> • Last night, he felt so tired that he couldn't do his homework.
> = Last night, he felt ___________ tired ___________ do his homework.

3 괄호 안에 주어진 동사를 알맞은 형태로 바꾸어 빈칸에 쓰세요.

> The best thing about visiting foreign countries is ______________ about their way of life. (learn)

4 두 문장이 같은 뜻이 되도록 빈칸에 알맞은 말을 쓰세요.

> • You're supposed to teach me how I should use the machine tonight.
> = You're supposed to teach me _________ ___________ ___________ the machine tonight.

5 다음 중 어법상 <u>어색한</u> 것은?

① I'd like you think about my suggestion.
② It takes time to get a good job.
③ I want to improve my writing ability.
④ Do you know how to make a homepage?
⑤ Let him decide what to do with the reward.

6 다음 중 밑줄 친 to부정사가 같은 용법으로 쓰인 것끼리 묶인 것을 <u>있는 대로</u> 고르세요.

> (A) I put my hand out of the window <u>to touch</u> the rain.
> (B) Do you have enough time <u>to help</u> me?
> (C) Please come in and have something <u>to eat</u>.
> (D) He went to the department store <u>to buy</u> a new vacuum cleaner.
> (E) Suji didn't promise <u>to send</u> an email to John.

① (A), (D) ② (A), (E) ③ (B), (C)
④ (B), (D) ⑤ (D), (E)

7 주어진 〈보기〉와 뜻이 같도록 문장을 영작하세요. (단, 'It seems that ~' 표현을 사용하여 총 12단어로 쓸 것.)

> 보 기 | He seems to need some rest after all that hard work.

➡ _______________________________________

____

8 우리말과 같은 뜻이 되도록 괄호 안에 주어진 단어들을 배열하세요.

> • 우리가 계곡에 도착하는 데 4시간이 걸렸다.
> (the, took, it, get, for, valley, hours, to, us, four, to)

➡ _______________________________

____

9 다음 문장의 밑줄 친 to부정사와 용법이 같은 것은?

> It was the best time <u>to send</u> her back to her parents.

① He wants <u>to be</u> a real engineer.
② It is hard <u>to know</u> whether the article is true.
③ My hobby is <u>to collect</u> miniature cars.
④ Wouldn't it be better <u>to invite</u> her brother?
⑤ She came up with a creative way <u>to catch</u> fish.

10 다음 중 어법상 옳은 것은?

① They decided forming study groups like ours.
② I want you find out who broke the window.
③ The physical activity you choose to do will help you lose weight.
④ I expect see Jim again at school.
⑤ What are you planning doing on your vacation?

11 다음 문장의 빈칸에 들어갈 동사의 형태로 옳은 것은?

> I like Harry, but I'm scared _______ and talk with him for now.

① go   ② going   ③ gone
④ to go   ⑤ to have gone

12 괄호 안에 주어진 동사를 알맞은 형태로 바꾸어 빈칸에 쓰세요.

> I decided _______ the literal meaning of poems first. (understand)

13 다음 문장의 빈칸에 들어갈 동사의 형태로 옳은 것은?

> The woman just told me _______ friends who will run away when I am in trouble.

① not have   ② have not
③ to not having   ④ not to have
⑤ to have not

14 우리말과 일치하도록 괄호 안에 주어진 단어를 모두 배열하여 문장을 완성하세요.

> • 난 나의 첫 번째 마라톤을 완주하는 것이 보람차다고 느꼈다.
> (to, marathon, it, complete, my, rewarding, first)

➡ I found _______________________________

_______________________________.

15 나머지 넷과 의미가 <u>다른</u> 하나는?

① He came home early in order to see the children before they went to bed.
② He came home early so as to see the children before they went to bed.
③ He came home early so that he could see the children before they went to bed.
④ He came home early to see the children before they went to bed.
⑤ He came home so early that he could see the children before they went to bed.

16 다음 중 밑줄 친 to부정사가 부사적 용법으로 쓰이지 <u>않은</u> 것은?

① What do I need <u>to borrow</u> some books?
② He worked hard not <u>to fail</u> in the exam.
③ Your mechanical pencil is hard <u>to write with</u>.
④ My father put the nets in the river <u>to catch</u> fish.
⑤ It is better <u>to</u> completely <u>finish</u> a thing than to partly finish two things.

17 다음 문장에서 <u>잘못된</u> 부분을 찾아 올바른 문장으로 쓰세요.

1) I heard my brother to go upstairs.

➡ _______________________________

____

2) Would you like me pick you up in the morning?

➡ _______________________________

____

18 다음 문장에서 밑줄 친 단어의 올바른 형태가 차례대로 짝지어진 것은?

> • He won't let his daughter <u>go</u> out late at night.
> • She asked her husband <u>fix</u> the washing machine.

① gone – to fix　　② gone – fixing
③ to go – to fix　　④ go　 – fixing
⑤ go　 – to fix

19 다음 중 빈칸에 들어갈 말이 나머지와 <u>다른</u> 하나는?

① I was ___________ nervous to make a good impression during the interview.
② The corridor I just mopped is ___________ slippery to walk on.
③ The Americano is still ___________ bitter for me to drink.
④ Her new novel is simple ___________ to read in a day.
⑤ The music played in the café is ___________ loud to concentrate.

20 밑줄 친 동사의 형태가 옳지 <u>않은</u> 것은?

① I had to force myself <u>get</u> up this morning.
② The teacher noticed students <u>looking</u> puzzled.
③ I'll have my assistant <u>schedule</u> another appointment for you.
④ I sometimes sit by the window and watch people <u>walking</u> past.
⑤ The power failure caused the whole computer system <u>to shut</u> down.

21 다음 문장의 밑줄 친 부분과 용법이 같은 것은?

> All pets brought into this park <u>are to</u> be kept on a leash at all times. Owners must clean up after their animals immediately.

① The concert <u>is to</u> begin at 6 p.m. tonight.
② Mr. Brown <u>is to</u> give a speech at the conference.
③ Students <u>are to</u> submit their homework by Monday.
④ Minor errors <u>are to</u> occur when you type too quickly.
⑤ She <u>was to</u> become a world-famous scientist one day.

22 밑줄 친 단어의 형태가 옳은 것은?

① I recited the poem my teacher had asked me to <u>memory</u>.
② You'll find these meals quick and convenient to <u>preparation</u>.
③ Leonardo da Vinci is celebrated as both an artist and an <u>inventor</u>.
④ Proper stretching helps <u>prevention</u> muscle injuries during workouts.
⑤ Emily was chosen to <u>representative</u> the company at the conference.

23 〈보기〉에서 어법상 틀린 문장의 개수는?

> 보 기
> ⓐ You must do what I told you to do it.
> ⓑ He felt his dog to touch his legs.
> ⓒ I saw a woman to walk across the road.
> ⓓ We'll have him study English after class.
> ⓔ We tried our best not to lose the game.

① 1개　② 2개　③ 3개　④ 4개　⑤ 5개

24 두 문장이 같은 뜻이 되도록 빈칸에 알맞은 말을 쓰세요.

> • To be honest, I'm too busy to think about anything else.
> = To be honest, I'm ＿＿＿＿＿ ＿＿＿＿＿ ＿＿＿＿＿ ＿＿＿＿＿ ＿＿＿＿＿ think about anything else.

25 다음 중 어법상 어색한 것은?

① It's foolish of him to make such an excuse.
② It's very smart of her to learn a new language so fast.
③ It's exciting for me to see the big game in person!
④ It's kind for you to give me a place to sleep.
⑤ It's difficult for me to choose a name for my son.

26 두 문장이 같은 뜻이 되도록 빈칸에 알맞은 말을 쓰세요.

> • My son is so smart that he can decide what he wants to be in the future.
> = My son is ＿＿＿＿＿ ＿＿＿＿＿ ＿＿＿＿＿ decide what he wants to be in the future.

27 다음 중 주어진 문장과 의미가 같은 것은?

> They arrived so late that they couldn't find a parking spot anywhere near the venue.

① They arrived late enough to find a parking spot anywhere near the venue.
② Although they arrived so late, they could find a parking spot anywhere near the venue.
③ They arrived too late to find a parking spot anywhere near the venue.
④ They didn't arrive late, but they couldn't find a parking spot anywhere near the venue.
⑤ They arrived very late so they could find a parking spot far from the venue.

28 빈칸에 들어갈 말로 알맞은 것은?

> It will be very stupid ___________ you not to take the chance to go abroad for free.

① of ② on ③ to
④ for ⑤ from

29 다음 빈칸에 들어갈 말이 바르게 짝지어진 것은?

> • I run along the Han River regularly ___________ stay healthy.
> • We should keep quiet ___________ my brother doesn't wake up.

① in order to — so as to
② in order to — so that
③ so as to — in order for
④ so that — in order that
⑤ so as that — in order for

30 빈칸에 들어갈 수 <u>없는</u> 것은?

> Nobody ___________ me break the mirror in my classroom.

① let ② told ③ made
④ saw ⑤ watched

31 빈칸에 들어갈 말로 알맞은 것은?

> Kimberly told me that this place made her ___________ of her hometown – quiet, clean and beautiful.

① think ② thinking ③ thought
④ to think ⑤ to thinking

32 주어진 우리말과 같은 뜻이 되도록 빈칸에 알맞은 말을 쓰세요.

> • 어떤 학생들에게는 그들 자신만의 결정을 내리는 것이 어렵다.
> = ___________ is difficult ___________ some students ___________ make their own decisions.

33 두 문장이 같은 뜻이 되도록 빈칸에 알맞은 말을 쓰세요.

> • It seems that Jeff and David are surprised at the news.
> = Jeff and David ___________ ___________ ___________ surprised at the news.

34 빈칸에 들어갈 단어가 차례대로 짝지어진 것은?

Since the automation system was introduced in the early 1900s, it has made our productivity __________ rapidly. However, workers feel tired of __________ the same thing over and over again.

① to increase – to do
② to increase – doing
③ to increase – do
④ increase – to do
⑤ increase – doing

35 다음 중 어법상 틀린 것을 모두 고르세요.

① It's often hard to find someone to trust.
② He felt alone with no one to talk.
③ Sam brought me some pieces of paper to write on.
④ There's interesting nothing to read.
⑤ To reach the shelf, I need something to step on.

36 다음 중 to부정사의 용법이 나머지 넷과 다른 것은?

① They did their best to win the prize.
② She grew up to be an English teacher.
③ I was pleased to get your text message.
④ She wants to become a famous TV show host.
⑤ He must be a fool to believe such a silly rumor.

37 다음 밑줄 친 to를 in order to로 바꾸어 쓸 때 문맥상 가장 자연스러운 것은?

① This book is hard to understand.
② Just press the button to take a picture.
③ I'm happy to tell you an interesting story.
④ His son grew up to be a famous doctor.
⑤ This room is too small to put a desk.

38 두 문장이 같은 뜻이 되도록 빈칸에 알맞은 말을 쓰세요.

• She had a hard time keeping a diary in English.
= It was hard _______ _______ _______ a diary in English.

39 다음 우리말을 적절하게 영작한 것은?

• 이제 우리가 새 학년을 시작할 시간이다.

① It is time to start for us a new school year.
② It is for us time to start a new school year.
③ It is time for us to start a new school year.
④ It is for time us to start a new school year.
⑤ It is time us to start for a new school year.

40 다음 각 문장에서 어법상 어색한 부분을 찾아 바르게 고치지 못한 사람은? (2명)

ⓐ She found it difficult finish the project on time.
ⓑ We think important it to protect the environment.
ⓒ The water is too cold for the children to swim in it.
ⓓ My parents reminded me to not forget my passport.
ⓔ It was generous them to donate so much money.

① 혜빈: ⓐ의 finish를 to finish로 고쳐야 해.
② 상우: ⓑ의 important it을 it important로 고쳐야 해.
③ 소연: ⓒ의 swim in it을 swim it in으로 고쳐야 해.
④ 민정: ⓓ의 to not forget을 not to forget으로 고쳐야 해.
⑤ 은찬: ⓔ의 them 앞에 for를 추가해야 해.

41 다음 중 어법상 어색한 것은?

① He has always wanted to travel around the world.
② Did you know that he managed to finish the marathon?
③ I made a promise to myself to develop my own talent.
④ The program will teach you how deal with people.
⑤ Could you help me carry these bags to my car?

42 글의 흐름을 고려할 때, (A)~(E)를 어법상 바르게 고친 것으로 적절하지 않은 것은?

> ### *Volunteer Work Diary*
>
> Name: Brooklyn Rose
> Date: Friday, August 18th
>
> I volunteered at Forest Nursing Home. What I had to do first was (A) <u>washed</u> the residents' clothes and bedclothes. It was a lot of work but I tried (B) <u>doing</u> my best. After I finished the laundry, the manager let me (C) <u>to spend</u> the rest of my time chatting with the elderly, learning about their lives and experiences. They seemed to be happy to have someone (D) <u>to talk to</u>. It was a valuable experience. If there's a chance, I'd like (E) <u>go</u> there again.

① (A) washed → wash
② (B) doing → to do
③ (C) to spend → spend
④ (D) to talk to → to talk
⑤ (E) go → to go

43 다음 중 어법상 옳은 것은?

① The color of the clothes is too dark of me to wear.
② It's time of you to make up your mind about the problem.
③ It's nice for you to show me the way to the post office.
④ Being a volunteer made it possible me to see famous sports players.
⑤ It is wise of you not to buy such an expensive computer.

44 주어진 우리말을 참고하여 다음 대화의 빈칸에 알맞은 말을 쓰세요.

> A: What's your opinion about the movie?
> B: I really don't know ___________
> ________________________.
> (뭐라고 말해야 할지)

45 다음 문장의 빈칸에 들어갈 말로 알맞은 것은?

> A sheet of paper is not enough for me ___________ about my dreams.

① to write
② to write on
③ to write with
④ writing
⑤ writing on

46 주어진 〈보기〉와 뜻이 같도록 문장을 영작하세요. (단, too를 포함하여 총 10단어로 쓸 것.)

> 보 기 | The plane ticket is so expensive that she can't afford it.

➡ _______________________________

____

47 〈보기〉의 문장은 모두 어법상 <u>어색한</u> 문장들이다. 바르게 고치지 <u>못한</u> 사람은?

> 보 기
>
> ⓐ My son found it difficult make friends at his new school.
> ⓑ This machine made possible it to keep food fresh in summer.
> ⓒ Sharon believes it importantly to respect other people's cultures.
> ⓓ I made it a rule take a walk for 30 minutes every morning.
> ⓔ Chris thought this a good idea to take a rest for a moment.

① 채영: ⓐ문장에서 make를 to make로 고쳐야 해.
② 지성: ⓑ문장에서 possible it을 it possible로 고쳐야 해.
③ 정인: ⓒ문장에서 importantly를 important로 고쳐야 해.
④ 승민: ⓓ문장에서 take를 to take로 고쳐야 해.
⑤ 지효: ⓔ문장에서 to take a rest를 to take it a rest로 고쳐야 해.

48 우리말을 영어로 바르게 옮긴 것은?

① 돈을 낭비하다니 그는 어리석었다.
  → It was foolish of he to waste money.
② 그녀가 진실을 믿는 것은 어려웠다.
  → It was hard for her to believe the truth.
③ 아이들이 혼자 수영하는 것은 위험하다.
  → It is dangerous of children to swim alone.
④ 언니가 나에게 준 드레스는 입기에 너무 컸다.
  → The dress my sister gave me was too big for me to wear it.
⑤ 내 생일을 기억하다니 당신은 사려 깊다.
  → It is thoughtful for you to remember my birthday.

49 두 문장의 의미가 같도록 어법에 맞게 바꿔 쓴 것으로 가장 적절한 것은?

① The noodles were so spicy that I couldn't eat them.
  → The noodles were too spicy for me to eat them.
② I go to school early so that I can prepare for my class.
  → I go to school so early that I can prepare for my class.
③ You should wear a swimming cap so as to use our pool.
  → You should wear a swimming cap in order to use our pool.
④ The teacher made his students clean the classroom again.
  → The teacher made his students to clean the classroom again.
⑤ Ryan watched his daughter play with dolls with her friends.
  → Ryan watched his daughter to play with dolls with her friends.

50 빈칸에 들어갈 알맞은 말을 〈보기〉에서 찾을 수 <u>없는</u> 것은?

> 보 기　　when, how, what, where

① I have no idea ________ to write for the essay.
② I learned ________ to drive a car from my father.
③ She showed me ________ to put my coat in her house.
④ I don't know ________ to talk to about my secret.
⑤ The alarm clock lets me know ________ to wake up.

CHAPTER 8
동명사

Problem Solving Skill	페이지	성취도				
		100%	99~75%	74~50%	49~25%	24~0%
PSS 1 주어와 보어로 쓰이는 동명사	168					
PSS 2 동사의 목적어로 쓰이는 동명사	페이지	성취도				
		100%	99~75%	74~50%	49~25%	24~0%
PSS 2-1 동사+동명사	169					
PSS 2-2 동사+동명사/to부정사 Ⅰ	170					
PSS 2-3 동사+동명사/to부정사 Ⅱ	171					
PSS 3 전치사의 목적어로 쓰이는 동명사	173					
PSS 4 동명사의 관용 표현	175					
PSS 5 동명사의 부정형	176					
PSS 6 동명사의 의미상의 주어	177					
중간·기말고사 대비문제	179					

PSS 1 주어와 보어로 쓰이는 동명사

동명사는 「동사원형+-ing」의 형태로, '～하기, ～하는 것'이라고 해석되며 문장에서 주어, 보어, 목적어의 역할을 한다.

1. 주어로 쓰이는 동명사

Having to sing in public was so embarrassing.
대중 앞에서 노래해야 하는 것은 매우 당황스러웠다.

= **It** was so embarrassing **having** to sing in public.
가주어 · 진주어

= **It** was so embarrassing **to have** to sing in public.
가주어 · 진주어

cf. 주어로 쓰인 동명사는 단수로 취급한다. 진주어로 쓰인 동명사는 to부정사로도 바꾸어 쓸 수 있다. 진주어로는 동명사보다 to부정사가 더 많이 쓰인다.

2. 보어로 쓰이는 동명사

The children's favorite activity is **playing** with a ball.
그 아이들이 가장 좋아하는 활동은 공을 가지고 노는 것이다.
= The children's favorite activity is **to play** with a ball.
cf. 보어로 쓰이는 동명사 역시 to부정사로 바꾸어 쓸 수 있다.

정답 p.37

PRACTICE 1

우리말 해석과 일치하도록 괄호 안의 말을 바르게 배열하고, 동명사가 문장에서 어떤 역할을 하는지 쓰세요.

1 그의 소원은 그의 30번째 생일 전에 전 세계를 여행하는 것이다.
(the world, is, around, traveling, his wish)
= _________________________________ before his 30th birthday.　(　　　)

2 불가능한 것을 기원해 봐야 소용없다.
(use, the impossible, it's, wishing, for, no)
= _________________________________　(　　　)

3 가기 전에 약속을 하는 게 좋다.
(an appointment, worth, it's, making)
= _________________________________ before you go.　(　　　)

4 각각의 구성원들이 서로 알게 하는 것이 이 모임의 목적이다.
(each, is, getting, the purpose, to know, member)
= _________________________________ of this meeting.　(　　　)

5 마지막 단계는 손님들의 수를 확인하는 것이다.

(checking, the last, the number, is, of, step, guests)

= ______________________________________ (   )

PSS 2 동사의 목적어로 쓰이는 동명사

PSS 2-1 동사 + 동명사

다음 동사들 뒤에 다른 동사가 목적어로 오면, 목적어로 쓰이는 동사는 동명사의 형태로 쓴다.

enjoy	keep	stop	finish	mind	practice	put off	deny	give up
suggest	dislike	avoid	quit	consider	imagine	postpone		

Junho **enjoys jogging** with his dog. 준호는 그의 개와 함께 조깅하는 것을 즐긴다.

I just **finished making** the client list. 나는 고객 명단을 만드는 것을 방금 끝냈다.

Would you **mind taking** off your cap? 괜찮으시다면 모자를 벗으시겠습니까?

He **put off starting** a new project. 그는 새 프로젝트를 시작하는 것을 연기했다.

I **gave up repairing** the motorcycle. 나는 오토바이 수리하는 것을 포기했다.

He **suggested reading** this article. 그는 이 기사를 읽어보는 것을 제안했다.

I **considered taking** a bus to the station. 나는 역까지 버스를 타는 것을 고려했다.

Can you **imagine being** 100 years old? 100살이 되는 것을 상상할 수 있어?

정답 p.37

PRACTICE 2 [1-15]

괄호 안의 동사를 알맞은 형태로 바꾸어 빈칸에 쓰세요.

1 The woman avoided ________________ the detective's questions. (answer)

2 The wise man pretended ________________ dead before the bear. (be)

3 I enjoy ________________ quiz shows on TV at 9 p.m. on Mondays. (watch)

4 He just finished ________________ the thrilling mystery novel he had picked up at the bookstore yesterday. (read)

5 All of us agreed ________________ rules for the game. (make)

6 She gave up ________________ to all the lectures. (listen)

7 He practiced ________________ Chinese for the Chinese speaking contest. (speak)

8 She imagined _________________ a mom after she got married. (be)

9 I chose _________________ at home rather than go out with him on Saturday night. (stay)

10 My brothers kept _________________ me while I was talking with Jane on the phone. (interrupt)

11 He decided _________________ an e-mail to his boss. (send)

12 Would you mind _________________ off the radio? (turn)

13 They put off _________________ their summer holiday. (plan)

14 The members are considering _________________ him to be their manager. (elect)

15 We planned _________________ cabbages and carrots in our garden. (plant)

PSS 2-2 동사 + 동명사 / to부정사 Ⅰ

다음은 동명사와 to부정사를 모두 목적어로 취하되, 그 중 어느 것을 목적어로 취하든지 뜻이 달라지지 않는 동사들이다.

| like | love | hate | start | begin | continue | intend | prefer |

I don't **like eating** only vegetables. 나는 야채만 먹는 것을 좋아하지 않는다.
= I don't **like to eat** only vegetables.

The baby **began crying** as soon as his mother left. 그 아기는 엄마가 나가자마자 울기 시작했다.
= The baby **began to cry** as soon as his mother left.

The crowd **continued shouting** for joy. 군중들은 계속해서 환호했다.
= The crowd **continued to shout** for joy.

John **intends going** to England to study. John은 공부를 하러 영국에 갈 작정이다.
= John **intends to go** to England to study.

정답 p.38

PRACTICE 3

괄호 안에 들어갈 알맞은 말을 <u>모두</u> 골라 동그라미 하세요.

1 I like (to live, living) in a big city rather than a small town.

2 I expected (to buy, buying) a new bicycle this week.

3 Congress continued (to take, taking) the next step to pass the law.

4 My sister learned (to drive, driving) when she was 21.

5 They started (to study, studying) for the final exam.

6 Tony didn't mean (to cause, causing) such a problem.

7 He practiced (to make, making) kimchi as my mom did.

8 Jina loves (to read, reading) storybooks to her brothers.

9 She quit (to learn, learning) to write English essays.

10 She dislikes (to take, taking) the crowded subway.

11 The hairdresser began (to cut, cutting) the man's hair fast.

12 Don't you hate (to listen, listening) to loud music?

13 She prefers (to wear, wearing) glasses to contact lenses.

14 Does he intend (to take, taking) part in the fair?

15 Can you imagine (to go, going) to the Moon and other planets?

16 You need (to find, finding) some information about where you can work.

PSS 2-3 동사 + 동명사 / to부정사 Ⅱ

다음의 동사들은 동명사와 to부정사 모두를 목적어로 취한다. 그러나 어떤 것을 목적어로 취하느냐에 따라 다음과 같이 뜻이 달라진다.

> try   remember   forget

1. try+동명사 '(시험 삼아) ~해 보다' / try+to부정사 '~하려고 노력하다, 애쓰다'

   I **tried turning** on the machine again, but it still didn't work.
   나는 그 기계를 다시 켜 봤지만, 여전히 작동하지 않았다.
   I **tried to turn** on the machine again, but it wasn't turned on.
   나는 그 기계를 다시 켜 보려고 노력했지만, 켜지지 않았다.

2. remember+동명사 '~한 것을 기억하다' / remember+to부정사 '~할[하는] 것을 기억하다'

   I **remember locking** the door when I left home. 나는 내가 집을 나올 때 문을 잠근 것을 기억한다.
   I **remember to lock** the door when I leave home.
   나는 내가 집을 나설 때 문을 잠가야 하는 것을 기억한다.

3. forget+동명사 '~한 것을 잊다' / forget+to부정사 '~할[하는] 것을 잊다'

I **forgot having** a meeting last Friday. 나는 지난 금요일에 회의를 한 것을 잊었다.

I **forgot to have** a meeting tomorrow morning. 나는 내일 아침에 회의하는 것을 잊었다.

cf. stop 뒤에는 동명사와 to부정사가 모두 올 수 있지만, 목적어로는 동명사만 취할 수 있다. stop 뒤에 오는 to부정사는 stop의 목적어가 아니라 부사구이다.

stop+동명사 '~하는 것을 멈추다, 그만두다' / stop+to부정사 '~하기 위해 멈추다'

Susan **stopped telling** them what happened last night.

Susan은 그들에게 지난밤에 무슨 일이 일어났는지 말하는 것을 그만두었다.

Susan **stopped to tell** them what happened last night.

Susan은 그들에게 지난밤에 무슨 일이 일어났는지 말해 주기 위해 멈추었다.

정답 p.38

PRACTICE 4

괄호 안의 단어를 알맞은 형태로 바꾸어 빈칸에 쓰세요.

1 Jim forgot ________________ the paper before, so he did it again. (copy)

2 I remember ________________ the accident last year. (watch)

3 They failed ________________ the correct answer to the question. (find)

4 Would you mind ________________ what you just said? (repeat)

5 Have you tried ________________ your hair color? (change)

6 Did you finish ________________ the report about global warming? (write)

7 We planned ________________ badminton at the park on weekends. (play)

8 Rosie stopped ________________ and told me what happened to her. (cry)

9 What kind of club activity did you choose ________________ part in? (take)

10 She forgot ________________ for the program, so she has to wait for another month. (apply)

11 I stopped ________________ a bottle of water at the supermarket. (buy)

12 I tried ________________ him until he accepted my proposal. (persuade)

13 The boys kept ________________ their mother while she was working. (bother)

14 He will remember ________________ me the box by this Thursday. (send)

15 I'd love ________________ those puppies to my house. (bring)

PSS 3 전치사의 목적어로 쓰이는 동명사

1. **by+-ing** '~함으로써'

   By recycling paper and bottles, we can preserve the Earth.
   종이와 병들을 재활용함으로써, 우리는 지구를 보존할 수 있다.

2. **on[upon]+-ing** '~하자마자'

   On seeing the famous actress, they began to run after her.
   그 유명한 여배우를 보자마자, 그들은 그녀를 쫓아 달려가기 시작했다.
   = **As soon as** they saw the famous actress, they began to run after her.

3. **thank … for+-ing** '~에 대해 …에게 감사하다'

   Thank you **for giving** me the opportunity. 제게 기회를 주셔서 감사합니다.

4. **use … for+-ing** '~하는 데 …를 쓰다'

   Did they **use** the chopsticks **for eating** noodles? 그들이 국수를 먹는 데 젓가락을 이용했니?

5. **feel like+-ing** '~하고 싶다'

   I **feel like getting** an autograph from the author of that book.
   나는 저 책의 저자에게서 사인을 받고 싶다.

6. **be in favor of+-ing** '~에 찬성하다'

   Daniel **is in favor of changing** the school uniform. Daniel은 교복을 바꾸는 것에 찬성한다.

7. **instead of+-ing** '~ 대신에'

   Instead of giving up, I practiced hard until I could do it.
   포기하는 것 대신에, 나는 내가 그것을 할 수 있을 때까지 열심히 연습했다.

8. **without+-ing** '~하지 않고'

   She walked out of the room **without saying** anything. 그녀는 아무 말도 하지 않고 방을 나갔다.

9. **succeed in+-ing** '~하는 데 성공하다'

   Jason is going to **succeed in finding** a new job. Jason은 새로운 직업을 구하는 데 성공할 것이다.

10. **prevent[prohibit/protect/keep/stop] … from+-ing** '…가 ~하는 것을 막다'

    This alarm system will **prevent** a thief **from breaking** into the house.
    이 경보 시스템은 도둑이 집 안으로 침입하는 것을 막을 것이다.

11. **be capable of+-ing** '~할 능력이 있다'

    He **is capable of running** a marathon in under three hours.
    그는 3시간 이내에 마라톤을 달릴 능력이 있다.

12. **apologize for+-ing** '~에 대해 사과하다'

    I **apologize for being** late again. 저는 또 다시 늦은 것에 대해 사과 드립니다.

PRACTICE 5

괄호 안의 단어를 알맞은 형태로 바꾸어 빈칸에 쓰세요.

1 His injury prevented him from ________________ in the soccer match. (participate)

2 I opened all of the windows instead of ________________ on the air conditioner. (turn)

3 By ________________ public transportation, we can reduce air pollution. (use)

4 Mike apologized to me for ________________ his word. (break)

5 Thank you for ________________ me to dinner. (invite)

6 On ________________ his name called, he raised his hand and answered. (hear)

PRACTICE 6

그림을 보고, 빈칸에 들어갈 말을 〈보기〉에서 골라 알맞은 형태로 바꾸어 쓰세요.

1

2

3

4

5

6

보 기	let the bird out	turn off the stove	have steak for dinner
	keep my child's old toys	do every kind of housework	save 20,000 won in a week

1 She left the kitchen without ____ .

2 Mike is in favor of ____ .

3 I used the box for ____ .

4 This robot is capable of ____ .

5 Tony succeeded in ____ .

6 I feel like ____ .

PSS 4 동명사의 관용 표현

1. **be used to+-ing** '～에 익숙하다'
   I **am used to walking** to school. 나는 학교까지 걸어가는 데 익숙하다.

2. **cannot help+-ing** '～하지 않을 수 없다'
   I **cannot help thinking** that I was really stupid. 나는 내가 정말 어리석었다고 생각하지 않을 수 없다.
   = I **cannot but think** that I was really stupid.

3. **go+-ing** '～하러 가다'
   Will you **go hiking** with us tomorrow? 내일 우리와 함께 하이킹 하러 갈래?
   My hobby is **going fishing** with my dad. 내 취미는 아빠와 함께 낚시를 하러 가는 것이다.

4. **need[want]+-ing** '～되어야 할 필요가 있다'
   I think your computer **needs formatting**.
   나는 너의 컴퓨터가 포맷될 필요가 있다고 생각한다.
   = I think your computer **needs to be formatted**.

5. **be busy+-ing** '～하느라고 바쁘다'
   Mina **is busy preparing** for the party. 미나는 파티 준비를 하느라고 바쁘다.

6. **have trouble[difficulty/a hard time]+-ing** '～하는 데 어려움을 겪다'
   Tom **had trouble making** new friends. Tom은 새로운 친구들을 사귀는 데 어려움을 겪었다.

7. **It is no use+-ing** '～해도 소용없다'
   It is no use crying over spilt milk. 엎질러진 우유 때문에 울어 봐야 소용없다.
   = **It is of no use to cry** over spilt milk.
   = **It is useless to cry** over spilt milk.

8. **spend+시간[돈]+-ing** '～하느라 …를 소비하다'
   He **spent** a lot of time **reading** history books.
   그는 역사책을 읽는 데 많은 시간을 소비했다.

9. **be worth+-ing** '～할 가치가 있다'= be worthwhile to+동사원형 = be worthy of -ing
   This book **is worth reading**. 이 책은 읽을 가치가 있다.
   = This book **is worthwhile to read**. = This book **is worthy of reading**.

10. **look forward to+-ing** '～을 고대하다'
    I'm **looking forward to hearing** from you soon. 곧 네게서 소식을 듣기를 고대하고 있다.

PRACTICE 7

우리말과 일치하도록 괄호 안의 단어를 이용하여 빈칸에 알맞은 말을 쓰세요.

1 나는 내 아들의 축구 경기에 가는 것을 고대한다.

= I ________________________ to my son's soccer game. (go)

2 그 빈 방들은 페인트칠해질 필요가 있다.

= Those empty rooms ________________________. (paint)

= Those empty rooms ________________________.

3 Jennifer는 스페인어를 말하는 데 어려움을 겪고 있다.

= Jennifer is ________________________ Spanish. (speak)

4 그는 아침 식사를 거르는 것에 익숙하다.

= He is ________________________ breakfast. (skip)

5 그녀는 학교에서 새 친구들을 사귀느라고 바빴다.

= She was ________________________ new friends in the school. (make)

6 내 친구는 새 휴대전화를 사는 데 많은 돈을 썼다.

= My friend ________________ a lot of money ________________ a new cell phone. (buy)

7 그의 콘서트는 환상적인 무대 때문에 볼 만한 가치가 있다.

= His concert is ________________________ because of the fantastic staging. (watch)

= His concert is ________________________ because of the fantastic staging.

8 나는 그 약속을 지키지 못했다. 나는 민호에게 미안해하지 않을 수 없었다.

= I didn't keep the promise. I ________________________ sorry for Minho. (feel)

= I didn't keep the promise. I ________________________ sorry for Minho.

9 내게 무슨 말을 해도 소용없다. 나는 네가 말하는 어떤 것도 믿지 않을 것이다.

= It is ________________________ me anything. I won't believe anything you say. (tell)

= It is ________________________ me anything. I won't believe anything you say.

= It is ________________________ me anything. I won't believe anything you say.

10 나는 이번 주 일요일에 명동으로 쇼핑하러 갈 계획이다.

= I'm planning to ________________________ to Myeong-dong this Sunday. (shop)

PSS 5 동명사의 부정형

동명사의 부정형을 만들 때는 동명사 바로 앞에 not이나 never를 쓴다.

I'm sorry for **not being** ready in time. 제시간에 준비가 안 된 것에 대해 미안하다.

Never ignoring small problems can prevent bigger ones later.

작은 문제를 무시하지 않는 것이 나중에 더 큰 문제를 막을 수 있다.

Henry imagined **not having** the final exam tomorrow.

Henry는 내일 기말고사를 보지 않는 것을 상상했다.

PRACTICE 8

괄호 안의 단어를 알맞은 형태로 바꾸어 문장을 완성하세요.

1 Thank you for ________________ this to anyone. (not, tell)

2 I'm sorry for ________________ able to talk with you. (not, be)

3 My brother wanted me ________________ his room without permission. (never, enter)

4 Mom still remembers ________________ me a birthday present last year. (not, give)

5 I apologize for ________________ your camera carefully. (not, handle)

6 Taxi fares have gone up a lot, so I suggested ________________ a taxi. (not, take)

7 Mary promised ________________ him again. (never, see)

8 One of the members suggested ________________ camping this summer. (not, go)

9 I decided ________________ Sam before he apologizes to me. (not, call)

10 My husband and I are considering ________________ our son to the school abroad. (not, send)

CH
8
동명사

PSS 6 동명사의 의미상의 주어

PROBLEM
SOLVING
SKILL

1. **의미상의 주어를 나타내지 않는 경우**

   ① 일반인이거나 문맥상 뚜렷한 경우

   Hunting in national parks is not allowed.

   국립 공원에서 사냥을 하는 것은 허용되지 않는다.

   ② 문장의 주어와 같은 경우

   I like **listening** to his music. 나는 그의 음악을 듣는 것을 좋아한다.

   ③ 문장의 목적어와 같은 경우

   He praised me for **working** hard. 그는 내가 열심히 일한 것에 대해 칭찬했다.

2. **의미상의 주어를 나타내는 경우**

   ① 행위의 주체가 주어나 목적어와 다른 경우에는 의미상의 주어를 소유격으로 쓰는 것이 원칙이다. 하지만 구어체에서는 목적격으로 쓰기도 한다.

   Do you mind **my[me] practicing** the flute here?

   제가 여기에서 플루트를 연습해도 괜찮으시겠어요?

   I'm not used to **your[you] acting** like that. 나는 네가 그렇게 행동하는 것에 익숙하지 않다.

   ② 의미상의 주어가 부정대명사나 무생물, 추상명사일 때는 목적격으로 쓴다.

   There is little chance of **the train** being late. 그 기차가 늦을 가능성은 거의 없다.

   I imagine **this old telephone working** again.

   나는 이 오래된 전화기가 다시 작동하는 것을 상상한다.

PRACTICE 9

다음 문장에서 동명사의 의미상의 주어가 일반인이거나 문맥상 뚜렷한 경우이면 ①, 문장의 주어와 같은 경우이면 ②, 문장의 목적어와 같은 경우이면 ③을 쓰세요.

1 Watching English TV programs is good for your English. [   ]

2 Persuading somebody is sometimes not easy. [   ]

3 Thank you for letting me know about the show beforehand. [   ]

4 He took the necklace without telling anybody. [   ]

5 I'm sorry for bothering you again. [   ]

6 I have to prevent the worker from leaving the company. [   ]

PRACTICE 10

다음을 동명사를 이용한 문장으로 바꾸세요.

1 I don't mind that my sister wears my clothes.
➡ I don't mind ______________________________________.

2 Those facts suggest that something is wrong with the engine.
➡ Those facts suggest ______________________________________.

3 She forgot that he said hello to her family.
➡ She forgot ______________________________________.

4 I want Minsu to be the chairman.
➡ I'm in favor of ______________________________________.

5 Jenny couldn't imagine that her teacher had cancer.
➡ Jenny couldn't imagine ______________________________________.

6 We remember that the man entered when we were having dinner.
➡ We remember ______________________________________.

7 I expect him to do his best on the stage.
➡ I'm looking forward to ______________________________________.

8 I'm sorry for him that my son doesn't follow his directions all the time.
➡ I should apologize to him for ______________________________________.

9 I feel good because my works are well-known among people.
➡ I feel good about ______________________________________.

10 She was very proud that I won first prize in this competition.
➡ She was very proud of ______________________________________.

중간·기말고사 대비문제

1 밑줄 친 부분의 용법이 나머지 넷과 다른 것은?

① <u>Seeing</u> is believing.
② <u>Judging</u> from his behavior, he seems like a nice guy.
③ <u>Sleeping</u> too much might make you dizzy.
④ <u>Having</u> a good friend is one of the most valuable assets.
⑤ <u>Playing</u> soccer every weekend keeps me energetic.

2 빈칸 (A)와 (B)에 들어갈 말끼리 알맞게 짝지은 것은?

> Sangjin gave up ______(A)______ the computer and decided ______(B)______ a new one.

　　　　(A)　　　　(B)　　　　　(A)　　　(B)
① to fix　　– to buy　② to fix – buying
③ fixing　　– to buy　④ fixing – buying
⑤ being fixed – buy

3 밑줄 친 부분의 용법이 나머지 넷과 다른 것은?

① My hobby is <u>collecting</u> foreign stamps.
② Her wish is <u>having</u> a baby of her own.
③ My dream is <u>coming</u> true right now.
④ His goal is <u>getting</u> an A⁺ in every subject.
⑤ My concern is <u>being</u> back at work soon.

4 다음 중 밑줄 친 부분의 쓰임이 잘못된 것은?

① They suddenly began <u>to cry</u> at his funeral.
② I stopped <u>drinking</u> Coke a month ago.
③ Would you mind <u>to step</u> aside a little bit?
④ I enjoy <u>reading</u> novels before bedtime.
⑤ She decided <u>to apply</u> for the part-time job.

5 다음 중 밑줄 친 부분의 쓰임이 올바른 것은?

① He continued <u>to search</u> for the herb.
② I remember <u>to see</u> her yesterday.
③ He considers <u>to move</u> to New York.
④ She has postponed <u>to meet</u> the journalists.
⑤ I dislike <u>to be</u> regarded as an outsider.

6 다음 두 문장의 뜻이 같게 할 때 밑줄에 알맞은 것은?

> She forgot that she had locked the door and had to go back to check.
> = She forgot ____________ the door and had to go back to check.

① lock　　　　　　② to lock
③ to have locked　④ locking
⑤ being locked

7 다음 중 밑줄 친 부분의 쓰임이 올바른 것은?

① I planned <u>studying</u> architecture in Paris.
② She pretended not <u>being</u> sad.
③ We agreed <u>taking</u> part in the project.
④ You must quit <u>teasing</u> your little brother.
⑤ I'd like <u>selling</u> it to make money.

8 다음 중 어법상 어색한 것은?

① She forgot to book a ticket for the movie.
② Countries can make money by trading.
③ They stopped to wait for the train to Seoul.
④ He remembers to turn off the TV before sleep.
⑤ Learning foreign languages are not easy.

9 다음 중 밑줄 친 부분의 쓰임이 잘못된 것은?

① I hope to go on a vacation soon.
② She put off to buy a new jacket.
③ They agreed to sign the treaty.
④ Because she was nervous, she refused to speak.
⑤ They will attempt to rescue the victims.

10 빈칸에 들어갈 말이 차례대로 짝지어진 것은?

> I look forward to ___________ you when you come to Seoul for the purpose of ___________ in the conference.

① seeing – participating
② see　 – participating
③ seeing – participate
④ see　 – participate
⑤ seen　 – participating

11 다음 중 어법상 틀린 문장의 개수는?

> ⓐ To avoid arguing with her, I rushed out of the room.
> ⓑ Alice had trouble to get along with others when she was young.
> ⓒ I remember meeting her for the first time at the airport.
> ⓓ Collecting artworks are an expensive hobby.
> ⓔ The team was proud of their winning the competition.

① 1개　　　　② 2개　　　　③ 3개
④ 4개　　　　⑤ 5개

12 다음 우리말을 바르게 영작한 것은?

> • 새로운 것을 배우는 것은 쉽지 않은데, 그것에 능숙해지는 것은 훨씬 더 어렵다.

① Learning new things are not easy, but get better at them is even more difficult.
② Learning new things is not easy, but getting better at them are even more difficult.
③ Learning new things are not easy, but getting better at them are even more difficult.
④ Learning new things is not easy, but get better at them is even more difficult.
⑤ Learning new things is not easy, but getting better at them is even more difficult.

13 두 문장이 같은 뜻이 되도록 빈칸에 알맞은 말을 쓰세요.

> • As soon as they are born, children learn from what they see, hear and experience.
> = ___________ being born, children learn from what they see, hear and experience.

14 밑줄 친 부분이 어법상 옳은 것은?

① I don't suggest to take that medicine for headaches.
② Both parties agreed holding more talks this year.
③ Three weeks ago, he promised going on a diet.
④ The man kept to call, but we failed to locate him.
⑤ Practicing speaking slowly and clearly will help you communicate better with others.

15 흐름상 빈칸에 들어갈 말로 가장 알맞은 것은?

> Nina travels alone to foreign countries. She doesn't feel lonely because she has done it many times before. She truly enjoys meeting new people and experiencing different cultures. ______________________.

① She uses to travel alone.
② She used to travel alone.
③ She used to traveling alone.
④ She is used to traveling alone.
⑤ She gets used to travel alone.

16 다음 문장에서 틀린 곳을 찾아 바르게 고치세요.

> Humans continued to do research and finally succeeded to launch satellites.

______________ ➡ ______________

17 다음 Mary의 일정표를 보고, 어법에 맞게 표현한 문장을 고르세요.

Yesterday	Tomorrow
17:00-18:00 take a walk	17:30-19:30 visit grandparents
20:00-20:40 do homework	20:00-20:30 do yoga
21:00-22:30 watch TV	21:00-22:00 study English

① She spent an hour take a walk.
② She will spend 30 minutes to do yoga.
③ She will spend an hour to studying English.
④ She stopped to watch TV before midnight.
⑤ She was busy doing her homework at around 8 p.m. yesterday.

18 다음 글의 밑줄 친 ⓐ~ⓔ를 바르게 고친 것을 모두 고르세요.

> While walking through the park, Olivia stopped ⓐ take pictures of the flowers. The gentle aroma surrounding her made her eager ⓑ taking the shot. She enjoyed ⓒ to spend her afternoon in the fresh air, but she had to leave early to avoid meeting her ⓓ noise neighbors. Before going home, she considered ⓔ to buy some bread from the bakery, and planned to bake a cake for her family that evening.

① ⓐ take → taking
② ⓑ taking → to take
③ ⓒ to spend → spending
④ ⓓ noise → noisily
⑤ ⓔ to buy → bought

19 다음 대화의 빈칸에 들어갈 말이 차례대로 짝지어진 것은?

> *Jane*: What do you plan ________ this weekend?
> *Josh*: I'm thinking of going ________ to the lake with my brother. Will you join us?
> *Jane*: That'll be great! Since I moved to this town, I've been looking forward to ________ the beautiful lake.

① to do – to fish – seeing
② to do – fishing – see
③ to do – fishing – seeing
④ doing – fish – see
⑤ doing – fishing – seeing

20
〈보기〉와 같은 형식의 문장이 되도록 주어진 우리말을 참고하여 빈칸에 알맞은 말을 쓰세요.

보 기 | Playing soccer is always interesting.

• _________ _________ _________
_________ a fun and healthy way to
stay active.
(스포츠에 참여하는 것은 즐겁고 건강한 방식으로 활동적으로 지내는 것이다.)

21
빈칸에 알맞은 단어를 쓰세요.

If you want to succeed _________
getting the right answers, read the book
thoroughly instead _________ asking
your friends.

22
주어진 우리말 뜻과 같도록 빈칸을 채워 문장을 완성하세요. (단, used to를 포함하여 총 6단어로 쓸 것.)

나는 지금 도쿄에서 운전하는 것에 익숙하지만 처음에는 어려웠다.
= _________ _________ _________
_________ _________ _________
now, but it was hard at the beginning.

23
다음 중 밑줄 친 부분의 쓰임이 잘못된 것은?

① She left me even without saying good-bye.
② The firewall prevents other computers from accessing your computer.
③ Few students are in favor with wearing school uniforms.
④ He apologized for being mean to me.
⑤ I felt like crying when I heard the sad news.

24
다음 문장을 아래와 같이 바꾸어 쓸 때 빈칸에 알맞은 단어를 쓰세요.

She couldn't go out of the house because the wind was very strong.

➡ The strong wind kept _________
_________ _________ out of the house.

25
다음 중 어법상 맞는 문장의 개수는?

(a) Please don't forget calling me when you arrive.
(b) They admitted breaking the classroom window.
(c) Do you remember lending me this book last month?
(d) My brother dreams of travel around the world someday.
(e) The museum is worth to visit if you're interested in history.

① 1개　② 2개　③ 3개　④ 4개　⑤ 5개

26
다음 문장을 아래와 같이 바꾸어 쓸 때 빈칸에 알맞은 말을 쓰세요.

This company needs changing on a large scale.

➡ This company needs _________
_________ _________ on a large scale.

27
다음 중 어법상 어색한 것은?

① I have been busy looking for a new office.
② She spent most of her time preparing for dinner.
③ He had difficulty focusing on details.
④ I feel like to taking a walk in the park.
⑤ They have trouble making decisions.

28 두 문장의 뜻이 같아지도록 빈칸에 알맞은 말을 쓰세요.

- The scenery was so beautiful that I couldn't help taking a lot of photos.
  = The scenery was so beautiful that I
  ___________ ___________ ___________
  a lot of photos.

29 〈보기〉에서 어법상 틀린 문장의 개수는?

보 기

ⓐ I am used to go skiing every winter.
ⓑ He could not but accept the proposal.
ⓒ We are looking forward to see the match.
ⓓ She is accustomed to be a leader.
ⓔ Her life has been devoted to helping the poor.

① 1개　② 2개　③ 3개　④ 4개　⑤ 5개

30 세 문장의 뜻이 같아지도록 빈칸에 알맞은 말을 쓰세요.

- It was useless to speak in soft and gentle tones because everyone else was shouting.
  = It was ___________ ___________ ___________
  ___________ to speak in soft and gentle tones because everyone else was shouting.
  = It was ___________ ___________ ___________
  ___________ in soft and gentle tones because everyone else was shouting.

31 다음 중 밑줄 친 부분의 쓰임이 잘못된 것은?

① We spent some time making Christmas cards.
② My house used to standing on the hill.
③ What do you feel like seeing there?
④ It is no use saying that IQ scores can be wrong.
⑤ How about going hiking to the mountain?

32 다음 중 어법상 옳은 것은?

① I enjoy to be friends with strangers.
② I want to sleep instead of eat something.
③ No one imagined to meet Mr. Lee there.
④ I prefer dying to living in dishonor.
⑤ He apologized not for joining the team.

33 다음 중 어법상 틀린 것은?

① Now I'm not as shy as I used to be.
② Music is sometimes used to relaxing people.
③ She got used to living in such a new environment.
④ The boy was not used to someone telling him what to do.
⑤ There used to be a bench under this tree.

34 다음의 밑줄 친 부분을 올바른 형태로 바꾸어 쓰세요.

(1) We need to stop by the gas station fill up the gas.
(2) Bob is not used to get up early in the morning.

(1) ___________________________________
(2) ___________________________________

35 다음 중 어법상 <u>어색한</u> 문장의 개수는?

ⓐ It is of no use telling him the truth.
ⓑ I don't like his singing aloud at night.
ⓒ He apologized for doing not return my book earlier.
ⓓ These days James has trouble falling asleep.
ⓔ Would you mind to turn the volume down on the radio?
ⓕ Remember dropping by the grocery store for dinner tonight.
ⓖ Making good friends are more important than getting good grades.

① 2개　　② 3개　　③ 4개
④ 5개　　⑤ 6개

36 다음은 건강을 지키는 방법을 메모한 것입니다. 밑줄 친 내용을 영어로 표현할 때 빈칸에 알맞은 말을 한 칸에 한 단어씩 쓰세요.

- (1) <u>하루에 8시간을 자는 것은 정신적·신체적 휴식에 필수적이다.</u>
- (2) <u>건강에 좋은 음식을 먹음으로써 필수 영양소를 섭취할 수 있다.</u>
- 주 3회 30분 운동으로 신체의 활력을 찾을 수 있다.
- 스트레스를 해소할 취미 활동을 가져야 한다.

(1) ________ ________ ________ ________ ________ ________ necessary for your mental and physical rest.

(2) You can take essential nutrients ________ ________ ________ ________ ________.

37 다음 주어진 우리말을 바르게 영작한 것은?

나는 그에게 그것을 거절하지 말라고 계속 얘기할 거야.

① I'll continue telling him to not turn it down.
② I'll keep telling him not to turn it down.
③ I'll keep to tell him to turn it up.
④ I'll continue to tell him to turn it up.
⑤ I'll keep telling him not to turn down it.

38 다음 글의 밑줄 친 우리말을 괄호 안의 표현을 이용하여 영작하세요. (단, 필요하면 형태를 바꾸세요.)

Suddenly, it started to rain with lots of thunder and lightning. Although I had some books to return to the library, <u>나는 외출하는 대신 집에 있기로 결심했다.</u>

➡ I ________________________________

________________________________.

(decide, stay, to, instead of, go out, home)

39 주어진 단어를 활용하여 우리말과 같은 뜻이 되도록 영작하세요.

조 건 ┃ 1. 필요한 경우 어형을 변형시킬 것.
　　　　2. 동명사 표현을 반드시 사용할 것.
　　　　3. 총 5단어가 되게 쓸 것.

만약 네가 좋은 자리를 원한다면, 거기에 일찍 가는 것이 좋다. (worth, get)

= ________________________________

if you want a good seat.

CHAPTER 9
분사

PSS 1 분사의 역할	페이지	성취도				
		100%	99~75%	74~50%	49~25%	24~0%
PSS 1-1 한정적 용법	186					
PSS 1-2 서술적 용법	188					
PSS 2 현재분사와 동명사	189					
PSS 3 감정을 나타내는 분사	190					

PSS 4 분사구문	페이지	성취도				
		100%	99~75%	74~50%	49~25%	24~0%
PSS 4-1 분사구문 만드는 법	192					
PSS 4-2 완료형 분사구문	194					
PSS 4-3 with+명사+분사	195					
PSS 4-4 분사구문의 관용적 표현	197					
중간·기말고사 대비문제	198					

PSS 1 분사의 역할

	현재분사	과거분사
형태	동사원형+-ing	동사원형+-ed (동사의 과거분사형)
의미	**진행** (~하고 있는) The **sleeping** baby is my nephew. 자고 있는 아기는 내 남자조카이다. The baby is **sleeping**. 아기는 자고 있다.	**완료** (~한) I have to sweep the **fallen** leaves. 나는 떨어진 나뭇잎들을 쓸어야 한다. The leaves have **fallen**. 나뭇잎들이 떨어졌다.
	능동 (~하게 하는) I was watching the **shocking** news. 나는 그 충격적인 뉴스를 보고 있었다. The news was **shocking**. 그 뉴스는 충격적이었다.	**수동** (~된, ~해진) The thief escaped through the **broken** window. 그 도둑은 깨진 창문을 통해 탈출했다. The window was **broken**. 그 창문은 깨져 있었다.

PSS 1-1 한정적 용법

1. 분사가 단독으로 쓰일 때는 명사의 앞에서 명사를 수식한다.

   Do you know the <u>**shouting man**</u> over there? 저쪽에서 소리치고 있는 남자를 아니?

   I threw away the <u>**broken glasses**</u>. 나는 깨진 유리잔들을 버렸다.

2. 분사가 구를 이루어 명사를 수식할 때는 명사의 뒤에서 명사를 수식한다.

   The <u>**girls chatting in the classroom**</u> are twins. 교실에서 이야기하고 있는 소녀들은 쌍둥이이다.

   I'm reading a <u>**novel written by George Orwell**</u>. 나는 George Orwell에 의해 쓰여진 소설을 읽고 있다.

정답 p.42

PRACTICE 1

빈칸에 들어갈 단어로 알맞은 것을 골라 동그라미 하세요.

1   The room (painting, painted) in light pink is my baby's.

2   The boys chased the (running, run) dog.

3   The girl (dancing, danced) on the stage is very pretty.

4   A new car is more expensive than a (using, used) car.

5   Those expressions are only used in (speaking, spoken) English.

6   Listen to the birds (singing, sung) in the woods.

7   She works for a company (founded, founding) by her grandfather.

8   I think bungee jumping was a (terrifying, terrified) experience.

정답 p.42

PRACTICE 2

〈보기〉와 같이 분사를 이용하여 두 문장을 한 문장으로 연결하세요.

보 기   Do you know the boy? He is sitting next to Mina.
➡ Do you know the boy _sitting next to Mina_?

1   I'm listening to several songs. They are sung by kids.
➡ I'm listening to several songs ________________________________.

2   Let's pick up those leaves. They have fallen under the tree.
➡ Let's pick up those leaves ________________________________.

3   Those students came here to do volunteer work. They are taking a break.
➡ Those students ________________________ came here to do volunteer work.

4   I saw a wounded soldier. He was lying on the grass.
➡ I saw a wounded soldier ________________________________.

5   My cat's house is over there. It is covered with snow.
➡ My cat's house ________________________ is over there.

6   The man is my Japanese teacher. He is standing in front of the gate.
➡ The man ________________________ is my Japanese teacher.

7   The portrait was painted in the 1960s. It is hanging on the wall.
➡ The portrait ________________________ was painted in the 1960s.

8   My mother-in-law gave me the pink bowl. It was filled with blueberries.
➡ My mother-in-law gave me the pink bowl ________________________________.

1. **주어의 상태나 행위를 설명하는 주격 보어로 쓰인다.**

   ① 주어와 주격 보어가 능동의 관계일 때는 현재분사를 쓰고 '~하면서, ~하게 하는'으로 해석한다.

   Mom was seated **knitting** a sweater. 엄마는 앉아서 스웨터를 짜고 계셨다.
   ↑능동

   ② 주어와 주격 보어가 수동의 관계일 때는 과거분사를 쓰고 '~한, ~된, ~해진'으로 해석한다.

   The roof was **damaged** because of the thunderstorm. 뇌우 때문에 지붕이 손상되었다.
   ↑수동

2. **목적어의 상태나 행위를 설명하는 목적격 보어로 쓰인다.**

   ① 목적어와 목적격 보어가 능동의 관계일 때는 현재분사를 쓰고 '(목적어가) ~하는 것을'로 해석한다.

   We saw **a big eagle flying** above us. 우리는 큰 독수리가 우리 위로 날아가는 것을 보았다.
   ↑능동

   ② 목적어와 목적격 보어가 수동의 관계일 때는 과거분사를 쓰고 '(목적어가) ~되는 것을'로 해석한다.

   She had **all her money stolen** on the subway. 그녀는 지하철에서 모든 돈을 도난당했다.
   ↑수동

정답 p.42

PRACTICE 3

괄호 안의 동사를 올바른 분사의 형태로 바꾸어 빈칸에 쓰세요.

1 A traveler stood at the information center ＿＿＿＿＿＿＿ a guidebook. (read)

2 Did you hear a woman ＿＿＿＿＿＿＿ there? (scream)

3 The child was crying hard ＿＿＿＿＿＿＿ for her mom. (look)

4 Mr. Thomas sat ＿＿＿＿＿＿＿ by his students. (surround)

5 I saw a man ＿＿＿＿＿＿＿ by a car in the middle of the road. (hit)

6 She looked a little ＿＿＿＿＿＿＿ at his sudden announcement. (surprise)

7 My friend came to me ＿＿＿＿＿＿＿ my name. (call)

8 I want my broken computer ＿＿＿＿＿＿＿ right now. (fix)

9 I'm sorry to keep you ＿＿＿＿＿＿＿ alone for a long time. (wait)

10 Lucy had her eyes ＿＿＿＿＿＿＿ yesterday. (test)

PSS 2 현재분사와 동명사

현재분사	동명사
현재분사는 '~하고 있는, ~하게 하는'의 의미를 가지며 형용사 역할을 한다. A **rolling** stone gathers no moss. (= A stone which is rolling) 구르는 돌에는 이끼가 끼지 않는다. Her **singing** voice is really **amazing**. 그녀의 노래하는 목소리는 정말로 놀랍다.	동명사는 '~하기 위한, ~하는 것'의 의미를 가지며 명사 역할을 한다. We have a **fitting** room in our store. (= a room for fitting) 우리 가게에는 탈의실이 있다. My dream is **becoming** a flight attendant. 내 꿈은 승무원이 되는 것이다.

정답 p.42

PRACTICE 4

다음 문장의 밑줄 친 부분의 용법이 〈보기〉의 A와 같으면 A, B와 같으면 B를 쓰세요.

> 보 기
> A. Mr. Lee is waiting for you in the <u>dining</u> room.
> B. Do you know the boy <u>smiling</u> at you?

1 My grandfather went for a walk with a <u>walking</u> stick. [   ]

2 Who is that woman <u>waving</u> her hand toward you? [   ]

3 Jiho was <u>painting</u> the wall when I went to see him. [   ]

4 We slept in <u>sleeping</u> bags during the camping. [   ]

5 I could see the monster <u>attacking</u> people in the movie. [   ]

6 Isn't the <u>sleeping</u> cat so cute? [   ]

7 Ms. Scott is the most <u>interesting</u> person I've ever met. [   ]

8 I am very proud of <u>being</u> his son. [   ]

9 Hana is going to buy a pair of <u>running</u> shoes. [   ]

10 He is good at <u>speaking</u> four foreign languages. [   ]

PSS 3 감정을 나타내는 분사

다음은 감정을 나타내는 동사의 분사형이다. '～한 감정을 느끼게 하는'의 뜻일 때는 현재분사를, '～한 감정을 느끼는'의 뜻일 때는 과거분사를 쓴다.

amazing – amazed 놀라운　　놀란	boring – bored 지루한　지루함을 느끼는
confusing – confused 혼란스럽게 하는　혼란스러운	depressing – depressed 우울하게 하는　　우울한
disappointing – disappointed 실망스러운　　실망한	embarrassing – embarrassed 당황하게 하는　　당황한
exciting – excited 흥미진진한　흥분한	fascinating – fascinated 매혹적인　　매료된
frightening – frightened 깜짝 놀라게 하는　깜짝 놀란	interesting – interested 흥미로운　흥미를 느끼는
moving – moved 감동적인　감동한	satisfying – satisfied 만족시키는　만족한
shocking – shocked 충격적인　충격받은	surprising – surprised 놀라운　　놀란

The first day of the school was **confusing**. 등교 첫날은 혼란스러웠다.

I was **confused** on the first day of the school. 등교 첫날에 나는 혼란스러웠다.

My grandmother used to tell me **interesting** stories.

나의 할머니는 내게 흥미로운 이야기를 해 주시곤 했다.

I was **interested** in my grandmother's stories. 나는 나의 할머니의 이야기에 흥미를 느꼈다.

My presentation was quite **satisfying** to the teacher. 내 발표는 선생님에게 꽤 만족스러웠다.

The teacher was quite **satisfied** with my presentation.

선생님은 내 발표에 꽤 만족스러워하셨다.

정답 p.42

PRACTICE 5 [1-14]

〈보기〉와 같이 분사를 이용하여 빈칸을 채우세요.

보 기	Bill's report satisfied the manager.
	➡ Bill's report was ___*satisfying*___ to the manager.
	➡ The manager was ___*satisfied*___ with Bill's report.

1 The motorcycle race excited all the audience.
➡ All the audience was _________________ about the motorcycle race.
➡ The motorcycle race was _________________ to all the audience.

2 The result disappointed my family and friends.
➡ The result was _________________ to my family and friends.
➡ My family and friends were _________________ at the result.

3 His new movie bored the audience.
➡ His new movie was _________________ to the audience.
➡ The audience was _________________ with his new movie.

4 The news surprised all of the TV viewers.
➡ All of the TV viewers were _________________ at the news.
➡ The news was _________________ to all of the TV viewers.

5 His stories about the universe always amaze us.
➡ We are always _________________ by his stories about the universe.
➡ His stories about the universe are always _________________ to us.

6 The manager's instructions confused me.
➡ The manager's instructions were _________________ to me.
➡ I was _________________ by the manager's instructions.

7 The singer's costume shocked the people.
➡ The singer's costume was _________________ to the people.
➡ The people were _________________ by the singer's costume.

8 The rainy weather depresses some people.
➡ Some people are _________________ by the rainy weather.
➡ The rainy weather is _________________ to some people.

9 The article about space travel fascinated us.
➡ The article about space travel was _________________ to us.
➡ We were _________________ by the article about space travel.

10 Watching sports games interests Minho.
➡ Minho is _________________ in watching sports games.
➡ Watching sports games is _________________ to Minho.

11 The sad story of his childhood moved us deeply.
➡ The sad story of his childhood was deeply _________________ to us.
➡ We were deeply _________________ by the sad story of his childhood.

12 The loud noise frightened the Kims.
➡ The Kims were _________________ by the loud noise.
➡ The loud noise was _________________ to the Kims.

13 The total score of this test satisfied me.

➡ I was ________________ with the total score of this test.

➡ The total score of this test was ________________ to me.

14 The mayor's speech embarrassed the public.

➡ The public was ________________ by the mayor's speech.

➡ The mayor's speech was ________________ to the public.

PSS 4 분사구문

PSS 4-1 분사구문 만드는 법

분사구문은 분사를 이용하여 부사절을 부사구로 바꾼 구문을 말한다.

When I knew the truth, I could be relieved. 그 사실을 알았을 때, 나는 안심할 수 있었다.
　　부사절　　　　　　　　주절

① 부사절의 접속사를 뺀다.

　When I knew the truth, I could be relieved.

② 주절의 주어와 같은 부사절의 주어를 뺀다.

　I knew the truth, I could be relieved.

③ 부사절의 동사를 -ing 형태로 바꾼다.

　➡ **Knowing** the truth, I could be relieved.

cf. 분사구문에서 문장의 의미를 분명히 하기 위해 분사 앞에 접속사를 쓰기도 한다.

1. 시간

After I graduated from college, I could make my dream come true.

대학을 졸업하고 난 후에, 나는 내 꿈을 실현할 수 있었다.

➡ **Graduating from college**, I could make my dream come true.

2. 원인, 이유

Because she didn't live with her family, she missed them a lot.

그녀는 가족과 함께 살지 않았기 때문에, 그녀는 그들을 많이 그리워했다.

➡ **Not living with her family**, she missed them a lot.

cf. not이나 never와 같은 부정어는 분사 앞에 붙인다.

3. 동시동작

All of the people watched the sunrise, **while they were drinking hot coffee**.

그 사람들 모두는 뜨거운 커피를 마시는 동안 해가 뜨는 것을 보았다.

➡ All of the people watched the sunrise, **drinking** hot coffee.

cf. All of the people watched the sunrise, **being drinking hot coffee**. (X)

부사절이 주절의 뒤에 올 경우, 진행형이 포함된 경우라고 하더라도 분사구문에서는
「being+-ing」 형태로 쓰지 않는다.

4. 연속동작

She walked to the garden, **and watered the trees**.

그녀는 정원으로 걸어가서 나무에 물을 주었다.

➡ She walked to the garden, **watering** the trees.

5. 양보

Although they had little money, they were still happy together.

비록 그들은 돈이 거의 없었지만, 여전히 함께 행복했다.

➡ **Having little money**, they were still happy together.

6. 조건

If you are left alone at home, you might feel lonely.

집에 홀로 남겨진다면, 넌 외로움을 느낄지도 모른다.

➡ **(Being) Left alone at home**, you might feel lonely.

cf. 수동형의 분사구문에서는 being을 생략할 수 있다.

정답 p.42

PRACTICE 6 [1-12]

다음 문장의 부사절을 분사구문으로 바꾸어 빈칸을 채우세요.

1 Because he felt tired, he lay down on the grass.

➡ ____, he lay down on the grass.

2 While I was walking along the street, I met a friend of mine.

➡ ____, I met a friend of mine.

3 Although I know it's her mistake, I still don't blame her.

➡ ____, I still don't blame her.

4 Since he doesn't have a car anymore, he has to use public transportation.

➡ ____, he has to use public transportation.

5 While he was waiting for a taxi, he was hit by a truck.

➡ ___________________________, he was hit by a truck.

6 The train left Seoul at 8:00, and arrived in Daejeon at 10:30.

➡ The train left Seoul at 8:00, ___________________________.

7 If you open the box, you will find something surprising.

➡ ___________________________, you will find something surprising.

8 When she was given the prize, she felt so happy.

➡ ___________________________, she felt so happy.

9 Although he is not very old, he is very wise and thoughtful.

➡ ___________________________, he is very wise and thoughtful.

10 If you turn right, you'll find the restaurant on your left.

➡ ___________________________, you'll find the restaurant on your left.

11 After she told me her plans, she went into her room.

➡ ___________________________, she went into her room.

12 Mr. and Mrs. Martin welcomed us, and served us some tea.

➡ Mr. and Mrs. Martin welcomed us, ___________________________.

PSS 4-2 완료형 분사구문

부사절의 시제가 주절의 시제보다 앞설 때는 「having+과거분사」를 써서 분사구문을 만든다.

Since I stayed up late last night, I feel sleepy now.

나는 어젯밤 늦게까지 깨어 있었기 때문에 지금 졸리다.

➡ **Having stayed** up late last night, I feel sleepy now.

After she had found the purse, she brought it to the police.

지갑을 발견한 후에, 그녀는 그것을 경찰에게 가져갔다.

➡ **Having found** the purse, she brought it to the police.

As he had not met her before, he didn't know her.

전에 그녀를 만난 적이 없기 때문에, 그는 그녀를 몰랐다.

➡ **Not having met** her before, he didn't know her.

cf. 완료형 분사구문에 not이나 never와 같은 부정어를 쓸 때는 having 앞에 쓴다.

Because she was raised in a musical family, Maria plays multiple instruments.

음악적인 가정에서 길러졌기 때문에, Maria는 여러 악기들을 연주한다.

➡ **(Having been) Raised** in a musical family, Maria plays multiple instruments.

cf. 수동형의 분사구문에서는 having been을 생략할 수 있다.

PRACTICE 7

빈칸에 알맞은 말을 써 넣어 분사구문은 부사절로, 부사절은 분사구문으로 바꾸세요.

1 Although they had just eaten pizza, they still felt hungry.

➡ ____, they still felt hungry.

2 After I had read the paper, I got rid of it.

➡ ____, I got rid of it.

3 Having lost my bag, I can't hand in the report.

➡ ____, I can't hand in the report.

4 Not having heard from her for a long time, I wasn't surprised to see her.

➡ ____, I wasn't surprised to see her.

5 After his car had been repaired by Greg, it worked as he expected.

➡ ____, his car worked as he expected.

6 Not having read the book, she couldn't join the discussion.

➡ ____, she couldn't join the discussion.

7 As he had bought a brand-new car, he gave his old car to me.

➡ ____, he gave his old car to me.

8 Not finding me, he reported to Thomas on the case.

➡ ____, he reported to Thomas on the case.

9 When I don't know what to do, I always ask Mr. Kim for a piece of advice.

➡ ____, I always ask Mr. Kim for a piece of advice.

10 Having heard the truth about him, I still don't believe it.

➡ ____, I still don't believe it.

PSS 4 - 3 with + 명사 + 분사

「with+명사+분사」는 '~을 …한 채로'의 뜻으로 동시상황을 나타낸다. 이때 명사와 분사의 관계가 능동이면 현재분사를, 수동이면 과거분사를 쓴다. 또한, 묘사하고 있는 상황이 진행·지속 중임을 나타낼 때는 현재분사, 이미 완료된 상황을 나타낼 때는 과거분사를 쓴다.

She turned around as tears were running down her cheeks.

➡ She turned around, **with tears running** down her cheeks.
       ↑ 진행

그녀는 눈물이 볼에 흘러 내리는 채로 돌아섰다.

John lay down on his bed, and his arms were folded.

➡ John lay down on his bed, **with his arms folded**.
       ↑ 수동

John은 팔짱을 긴 채로, 침대에 누웠다.

cf. 「with+명사+형용사/부사(구)」도 동시동작을 나타낸다.

Don't study **with your computer on**. 컴퓨터를 켠 채로 공부하지 마라.

정답 p.43

PRACTICE 8

그림을 보고 짝지어진 두 문장의 의미가 같도록 「with+명사+분사」를 이용하여 빈칸을 채우세요.

1

2

3

4

5

6

1 The lady was sitting on the sofa, and she was crossing her legs.

= The lady was sitting on the sofa, ________________________________.

2 Cathy went to sleep, and the light was turned on.

= Cathy went to sleep, ________________________________.

3 Jack was reading a newspaper, and his wife was knitting a sweater.

= Jack was reading a newspaper, ________________________________.

4 I was walking home, and my dog was following me.

= I was walking home, ________________________________.

5 Ted practiced the piano, and the door was closed.

= Ted practiced the piano, ________________________________.

6 Susan was watching TV while her daughter was sitting beside her.

= Susan was watching TV, ________________________________.

분사구문의 의미상의 주어가 주절의 주어와 다르고, you, we, they, people과 같은 일반인을 나타낼 경우, 의미상의 주어가 생략되어 숙어처럼 관용적으로 쓰인다.

If **we speak generally**, learning Chinese is not easy.

➡ **Generally speaking**, learning Chinese is not easy.

일반적으로 말하면, 중국어를 배우는 것은 쉽지 않다.

If **we consider** global warming, I can understand why the temperature is so high.

➡ **Considering** global warming, I can understand why the temperature is so high.

지구 온난화를 고려하면, 기온이 매우 높은 것이 이해가 된다.

cf. frankly speaking (솔직히 말하면), strictly speaking (엄밀히 말하면), judging from (~으로 판단할 때), compared with (~와 비교하면), speaking of (~에 관해 말하면)

정답 p.43

PRACTICE 9

괄호 안에 들어갈 알맞은 말을 골라 동그라미 하세요.

1 Frankly (speak / speaking), I don't want to go hiking, but I have to.

2 Strictly (speaking / speak), you are late. You arrived at 9:01.

3 (Compared / Compare) with textbooks, comic books are easy to read.

4 (To judge / Judging) from her accent, she must be from Japan.

5 Generally (speaking / to speak), there are more right-handed people in Korea.

6 (Spoken / Speaking) of music, do you like classical music?

정답 p.43

PRACTICE 10

다음 두 문장이 같은 뜻이 되도록 빈칸에 알맞은 말을 쓰세요.

1 If we speak generally, the harder you work, the more you earn.

= ___________ ___________, the harder you work, the more you earn.

2 If we compare them with cities, rural areas are less crowded and polluted.

= ___________ ___________ cities, rural areas are less crowded and polluted.

3 If we speak strictly, the accident has nothing to do with him.

= ___________ ___________, the accident has nothing to do with him.

4 If we consider his age, his memory is still sharp and impressive.

= ___________ his age, his memory is still sharp and impressive.

5 If we speak frankly, neither Mina nor you are invited to Jinny's party.

= ___________ ___________, neither Mina nor you are invited to Jinny's party.

1 다음 빈칸에 들어갈 말이 차례대로 짝지어진 것은?

> • He worked with the parrot for two weeks,
> ___________ it to talk.
> • I imagined ___________ the piano in front
> of many people.

① teaching – to play　② taught – to play
③ teaching – playing　④ taught – playing
⑤ teaching – play

2 다음 중 밑줄 친 부분을 문맥에 맞게 절로 고친 것은?

> Doing his best, he failed in the exam.

① As he did his best
② Since he did his best
③ If he did his best
④ Though he did his best
⑤ Because he did his best

3 올바른 문장을 모두 고르세요. (정답 2개)

① I saw some birds flying across the lake.
② The cake bake by my sister tastes delicious.
③ The flowers planted last spring is blooming
now.
④ The students preparing for the test look
nervous.
⑤ She picked up a glove lay near the bus stop.

4 다음 중 밑줄 친 부분의 형태가 올바른 것은?

① She wants to buy a <u>using</u> car at a low price.
② The girl <u>helping</u> my mom is Sandy.
③ I have the bag <u>giving</u> to me by my sister.
④ The boy <u>played</u> on the beach is Scott.
⑤ I have to read the book <u>writing</u> in Japanese.

5 다음 우리말과 같은 뜻이 되도록 주어진 단어들 중 일부를 변형시켜 문장을 완성하세요.

> • 이틀이 지난 후에 우리에게 남은 물은 전혀 없었다.
> = After two days we had ___________.
> (leave, water, no)

6 다음을 영작하려고 할 때 가장 알맞은 것은?

> "핸드폰을 꺼주세요"라는 팻말이 있다.

① There is a sign said "Please turn off your
cellphone."
② There is a sign saying "Please turn off your
cellphone."
③ There is a sign writing "Please turn off your
cellphone."
④ There is a sign written "Please turn off your
cellphone."
⑤ There is a signature saying "Please turn off
your cellphone."

7 빈칸에 들어갈 말로 알맞은 것은?

> I met an old man ____________ his hometown after 52 years of absence.

① visit
② to visiting
③ visited
④ to be visited
⑤ visiting

8 다음 밑줄 친 부분을 문맥에 맞게 절로 고친 것은?

> <u>Tired</u> from the work, he went to bed as soon as he got home.

① As he was tired
② Though he was tired
③ Before he was tired
④ While he was tired
⑤ After he was tired

9 다음 문장에서 밑줄 친 부분을 바르게 고치세요.

(1) I was born and <u>raise</u> a city boy.

➡ ________________________________

(2) Tom saw a trailer <u>to block</u> the narrow road to his house.

➡ ________________________________

10 다음 중 어법상 옳은 것은?

① He was surprising by what he saw with his friend.
② I noticed her wallet to lie on the floor under the table.
③ He decided taking the money to the police station.
④ I read a book about a woman's life, and I was very moved.
⑤ I spent my weekend prepared for the presentation.

11 다음 중 밑줄 친 동사를 바르게 고친 것은?

> In many English dictionaries <u>publish</u> lately, we can find a number of new words.

① are published
② have been published
③ to publish
④ published
⑤ publishing

12 다음 문장에서 어법상 틀린 부분을 찾아 바르게 고치세요.

> People often have names taking from good and beautiful things.

________________ ➡ ________________

13 다음 분사구문을 부사절로 바꿀 때 빈칸에 들어갈 수 있는 것을 모두 고르세요.

> • Being good at painting, he could easily learn how to draw cartoons.
> ➡ ____________ he was good at painting, he could easily learn how to draw cartoons.

① Because
② Before
③ Though
④ As
⑤ While

14 다음 우리말과 같은 뜻이 되도록 주어진 단어들을 바르게 배열하여 문장을 완성하세요. (단, 필요시 어형을 변형시킬 것.)

> • 나를 향해 미소 짓고 있는 저 아기를 보아라.
> = ________________________________
>
> ________________________________
> (at, at, the, look, me, baby, smile)

CH
9
분사

 다음 밑줄 친 부분 중 어법상 옳지 <u>않은</u> 것을 모두 고르세요.

> ① <u>A number of</u> great ② <u>speeches</u> ③ <u>have been delivering</u> by famous speakers in the world. Anyone ④ <u>can be</u> a good speaker if he or she makes an effort. So, stand up and make your voice ⑤ <u>hearing</u>!

16 다음 일기에서 틀린 부분 세 곳을 찾아 어법에 맞게 고치세요.

> *Sunday, October 28th, Cloudy*
> My sister and I swept the falling leaves on the ground in the morning. After that, we drank tea in the dining room while my dog, Charli, was slept beside me. Wanting not to wake him up, we talked to each other quietly.

(1) ______________ ➡ ______________

(2) ______________ ➡ ______________

(3) ______________ ➡ ______________

17 다음 문장의 밑줄 친 부분과 쓰임이 <u>다른</u> 것은?

> I found that <u>knowing</u> myself is very important.

① <u>Speaking</u> English fluently is my wish.
② Instead of <u>punishing</u> me, he forgave me.
③ A proverb says a <u>barking</u> dog seldom bites.
④ <u>Working</u> as a reporter was a wonderful experience.
⑤ Do you mind <u>turning</u> down the volume a little, please?

18 ⓐ~ⓔ 중 어법상 틀린 것을 있는 대로 고른 것은?

> ⓐ I could see red and yellow leaves falling.
> ⓑ Did you get a portable bluetooth speaker sending from China?
> ⓒ The lights must turn off if they are unnecessary.
> ⓓ I was so excited to hearing the news.
> ⓔ You must attend the meeting holding in Gwangju.

① ⓐ, ⓑ   ② ⓑ, ⓒ   ③ ⓐ, ⓑ, ⓒ
④ ⓐ, ⓓ, ⓔ   ⑤ ⓑ, ⓒ, ⓓ, ⓔ

19 다음 문장의 밑줄 친 부분과 쓰임이 <u>다른</u> 것은?

> We need to take care of that <u>sleeping</u> child.

① People enjoyed <u>eating</u> the sausages in buns.
② Where did you see the <u>sleeping</u> dog?
③ Some children sat <u>crying</u> in the classroom.
④ The girl <u>dancing</u> on the stage is my sister, Mary.
⑤ Do you know that girl <u>living</u> on the island?

20 빈칸에 들어갈 말이 차례대로 짝지어진 것은?

> Green and blue have a ___________ effect, while dark gray and black create a ___________ effect.

① relax – depressing
② relaxing – depressing
③ relaxed – depressed
④ relaxing – depressed
⑤ relaxed – depress

21 다음 중 어법상 옳은 것은?

① Do you know the girl talk with Jim?
② Read classical literature is very important.
③ I was put away some groceries, when he entered the room.
④ After she finished to read, she went shopping.
⑤ Look at that boy running towards the deck.

22 다음 밑줄 친 부분의 어법이 틀린 것은?

① Mary was watching a movie <u>with tears rolling down her face</u>.
② He read a book <u>with his legs crossing</u>.
③ Why do you study <u>with the music on</u>?
④ Don't speak <u>with your mouth full</u>.
⑤ He waited for her <u>with his back against the wall</u>.

23 주어진 문장의 분사구문의 용법과 같은 것은?

Being old, she couldn't cross the desert.

① Being old, he is full of energy and confidence.
② Walking to school, I found a strange man.
③ Being a young kid, she often makes some mistakes.
④ Turning to the right, you'll find the building on your right.
⑤ Watching TV, he was thinking about his brother.

24 다음 중 어법상 옳은 문장은 몇 개인가?

ⓐ I was looking at the fire burned brightly.
ⓑ You should make a sentence with giving words.
ⓒ Do you know the bell called Big Ben?
ⓓ She put me in a very embarrassing situation.
ⓔ What is the language speaking in Iraq?
ⓕ The researchers found some treasure hiding in the woods.
ⓖ Frankly speaking, I don't know who she is.

① 2개 ② 3개 ③ 4개
④ 5개 ⑤ 6개

25 다음 밑줄 친 부분의 쓰임이 나머지 넷과 다른 것은?

① How about <u>electing</u> the leader among them?
② Her favorite pastime is <u>riding</u> a bike with her friends.
③ Although he was old, he never stopped <u>learning</u>.
④ We are <u>making</u> some paper flowers for our parents.
⑤ <u>Entertaining</u> many people is important to us.

26 우리말과 일치하도록 괄호 안에 주어진 말을 바르게 배열하세요. (필요시, 어형변화 가능)

• 다른 사람들의 문제들과 비교해 보면 내 자신의 문제는 대수롭지 않아 보인다.
(other, seem, compare, my own, with, problems, insignificant, people's)

➡ _______________________________________

____

27 다음 중 어법상 옳은 것은?

① We heard some shocked news from the teacher.
② It is an excited movie about adventure.
③ The teacher's explanation is so fascinated.
④ She was disappointed at the result.
⑤ It's amazed that he became a doctor.

28 빈칸에 들어갈 말이 차례대로 짝지어진 것은?

> I can't understand this story __________ in English perfectly. There are some parts that make me __________ .

① writing – confusing
② writing – confused
③ written – confuse
④ written – confused
⑤ written – confusing

29 밑줄 친 부분의 쓰임이 나머지와 다른 것은?

① They got on their bikes and rode off.
② He led a full and varied life as an artist.
③ She opened her mouth to say something.
④ The large bag carried by the man is mine.
⑤ Anything to do with planes and flying amused him.

30 다음 중 어법상 어색한 것은?

① This map is confusing. I don't know where I am.
② I'm interested in cooking Chinese food.
③ The grade was not very satisfying because I didn't study enough.
④ The noise was very annoyed to me.
⑤ He was surprised by my dirty room.

31 다음 밑줄 친 부분이 어법상 어색한 것은?

① Tom wore a scary mask and costume to make his classmates get scared.
② The news that we were still at the forefront of the computer software field was amazing.
③ It will be excited to see many beautiful places with you in Rome.
④ Why are you interested in working with us?
⑤ His lecture on politics was so boring that students started to feel bored.

32 다음 문장을 분사구문으로 바꿀 때 빈칸에 알맞은 말을 쓰세요.

> After my mom watched TV with me, she went to bed.

➡ __________ TV with me, __________ went to bed.

33 다음 중 밑줄 친 분사구문의 용법이 나머지 넷과 다른 것은?

① Written by a child, the poem was well-written and moving.
② Being young, she is a world-famous superstar.
③ Knowing how to solve the problem, he pretended not to know about it.
④ Being poor, she was a very talented writer.
⑤ Reading a newspaper in the kitchen, I fell asleep.

34 밑줄 친 동사를 알맞은 형태로 바꾼 것이 차례대로 짝지어진 것은?

> Julie was listening to music, with her eyes <u>close</u>. To her, listening to music and <u>watch</u> TV are very relaxing.

① close – watch
② closed – watched
③ closed – watching
④ closing – watching
⑤ closed – watch

35 다음 분사구문을 부사절로 바꾼 것 중 옳은 것은?

① Not knowing what to say, I remained silent.
➡ Though I didn't know what to say, I remained silent.
② Finishing my homework, I went to Michael's party.
➡ After I finished my homework, I went to Michael's party.
③ Living near the park, I have seldom been there.
➡ As I live near the park, I have seldom been there.
④ Being tired, I would rather sleep than go out.
➡ Though I am tired, I would rather sleep than go out.
⑤ Arriving home, I noticed I had lost the key.
➡ If I arrived home, I noticed I had lost the key.

36 다음 문장을 분사구문으로 바꿀 때 빈칸에 알맞은 말을 쓰세요.

> Because he had not brought his umbrella, he got wet in the rain.

➡ _________ _________ _________ his umbrella, he got wet in the rain.

37 다음 문장을 분사구문으로 바꿀 때 빈칸에 들어갈 말로 알맞은 것은?

> • As I was surprised at the news, I fell down on the floor.
> ➡ _________ at the news, I fell down on the floor.

① Being surprising
② Having surprised
③ Surprised
④ Surprising
⑤ To surprise

38 우리말을 영어로 쓸 때 맞는 문장의 개수는?

> ⓐ 이 책은 너에게 영감을 줄 것이다.
> → This book will give you inspiration.
> ⓑ 그는 보람 있는 직업을 갖고 싶어 한다.
> → He wants to have a rewarded job.
> ⓒ 겨울에 곰들은 겨울잠을 잔다.
> → In the winter, bears go into hibernate.
> ⓓ 이 박물관은 1956년에 설립되었다.
> → This museum was found in 1956.
> ⓔ 성공은 두 손을 주머니에 넣고는 오를 수 없는 사다리다.
> → Success is a ladder that cannot be climbed with your hands in your pockets.

① 1개   ② 2개   ③ 3개   ④ 4개   ⑤ 5개

39 빈칸에 들어갈 말이 차례대로 짝지어진 것은?

> _________ out the window, she happened to see a swallow _________ by.

① Look – flew
② Looking – flew
③ Looked – fly
④ Looking – flying
⑤ To look – flying

40 다음 분사구문을 부사절로 바꿀 때 빈칸에 알맞은 말을 쓰세요.

Having been to his house several times, Jane still couldn't remember how to get there.

➡ _______________ Jane _______________ _______________ to his house several times, she still couldn't remember how to get there.

41 (A)~(C)에서 어법상 옳은 것끼리 짝지어진 것은?

A farmer's son was walking home from the market (A) carried / carrying a box. The box was full of chickens (B) giving / given by his father. Then, he tripped and the box fell. The boy tried to chase all of the chickens and put them into the box. However, he was unsure if he had caught all of them. When he got home, he said to his father, "I'm sorry, Dad. The chickens escaped but I caught 10 of them."
(C) Surprising / Surprised, his father said, "That's good, Son! I gave you only seven chickens!"

	(A)		(B)		(C)
①	carrying	–	giving	–	Surprised
②	carrying	–	given	–	Surprising
③	carrying	–	given	–	Surprised
④	carried	–	giving	–	Surprised
⑤	carried	–	giving	–	Surprising

42 다음 중 어법상 옳은 문장의 개수는?

(a) The book written by Jason Carter is popular worldwide.
(b) The girl which is playing the piano is my sister.
(c) I saw a dog barking loudly at the stranger.
(d) The homework doing by Jake was difficult.
(e) The students standing near the gate are waiting for the bus.
(f) The birds flying in the sky look beautiful.
(g) We visited a museum that displays ancient paintings.
(h) The man who wearing a hat is my uncle.

① 3개　② 4개　③ 5개　④ 6개　⑤ 7개

43 다음의 밑줄 친 부분을 절로 바꾸세요.

<u>Having stage fright</u>, he sang his songs powerfully in front of the audience.

➡ _______________________________________

44 어법상 <u>어색한</u> 문장은?

① The children were playing happily, with toys scattered all around the room.
② My family decided to stay at home with the rain pouring outside.
③ The picture shows a woman seated with her legs crossed.
④ They hiked silently, with the forest surrounding them.
⑤ He ran swiftly, with his dog raced alongside him.

CHAPTER 10
형용사

Problem Solving Skill	페이지	성취도				
		100%	99~75%	74~50%	49~25%	24~0%
PSS 1 형용사의 쓰임	206					
PSS 2 -thing, -one, -body, -where+형용사	208					
PSS 3 the+형용사	209					
PSS 4 형용사의 어순	210					
PSS 5 부정수량형용사	페이지	성취도				
		100%	99~75%	74~50%	49~25%	24~0%
PSS 5-1 many, much	211					
PSS 5-2 few, a few, little, a little	213					
PSS 5-3 some, any	215					
PSS 6 수사	페이지	성취도				
		100%	99~75%	74~50%	49~25%	24~0%
PSS 6-1 기수와 서수	217					
PSS 6-2 정수	218					
PSS 6-3 분수와 소수	219					
PSS 6-4 연도와 날짜	220					
PSS 6-5 배수사	221					
PSS 6-6 시각	222					
중간·기말고사 대비문제	223					

PSS 1 형용사의 쓰임

한정적 용법

1. 형용사는 명사의 앞에서 명사를 수식한다.

I want to live in a **peaceful village**. 나는 평화로운 마을에서 살기를 원한다.

He must be an **active person**. 그는 활동적인 사람임이 틀림없다.

2. 다음의 형용사는 한정적 용법으로만 사용된다.

> only   main   elder   inner   outer   former   mere   upper

Sujin is the **only person** I know here.

수진이가 내가 여기에서 아는 유일한 사람이다.

cf. Sujin is **only**. (×)

Mr. Green was the **former chairman**. Green 씨는 전직 의장이었다.

cf. Mr. Green was **former**. (×)

서술적 용법

1. 형용사는 주격 보어나 목적격 보어로 쓰여 주어나 목적어에 대한 설명을 한다.

I felt **satisfied** to hear the news. 나는 그 소식을 듣고 만족스러웠다.
주격 보어

The music made **the students sleepy**. 그 음악은 학생들을 졸리게 만들었다.
목적격 보어

2. 다음의 형용사는 서술적 용법으로만 사용된다.

> afraid   alike   alive   alone   ashamed
> asleep   glad   sorry   pleased   worth

Paul was **afraid** of the bear. Paul은 그 곰이 두려웠다.
cf. Paul was an **afraid** boy. (×)

The performance was **worth** watching. 그 공연은 볼만한 가치가 있었다.
cf. That was a **worth** performance. (×)

정답 p.47

PRACTICE 1

괄호 안에 주어진 형용사를 어법이나 문맥상 알맞은 곳에 넣어 문장을 다시 쓰세요.

1 Golf is a game. (outdoor)

➡ ___________________________________

2 I'm sorry that you missed a lesson. (important)

➡ ___________________________________

3 I did my best to avoid mistakes. (similar)

➡ ____

4 My sister is a singer in Japan. (famous)

➡ ____

5 They played a game and the spectators enjoyed it. (exciting)

➡ ____

6 James was the person I talked to last night. (only)

➡ ____

7 The woman standing there is the leader. (former)

➡ ____

8 No one could move the rock. (heavy)

➡ ____

9 Where did you meet the kids? (lovely)

➡ ____

10 Jenny was very shocked by her dad's death. (sudden)

➡ ____

정답 p.47

PRACTICE 2

괄호 안에 들어갈 알맞은 단어를 골라 동그라미 하세요.

1 It's amazing that the fish that I caught two hours ago is still (alive, live).

2 I met a lot of (alone, lone) travelers in Europe.

3 You shouldn't skip chapter two because it's (important, main).

4 Mr. Carter looks like a (glad, cheerful) person.

5 The (sleeping, asleep) baby is my youngest son, Jiho.

6 Everyone thought that his personality was (unique, only).

7 I'm (scaring, afraid) of flying birds.

8 That was such a (worth, great) movie.

9 Minho and Junho are very (alike, like).

10 That (angry, alone) man is my boss.

PSS 2 -thing, -one, -body, -where + 형용사

-thing, -one, -body, -where로 끝나는 단어는 형용사가 뒤에서 수식한다.

Don't you want to drink **anything cold**? 찬 것을 마시고 싶지 않니?

Do you know **anyone generous** like Mr. Roberts? Roberts 씨처럼 마음이 너그러운 누군가를 아니?

There was **nobody funny** at the party. 파티에는 재미있는 사람이 아무도 없었다.

I'd like to go **somewhere warm**. 나는 따뜻한 어딘가에 가고 싶다.

cf. 한 단어인 명사 thing은 형용사가 앞에서 수식한다.

Bad things kept happening to me. 나쁜 일들이 내게 계속해서 일어났다.

정답 p.47

PRACTICE 3

괄호 안에 주어진 단어를 바르게 배열하여 빈칸에 쓰세요.

1 Bob bought the woman ___________________________. (something, expensive, very)

2 ___________________________ came to the theater for the contest. (someone, famous)

3 Police found ___________________________ in the airport. (a, thing, strange)

4 Nobody is allowed to carry ___________________________ here. (dangerous, anything)

5 I'm going to do ___________________________ for my best friend's birthday. (special, something)

6 We're planning ___________________________ for our students. (party, a, meaningful)

7 Do you have ___________________________? (anything, to, say, else)

8 I met ___________________________ during my trip to India. (people, a lot of, nice)

9 I've seen ___________________________ like Mr. Jackson. (no one, humorous)

10 ___________________________ is that you should not give it up. (the, thing, important)

11 I don't know why I can't find ___________________________ to me. (anybody, attractive)

12 She had to take a risk to go ___________________________. (very, somewhere, dangerous)

13 I have ___________________________ you. (new, to, nothing, tell)

14 Let's go ___________________________ so we won't be disturbed. (quiet, talk, somewhere, to)

PSS 3 the + 형용사

「the+형용사[분사]」는 '~한 사람들'의 뜻으로 복수 명사처럼 쓰인다.

The rich seem to have a desire to get richer. 부유한 사람들은 더 부유해지려는 욕망을 가지고 있는 것처럼 보인다.
(= Rich people)

The old also want to have their private lives. 노인들 또한 그들의 사생활을 가지기를 원한다.
(= Old people)

The young are interested in new trends. 젊은 사람들은 새로운 경향에 관심이 있다.
(= Young people)

The injured were taken to the hospital in an ambulance. 부상을 입은 사람들은 구급차를 타고 병원으로 옮겨졌다.
(= Injured people)

정답 p.48

PRACTICE 4

밑줄 친 부분에 유의하여 주어진 문장을 〈보기〉와 같이 바꾸어 쓰세요.

> 보 기
> Children should learn to respect the elderly.
> ➡ Children should learn to respect elderly people.

1 We collected some money for the homeless last year.
   ➡ ____

2 My sister went to Africa to help the doctor cure the sick.
   ➡ ____

3 We should provide some more convenient services for the disabled.
   ➡ ____

4 The city is planning to build a school for the deaf.
   ➡ ____

5 We need to find a solution for the young who don't have jobs.
   ➡ ____

6 There's a special class for the blind in this center.
   ➡ ____

7 Do you think the rich should pay more taxes to help the poor?
   ➡ ____

8 The battlefield was covered with the dead and the injured.
   ➡ ____

PSS 4 형용사의 어순

1. 명사 앞에 2개 이상의 형용사가 함께 올 때는 다음의 어순으로 쓴다.

서수	기수	성질	크기	신구	색깔	국적	재료
first	three	polite	big	new	black	Korean	plastic
seventh	five	gorgeous	small	old	pink	German	metal
twelfth	eleven	hard	large	young	green	American	wooden

2. 형용사 앞에 다른 수식어가 올 때는 다음의 어순으로 쓴다.

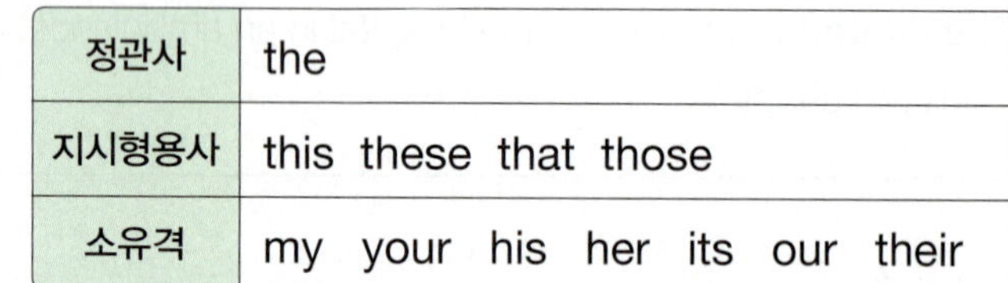

all	both
double	half

+

정관사	the
지시형용사	this these that those
소유격	my your his her its our their

I'm going to throw away **all those old plastic** toys.
나는 그 모든 오래된 플라스틱 장난감들을 버릴 것이다.
Both the pretty Korean girls are my friends from elementary school.
그 예쁜 한국 소녀 둘 다 내 초등학교 친구들이다.

정답 p.48

PRACTICE 5

다음 문장의 밑줄 친 부분을 바르게 고쳐 쓰세요.

1 The parents bought <u>purple two silk</u> dresses for the twins. _______________

2 I didn't know that this is <u>your Italian favorite</u> food. _______________

3 My dad bought <u>those small all</u> tables when he went to China. _______________

4 You have to clean <u>these plastic dirty half</u> dishes. _______________

5 <u>My gorgeous both</u> daughters are famous singers in Japan. _______________

6 <u>The all smart</u> students applied for our computer programming club. _______________

7 People will buy the ticket even if we sell it at <u>the regular double</u> price. _______________

8 Sungjin invited <u>his both new Canadian</u> friends to the party. _______________

9 Jason read <u>first three the</u> lines of the page and gave up. _______________

10 She used to like to wear <u>these yellow two large</u> shirts. _______________

PSS 5 부정수량형용사

PSS 5 - 1 many, much

many cars

much rain

| many+셀 수 있는 명사의 복수형 | much+셀 수 없는 명사 |

1. many와 much는 '많은'의 뜻으로 주로 부정문과 의문문에 쓰인다.

   Were there **many people** in the stadium? 경기장에 사람들이 많았니?
   You'd better not spend **much money** while you're traveling.
   너는 여행하는 동안에 많은 돈을 쓰지 않는 게 낫다.

2. 긍정문에서도 쓸 수 있지만, 긍정문에는 보통 many와 much 대신 a lot of, lots of, plenty of를 더 많이 쓴다.

   Many Hollywood films sell to all the world. 많은 할리우드 영화들이 전 세계로 팔린다.
   = **A lot of Hollywood films** sell to all the world.
   = **Lots of Hollywood films** sell to all the world.
   = **Plenty of Hollywood films** sell to all the world.

3. 긍정문에 쓰일 때는 many와 much 앞에 그 의미를 강조하는 so나 too를 함께 쓰기도 한다.

   There are **so many restaurants** near my new apartment.
   내 새로운 아파트 근처에는 아주 많은 식당들이 있다.
   I put **too much sugar** in my coffee. 나는 내 커피에 너무 많은 설탕을 넣었다.

정답 p.48

PRACTICE 6 [1-12]

다음 문장의 빈칸에 many나 much 중 알맞은 것을 쓰세요.

1 I haven't saved ______________ money for the last few years.

2   There were so ________________ fallen leaves on the street.

3   We didn't have ________________ rain last summer.

4   There are ________________ rooms in the new dormitory.

5   Junho used to collect so ________________ stamps when he was young.

6   I don't make ________________ new friends at school these days.

7   I drank too ________________ water after exercising hard.

8   She spent so ________________ time looking for her lost dog.

9   We found ________________ famous people gathered at the party.

10 Dana ate too ________________ food and her stomach is upset now.

11 Did you have ________________ chances to talk to foreigners at the meeting?

12 Was there ________________ information about the law firm you applied for?

정답 p.48

PRACTICE 7

〈보기〉에서 알맞은 단어를 골라 a lot of와 함께 써서 문장을 완성하세요. (필요하면 보기의 단어를 복수형으로 바꾸세요.)

보 기	world-famous dish	worker	work	evidence	time
	interesting story	chance	salt	weight	water

1   I could try ________________________ at the Food Festival.

2   We had ________________________ to meet new people in the city.

3   Mr. Park always uses ________________________ when he cooks.

4   There is ________________________ to support his idea.

5   Jina has lost ________________________ since she started to jog.

6   There were ________________________ at the construction site.

7   Grandmother knows ________________________ to tell us.

8   I had ________________________ to do when he visited my office.

9   Does it take ________________________ to get there on foot?

10 Should I give the plants ________________________ ?

PSS 5-2 few, a few, little, a little

few students

few + 셀 수 있는 명사의 복수형

a few students

a few + 셀 수 있는 명사의 복수형

1. few는 '거의 ~ 없는'의 뜻을, a few는 '약간의'의 뜻으로 셀 수 있는 명사의 수를 나타낸다.

There were **few portraits** in the gallery. 그 미술관에는 초상화가 거의 없었다.
There were **a few portraits** in the gallery. 그 미술관에는 약간의 초상화가 있었다.

cf. only a few '극소수의', quite a few '상당수의'
Only a few people lived on the island at first. 극소수의 사람들만이 처음에 그 섬에 살았다.
Quite a few people lived on the island at first. 상당수의 사람들이 처음에 그 섬에 살았다.

little sugar

little + 셀 수 없는 명사

a little sugar

a little + 셀 수 없는 명사

2. little은 '거의 ~ 없는'의 뜻을, a little은 '약간의'의 뜻으로 셀 수 없는 명사의 양을 나타낸다.

I had **little money** left in my wallet. 나는 지갑에 남은 돈이 거의 없었다.
I had **a little money** left in my wallet. 나는 지갑에 남은 약간의 돈이 있었다.

cf. only a little '아주 약간의', quite a little '많은, 다량의, 상당한'
There is **only a little traffic** today for a Sunday. 일요일치고는 오늘 교통이 거의 없다.
There is **quite a little traffic** today for a Sunday. 일요일치고는 오늘 교통이 꽤 많다.

PRACTICE 8

다음 문장의 빈칸에 few, a few, little, a little 중 가장 알맞은 것을 쓰세요.

1 Could you lend me _______________ money? I'll give it back by tomorrow.

2 I'm planning to teach students _______________ foreign languages.

3 There is nothing to do in this town, so _______________ tourists visit here.

4 The man couldn't read and write because he had _______________ education.

5 We are having _______________ difficulty, but the problem is not so serious.

6 I'll give you another phone call in _______________ days.

7 Due to the sudden rainstorm, _______________ people arrived at the meeting on time.

8 We had _______________ free time, so I couldn't call my parents.

9 Can I have _______________ talk with you now? I've got something important to tell you.

10 There were _______________ suggestions that I couldn't accept. I'd like to talk about them now.

11 No one knew that it was Tom's birthday. He had _______________ friends in his class.

12 My brother had a stomachache this morning, so he could have _______________ food.

PRACTICE 9

〈보기〉에서 알맞은 단어를 골라 only a few 또는 only a little과 함께 써서 문장을 완성하세요.

보 기	information applicant friend practice hour pepper

1 Sometimes I feel lonely because I have _______________.

2 We'll have to look it up on the Internet if we have _______________.

3 I needed _______________ to use it.

4 Everyone will get to know the truth in _______________.

5 _______________ could get an interview for the position.

6 If you put _______________ in it, it will taste much better.

PSS 5-3 some, any

some

1. **일반적으로 긍정문에 쓰인다.**

   ① some+셀 수 있는 명사의 복수형: '몇몇의, 약간의'
   Some farmers were working on the field.
   몇 명의 농부들이 들판에서 일하고 있었다.

   ② some+셀 수 없는 명사: '몇몇의, 약간의'
   My teacher gave me **some advice**. 나의 선생님은 내게 약간의 조언을 해 주셨다.

   ③ some+셀 수 있는 명사의 단수형/셀 수 없는 명사: '어떤, 무슨'
   I heard **some woman** shouting near the beach.
   나는 해변 근처에서 어떤 여자가 소리치고 있는 것을 들었다.
   I ate **some food** but I don't know its name.
   나는 어떤 음식을 먹었지만 그것의 이름을 모른다.

   ④ some of+셀 수 있는 명사의 복수형+복수 동사
   some of+셀 수 없는 명사+단수 동사: '~중의 몇몇'
   Some of the students have to prepare for the festival.
   학생들 중 몇몇은 축제를 준비해야 한다.
   Some of his information is not right. 그의 정보 중 몇몇은 옳지 않다.

2. **권유나 요구를 나타내는 의문문에 쓰인다.**

   Why don't you eat **some** cookies? 쿠키 좀 먹는 게 어때?
   Can I have **some** more juice? 주스 좀 더 마셔도 될까요?

3. **긍정의 대답을 예상하는 의문문에 쓰인다.**

   Aren't there **some** people waiting for me? 나를 기다리는 몇 명의 사람들이 있지 않나요?

4. **some이 불특정한 일부를 나타낼 때는 부정문에 쓸 수 있다.**

   Some students didn't follow the rule. 몇 명의 학생들은 규칙을 따르지 않았다.

any

1. **일반적으로 부정문과 의문문에 쓰인다. 부정문에서는 '조금도', 의문문에서는 '얼마간의, 몇몇의'의 뜻으로 쓰인다.**

   ① any+셀 수 있는 명사의 복수형
   I didn't find **any errors**. 나는 아무런 잘못도 발견하지 못했다.

   ② any+셀 수 없는 명사
   Do we have to buy **any bread**? 우리가 빵을 좀 사야 하나요?

2. **'어떠한 ~라도'의 뜻으로 긍정문에 쓰인다.**

   You can choose **any color** that you want. 네가 원하는 어떤 색이라도 고를 수 있다.

3. **조건을 나타내는 if절에 쓰인다.**

   If you have **any** trouble, ask Mr. Kim for help.
   문제가 있으면 김 선생님에게 도움을 요청해.

PRACTICE 10

다음 문장의 빈칸에 some이나 any 중 알맞은 것을 쓰세요.

1 He has never received _________________ salary from his boss.

2 Don't worry about it. _________________ child can deal with it.

3 My father donated _________________ money to our school's scholarship fund to help deserving students.

4 Would you have _________________ more chocolate?

5 There won't be _________________ traffic jam during the holiday.

6 Will you give me _________________ cereal for breakfast?

7 If you have _________________ butter left, I'd like you to give it to me.

8 _________________ kids weren't listening to their teacher.

9 Do you have _________________ bags to be checked?

10 Were there _________________ phone calls for me? Nancy was supposed to call me.

PRACTICE 11

〈보기〉의 단어를 some이나 any와 함께 한 번씩만 써서 문장을 완성하세요.

보 기	rice water situation interest help souvenir pride money people medicine

1 Don't you have _________________ in yourself?

2 He mixed the leftover vegetables with _________________ to create a quick and delicious fried rice.

3 In _________________, don't lose courage.

4 If you don't need _________________, I'll just leave.

5 I can't believe that she didn't buy _________________ for us in Canada.

6 Can I have _________________? I'm very thirsty.

7 _________________ couldn't believe that David was elected as president.

8 If you have _________________ in baking, ask Minji for details.

9 Mina must save _________________, so she can buy a new bicycle.

10 The dentist gave me _________________. It made me feel better.

PSS 6 수사

PSS 6 - 1 기수와 서수

수	기수	서수	수	기수	서수
1	one	first (1st)	15	fifteen	fifteenth (15th)
2	two	second (2nd)	16	sixteen	sixteenth (16th)
3	three	third (3rd)	17	seventeen	seventeenth (17th)
4	four	fourth (4th)	18	eighteen	eighteenth (18th)
5	five	fifth (5th)	19	nineteen	nineteenth (19th)
6	six	sixth (6th)	20	twenty	twentieth (20th)
7	seven	seventh (7th)	21	twenty-one	twenty-first (21st)
8	eight	eighth (8th)	22	twenty-two	twenty-second (22nd)
9	nine	ninth (9th)	30	thirty	thirtieth (30th)
10	ten	tenth (10th)	40	forty	fortieth (40th)
11	eleven	eleventh (11th)	70	seventy	seventieth (70th)
12	twelve	twelfth (12th)	90	ninety	ninetieth (90th)
13	thirteen	thirteenth (13th)	100	a[one] hundred	a[one] hundredth (100th)
14	fourteen	fourteenth (14th)	1000	a[one] thousand	a[one] thousandth (1000th)

정답 p.49

PRACTICE 12 [1-20]

다음 숫자의 기수와 서수 형태를 쓰세요.

1 1 ➡ _____one – first_____

2 2 ➡ __________

3 3 ➡ __________

4 5 ➡ __________

5 9 ➡ __________

6 12 ➡ __________

7 15 ➡ __________

8 20 ➡ __________

9 22 ➡ __________

10 26 ➡ __________

11 30 ➡ __________

12 31 ➡ __________

13 40 ➡ __________

14 57 ➡ __________

15 69 ➡ _______________

16 73 ➡ _______________

17 84 ➡ _______________

18 99 ➡ _______________

19 100 ➡ _______________

20 1000 ➡ _______________

PSS 6-2 정수

정수는 세 자리씩 끊어서 읽고, 백 자리 수 뒤에는 and를 써서 연결하지만 구어체에서는 생략하기도 한다. hundred와 thousand, million 앞에 복수를 나타내는 수사가 오더라도 hundred, thousand, million은 복수형으로 쓰지 않는 것에 주의한다.

139 ➡ a[one] hundred (and) thirty-nine

427 ➡ four hundred (and) twenty-seven

1,904 ➡ a[one] thousand, nine hundred (and) four

5,186 ➡ five thousand, a[one] hundred (and) eighty-six

83,015 ➡ eighty-three thousand, (and) fifteen

269,488 ➡ two hundred (and) sixty-nine thousand, four hundred (and) eighty-eight

6,117,093 ➡ six million, a[one] hundred (and) seventeen thousand, (and) ninety-three

정답 p.49

PRACTICE 13

다음 숫자를 영어로 읽을 때의 표기법을 쓰세요.

1 195 ➡ _______________

2 374 ➡ _______________

3 501 ➡ _______________

4 918 ➡ _______________

5 2,116 ➡ _______________

6 4,087 ➡ _______________

7 5,302 ➡ _______________

8 9,703 ➡ _______________

9 11,090 ➡ _______________

10 34,815 ➡ _______________

11 70,302 ➡ _______________

12 86,240 ➡ _______________

13 102,369 ➡ _______________

14 280,166 ➡ _______________________________

15 602,801 ➡ _______________________________

16 911,300 ➡ _______________________________

17 3,744,000 ➡ _______________________________

18 5,018,799 ➡ _______________________________

19 16,950,541 ➡ _______________________________

20 28,227,846 ➡ _______________________________

PSS 6-3 분수와 소수

1. 분수 – 분자는 기수로, 분모는 서수로 읽고, 분자가 2 이상이면 분모에 '-s'를 붙여 읽는다.

    1/3 ➡ a third 또는 one-third   2/7 ➡ two-sevenths

    4 5/6 ➡ four and five-sixths   8 3/4 ➡ eight and three-fourths[three-quarters]

    cf. 1/2 ➡ a half 또는 one-half   1/4 ➡ a quarter 또는 one-quarter

2. 소수 – 모두 기수로 읽되, 소수점 이하는 한 자리씩 읽는다. 소수점은 point라고 한다.

    0.39 ➡ zero point three nine   1.07 ➡ one point zero seven

    5.16 ➡ five point one six   23.85 ➡ twenty-three point eight five

정답 p.50

PRACTICE 14

다음 분수와 소수를 영어로 읽을 때의 표기법을 쓰세요.

1 4/7 ➡ _________________________   **2** 7/10 ➡ _________________________

3 5 2/5 ➡ _________________________   **4** 2/3 ➡ _________________________

5 3/4 ➡ _________________________   **6** 16 1/2 ➡ _________________________

7 25 8/9 ➡ _________________________   **8** 6 1/4 ➡ _________________________

9 1/7 ➡ _________________________   **10** 9 3/8 ➡ _________________________

11 2.76 ➡ _________________________   **12** 31.04 ➡ _________________________

13 0.12 ➡ _________________________   **14** 3.5 ➡ _________________________

15 52.93 ➡ _________________________   **16** 10.01 ➡ _________________________

17 0.89 ➡ _________________________   **18** 1.39 ➡ _________________________

19 14.251 ➡ _________________________   **20** 275.19 ➡ _________________________

PSS 6-4 연도와 날짜

1. **연도 – 두 자리씩 끊어 읽는다.**

    1993년 ➡ nineteen ninety-three   1700년 ➡ seventeen hundred

    cf. 2003년 ➡ two thousand (and) three   2023년 ➡ two thousand (and) twenty-three

2. **날짜 – 서수를 이용한다.**

    3월 28일 ➡ March (the) twenty-eighth 또는 the twenty-eighth of March

    8월 15일 ➡ August (the) fifteenth 또는 the fifteenth of August

    2021년 4월 7일 ➡ April (the) seventh, two thousand (and) twenty-one 또는

       the seventh of April, two thousand (and) twenty-one

정답 p.50

PRACTICE 15

다음 연도와 날짜를 영어로 읽을 때의 표기법을 쓰세요.

1 2006년   ➡ ____

2 1990년   ➡ ____

3 1884년   ➡ ____

4 6월 5일   ➡ ____

5 11월 19일 ➡ ____

6 2월 24일   ➡ ____

7 2020년 12월 1일 ➡ ____

       ➡ ____

8 2024년 9월 15일 ➡ ____

       ➡ ____

9 1582년 1월 20일 ➡ ____

       ➡ ____

10 1735년 4월 9일 ➡ ____

       ➡ ____

PSS 6-5 배수사

배수사는 quarter(1/4), half(반), once(1배, 한 번), twice(2배, 두 번), 그 이후부터는 「기수+times (three times, four times, five times …)」(~배, ~번)로 나타낸다.

My family has taken a trip with Cathy's family **twice**.
나의 가족은 Cathy의 가족과 두 번 여행을 갔다.
My room is **three times** as large as my brother's room. 내 방은 내 남동생의 방보다 3배 크다.
= My room is **three times** larger than my brother's room.
Could you cut this hamburger in **half**? 이 햄버거를 반으로 잘라 주시겠어요?
Hana ate **a quarter** of the pizza. 하나는 피자의 1/4을 먹었다.

정답 p.50

PRACTICE 16

우리말과 같은 뜻이 되도록 빈칸에 알맞은 말을 쓰세요.

1 나는 선생님 댁에 한 번 갔다 온 적이 있다.
= I have been to my teacher's house ________________.

2 이 수화물이 그 수화물보다 3배 더 무겁다.
= This baggage is ________________ heavier than that baggage.

3 나의 집은 Brown 씨 집의 반만 하다.
= My house is ________________ as large as Mr. Brown's.

4 Bob의 옷은 내 옷보다 10배 많다.
= Bob has ________________ as many clothes as I have.

5 나는 오늘 Sam과 최소 4번은 우연히 마주쳤다.
= I came across Sam at least ________________ today.

6 엄마는 형을 보기 위해 한 달에 두 번 부산에 가신다.
= Mom goes to Busan ________________ a month to see my brother.

7 Taylor는 피자의 4분의 3을 먹었다.
= Taylor ate three ________________ of the pizza.

8 우리 아버지는 일주일에 5번 수영하러 가신다.
= My dad goes swimming ________________ a week.

9 나는 그 방을 절반으로 나눴다.
= I have divided the room in ________________.

10 저 차는 다른 차들보다 세 배 빠르다.
= That car is ________________ faster than the others.

PSS 6-6 시각

1. **시간과 분을 끊어서 읽는다.**

    6:30 ➡ six thirty   8:25 ➡ eight twenty-five

    11:08 ➡ eleven-o-eight   12:40 ➡ twelve forty

    3:55 ➡ three fifty-five   1:15 ➡ one fifteen

2. **'~을 지나서'를 뜻하는 after[past]와 '~전에'를 뜻하는 to를 사용하여 읽기도 한다. after[past]와 to는 주로 a quarter(15분)나 half(30분) 또는 분을 나타내는 수가 5의 배수인 경우에 쓰인다. 30분을 기준으로 하여 30분 이전을 나타내는 분에는 after[past]를, 30분은 past를, 30분 이후를 나타내는 분에는 to를 이용한다.**

    7:10 ➡ ten after[past] seven   4:30 ➡ half past four

    12:15 ➡ a quarter after[past] twelve   2:45 ➡ a quarter to three

    5:20 ➡ twenty after[past] five   9:55 ➡ five to ten

정답 p.51

PRACTICE 17

다음 시각을 영어로 읽을 때의 표기법을 쓰세요.

1   1:20 ➡ __________________________

2   5:16 ➡ __________________________

3   4:05 ➡ __________________________

4   7:56 ➡ __________________________

5   8:45 ➡ __________________________

6   2:15 ➡ __________________________

7   12:50 ➡ __________________________

8   6:13 ➡ __________________________

9   11:35 ➡ __________________________

10 9:17 ➡ __________________________

11 4:09 ➡ __________________________

12 3:30 ➡ __________________________

13 8:23 ➡ __________________________

14 9:48 ➡ __________________________

15 10:40 ➡ __________________________

중간·기말고사 대비문제 

1 다음 문장의 빈칸에 들어갈 수 <u>없는</u> 단어는?

> On my way home, I saw a __________ girl in red.

① cute ② blind ③ unique
④ glad ⑤ strange

2 빈칸에 들어갈 말로 알맞은 것은?

> Bats and owls are __________ at night.

① act ② action ③ active
④ activity ⑤ actively

3 〈보기〉의 표현 중 올바른 것을 <u>모두</u> 고른 것은?

> 보 기
>
> ⓐ Drinking something hot can be helpful to soothe a sore throat.
> ⓑ There is harmful nothing in our perfume.
> ⓒ She had little time to spare as she rushed to catch her flight at the airport.
> ⓓ Every people were offered lunch after the meeting.
> ⓔ I need to buy any new clothes to stay fashionable.
> ⓕ He doesn't have any experience in this field, but he's willing to learn.

① ⓐ, ⓒ ② ⓑ, ⓓ ③ ⓐ, ⓒ, ⓕ
④ ⓑ, ⓒ, ⓕ ⑤ ⓒ, ⓓ, ⓔ, ⓕ

4 빈칸에 들어갈 형용사로 알맞은 것은?

> We have heard that a lot of innocent people have died in the military operation. Do you think that the price is __________ it?

① worthy ② valuable ③ worth
④ valued ⑤ worthwhile

5 다음 밑줄 친 부분 중 그 쓰임이 <u>어색한</u> 것은?

① She has <u>something different</u> from other girls.
② There's <u>nothing comparable</u> to his work.
③ You are blessed with <u>something precious</u>.
④ I have eaten nearly <u>everything imaginable</u>.
⑤ <u>Things bad</u> can happen to good people.

6 주어진 우리말과 같은 뜻이 되도록 괄호 안의 단어를 활용하여 문장을 완성하세요. (단, Give me를 포함하여 총 9단어가 되도록 쓸 것.)

> 내게 중요한 무언가를 검토할 몇 분을 줘.
> (something, few, review)

➡ Give me __________________
__________________________.

7 빈칸에 들어갈 말로 알맞은 것은?

I haven't noticed __________ about this picture yet.

① interesting something
② something interesting
③ interesting anything
④ anything interesting
⑤ interesting thing

8 밑줄 친 단어와 같은 의미로 쓰인 것은?

A: We nearly missed the last train. We got to the platform just as the doors were closing.
B: That was close! It's a good thing we hurried, or we'd still be at the station.

① He kept a close watch on the children.
② My brother and I have always been close.
③ The library will close for renovations next month.
④ Don't forget to close your eyes during the surprise.
⑤ The election was close, with only 200 votes apart.

9 다음 중 빈칸에 공통으로 알맞은 것은?

• Would you like to have __________ snacks before the movie starts?
• My American friends like __________ of Korean food.

① any   ② some   ③ little
④ much   ⑤ few

10 다음 밑줄 친 부분의 용법이 나머지 넷과 다른 것은?

① Parking spaces for the disabled are also available.
② The young tend to be more idealistic than the old.
③ The kind police officer helped me find the station.
④ More jobs need to be made for the jobless.
⑤ The clever are not greedy and the greedy are not clever.

11 다음 대화의 빈칸에 들어갈 말이 바르게 짝지어 진 것은?

A: If you don't get __________ sleep, you can hardly stay awake during the day.
B: Don't worry. I'm strong __________ to do without __________ sleep at all for a couple of days.
A: I understand your confidence, but even strong people need enough sleep for optimal health and performance. Take care of yourself and get __________ rest.

① some   –   much   –   any   –   any
② enough – enough – some – some
③ any   –   enough – some – any
④ enough – enough – any   – some
⑤ any   –   much   – some – any

12 다음 우리말 뜻에 맞게 주어진 단어를 활용하여 영작하세요. (단어 변형 가능, 6단어로 쓸 것.)

• 우리는 쓸모 없는 무언가를 유용한 무엇으로 바꾸고 있다. (turn, something, use)
➡ We're ______________________
________________________________ .

13 괄호 안에 주어진 단어가 순서대로 바르게 배열된 것은?

> The last time I saw her, she looked so sick and (blue, her, famous) scarf was torn.

① blue her famous
② blue famous her
③ her blue famous
④ her famous blue
⑤ famous blue her

14 다음 대화의 빈칸에 들어갈 말이 차례대로 짝지어진 것은?

> *Jack*: How ___________ money do you have?
>
> *Jane*: I have fifty dollars.
>
> *Jack*: Is it ___________ money to buy a nice pair of running shoes?
>
> *Jane*: No, it is not ___________.

① many – some – any
② many – any – enough
③ much – some – any
④ much – any – enough
⑤ much – enough – enough

15 다음 밑줄 친 부분 중 그 쓰임이 잘못된 것은?

① I did well for my first two years of high school.
② Raise right your hand and sing along with me.
③ Another two pages have been added.
④ Where did you buy all those lovely clothes?
⑤ The restaurant is famous for its delicious Chinese food.

16 다음 문장의 빈칸 중 어떤 위치에도 들어갈 수 없는 단어는?

> ⓐ He made some important announcements during the ___________.
>
> ⓑ He tried to chew gum to avoid falling ___________ during the long car drive.
>
> ⓒ She was ___________ engaged in the class meeting as a class president.
>
> ⓓ The dog is often described as ___________, dependable, and adorable.
>
> ⓔ There is a high ___________ for AI technology in the field.

① loyal
② sleep
③ demand
④ break
⑤ actively

17 밑줄 친 (a)~(e) 중 어법상 틀린 것을 모두 고르세요.

> Last weekend, our volunteer group was invited (a) to clean up the riverbank. We collected litter and (b) planting new trees along the walking path. Everyone enjoyed themselves and took (c) a lot of photos of the beautiful scenery. To protect the environment for future generations (d) is our main mission. Unfortunately, several bags of litter were left behind by mistake. We felt (e) disappointing but promised to do better next time.

① (a)　② (b)　③ (c)　④ (d)　⑤ (e)

18 다음 글의 빈칸에 들어갈 알맞은 단어를 〈보기〉에서 찾아 쓰세요.

> 보 기 ｜ few little many much

> The city is very old and does not have _________ modern buildings. Its citizens do not make _________ money. And they have _________ contact with the other part of the country due to high mountains surrounding the city. The roads aren't very good. There are _________ cars on the roads.

19 빈칸에 들어갈 말로 알맞은 것은?

> There were _________ women who had professional jobs in the past, since they had to do a lot of housework all by themselves.

① much   ② little   ③ few
④ many   ⑤ a lot of

20 다음 밑줄 친 부분 중, 문맥상 쓰임이 자연스러운 것은?

> Today, Michael and I went to the theater together. It was ① <u>crowd</u> with people. The movie was boring and I felt ② <u>sleep</u>. When the movie ended, we got ③ <u>hungry</u>. So, we went to a fast-food restaurant. We ate burgers and French fries for dinner. I added fried onions to my burger and more ④ <u>salty</u> on my fries. The food was really ⑤ <u>taste</u>.

21 빈칸에 들어갈 말이 차례대로 짝지어진 것은?

> Because I had _________ particular to do, I walked the street looking for _________ funny.

① much   – nothing
② something – anything
③ nothing   – something
④ nothing   – anything
⑤ something – much

22 다음 문장을 아래와 같이 바꿀 때 빈칸에 알맞은 말을 쓰세요.

> We are expected to help the sick, the disabled, and the disadvantaged.

➡ We are expected to help _________ people, _________ people, and _________ people.
➡ We are expected to help those who are _________, those who are _________, and those who are _________.

23 빈칸에 들어갈 말이 차례대로 짝지어진 것은?

> I'd like to have _________ more coffee, if there is _________.

① some – little   ② any   – some
③ little   – some   ④ some – any
⑤ any   – little

24 (A), (B), (C)에 들어갈 말로 적절한 것은?

Carl recently got his first job. He is satisfied with his job, but there's one problem. His company is located in downtown Seoul, so it takes about 2 hours to get there from his home. He spends a lot of time (A)[to drive / driving] his car on weekdays. It is (B)[stress / stressful] to be stuck in a traffic jam. Sometimes, it makes him feel (C)[tired / tiring] and affects his work. He's thinking about moving closer to his company.

	(A)	(B)	(C)
①	driving	– stressful	– tired
②	to drive	– stress	– tiring
③	driving	– stress	– tired
④	to drive	– stress	– tired
⑤	driving	– stressful	– tiring

25 다음 중 영어로 읽을 때의 표기법이 **틀린** 것은?

① 2007년 7월 1일 : July first, two thousand seven

② 수십만 : hundreds of thousands

③ 8 1/2 : eight and a half

④ 2시 45분 : a quarter to three

⑤ 34.14 : three four point one four

26 다음 문장의 밑줄 친 the brave가 의미하는 바를 영어로 쓰세요. (2단어)

Even the brave are scared by a lion three times: first by its tracks, again by its roar, and one last time face to face.

➡ ___________________________

27 〈보기〉의 밑줄 친 mean과 뜻이 같은 문장끼리 짝지어진 것은?

보 기	Don't be so mean to your little sister!

ⓐ I didn't mean to do any harm.
ⓑ Why are you being so mean to me?
ⓒ The mean annual rainfall was 1400mm.
ⓓ Her children mean the world to her.
ⓔ Those clouds mean that it's going to rain.
ⓕ She played a mean stepmother in the movie.

① ⓐ, ⓕ ② ⓑ, ⓔ ③ ⓑ, ⓕ
④ ⓒ, ⓔ ⑤ ⓓ, ⓔ

28 ⓐ, ⓑ 안에 들어갈 말로 알맞은 것은?

A: Don't make such a noise around here. We have a ___ⓐ___ baby inside.
B: Sorry. I didn't know that. When did he fall ___ⓑ___ ?

	ⓐ	ⓑ
①	sleeping	– sleeping
②	sleeping	– asleep
③	asleep	– sleeping
④	asleep	– asleep
⑤	sleeping	– slept

29 다음 중 어법상 어색한 것을 고르세요.

① All the children looked happy.
② Who gave you these two red roses?
③ Both her parents are proud of her.
④ Let me introduce my French two friends.
⑤ I don't need this big old black shirt.

[30 – 31] 다음 글을 읽고, 물음에 답하세요.

One of the best ways to spend summer vacation is to visit places ⓐ where you've never been to. As many of us ⓑ are known, Busan and Jeju Island are popular options for a nice vacation. Or if you want ⓒ quiet somewhere, Geoje Island is another good choice. You don't have to visit ⓓ other country to enjoy your vacation. Ⓐ 휴식을 취하고 재미있게 놀 수 있는 장소라면 어디든 될 것이다. Many people think traveling abroad is the only way to enjoy the best vacation. However, there ⓔ is a lot of beautiful places to visit in Korea!

30 윗글의 ⓐ~ⓔ를 어법상 잘못 고친 것은?

① ⓐ where → that
② ⓑ are known → know
③ ⓒ quiet somewhere → quiet anywhere
④ ⓓ other country → other countries
⑤ ⓔ is → are

31 밑줄 친 Ⓐ와 같은 뜻이 되도록 문장을 완성하세요.

➡ ___________ place where you can
___________ and have fun will ___________.

32 빈칸 ⓐ~ⓕ에 주어진 숫자 표현을 영어로 바르게 써넣어 Jenny의 일기를 완성하세요.

Jenny's diary

March, ⓐ ___________ (12일)
I arranged the books in the library with my friends this afternoon. This was my
ⓑ ___________ (5번째) volunteering in the library. My friends and I classified and arranged about 150 books, which were
ⓒ ___________ (3배) more than we did last time. We finished all the work at
ⓓ ___________ to ⓔ ___________ (3시 55분) and we went to eat pizza. I ate
ⓕ ___________ (1/4) of large size pizza with mushrooms. It was really delicious.

33 ⓐ~ⓔ 중 어법상 올바른 것끼리 모두 묶인 것은?

ⓐ A lot of olive oil are produced in Greece.
ⓑ Two-thirds of my furniture is made of wood.
ⓒ The rich are not always happier than the poor.
ⓓ She has blue eyes alike mine.
ⓔ Economics are often called the study of choice.

① ⓐ, ⓔ   ② ⓑ, ⓒ   ③ ⓒ, ⓔ
④ ⓐ, ⓒ, ⓓ   ⑤ ⓑ, ⓓ, ⓔ

CHAPTER 11
부사

PSS 1 부사의 형태	페이지	성취도				
		100%	99~75%	74~50%	49~25%	24~0%
PSS 1-1 형용사를 부사로 만드는 법 Ⅰ	230					
PSS 1-2 형용사를 부사로 만드는 법 Ⅱ	231					
PSS 1-3 형용사와 형태가 같은 부사	232					
PSS 1-4 형용사 형태의 부사에 '-ly'를 붙이면 다른 뜻이 되는 부사	235					
PSS 2 여러 가지 부사의 용법	페이지	성취도				
		100%	99~75%	74~50%	49~25%	24~0%
PSS 2-1 빈도부사	237					
PSS 2-2 already, yet, still	239					
PSS 2-3 too, either, neither	241					
PSS 2-4 very, much	242					
PSS 2-5 else, even	243					
PSS 2-6 ago, before	245					
PSS 2-7 「타동사+부사」의 어순	246					
중간·기말고사 대비문제	248					

PSS 1 부사의 형태

PSS 1-1 형용사를 부사로 만드는 법 I

일반적인 경우	형용사+ly	actual – actual**ly** 실제의 실제로 certain – certain**ly** 확실한 확실히 effective – effective**ly** 효과적인 효과적으로 moral – moral**ly** 도덕적인 도덕적으로 similar – similar**ly** 비슷한 비슷하게	attentive – attentive**ly** 주의 깊은 주의 깊게 constant – constant**ly** 끊임없는 끊임없이 immediate – immediate**ly** 즉시의 즉시, 당장 private – private**ly** 사적인 사적으로 sudden – sudden**ly** 갑작스러운 갑자기
자음+y로 끝나는 경우	자음+i+ly	angry – angr**ily** 화난 노하여 happy – happ**ily** 행복한 행복하게 busy – bus**ily** 바쁜 바쁘게	easy – eas**ily** 쉬운 쉽게 lucky – luck**ily** 운 좋은 운 좋게도 heavy – heav**ily** 무거운 무겁게

정답 p.53

PRACTICE 1

다음 형용사의 부사형을 쓰세요.

1 free ➡ _______________

2 fair ➡ _______________

3 creative ➡ _______________

4 firm ➡ _______________

5 angry ➡ _______________

6 wise ➡ _______________

7 effective ➡ _______________

8 soft ➡ _______________

9 quick ➡ _______________

10 willing ➡ _______________

11 fortunate ➡ _______________

12 heavy ➡ _______________

13 certain ➡ _______________

14 private ➡ _______________

15 lucky ➡ _______________

16 essential ➡ _______________

17 similar ➡ _______________

18 easy ➡ _______________

19 serious ➡ _______________

20 main ➡ _______________

21	actual	➡ __________	22	complete	➡ __________
23	final	➡ __________	24	global	➡ __________
25	natural	➡ __________	26	safe	➡ __________
27	necessary	➡ __________	28	colorful	➡ __________
29	formal	➡ __________	30	hopeful	➡ __________
31	equal	➡ __________	32	frequent	➡ __________
33	special	➡ __________	34	attentive	➡ __________
35	careless	➡ __________	36	contrary	➡ __________
37	negative	➡ __________	38	original	➡ __________
39	direct	➡ __________	40	international	➡ __________

PSS 1-2 형용사를 부사로 만드는 법 Ⅱ

-le로 끝나는 경우	-le ➡ -ly	probable – probab**ly** 있을 법한　아마도 possible – possib**ly** 가능한　혹시 reasonable – reasonab**ly** 합리적인　　합리적으로	gentle – gent**ly** 온화한　온화하게 simple – simp**ly** 간단한　간단히 comfortable – comfortab**ly** 편안한　　　편안하게
-ue로 끝나는 경우	-ue ➡ -uly	true – tr**uly** 진실인 진실로	*cf.* unique – uniqu**ely** 독특한　　독특하게
-ll로 끝나는 경우	-ll ➡ -lly	full – fu**lly** 충분한 충분히	dull – du**lly** 우둔한 우둔하게

정답 p.53

PRACTICE 2 [1-50]

다음 형용사의 부사형을 쓰세요.

1	terrible	➡ __________	2	personal	➡ __________
3	definite	➡ __________	4	full	➡ __________
5	happy	➡ __________	6	unique	➡ __________
7	successful	➡ __________	8	gentle	➡ __________

9	sure	➡	__________		10	real	➡	__________

9 sure	➡	____________________	10 real	➡	____________________
11 current	➡	____________________	12 probable	➡	____________________
13 sudden	➡	____________________	14 bright	➡	____________________
15 reasonable	➡	____________________	16 active	➡	____________________
17 simple	➡	____________________	18 busy	➡	____________________
19 sharp	➡	____________________	20 different	➡	____________________
21 dull	➡	____________________	22 polite	➡	____________________
23 tight	➡	____________________	24 genuine	➡	____________________
25 proud	➡	____________________	26 rare	➡	____________________
27 true	➡	____________________	28 moral	➡	____________________
29 normal	➡	____________________	30 possible	➡	____________________
31 foolish	➡	____________________	32 anxious	➡	____________________
33 general	➡	____________________	34 mental	➡	____________________
35 casual	➡	____________________	36 official	➡	____________________
37 cheerful	➡	____________________	38 nice	➡	____________________
39 perfect	➡	____________________	40 whole	➡	____________________
41 incredible	➡	____________________	42 practical	➡	____________________
43 proper	➡	____________________	44 responsible	➡	____________________
45 sensitive	➡	____________________	46 pleasant	➡	____________________
47 exact	➡	____________________	48 severe	➡	____________________
49 emotional	➡	____________________	50 sensible	➡	____________________

PSS 1-3 형용사와 형태가 같은 부사

fast	빠른	David was so **fast** that nobody could catch him. David는 아주 빨라서 아무도 그를 잡을 수 없었다.
	빨리	The train was moving very **fast**. 기차는 매우 빠르게 움직이고 있었다.

late	늦은	The shuttle bus was **late** again this morning. 셔틀버스는 오늘 아침에 또 늦었다.
	늦게	I went to bed **late** last night. 나는 어젯밤 늦게 잠자리에 들었다.
hard	열심인, 단단한	Mr. White is such a **hard** worker. White 씨는 정말 열심히 일하는 사람이다.
	열심히, 단단하게	She tried **hard** to achieve her goal. 그녀는 목표를 달성하기 위해 열심히 노력했다.
most	가장 많은, 가장 ~한	Mrs. Brown got the **most** kids. Brown 부인이 가장 많은 아이들을 가졌다.
	가장 많이, 제일	What part of the play did you like **most**? 너는 연극의 어떤 부분이 가장 좋았니?
last	마지막인, 마지막의	Kevin and I missed the **last** subway. Kevin과 나는 마지막 지하철을 놓쳤다.
	마지막으로	Yuri is the girl who talked to Mihye **last**. 유리는 미혜와 마지막으로 이야기를 한 소녀이다.
long	오래된, 긴	I talked to him on the phone for a **long** time. 나는 오랫동안 그와 전화로 이야기했다.
	오래, 길게	She's been staying there too **long**. 그녀는 거기에 너무 오래 머물러왔다.
early	이른	The **early** bird catches the worm. 일찍 일어나는 새가 벌레를 잡는다.
	일찍	I left work **early** to pick him up at the airport. 나는 공항으로 그를 데리러 가기 위해 회사를 일찍 나왔다.
near	가까운, 근처의	In the **near** future, I hope to be able to see him again. 가까운 미래에 나는 그를 다시 볼 수 있기를 희망한다.
	가까이	The long holiday is coming **near**. 긴 연휴가 가까이 오고 있다.
high	높은	The city is full of **high** buildings. 도시는 높은 건물들로 가득하다.
	높이	He was holding the ball **high** so that I couldn't grab it. 그는 내가 공을 잡지 못하도록 공을 높이 들고 있었다.
right	옳은	What he says seems always **right**. 그가 말하는 것은 항상 옳은 것 같다.
	바르게, 바로, 곧	If I remember **right**, he's the one I saw that night. 내가 바르게 기억한다면, 그는 내가 그날 밤 보았던 사람이다.

PRACTICE 3

밑줄 친 부분의 역할이 〈보기〉의 (A)와 같으면 A, (B)와 같으면 B라고 쓰세요.

보 기   (A) My mom is not <u>well</u>, so she's in bed.

              (B) Tony is doing <u>well</u> at school like his brother.

1   The <u>last</u> performance tickets were already sold out. [   ]

2   I'm sick of his being <u>late</u> for work. [   ]

3   The boy wanted to fly <u>high</u> in the sky like a bird. [   ]

4   Surprisingly, Hana got the <u>most</u> votes. [   ]

5   I work <u>hard</u> to make my dream come true. [   ]

6   I could see the hospital in the <u>near</u> distance. [   ]

7   I had to walk <u>fast</u> to be there on time. [   ]

8   I guess this rain will last <u>long</u>. [   ]

9   In the <u>early</u> morning, I got a call from my friend in Canada. [   ]

10   I had the machine repaired since it didn't work <u>right</u>. [   ]

PRACTICE 4

괄호 안에 주어진 단어를 활용하여 빈칸을 채우세요.

1   He drove the taxi so ________________ that I felt dizzy when I got off. (fast)

2   Listen ________________ to what the speaker says. (careful)

3   Raise your arms ________________ and take a deep breath. (high)

4   I was angry that the delivery arrived ________________. (late)

5   The constant exercises will ________________ improve their skills. (sure)

6   If you blow ________________, you can put out all the candles. (hard)

7   Bill's grandfather lived very ________________. (long)

8   The meeting will start at 9 a.m. ________________, so please be on time. (exact)

9   Where did you see him ________________? (last)

10   She was ________________ absorbed in the book and lost track of time. (complete)

close	가까이에	She came to me and sat **close**. 그녀는 내게 와서 가까이에 앉았다.
closely	주의 깊게, 면밀히	The police read the letters on the wall **closely**. 경찰은 벽에 있는 글자들을 주의 깊게 읽었다.
hard	열심히	I need to exercise **hard** to lose weight. 나는 몸무게를 줄이기 위해 운동을 열심히 할 필요가 있다.
hardly	거의 ~ 않는	When I heard the news, I could **hardly** believe it. 나는 그 소식을 들었을 때, 거의 그것을 믿을 수가 없었다.
high	높이	Raise your glasses **high**. 잔을 높이 드세요.
highly	크게, 매우 (= very)	Education is **highly** important in Korea. 교육은 한국에서 매우 중요하다.
late	늦게	Everyone at the party left **late** at night. 파티에 있던 모든 사람들은 밤늦게 떠났다.
lately	최근에	I haven't had enough sleep **lately**. 나는 최근에 충분한 잠을 자지 못했다.
near	가까이	I was scared when the group of boys came **near**. 나는 그 소년들 일당이 가까이 왔을 때 무서웠다.
nearly	거의	Our team has a match **nearly** every weekend. 우리 팀은 거의 주말마다 시합이 있다.
most	가장 많이	Among ten people, I pulled out the weeds **most**. 10명의 사람들 중에 내가 잡초를 가장 많이 뽑았다.
mostly	대체로	Chopsticks are **mostly** used in Asia. 젓가락은 대체로 아시아에서 쓰인다.

정답 p.54

PRACTICE 5 [1-15]

괄호 안에 들어갈 알맞은 단어를 골라 동그라미 하세요.

1 My team members had to work until (late, lately) last night.

2 The dog came (close, closely) to the box and looked for something to eat.

3 Jieun stayed (most, mostly) at the cheap hotels during her trip.

4 I could (hard, hardly) believe what he was saying.

5 The report said that (near, nearly) 50% of the students felt unhappy.

6 The police officer who is controlling traffic over there looks (friend, friendly).

7 Look at these questions (close, closely).

8 Let's discuss some (high, highly) interesting facts about dinosaurs.

9 The temperature has gone so (high, highly) because of global warming.

10 I've practiced the flute very (hard, hardly) for three years.

11 A lot of foreigners are moving to this city (late, lately).

12 The story that Minji told me sounded (strange, strangely).

13 I heard the news that the typhoon is coming (near, nearly).

14 I can't tell him (direct, directly) how much I like him.

15 The person who gets the (most, mostly) right answers is going to win.

정답 p.55

PRACTICE 6

〈보기〉와 같이 주어진 단어를 이용하여 빈칸을 채우세요.

> 보 기
>
> serious
> ① I'm responsible for making the _serious_ mistake.
> ② Don't take the matter so _seriously_.

1 hard
① I've never seen him working so _______________.
② I could _______________ breathe at the top of the mountain.

2 regular
① The doctor said that I should eat on a _______________ basis.
② I'm going to exercise _______________ for my health.

3 logical
① You should think _______________ when you make a decision.
② His idea sounds very _______________.

4 fast
① I was impressed by their _______________ service.
② We'd better walk _______________ in order to get there on time.

5 late
① Have you heard from Chris _______________?
② I heard the thunderstorm when I was reading _______________ at night.

6 effective

① We can communicate with each other ________________ with this method.

② I have a few suggestions for ________________ study.

7 high

① He held his head ________________ with confidence.

② My 2-year-old baby is very sick with a ________________ fever.

8 close

① Read the article ________________ and find the topic.

② I became so ________________ to his family after I rescued his son from deep water.

PSS 2 여러 가지 부사의 용법

PSS 2-1 빈도부사

빈도부사는 일반동사 앞, be동사나 조동사 뒤에 위치한다.

cf. sometimes, often, usually는 문장의 맨 앞이나 맨 뒤에 올 수도 있다.

Sometimes listening to his lectures was boring. 때때로 그의 강의를 듣는 것은 지루했다.

= Listening to his lectures was boring **sometimes**.

PRACTICE 7

다음 괄호 안에 주어진 말을 바르게 배열하여 문장을 완성하세요. (단, 빈도부사를 문장 맨 앞, 뒤에는 오게 하지 말 것.)

1 (often, you, movie stars, in this district, will, see)
➡ ____

2 (sometimes, feel, with Mr. Jung, I, uncomfortable)
➡ ____

3 (seldom, the Korean language, easily, foreigners, learn)
➡ ____

4 (always, is, the weather, unpredictable)
➡ ____

5 (rarely, when, I, in the town, it, rained, was staying)
➡ ____

6 (never, I'll, what happened, yesterday, to you, tell, him)
➡ ____

7 (usually, my sister, more impulsive, my brother and I, is, than)
➡ ____

PRACTICE 8

다음 밑줄 친 부분을 바르게 고쳐 쓰세요.

1 The music that she listens to always is too loud. ➡ _______________________

2 My brother rides seldom his motorcycle after the accident. ➡ _______________________

3 I got often lost while I was traveling in India. ➡ _______________________

4 His team never can win the game without my help. ➡ _______________________

5 Despite living close to the beach, rarely Eric goes for a swim in the ocean. ➡ _______________________

6 I shake usually hands when I meet somebody new. ➡ _______________________

7 It sometimes is difficult to be kind to everyone. ➡ _______________________

8 Over the years, she would spend often Christmas at my house. ➡ _______________________

PSS 2-2 already, yet, still

already	이미, 벌써	already는 긍정문과 놀람을 나타내는 의문문에 쓰이고 문장의 중간이나 끝에 위치한다. I have **already** washed the dishes. 나는 이미 설거지를 했다. Has the movie finished **already**? 영화가 벌써 끝났니?
yet	이미, 벌써, 이제, 아직	yet은 주로 의문문과 부정문에 쓰인다. 의문문에서는 '이미, 벌써, 이제'의 뜻으로 해석되고, 놀람을 나타내는 의문문에서는 already를 대신하여 쓸 수 있다. 부정문에서는 '아직'의 뜻으로 해석되고 보통 문장의 끝에 위치한다. Have the Stuarts moved to Paris **yet**? Stuart 씨네 가족은 벌써 파리로 이사 갔니? He might not know about it **yet**. 그는 그것에 대해 아직 모를지도 모른다.
still	여전히, 아직도	still은 긍정문과 의문문에 쓰이며 보통 문장의 중간에 위치한다. 계속되는 행위를 강조하고자 할 때는 부정문에도 쓰인다. I **still** work part-time as a waitress. 나는 여전히 웨이트리스로 아르바이트 일을 한다. Are you **still** upset about my mistake? 넌 아직도 내 실수에 화가 나 있니? The students **still** don't know that the basketball game is cancelled. 학생들은 아직도 농구 경기가 취소되었다는 것을 알지 못한다. ***cf.*** still이 부정문에 쓰일 때는 부정어보다 앞에 온다.

정답 p.55

PRACTICE 9 [1-5]

〈보기〉와 같이 빈칸에 already, yet, still 중 알맞은 것을 쓰세요.

> 보기
> ① I _already_ decided what to study in college.
> ② I'm _still_ thinking about what to study in college.
> ③ I haven't decided what to study in college _yet_.

1 ① She _______________ doesn't want to start her holiday task.
② She hasn't even started her holiday task _______________.
③ Did she _______________ start her holiday task?

2 ① The company's shares have ________________ been listed.

② The company's shares are ________________ being listed.

③ The company's shares have not been listed ________________ .

3 ① I've ________________ received an annual flu vaccination.

② Have you received an annual flu vaccination ________________ ?

③ Do you ________________ need to receive an annual flu vaccination?

4 ① Has the art complex been completed ________________ ?

② The art complex is ________________ completed.

③ The art complex ________________ needs a few months to be completed.

5 ① My mom has ________________ made the main dish for the dinner party.

② My mom is ________________ busy making the main dish for the dinner party.

③ My mom has not made the main dish for the dinner party ________________ .

정답 p.55

PRACTICE 10

괄호 안에 들어갈 알맞은 단어를 골라 동그라미 하세요.

1 I haven't seen Mike in an hour. Did he go to bed (already, still)?

2 He (already, yet) made up his mind to be a chef after graduating from college.

3 Mandy (still, yet) feels hungry after having the sandwich.

4 The famous rock band is (yet, still) on its world tour.

5 Most of my friends don't have their own blog (already, yet).

6 Have you finished doing the laundry (still, yet)?

7 The tigers are (yet, still) wandering in the forest.

8 Your aunt hasn't got married (already, yet), has she?

9 Keep up the good work! You (already, still) have one more chance!

10 Karen (already, yet) knows how the fight got started.

11 Have you decided if you're staying in Europe for the winter (still, yet)?

12 The film was intended for those who were not there or not even born (yet, already).

13 Owen is bigger than I was at his age, but he (still, already) doesn't weigh that much.

PSS 2-3 too, either, neither

too	～ 또한	too는 긍정문에 쓰인다. If your mom allows, I'll allow, **too**. 네 엄마가 허락하시면 나도 허락하겠다. Jihye finished the homework in time. I finished the homework in time, **too**. (= Me, **too**.) 지혜는 시간 내에 숙제를 끝냈다. 나도 시간 내에 숙제를 끝냈다.
either	～ 또한 (아니다)	either는 부정문에 쓰인다. 「not ～ either」를 neither로 바꾸어 쓸 수 있다. Since she's not going to leave, I won't, **either**. 그녀가 떠나지 않을 것이므로, 나 또한 떠나지 않을 것이다. = Since she's not going to leave, **neither** will I. ***cf.*** 이때의 neither는 「Neither+조동사+주어」의 어순으로 쓴다. I don't like horror movies. – I don't like horror movies, **either**. 나는 공포영화를 좋아하지 않아. – 나 또한 공포영화를 좋아하지 않아. = I don't like horror movies. – **Neither** do I. (= Me, **neither**.)

정답 p.56

PRACTICE 11

빈칸에 too, either, neither 중 알맞은 것을 넣어 문장을 완성하세요.

1 If you don't accept my proposal, I won't accept your proposal, _______________.

2 My father has a big mole on his back, and I have one, _______________.

3 If Brian is going to the mall this Friday, I will, _______________.

4 I can't wait to see the comedy show! – _______________ can I.

5 Since you didn't do him a favor, I won't, _______________.

6 Don't talk like that! She is having a hard time, _______________.

7 I should not have spicy food. – Me, _______________.

8 Be polite to others, and they will be polite to you, _______________.

9 I've never been to a foreign country yet. – I haven't, _______________.

10 My sister often comes home late, and I do, _______________.

11 Yuna didn't make good marks at school, _______________.

12 I'll have a chicken burger and a Coke. – Me, _______________.

PSS 2-4 very, much

very	매우	형용사나 부사의 원급을 수식한다. The buildings in that city were **very modern**. 그 도시에 있던 건물들은 매우 현대적이었다. The fire could spread **very quickly**. 불은 매우 빠르게 번질 수 있었다.
much	훨씬	형용사나 부사의 비교급을 수식한다. Vancouver was a **much smaller** city than I expected. 밴쿠버는 내가 기대한 것보다 훨씬 더 작은 도시였다. I can speak English **much more fluently** than Jinyoung. 나는 진영이보다 영어를 훨씬 더 유창하게 말할 수 있다.

정답 p.56

PRACTICE 12

괄호 안에 들어갈 알맞은 말을 골라 동그라미 하세요.

1 I clean the house much (frequently, more frequently) than my brother does.

2 The teacher explained the topic (very, much) thoroughly in the first class.

3 The blue whale is a very (large, larger) mammal living today.

4 Seafood in that restaurant is very (expensive, more expensive).

5 This film is (very, much) more realistic than the other films.

6 My baby sister cries (very, much) loudly whenever she is hungry.

7 The cheetah runs much (fast, faster) than the elephant.

8 The clothes are made with a special fabric that is very (smooth, smoother).

9 The comedy show is (very, much) funnier than I expected.

10 It's very (easy, easier) to find our house.

11 He is much (experienced, more experienced) than you in the field of classical music.

12 Jasmine was always (very, much) good at art.

13 Going away to college has made me (very, much) more independent.

PSS 2-5 else, even

else	그 밖에	else는 수식하는 말 뒤에 온다. We couldn't find **anywhere** else but here. 우리는 여기 말고 그 밖의 어떤 곳도 찾을 수 없었다. **How** else can I get in touch with Mr. Brown? 그 밖에 어떻게 제가 Brown 씨와 연락할 수 있습니까? ***cf.*** else가 의문대명사나 부정대명사 뒤에 올 때, else의 품사는 형용사이다. **What** else can you tell me about the theory? 그 이론에 대해 내게 그 밖에 무엇을 말해 줄 수 있니? **No one** else wanted to do it instead of me. 그 밖에 아무도 나 대신 그것을 하기를 원하지 않았다.
even	~조차	even은 수식하는 말 앞에 온다. He doesn't even **know** that I am his cousin. 그는 내가 그의 사촌이라는 것을 알지도 못한다. Sometimes even **my brother** doesn't understand what I'm saying. 가끔씩은 내 남동생조차도 내가 하는 말을 이해하지 못한다. My dog tries to follow me even **when I go to the bathroom**. 나의 강아지는 내가 화장실에 갈 때조차 나를 따라오려고 한다. The girl always smiled even **in difficult situations**. 그 소녀는 어려운 상황에서조차 항상 웃었다. The new product I bought is even **cheap**. 내가 산 그 신상품은 저렴하기까지 하다.

정답 p.56

PRACTICE 13 [1-8]

괄호 안에 주어진 단어가 밑줄 친 부분을 수식하도록 문장을 다시 쓰세요.

1 <u>Who</u> should we pick up at the airport? (else)

➡ ____

2 His <u>kind words</u> couldn't calm me down. (even)

➡ ____

3 Jason couldn't talk to <u>anyone</u> about his problem. (else)

➡ ____

4 He <u>resembles</u> my father's personality. (even)

➡ ____

5 I want <u>nothing</u> except a bicycle for my birthday. (else)

➡ ____

6 She goes jogging <u>when the weather is bad</u>. (even)

➡ ____

7 <u>What</u> did your professor advise you to do? (else)

➡ ____

8 One of my friends calls me <u>in the middle of the night</u>. (even)

➡ ____

정답 p.56

PRACTICE 14

괄호 안에 들어갈 알맞은 말을 골라 동그라미 하세요.

1 I won't be able to accept it if someone (else, even) wins.

2 After suffering from a stroke, he could not talk and (else, even) hear.

3 I am fed up with the same food. I want to try something (else, even).

4 The fact that (else, even) you criticized me makes me sad.

5 (Else, Even) Jina couldn't stop me from falling asleep.

6 He is sure to win the dance contest. Who (else, even) can dance better than him?

7 Is there anyone (else, even) who wants to help Tom?

8 My uncle didn't (else, even) recognize my brother and me.

9 What (else, even) do you want me to do? I'm willing to do anything for you.

10 How (else, even) can I get there in thirty minutes?

11 When an elephant is in trouble, (else, even) a frog will kick him.

12 (Else, Even) when his children are noisy in public, he never scolds them.

PSS 2-6 ago, before

ago	~ 전에	ago는 현재를 기준으로 하여 과거의 한 시점에 일어난 일을 나타낼 때 쓰인다. ago는 홀로 쓸 수 없으며 항상 시간을 나타내는 말과 함께 오고, 과거 시제와 함께 사용된다. There were a lot of volcanoes in this area a long time **ago**. 오래 전에 이 지역에는 많은 화산이 있었다. I moved to Suwon from Gwangju two years **ago**. 나는 2년 전에 광주에서 수원으로 이사했다.
before		before는 한 시점을 기준으로 하여 그 이전 시점에 일어난 일을 나타내고, 주로 완료 시제와 함께 사용된다. Someone told me that Mr. Smith had left Korea three years **before**. 누군가가 내게 Smith 씨가 3년 전에 한국을 떠났다고 말했다. I heard that you had traveled in India a few months **before**. 나는 네가 몇 달 전에 인도에서 여행을 했다는 것을 들었다. *cf.* before는 ago와 달리 시간을 나타내는 말 없이 홀로 쓰일 수 있고, 이때는 현재완료, 과거, 과거완료 시제와 함께 사용될 수 있다. I**'ve** never **seen** those people **before**. 나는 그 사람들을 전에 본 적이 없다. It was humid because it **had rained before**. 전에 비가 왔기 때문에 날씨가 습했다.

정답 p.56

PRACTICE 15 [1-12]

괄호 안에 들어갈 알맞은 말을 골라 동그라미 하세요.

1 Have the boys talked to each other (ago, before)?

2 He was very poor (ago, before), but now he is a successful businessman.

3 Two years (ago, before), I learned how to scuba dive.

4 He wanted to be a diplomat (ago, before), but now he wants to be a movie director.

5 I heard that he had gone to Africa to go on a safari two months (ago, before).

6 I've read the article about school violence (ago, before).

7 People used to live a peaceful life (ago, before), but now everything has changed.

8   Jenny and Mike broke up three weeks (ago, before).

9   The government began to build new expressways across the nation three years (ago, before).

10   We went to see the Maya ruins six months (ago, before).

11   Jane told me that she had worked as a nurse ten years (ago, before).

12   My dog ran away from home but came back two days (ago, before).

PSS 2-7 「타동사 + 부사」의 어순

in, out, on, off, up, down, away, over, through와 같은 부사가 동사와 함께 쓰여 동사구를 이룰 때는 목적어에 따라 어순이 달라진다.

1. 목적어가 명사일 때, 목적어는 부사의 뒤에 오거나 동사와 부사의 사이에 온다. 즉, 「동사+부사+목적어」나 「동사+목적어+부사」의 어순 둘 다 가능하다.

    Could you **fill out** this form? 이 양식을 기입해 주시겠습니까?
    = Could you **fill** this form **out**?

2. 목적어가 대명사일 때, 목적어는 반드시 동사와 부사의 사이에 온다. 즉, 「동사+목적어+부사」의 어순만 가능하다.

    Did you forget to **hand** it **in** by this afternoon? 오늘 오후까지 그것을 제출하는 것을 잊었니?
    Did you forget to **hand in** it by this afternoon? (×)

    cf. 자동사 뒤에 전치사가 올 때, 전치사의 목적어는 반드시 전치사 뒤에 온다. 즉, 「동사+전치사+목적어」의 어순만 가능하다.
    I won't **care about** the rumor. 나는 그 소문에 대해 신경 쓰지 않을 것이다.
    I won't **care** the rumor **about**. (×)
    I won't **care about** it. 나는 그것에 대해 신경 쓰지 않을 것이다.
    I won't **care** it **about**. (×)

정답 p.56

PRACTICE 16

괄호 안에 들어갈 알맞은 말을 골라 동그라미 하세요.

1   I want you to wake (up your sister, up her).

2   She tried to put (on it, it on), but it was too small.

3   Please check (out the gas, out it) before driving.

4 He ironed (out the wrinkles, out them) on his shirt.

5 Do you mind if I turn (on the TV, on it) in the living room?

6 The man used to throw (away it, it away) illegally.

7 If you go (your room into, into your room), you'll find something surprising.

8 I figured (out how to operate the machine, out it) by myself.

9 She carried (the experiment out, out it) with care.

10 I looked (the keys for, for the keys) to the door.

11 She stopped to fill (up her car, up it).

12 I don't agree (him with, with him), but I have to follow him.

13 Will you pick (up the phone, up it) while I'm in the bathroom?

14 Let's talk (the problem about, about it) tomorrow morning.

15 Do you remember when you handed (in it, it in)?

정답 p.57

PRACTICE 17

우리말에 맞게 괄호 안에 주어진 말을 바르게 배열하여 빈칸에 쓰세요.

1 너는 건강에 신경을 써야 한다.
➡ ____ (you, care, your health, about, should)

2 그것을 금요일까지 미루지 마라.
➡ ____ (put, off, don't, it, Friday, until)

3 그는 그 메모를 보았니?
➡ ____ (look, did, he, the memo, at)

4 그것을 벗고 이것을 입어봐.
➡ ____ (try, on, this, take, and, off, it)

5 나는 내 차례를 기다리고 있다.
➡ ____ (I, waiting, my turn, for, am)

6 나는 그것들을 도서관에서 대출했다.
➡ ____ (checked, at, I, them, the library, out)

7 그 고양이는 그 의자 위에 앉아 있었다.
➡ ____ (on, the cat, sitting, was, the chair)

8 나를 위해 그것을 주워 주겠니?
➡ ____ (for, pick, will, it, up, me, you)

1 다음 중 짝지어진 두 단어의 관계가 나머지 넷과 다른 것은?

① effective – effectively
② moral – morally
③ actual – actually
④ constant – constantly
⑤ friend – friendly

2 빈칸에 들어갈 말로 알맞은 것은?

> *Chulsu* : Inho, hurry up, or we will be late for class.
> *Inho* : I'm not ready __________. Can you wait for another five minutes?

① still ② yet ③ even
④ seldom ⑤ already

3 다음 우리말을 영어로 바르게 옮긴 것은?

> 그들 역시 할 말을 찾지 못하는 것 같았다.

① They couldn't seem to find any words, too.
② They couldn't seem to find any words, neither.
③ They couldn't seem to find any words, also.
④ They couldn't seem to find any words, either.
⑤ They could seem not to find any words, too.

4 다음 문장의 밑줄 친 부분 중 어법상 잘못된 것은?

> If you don't ① do the housework, I ② won't, ③ neither. I'm sick of ④ doing it all by ⑤ myself.

5 우리말을 영어로 바르게 영작한 것은?

① 우리는 짙은 안개 때문에 길을 거의 볼 수 없었다.
➡ We couldn't hardly see the road because of the thick fog.
② 그 소문이 학교 전체에 널리 퍼졌다.
➡ The rumor spread wide across the school.
③ 그 교사는 수업 중 학생들이 휴대폰을 사용하는 것에 반대했다.
➡ The teacher objected students using their phones in class.
④ 그들이 공항에서 우리를 정말 따뜻하게 맞아주는구나!
➡ How warm they welcomed us at the airport!
⑤ 그 낡은 차를 고치는 것은 새 차를 사는 것보다 더 비쌀 수 있다.
➡ Repairing the old car could be more costly than buying a new one.

6 ⓐ~ⓔ 중 어법상 틀린 것을 있는 대로 고른 것은?

> ⓐ Take an umbrella since it's raining hardly outside.
> ⓑ Take off your gloves and throw away them.
> ⓒ Exercise regularly, and you'll be much healthy.
> ⓓ Fill this form out and hand in it to me.
> ⓔ Put it off and you don't have to care about it.

① ⓐ, ⓔ ② ⓑ, ⓓ ③ ⓐ, ⓑ, ⓒ
④ ⓒ, ⓓ, ⓔ ⑤ ⓐ, ⓑ, ⓒ, ⓓ

7 다음 중 어법상 어색한 것은?

① The picture has always caught people's imagination.
② John's brother often came to the game.
③ When you touch it, it feels usually slippery.
④ I sometimes arrange flowers to relax.
⑤ I have never thought about that problem.

8 밑줄 친 곳에 한 번도 활용될 수 없는 것은?

- She always thinks __________ about how others feel. She's very considerate.
- Don't worry. Everything is completely __________ control now.
- The writer ran __________ of ideas and couldn't finish the last chapter.
- I __________ recommend that you try the local seafood restaurant.
- Everyone was __________ after hearing the shocking news.

① out   ② under   ③ deeply
④ upset   ⑤ strong

9 ⓐ~ⓔ에서 어법상 틀린 문장의 개수는?

ⓐ All the shops in the area are open late.
ⓑ About 40 years ago, only a few houses had televisions because of the highly price.
ⓒ They were trying very hard to save the ship from the storm.
ⓓ The park is closely to the downtown area.
ⓔ The residents in the building are mostly elderly.

① 1개   ② 2개   ③ 3개   ④ 4개   ⑤ 5개

10 다음 문장에서 어법상 틀린 곳을 찾아 바르게 고치세요.

It has snowed near every day and everything is frozen.

__________ ➡ __________

11 다음 중 밑줄 친 much의 쓰임이 나머지와 다른 것은?

① How _much_ money will the performance need?
② We already have too _much_ work to do.
③ Unfortunately, they don't have _much_ food left.
④ It takes _much_ time to train for a marathon.
⑤ There is _much_ more homework to do.

12 다음 중 어법상 어색한 것은? (정답 2개)

① He is nearly as diligent as you are.
② I've been really busy lately.
③ They found strange something.
④ Sean carefully took out it and carried back it to his room.
⑤ Why don't you tidy up the desk before she gets back home?

13 빈칸에 들어갈 수 있는 것을 모두 고르세요.

Minhee : I'm not very good at math and science. How about you?
Jiho   : __________ I want to know how to study them effectively.

① Neither am I. ② Me, too.   ③ I do, either.
④ Me, neither. ⑤ Neither do I.

14 다음 중 어법상 <u>어색한</u> 것을 <u>모두</u> 고르세요.

① Turn the light off when it is bright outside.
② She threw away her old clothes into the waste bag.
③ When I heard the news, I couldn't figure out it.
④ I went out to the field to look him for.
⑤ Their team didn't win the match, either.

15 주어진 우리말과 같은 뜻이 되도록 빈칸을 채울 때 알맞은 말은?

> • 이제 우리는 전과 같이 좋은 이웃이다.
> = Now we are good neighbors again, just as ___________ .

① ago ② before ③ former
④ same ⑤ since

16 다음 문장의 밑줄 친 부분 중 어법상 <u>잘못된</u> 것은?

> Seoul ① <u>is</u> the city ② <u>where</u> things ③ <u>change</u> ④ <u>faster</u> than ⑤ <u>else anywhere</u> in Korea.

17 다음 우리말과 같은 뜻이 되도록 괄호 안에 주어진 단어를 포함시켜 빈칸을 완성하세요.

> • 사막에서는 거의 비가 오지 않고 태양이 계속 내리쬔다.
> = In deserts, ___________ ___________ ___________ and the Sun keeps shining. (rarely)

18 다음 중 밑줄 친 부분을 어법상 옳게 고친 것은?

① The dog was too fat to run <u>fast</u>(→ fastly).
② She climbed <u>highly</u>(→ high) up the mountain by herself.
③ A friend of mine really studies <u>hard</u>(→ hardly).
④ I <u>strongly</u>(→ strong) advise you to wash your hands thoroughly.
⑤ We <u>mostly</u>(→ most) eat out on Saturday evenings.

19 빈칸에 공통으로 들어갈 단어로 알맞은 것은?

> • Some students began to show ________ as early as 6 o'clock.
> • Their friends came to pick them ________ .
> • You'd better get ________ early not to miss the train.

① on ② in ③ up
④ out ⑤ at

20 주어진 우리말과 같은 뜻이 되도록 괄호 안에 주어진 말을 활용하여 부분영작하세요.

> • 재훈이는 보통 한 달에 한 번 미술관에 방문한다.
> = Jaehoon ___________________________
> ___________________________ once a month.
> (pay a visit, gallery, usually)

21 다음 중 어법상 <u>어색한</u> 것은?

① I'm much taller than my brother.
② The rain was too heavy for me to go for a walk outside.
③ Max is not a pilot, either.
④ She doesn't like milk. Either do I.
⑤ I thought it was impossible to jump that high.

22 A의 마지막 응답이 같은 의미를 갖도록 ⓐ, ⓑ에 들어갈 알맞은 말을 쓰세요.

A: I heard that Hana won first prize in the contest.
B: Did she? I can't believe it.
A: I can't, _______ⓐ_______ .
  = Neither _______ⓑ_______ I.

ⓐ : _______________ ⓑ : _______________

23 다음 문장에서 seldom이 들어갈 위치로 알맞은 것은?

They do ① not know ② each other ③ well because they ④ spend ⑤ time together.

24 다음 문장의 밑줄 친 부분 중 그 쓰임이 잘못된 것은?

① Has he finished his homework <u>still</u>?
② It's <u>already</u> been two months since he left.
③ Most of them don't know what they want to be <u>yet</u>.
④ I found they did not use spoons <u>even</u> when they ate soup.
⑤ What <u>else</u> can you tell me about the woman?

25 다음 문장에서 어법상 어색한 부분을 찾아 바르게 고치세요.

After staying up all night, I could hard keep my eyes open during the morning meeting.

_______________ ➡ _______________

26 다음 중 밑줄 친 still의 뜻이 나머지 넷과 다른 것은?

① Are you <u>still</u> waiting for me?
② Sumi sat <u>still</u>, looking out the window.
③ That material is <u>still</u> used in making medicines.
④ My grandfather <u>still</u> goes to law school seminars.
⑤ I <u>still</u> have a question about the theory.

27 빈칸에 들어갈 말이 바르게 짝지어진 것은?

• Have you ___________ been to America?
• I ___________ lived in Jeju Island.
• I ___________ can't believe he's guilty.

① once　　– still　　– already
② always – still　　– ever
③ ever　　– once　　– still
④ always – once　　– yet
⑤ ever　　– already – yet

28 밑줄 친 (a)~(e) 중 어법상 틀린 것을 모두 고르면? (정답 2개)

Bananas are popular fruits around the world. They help your body with (a) <u>digestion</u>. Bananas give many health benefits. They are healthy and taste (b) <u>great</u>. Bananas grow in warm climates and (c) <u>harvested</u> all year round. Farmers pack the fresh bananas (d) <u>careful</u> to keep them safe. After (e) <u>being picked</u>, they are moved to stores for sale. Many people like to include bananas in smoothies, sweet recipes, and different breakfast meals.

① (a)　　② (b)　　③ (c)　　④ (d)　　⑤ (e)

29 다음 중 어법상 옳은 것은?

① He was much happy to see his family.
② People agreed that this had been a much good garden.
③ Do you think David is very taller than Jason?
④ She has bought the book a week ago.
⑤ He predicts that life will be very different in 50 years.

30 빈칸에 들어갈 말로 알맞은 것은?

> I haven't seen her ___________ . I wonder what happened to her.

① hardly   ② late   ③ lately
④ close   ⑤ random

31 어법상 틀린 곳을 찾아 바르게 고치세요.

> When you first learn Taekwondo, you should learn to turn over and kick highly.

➡ _________________________________

32 밑줄 친 even이 같은 뜻으로 쓰인 문장끼리 짝 지어진 것은?

> ⓐ 2, 4, and 6 are even numbers.
> ⓑ It was cold there even in summer.
> ⓒ Mom divided the cake into three even amounts.
> ⓓ It was quite difficult to see, even with the light on.
> ⓔ Her first book was good, but this one is even better.
> ⓕ The student representative spoke in a steady, even voice.

① ⓐ, ⓕ   ② ⓑ, ⓓ   ③ ⓑ, ⓕ   ④ ⓒ, ⓔ   ⑤ ⓓ, ⓕ

33 다음 단어를 어법에 맞게 빈칸에 넣었을 때, ⓐ와 ⓑ의 관계가 나머지 넷과 <u>다른</u> 하나는?

①	difficult	• The math problem was so ⓐ _________ that I couldn't solve it. • He completed the task with great ⓑ _________ .
②	hard	• His handwriting is ⓐ _________ to understand. • He ⓑ _________ ate anything at the party.
③	loud	• She has such a ⓐ _____ voice that I could hear her from the hall. • The phone rang ⓑ _____ in the middle of the meeting.
④	close	• We only invited ⓐ _____ friends to our wedding. • The kids sat ⓑ _____ together on the bench.
⑤	true	• The movie was based on a ⓐ _____ story. • Dan Smith is ⓑ _____ a great actor.

34 다음 중 어법상 <u>어색한</u> 것은?

① We have to pick up the man who will clean this building.
② You look gorgeous dressed up like that.
③ It is Jimmy that broke down it.
④ The manager called off the meeting again.
⑤ As soon as they heard about the idea, they objected to it.

CHAPTER 12
가정법

Problem Solving Skill	페이지	성취도				
		100%	99~75%	74~50%	49~25%	24~0%
PSS 1 조건을 나타내는 if	254					
PSS 2 가정법 과거	페이지	성취도				
		100%	99~75%	74~50%	49~25%	24~0%
PSS **2-1** if+가정법 과거	256					
PSS **2-2** I wish+가정법 과거	258					
PSS **2-3** as if[though]+가정법 과거	260					
PSS **2-4** without	261					
PSS 3 가정법 과거완료	페이지	성취도				
		100%	99~75%	74~50%	49~25%	24~0%
PSS **3-1** if+가정법 과거완료	262					
PSS **3-2** I wish+가정법 과거완료	263					
PSS **3-3** as if[though]+가정법 과거완료	265					
PSS **3-4** without	266					
PSS 4 혼합가정법	267					
PSS 5 가정법 현재 명사절	268					
PSS 6 if의 생략	269					
중간·기말고사 대비문제	271					

PSS 1 조건을 나타내는 if

If you clean the dishes, I can iron your suit.
당신이 설거지를 한다면, 나는 당신의 양복을 다려 줄 수 있어요.

1. if는 '~한다면, ~라면'의 뜻으로 현재나 미래에 실제로 일어날 수 있는 상황에 대한 조건을 나타낸다.

   If Brian calls, just say I'll be back in the office at two o'clock.
   Brian이 전화하면, 내가 2시에 사무실에 돌아온다고 말하세요.
   If Mom comes to pick me up tomorrow, I'll be very happy.
   엄마가 내일 나를 데리러 오신다면, 나는 매우 행복할 거야.

   cf. 미래의 일을 나타낸다고 하더라도 if절의 동사는 항상 현재형으로 쓴다.
   If Mom **will come** to pick me up tomorrow, I'll be very happy. (×)

2. 조건을 나타내는 if절은 과거에 실제로 일어난 사실에 대한 조건을 나타낼 수도 있다.

   If he acted like that, he was such an idiot. 그가 그렇게 행동했다면, 그는 정말 바보였다.

   cf. 의미상 현재 일어날 가능성이 희박한 상황을 가정하는 문장이라면, 조건을 나타내는 if절이 아니라 현재 사실에 반대되는 일을 가정하는 가정법 과거이다.
   If he acted like that, Julie would be very upset.
   그가 그렇게 행동한다면, Julie는 매우 화가 날 것이다.

3. if와 when

   If I meet Daniel, I'll let him know that you're in the hospital.
   내가 Daniel을 만난다면, 그에게 네가 병원에 있다는 것을 알려줄게.
   (Daniel을 만날지 만나지 않을 것인지 확실하지 않으므로 if를 쓴다.)
   When I meet Daniel, I'll let him know that you're in the hospital.
   내가 Daniel을 만날 때, 그에게 네가 병원에 있다는 것을 알려줄게.
   (Daniel을 만날 것이 확실하므로 when을 쓴다.)

PRACTICE 1

괄호 안에 주어진 말을 이용하여 조건을 나타내는 if절을 완성하세요.

1 If you _______________ a package tomorrow, it will arrive by Friday. (send)

2 If you _______________ the last person to leave the room, turn the lights off. (be)

3 If she _______________ the machine, she was a real genius. (invent)

4 If you _______________ cookies to the dog, it keeps begging you for food. (give)

5 If a forest fire _______________ , it can spread very quickly. (break out)

6 If you _______________ breakfast, you will be full of energy during the day. (have)

7 If I _______________ newspapers for a few hours a day, I can make some money. (deliver)

8 If she _______________ the quiz in ten minutes, she was a very smart girl. (solve)

9 If my parents _______________ me go to the concert, I'll do the laundry for this month. (let)

10 If I _______________ rich, I will spend my fortune on helping homeless people. (become)

PRACTICE 2

〈보기〉에서 적당한 단어를 골라 알맞은 형태로 바꾸어 빈칸에 쓰세요.

| 보 기 | rain / know / answer / not. feel / eat / go / smell |

1 If it _______________ , we can't go camping tomorrow.

2 If she _______________ to the island, she will spend all day swimming.

3 If you _______________ hot, you can turn off the air conditioner.

4 If you _______________ my questions, I'll give you more points.

5 If she _______________ enough, she wouldn't feel hungry that often.

6 If you _______________ gas, turn off the gas and open all the doors and windows.

7 If we _______________ a country's language, we could understand its culture more easily.

PSS 2 가정법 과거

PSS 2 - 1 if + 가정법 과거

If I **had** wings, I **could follow** the bird.
내가 날개가 있다면, 그 새를 따라갈 수 있을 텐데.

1. 가정법 과거는 '만약 ～한다면 …할 텐데'의 뜻으로 현재 사실에 반대되거나 실현 가능성이 거의 없는 일을 가정할 때 쓴다.

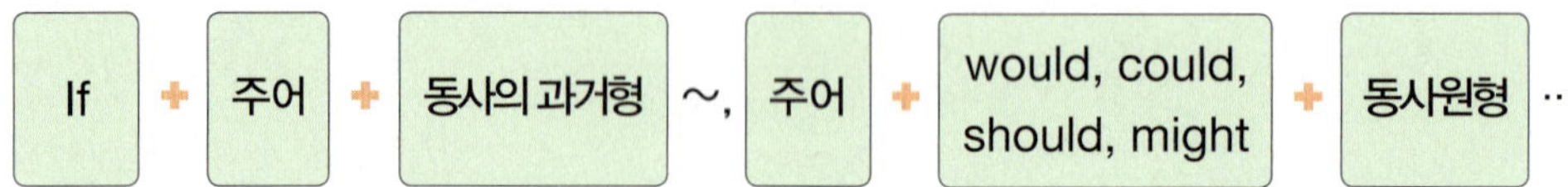

If we **knew** how to swim, we **could have** more fun.
만약 우리가 수영을 어떻게 하는지 안다면, 우리는 더 재미있을 텐데.

➡ As we don't know how to swim, we can't have more fun.
우리가 수영을 어떻게 하는지 알지 못하므로, 우리는 더 재미있을 수 없다.

> *cf.* were to 가정법: 실제로 일어날 가능성이 낮거나 전혀 없는 일, 혹은 상상 속의 상황을 나타낼 때 쓴다.
>
> If + 주어 + were to + 동사원형, 주어 + would[could/should/might] + 동사원형
>
> **If** I **were to meet** him again, I **would apologize**.
>
> (혹시라도 또는 거의 일어날 가능성이 없지만) 그를 다시 만나게 된다면 나는 사과할 것이다.
>
> **If** I **met** him again, I **would apologize**.
>
> 만약 내가 그를 다시 만난다면, 사과할 것이다. (가능성에 대한 특별한 강조 없음)

2. if절의 be동사는 주어의 수나 인칭에 상관없이 were를 쓰는 것이 원칙이지만, 구어체에서는 was를 쓰기도 한다.

If **I were** in Paris, I could attend my cousin's wedding.
만약 내가 파리에 있다면, 나는 내 사촌의 결혼식에 참석할 수 있을 텐데.

➡ As I am not in Paris, I can't attend my cousin's wedding.
나는 파리에 있지 않으므로, 내 사촌의 결혼식에 참석할 수 없다.

PRACTICE 3

괄호 안의 단어를 알맞은 형태로 바꾸어 빈칸에 쓰세요.

1   If I ________________ up a wallet with a lot of money, I would take it to the police. (pick)

2   What would you do if you ________________ in my shoes? (be)

3   If you ________________ your health, you can't do what you like. (lose)

4   If you ________________ the cello well, you could take part in the contest. (play)

5   If you ________________ home now, you'll arrive here in 30 minutes. (leave)

6   If I ________________ Chinese well, I could guide the Chinese tourists. (speak)

7   If you ________________ lucky enough to see this sunrise, you will have a good memory. (be)

8   If he ________________ sick, he could go mountain climbing. (not, be)

9   If you ________________ enough sleep, you can concentrate on this better. (get)

10 If we often ________________ public transportation, there will be less air pollution. (use)

PRACTICE 4

다음 문장을 if를 이용한 가정법 문장으로 바꾸어 쓰세요.

1   As I like golf very much, my dream is to be a professional golf player.
    ➡ If I didn't like golf very much, my dream wouldn't[couldn't] be to be a professional golf player.

2   As I don't know her email address, I can't write to her.
    ➡ ____

3   As he tells lies all the time, we don't like him.
    ➡ ____

4   As she isn't in the office, I can't meet her.
    ➡ ____

5   As I am appointed as principal of this school, I won't leave this city.
    ➡ ____

6   As Ms. Kim can't find another apartment, she will stay here for one more month.
    ➡ ____

7   As she does not love the boy, she doesn't pay attention to him.
    ➡ ____

8   As we don't have a time machine, we don't know exactly what happened to dinosaurs.
    ➡ ____

CH
12
가
정
법

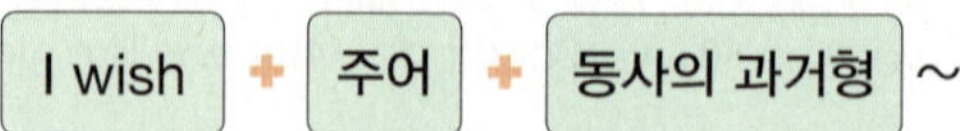

PSS 2-2 I wish + 가정법 과거

「I wish+가정법 과거」는 '~라면 좋을 텐데'의 뜻으로 현재의 사실과 반대되거나 이룰 수 없는 일을 소망할 때 쓴다.

I wish + 주어 + 동사의 과거형 ~

I wish (that) I **had** the opportunity to travel around the world.
세계 여행을 할 기회가 있으면 좋을 텐데.

➡ I'm sorry that I don't have the opportunity to travel around the world.
나는 세계 여행을 할 기회가 없어서 유감이다.

I wish (that) we **were** on vacation right now. 우리가 지금 당장 방학 중이라면 좋을 텐데.

➡ I'm sorry that we are not on vacation right now.
나는 우리가 지금 당장 방학이 아니어서 유감이다.

cf. 미래에 있을 일에 대한 소망을 나타낼 때는 종속절에 will 대신 would를 쓴다.
I wish (that) the weather **would** be better tomorrow. 내일 날씨가 더 좋았으면 좋겠다.

정답 p.60

PRACTICE 5

다음 「I wish+가정법 과거」 문장을 〈보기〉와 같이 직설법 문장으로 바꾸어 쓰세요.

> 보 기
> I wish I had a twin brother.
> ➡ I'm sorry that ___I don't have a twin brother___.

1 I wish I spent more time with my family.
➡ I'm sorry that ___________________________________.

2 I wish I could play tennis like him.
➡ I'm sorry that ___________________________________.

3 I wish you fell into a deep sleep.
➡ I'm sorry that ___________________________________.

4 I wish I could meet an angel in heaven.
➡ I'm sorry that ___________________________________.

5 I wish I were the tallest among my friends.
➡ I'm sorry that ___________________________________.

6 I wish I were good at cooking.
➡ I'm sorry that ___________________________________.

7 I wish I didn't know the truth about Emma.

➡ I'm sorry that ___________________________________ .

8 I wish I weren't disappointed with my grade.

➡ I'm sorry that ___________________________________ .

9 I wish it weren't raining right now.

➡ I'm sorry that ___________________________________ .

10 I wish I didn't wear these uncomfortable jeans.

➡ I'm sorry that ___________________________________ .

정답 p.60

PRACTICE 6

주어진 문장과 의미가 통하도록 빈칸에 알맞은 말을 쓰세요.

1 I'm sorry that I don't have money to buy that luxurious car.

➡ I wish _____*I had money to buy that luxurious car*_____ .

2 I'm sorry that I don't speak Spanish fluently enough to travel alone.

➡ I wish ___________________________________ .

3 I'm sorry that I am not good at painting like my sister.

➡ I wish ___________________________________ .

4 I'm sorry that he is not strong enough to knock the boy down.

➡ I wish ___________________________________ .

5 I'm sorry that we don't live in a world free from wars.

➡ I wish ___________________________________ .

6 I'm sorry that my parents don't let me ride a motorbike.

➡ I wish ___________________________________ .

7 I'm sorry that I will need to take a math test next week.

➡ I wish ___________________________________ .

8 I'm sorry that I am not allowed to go out after 9 o'clock.

➡ I wish ___________________________________ .

9 I'm sorry that he doesn't know how to fix a car.

➡ I wish ___________________________________ .

10 I'm sorry that the weather will be freezing cold tomorrow.

➡ I wish ___________________________________ .

PSS 2-3 as if[though] + 가정법 과거

「as if[though]+가정법 과거」는 '마치 ~인 것처럼'의 뜻으로 현재의 사실과 반대되는 가정을 나타낸다. as if절에서 나타내는 일의 시제는 주절의 시제와 같다.

동사의 현재형/과거형 **+** as if[though] **+** 주어 **+** 동사의 과거형 ~

I **feel** as if[though] I **were** a real police officer. 나는 마치 내가 진짜 경찰관인 것처럼 느낀다.
➡ In fact, I'm not a real police officer. 사실, 나는 진짜 경찰관이 아니다.
I **felt** as if[though] I **were** a real police officer. 나는 마치 내가 진짜 경찰관인 것처럼 느꼈다.
➡ In fact, I was not a real police officer. 사실, 나는 진짜 경찰관이 아니었다.

They **look** as if[though] they **knew** each other. 그들은 마치 서로를 알고 있는 것처럼 보인다.
➡ In fact, they don't know each other. 사실, 그들은 서로를 알지 못한다.
They **looked** as if[though] they **knew** each other. 그들은 마치 서로를 알고 있는 것처럼 보였다.
➡ In fact, they didn't know each other. 사실, 그들은 서로를 알지 못했다.

정답 p.60

PRACTICE 7

〈보기〉와 같이 주어진 문장을 as if를 이용한 가정법 과거 문장으로 바꾸어 쓰세요.

보 기	In fact, my dad doesn't climb the mountain during the weekdays.
	➡ My dad sounds _____as if he climbed the mountain during the weekdays_____ .

1 In fact, he is not a professional dancer.
➡ He dances ____ .

2 In fact, she was not a celebrity.
➡ She behaved ____ .

3 In fact, he didn't do everything by himself.
➡ He pretended ____ .

4 In fact, he was not a brave soldier at that time.
➡ He fought ____ .

5 In fact, she didn't have a good relationship with her brother.
➡ She behaved ____ .

6 In fact, she didn't write the report by herself.
➡ She pretended ____ .

7 In fact, he is responsible for the terrible accident.

➡ He sounds ____.

8 In fact, his father is not a successful businessman.

➡ It appears ____.

9 In fact, she didn't know the whole story.

➡ She pretended ____.

10 In fact, he doesn't help me make the bed every morning.

➡ He pretends ____.

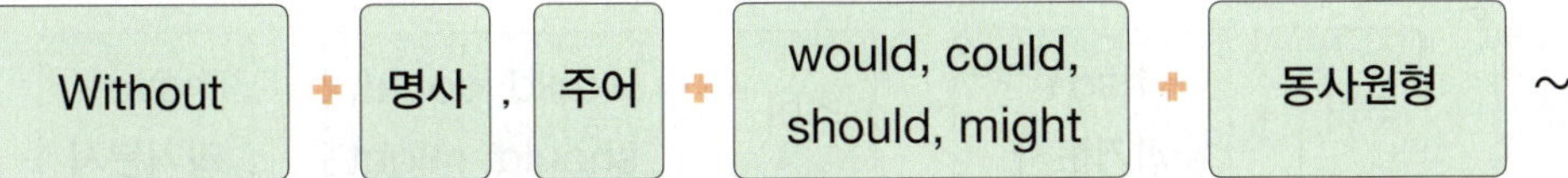

PSS 2-4 without

「without+명사, 가정법 과거」는 '~이 없다면 …할 것이다'의 뜻으로 현재의 사실과 반대되는 일을 나타내며 without은 「if it were not for」와 바꿔 쓸 수 있다.

| Without | + | 명사 | , | 주어 | + | would, could, should, might | + | 동사원형 | ~ |

Without air pollution, we **could have** fresh air.

대기 오염이 없다면, 우리는 신선한 공기를 마실 것이다.

➡ **If it were not for** air pollution, we **could have** fresh air.

= **Were it not for** air pollution, we **could have** fresh air.

= **But for** air pollution, we **could have** fresh air.

PRACTICE 8

괄호 안에 들어갈 알맞은 말을 골라 동그라미 하세요.

1 If it (were, were not) for love, life would be of no meaning.

2 If it were not for Jack, class (will, would) be very boring.

3 If it (are, were) not for soccer, my life would not be fun.

4 If (that, it) were not for electricity, I wouldn't be able to watch TV.

5 Without her, I (could, couldn't) study English harder. She teaches me English very well.

6 Without stress, she (could, couldn't) be much healthier.

7 Without food, no one (could, couldn't) live.

8 If it were not for my smartphone, I (won't, wouldn't) waste so much time.

PSS 3 가정법 과거완료

PSS 3-1 if + 가정법 과거완료

If I **had left** home earlier, I **would have arrived** on time.

내가 좀 더 일찍 집에서 출발했다면, 난 제때에 도착했었을 텐데.

가정법 과거완료는 '만약 ~했다면 …했을 텐데'의 뜻으로 과거 사실에 반대되는 일을 가정할 때 쓴다.

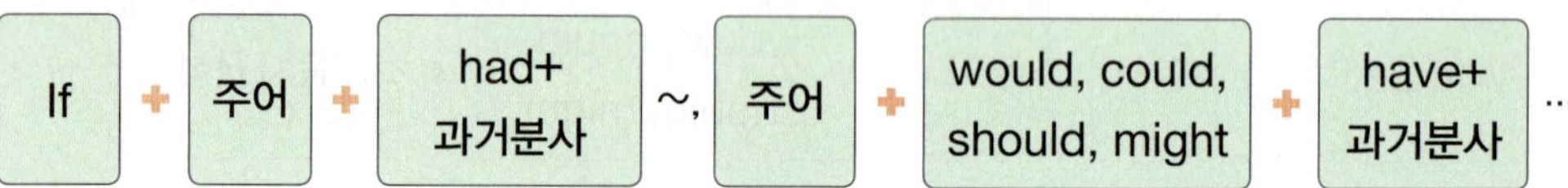

| If | + | 주어 | + | had+
과거분사 | ~, | 주어 | + | would, could,
should, might | + | have+
과거분사 | … |

If he **had followed** the recipe correctly, the cake **wouldn't have turned** out burnt.

만약 그가 그 조리법을 올바르게 따랐다면, 그 케이크는 타지 않았을 텐데.

➡ As he didn't follow the recipe correctly, the cake turned out burnt.

그가 조리법을 올바르게 따르지 않았기 때문에, 그 케이크는 타 버렸다.

If I **had made** a different choice, I **would have regretted** it.

만약 내가 다른 선택을 했다면, 나는 그것을 후회했을 것이다.

➡ As I didn't make a different choice, I didn't regret it.

내가 다른 선택을 하지 않았기 때문에, 나는 그것을 후회하지 않았다.

정답 p.60

PRACTICE 9

다음 문장을 if를 이용한 가정법 문장으로 바꾸어 쓰세요.

1 As I didn't move to Daegu last year, I couldn't meet his family more often.

➡ _If I had moved to Daegu last year, I could have met his family more often._

2 As I didn't know you were so busy, I called on you.

➡ ____

3 As we don't try to keep our great traditions, many of them will disappear.

➡ ____

4 As I met a good English teacher, I became interested in English.

➡ ____

5 As I don't play the flute well enough, the symphony orchestra won't accept me as a member.

➡ ____

6 As I was an only child in my family, I wanted brothers and sisters.

➡ ____

7 As I worked part-time after school, I could earn extra money.

➡ ____

8 As Mike was born and raised in such a cold area, he couldn't stand the hot weather here.

➡ ____

9 As Susan saw a scary movie at night by herself, she couldn't fall asleep.

➡ ____

10 As he doesn't run an anti-virus program regularly, his computer crashes frequently.

➡ ____

11 As my grandfather knew how to send an e-mail, we could keep in touch more often.

➡ ____

CH
12
가정법

PSS 3-2 I wish + 가정법 과거완료

「I wish+가정법 과거완료」는 '~했더라면 좋았을 텐데'의 뜻으로, 과거의 사실과 반대되는 일을 소망할 때 쓴다.

I wish ＋ 주어 ＋ had+과거분사 ~

I wish we **had taken** the subway last night. 우리가 지난밤에 지하철을 탔더라면 좋았을 텐데.

➡ I regret that we didn't take the subway last night.

나는 우리가 지난밤에 지하철을 타지 않은 것을 후회한다.

I wish I **had brought** my cat to the vet when he first got sick.

내 고양이가 처음 아팠을 때 수의사에게 데려왔더라면 좋았을 텐데.

➡ I regret that I didn't bring my cat to the vet when he first got sick.

나는 내 고양이가 처음 아팠을 때 수의사에게 데려오지 않은 것을 후회한다.

PRACTICE 10

다음 문장을 I wish를 이용한 가정법 문장으로 바꾸어 쓰세요.

1 I regret that I didn't complete this course last year.

➡ _I wish I had completed this course last year._

2 My mom doesn't give me chocolate chip cookies at night, but I want her to.

➡ ____

3 I regret that I didn't read many good books in my school days.

➡ ____

4 I am not talented at all kinds of martial arts, but I want to be.

➡ ____

5 I regret that I complained to my mother about everything.

➡ ____

6 James will leave Korea after he finishes this semester, but I don't want him to.

➡ ____

7 I regret that I did not accept my friend's sincere advice then.

➡ ____

8 I regret that I did not buy the concert ticket on the first day of selling.

➡ ____

9 I am sorry that her new album doesn't sell well.

➡ ____

10 I regret that I did not prepare for the performance better.

➡ ____

11 I did not pay attention to what was going on around me. I regret it.

➡ ____

12 I made fun of one of our classmates at all times. I regret it.

➡ ____

13 There are not many national museums in my city, but I want many national museums in it.

➡ ____

14 I didn't travel around the country when I was young and healthy. I regret it.

➡ ____

15 I didn't accept the best candidate as a member of the committee. I regret it.

➡ ____

PSS 3-3 as if[though] + 가정법 과거완료

「as if[though]+가정법 과거완료」는 '마치 ~였던 것처럼'의 뜻으로 주절보다 더 과거에 일어난 사실과 반대되는 가정을 나타낸다. as if절에서 나타내는 일의 시제는 주절의 시제보다 한 시제 앞선다.

동사의 현재형/과거형 + **as if[though]** + **주어** + **had+과거분사** ~

He **talks as if[though]** he **had finished** the work by himself.

그는 마치 그가 혼자서 그 일을 끝낸 것처럼 말한다.

➡ In fact, he didn't finish the work by himself. 사실, 그는 혼자서 그 일을 끝내지 않았다.

He **talked as if[though]** he **had finished** the work by himself.

그는 마치 그가 혼자서 그 일을 끝냈던 것처럼 말했다.

➡ In fact, he hadn't finished the work by himself. 사실, 그는 혼자서 그 일을 끝내지 않았었다.

Jenny **acts as if[though]** she **had never met** me before.

Jenny는 마치 전에 나를 만난 적이 없는 것처럼 행동한다.

➡ In fact, Jenny met me before. 사실, Jenny는 전에 나를 만났다.

Jenny **acted as if[though]** she **had never met** me before.

Jenny는 마치 전에 나를 만난 적이 없었던 것처럼 행동했다.

➡ In fact, Jenny had met me before. 사실, Jenny는 전에 나를 만났었다.

정답 p.61

PRACTICE 11 [1-10]

주어진 문장을 as if를 이용한 가정법 문장으로 바꾸어 쓰세요.

1 In fact, she wasn't a very popular singer in Korea.

➡ She sounds ___as if she had been a very popular singer in Korea___ .

2 In fact, she doesn't feel guilty about herself.

➡ She talks _______________ .

3 In fact, he worked for the company as a sales manager.

➡ He sounds _______________ .

4 In fact, the police had made much effort to find the lost child.

➡ The news anchor talked _______________ .

5 In fact, he didn't study computer science in college.

➡ He pretends _______________ .

6 In fact, the reporter didn't interview the professor regarding the issue.

➡ The reporter acts _______________ .

7 In fact, she couldn't afford to buy a house near the beach at that time.

➡ She acted ____.

8 In fact, he hadn't witnessed the car accident.

➡ He pretended ____.

9 In fact, the secretary didn't send the papers to the right place.

➡ The secretary talks ____.

10 In fact, the girl had not been to Australia and had not seen kangaroos.

➡ It sounded ____.

PSS 3-4 without

「without+명사, 가정법 과거완료」는 '~이 없었다면 …했을 것이다'의 뜻으로 과거의 사실
과 반대되는 일을 나타내며 without은 「if it had not been for」와 바꿔 쓸 수 있다.

| Without | + | 명사 , | 주어 | + | would, could, should, might | + | have+ 과거분사 | ~ |

Without her help, I **couldn't have finished** my homework.
그녀의 도움이 없었다면, 나는 숙제를 끝낼 수 없었을 것이다.

➡ **If it had not been for her help**, I **couldn't have finished** my homework.
  = **Had it not been for her help**, I **couldn't have finished** my homework.
  = **But for her help**, I **couldn't have finished** my homework.

정답 p.62

PRACTICE 12

다음 두 문장의 뜻이 같도록 빈칸에 if로 시작하는 알맞은 말을 쓰세요.

1 Without you, I could not have enough information.

= ____, I could not have enough information.

2 Without the movie, I would have felt bored in the train.

= ____, I would have felt bored in the train.

3 Without the accident, we could arrive earlier.

= ____, we could arrive earlier.

4 Without his effort, we might have failed.

= ____, we might have failed.

5 Without this navigation app, we would get lost.

= ____, we would get lost.

6 What would have happened without this?

= What would have happened ____?

PSS 4 혼합가정법

혼합가정법은 '~했더라면, …할 텐데'의 뜻으로 과거 사실에 반대되는 일을 가정하고, 과거 사실이 현재까지 영향을 미치는 경우에 쓰인다.

| If | + | 주어 | + | had+과거분사 | ~, | 주어 | + | would, could, should, might | + | 동사원형 | … |

If you **had stayed** up late last night, you **would be** sleepy now.

만약 네가 지난밤에 늦게까지 깨어 있었더라면, 너는 지금 졸릴 텐데.

➡ As you didn't stay up late last night, you are not sleepy now.

너는 지난밤에 늦게까지 깨어있지 않았기 때문에, 지금 졸리지 않다.

If he **had not broken** his leg, he **could be** skating here in this contest.

만약 그의 다리가 부러지지 않았더라면, 그는 여기 이 대회에서 스케이트를 타고 있을 텐데.

➡ As he broke his leg, he can't be skating here in this contest.

그는 다리가 부러졌기 때문에, 이 대회에서 스케이트를 타고 있을 수 없다.

정답 p.62

PRACTICE 13

괄호 안에 들어갈 알맞은 말을 골라 동그라미 하세요.

1 If you (didn't help, hadn't helped) me for the last three days, I couldn't be standing here now.

2 If you (took, had taken) the small old plane at that time, you could not be alive now.

3 If she really (loves, had loved) him, she won't do such a horrible thing to him.

4 If we (didn't set, hadn't set) the alarm, we would have been late for the meeting.

5 If we (invent, invented) working robots, our life would be more convenient.

6 If I (drove, had driven) safely, I would not be in the hospital now.

7 If you (know, knew) what situation he is in, you can understand why he acts like that.

8 If I (studied, had studied) harder for the exam, I would be a lawyer now.

9 If a dam (was constructed, had been constructed), the town would not have been destroyed.

10 If I (win, won) the lottery, I would give 100 dollars to each one of you.

11 If she (took, had taken) a closer look at the picture, she would have known the man was lying.

12 If he (exercised, had exercised) regularly when he was young, he would be much healthier now.

PSS 5 가정법 현재 명사절

제안, 주장, 명령, 요구, 권고 등을 나타내는 동사 뒤에 이어지는 that절에는 「should+동사원형」이 올 수 있는데, 이때 should를 생략하고 동사원형만 쓸 수 있다.

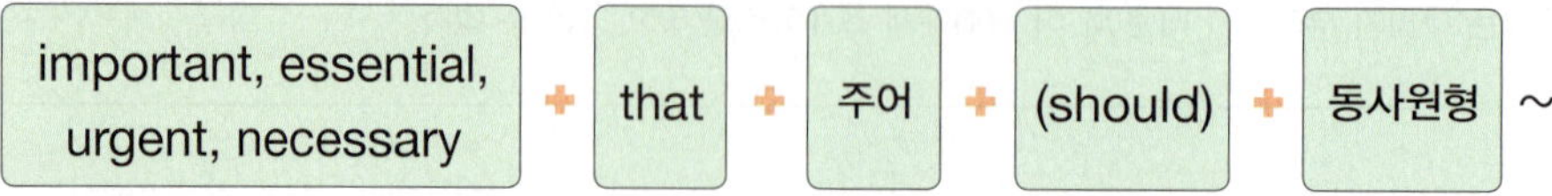

He **suggested** that I **(should) go** to the doctor right away.
그는 내가 즉시 의사에게 가야 한다고 제안했다.
Mr. Scott **recommended** that the store **(should) provide** more service.
Scott 씨는 그 상점이 더 많은 서비스를 제공해야 한다고 권고했다.

다음과 같은 형용사 뒤에 이어지는 that절에는 「should+동사원형」이 올 수 있는데, 이때 should를 생략하고 동사원형만 쓸 수 있다.

It is **important** that my team **(should) finish** the project by this month.
우리 팀이 이번 달까지 그 프로젝트를 끝내야 하는 것은 중요하다.
It is **essential** that the contract **(should) be** extended.
그 계약이 연장되어야 하는 것은 꼭 필요하다.

cf. that절의 내용에 '~해야 한다'의 의미가 포함되어 있지 않고, 단지 단순한 사실만을 언급할 때는 위의 원칙에 따르지 않는다. 즉, that절의 시제는 주절의 시제에 따라 바꾸어 써야 한다.
He **insisted** that he **had witnessed** the robbery that night.
그는 그날 밤 그 강도 사건을 목격했다고 주장했다.

정답 p.62

PRACTICE 14

괄호 안에 주어진 단어를 이용하여 문장을 완성하세요. (단, should를 생략할 수 있으면 반드시 생략할 것)

1 엄마는 내가 나가는 길에 우산 하나를 가지고 가도록 권했다.
= Mom recommended that ________________________________ on the way out. (bring)

2 네가 이 발표를 잘 준비하는 것은 꼭 필요하다.
= It is essential that ________________________________ well. (prepare)

3 우리가 다른 사람들의 의견을 존중하는 것은 중요하다.
= It is important that ________________________________ of others' opinions. (respectful)

4 그 고객은 그 가방이 좋지 않은 상태로 배송되었다고 주장했다.

= The customer insisted that ________________________ in poor condition. (deliver)

5 그녀는 우리가 공항에 버스를 타고 갈 것을 제안했다.

= She suggested that ________________________ the bus to go to the airport. (take)

6 그녀가 그녀의 사랑하는 사람들의 안부를 걱정하는 것을 표현하는 것은 자연스러운 일이다.

= It is natural that ________________________ concern for her loved ones' well-being. (express)

7 그는 그녀가 내일 회의에 참석하기를 요구했다.

= He demanded that ________________________ tomorrow. (attend)

8 그 용의자는 그가 그 살인사건과 관련이 없다고 주장했다.

= The suspect insisted that ________________________ to the murder case. (relevant)

9 학생들은 그들의 학교 교복들의 디자인이 변경되길 요청한다.

= The students request that the design of their ________________________ . (change)

PSS 6 if의 생략

가정법 문장의 if가 생략되면 be동사(또는 조동사)가 주어 앞으로 옮겨져 도치구문이 된다.

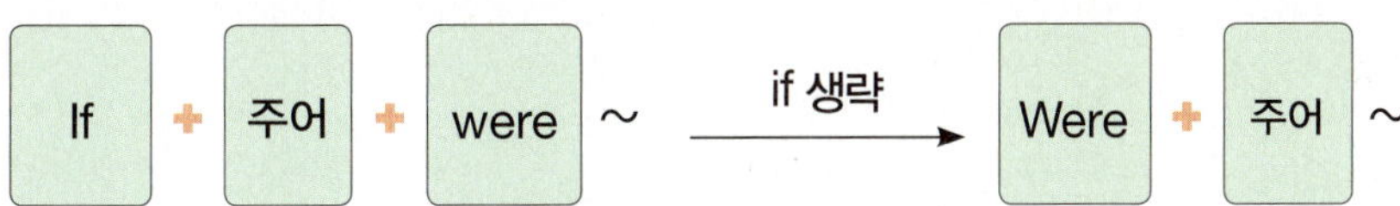

If John were here, he would eat dinner with us.

➡ **Were John** here, he would eat dinner with us.

John이 여기에 있다면, 그는 우리와 함께 저녁을 먹을 것이다.

If we were to announce the truth, we would receive a lot of criticism.

➡ **Were we** to announce the truth, we would receive a lot of criticism.

우리가 진실을 알린다면, 우리는 많은 비난을 받을 것이다.

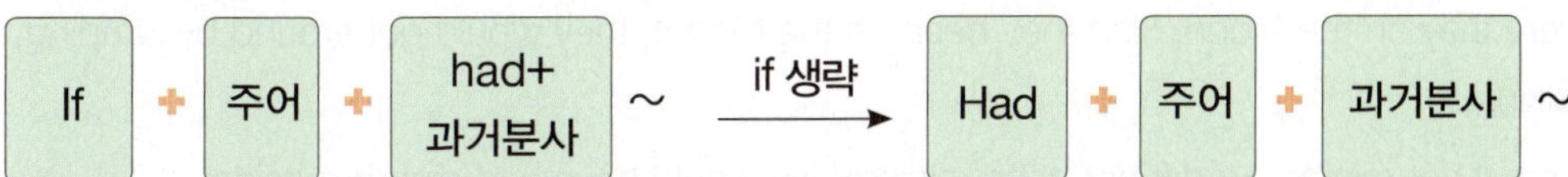

If I had woken up earlier, I wouldn't have missed the bus.

➡ **Had I** woken up earlier, I wouldn't have missed the bus.

내가 더 일찍 일어났다면, 나는 버스를 놓치지 않았을 것이다.

cf. 가정법 조건절에 if가 생략되어 있더라도 주절의 형태는 그대로 남아있기 때문에 주절의 조동사 would(could, should, might) 뒤의 동사의 형태를 보면 가정법 과거인지 과거완료인지 알 수 있다.

PRACTICE 15

〈보기〉와 같이 다음 밑줄 친 가정법 문장의 조건절을 if를 생략하여 쓰세요.

> 보 기　　　　If I had known you were so busy, I would not have called on you.
> ➡ _______Had I known you were so busy_______

1　If I were as big as an elephant, I could lift heavy things! ➡ _______________

2　If I were you, I would listen to the people around you.　➡ _______________

3　If I had known him better, I would not have left him.　➡ _______________

4　If she had not been here, I would have been lonely.　➡ _______________

5　If a satellite were destroyed, we would face a lot of serious problems.

　➡ _______________

6　If he had eaten breakfast, he would have done better on his test.

　➡ _______________

7　If you had painted the walls in your room light green, you would have felt more comfortable.

　➡ _______________

8　If you were interested in living at the North Pole, you could come and join us.

　➡ _______________

PRACTICE 16

괄호 안에 들어갈 알맞은 말을 골라 동그라미 하세요.

1　(Were it not for, Had it not been for) water, no one could live.

2　(Were they successful, Had they been successful), they would have been given a present.

3　(Had he been here, Were he here), I would ask for his advice on the matter.

4　(Were there, Had there been) nothing to slow down the car, it would have crashed.

5　(Were they on the Moon, Had they been on the Moon), they would get around by jumping, not walking.

6　(Were it not raining, Had it not been raining), we would have had dinner outside.

7　(Were we in outer space, Had we been in outer space), we would experience zero gravity.

8　(Had the train arrived, Were the train) on time, we would not have been late.

중간·기말고사 대비문제 📝

가정법

1 주어진 동사를 이용하여 빈칸에 알맞은 형태를 쓰세요.

> If the sun ___________ tomorrow, I'll take the children to the park. (shine)

2 다음 중 의미가 서로 같은 문장끼리 연결된 것은?

① The monster in the film looks as if it were real.

= In fact, the monster was not real.

② Mom suggested that I go abroad to study English.

= Mom believed I could go abroad to study English.

③ If I had stayed at the beach, I could have seen that beautiful sunset.

= As I don't stay at the beach, I can't see that beautiful sunset.

④ He makes it seem as if he had written the song.

= In fact, he didn't write the song.

⑤ Were I in your shoes, I would say sorry to him first.

= As I was in your shoes, I didn't say sorry to him first.

3 다음 중 밑줄 친 if의 용법이 나머지 넷과 다른 하나는?

① We'll be happy if you kindly accept our invitation.

② If my dog dies, I will make a grave for it.

③ I still wonder if she really loved her fiancé.

④ If you want to be a pilot, you must have good eyesight.

⑤ You can choose her if you think she's the best.

4 ㉮, ㉯에 들어갈 말로 알맞은 것은?

> If it ___㉮___ , the harvest ___㉯___ good.

	㉮		㉯
①	rained	–	would have been
②	has rained	–	would be
③	had rained	–	would have been
④	rained	–	will be
⑤	had rained	–	will be

5 다음 밑줄 친 부분 중 그 쓰임이 <u>잘못된</u> 것은?

① If she had wanted to, she could have become an actress.

② He would not be what he is if his mother didn't support him when he was young.

③ It is important that he arrive at the meeting on time.

④ If I were you, I would not make such a decision.

⑤ I wish my late mother could be here with me now.

6 빈칸에 들어갈 말로 알맞은 것은?

> If he had not died in the tragic accident, he ___________ 27 years old now.

① will be　　② is　　③ would be

④ was　　⑤ would have been

7 주어진 가정법 문장을 직설법 문장으로 바르게 바꾼 것은?

> If he had been qualified for the job, he could have been recruited.

① As he was qualified for the job, he could be recruited.
② As he had been qualified for the job, he could have been recruited.
③ As he was not qualified for the job, he could not be recruited.
④ As he had not been qualified for the job, he could not be recruited.
⑤ As he is not qualified for the job, he cannot be recruited.

8 〈보기〉에서 어법상 틀린 문장의 개수는?

> 보 기
> ⓐ I'll tell him everything when he will come back here.
> ⓑ I don't know if he helps me move tomorrow.
> ⓒ If she is a goddess, I would be her messenger.
> ⓓ My life would be different now if I had not married her.
> ⓔ It is necessary that he keep his word in any case.

① 1개　② 2개　③ 3개　④ 4개　⑤ 5개

9 다음 문장의 밑줄 친 부분 중 그 쓰임이 <u>잘못된</u> 것은?

> ① If Sujin ② had been at the shopping mall, ③ she ④ could buy the pants ⑤ more cheaply.

10 다음은 Rose가 Tim에게 제안한 내용입니다. 주어진 단어를 사용하여 조건에 맞게 문장을 완성하세요.

> 조 건 │ • 주어진 단어의 형태를 변형해서 사용할 수 있음. 한 칸에 한 단어만 쓸 것.
> • 우리말 해석: Rose는 Tim에게 좋은 연설자가 되기 위해서 천천히 말하는 것을 연습하라고 제안했다.

> slowly, speak, practice

➡ Rose suggested that Tim ___________ ___________ ___________ to be a good speaker.

[11-12] 다음 빈칸에 들어갈 be동사의 형태로 가장 알맞은 것을 고르세요.

11

> If I ___________ 10 years younger, I would invest all the money I have in that project.

① be　　② is　　③ had been
④ are　　⑤ were

12

> He demanded that Ms. Lee ___________ hired as soon as possible.

① be　② is　③ was　④ are　⑤ were

13 주어진 문장과 동일한 의미가 되도록 밑줄 친 부분을 바꿔 쓰세요.

> • Without him, we would lose the game.
> = ___________________________, we would lose the game.

14 다음 가정법 문장을 직설법 문장으로 바르게 바꾼 것은?

> He pretends as if he were not interested in the conversation.

① In fact, he was interested in the conversation.
② In fact, he was not interested in the conversation.
③ In fact, he is interested in the conversation.
④ In fact, he is not interested in the conversation.
⑤ In fact, he had been interested in the conversation.

15 주어진 문장을 가정법 문장으로 바꿀 때 빈칸에 알맞은 말을 쓰세요.

> He didn't join my birthday party due to his busy schedule.

➡ I wish he ___________ ___________ my birthday party in spite of his busy schedule.

16 주어진 문장을 as if를 이용한 가정법 문장이 되도록 문장을 완성하세요.

> In fact, he didn't make the choice by himself.

➡ He sounds ________________________
________________________.

17 다음 우리말과 같은 뜻이 되도록 괄호 안에 주어진 동사를 활용하여 빈칸에 알맞은 말을 쓰세요.

> 만약 그가 여자로 태어났다면, 대단한 미인일 것이다.

➡ If he ___________ ___________ born a woman, he would be a great beauty. (be)

18 짝지은 두 문장의 의미가 같지 <u>않은</u> 2개는?

① I'm very sorry that I can't play the piano well.
= I wish I could play the piano well.
② He can't decide where to go for his summer vacation.
= He can't decide where he should go for his summer vacation.
③ David isn't rich, but he wants to be.
= David wishes he becomes rich.
④ If I studied harder, I could get better grades.
= Because I don't study hard, I couldn't get better grades.
⑤ My uncle gave me this watch last year.
= My uncle gave this watch to me last year.

19 〈보기〉에서 알맞은 말을 골라 빈칸에 쓰세요.

> 보 기   if / what / as if / though / when

> Even if you don't lose all your friends, you may lose some of them ___________ you act ___________ you were the smartest guy in the world.

20 다음 우리말을 영작할 때 빈칸에 적절한 말을 쓰세요. (빈칸 하나에 한 단어만 쓸 것.)

> 네 격려가 없었다면 나는 대회를 그만두었을 것이다.

➡ (A) ___________ your encouragement, I would (B) ___________ ___________ the competition.

21 다음 가정법 문장을 〈조건〉에 맞게 직설법 문장 (실제로 일어난 상황)으로 전환하세요.

> If I had known how to use this machine, I could have baked cookies easily.
>
> ➡ ⓐ ______________________________ ,
> so ⓑ ______________________________ .

> 조 건
> 1. ⓐ는 8단어, ⓑ는 5단어로 쓸 것.
> 2. 문장 전환에 불필요한 단어를 추가할 수 없음.

22 다음 문장의 밑줄 친 부분 중 그 쓰임이 잘못된 것은?

① He suggested that he <u>had met</u> that friend of mine.
② The captain ordered that the flag <u>be</u> raised.
③ They requested that I <u>looked</u> for the missing cat.
④ It is necessary that the law <u>be</u> kept by everybody.
⑤ She insisted that we <u>trust</u> the local people.

23 다음 우리말을 영작하세요.

> • 너의 성원이 없다면, 우리는 이 프로젝트를 진행할 수 없을 것이다. (support / carry out)

(1) Were로 시작

➡ ______________________________

____

(2) But for로 시작

➡ ______________________________

____

24 (A)~(C)에 들어갈 말이 차례대로 알맞게 짝지어진 것은?

> *Amy*: It's a shame that you couldn't watch the movie. If you ____(A)____ to the cinema with me, I would have bought popcorn for you.
> *Lewis*: But my mom ordered that I ____(B)____ my homework after school. So I had no choice.
> *Amy*: I wish we ____(C)____ the movie together. The movie was so great.

	(A)	(B)	(C)
①	had gone	finish	watched
②	went	finish	watched
③	had gone	finish	had watched
④	went	finished	had watched
⑤	had gone	finished	watch

25 다음 우리말을 영어로 옮긴 것 중 옳은 것을 2개 고르면?

> 용의자는 그에게 변호사가 선임되어야 한다고 주장했다.

① The suspect insisted that he is given a lawyer.
② The suspect insisted that he be given a lawyer.
③ The suspect insisted he has been given a lawyer.
④ The suspect insisted he should be given a lawyer.
⑤ The suspect insisted that he would be given a lawyer.

CHAPTER 13
비교구문

PSS 1 비교급과 최상급 만드는 법	페이지	성취도				
		100%	99~75%	74~50%	49~25%	24~0%
PSS 1-1 규칙 변화 I	276					
PSS 1-2 규칙 변화 II	277					
PSS 1-3 규칙 변화 III	278					
PSS 1-4 불규칙 변화	282					

PSS 2 원급을 이용한 비교	페이지	성취도				
		100%	99~75%	74~50%	49~25%	24~0%
PSS 2-1 as+원급+as	283					
PSS 2-2 as+원급+as+주어+can[could]	286					

PSS 3 비교급을 이용한 비교	페이지	성취도				
		100%	99~75%	74~50%	49~25%	24~0%
PSS 3-1 비교급+than I	288					
PSS 3-2 비교급+than II	289					
PSS 3-3 비교급 강조	291					
PSS 3-4 less+원급+than	292					
PSS 3-5 the+비교급, the+비교급	293					
PSS 3-6 비교급+and+비교급	294					

PSS 4 최상급을 이용한 비교	페이지	성취도				
		100%	99~75%	74~50%	49~25%	24~0%
PSS 4-1 the+최상급	295					
PSS 4-2 one of+the+최상급+복수 명사	296					
PSS 4-3 There is nothing ~ 비교급+than …	297					
PSS 4-4 최상급의 다른 표현	299					
중간·기말고사 대비문제	301					

PSS 1 비교급과 최상급 만드는 법

PSS 1 - 1 규칙 변화 I

일반적인 경우	원급+er, est	high – high**er** – high**est** deep – deep**er** – deep**est** great – great**er** – great**est** cheap – cheap**er** – cheap**est** fast – fast**er** – fast**est** small – small**er** – small**est**
-e로 끝나는 경우	원급+r, st	large – larger – largest strange – stranger – strangest close – closer – closest nice – nicer – nicest

정답 p.66

PRACTICE 1

다음 형용사나 부사의 비교급과 최상급을 쓰세요.

1 small – _________ – _________
2 weak – _________ – _________
3 nice – _________ – _________
4 deep – _________ – _________
5 cheap – _________ – _________
6 dark – _________ – _________
7 fast – _________ – _________
8 wide – _________ – _________
9 cute – _________ – _________
10 safe – _________ – _________
11 low – _________ – _________
12 huge – _________ – _________
13 large – _________ – _________
14 short – _________ – _________
15 great – _________ – _________
16 high – _________ – _________
17 cold – _________ – _________
18 close – _________ – _________
19 sweet – _________ – _________
20 warm – _________ – _________
21 kind – _________ – _________
22 rude – _________ – _________
23 tall – _________ – _________
24 loud – _________ – _________
25 strange – _________ – _________
26 cool – _________ – _________

27 soft	– _______ – _______	28 long	– _______ – _______
29 thick	– _______ – _______	30 smart	– _______ – _______

PSS 1-2 규칙 변화 Ⅱ

자음+y로 끝나는 경우	자음+i+er, est	easy – eas**ier** – eas**iest** pretty – prett**ier** – prett**iest** lazy – laz**ier** – laz**iest** funny – funn**ier** – funn**iest** dirty – dirt**ier** – dirt**iest** lucky – luck**ier** – luck**iest**
단모음+단자음으로 끝나는 경우	원급+마지막 자음+er, est	hot – hot**ter** – hot**test** big – big**ger** – big**gest** thin – thin**ner** – thin**nest**

정답 p.66

PRACTICE 2 [1-30]

다음 형용사나 부사의 비교급과 최상급을 쓰세요.

1 heavy	– _______ – _______	2 funny	– _______ – _______
3 big	– _______ – _______	4 curly	– _______ – _______
5 happy	– _______ – _______	6 hot	– _______ – _______
7 hungry	– _______ – _______	8 strict	– _______ – _______
9 healthy	– _______ – _______	10 flat	– _______ – _______
11 easy	– _______ – _______	12 new	– _______ – _______
13 thin	– _______ – _______	14 tasty	– _______ – _______
15 fresh	– _______ – _______	16 pretty	– _______ – _______
17 fat	– _______ – _______	18 dry	– _______ – _______
19 hard	– _______ – _______	20 lucky	– _______ – _______
21 brave	– _______ – _______	22 poor	– _______ – _______
23 noisy	– _______ – _______	24 early	– _______ – _______

25 lazy	– _____ – _____	26 ugly	– _____ – _____
27 sunny	– _____ – _____	28 dirty	– _____ – _____
29 crazy	– _____ – _____	30 light	– _____ – _____

PSS 1-3 규칙 변화 Ⅲ

-y, -er, -ow로 끝나는 형용사를 제외한 대부분의 2음절 이상의 형용사	more+원급, most+원급	formal – **more** formal – **most** formal curious – **more** curious – **most** curious similar – **more** similar – **most** similar difficult – **more** difficult – **most** difficult
분사 형태의 형용사	more+원급, most+원급	boring – **more** boring – **most** boring shocked – **more** shocked – **most** shocked pleasing – **more** pleasing – **most** pleasing tired – **more** tired – **most** tired
'형용사+ly' 형태의 부사	more+원급, most+원급	easily – **more** easily – **most** easily quickly – **more** quickly – **most** quickly slowly – **more** slowly – **most** slowly fluently – **more** fluently – **most** fluently

정답 p.66

PRACTICE 3 [1-90]

다음 형용사나 부사의 비교급과 최상급을 쓰세요.

1 mean – _____ – _____

2 easily – _____ – _____

3 bright – _____ – _____

4 slim – _____ – _____

5 shocked – _____ – _____

6 effective – _____ – _____

7 friendly – _____ – _____

8 famous – _____________ – _____________

9 curious – _____________ – _____________

10 logical – _____________ – _____________

11 quickly – _____________ – _____________

12 surprised – _____________ – _____________

13 pleasing – _____________ – _____________

14 quiet – _____________ – _____________

15 formal – _____________ – _____________

16 dull – _____________ – _____________

17 nervous – _____________ – _____________

18 slowly – _____________ – _____________

19 difficult – _____________ – _____________

20 creative – _____________ – _____________

21 fluently – _____________ – _____________

22 comfortable – _____________ – _____________

23 complicated – _____________ – _____________

24 similar – _____________ – _____________

25 rich – _____________ – _____________

26 diligent – _____________ – _____________

27 boring – _____________ – _____________

28 exactly – _____________ – _____________

29 tired – _____________ – _____________

30 artistic – _____________ – _____________

31 practical – _____________ – _____________

32 scary – _____________ – _____________

33 upset – _____________ – _____________

34 enjoyable – _____________ – _____________

35 lovely – _____________ – _____________

36 wonderful – _____________ – _____________

37 delicious – _____________ – _____________

38 depressed – __________ – __________

39 intelligent – __________ – __________

40 powerful – __________ – __________

41 familiar – __________ – __________

42 convenient – __________ – __________

43 useless – __________ – __________

44 skillful – __________ – __________

45 generous – __________ – __________

46 impressive – __________ – __________

47 foolish – __________ – __________

48 insistent – __________ – __________

49 dangerous – __________ – __________

50 nutritious – __________ – __________

51 serious – __________ – __________

52 peaceful – __________ – __________

53 colorful – __________ – __________

54 ambitious – __________ – __________

55 negative – __________ – __________

56 amazing – __________ – __________

57 natural – __________ – __________

58 valuable – __________ – __________

59 awkward – __________ – __________

60 urgent – __________ – __________

61 often – __________ – __________

62 sensitive – __________ – __________

63 common – __________ – __________

64 challenging – __________ – __________

65 abstract – __________ – __________

66 active – __________ – __________

67 mild – __________ – __________

68 helpful – _______________ – _______________

69 attractive – _______________ – _______________

70 awesome – _______________ – _______________

71 cheerful – _______________ – _______________

72 severe – _______________ – _______________

73 busy – _______________ – _______________

74 polite – _______________ – _______________

75 beautiful – _______________ – _______________

76 important – _______________ – _______________

77 harmful – _______________ – _______________

78 useful – _______________ – _______________

79 patient – _______________ – _______________

80 glad – _______________ – _______________

81 tough – _______________ – _______________

82 fantastic – _______________ – _______________

83 angry – _______________ – _______________

84 crowded – _______________ – _______________

85 recent – _______________ – _______________

86 hopeless – _______________ – _______________

87 loudly – _______________ – _______________

88 positive – _______________ – _______________

89 selfish – _______________ – _______________

90 embarrassed – _______________ – _______________

good – better – best 좋은	I'm going to set a goal to get **better** grades this time. 나는 이번에 더 좋은 점수를 얻기 위해 목표를 세울 것이다.
well – better – best 건강한, 잘	It's he who knows himself **best**. 그 자신을 가장 잘 아는 사람은 그다.
bad – worse – worst 나쁜	That was the **worst** thing that happened in my life. 그것은 내 인생에서 일어난 가장 나쁜 일이었다.
ill – worse – worst 병든, 건강이 나쁜	You'll feel **worse** unless you take your medicine. 너는 약을 먹지 않으면 몸 상태가 더 나빠질 것이다.
old – older – oldest 늙은, 오래된, 손위의	It was the **oldest** royal palace in Japan. 그것은 일본에서 가장 오래된 고궁이었다.
old – elder – eldest 손위의	I wanted to have an **elder** brother when I was young. 나는 어렸을 때 형이 있었으면 했다.
late – later – latest 〈시간〉 늦은	I wonder if there is a **later** train than this one. 나는 이것보다 더 늦은 기차가 있는지 궁금하다.
late – latter – last 〈순서〉 늦은	The horse came **last** in the race. 그 말은 경주에서 마지막으로 들어왔다.
far – farther – farthest 〈거리〉 먼	A bird that flies higher can see **farthest**. 더 높이 나는 새가 가장 멀리 본다.
far – further – furthest 〈정도〉 더욱, 한층	We must look **further** into the reasons for the failure. 우리는 실패의 원인에 대해 더 깊이 살펴봐야 한다. *cf.* '〈거리〉 먼'이라는 뜻도 있음
many – more – most 〈수〉 많은	I'll give a prize to someone who picks up the **most** leaves. 가장 많은 나뭇잎을 줍는 사람에게 상을 줄 것이다.
much – more – most 〈양〉 많은	We need to search for some **more** information. 우리는 더 많은 정보를 찾을 필요가 있다.
few – fewer – fewest 〈수〉 적은	I was surprised that **fewer** people showed up at the party. 나는 더 적은 사람들이 파티에 나타났다는 것에 놀랐다.
little – less – least 〈양〉 적은	What kind of food do you like **least**? 넌 어떤 종류의 음식을 가장 덜 좋아하니?

PRACTICE 4

괄호 안의 단어를 변형시켜 빈칸에 알맞은 말을 써 넣으세요.

1 We need some _________________ resources for teaching children Chinese. (many)

2 Sally speaks Japanese _______________ than Sam because she has a Japanese friend. (well)

3 As the population increases, the energy situation is getting _______________. (bad)

4 The reporter announced the _______________ news. (late)

5 I know the easiest way to do it in the _______________ amount of time. (little)

6 The library is the _______________ place for you to do your homework because it is quiet. (good)

7 I have one _______________ sister and one younger brother. (old)

8 He is widely known as the _______________ survivor of the shipwreck. (late)

9 The baby was born in bad condition, and his condition was getting _______________. (ill)

10 If you get _______________ education, you can have more chances to get a good job. (far)

11 In the future, people will work _______________ hours a day because of advanced technology. (few)

12 Cheomseongdae is known as the _______________ astronomical observatory in Asia. (old)

13 This website gives _______________ information about cooking. (much)

14 Jason lived the _______________ away from school of all of us. (far)

CH 13 비교구문

PSS 2 원급을 이용한 비교

PROBLEM SOLVING SKILL

PSS 2-1 as + 원급 + as

1. 「as+원급+as」 '~만큼 …한'

Kevin is **as heavy as** Chulsoo.
Kevin은 철수만큼 무겁다.

She speaks Chinese **as fluently as I do**.
그녀는 나만큼 중국어를 유창하게 말한다.
= She speaks Chinese **as fluently as me**.

cf. as나 than 뒤의 「주어+동사」는 목적격으로 바꾸어 쓸 수 있다.

2. 「not as[so]+원급+as」 '~만큼 …하지 않은'

Mrs. Smith is **not as[so] old as** Mrs. Jones.

Smith 부인은 Jones 부인만큼 나이가 많지 않다.

= Mrs. Jones is **older than** Mrs. Smith is.

Jones 부인은 Smith 부인보다 나이가 많다.

His first novel was **not as[so] popular as** the second one.

그의 첫 번째 소설은 두 번째 것만큼 인기 있지 않았다.

= His second novel was **more popular than** the first one.

그의 두 번째 소설은 첫 번째 것보다 더 인기 있었다.

3. 배수 표현+as+원급+as '~보다 …배 —한'

I have only **half as many books as** Minho does.

나는 민호가 가진 책의 절반밖에 가지고 있지 않다.

She earns **three times as much as** he does.

그녀는 그가 버는 것의 세 배를 번다.

His house is **four times as big as** our house.

그의 집은 우리 집보다 네 배 더 크다.

정답 p.68

PRACTICE 5

괄호 안의 단어와 as ~ as를 이용하여 빈칸을 채우세요.

1 Sujin gets up at 6:00. Minsu gets up at 6:00, too.

➡ Minsu gets up ______as early as______ Sujin. (early)

2 James studies 5 hours a day. David studies 1 hour a day.

➡ James studies ___________________ David. (long)

3 Tom goes jogging 5 days a week. Jordan goes jogging 5 days a week, too.

➡ Jordan goes jogging ___________________ Tom. (often)

4 That stick is 150 cm. This stick is 75 cm.

➡ This stick is ___________________ that stick. (half, long)

5 Mina is 170 cm. Yujin is 170 cm, too.

➡ Yujin is ___________________ Mina. (tall)

6 Yesterday was −15℃. Today is −15℃, too.

➡ Today is ___________________ yesterday. (cold)

7 My classroom has six windows. Hojung's classroom has six windows, too.

➡ My classroom has ___________________ Hojung's. (many)

8 John weighs 60 kg. His little sister weighs 20 kg.

➡ John is _________________________________ his little sister. (heavy)

9 That dress costs 1,000 dollars. This dress costs 100 dollars.

➡ That dress costs _____________________ this dress. (much)

10 I paid 400,000 won for my cell phone. Sam paid 100,000 won for his cell phone.

➡ My cell phone is _____________________________ Sam's. (expensive)

정답 p.68

PRACTICE 6

짝지어진 두 문장의 의미가 같도록 not as[so] ~ as를 이용하여 빈칸을 채우세요. (단, 축약이 가능할 경우, 축약형으로 쓸 것.)

1 Mary is richer than Jerry.

= Jerry __________ *isn't as[so] rich as* __________ Mary.

2 This sofa is more comfortable than that sofa.

= That sofa __________________________________ this sofa.

3 Minsu can read faster than Chulsu.

= Chulsu __________________________________ Minsu.

4 Minji writes English essays better than Jiho.

= Jiho __________________________________ Minji.

5 Sally's hair is longer than Sumi's.

= Sumi's hair __________________________________ Sally's.

6 My pig is fatter than your pig.

= Your pig __________________________________ my pig.

7 This street is more crowded than that street.

= That street __________________________________ this street.

8 Jungho speaks French more fluently than I do.

= I __________________________________ Jungho does.

9 I know about their history more than you.

= You __________________________________ I do.

10 The air in this city is more polluted than the air in that city.

= The air in that city __________________________________ the air in this city.

11 This map is more complicated than the other one.

= The other map __________________________________ this one.

12 My salary is higher than Bill's salary.

= Bill's salary __________________________________ my salary.

「as+원급+as+주어+can[could]」 = 「as+원급+as possible」 '~가 할 수 있는 한 …하게'

You'd better come back home **as early as you can**.
너는 할 수 있는 한 일찍 집에 돌아오는 게 낫겠다.
= You'd better come back home **as early as possible**.

Tell me about your plan **as specifically as you can**.
할 수 있는 한 자세하게 네 계획에 대해 말해 줘.
= Tell me about your plan **as specifically as possible**.

cf. 「as+원급+as can[could] be」 '더없이 ~한'
The winner looks **as happy as can be**. 그 승자는 더없이 행복해 보인다.
I ran to the doctor **as quickly as could be**. 나는 더없이 빨리 의사에게 달려갔다.

정답 p.68

PRACTICE 7

〈보기〉와 같이 괄호 안의 단어를 이용하여 as ~ as 문장을 완성하세요.

보 기	Try to be ___as brief as possible___ when you make a phone call. (brief)
	= Try to be ___as brief as you can___ when you make a phone call.

1 The policeman ran after the thief ________________________. (fast)
   = The policeman ran after the thief ________________________.

2 I tried to make the noodle soup ________________________. (spicy)
   = I tried to make the noodle soup ________________________.

3 We have to save energy ________________________. (much)
   = We have to save energy ________________________.

4 She tried to hide her wrinkles to look ________________________. (young)
   = She tried to hide her wrinkles to look ________________________.

5 I visit my grandparents ________________________ because they feel lonely. (often)
   = I visit my grandparents ________________________ because they feel lonely.

6 She is studying Spanish ________________________ to get a good grade. (hard)
   = She is studying Spanish ________________________ to get a good grade.

7 He tried to get home ________________________________ to watch the football game. (early)

   = He tried to get home ________________________________ to watch the football game.

8 The teacher made the quiz ________________________ to encourage her students. (easy)

   = The teacher made the quiz ________________________ to encourage her students.

정답 p.68

PRACTICE 8

괄호 안에 주어진 말을 바르게 배열하여 문장을 완성하세요.

1 The artist tried to make the painting look ________________________________.

(as, as, possible, real)

2 The kids giggled and played in the playground, ________________________________.

(as, enjoying, could, long, they, their, as, free time)

3 The doctor advised him to ________________________________.

(possible, as, as, hard, exercise)

4 Those volunteers vowed to ________________________________.

(as, other people, possible, much, as, help)

5 The girl ________________________________ to watch the TV program.

(as, she, her homework, could, fast, finished, as)

6 He ________________________________ because he wants to be a good father.

(with, his children, often, he, can, as, talks, as)

7 I didn't want to wake up my parents, so I ________________________________.

(as, came in, possible, quietly, as)

8 You should ________________________________ to be a good writer.

(as, write down, many things, as, possible)

9 I ________________________________ to get people's attention.

(as, I, could, spoke, loudly, as)

10 I ________________________________ so that I won't be late for the concert.

(as, will, finish, my work, soon, can, as, I)

PSS 3 비교급을 이용한 비교

PSS 3-1 비교급 + than Ⅰ

Namsu: I think I spent too much money on my
shoes. They are almost 100,000 won.

Jiyeon : My shoes are only 30,000 won. They
were on sale.

「비교급+than」 '~보다 더 …한'

Namsu spent **more** money **than** **Jiyeon did** at the department store.

남수는 백화점에서 지연이보다 더 많은 돈을 썼다.

= Namsu spent **more** money **than** **Jiyeon** at the department store.

Jinoo is **kinder than** he was the last time I saw him.

진우는 지난 번에 내가 그를 봤을 때보다 더 친절하다.

정답 p.69

PRACTICE 9

주어진 문장을 「비교급+than」을 이용한 문장으로 바꾸세요.

1 The final exam was not as difficult as the midterm exam.
   ➡ The midterm exam was ________________________ the final exam.

2 The cat was not as big as the dog when they were young.
   ➡ The dog was ________________________ the cat when they were young.

3 The singer was not as popular as her husband a year ago.
   ➡ The singer's husband was ________________________ the singer a year ago.

4 Mike was not as smart as Jane when they were in first grade.
   ➡ Jane was ________________________ Mike when they were in first grade.

5 Her new novel is not as boring as her previous one.
   ➡ Her previous novel is ________________________ her new one.

6 Her recent ballet performance was not as amazing as the last one.
   ➡ Her last ballet performance was ________________________ the recent one.

7 Jane doesn't need this necklace as much as Susan.

➡ Susan needs this necklace ________________________ Jane.

8 Mr. Kim's speech was not as impressive as Ms. Park's.

➡ Ms. Park's speech was ________________________ Mr. Kim's.

9 Kelly is not as nervous as Sam about their first concert.

➡ Sam is ________________________ Kelly about their first concert.

10 Paper dictionaries are not as convenient as online dictionaries.

➡ Online dictionaries are ________________________ paper dictionaries.

11 His answer is not as logical as her answer.

➡ Her answer is ________________________ his answer.

12 This painting doesn't seem as beautiful as that painting to me.

➡ That painting seems ________________________ this painting to me.

PSS 3-2 비교급 + than Ⅱ

1. 비교의 대상이 같은 종류이면 소유대명사로 나타낼 수 있다.

My dog is quieter than **your dog**. 나의 개가 너의 개보다 더 조용하다.

= My dog is quieter than **yours**.

Mark's explanation was more confusing than **Jenny's explanation**.

Mark의 설명이 Jenny의 설명보다 더 혼란스러웠다.

= Mark's explanation was more confusing than **Jenny's**.

2. 비교급 문장에서 than 뒤에 나오는 명사가 앞에 있는 명사와 같은 경우 단수명사는 'that', 복수명사는 "those'로 대신한다. (내신빈출문법사항)

The area of Texas is larger than **that** of California.

텍사스의 면적은 캘리포니아의 그것보다 더 넓다.

3. 비교의 대상이 명확할 때는 than이 이끄는 구나 절을 생략할 수 있다.

I meant to bring you to a **more** interesting place. 나는 너를 더 재미있는 장소로 데려가려고 했었다.

= I meant to bring you to a **more** interesting place **than here**.

The teacher's voice is getting **louder**. 선생님의 목소리는 점점 더 커지고 있다.

= The teacher's voice is getting **louder than before**.

정답 p.69

PRACTICE 10 [1-10]

짝지어진 두 문장의 의미가 같도록 빈칸에 알맞은 말을 쓰세요.

1 Your report was more useful than Mihyun's report.

➡ Your report was more useful than ________________.

2 I concentrated on the quiz more than Hojung.

➡ I concentrated on the quiz more than ________________ ________________.

3 Your story sounds more real than Jihoon's story.

➡ Your story sounds more real than ________________.

4 Jane takes better care of her sister than Kim.

➡ Jane takes better care of her sister than ________________ ________________.

5 He got a better score on the math test than me.

➡ He got a better score on the math test than ________________ ________________.

6 This diamond's quality is better than that diamond's quality.

➡ This diamond's quality is better than that ________________.

7 She bakes better chocolate chip cookies than him.

➡ She bakes better chocolate chip cookies than ________________ ________________.

8 This doll's dress is more colorful than that doll's dress.

➡ This doll's dress is more colorful than that ________________.

9 Jenny usually drives faster than Heeyoung.

➡ Jenny usually drives faster than ________________ ________________.

10 Charlie's IQ is higher than Mike's IQ.

➡ Charlie's IQ is higher than ________________.

정답 p.69

PRACTICE 11

빈칸에 알맞은 단어를 that과 those 중에서 골라 쓰세요.

1 The questions on this test are easier than ________________ on the last test.

2 Are the animals in the zoo safer than ________________ in the wild?

3 It was a clearer presentation than ________________ of our team.

4 The opportunities you'll find abroad are broader than ________________ available here.

5 The atmosphere of Venus is thicker than ________________ of Earth.

6 It is true that the speed of light is much faster than ________________ of sound.

7 The stars in the countryside are far brighter than ________________ in the city.

8 Do you think the design of this phone is better than ________________ of the old one?

9 Compared with ________________ of the tiger, the roar of a lion is deeper and louder.

10 The theories of Einstein were more revolutionary than ________________ of his contemporaries.

다음은 비교급 앞에서 '훨씬'의 뜻으로 비교급을 강조하는 말이다.

> **much, still, even, far, a lot**

I felt **much** **more nervous** than I had imagined. 나는 내가 상상했던 것보다 훨씬 더 떨렸다.

This is **still** **more expensive** than the one that I bought him.

이것은 내가 그에게 사 준 것보다 훨씬 더 비싸다.

Finding a job was **even** **more difficult** than I had thought.

일자리를 구하는 것은 내가 생각했던 것보다 훨씬 더 어려웠다.

The adult was wounded **far** **more severely** than the child.

어린이보다 어른이 훨씬 더 심하게 다쳤다.

It's **a lot** **cheaper** to send the package by ship. 그 소포를 배로 보내는 것이 훨씬 더 싸다.

cf. very는 '매우'의 뜻으로 원급을 강조한다.

I felt **very** **relaxed** when I went into the room.

나는 그 방에 들어갔을 때 매우 편안함을 느꼈다.

A couple of kites were flying **very** **high** in the sky.

두세 개의 연이 하늘에서 매우 높이 날고 있었다.

cf. 비교급 뒤에 복수명사가 오면 much more가 아니라 many more를 씀에 유의한다.

I had **many more** **peaches** than Jenny. 나는 Jenny보다 훨씬 더 많은 복숭아를 가지고 있었다.

정답 p.69

PRACTICE 12

주어진 철자로 시작하는 비교급 강조 표현을 빈칸에 써 넣으세요.

1 His English was m _________ harder for me to understand.

2 My new sofa is f _________ more comfortable than the old one.

3 Christine is a _________ more skillful in fixing cars than Harry.

4 This sports magazine is e _________ more recent than that one.

5 This period was s _________ more peaceful than now.

6 His handwriting is f _________ more difficult for us to read.

7 My brother is e _________ braver than I was at his age.

8 This bread is m _________ more nutritious than those cupcakes.

9 I feel s _________ more tired than before when I get home from work.

10 The distance from my apartment to the supermarket was a _________ farther than you imagine.

PRACTICE 13

괄호 안에 들어갈 알맞은 말을 골라 동그라미 하세요.

1 The museum that we visited in Singapore was (a lot, very) more interesting than we had imagined.

2 The twins are (much, very) similar. Even their parents sometimes can't distinguish them.

3 The current issue is (far, very) more sensitive than many people think.

4 The situation is (much, very) urgent. We need to call an ambulance right away.

5 The adventure was (a lot, very) more challenging than we had thought.

6 Sophia is (even, very) friendlier to the newcomer than anyone else in the class.

7 He was (much, very) upset about his son's mistakes in the speaking contest.

8 I could solve these questions (far, very) more easily than before because I practiced a lot.

PSS 3-4 less + 원급 + than

It's nice to get some fresh air.
약간의 신선한 공기를 마시니 좋다.

The air here is not very good.
여기 공기는 매우 좋지 않다.

「less+원급+than」 '~보다 덜 …한'

The air in the country was **less polluted than** the air in the city.
시골의 공기가 도시의 공기보다 덜 오염되었다.

= The air in the country **wasn't as[so] polluted as** the air in the city.

> *cf.* 「less+원급+than」은 「not as[so]+원급+as」로 바꾸어 쓸 수 있는데, 「less+원급+than」 보다
> 는 「not+as[so]+원급+as」가 더 자주 쓰인다.
> The theater was **less crowded than** usual. 극장은 평소보다 덜 붐볐다.
> = The theater **wasn't as[so] crowded as** usual.

PRACTICE 14

주어진 문장을 less ~ than을 이용한 문장으로 바꾸어 쓰세요.

1 I don't help my mom clean the house as often as my sister does.

= *I help my mom clean the house less often than my sister does.*

2 The second series of the drama was not as mysterious as the first series.

= ____

3 Your English essay was not as impressive as your Korean essay.

= ____

4 He didn't react as sensitively to the matter as his wife did.

= ____

5 Sujin doesn't write a poem as creatively as other students in class.

= ____

6 The law wasn't put into practice as effectively as we had expected.

= ____

7 Karen doesn't speak Chinese and Japanese as fluently as Joey does.

= ____

8 Hiking is not as attractive as playing online games to me.

= ____

9 His new work is not as creative as his previous work.

= ____

10 My elder brother does not run as quickly as my father used to.

= ____

CH
13
비교구문

PSS 3-5 the + 비교급, the + 비교급

「the+비교급, the+비교급」 '~하면 할수록 더 …한'

The worse the weather is, **the more depressed** I feel.

날씨가 나쁘면 나쁠수록 나는 더 우울해진다.

The more I get to know the girl, **the more** I get to like her.

그 소녀를 알면 알수록 나는 그녀를 더 좋아하게 된다.

The longer you stay here, **the closer** you will get to each other.

너희들이 여기에 오래 머물면 머물수록 서로 더 친해질 것이다.

PRACTICE 15

〈보기〉와 같이 「the+비교급, the+비교급」을 이용하여 주어진 문장을 바꾸어 쓰세요.

> 보 기　　If you practice it harder, you'll get it sooner.
> ➡ The harder you practice it, the sooner you'll get it.

1 As the weather gets hotter, people have more cold drinks.

➡ ____

2 If you know the rules of the game better, you'll enjoy it more.

➡ ____

3 When you try to forget something harder, you remember it more clearly.

➡ ____

4 As our society becomes larger, crime occurs more.

➡ ____

5 When your energy level is higher, your body works more efficiently.

➡ ____

6 If the price becomes cheaper, the demand will be greater.

➡ ____

7 If you buy the plane ticket earlier, you can get a bigger discount.

➡ ____

8 As you expose your skin to the sun longer, you have higher chances to get a sunburn.

➡ ____

PSS 3-6 비교급 + and + 비교급

「비교급+and+비교급」 '점점 더 ~한'

The weather is getting **warmer and warmer**. 날씨가 점점 더 따뜻해지고 있다.

She started to eat **less and less** to lose weight.
그녀는 살을 빼기 위해 점점 더 적게 먹기 시작했다.

His health condition became **worse and worse**. 그의 건강 상태는 점점 더 악화되었다.

The audience felt **more and more confused** during his speech.
청중들은 그의 연설 중에 점점 더 혼란스러움을 느꼈다.

PRACTICE 16

〈보기〉에서 알맞은 단어를 골라 「비교급+and+비교급」의 형태로 바꾸어 문장을 완성하세요.

보 기	strong little colorful fast tired interesting loud fluently generous dark

1 She began to walk ________________________ after she saw the dog.

2 Her voice was getting ________________________ as he turned up the volume.

3 As the movie is drawing to a close, it becomes ________________________ .

4 As he walked a long distance, he grew ________________________ .

5 Jerry is getting ________________________ as he grows up.

6 As the sky was getting ________________________ , we hurried back to the camp.

7 He had to eat ________________________ to look thinner in the audition.

8 As he got older, he became ________________________ to his children.

9 The flowers became ________________________ as time went by.

10 She spoke Spanish ________________________ after she made many Spanish friends.

PSS 4 최상급을 이용한 비교

PSS 4-1 the + 최상급

「the+최상급」 '가장 ~한' – 최상급 뒤에는 비교의 대상을 한정하는 in이나 of가 이끄는 전치사구 또는 절이 나올 수 있다.

the+최상급	+	in+장소나 집단을 나타내는 단수 명사
		of+복수 명사 또는 복수의 의미를 나타내는 명사
		절

The most important thing to me now is to study. 내게 지금 가장 중요한 것은 공부하는 것이다.
Nancy is **the smartest** girl **in my class**. Nancy는 나의 반에서 가장 똑똑한 소녀이다.
This painting is **the most abstract** of all. 이 그림이 모든 그림 중 가장 추상적이다.
This is **the thickest** book **I have ever seen**. 이것은 내가 본 것 중 가장 두꺼운 책이다.

PRACTICE 17

괄호 안의 단어를 비교급 또는 최상급의 형태로 바꾸어 빈칸에 쓰세요.

1 That is _________________ story I've ever read. (strange)

2 The performance was _________________ than I heard from my friends. (funny)

3 We could overcome those difficult problems _________________ than we thought. (easily)

4 His theory has _________________ concept of all the theories. (familiar)

5 Minho is _________________ boy in our class. (diligent)

6 This fishing rod is _________________ one I've ever had. (convenient)

7 August of this year was _________________ than that of last year. (hot)

8 This necklace is _________________ one of all the jewelry. (valuable)

9 Christine's family is _________________ family I've ever met. (wealthy)

10 Jake got _________________ votes in the school election. (many)

11 Suyeon looked _________________ than the other players at the competition. (nervous)

12 His method is _________________ one I've ever heard. (practical)

13 Our team could get to the destination _________________ than we had planned. (early)

14 The director's movie was _________________ than the previous one. (fantastic)

15 A human being is considered to be _________________ creature of all on earth.
(intelligent)

PSS 4-2 one of + the + 최상급 + 복수 명사

「one of+the+최상급+복수 명사」 '가장 ~한 것 중의 하나'라고 해석하고, 주어 자리에 올 경우 단수 취급함에 유의한다.

One of the worst experiences during my travels **was** being pickpocketed in a foreign country. 나의 여행 중의 가장 나쁜 경험들 중의 하나는 외국에서 소매치기를 당한 것이었다.

One of the most common natural disasters is an earthquake.

가장 흔한 자연 재해 중 하나는 지진이다.

Susan is **one of the politest students** in the school.

Susan은 학교에서 가장 예의 바른 학생들 중 한 명이다.

My uncle is **one of the most famous movie directors** in Korea.

나의 삼촌은 한국에서 가장 유명한 영화 감독들 중 한 명이다.

PRACTICE 18

괄호 안에 주어진 단어 중 알맞은 것을 고르세요.

1 One of the most dangerous (animal, animals) in the world is the polar bear.

2 Scuba diving is one of the (good, best) experiences I've ever had.

3 Vincent van Gogh was one of the most influential (artist, artists) of the 19th century.

4 One of the most delicious desserts I had ever tried (was, were) French apple tart.

5 One of the most popular tourist attractions (in, of) Korea is the N Seoul Tower.

6 One of the most famous landmarks in the world (is, are) the Eiffel Tower in Paris.

7 One of the largest palaces in India (is, are) the Taj Mahal.

8 One of (the more important, the most important) leadership skills is the ability to motivate and inspire others.

9 One of the busiest (intersection, intersections) in the city is undergoing a major renovation.

10 *The Great Gatsby* is one of (most impressive novels, the most impressive novels) I've ever read.

CH
13
비교구문

PSS 4-3 There is nothing ~ 비교급 + than …

「There is nothing ~ 비교급+than …」은 '…보다 더 ~한 것은 없다'의 뜻으로 최상급의 의미를 나타낸다.

1. 「There is nothing + 비교급 + than …」

There is nothing greater than a challenge in the world.
세상에서 도전보다 더 위대한 것은 없다.
= A challenge is **the greatest** thing in the world. 도전은 세상에서 가장 위대한 것이다.

There is nothing more boring than waiting for somebody on the street.
길에서 누군가를 기다리는 것보다 더 지루한 것은 없다.
= Waiting for somebody on the street is **the most boring** thing to do.
길에서 누군가를 기다리는 것이 하기에 가장 지루한 일이다.

2. 「There is nothing + 주어 + 동사 + 비교급 + than …」

There is nothing I enjoy more than inline skating.

인라인 스케이트를 타는 것보다 내가 더 즐기는 것은 없다.

= I enjoy inline skating **the most**. 나는 인라인 스케이트를 타는 것을 가장 즐긴다.

There is nothing I can do better than swimming.

수영보다 내가 더 잘 할 수 있는 것은 없다.

= I can do swimming **the best**. 나는 수영하는 것을 가장 잘할 수 있다.

정답 p.70

PRACTICE 19

괄호 안의 말을 어법에 맞게 배열하여 문장을 완성하세요.

1 나는 뉴질랜드에서 살고 있는 내 아이들을 가장 걱정한다. (nothing, I, than, worry about, there's, more)

➡ ____ my kids living in New Zealand.

2 자유는 세상에서 가장 소중한 것이다. (than, more, nothing, there is, precious)

➡ ____ freedom in the world.

3 그녀의 최근 소설은 그녀의 모든 작품들 중에서 가장 재미있다. (there is, than, more interesting, nothing)

➡ ____ her recent novel of all her works.

4 나는 크리스마스 선물로 새 스마트폰을 가장 원한다. (there's, want, nothing, I, than, more)

➡ ____ a new smartphone as a Christmas gift.

5 내 인생에서 나의 가족이 가장 중요하다. (than, nothing, more important, there is)

➡ ____ my family in my life.

6 그녀가 가장 잘하는 것은 꽃을 그리는 것이다. (there's, she, nothing, can, better, do, than)

➡ ____ painting flowers.

7 나는 이 식당에서 하와이안 피자를 가장 좋아한다. (than, I, there's, more, like, nothing)

➡ ____ Hawaiian pizza in this restaurant.

8 내 생일에 혼자 있는 것이 가장 최악이다. (there is, than, nothing, worse)

➡ ____ being alone on my birthday.

9 그 옷가게에서 이 드레스가 가장 비싸다. (there is, than, nothing, more expensive)

➡ ____ this dress in the clothing shop.

10 수지는 외국어로서 중국어를 가장 유창하게 말한다. (more fluently, Suji, nothing, than, there's, speaks)

➡ ____ Chinese as a foreign language.

「No (other) ~ as[so]+원급+as」
= 「No (other) ~ 비교급+than」
= 「비교급+than any other+단수 명사」
= 「비교급+than all the other+복수 명사」

Mt. Everest is **the highest mountain** in the world.
에베레스트 산은 세계에서 가장 높은 산이다.

= **No (other) mountain** in the world is **as[so] high as** Mt. Everest.
세계에서 그 어떤 산도 에베레스트 산만큼 높지 않다.

= **No (other) mountain** in the world is **higher than** Mt. Everest.
세계에서 그 어떤 산도 에베레스트 산보다 높지 않다.

= Mt. Everest is **higher than any other mountain** in the world.
에베레스트 산은 세계에서 다른 어떤 산보다 더 높다.

= Mt. Everest is **higher than all the other mountains** in the world.
에베레스트 산은 세계에서 다른 모든 산들보다도 더 높다.

She is **the most attractive actress** in Korea.
그녀는 한국에서 가장 매력적인 여배우이다.

= **No (other) actress** in Korea is **as[so] attractive as** her.
한국에서 그 어떤 여배우도 그녀만큼 매력적이지 않다.

= **No (other) actress** in Korea is **more attractive than** her.
한국에서 그 어떤 여배우도 그녀보다 매력적이지 않다.

= She is **more attractive than any other actress** in Korea.
그녀는 한국에서 다른 어떤 여배우보다 더 매력적이다.

= She is **more attractive than all the other actresses** in Korea.
그녀는 한국에서 다른 모든 여배우들보다 더 매력적이다.

CH
13
비교구문

정답 p.70

PRACTICE 20 [1-6]

다음 문장들이 같은 뜻이 되도록 빈칸에 알맞은 말을 쓰세요.

1 This was the cheapest necklace in the shop.

= ___No (other) necklace___ in the shop was ___as[so] cheap as___ this necklace.

= ___No (other) necklace___ in the shop was ___cheaper than___ this necklace.

= This was ___cheaper than any other necklace___ in the shop.

= This was ___cheaper than all the other necklaces___ in the shop.

2 Lake Baikal is the deepest lake in the world.

= ________________________ in the world is ________________________ Lake Baikal.

= ________________________ in the world is ________________________ Lake Baikal.

= Lake Baikal is ____ in the world.

= Lake Baikal is ____ in the world.

3 This is the oldest dinosaur fossil up to now.

= ________________________ up to now is ________________________ this.

= ________________________ up to now is ________________________ this.

= This is ____ up to now.

= This is ____ up to now.

4 Mr. Kang is the luckiest person in the world.

= ________________________ in the world is ________________________ Mr. Kang.

= ________________________ in the world is ________________________ Mr. Kang.

= Mr. Kang is ____ in the world.

= Mr. Kang is ____ in the world.

5 Cathy is the most artistic student in my class.

= ________________________ in my class is ________________________ Cathy.

= ________________________ in my class is ________________________ Cathy.

= Cathy is ____ in my class.

= Cathy is ____ in my class.

6 That is the strictest policy in my company.

= ________________________ in my company is ________________________ that.

= ________________________ in my company is ________________________ that.

= That is ____ in my company.

= That is ____ in my company.

중간·기말고사 대비문제

1 다음 중 어법상 옳은 것은?

① Jiwon can't run as fastly as Yuna.
② I just want something more simpler.
③ The weather is very bad than yesterday.
④ I wish I could speak French as fluent as I speak Korean.
⑤ He doesn't read as many books as his classmates.

2 Which is proper for the blank?

> If you eat __________ calories than you use, you will lose weight by using the stored calories.

① little　　② less　　③ few
④ fewer　　⑤ least

3 Which is NOT proper for the blank in the following sentence?

> On the contrary, producers want __________ higher prices for their goods.

① very　　② still　　③ far
④ even　　⑤ much

4 다음 문장과 같은 뜻이 되도록 빈칸에 들어갈 알맞은 말을 쓰세요.

> I decided to make the computer graphics seem as real as I could.
> = I decided to make the computer graphics seem __________ __________.
> __________ __________.

5 주어진 문장의 밑줄 친 much와 의미가 같은 것은?

> Then they will produce fruit and vegetables which are much more nutritious.

① I was able to learn much about the different cultures of other countries.
② Be careful not to change too much at once.
③ If we had no body language, it would be much harder to communicate.
④ Thank you so much for accepting my proposal.
⑤ He said that he had a habit of eating too much.

6 우리말 해석에 맞게 주어진 단어를 활용하여 빈칸을 완성하세요. (단, 필요시 어형을 변화시킬 것)

> • 그녀는 나만큼 그 농담에 웃었다. (as, do)
> = She laughed at the joke __________.

7 빈칸에 들어갈 말로 알맞은 것은?

> We want our services to be __________ they can be for every customer.

① as great　　　② as great as
③ as greater　　④ as great that
⑤ as greater than

8 짝지어진 두 문장의 의미가 서로 같지 <u>않은</u> 것은?

① He is too short to reach the top shelf.

= He is so short that he cannot reach the top shelf.

② The English book is much harder than the one we learned last year.

= The English book is as hard as the one we learned last year.

③ My sister is not so tall as you.

= You are taller than my sister.

④ Since I had decided to become a writer, I started to write as much as possible.

= Having decided to become a writer, I started writing as much as I could.

⑤ You were so smart that you could solve it.

= You were smart enough to solve it.

9 ⓐ~ⓒ를 문맥에 맞도록 바르게 활용한 것끼리 짝지은 것은?

Since my family moved to the countryside three years ago, we ⓐ <u>enjoy</u> a more relaxed and peaceful life. Last winter, we built a small greenhouse in the backyard to grow vegetables. So far, we've harvested tomatoes, cucumbers, and even strawberries. Living here has ⓑ <u>true</u> changed the way we think about food and nature. Most importantly, it has brought our family ⓒ <u>close</u> together than ever before.

	ⓐ		ⓑ		ⓒ
①	enjoyed	–	truly	–	closest
②	have enjoyed	–	truly	–	closer
③	have enjoyed	–	true	–	closest
④	have enjoyed	–	truly	–	closest
⑤	enjoyed	–	true	–	closer

10 보기를 참고하여 아래 우리말을 주어진 조건에 맞게 영작하세요.

보 기	When you feel comfortable, you look natural in photos.

조 건	1. 반드시 "the 비교급, the 비교급" 사용 2. 현재형 동사 사용

당신이 더 편안하게 느낄수록, 사진에 더욱 자연스럽게 나온다.

➡ ________________________________

____

11 괄호 안에 주어진 단어를 이용하여 우리말과 같은 뜻이 되도록 빈칸에 알맞은 말을 쓰세요.

• 기술자를 고용하는 것이 네가 혼자서 컴퓨터를 고치는 것보다 덜 복잡하다.

= Hiring a technician is ___________ ___________ ___________ fixing the computer by yourself. (complicated)

12 다음 우리말과 같은 뜻이 되도록 괄호 안에 주어진 단어를 바르게 배열하세요. (필요시 어형 변화 가능)

• 가장 많이 배운 사람이 가장 현명한 사람은 아니다.

= ________________________________

____

(be, the, not, wisest, the most, learned)

13 어법상 올바르지 <u>않은</u> 것들로 짝지어진 것은?

The pot-in-pot Cooler is one of ⓐ <u>the cleverest inventions</u>. You only need two earthen pots and wet sand to make it work. One pot is smaller than ⓑ <u>another</u> one. The smaller pot is put into the larger one. The wet sand is poured between the two pots. Then the food is placed into the smaller one. When the water in the sand ⓒ <u>evaporates</u>, it takes away heat from the smaller pot. You can keep fruits and vegetables ⓓ <u>fresh</u> this way. The Cooler is simpler ⓔ <u>than any other inventions</u>.

① ⓐ, ⓒ
② ⓐ, ⓓ
③ ⓑ, ⓔ
④ ⓐ, ⓒ, ⓔ
⑤ ⓑ, ⓒ, ⓓ

14 다음 우리말과 같은 뜻이 되도록 괄호 안에 주어진 말을 배열하세요.

- 그녀가 서울에 머무는 시간이 길어질수록, 그녀는 그 도시의 사람들이 더 좋아졌다.

(in Seoul / the people / like / the more / the longer / she / stayed / got to / in the city / she)

➡ _______________________

____

15 다음 우리말과 같은 뜻이 되도록 빈칸을 채울 때 알맞은 것은?

- 상황이 위험하면 할수록, 나는 그것을 더 즐긴다.
  = __________ it is, the more I enjoy it.

① Dangerous
② Dangerouser
③ The dangerouser
④ More dangerous
⑤ The more dangerous

16 주어진 문장과 같은 의미가 되도록 빈칸을 채우세요.

(1) Cooking for yourself is healthier than ordering food.
= Ordering food _______ _______

_______ _______ _______ cooking for yourself.

(2) He answered the question as honestly as possible.
= He answered the question _______

_______ _______ _______ _______.

17 다음 글을 읽고, 빈칸에 들어갈 알맞은 어구를 〈조건〉에 맞게 완성하세요.

Think of your mind as a garden. The more you feed it positive thoughts, the more it flourishes. Each day, your actions, words, and attitudes plant seeds that shape it. Seeds of kindness, gratitude, and focus grow into happiness, productivity, and peace. However, the more you focus on negativity and stress, ________________, and the harder it becomes to find peace. Like a garden, your mind thrives with daily care and positive habits, bringing resilience, clarity, and peace. *resilience 회복력

조 건
- 〈보기〉에서 4개의 단어나 어구를 골라 작성할 것
- 〈보기〉의 단어나 어구를 변형하지 말 것
- 〈보기〉의 단어나 어구 외에는 사용하지 말 것

보 기 | weeds, the more, you'll, cultivate, the less, remove

➡ _______________________

18 다음 중 주어진 문장과 의미가 같은 것은?

Seoul is the most crowded city in Korea.

① Every city in Korea is more crowded than Seoul.
② Every city in Korea is as crowded as Seoul.
③ Seoul is as crowded as other cities in Korea.
④ No city in Korea is as crowded as Seoul.
⑤ Seoul is not so much crowded as other cities in Korea.

19 다음 문장의 밑줄 친 부분 중 어법상 잘못된 것은?

The director's new movie ① is ② more fantastic ③ than any other ④ movies ⑤ in Korea.

20 우리말 해석에 맞게 주어진 단어를 활용하여 빈칸을 완성하세요. (단, 필요시 어형을 변화시킬 것)

• 날씨가 시원해질수록, 나는 기분이 더 좋아진다. (cool, good)

= _______________ the weather is, _______________ I feel.

21 주어진 우리말과 같은 뜻이 되도록 빈칸에 알맞은 말을 한 단어로 쓰세요.

• 네 보고서는 가능한 한 구체적으로 쓰여져야 한다.
= Your report should be written as specifically as __________.

22 다음 중 어법상 옳은 것은?

① I prefer watching TV to play outside.
② His son was in the most famous football team.
③ He is one of the best singer in Korea.
④ Your artwork is more creative than him.
⑤ Unfortunately, the little bird got bad and bad.

23 주어진 우리말과 같은 뜻이 되도록 빈칸에 알맞은 말을 쓰세요.

• 내가 그녀를 방문할 때마다, 그녀는 점점 더 혼란스러워했다.
= Every time I visited her, she became __________ __________ __________ confused.

24 다음 중 주어진 우리말을 영어로 바르게 옮긴 것은?

① 더 많이 연습할수록, 그들은 더 잘하게 되었다.
= The more practice they were, the better they got.
② 더 높이 올라갈수록, 그는 더 무서움을 느꼈다.
= The higher he climbed, the scared he felt.
③ 그녀는 나이가 들어갈수록, 더 현명해졌다.
= The older she grew, the wiser she became.
④ 더 오래 일할수록, 나는 더 피곤했다.
= The longer I worked, the more tired I did.
⑤ 우리는 더 많은 책을 읽을수록, 더 많이 배운다.
= The more we read books, the more we learn.

25 주어진 두 문장이 같은 뜻이 되도록 빈칸에 알맞은 말을 쓰세요.

- Making a dress is not as difficult as I thought.
  = Making a dress is __________ difficult __________ I thought.

26 다음 중 어법상 어색한 것은?

① Tony is much more polite than any other boy in his class.
② I think your doll is prettier than mine.
③ Left-handed people tend to be better at driving.
④ Do you think line A is longer than line B?
⑤ The windows of that house are much larger than that of my house.

27 다음 문장 중 나머지 넷과 의미가 다른 것은?

① Russia is the largest country in the world.
② No country in the world is larger than Russia.
③ Russia is not as large as any other country in the world.
④ Russia is larger than any other country in the world.
⑤ No country in the world is as large as Russia.

28 두 문장이 같은 뜻이 되도록 빈칸에 알맞은 말을 쓰세요.

- My favorite sport is soccer.
  = There's __________ sport that I like __________ soccer.

29 다음 대화의 빈칸에 들어갈 말로 올바르지 않은 것은?

Mark : To me, __________________. How about you?
Jenny: I agree with you, Mark. I really love music.

① nothing is more important than music
② nothing is as important as music
③ music is the most important thing in my life
④ music is not so important as anything else
⑤ music is more important than anything else

30 빈칸에 들어가기에 어법상 어색한 말을 2개 고르면?

As the story develops, it's getting __________________.

① worse and worse
② more uninteresting and more uninteresting
③ still more exciting
④ better and better
⑤ more and more duller

31 주어진 문장과 의미가 같은 것 두 개를 고르세요.

Kimchi is the hottest food in my home.

① Kimchi is very hot in my home.
② Kimchi is hotter than any other food in my home.
③ No food in my home is hotter than Kimchi.
④ Kimchi is less hot than any other food in my home.
⑤ Kimchi is not as hot as any other food in my home.

32 밑줄 친 ⓐ~ⓔ 중 어법상 <u>어색한</u> 것은? (정답 2개)

Last Friday, I thought – ⓐ <u>what an useful project this was!</u> Our club was ⓑ <u>in charge</u> of organizing a book donation. The donated books ⓒ <u>were delivered</u> to the children's library in our town. ⓓ <u>Even better, many children who didn't have books now enjoy reading.</u> The reading room has grown ⓔ <u>very more popular than before</u>, and parents truly appreciate it.

① ⓐ　　② ⓑ　　③ ⓒ　　④ ⓓ　　⑤ ⓔ

33 괄호 안에 주어진 단어를 활용하여 두 문장이 같은 뜻이 되도록 빈칸에 알맞은 말을 쓰세요.

• Minho is the most intelligent boy in the science club.

= Minho ______________ ______________

______________ ______________ ______________

______________ ______________ in the science club. (than / any)

34 두 문장이 같은 뜻이 되도록 빈칸에 알맞은 말을 쓰세요.

• He tried to read as much as me.

= He tried to read as much as ______________

______________ .

35 다음 글의 밑줄 친 (A)~(E) 중 어법상 <u>틀린</u> 것은?

Recently, we talked to a nutrition specialist. (A) <u>She told us that unhealthy eating habits are more dangerous than our health to we often realize.</u> (B) <u>Many people suffer from preventable diseases due to poor diets.</u> (C) <u>Unhealthy eating can have a greater impact on our well-being than lack of exercise.</u> After we came home, we created an educational project about how to maintain a balanced diet. (D) <u>Our organization also does other projects to promote healthy living.</u> Even though we started small, we are making a big difference. (E) <u>What you do today can change your life.</u> So, take that first step!

① (A)　　② (B)　　③ (C)　　④ (D)　　⑤ (E)

36 다음 중 어법상 올바른 것은?

① You are smartest student that I've ever seen.
② There is nothing visitors enjoy more as the game.
③ No other dictionary is as more specific as this one.
④ Mr. Kim is more generous than any other teachers.
⑤ He is more popular than all the other politicians in Korea.

37 다음 문장이 자연스러워지도록 괄호 안에 주어진 말을 바르게 배열할 때 <u>네 번째</u>에 올 단어는?

They thought that I was (the, famous, most, one, of, painters) in the world.

① the　　② most　　③ famous
④ one　　⑤ of

CHAPTER 14
관계사

PSS 1 관계대명사	페이지	성취도				
		100%	99~75%	74~50%	49~25%	24~0%
PSS 1-1 who	308					
PSS 1-2 which	310					
PSS 1-3 that	312					
PSS 1-4 what	314					
PSS 1-5 계속적 용법	315					
PSS 1-6 전치사+관계대명사	317					
PSS 1-7 관계대명사의 생략	318					
PSS 1-8 복합관계대명사	319					
PSS 2 관계부사	페이지	성취도				
		100%	99~75%	74~50%	49~25%	24~0%
PSS 2-1 관계부사의 종류	321					
PSS 2-2 관계부사의 주의해야 할 용법	323					
PSS 2-3 복합관계부사	326					
중간·기말고사 대비문제	328					

PSS 1 관계대명사

관계대명사는 앞에 오는 선행사를 수식하며, 「접속사+대명사」의 역할을 한다.

선행사　　　　격	주격	소유격	목적격
사람	who	whose	who(m)
사물, 동물	which	whose[of which]	which
사물, 동물, 사람	that	–	that
사물(선행사 포함)	what	–	what

PSS 1-1 who

관계대명사절은 수식하는 선행사의 뒤에 위치한다. 주격 관계대명사의 동사의 수는 선행사에 따라 결정된다.

1. 주격

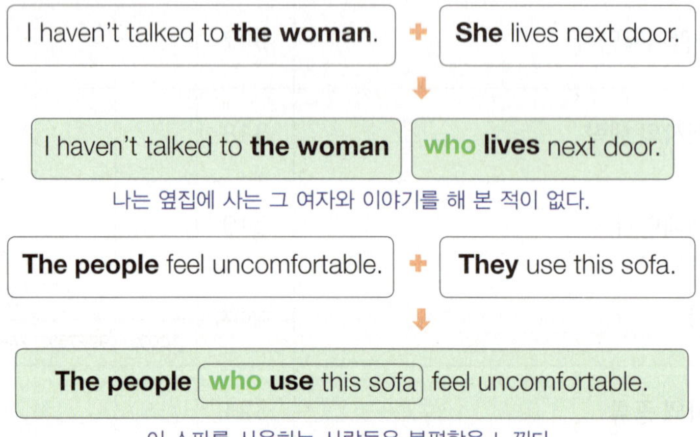

2. 소유격

I saved **a kid**. **His** life was in danger.

➡ I saved **a kid whose** life was in danger. 나는 목숨이 위태로운 한 아이를 구했다.

Have you heard about **the girl**? **Her** name is Andrea.

➡ Have you heard about **the girl whose** name is Andrea?

이름이 Andrea라는 소녀에 대해 들어봤니?

3. 목적격

The police officer is my uncle's friend. I asked **him** for directions.
➡ **The police officer** who(m) I asked for directions is my uncle's friend.
내가 길을 물었던 그 경찰관은 내 삼촌의 친구이다.

I invited **the young businessmen**. I met **them** at the party.
➡ I invited **the young businessmen** who(m) I met at the party.
나는 파티에서 만난 젊은 사업가들을 초대했다.

정답 p.74

PRACTICE 1

관계대명사 who, whose, whom 중 알맞은 것을 이용하여 문장을 완성하세요.

1 The students don't have to wear uniforms on Friday. They go to this school.
➡ The students ___________________________.

2 I don't trust the doctor. His office plants are not taken good care of.
➡ I don't trust the doctor ___________________________.

3 We like friends. They support us when we are having a hard time.
➡ We like friends ___________________________.

4 I met a pretty girl. Her parents run a big bakery downtown.
➡ I met a pretty girl ___________________________.

5 The man was not in the office. I wanted to see him because of an interview.
➡ The man ___________________________.

6 This movie is about a girl. She was raised by wolves in the jungle.
➡ This movie is about a girl ___________________________.

7 The students are likely to get low grades. They have poor concentration.
➡ The students ___________________________.

8 The burglar was arrested. He broke into my neighbor's house last night.
➡ The burglar ___________________________.

9 The people are very diligent. They work for the law firm.
➡ The people ___________________________.

10 We had a chef. His recipes could meet our expectations.
➡ We had a chef ___________________________.

11 The person is welcomed by everyone. His or her character is open and kind.
➡ The person ___________________________.

12 My uncle lives near my house. I visit him twice a month with some cookies.
➡ My uncle ___________________________.

CH
14
관계사

PSS 1-2 which

1. 주격

No one followed **the rules**. **They** had been made by Mr. Green.

➡ No one followed **the rules which** had been made by Mr. Green.

아무도 Green 씨에 의해 만들어진 그 규칙들을 따르지 않았다.

A new machine was invented two years ago. **It** had a cleaner inside.

➡ **A new machine which** had a cleaner inside was invented two years ago.

내부에 청소기가 있는 새로운 기계가 2년 전에 발명되었다.

2. 소유격

I wanted to buy **the table**. **Its** legs looked very strong.

➡ I wanted to buy **the table whose** legs looked very strong.

나는 다리가 매우 튼튼하게 보였던 그 탁자를 사고 싶었다.

I am reading **the book**. **Its** author is my friend from high school.

➡ I am reading **the book whose** author is my friend from high school.

나는 저자가 고등학교 때 내 친구인 그 책을 읽고 있다.

cf. which의 소유격으로 of which를 사용하기도 한다.

1. of which the 명사 (격식을 갖춘 문장이나 문어체에서 주로 사용)

   He bought a house, **of which the garden** is very large.

2. the 명사 of which (회화나 일반 글쓰기에서 주로 사용)

   He bought a house, **the garden of which** is very large.

3. 목적격

I bought **the digital watch**. My brother wanted to have **it**.

➡ I bought **the digital watch which** my brother wanted to have.

나는 내 남동생이 가지고 싶어 했던 그 디지털 시계를 샀다.

Jenny found **her books**. She had lost **them** in the subway.

➡ Jenny found **her books which** she had lost in the subway.

Jenny는 그녀가 지하철에서 잃어버린 책들을 찾았다.

정답 p.74

PRACTICE 2

관계대명사 which, whose 중 알맞은 것을 이용하여 두 개의 문장을 한 개의 문장으로 바꾸어 쓰세요.

1 The pictures were taken in Eastern Europe. The pictures are hanging on the wall.

➡ ____

2 Students can develop self-confidence through the program. The program is provided by some counselors.

➡ ____

3 The bicycle was invented in the 1860s. It had pedals.

➡ ____

4 The farmer could produce a new kind of fruit. It was bigger than any other fruit.

➡ ____

5 There was a glass of water. Its temperature was under 5 degrees Celsius.

➡ ____

6 The bus runs every fifteen minutes. It goes to the airport via the city hall.

➡ ____

7 People try to remember some accidents. The accidents taught them an important lesson.

➡ ____

8 There are many animals. Their lives are in great danger.

➡ ____

9 The workers constructed the building. The building is the tallest in the city.

➡ ____

10 Cyberspace has given us a new kind of reality. It is called a virtual reality.

➡ ____

정답 p.74

PRACTICE 3

괄호 안에 들어갈 알맞은 말을 골라 동그라미 하세요.

1 I joined three clubs which (has, have) a lot of members.

2 I like the blue striped shirt (who, which) Tom is wearing.

3 The volunteer work (who, which) I had done during the last vacation changed me a lot.

4 The waitress who (serve, serves) at that restaurant is very kind.

5 Some of my friends (whom, whose) I had invited to my birthday party couldn't come.

6 Cynthia works for a company which (import, imports) foreign films.

7 The computer (which, whose) I had bought last week already broke down.

8 I don't like people who (don't, doesn't) keep their words.

9 Once upon a time, there lived a girl (who, whose) name was Gretel.

10 The police have caught the man (who, which) stole my money.

11 Where is my yogurt which (was, were) in the refrigerator?

12 Marie Curie was a scientist (who, whose) won the Nobel Prize in Chemistry in 1911.

13 What is the name of the boy (whose, whom) we met in the library yesterday?

14 Anyone who (want, wants) to see the show should buy a ticket as soon as possible.

15 I don't like singers who only (focus, focuses) on dancing rather than singing.

PSS 1-3 that

1. **that은 who의 주격과 목적격을 대신하여 쓸 수 있다.**

   My daughter married a guy **who** has blue eyes. 내 딸은 파란 눈을 가진 남자와 결혼했다.
   = My daughter married a guy **that** has blue eyes.

   That woman is the actress **whom** I wanted to meet. 저 여자가 내가 만나고 싶어 했던 그 여배우이다.
   = That woman is the actress **that** I wanted to meet.

2. **that은 which의 주격과 목적격을 대신하여 쓸 수 있다.**

   All of us went out to the beach **which** is covered with white sand.
   우리 모두는 흰 모래로 뒤덮인 해변으로 나갔다.
   = All of us went out to the beach **that** is covered with white sand.

   There are some cards **which** you can choose. 네가 고를 수 있는 몇 장의 카드가 있다.
   = There are some cards **that** you can choose.

3. **선행사에 다음이 포함되어 있을 경우에는 주로 that을 쓴다.**

형용사의 최상급	It is **the most embarrassing** experience **that** I've ever had. 그것은 내가 지금껏 겪은 것 중 가장 당황스러운 경험이다.
서수	**The first** person **that** was waiting in line was Bob. 줄을 서서 기다리고 있던 첫 번째 사람은 Bob이었다.
all, much, little, no, some	There wasn't **much** work **that** we had to deal with. 우리가 다루어야 했던 일이 많지 않았다. He had **little** information **that** was needed for the test. 그는 시험에 필요한 정보를 거의 가지고 있지 않았다.
something, anything, nothing	Is there **anything that** I can do for you? 내가 너를 위해 할 수 있는 일이 있니?
the same, the only, the very	This is **the same** problem **that** we faced last time. 이것은 우리가 지난번에 직면했던 그와 같은 문제다.

정답 p.74

PRACTICE 4

빈칸에 알맞은 관계대명사를 모두 써 넣으세요.

1 Jamie brought a ladder ________________ was over 2 meters long.

2 The lady ________________ lives next door has two daughters.

3 I don't drink anything _________________ contains artificial sweetener.

4 My sister doesn't like the puppies _________________ I brought home.

5 When I was in England, the best thing _________________ happened to me was meeting my current girlfriend.

6 A curator is someone _________________ is in charge of works of art in a museum or an art gallery.

7 Richard is a boy _________________ has great hope and passion.

8 There was no vacant room _________________ we could stay in on that rainy day.

9 The actress _________________ I wanted to see was waving her hand on the red carpet.

10 At a bus stop, I ran into a man _________________ went to the same elementary school with me.

11 I saw something _________________ was shining under the water come straight towards me.

12 Shane showed me some photos _________________ he had taken during the summer vacation.

13 I think the most serious problem _________________ we have to overcome in this century is pollution.

14 One of my friends _________________ I considered a best friend deceived me.

15 While I was in New Zealand, the first thing _________________ I missed about Korea was kimchi.

정답 p.75

PRACTICE 5

괄호 안에 들어갈 알맞은 말을 골라 동그라미 하세요.

1 The bench (that, who) my dad has just made will be sent to my uncle's house.

2 Mr. Green, (that, whose) shop had been broken into, called the police.

3 The man tried to make the greatest perfume (which, that) had ever been produced.

4 The package (that, who) I had sent to Jake was delivered to the wrong person.

5 The palace that (was, were) built in India is a symbol of great love.

6 I am meeting a woman (which, who) has a small art gallery near the river.

7 The last person (who, that) was in the swimming pool is Jacob.

8 If there is something (which, that) you need while I'm away, ask Ms. Lee.

9 We are looking for a person that (is, are) good at planning various events.

10 What is the name of the girl (whose, that) you spend time with every weekend?

PRACTICE 6

다음 문장의 밑줄 친 부분을 바르게 고치세요.

1 These vases are all <u>which</u> still remain. ________________

2 I met someone <u>whose</u> had a very friendly smile. ________________

3 An event <u>that it produce</u> stress is called a stressor. ________________

4 There is no option <u>which</u> satisfies everyone's needs. ________________

5 We stayed at a hotel which <u>John had recommended it to us</u>. ________________

6 Her voice is the most beautiful voice <u>which</u> I've ever heard. ________________

7 Laughter eases the fear and depression <u>who</u> happen in our lives. ________________

8 Our aunt couldn't give us anything <u>that we wanted to have it</u>. ________________

9 You must use every method that <u>you already know it</u>. ________________

10 They saw something big that <u>it looked</u> like a UFO. ________________

11 The building that <u>it was built</u> 100 years ago is going to be remodeled soon. ________________

12 Have you finished the work <u>who</u> Mr. Choi asked you to do? ________________

PSS 1-4 what

선행사를 자체에 포함하는 관계대명사 what은 선행사가 따로 없고 the thing(s) which[that] 와 바꿔 쓸 수 있다. what은 문장 내에서 주어, 목적어, 보어 역할을 하는 명사절을 이끌며 소 유격을 쓰지 않는다.

What I had to do was bring the kid back right away. (주어 역할의 명사절)

내가 해야 했던 것은 아이를 즉시 데려오는 것이었다.

= **The thing which[that]** I had to do was bring the kid back right away.

cf. 위의 예문에서 보어 자리에 to 부정사구(to bring the kid back right away)가 오는 게 어법 에 맞지 않나 의문을 가질 수 있다. 일상체에서 all you have to do나 이와 비슷한 구문(what I had to do)이 주어로 쓰인 문장의 보어 자리에는 대부분 원형부정사를 씀에 유의할 것.

I will remember **what** they have done for me. (목적어 역할의 명사절)

나는 그들이 나를 위해 한 것을 기억할 것이다.

= I will remember **the things which[that]** they have done for me.

Experience is **what** matters. (보어 역할의 명사절) 경험은 중요한 것이다.

PRACTICE 7

괄호 안에 들어갈 알맞은 말을 골라 동그라미 하세요.

1 (What, Which) you believe is not always right.

2 Many jobs (what, which) were needed in the past don't exist now.

3 My younger sister does only (what, which) she must not do when our parents are out.

4 Some people use their left hands to handle things (what, which) are not clean.

5 (What, Which) I don't understand is the reason why she left me without saying good-bye.

6 You got me wrong. That was not (what, which) I meant to say.

7 Mountain climbing is a hobby (what, which) gives you more energy in your everyday life.

8 Scientists are developing the robots (what, which) might be able to think like us.

9 The soldiers were supposed to do (what, which) the general ordered them to do.

10 I have studied about genes (what, which) determine physical appearance.

11 When you make a plan of something, think about (what, which) really counts.

12 Animal documentaries are (what, which) I enjoy watching.

PSS 1-5 계속적 용법

1. 「접속사+대명사」의 역할을 하는 관계대명사의 계속적 용법은 형태상으로 볼 때 관계대명사 앞에 ,(comma)가 있어 일반적인 관계대명사의 용법과 구별되며 선행사에 대해 부가적인 설명을 덧붙이고자 할 때 사용한다.

   I'll introduce our new program, **which** will help you lose weight.
   저는 우리의 새로운 프로그램을 소개하겠는데, 그것은 당신의 몸무게를 줄이는 것을 도와줄 것입니다.
   = I'll introduce our new program, **and it** will help you lose weight.

2. 선행사가 특정한 사람이나 사물, 고유명사일 때는 관계대명사절이 빠져도 의미가 전달되므로 계속적 용법을 쓴다.

   Jimmy, **who** is my friend from middle school, went to the States to study.
   Jimmy는 나의 중학교 때 친구이고, 공부를 하러 미국에 갔다.
   I stayed at the Plaza hotel, **which** Suji's dad owns.
   나는 Plaza 호텔에서 머물렀는데, 그것은 수지의 아버지가 소유하고 있다.

3. 계속적 용법의 관계대명사 who(m)나 which는 that으로 바꾸어 쓸 수 없다.

   My aunt, **who** gave birth to twins last month, is still in the hospital.
   나의 고모는 지난달에 쌍둥이를 낳았는데, 아직도 병원에 계신다.
   cf. My aunt, that gave birth to twins last month, is still in the hospital. (×)

4. 계속적 용법의 관계대명사는 단어뿐만 아니라 절을 설명하기도 한다.

   The flight was delayed for another 30 minutes, **which** made everyone annoyed.
   비행기는 30분이 더 지연되었고, 그것은 모두를 화나게 만들었다.
   cf. 이 경우 주격 관계대명사 뒤에 오는 절의 시제가 현재일 때는 단수 동사를 쓴다.
   She didn't take the job, **which** still **remains** a mystery.
   그녀는 그 일을 맡지 않았는데, 그것은 여전히 수수께끼로 남아있다.

PRACTICE 8

관계대명사의 계속적 용법을 이용하여 두 개의 문장을 한 개의 문장으로 바꾸어 쓰세요.

1 My teacher bought me this book. It has influenced me a lot.

➡ ____

2 I sometimes ask my grandmother for advice. It has been very helpful.

➡ ____

3 An old lady gave me some cookies that she had made. She lives next door.

➡ ____

4 He made a number of cartoons and movies. They have been loved by children.

➡ ____

5 Last Friday, I met Chris. I hadn't seen him for a long time.

➡ ____

6 We will fly to Busan. It means we won't have to worry about traffic jams.

➡ ____

7 Thomas Edison was born in 1847. He is called the Father of Invention.

➡ ____

8 Taekwondo requires both mental and physical training. It is a kind of martial arts.

➡ ____

9 Jay couldn't do his homework. His computer broke down yesterday.

➡ ____

10 The game was shown on TV. It greatly helped the game to sell well.

➡ ____

PRACTICE 9

괄호 안에 들어갈 알맞은 관계대명사를 <u>모두</u> 골라 동그라미 하세요.

1 I added some maple syrup, (which, that) made the tea special.

2 Jamie told me about his new girlfriend (who, that) lives in California.

3 A nurse, (who, that) didn't wear a uniform, was taking care of a sick baby.

4 Is he the man (who, that) speaks five foreign languages?

5 The exchange students (who, that) live downstairs are from Malaysia.

6 He was a famous architect, (who, that) designed the Eiffel Tower.

7 The woman (whom, that) I wanted to talk with looked proud of herself.

8 There will be another new hotel, (which, that) will help villagers earn more money.

9 I met a guy (who, that) wishes to climb Mt. Everest someday.

10 The U.S. Constitution, (which, that) was made in 1787, emphasizes human rights.

PSS 1-6 전치사 + 관계대명사

관계대명사가 전치사의 목적어로 쓰일 때는 전치사를 문장의 맨 끝에 두거나 관계대명사 바로 앞에 둘 수 있다. 단, 관계대명사 that 앞에는 전치사를 쓸 수 없고, 전치사가 관계대명사 바로 앞에 올 때는 whom 대신 who를 쓸 수 없다.

She's the rude girl. I talked about her.
➡ She's the rude girl **who(m)** I talked **about**. 그녀가 내가 이야기했던 무례한 소녀이다.
➡ She's the rude girl **about whom** I talked.
➡ She's the rude girl **about who** I talked. (×)
➡ She's the rude girl **that** I talked **about**.
➡ She's the rude girl **about that** I talked. (×)

This is the house. He was born in it.
➡ This is the house **which** he was born **in**. 여기가 그가 태어난 집이다.
➡ This is the house **in which** he was born.
➡ This is the house **that** he was born **in**.

정답 p.76

PRACTICE **10** [1-10]

관계대명사를 이용하여 두 문장을 한 문장으로 바꾸세요.

1 I found the Japanese comic book. You were looking for it.
➡ I found the Japanese comic book which[that] you were looking for.
➡ I found the Japanese comic book for which you were looking.

2 Do you know the boy? Tom is talking to him with a big smile.
➡
➡

3 The bed was very comfortable. I slept in it last night.
➡
➡

4 These are the great inventions. He is well-known for them.
➡
➡

5 Before it is too late, we need to protect the Earth. We live on the Earth.

  ➡ ____

  ➡ ____

6 Soccer is a sport. My friends and I are very fond of it.

  ➡ ____

  ➡ ____

7 What is the title of the movie? You told me about it yesterday.

  ➡ ____

  ➡ ____

8 We couldn't go to the birthday party. We were invited to it.

  ➡ ____

  ➡ ____

9 This is the port. Millions of immigrants from Europe entered America through it.

  ➡ ____

  ➡ ____

10 I've never seen Susan. Mark fell in love with her two years ago.

  ➡ ____

  ➡ ____

PSS 1-7 관계대명사의 생략

1. **목적격 관계대명사 who(m), which, that은 생략 가능하다.**

   I couldn't trust some people **(whom)** I worked with.
   나는 내가 같이 일했던 몇몇 사람들을 신뢰할 수 없었다.
   You can't cancel the meeting **(which)** you arranged. 너는 네가 준비했던 회의를 취소할 수 없다.
   Everything **(that)** she told me was unbelievable. 그녀가 내게 말한 모든 것은 믿을 수 없었다.

   cf. 관계대명사 앞에 전치사가 오는 경우에는 목적격 관계대명사를 생략할 수 없다.
   I couldn't trust some people **with** I worked. (×)
   I couldn't trust some people **with whom** I worked. (○)

2. **주격 관계대명사 뒤에 be동사가 있고 그 뒤에 분사, 형용사구, 전치사구가 오면, 「관계대명사+be동사」를 생략할 수 있다. 단, 이때 관계대명사와 be동사는 반드시 함께 생략되어야 한다.**

   Those kids **(who are)** **standing** in front of that building are waiting for the famous singer. 저 건물 앞에 서 있는 저 아이들은 그 유명한 가수를 기다리고 있다.
   The teapot **(which was)** **put** on the stove was handmade.
   가스레인지에 올려진 그 찻주전자는 수공예로 만들어졌다.

PRACTICE 11

다음 문장에서 생략해도 되는 부분이 있으면 그 부분에 괄호로 표시하세요.

1 Have you found the luggage that you lost at the airport?

2 Look at those giraffes which are eating treetop leaves so peacefully.

3 We tend to like the music to which we often listen.

4 The woman who you see at the park every morning is my best friend, Jennifer.

5 You know what? The pajamas which Steve wore last night are actually mine.

6 The people who we met in Vancouver were very friendly.

7 The people who work for the company are very diligent.

8 Don't watch the movie. It is the most boring movie that I've seen lately.

9 Who was the lady whom I saw at the graduation ceremony?

10 The blond boy who is sitting next to my teacher is James.

11 The people who were injured in the accident were taken to a nearby hospital.

12 I live in a nice house which is overlooking the river and the bridges.

PSS 1-8 복합관계대명사

복합관계대명사는 「관계대명사+ever」의 형태로 그 자체에 선행사를 포함한 명사절과 양보를 나타내는 부사절을 이끈다.

whatever	~하는 것은 무엇이든지 (= anything that) You can choose **whatever** you want. 너는 네가 원하는 무엇이든지 고를 수 있다.
	무엇을 ~하더라도 (= no matter what) **Whatever** I do, I'll try my best. 나는 무슨 일을 하더라도, 최선을 다할 것이다.
whoever	~하는 누구든지 (= anyone who[that]) **Whoever** is happy will make others happy, too. 행복한 사람은 누구든지 다른 사람들도 행복하게 만들 것이다.
	누가 ~하더라도 (= no matter who) **Whoever** he is, I don't want to meet him. 그가 누구더라도, 나는 그를 만나고 싶지 않다.

<table>
<tr><td rowspan="2">whichever</td><td>~하는 어느 것이든지 (= anything that)
He can buy **whichever** he wants.
그는 원하는 어느 것이든지 살 수 있다.</td></tr>
<tr><td>어느 것을 ~하든지 (= no matter which)
Whichever you take, you will be satisfied.
너는 어느 것을 취하든지, 만족할 것이다.</td></tr>
</table>

cf. whoever가 목적어로 쓰이면 whomever로도 쓸 수 있으나 현대 영어에서는 거의 쓰지 않는다.
She doesn't care **whomever he likes**. 그녀는 그가 누구를 좋아하든지 상관하지 않는다.

정답 p.76

PRACTICE 12

다음 두 문장의 뜻이 같도록 빈칸에 알맞은 말을 쓰세요.

1 Whatever you do, love what you are doing.
= ___________________________________, love what you are doing.

2 Whoever wants some cookies may eat them.
= ___________________________________ may eat them.

3 I will give her whatever she needs.
= I will give her ___________________________________.

4 He will buy you whichever you choose among these clothes.
= He will buy you ___________________________________ among these clothes.

5 How about asking whoever you meet?
= How about asking ___________________________________?

6 Whichever you buy, you will not regret it.
= ___________________________________, you will not regret it.

7 Whatever I asked, the man didn't say a word.
= ___________________________________, the man didn't say a word.

8 Whoever may say so, I don't care.
= ___________________________________, I don't care.

9 I will follow whatever you decide.
= I will follow ___________________________________.

10 Whatever he hears, he doesn't give up his plan.
= ___________________________________, he doesn't give up his plan.

PSS 2 관계부사

PSS 2-1 관계부사의 종류

관계부사는 선행사를 수식하는 절을 이끌며, 접속사와 부사의 역할을 동시에 한다. 관계부사는 「전치사+관계대명사」로 바꾸어 쓸 수 있다.

	선행사	관계부사	전치사+관계대명사
장소	the place, the country, the city, the house…	where	at/in/to which
시간	the time, the year, the month, the day…	when	at/in/on which
이유	the reason	why	for which
방법	(the way)	how	in which

This is the place. I used to hide my money in it.
➡ This is **the place in which** I used to hide my money.
➡ This is **the place where** I used to hide my money. 이곳은 내가 돈을 숨겨 놓곤 하던 장소이다.

May 5th is the day. I was born on the day.
➡ May 5th is **the day on which** I was born.
➡ May 5th is **the day when** I was born. 5월 5일은 내가 태어난 날이다.

I will tell you the reason. He lied to his friends for the reason.
➡ I will tell you **the reason for which** he lied to his friends.
➡ I will tell you **the reason why** he lied to his friends.
그가 그의 친구들에게 거짓말을 한 이유를 네게 말해 줄게.

I don't know the way. The student came into the room in the way.
➡ I don't know **the way in which** the student came into the room.
➡ I don't know **how** the student came into the room.
나는 그 학생이 어떻게 그 방에 들어왔는지 모른다.
cf. the way와 how는 함께 쓸 수 없으므로 둘 중 하나를 생략해야 한다.
I don't know **the way** the student came into the room. (○)
I don't know **the way how** the student came into the room. (×)

정답 p.76

PRACTICE 13 [1-15]

다음 두 문장이 같은 뜻이 되도록 관계대명사나 관계부사를 이용하여 빈칸을 채우세요.

1 Tom won't tell anyone the reason for which he missed the test.

= Tom won't tell anyone the reason ________________________.

2 I can clearly remember the day when Henry and I first met.

= I can clearly remember the day ____ .

3 Where is the nearest place at which the bus picks up passengers?

= Where is the nearest place ____ ?

4 My uncle showed me the way in which I could repair a bicycle tire.

= My uncle showed me ____ .

5 This book explains the reason why the war broke out.

= This book explains the reason ____ .

6 Australia is the country where there live various kinds of animals.

= Australia is the country ____ .

7 1969 was the historic year in which a man first landed on the Moon.

= 1969 was the historic year ____ .

8 I like the way the teacher deals with students.

= I like the way ____ .

9 Thanksgiving is known as the day on which people eat turkey.

= Thanksgiving is known as the day ____ .

10 I could not even find the house where I had lived with my parents.

= I could not even find the house ____ .

11 Eating insects is common in some areas in which people cannot take protein easily.

= Eating insects is common in some areas ____ .

12 Yoga teaches us the way in which we can relax our mind and body.

= Yoga teaches us ____ .

13 I haven't seen some of my friends since the day when we graduated.

= I haven't seen some of my friends since the day ____ .

14 The reason why I'm listening to this radio show is that it is educational.

= The reason ____

is that it is educational.

15 The way you talk and behave can indicate your personal character.

= ____

can indicate your personal character.

정답 p.77

PRACTICE 14

빈칸에 들어갈 알맞은 관계부사를 써 넣으세요.

1 Would you recommend a restaurant ____________ we can have nice seafood?

2 In May, ____________ we went to the area, the weather was so bad that we couldn't do anything.

3 I asked the villagers ____________ I could reach the nearest hospital, but no one answered me correctly.

4 I remember the day ____________ you joined my class for the first time.

5 I want to visit a town ____________ the artist was born and raised.

6 She never told me the reason ____________ she kept on doing the experiment by herself.

7 Many tourists take pictures in the city ____________ there is the Eiffel Tower.

8 The diary clearly describes the days ____________ all of her family lived in fear.

9 I tried to explain the reason ____________ my homework was incomplete, but the teacher gave me a low grade.

10 I don't know ____________ he reached me. I never told him my phone number.

PSS 2-2 관계부사의 주의해야 할 용법

선행사의 생략	관계부사의 선행사는 the time, the place, the reason과 같이 일반적일 때 생략할 수 있다. Friday is **(the day) when** I am the busiest of the week. 금요일은 내가 일주일 중 가장 바쁜 날이다. I don't know **(the reason) why** I have to keep doing this. 나는 내가 왜 계속해서 이것을 해야 하는지를 알 수 없다. ***cf.*** 특정한 때나 장소를 나타내는 선행사는 생략할 수 없다. Welcome to (New York) where you'll have an unforgettable experience. (×) 잊지 못할 경험을 하실 뉴욕에 오신 것을 환영합니다.
관계부사의 생략	일반적인 선행사(time / day / place(somewhere / anywhere / everywhere) / reason) 뒤에 오는 관계부사는 생략할 수 있다. Do you know **the time (when)** the newspaper is delivered? 너는 신문이 배달되는 시간을 아니? I need **a place (where)** I can stay during my holidays. 나는 내 휴가 동안 머무를 수 있는 장소가 필요하다. I need **a small apartment where** I can stay during my holidays. (생략 불가능) 나는 내 휴가 동안 머무를 수 있는 작은 아파트가 필요하다.

<table>
<tr><td>관계부사의 생략</td><td>관계부사 where를 「전치사+관계대명사」 형태로 바꾸고 전치사를 관계사절의 맨 뒤로 보낸 후 남은 목적격 관계대명사는 생략할 수 있다.

That is the building my parents lived. (×)
저곳은 나의 부모님이 거주하셨던 건물이다.
➡ That is the building **where(=in which)** my parents lived. (○)
= That is the building **(which)** my parents lived **in**. (○)
= That is the building **(that)** my parents lived **in**. (○)</td></tr>
<tr><td>관계부사와
관계대명사의 구분</td><td>관계부사는 뒤에 완전한 절이, 관계대명사 뒤에는 주어나 목적어가 빠진 불완전한 절이 온다.

This building is a place where **smoking is forbidden**.
2형식의 완전한 절
이 건물은 흡연이 금지된 장소이다.
My teacher introduced a new classmate who **moved from L.A.**
주어가 없는 불완전한 절
나의 선생님이 L.A.에서 이사 온 새 학급 친구를 소개했다.</td></tr>
</table>

정답 p.77

PRACTICE 15

다음 문장들이 같은 뜻이 되도록 빈칸에 알맞은 단어를 쓰세요.

1 This is the place where I used to work with my best friend.

= This is ___*where*___ I used to work with my best friend.

= This is ___*the*___ ___*place*___ I used to work with my best friend.

2 Do you remember the time when your little sister was born?

= Do you remember ___________ your little sister was born?

= Do you remember ___________ ___________ your little sister was born?

3 Mike tried to tell me the reason why he didn't show up.

= Mike tried to tell me ___________ he didn't show up.

= Mike tried to tell me ___________ ___________ he didn't show up.

4 England is the country where I went to college.

= England is the country ___________ ___________ I went to college.

= England is ___________ ___________ I went to college in.

5 September is the month when a new semester starts.

= September is ___________ a new semester starts.

= September is ___________ ___________ a new semester starts.

6 Please tell me the reason why you want to change your partner.

= Please tell me ___________ you want to change your partner.

= Please tell me ___________ ___________ you want to change your partner.

7 I need to move somewhere where nobody can find me.

   = I need to move _______________ nobody can find me.

   = I need to move _______________ nobody can find me.

정답 p.77

PRACTICE 16

다음 중 밑줄 친 부분을 생략해도 되는 것에 ○표 하세요.

1 That is the reason why she left our club without any explanation.

2 Have you stayed at the hotel that I mentioned before?

3 The boy whose father is a famous writer drives a fancy car.

4 Please teach me the way that I can bake a nice birthday cake.

5 Amy, whose sister lives in Korea, visits the country every summer.

6 The Italian restaurant where we can have delicious pizza is next to the bank.

7 She needs to know the way that she can get along with her friends.

8 Do you know the lady who is reading a newspaper next to John?

9 I am sorry that he doesn't remember the day when we first met.

10 Please return the dictionary that you borrowed from me last week.

11 I can't understand the reason why he told her my secret.

정답 p.77

PRACTICE 17

괄호 안에 들어갈 알맞은 말을 골라 동그라미 하세요.

1 This was the reason (which, why) I lied to you.

2 I met an old lady (where, who) took care of a stray dog.

3 India is a country (where, which) the population is over one billion.

4 I've decided to accept the offer (how, which) my boss made me yesterday.

5 2018 was a historic year (when, which) the Winter Olympic Games was held in Pyeongchang.

6 I don't care (how, which) you treat people around you.

7 He didn't tell me the reason (why, which) he canceled the appointment.

8 Since 2021 he has lived in Cambodia, (which, where) he works for the United Nations.

9 Children's Day, (which, when) my daughter looks forward to, was established by Bang Jeong-Hwan.

10 I know a bakery (which, where) you can buy good brownies.

PSS 2-3 복합관계부사

복합관계부사는 「관계부사+ever」의 형태로 그 자체에 선행사를 포함한 시간, 장소의 부사절과 양보의 부사절을 이끈다.

whenever	~할 때는 언제나 (= at any time when ~) I feel happy **whenever** I meet my friends. 나는 나의 친구들을 만날 때는 언제나 행복하다. 언제 ~을 하더라도 (= no matter when ~) I'll help you, **whenever** you ask. 나는 네가 요청할 때 언제라도 너를 도울 것이다.
wherever	~하는 어디든지 (= at any place where ~) He got good service **wherever** he visited. 그는 방문했던 곳마다 좋은 서비스를 받았다. 어디에서 ~하더라도 (= no matter where ~) Do your best **wherever** you may work. 너는 어디에서 일하더라도 최선을 다해라.
however	~하는 어떤 방식이든지 (= in any way) You can arrange the chairs **however** you want. 네가 원하는 방식대로 의자들을 배치해도 된다. 아무리/어떻게 ~하더라도 (= no matter how ~) **However** high the price is, I will buy the computer. 가격이 아무리 비싸더라도, 나는 그 컴퓨터를 사겠다.

정답 p.78

PRACTICE 18

다음 빈칸에 알맞은 복합관계부사를 쓰세요.

1   I will be with you _______________ you go.

2   How do you feel _______________ you read the book?

3   _______________ hard he tries, he can't get the prize.

4   _______________ she lives, I will find her.

5   _______________ rich she is, she can't get everything.

6   _______________ you come, I will welcome you.

7 ______________ tired you may be, you must finish the work.

8 He meets his friends ______________ he has free time.

9 You can sit ______________ you want.

10 I feel happy ______________ I talk with him.

정답 p.78

PRACTICE **19**

괄호 안에 들어갈 알맞은 말을 골라 동그라미 하세요.

1 (Whenever, Whatever) may happen, I will help you.

2 I feel scared (however, whenever) I see the movie.

3 (However, Wherever) she goes, she is warmly welcomed.

4 (Whoever, Whenever) wins this game will get 20,000 dollars.

5 (Whatever, However) good it is, I don't want to get it.

6 (Wherever, Whenever) I have an exam, I study in the library.

중간·기말고사 대비문제 📝

1 다음 두 문장을 관계대명사를 이용하여 한 문장으로 바꿀 때 빈칸에 알맞은 말을 쓰세요.

- Do you know the lady?
- She is parking her car in front of the restaurant.

➡ Do you know the lady ＿＿＿＿＿＿ ＿＿＿＿＿＿ parking her car in front of the restaurant?

2 다음 중 문법적으로 옳은 것만을 있는 대로 고른 것은?

(A) Is this the book what you told me to buy?
(B) Look at this car whose tires are all flat.
(C) They work for a company which sells sneakers.
(D) I have no idea which this word means.
(E) Sam is a singer whose first album was a big hit.

---

① (A), (B)　　② (C), (D)　　③ (A), (B), (D)
④ (B), (C), (E)　⑤ (B), (D), (E)

3 빈칸에 들어갈 알맞은 말을 고르세요.

I want to enter the university, ＿＿＿＿＿＿ hard it may be.

---

① wherever　② whoever　③ however
④ whichever　⑤ whenever

4 [A]～[E] 중 어법상 올바른 것은?

People usually celebrate their birthday with a delicious cake and birthday candles. [A]Have you ever wonder why people blow out candles on birthday cakes? [B]There is several theories regarding the origin of birthday candles. [C]Some believe that the tradition of birthday candles were begun in Ancient Greece. [D]People brought cakes adorned with lit candles to the temple of Artemis, who was the goddess of the hunt. [E]The reason why the candles were lit was to make them glow like the moon, who was a popular symbol related to Artemis.

---

① [A]　② [B]　③ [C]　④ [D]　⑤ [E]

5 〈보기〉에서 밑줄 친 부분이 어법상 틀린 문장의 개수는?

보 기

ⓐ She spent all the money that I had earned.
ⓑ I grew up in a city in that everything was out-of-date.
ⓒ He founded the company, that is now producing microscopes.
ⓓ This is that the team has won the championship.
ⓔ Can you recognize the boy that father died of cancer last year?

---

① 1개　② 2개　③ 3개　④ 4개　⑤ 5개

6 다음 중 어법상 틀린 문장은?

① I have two brothers who are older than I am.
② He owns a building which is very expensive.
③ She loves the man who are working at the café.
④ Who brought the dog that is sleeping over there?
⑤ She went to the college which is famous for its beautiful campus.

7 다음 두 문장을 관계대명사를 이용하여 한 문장으로 바꾸세요.

- Look at the old lady.
- Her son is a famous actor.

➡ ______________________________________

____

8 빈칸에 알맞은 관계사를 쓰세요.

The statue, ___________ was covered all over with thin leaves of fine gold, stood on top of the hill.

9 다음 문장의 빈칸에 공통으로 들어갈 관계사로 알맞은 것은?

- I've booked the tickets for the concert, ___________ were almost sold out.
- She has been to Paris in ___________ she had her purse stolen.

① that ② where ③ which
④ who ⑤ whose

10 다음 두 문장을 한 문장으로 바꿀 때 빈칸에 알맞은 말을 각각 쓰세요.

- The university runs the hospital.
- The nurses have been on strike for a month at the hospital.

➡ The university runs the hospital ___________ ___________ the nurses have been on strike for a month.
➡ The university runs the hospital ___________ the nurses have been on strike for a month.

11 다음 우리말을 영어로 옮긴 것 중 어법상 어색한 것 2개는?

저 남자가 내가 어제 길에서 마주친 사람이다.

① He is the man I ran into on the street yesterday.
② He is the man that I ran into on the street yesterday.
③ He is the man whom I ran into on the street yesterday.
④ He is the man to whom I ran into on the street yesterday.
⑤ He is the man into who I ran on the street yesterday.

12 우리말 해석에 맞게 괄호 안에 주어진 말을 활용하여 영작하세요. (단, 필요시 어형을 변화시킬 것)

- 누구든지 법을 어기는 사람은 처벌받을 것이다. (punish, break, the law).

= ______________________________________

____

CH
14
관계사

13 다음 우리말을 가장 바르게 영작한 것은?

> 비행기는 라이트 형제에 의해 발명되었는데, 그들은 19세기 후반에 미국에서 태어났다.

① The airplane was invented by the Wright brothers, which were born in the United States in the late 19th century.
② The airplane was invented by the Wright brothers, whom were born in the United States in the late 19th century.
③ The airplane was invented by the Wright brothers so they were born in the United States in the late 19th century.
④ The airplane was invented by the Wright brothers, that were born in the United States in the late 19th century.
⑤ The airplane was invented by the Wright brothers, who were born in the United States in the late 19th century.

14 다음은 한 스포츠 팀의 코치가 선수들에게 한 말입니다. 빈칸에 들어갈 말이 차례대로 짝지어진 것은?

> __________ makes me angry is not that you lost the game but that you played without thinking. The only thing __________ I am telling you now is to use your head as well as your body. Do you understand __________ I mean?

① What – that – that
② That – what – that
③ What – that – what
④ That – that – what
⑤ What – what – that

15 Which ones are grammatically correct? (정답 2개)

① This is the reason in which she was late for school.
② The bed in which I slept last Saturday was comfortable.
③ He didn't want to tell the location in which he had hidden his jewelry.
④ My sister met a man with who she fell in love when she was 20.
⑤ Jackson needs someone to whom he can rely when he makes decisions.

16 다음 밑줄 친 that의 성격이 나머지 넷과 다른 것은?

① All <u>that</u> glitters is not gold.
② He realized <u>that</u> he had left his wallet at home.
③ Don't do something <u>that</u> doesn't seem right.
④ He hated the book <u>that</u> she was reading.
⑤ She entered the room <u>that</u> nobody wanted to enter.

17 다음 우리말을 영어로 바르게 옮긴 것을 <u>모두</u> 고르세요.

> 이것이 내가 본 것 중 가장 높은 건물이다.

① This is the tallest building I have ever seen.
② This is the tallest building where I have ever seen.
③ This is the tallest building what I have ever seen.
④ This is the tallest building that I have ever seen.
⑤ This is the tallest building in which I have ever seen.

[18-19] 다음 글을 읽고, 물음에 답하세요.

Did you know ⓐthe fact which the hot chocolate we enjoy today is different from the original drink? It wasn't hot and sweet, for a start. Its origin traces back to the Maya civilization. To make the chocolate drink, ⓑwhich was served cold, the Maya ground cocoa seeds and mixed them with water, chili peppers, and other ingredients. The drink tasted spicy and bitter as opposed to the sweet hot chocolate we enjoy today. ⓒSweet hot chocolate and bar chocolate were yet to invent. In the 15th century, the Aztecs believed chocolate drinks gave strength and vitality, and used them to show their high status. ⓓOnce handing over to the Spanish, hot chocolate became a popular drink with the Spanish upper class. In the 17th century, sweet-tasting hot chocolate made by using sugar was invented. It became a luxury item among the European nobility ⓔwhen the English decided to make it used milk instead of water. Now, hot chocolate is consumed throughout the world and comes in multiple variations. As (가) 날이 더 추워질수록 핫초코 한 잔보다 더 좋은 것은 없다.

18 ⓐ~ⓔ 중 어법상 옳은 것은?

① ⓐ　　② ⓑ　　③ ⓒ　　④ ⓓ　　⑤ ⓔ

19 〈보기〉의 단어를 모두 배열하여 우리말 의미에 맞게 (가)를 완성하였을 때, 일곱 번째로 오는 단어는?

보 기

than, colder, hot, the, a, days, cup, chocolate, get, better, there's, of, nothing

① there's　　② hot　　③ better
④ nothing　　⑤ than

20 어법상 틀린 곳을 찾아 바르게 고치세요.

I have much work that need to be done before I leave for Europe next week.

⟶

21 주어진 문장을 같은 의미가 되도록 고친 것 중 어법상 틀린 것은?

① I went to the movie theater, which was closed for renovations.
　⟶ I went to the movie theater, but it was closed for renovations.
② I saw someone who looked just like James yesterday.
　⟶ I saw someone that looked just like James yesterday.
③ I needed a biology textbook, which I didn't bring.
　⟶ I needed a biology textbook, but I didn't bring it.
④ My friend gave me a gift, which was wrapped and tied with a ribbon.
　⟶ My friend gave me a gift, and it was wrapped and tied with a ribbon.
⑤ Uncle Sam, who we had been talking about earlier, walked in.
　⟶ Uncle Sam, what we had been talking about earlier, walked in.

22 다음 영단어의 뜻풀이에서 밑줄 친 부분 중 생략이 가능한 것은?

①	success	*n.* the achievement of a goal or aim for <u>which</u> someone has worked hard
②	freedom	*n.* the state <u>that</u> allows someone to act or speak without restriction
③	effort	*n.* the energy <u>that</u> someone uses to try to get something
④	diligence	*n.* the careful and persistent effort with <u>which</u> someone works on their tasks
⑤	achievement	*n.* something <u>that</u> has been done or achieved through effort

23 밑줄 친 부분을 의미가 같은 말로 바꿀 때 잘못된 것은?

① You can work with <u>whomever</u> you like.
  = anyone whom
② <u>However</u> busy you are, take time to exercise.
  = Anytime how
③ You can learn something from <u>whatever</u> you do.
  = anything that
④ <u>Whoever</u> wins the game, it makes no difference to me.
  = No matter who
⑤ <u>Whoever</u> has a talent is welcome to join the contest.
  = Anyone who

24 다음 주어진 단어를 우리말에 맞게 배열하세요.

> • 그 문제가 아무리 어려워도, 그는 쉽게 풀 것이다. (difficult, however, is, the problem), he will solve it easily.

➡ ___________________________

25 다음 밑줄 친 부분 중 생략할 수 <u>없는</u> 것은?

① The woman <u>whom</u> I wanted to meet was on vacation.
② There's the old oak tree <u>which was</u> standing in front of my home.
③ He's watching the bird <u>that is</u> sitting on the wire.
④ I had to do <u>what was</u> to be done.
⑤ I'm not the only one <u>that is</u> dreaming of a different world.

26 두 문장이 같은 뜻이 되도록 빈칸을 채우세요.

> • Oxygen and moisture are what are needed for a faster recovery from the skin damage.
> = Oxygen and moisture are the things ___________ ___________ needed for a faster recovery from the skin damage.

27 어법상 옳은 것 2개는?

① This is the house in which my grandparents lived.
② I know a place where we can swim there in summer.
③ She met the writer who books are on the bestseller list.
④ He is the person to which I talked about my problem.
⑤ That is the restaurant where we ate dinner yesterday.

28 각 빈칸에 빠짐없이 단어를 하나씩 넣어 영작할 때, 빈칸 (B), (D), (G)에 들어갈 적절한 단어로 짝지어진 것은? (단, 축약하지 말 것)

> 그 카페는 항상 노트북으로 작업하는 프리랜서들로 가득하다.
> ➡ The coffee shop (A) (B) (C) (D) (E) (F) (G) on their laptops.

① always, with, who
② is, filled, freelancers
③ is, with, always
④ always, with, work
⑤ always, filled, who

29 다음 중 주어진 문장의 밑줄 친 when과 쓰임이 같은 것은?

> Monday is the day when I don't like to wake up in the morning.

① Do you know when we have a meeting?
② I love winter when I can go skiing.
③ She was watching TV when we visited her last night.
④ When do you think you can drop by here?
⑤ I used to play soccer after school when I was a middle school student.

30 빈칸에 공통으로 들어갈 말로 알맞은 것은?

> __________ makes a boy become a man is quite different from __________ makes a girl become a woman.

① where ② which ③ who
④ what ⑤ that

31 다음 밑줄 친 부분 중 그 쓰임이 잘못된 것은?

① The cat that is sleeping on the chair is called Jude.
② The hotel where I'm staying at is located in the center of Tokyo.
③ A comet has a tail which is made of frozen gases.
④ Next summer is when I plan to go to Italy.
⑤ That is why his record can hardly be recognized.

32 다음 두 문장을 한 문장으로 바꾸어 쓸 때 어법상 옳지 않은 것은?

> • He bought the studio.
> • A famous painter had lived in the studio.

① He bought the studio which a famous painter had lived in.
② He bought the studio that a famous painter had lived in.
③ He bought the studio in which a famous painter had lived.
④ He bought the studio in that a famous painter had lived.
⑤ He bought the studio where a famous painter had lived.

33 다음 중 어법상 틀린 문장을 고른 것은?

① Tell me what you see when you get there.
② I don't know whom she invited to the party.
③ Do you know the person who won the competition?
④ He showed me the things what he bought yesterday.
⑤ I decided to buy the car which my parents recommended.

CH
14
관계사

34 다음 중 주어진 문장의 밑줄 친 how와 쓰임이 같은 것은?

> I really respect how you spoke up when they asked for your opinion.

① How did you make him decide it so quickly?
② How am I supposed to live without you?
③ She told me how nice her new neighbors are.
④ How do you usually spend your weekends?
⑤ They are not much interested in how other people live and think.

35 다음 문장의 빈칸에 들어갈 말이 차례대로 짝지어진 것은?

> • Many countries in Asia are learning ________ Korea has developed its economy.
> • I visited Rome last year ________ it was very hot.
> • I graduated from the college ________ I learned a lot about chemistry.

① how – when – which
② why – which – which
③ how – when – where
④ why – when – which
⑤ how – why – where

36 다음 문장의 빈칸에 들어갈 말이 차례대로 짝지어진 것은?

> My brother __________ wife is a Canadian studied at the University of Ottawa, __________ is located in the heart of Canada's capital.

① that – where
② who – where
③ whose – where
④ who – which
⑤ whose – which

37 아래 그림은 Yoon이라는 음악가가 살았던 집을 소개하는 장면입니다. 집을 소개한 설명 중 표현이 어색한 것을 고르세요.

> "This is the house in which Yoon, a famous musician from the early-1900s, lived."

① Here is the room in which he stayed most of the time.
② It is the piano with which he worked.
③ That is the chair on which he usually sat.
④ The music to which we're now listening is his last work.
⑤ This is the pen on which he wrote.

38 다음 우리말에 맞게 영작하세요. (단, 관계대명사와 주어진 단어를 반드시 사용할 것)

(1)
> 나는 네가 어젯밤에 연주한 그 노래를 듣고 싶어. (play)

➡ I want to listen to the song __________

__________________ .

(2)
> 나는 다른 사람들을 구하기 위해 그의 목숨을 거는 소방관을 존경한다. (risk, save)

➡ I respect the firefighter __________

__________________ .

CHAPTER 15
접속사

Problem Solving Skill	페이지	성취도				
		100%	99~75%	74~50%	49~25%	24~0%
PSS 1 and, but, or	336					
PSS 2 명령문+and/or	337					
PSS 3 not only A but also B	338					
PSS 4 both A and B, either A or B, neither A nor B	340					
PSS 5 because, so	342					
PSS 6 as	344					
PSS 7 조건을 나타내는 접속사	345					
PSS 8 so that ~, so ~ that …	347					

PSS 9 명사절을 이끄는 접속사	페이지	성취도				
		100%	99~75%	74~50%	49~25%	24~0%
PSS 9-1 that	349					
PSS 9-2 whether	351					
PSS 10 시간을 나타내는 접속사 I	353					
PSS 11 시간을 나타내는 접속사 II	355					
PSS 12 even though, even if	356					
PSS 13 접속부사 I	357					
PSS 14 접속부사 II	359					
중간·기말고사 대비문제	361					

PSS 1 and, but, or

and, but, or는 대등한 내용과 형태의 낱말과 낱말, 구와 구 또는 절과 절을 연결한다. 세 개 이상의 단어가 나열될 때는 마지막 단어 앞에 접속사를 쓴다.

and	~와, 그리고, ~하고 나서	and는 앞뒤의 내용이 대등하거나 비슷한 것, 또는 이어지는 행위를 나타내는 말을 연결한다. We should learn English **and** another foreign language. 우리는 영어와 또 다른 외국어를 배워야 한다. Get out a pencil **and** write down your wishes on the paper. 연필을 꺼내서 종이에 네 소원들을 적어 봐. *cf.* 접속사의 앞뒤 절의 주어가 같을 때는 접속사 뒤에 나오는 주어를 생략할 수 있다. He finally found his talents **and (he)** developed them. 그는 결국 그의 재능을 찾아서 그것들을 개발했다.
but	하지만, 그러나	앞뒤의 내용이 반대되는 것을 연결한다. We did our best, **but** we lost the game again. 우리는 최선을 다했지만, 게임에 또다시 지고 말았다. The food was delicious, **but** it was too expensive. 음식은 맛있었지만 너무 비쌌다. *cf.* not A but B 'A가 아니라 B' My brother is **not** in Paris **but** in London. 내 남동생은 파리가 아니라 런던에 있다.
or	또는, 아니면	Jordan usually goes to a library **or** a museum on Saturday. Jordan은 토요일에는 대개 도서관이나 박물관에 간다. Does she work at a radio station **or** a post office? 그녀는 라디오 방송국에서 일하니 아니면 우체국에서 일하니? You can use a book, a magazine, **or** a newspaper. 너는 책, 잡지 또는 신문을 이용할 수 있다.

정답 p.80

PRACTICE 1

괄호 안에 들어갈 알맞은 접속사를 골라 동그라미 하세요.

1 Is that frog alive (and, but, or) dead?

2 I've tried hard, (and, but, or) I'm still not good at playing the violin.

3 Do you still live in Arizona (and, but, or) have you moved to another state?

4 I think I am responsible for myself (and, but, or) I can take good care of myself.

5 At first, I couldn't remember her name, (and, but, or) later it occurred to me.

6 I'm not sure whether I'll work at home (and, but, or) abroad after graduation.

7 She always talks a lot (and, but, or) wants to know everything.

8 The secret to success is not luck (and, but, or) hard work.

9 Please write the number of the correct answer (and, but, or) circle the correct answer.

10 I ate an apple, chicken salad, (and, but, or) some pudding for lunch.

11 She got very angry, (and, but, or) she tried not to show it.

12 Students can submit their assignments online, in person (and, but, or) via email.

13 He practiced really hard for the match (and, but, or) finally won the championship.

14 You have to call the police right away (and, but, or) describe what you saw.

15 He needed the book not because he had to do homework with it, (and, but, or) because he had to return it.

PSS 2 명령문 + and / or

명령문 + and	~해라, 그러면	Go to the airport to pick her up, **and** she'll be very happy. 그녀를 데리러 공항에 가라, 그러면 그녀는 매우 기뻐할 것이다. = If you go to the airport to pick her up, she'll be very happy. 만약 네가 그녀를 데리러 공항에 간다면, 그녀는 매우 기뻐할 것이다.
명령문 + or	~해라, 그렇지 않으면	Hand in the report by tomorrow, **or** you'll be given extra homework. 내일까지 보고서를 제출해라, 그렇지 않으면 너에게는 추가 숙제가 주어질 것이다. = If you don't hand in the report by tomorrow, you'll be given extra homework. 만약 네가 내일까지 보고서를 제출하지 않는다면, 너에게는 추가 숙제가 주어질 것이다.

PRACTICE 2

두 문장이 같은 뜻이 되도록 빈칸에 and나 or 중 알맞은 것을 쓰세요.

1 If you take a shuttle bus, you can save time and energy.

= Take a shuttle bus, ____________ you can save time and energy.

2 If you don't try to keep a promise, she will be disappointed in you.

= Try to keep a promise, ____________ she will be disappointed in you.

3 If you get up early in the morning, you will be able to see the beautiful sunrise.

= Get up early in the morning, ____________ you will be able to see the beautiful sunrise.

4 If you don't spend more time with your family, you'll grow apart from them.

= Spend more time with your family, ____________ you'll grow apart from them.

5 If you are not quiet, your baby sister will wake up and cry.

= Be quiet, ____________ your baby sister will wake up and cry.

6 If you finish the report before this Wednesday, you'll get bonus points.

= Finish the report before this Wednesday, ____________ you'll get bonus points.

7 If you don't write down every detail you see, you won't be able to remember them.

= Write down every detail you see, ____________ you won't be able to remember them.

8 If you go to the public library on Saturday afternoon, you can meet Jane.

= Go to the public library on Saturday afternoon, ____________ you can meet Jane.

9 If you don't read as many good books as possible when you have time, you'll regret it.

= Read as many good books as possible when you have time, ____________ you'll regret it.

10 If you are not responsible for your acts, nobody will trust you.

= Be responsible for your acts, ____________ nobody will trust you.

PSS 3 not only A but also B

PROBLEM
SOLVING
SKILL

「not only A but also B」는 'A뿐만 아니라 B도'의 의미로 「B as well as A」로 바꾸어 쓸 수 있다. 이때 A와 B는 병렬 구조를 이룬다. (also는 생략 가능)

Bright colors **not only** make you feel good **but also** calm you down.

밝은 색은 당신을 기분 좋게 만들 뿐만 아니라 진정시킨다.

= Bright colors **calm you down as well as** make you feel good.

The information includes **not only** their history **but also** their traditional customs.

그 정보는 그들의 역사뿐만 아니라 전통적인 관습도 포함한다.

= The information includes **their traditional customs as well as** their history.

> ***cf.*** 「not only A but also B」와 「B as well as A」 뒤에 나오는 동사의 수는 B에 일치시킨다.
> **Not only** you **but also he** is going to join our club.
>
> 너뿐만 아니라 그도 우리의 클럽에 가입할 것이다.
> = **He as well as** you is going to join our club.
>
> ***cf.*** 「not only A but also B」에서 also가 생략될 경우 문장 끝에 as well을 쓸 수 있다.
> **Not only** you **but** he is going to join our club **as well**. (○)

정답 p.81

PRACTICE 3

주어진 문장과 같은 뜻이 되도록 문장을 바꾸어 쓰세요.

1 Not only the United States but also some other countries use English as their first language.
= Some other countries as well as the United States use English as their first language.

2 I'd like to study Chinese as well as English to become a competent translator.
=

3 You have to consider your talents as well as your interests to find a good job for yourself.
=

4 I not only work hard but also do things that others don't want to do.
=

5 We need to hire a new secretary as well as a new salesperson.
=

6 Sally as well as I wants to succeed in losing weight and being more confident.
=

7 You should not only set a goal but also do your best.
=

8 It is not only a waste of money but also a waste of time.
=

9 A clean environment is good for our economy as well as essential for our health.
=

10 Not only the students but also the teachers were shocked by the principal's final decision.
=

11 Human genes determine not only what people look like but also what diseases they may get.
=

12 Humans have explored the universe as well as have researched the Earth.
=

PSS 4   both A and B, either A or B, neither A nor B

1. 「both A and B」 'A와 B 둘 다'

This sign represents **both** love **and** peace. 이 기호는 사랑과 평화 둘 다를 나타낸다.
Both Jisu **and** Hoyoung **are** planning to go to Japan during the vacation.
지수와 호영이 둘 다 방학 동안에 일본에 갈 계획이다.

   cf. 「both A and B」가 주어일 때는 항상 복수 동사가 뒤따라 온다.

2. 「either A or B」 'A와 B 중 어느 하나'

I'm going to take **either** Sam **or** Laura to the party.
나는 Sam과 Laura 중 어느 한 명을 파티에 데려갈 것이다.

   cf. 「either A or B」 뒤에 오는 동사는 동사에 더 가까이 있는 B의 수에 일치시킨다.

Either he **or** I **have** to exchange e-mails with the company.
그와 나 가운데 한 명은 그 회사와 이메일을 주고받아야 한다.

3. 「neither A nor B」 'A도 B도 ~ 아닌'

My brother resembles **neither** my mom **nor** my dad. 내 남동생은 엄마도 아빠도 닮지 않았다.

   cf. 「neither A nor B」 뒤에 오는 동사는 동사에 더 가까이 있는 B의 수에 일치시킨다.

Neither Suji **nor** you **are** invited to Mr. Scott's new house.
수지도 너도 Scott 씨의 새 집에 초대되지 않았다.

정답 p.81

PRACTICE 4

다음 문장의 빈칸에 both ~ and, either ~ or, neither ~ nor 중 알맞은 접속사를 쓰세요.

1   Mr. Kim bought a luxurious car last year. Ms. Lee bought a luxurious car last year, too.

➡ ___________ Mr. Kim ___________ Ms. Lee bought a luxurious car last year.

2   This woman cannot be a suspect. That old lady cannot be a suspect, either.

➡ ___________ this woman ___________ that old lady can be a suspect.

3   You were supposed to take part in the contest. Or she was supposed to take part in the contest.

➡ ___________ you ___________ she was supposed to take part in the contest.

4 Teachers had fun at the amusement park. Students had fun at the amusement park, too.

➡ ___________ teachers ___________ students had fun at the amusement park.

5 Too much food is not good for your body. Too little food is not good for your body, either.

➡ ___________ too much food ___________ too little food is good for your body.

6 I'd like to study English in England. Or I'd like to study English in Australia.

➡ I'd like to study English ___________ in England ___________ in Australia.

7 Mike doesn't enjoy going to the movies. He doesn't enjoy listening to music, either.

➡ Mike enjoys ___________ going to the movies ___________ listening to music.

8 The 2002 World Cup was held in Korea. It was held in Japan, too.

➡ The 2002 World Cup was held ___________ in Korea ___________ in Japan.

9 The game can be played by six people. Or it can be played by nine people.

➡ The game can be played by ___________ six people ___________ nine people.

10 The new technology developed recently is simple. It is effective, too.

➡ The new technology developed recently is ___________ simple ___________ effective.

정답 p.81

PRACTICE 5

괄호 안의 동사를 이용하여 빈칸에 알맞은 말을 써 넣으세요. (단, 현재형으로 쓰세요.)

1 Either my wife or I ___________ to stay home and wait for my parents. (have)

2 Neither he nor his friends ___________ allowed to go out after 9 in the evening. (be)

3 I found out that both Jill and Shane ___________ good at painting portraits. (be)

4 Either my sister or I ___________ public transportation every Monday. (use)

5 Both the book and the movie ___________ about a young girl growing up in America. (be)

6 Neither Dorothy nor I ___________ to get along with unfamiliar people. (like)

7 Both Susan and Peter ___________ to know more about the Korean language. (want)

8 Either my brothers or my mom ___________ care of my dog while I'm away. (take)

9 Neither Sally nor Peter usually ___________ time in the library after school. (spend)

10 Either my classmates or my teacher ___________ me walk up the stairs. (help)

PSS 5 because, so

because	~ 때문에	**because가 이끄는 절은 원인을 나타낸다.** I'm going to learn their language **because** the language is a part of their culture. 언어는 그들 문화의 일부이기 때문에 나는 그들의 언어를 배울 것이다. **Because** the sign was written in Chinese, I couldn't read it. 표지판이 중국어로 쓰여 있었기 때문에, 나는 그것을 읽을 수 없었다. ***cf.*** because와 달리 because of 뒤에는 명사(구)가 온다. Consumers tend to buy things more **because of the ads**. 소비자들은 광고 때문에 물품들을 더 많이 사는 경향이 있다.
so	그래서, 그러므로	**so가 이끄는 절은 결과를 나타낸다.** The language is a part of their culture, **so** I'm going to learn their language. 언어는 그들 문화의 일부이므로 나는 그들의 언어를 배울 것이다. The sign was written in Chinese, **so** I couldn't read it. 표지판이 중국어로 쓰여 있어서 나는 그것을 읽을 수 없었다.

정답 p.81

PRACTICE 6

다음 문장을 바르게 해석하고, 밑줄 친 부분이 원인을 의미하는지 결과를 의미하는지 쓰세요.

> 보 기 Junho couldn't find his little sister anywhere, so he went to the police station.
> ➡ 준호는 그의 여동생을 어디서도 찾을 수 없어서 그는 경찰서에 갔다. [결과]

1 Because the royal family in Europe played golf, it began to become popular among rich people.

 ➡ ____ [   ]

2 Strong winds blow from the sea, so most walls around the houses in Jeju Island are built with stones.

 ➡ ____ [   ]

3 Because people grow up in different environments, they can never be the same as someone else.

 ➡ ____ [   ]

4 Because the museum was burnt down during the German invasion, <u>we couldn't see the original one.</u>

➡ ____ [   ]

5 <u>I know what it is like to be a new student in a strange school</u>, so I want to help him fit in.

➡ ____ [   ]

6 The water is clean, and the air is fresh, so <u>I prefer living in the countryside to living in the city.</u>

➡ ____ [   ]

7 Because <u>keeping a diary helps me think about my everyday life</u>, I try to write in it every day.

➡ ____ [   ]

8 <u>I like to observe different kinds of fish</u>, so I am planning to visit the aquarium in Singapore.

➡ ____ [   ]

9 Because we live in the age of information technology, <u>many jobs require us to have computer skills.</u>

➡ ____ [   ]

10 <u>The chocolate cake was very delicious</u>, so I couldn't stop myself from eating too much of it.

➡ ____ [   ]

정답 p.81

PRACTICE 7

다음 문장의 빈칸에 because나 because of 중 알맞은 것을 쓰세요.

1 The time of departure is delayed _______________ the thunderstorm.

2 I couldn't concentrate on my work _______________ I didn't get enough sleep last night.

3 I feel sorry that she had to quit her work _______________ her illness.

4 The polluted water looked green _______________ plankton.

5 We couldn't make it on time _______________ there were so many cars on the road.

6 I couldn't go to the concert _______________ I had to help my mom.

7 Some teenagers tend to do what they don't want to do _______________ the pressure from their parents.

8 The meeting couldn't help but be delayed _______________ the plane arrived late.

PSS 6 as

as	~처럼, ~대로	I just entered the room through the window **as** he did. 나는 단지 그가 한 것처럼 창문을 통해 방으로 들어갔다. I have to work on history more than any other subject **as** my teacher said. 나는 선생님이 말씀하신 대로 다른 과목보다 역사를 더 열심히 해야 한다.
	~함에 따라, ~할수록	**As** you experience many things, your interests may change. 네가 많은 것을 경험함에 따라, 네 관심사가 변할 수도 있다. **As** we went up the mountain, we got tired and thirsty. 우리는 산 위로 올라갈수록 피곤해지고 목이 말랐다.
	~ 때문에	**As** it was very hot and humid, I was exhausted before I got there. 매우 덥고 습했기 때문에, 나는 그곳에 도착하기 전에 지쳤다. **As** it was a traditional holiday, I went to my grandparents' house. 명절이었기 때문에, 나는 조부모님 댁에 갔다.

정답 p.82

PRACTICE 8

밑줄 친 as의 의미가 〈보기〉의 (A)와 같으면 A, (B)와 같으면 B, (C)와 같으면 C를 쓰세요.

> 보 기
> (A) As Mark moved to the city, I have to visit the city to meet him.
> (B) I took five pills at a time for two weeks as the doctor ordered.
> (C) As time passed, my dog began to recover.

1   As it's definitely going to rain tomorrow, we should postpone the field trip. [   ]

2   As the show went on, the audience got more and more excited. [   ]

3   I went to the garden and dug a big hole as I was told. [   ]

4   As summer nears, the sun rises earlier. [   ]

5   All the furniture has been placed in the right place as I asked. [   ]

6   As Mom was not home during the weekend, I had to take care of my little brother. [   ]

7   As the man walked away, the sound of his footsteps gradually disappeared. [   ]

8 I had to walk home <u>as</u> the bus drivers were on strike. [   ]

9 If you want to impress the boss, just do <u>as</u> Jenny does. [   ]

10 <u>As</u> the electricity bill was too high last month, we decided to save the electricity. [   ]

PSS 7 조건을 나타내는 접속사

if	～한다면	**If** we do something about it now, they won't leave the town. 우리가 지금 그것에 대해 무언가를 한다면, 그들은 도시를 떠나지 않을 것이다. **If** we **don't** do something about it now, they will leave the town. = **Unless** we do something about it now, they will leave the town. 우리가 지금 그것에 대해 무언가를 하지 않는다면, 그들은 도시를 떠날 것이다. *cf.* 「if ~ not」은 unless로 바꾸어 쓸 수 있다.
once	일단 ～하면	**Once** you try bibimbap, you will like it. 너는 일단 비빔밥을 먹어보면, 그것을 좋아하게 될 것이다.
as long as	～하는 한	**As long as** it doesn't rain, I will ride a bike. 비가 오지 않는 한, 나는 자전거를 탈 것이다.
in case	～할 경우에 대비해서	Take this medicine with you **in case** you feel sick during the trip. 여행 중에 네가 아플 경우를 대비해서 이 약을 챙겨라.

cf. 조건을 나타내는 부사절에서는 현재형이 미래형을 대신한다.

  If you will buy a shirt, you'll get another shirt for free. (X)

  ➡ If you **buy** a shirt, you'll get another shirt for free. (O)

  셔츠 한 개를 사면 공짜로 셔츠를 하나 더 얻게 될 것이다.

PRACTICE 9

주어진 문장을 unless를 이용하여 다시 쓰세요.

1 I'll just walk there if it's not far from my house.

= ____

2 The door won't open if you don't know the exact password.

= ____

3 If you are not careful with it, you might get into trouble.

= ____

4 If you don't stop spending too much money, you'll be broke soon.

= ____

5 Her heart disease will get worse if she doesn't go on a diet.

= ____

6 You will get soaked on the way home if you don't bring your umbrella with you.

= ____

7 If you don't say anything when you need help, no one can help you.

= ____

8 You cannot build a good relationship if you don't try to listen to others.

= ____

9 If you don't have much experience in that field, you won't get the job.

= ____

10 If you don't follow the directions, you will get lost in a strange city.

= ____

PRACTICE 10

괄호 안에 주어진 말을 바르게 배열하여 문장을 완성하세요.

1 ____, he will fall in love with her.
(he, once, her, sees)

2 ____, you won't regret.
(long, your best, as, you, as, do)

3 ____, let me know.
(change, you, if, your mind)

4 ____, you can solve any problems.
(long, yourself, as, you, as, believe in)

5 _________________________________, people will like you, too.

    (you, once, yourself, like)

6 _________________________________, you will be hungry later.

    (now, unless, eat, you)

7 _________________________________, you need to spend much time on it.

    (you, want, if, to speak, well, English)

8 _________________________________, he doesn't stop reading it.

    (a book, he, starts, to read, once)

9 _________________________________, we can arrive there on time.

    (as, snow, as, it, long, doesn't)

10 _________________________________, you can play the game easily.

    (the rules, once, learn, you)

11 _________________________________, invite your friend or neighbor to join you.

    (you, if, like, exercising, alone, don't)

12 _________________________________, you'll be late for the meeting.

    (you, quickly, unless, walk, more)

PSS 8   so that ~, so ~ that …

so that ~	~하기 위해서, ~하도록	목적을 나타낼 때 쓰며, in order to[so as to]와 같은 의미를 나타낸다. Manage your time **so that** you can do important things first. 중요한 것들을 먼저 할 수 있도록 너의 시간을 관리해라. = Manage your time **in order to** do important things first. Turn around **so that** you can see Mike standing behind you. Mike가 네 뒤에 서 있는 것을 볼 수 있도록 뒤로 돌아라. = Turn around **in order to** see Mike standing behind you.

		결과를 나타낼 때 쓰고 because와 같은 의미를 나타낸다. so 뒤에는 형용사나 부사가 온다. Ted was injured **so** badly **that** he had to stay in bed for a few months. Ted는 매우 심하게 다쳐서 몇 달 동안 침대에 누워 있어야 했다. = **Because** Ted was injured so badly, he had to stay in bed for a few months. I became **so** close to his family **that** it was hard to say good-bye. 나는 그의 가족과 매우 가까워져서 작별 인사를 하기가 힘들었다. = **Because** I became so close to his family, it was hard to say good-bye. ***cf.*** 형용사/부사가 아닌 「(a/an)+형용사+명사」가 원인이 되는 경우에는 so 대신 such를 쓴다. He was **such** a nice friend **that** I'll always remember him. 그는 매우 멋진 친구여서 나는 항상 그를 기억할 것이다.
so ~ that …	매우 ~해서 …한	

정답 p.82

PRACTICE 11

〈보기〉와 같이 「so that ~」이나 「so ~ that …」을 이용하여 두 문장을 한 문장으로 바꾸어 쓰세요.

보 기	She made him a cup of tea. She hoped it would help him relax.
	➡ *She made him a cup of tea so that it could help him relax.*

1 Throw the ball softly. I want to hit it well.

➡ ____

2 Mr. Park spoke slowly. He wanted everyone to write down what he was saying.

➡ ____

3 Make your plan as specific as possible. We want you to follow it step by step.

➡ ____

4 The fishermen start the morning by mending their nets. They want to fish with them.

➡ ____

5 Review your notes every day. We hope you don't have to study all night before the exam.

➡ ____

➡ <u>I was so exhausted that I couldn't go up to the top of the mountain.</u>

6　I had become close to my teacher. It became easier for me to talk with him.

➡ ____

7　Taekwondo is popular. Thousands of its practitioners visit Korea every year.

➡ ____

8　I'm terrible at drawing. I don't think I am talented in art.

➡ ____

9　Information is easily accessible on the Internet. You can get anything you want.

➡ ____

10　My father is busy with his work. He can't take summer holidays this year.

➡ ____

PSS 9　명사절을 이끄는 접속사

PROBLEM SOLVING SKILL

PSS 9-1 that

주어	~라는 것은	that절이 주어 역할을 할 때는 주로 문장의 맨 앞에 가주어 it을 쓰고 진주어인 that절은 뒤로 보낸다. **That children resemble their parents** is natural. 자녀들이 그들의 부모를 닮는 것은 당연하다. = **It** is natural **that children resemble their parents**. 　가주어　　　　　　　　　　　　　　　　진주어 **It** is amazing **that it took only two days by ship**. 배로 겨우 이틀 걸렸다는 것은 놀랍다.
목적어	~라는 것을	목적어 역할을 하는 명사절을 이끄는 that은 생략할 수 있다. The research shows **(that)** it is because of the high temperature. 연구는 그것이 높은 온도 때문이라는 것을 보여준다. I've heard **(that)** you worked at the White House. 나는 당신이 백악관에서 일했다는 것을 들었다.

CH **15** 접속사

보어	~라는 것인	The important thing is **that** he doesn't know a lot about the car yet. 중요한 것은 그가 아직 그 차에 대해 많이 알지 못한다는 것이다. The problem is **that** they can break the songwriter's copyright. 문제는 그들이 그 작곡가의 저작권을 침해할 수 있다는 것이다.
동격	~라는	We often forget **the fact that health is important**. 우리는 종종 건강이 중요하다는 사실을 잊는다. ***cf.*** 동격의 that은 fact, rumor, news, idea와 같은 명사와 함께 쓰이는 경우가 많다.

정답 p.83

PRACTICE 12

〈보기〉와 같이 주어진 문장을 바꾸어 쓰세요.

> 보 기 Art has the power to evoke strong emotions and convey messages. It is amazing.
> ➡ *It is amazing that art has the power to evoke strong emotions and convey messages.*

1 Sound travels much faster in steel than in water. It is interesting.

➡ ____

2 A lot of workers in the factory died because of the fire. It is a pity.

➡ ____

3 We survived the car crash. It was unbelievable.

➡ ____

4 We must do something to help the town. It is very important.

➡ ____

> 보 기 Mr. Kim is a well-mannered person. (They don't think)
> ➡ *They don't think that Mr. Kim is a well-mannered person.*

5 His arm was badly injured. (The young man said)

➡ ____

6 I could take English and other language courses. (I was excited to know)

➡ ____

7 I may have made a lot of mistakes. (I'm afraid)

➡ ____

8 The baby hardly eats all day long. (Mother is worried)

➡ ____

9 Millions of years ago there were many volcanoes in this area. That is the fact.

➡ ____

10 There are no magazines that you can read in this cafe. That is the difference between them.

➡ ____

11 Our flight to Canada would be expensive. That was the problem.

➡ ____

12 You should respect other people's cultures. That is the important thing.

➡ ____

정답 p.83

PRACTICE 13

밑줄 친 that의 용법을 주어, 목적어, 보어, 동격 중에 골라서 쓰세요.

1 We like the idea that we can start the morning with music. [   ]

2 I knew that I had to follow the rules. [   ]

3 Did you hear the news that a 15-year-old boy entered university? [   ]

4 The worst thing is that you waste too much money. [   ]

5 It is essential that we recycle bottles and cans. [   ]

PSS 9-2 whether

주어	~인지 (어떤지)는	**Whether** you agree or disagree isn't important. 네가 동의하는지 동의하지 않는지는 중요하지 않다. **Whether** you are rich or not doesn't matter. 네가 부유한지 아닌지는 문제가 되지 않는다.
목적어	~인지 (어떤지)를	목적어로 쓰인 명사절을 이끄는 whether는 if와 바꾸어 쓸 수 있다. We can't predict **whether** the weather is going to be fine. 우리는 날씨가 좋을 것인지 어떨 것인지 예측할 수가 없다. = We can't predict **if** the weather is going to be fine.

<table>
<tr><td rowspan="2" style="text-align:center"></td><td rowspan="2" style="text-align:center"></td><td>I was just wondering whether you were in favor of it or against it.
나는 그냥 네가 그것에 찬성하는지 반대하는지 궁금했어.
= I was just wondering if you were in favor of it or against it.</td></tr>
<tr><td style="text-align:center">보어</td><td style="text-align:center">~인지 아닌지,
~ 여부</td><td>The question is whether they will support us.
문제는 그들이 우리를 지지할 것인지의 여부이다.</td></tr>
</table>

cf. whether는 '~이든지 아니든지'의 뜻으로 양보절을 이끌기도 한다.
You should get started now **whether** you're prepared or not.
너는 준비가 되었든 아니든 지금 시작해야 한다.

정답 p.83

PRACTICE 14

〈보기〉와 같이 빈칸에 알맞은 말을 쓰세요.

> **보 기**
> Are you going to let him know it by e-mail or telephone?
> ➡ Have you decided _if you are going to let him know it by e-mail or telephone_?
> ➡ Have you decided _whether you are going to let him know it by e-mail or telephone_?

1 Is she going to study English literature or Asian history?
➡ Has she decided ____?
➡ Has she decided ____?

2 Is he going to go to graduate school or get a job?
➡ Has he decided ____?
➡ Has he decided ____?

3 Are you going to attend the party or study for the final exam?
➡ Have you decided ____?
➡ Have you decided ____?

4 Is she going to face the difficult situation or run away from it?
➡ Has she decided ____?
➡ Has she decided ____?

5 Are you going to keep working on the project or stop doing it?
➡ Have you decided ____?
➡ Have you decided ____?

6 Is he going to take part in the competition or keep practicing a little more?
➡ Has he decided ____?
➡ Has he decided ____?

7 Are they going to make apologies or stay mad at each other?

➡ Have they decided ____?

➡ Have they decided ____?

8 Is your brother going to return the shirt or keep it?

➡ Has your brother decided ____?

➡ Has your brother decided ____?

PSS 10 시간을 나타내는 접속사 Ⅰ

when	~할 때	**1. 특정 시점에 비교적 긴 다른 사건과 동시에 일어나고 있는 하나의 사건을 나타낸다.** Vicky was listening to music **when** her cell phone rang. Vicky는 휴대폰이 울렸을 때 음악을 듣고 있었다. **2. 과거의 일정 기간 동안에 일어난 사건을 나타낸다.** **When** I was a seven-year-old boy, this area began to be developed. 내가 7살 소년이었을 때, 이 지역이 개발되기 시작했다. **3. 한 가지의 사건 직후에 일어난 다른 사건을 나타낸다.** **When** Inho finished cleaning the garage, his friend came to his house. 인호가 차고 청소를 끝냈을 때, 그의 친구가 그의 집에 왔다.
as	~하고 있을 때, ~하면서, ~함에 따라	**1. 두 가지의 비교적 짧은 사건이 동시에 또는 연속적으로 일어날 때 쓰고, 이때의 as는 when으로 바꾸어 쓸 수 있다.** **As[When]** I heard his story, I could recall my childhood. 그의 이야기를 들으면서[들었을 때], 나는 내 어린 시절을 회상할 수 있었다. **2. 한 가지 사건에 변화가 생김에 따라 나머지 사건에도 변화가 생길 때는 as를 쓴다.** **As** she grew older, she became interested in astronomy. 그녀는 나이가 듦에 따라, 천문학에 관심을 갖게 되었다.

CH
15
접속사

<table>
<tr>
<td>while</td>
<td>~하는 동안</td>
<td>비교적 긴 두 가지 사건이 동시에 일어나고 있을 때 쓰고, 이때의 while은 as로 바꾸어 쓸 수 있다.

While[As] I was climbing up the mountain, I heard the sound of a waterfall. 산을 오르고 있는 동안에 나는 폭포 소리를 들었다.
While[As] my mom was cooking dinner, my puppy watched her cooking. 우리 엄마가 저녁식사를 준비하고 있는 동안에, 내 강아지는 그녀가 요리하는 것을 지켜보았다.
cf. while은 '~인 반면'이란 뜻으로 대조를 나타내는 접속사로도 쓰인다.
　　While I chose an orange, my brother chose a banana.
　　나는 오렌지를 고른 반면, 나의 형은 바나나를 골랐다.</td>
</tr>
</table>

> ***cf.*** 일반적으로 특정 기간 동안 두 가지 사건이 동시에 일어나고 있음을 나타낼 때는 when, as, while을 모두 쓸 수 있다.
> **When[As/While]** we were waiting for a bus, Paul saw us and stopped his car.
> 우리가 버스를 기다리고 있었을 때, Paul이 우리를 보고 그의 차를 멈추었다.

정답 p.83

PRACTICE 15

괄호 안에 들어갈 알맞은 접속사를 <u>모두</u> 골라 동그라미 하세요.

1　(As, While) you get older, you will gain a lot of experience.

2　The airplane exploded (while, when) it was taking off.

3　Even (when, as) paper was first invented, people still wrote on clay.

4　The situation worsened (as, when) time passed.

5　James bumped his head (while, as) he was getting off the car.

6　The desk broke (when, while) I put my new computer and printer on it.

7　I enjoy eating popcorn and drinking soda (while, as) I watch movies.

8　What do you usually do (when, as) you have free time?

9　(While, As) I was reading the article about the battlefield, I thought about the people who were living there.

10　Would you hold the dog for a moment (while, as) I examine it?

11　He ran away from home to New York (as, when) he was just a boy.

12　The mailman delivered the package (while, as) I was out.

13　(While, When) I got back home, I turned on the TV first.

14　(While, When) we were setting up a tent at the campsite, it started to rain.

15　(When, As) the helicopter flew over the Grand Canyon, I could see the beautiful landscape.

PSS 11 시간을 나타내는 접속사 Ⅱ

before	~ 전에	**Before** you hand in your answer sheet, make sure that you wrote your name on it. 답안지를 제출하기 전에 이름을 썼는지 확인해라.
after	~ 후에	**After** Kelly graduated from college, she married a police officer. Kelly는 대학을 졸업한 후에, 경찰관과 결혼을 했다.
until[till]	~까지	I had to wait **until[till]** the kid's parents came to pick him up. 나는 그 아이의 부모님이 그를 데리러 올 때까지 기다려야 했다.
since	~ 이후로	Her personality has changed a lot **since** she met Paul. 그녀가 Paul을 만난 이후로, 그녀의 성격은 많이 변했다. *cf.* since는 '~하기 때문에'라는 뜻의 이유를 나타내는 접속사로 쓰이기도 한다. **Since** the weather was terrible, we decided to stay indoors all day. 날씨가 매우 나빴기 때문에, 우리는 하루 종일 실내에 있기로 결정했다.
as soon as	~하자마자	**As soon as** he heard the news, he rushed to my house. 그는 그 소식을 듣자마자, 나의 집으로 서둘러 왔다.
every time	~할 때마다	**Every time** you feel depressed, remember that you're loved by many people around you. 기분이 침체될 때마다 네가 주위의 많은 사람들로부터 사랑 받고 있음을 기억해라.

CH
15
접속사

정답 p.84

PRACTICE 16 [1-15]

괄호 안에 들어갈 알맞은 접속사를 골라 동그라미 하세요.

1 I've been living here (until, since) our family moved to Korea in 2020.

2 The little boy started to cry (until, as soon as) his father boarded the airplane.

3 A friend of mine called me (while, as soon as) I was watching soccer on TV last night.

4 I must not eat anything (since, until) the doctor allows me to do so.

5 (After, Every time) I asked for directions in Seoul, I got different replies.

6 (Unless, When) the chicks cry for food, the mother bird flies away to catch worms.

7 This castle has been standing here (until, since) the king died.

8 The dog raced toward the door (until, as soon as) it heard the bell ring.

9 Why don't we talk about it (before, after) we eat dinner first? I'm so hungry.

10 (After, Before) the leaders of each party met last month, everything has been going well.

11 (Before, As) the day went on, Paul and I got more and more tired of it.

12 (As soon as, Every time) I play with my dog, I throw a Frisbee and my dog catches it.

13 (While, After) we were walking down the road, we found a wallet on the ground.

14 I don't think I can wait (since, until) he apologizes to me about what he did to me last night.

15 My cousin lived in Australia (before, after) he moved to England.

PSS 12 even though, even if

even though, although, though	비록 ~일지라도	even though 뒤에는 확실한 사실 또는 실제로 일어난 일을 나타내는 내용이 오며, 그 내용이 사실임을 강조할 때 쓴다. **Even though** I knew it was dangerous, I continued the experiment. 비록 나는 위험하다는 것을 알았지만, 실험을 계속했다. = **Although** I knew it was dangerous, I continued the experiment. = **Though** I knew it was dangerous, I continued the experiment. *cf.* even though가 although나 though보다 더 강한 양보의 뜻을 가지고 있다.
even if	가령 ~라 할지라도	even if는 확실하지 않은 일을 가정할 때 쓴다. **Even if** she wins the game this time, she will retire. 가령 그녀가 이번에 경기에서 이긴다 할지라도, 그녀는 은퇴할 것이다.

PRACTICE 17

빈칸에 even though 또는 even if 중 알맞은 것을 써 넣으세요.

1 Ms. Wilson enjoys eating kimchi very much, _______________ she is not a Korean.

2 I'm sure we will be proud of ourselves _______________ we lose in the final match.

3 I could still see children playing in the street _______________ it was raining outside.

4 They will lose everything _______________ they survive.

5 _______________ I had never tried Japanese food before, I quickly got used to it.

6 I don't think Dad will be angry at me _______________ I make a big mistake.

7 _______________ it rains tomorrow, we'll go on a picnic.

8 _______________ it was already April, the weather was rather cold.

9 I will have to tell her the news _______________ she doesn't want to hear about it.

10 None of the passengers complained _______________ the flight was delayed.

PSS 13 접속부사 I

접속부사는 접속사가 아니라 부사이므로 절과 절을 연결하지 못하며, 보통 뒤에 ,(콤마)를 찍는다.

for example (=for instance)	예를 들면	People use gestures in various ways. **For example**, the listeners nod when they want to show that they understand what the speakers talk about. 사람들은 다양한 방법으로 몸짓을 사용한다. 예를 들면, 청자는 그들이 화자가 말하는 것을 이해한다는 것을 보여주기를 원할 때 고개를 끄덕인다.
however (=nevertheless, yet)	그러나	When Charlie was young, he liked painting. **However**, he studied law in university and became a lawyer. Charlie는 어렸을 때, 그림 그리는 것을 좋아했다. 그러나 그는 대학교에서 법을 공부했고 변호사가 되었다.
therefore (=consequently, so, thus)	그러므로	The flight was delayed, resulting in them missing their connecting flight. **Therefore**, they had to spend an extra night in the airport. 비행편이 지연되어, 그 결과 그들은 연결편 비행기를 놓쳤다. 그러므로 그들은 공항에서 추가로 하룻밤을 보내야 했다.

in addition, besides, moreover, furthermore	게다가	I haven't made a flight reservation yet. **In addition [Besides]**, I have to extend the visa. 나는 아직 비행기 예약을 하지 못했다. 게다가, 나는 비자를 연장해야 한다.
on the other hand	반면에	My song completely satisfied the judges. **On the other hand**, they didn't like Jordan's at all. 내 노래는 심사위원들을 완전히 만족시켰다. 반면에, 그들은 Jordan의 노래는 조금도 좋아하지 않았다.

정답 p.84

PRACTICE 18

괄호 안에 들어갈 알맞은 말을 골라 동그라미 하세요.

1 You can tell how a dog feels by looking at its tail. (For example, In addition), wagging its tail means it is happy.

2 Many people think spiders are bad insects. (However, Therefore), the very opposite is true.

3 How you speak may affect your relationship with others. (In addition, Therefore), it is nice to say things that leave a good impression.

4 Fruit is a good source of vitamin C, minerals and carbohydrates. (In addition, On the other hand), they taste great, too!

5 Learning a new language can be challenging. (In addition, On the other hand), it opens up doors to new cultures and experiences.

6 Coins all over the world are produced in many shapes and sizes. (For example, However), some coins in Hong Kong have wavy edges.

7 Jane studied hard for the exams. (Therefore, However), her exam results weren't as good as she had expected.

8 Whenever I go shopping, I forget what I need to buy. (Therefore, On the other hand), I'll write a shopping list when I go shopping tomorrow.

9 Before going on a trip abroad, you should try to learn some useful English expressions. (For example, In addition), you'd better try to learn about local customs.

10 I'm good at English and poetry. (On the other hand, In addition), I'm not very good at math and science.

PSS 14 접속부사 Ⅱ

finally, eventually, in the end, at last	결국, 마침내	After one hour waiting, the mechanic arrived and fixed the car. **Finally**, it started to move again. 한 시간의 기다림 후에, 수리공이 도착했고 차를 고쳤다. 결국, 차는 다시 움직이기 시작했다.
in contrast, on the contrary	대조적으로	I have a twin sister. She is very outgoing and talkative. **In contrast**, I am very quiet and shy. 나는 쌍둥이 언니가 있다. 그녀는 매우 사교적이고 이야기하는 것을 좋아한다. 대조적으로, 나는 매우 조용하고 부끄러움을 탄다.
as a result	그 결과로	The typhoon swept the whole town. **As a result**, there were many victims of it. 태풍이 도시 전체를 휩쓸었다. 그 결과로, 많은 희생자가 생겨났다.
in other words, that is (to say)	다시 말해서	Several people who are supposed to lead the meeting are not going to attend the meeting. **In other words**, we have to arrange the meeting again. 회의를 이끌기로 한 몇몇 사람들이 회의에 참석하지 않을 것이다. 다시 말해서, 우리는 회의를 다시 준비해야 한다.

정답 p.84

PRACTICE 19 [1-13]

괄호 안에 들어갈 알맞은 말을 골라 동그라미 하세요.

1 We had to sail through many storms on our way to America. (In other words, Finally), after five weeks, we reached the land.

2 Most Asians use spoons and chopsticks when they eat. (In addition, In contrast), Westerners use forks and knives.

3 My father refused to take the medicine. (However, As a result), he became weaker day by day.

4 A sudden wind came from the open window and papers were all over the floor. (In other words, In contrast), the classroom was a mess.

5 We were worried that the snow would not stop. (As a result, Finally), on the eighth day, it stopped.

6 In the East, the dragon was considered a symbol of good luck. (For example, In contrast), Europeans thought it was a symbol of evil.

7 Since I wanted to lose weight, I started to walk to school instead of taking a bus. (However, As a result), I lost 5 kg in a month.

8 There is a saying "When in Rome, do as the Romans do." (In other words, On the other hand), you must follow local customs.

9 Many English words came from other languages. (On the other hand, For example), the words "restaurant" and "culture" came from French.

10 We were all ready to go. (However, As a result), as we got in the car, it started to rain.

11 Violent online games may affect your behavior. (However, Therefore), you must be careful of what games you play.

12 This robot can perform many household chores such as vacuuming the room. (In contrast, In addition), its price is quite reasonable.

13 This computer has a really nice graphics card. (For example, On the other hand), it has a poor sound card.

정답 p.84

PRACTICE 20

〈보기〉에서 알맞은 접속부사를 골라 빈칸에 쓰세요.

보 기	finally / in contrast / therefore / in other words / for example / besides

1 I didn't give up and kept running for two hours. ________________, I won second place in the marathon.

2 I couldn't go for a walk because it was raining outside. ________________, I had to finish reading a book for my literature class.

3 Mina was absent yesterday. ________________, she didn't hear the news.

4 He made a serious mistake at work and his boss asked him to leave. ________________, he was fired.

5 You can protect the environment in your daily life. ________________, you can turn off the water when you brush your teeth.

6 I can't go out because I have to do my math homework. ________________, I have to do chores at home.

7 I have been working very hard on this report for two weeks. ________________, I have finished it successfully.

8 If you live in the city, you can rarely see stars at night. ________________, if you live in the country, you can see many shining stars at night.

중간·기말고사 대비문제

1 주어진 문장을 다른 표현으로 올바르게 바꾼 것은?

① If you exercise every day, you will be able to stay healthy.
 → Exercise every day, or you will be able to stay healthy.
② Everyone is too busy studying. No one talks to each other.
 → Everyone is such busy studying that no one talks to each other.
③ We had a wonderful time. We ended up staying another night.
 → We had such a wonderful time that we ended up staying another night.
④ Because it was raining, I wore rain boots to school.
 → It was raining, but I wore rain boots to school.
⑤ Tom did a good job. His boss encouraged him to do more.
 → Tom did so a good job that his boss encouraged him to do more.

2 다음 문장의 빈칸에 공통으로 들어갈 말로 알맞은 것은?

> • Tell your mom about the secret, __________ she will get angry later.
> • Which do you like better, coffee __________ tea?

① and ② but ③ or
④ for ⑤ so

3 일의 발생순서가 명확히 드러나도록 다음을 바르게 영작한 것은?

> 나는 아침을 걸러서 배가 고팠다.

① I felt hungry because I skip breakfast.
② I felt hungry because I have been skipped breakfast.
③ I felt hungry because I had skipped breakfast.
④ I had felt hungry because I skipped breakfast.
⑤ I had felt hungry because I had skipped breakfast.

4 빈칸에 들어갈 말로 가장 알맞은 것은?

> Bad posture can be harmful to your back. __________, keep a good posture.

① In contrast ② However ③ For example
④ In addition ⑤ Therefore

5 빈칸에 들어갈 말로 알맞은 것은?

> There are so many important things young people should do. __________, they should read books, travel, learn new languages, and so on.

① In addition ② Therefore
③ However ④ For example
⑤ Otherwise

6 다음 우리말에 맞게 빈칸에 알맞은 말을 고르세요.

> • 만약 네가 매일 운동을 한다면, 건강해질 것이다.
> = If you ___________ every day, you'll become healthy.

① exercising   ② have exercised
③ exercise   ④ exercised
⑤ will exercise

7 주어진 두 문장이 같은 뜻이 되도록 빈칸에 알맞은 말을 쓰세요.

> • We communicate not only with verbal languages but also with body movements.
> = We communicate with ___________ ___________ ___________ ___________ with ___________ ___________ .

8 밑줄 친 곳의 if의 쓰임이 나머지 넷과 다른 것은?

① I don't know <u>if what I am saying makes any sense</u>.
② The police are investigating <u>if the crime was intentional</u>.
③ I'm questioning <u>if he has enough money to fund that project</u>.
④ We can have tea together <u>if you can't manage dinner tonight</u>.
⑤ Sally couldn't find the bus stop, so she asked a passerby <u>if he could direct her</u>.

9 ⓐ~ⓔ 중 어법상 틀린 것을 모두 고른 것은?

> ⓐ Either he or you has to go to the party instead of me.
> ⓑ Not only you but also Tom are responsible for the accident.
> ⓒ Both Sangmi and Minsu are famous in our school.
> ⓓ I as well as my sister is going to buy the clothes.
> ⓔ Neither Susan nor you is going to be promoted at work.

① ⓐ, ⓑ   ② ⓑ, ⓒ   ③ ⓐ, ⓑ, ⓒ
④ ⓐ, ⓓ, ⓔ   ⑤ ⓐ, ⓑ, ⓓ, ⓔ

10 빈칸에 들어갈 말로 알맞은 것은?

> Most parents worry about their children's online game habits. ___________, I am not that worried about it.

① Therefore   ② Besides   ③ However
④ For example ⑤ At last

11 〈보기〉에 있는 단어들을 배열하여 해석에 알맞은 문장을 완성하세요.

보 기	heavily, rained, he, slowly, so, drove, his, that, car

해 석	비가 너무 많이 내려서 그는 자동차를 천천히 운전했다.

➡ It ___________
___________ .

[12 – 13] 다음 글을 읽고, 물음에 답하세요.

I'm so overwhelmed with joy that I can't even grasp what's happening around us. I glance around. ① All of our members are crying and shouting with excitement over our first championship. The final match has just ended, and our fans are cheering for us. It's been a tough journey. ② There were times when I wanted to give up on preparing for the match. ③ The conditions were poor, and we grew more exhausting as time went on. We didn't perform well during the regular season. ④ Never had we imagined that we would win even a single game. The only thing I could do was to focus on the moment and keep trying. During the year, we were often underestimated. Some people even said (A) that our team would be eliminated early. ⑤ Every single day was an opportunity to prove ourselves. But in the end, we finally won the championship this year.

12 윗글의 (A)와 쓰임이 같은 것은?

① I can't trust the validity of that technology yet.
② In the café, the song that reminds me of my childhood was played.
③ My opinion is different from that of my teacher.
④ Scientists discovered that water once existed on Mars.
⑤ The building that overlooks the river is the highest in this city.

13 ①~⑤ 중 어법상 옳지 않은 것은?

①   ②   ③   ④   ⑤

14 주어진 문장의 밑줄 친 as와 뜻이 같은 것은?

As it was cloudy and windy, they couldn't go on a picnic.

① Imagine the whole class smiling and clapping as you dance.
② Your bodies become weaker as you become older.
③ As you enter the building, you will be impressed with its color.
④ He left work early as he was exhausted.
⑤ Many doors will open as you look for an answer.

15 주어진 문장의 밑줄 친 that과 용법이 같은 것은?

Then I figured out that the object seemed to be a little bigger than the airplane.

① After that, we started to work with computers.
② Sam pretended that he did not know where the book was.
③ The cost of living in London is higher than that of Seoul.
④ I bought the cap that my brother wanted to have.
⑤ This sword is for the person that can move the rock.

16 주어진 우리말과 뜻이 같도록 빈칸에 알맞은 말을 쓰세요.

• 당신은 당신 자신뿐만 아니라 당신의 가족을 위해서 최선을 다해야 한다.
= You should do your best ___________ ___________ for yourself ___________ ___________ for your family.

17 다음 문장의 빈칸에 들어갈 말로 알맞은 것은?

> The small parking lots were made not for
> us, ___________ for the disabled.

① and ② but ③ or
④ as ⑤ while

18 다음 문장의 빈칸에 들어갈 말이 순서대로 바르게 짝지어진 것은?

> They will help you find out ___________
> you're a negative thinker ___________ .

① which – or not ② that – or not
③ whether – or not ④ how – or so
⑤ if – or so

19 밑줄 친 접속사가 문맥상 어울리지 <u>않는</u> 것은?

① They had fixed up the house <u>before</u> they moved in.
② The streets were flooded <u>because</u> it had rained heavily.
③ Could you watch my bags for me <u>while</u> I buy some groceries?
④ He had practiced basketball <u>since</u> it was too dark to see the hoop.
⑤ <u>Though</u> she joined the company only a year ago, she's already been promoted twice.

20 다음 우리말과 일치하도록 괄호 안에 주어진 단어를 바르게 배열하세요.

> • 나는 그가 그의 휴대폰을 결코 사용하지 않는 것이 이상하다고 생각한다.
>
> ➡ ___________________________
>
> ___________________________
>
> (cellphone, I, never, his, it, that, he, find, uses, strange)

21 빈칸에 들어갈 말로 알맞은 것은?

> Every morning, her mom gives her a ride
> to school, ___________ the school is very
> close to her house.

① as if ② even though
③ when ④ while
⑤ whether

22 ⟨보기⟩에서 주어진 문장의 밑줄 친 부분과 쓰임이 같은 것을 있는 대로 고른 것은?

> You can decorate your room <u>as</u> you want.

보 기

ⓐ He wasn't as tall <u>as</u> me in the past.
ⓑ <u>As</u> the forecast predicted, the weather was freezing.
ⓒ It wasn't easy to buy a TV back then, <u>as</u> it was very expensive.
ⓓ <u>As</u> she grew older, she became smarter.
ⓔ I asked you to do that <u>as</u> I told you.

① ⓐ, ⓑ ② ⓑ, ⓔ ③ ⓐ, ⓑ, ⓒ
④ ⓐ, ⓓ, ⓔ ⑤ ⓑ, ⓒ, ⓓ, ⓔ

23 괄호 안에 들어갈 알맞은 단어를 고르세요.

> All animals aren't exactly the same. Some
> animals have hair, (while, as) others don't.

24 다음 문장에서 어법상 **틀린** 부분 **두 군데**를 찾아 바르게 고쳐 문장을 다시 쓰세요.

> • Not even many citizens but also the leader of the country support the new treaty.
>
> * treaty: 조약

➡ ______________________________________

____

25 주어진 두 문장이 같은 뜻이 되도록 빈칸에 알맞은 말을 쓰세요.

> • He went to bed early in order not to be late for class the next morning.
> = He went to bed early ___________ ___________ he wouldn't be late for class the next morning.

26 다음 중 문법적으로 옳은 것만을 **모두** 고른 것은?

> (A) In the night sky, the Moon as well as the twinkling stars is beautiful.
> (B) Not only my best friend but also I are interested in playing chess.
> (C) Neither I nor you were invited to her graduation ceremony.
> (D) Both Tom and Judy was satisfied with the result.
> (E) Either you or he has to attend the meeting on behalf of me.

① (A), (B) ② (C), (E) ③ (A), (B), (D)
④ (A), (C), (E) ⑤ (B), (D), (E)

27 다음 중 어법상 **어색한** 것은?

① She couldn't do her homework because she had a high fever.
② Do your best, and you will get what you want.
③ We often forget the fact which a healthy diet is more important than weight loss.
④ Tell the truth, or you will feel guilty every day.
⑤ She lost her laptop computer, so she couldn't work.

28 다음 우리말에 맞게 바르게 영작되지 **않은** 것은? (2개)

① 상점이 문을 열지 않으면, 우리는 오늘 식료품을 살 수 없다.
 : Unless the store isn't open, we can't buy groceries today.
② 그녀가 도착하자마자 비가 내리기 시작했다.
 : As soon as she arrived, it started to rain.
③ 버스가 늦게 오면 우리는 택시를 탈 것이다.
 : If the bus will come late, we will take a taxi.
④ 그는 피아노를 잘 치기 위해 매일 연습한다.
 : He practices every day so that he can play the piano well.
⑤ 네가 그 프로젝트를 그렇게 빨리 끝냈다는 것은 인상적이다.
 : That you finished the project so quickly is impressive.

29 빈칸에 들어갈 말로 알맞은 것은?

> ___________ you fail or succeed will depend on your thoughts.

① Whether ② When ③ What
④ That ⑤ If

30 다음 밑줄 친 that의 쓰임이 나머지 넷과 다른 것은?

① The chart shows that exercise makes the body healthy.
② Remember that you should solve the problem.
③ He knows that he should study hard for the test.
④ Ted said that he had lost his house because of the fire.
⑤ The energy that is not used is stored as fat in the body.

31 빈칸에 들어갈 말로 알맞은 것은?

> It is certain ____________ she can speak both Chinese and French.

① so   ② and   ③ while
④ that   ⑤ what

32 다음 문장의 빈칸에 공통으로 들어갈 말로 알맞은 것은?

> • I asked myself ____________ I really wanted to do this job.
> • Is it OK ____________ I use your mobile phone?

① but   ② if   ③ as
④ that   ⑤ since

33 다음 중 어법상 어색한 것은?

① I'm not sure if I can introduce you to her this weekend.
② Turn around so that you can face the fence.
③ The villagers have to decide whether they are in favor of the policy.
④ She said that her leg was broken yesterday.
⑤ You should not ask that he knows the fact or not.

34 다음 중 어법상 적절한 문장의 개수는?

> (A) Both my brother and my sister likes soccer very much.
> (B) Either you or your friends are responsible for this work.
> (C) The manager as well as his assistants has agreed to the new plan.
> (D) Neither the teacher nor the students was ready for the trip.
> (E) Not only Tom but also his parents have been invited.
> (F) I want both to visit Paris and London.

① 2개   ② 3개   ③ 4개   ④ 5개   ⑤ 6개

35 빈칸에 들어갈 말로 알맞은 것은?

> ____________ I am a teenager like my friends, sometimes even I cannot understand their acts.

① Besides   ② Because   ③ Although
④ When   ⑤ And

36 다음 문장의 빈칸에 공통으로 들어갈 말로 알맞은 것은? (대소문자 구분하지 않음.)

> • ___________ I was studying, my sister was watching TV.
> • She always eats breakfast, ___________ I usually skip it.

① that   ② if   ③ while
④ when   ⑤ since

37 다음 문장의 빈칸에 알맞은 단어들이 차례대로 바르게 짝지어진 것은?

> • I'll call you ________ I arrive at my house.
> • She caught a very bad cold. That's ___________ she didn't come to school today.

① why   – because
② why   – why
③ when – because
④ when – why
⑤ when – what

38 다음 문장의 빈칸에 들어갈 말이 순서대로 바르게 짝지어진 것은?

> • She can't bake the cake ___________ she ran out of flour.
> • There were few people on the street ___________ the cold weather.

① because of – though
② though – because of
③ because – though
④ because of – because
⑤ because – because of

39 다음 중 어법상 어색한 것은?

① We have to leave before it gets dark.
② I'm not sure when she will come back home.
③ Whenever he visits us, he brings some fruits.
④ As you didn't get up early, you will be late.
⑤ Though he is handsome and tall, many girls love him.

40 (A), (B), (C)에 들어갈 말로 알맞은 것은?

> Up until last year, most students preferred energy drinks to plain water. ______(A)______, a science teacher showed them how much sugar was in those drinks. The students watched a video ______(B)______ by the teacher about hidden sugar. After the lesson, they decided ______(C)______ fewer energy drinks and drink more water instead.

    (A)   (B)   (C)
① However – made   – buying
② However – made   – to buy
③ Besides – making – buying
④ However – making – to buy
⑤ Besides – made   – buying

41 다음 중 어법상 어색한 것은?

① We had so a nice time that I will never forget it.
② They are written in a language he doesn't know, so he can't read them.
③ Tom is American, but he likes Korean food.
④ Either he or I am going to visit Sumi's house.
⑤ Do you want to take a bus or a taxi?

CH
15
접속사

As many people can use computers, they don't need typists anymore. ____________, the growing interest in weight has led to the recent emergence of diet programmers that didn't exist in the past.

① Finally
② As a result
③ In other words
④ In contrast
⑤ In addition

43 다음 중 어법상 옳지 <u>않은</u> 것은?

① Set an alarm on your phone so that you can get up on time.
② They wore thick boots in order that they could walk on the snow.
③ She checked the data again not in order to make a mistake.
④ He started exercising after work so that he could lose weight.
⑤ The government has banned the use of plastic cups so as to reduce waste.

[44-45] 다음 글을 읽고, 물음에 답하세요.

The Battle of Myeongnyang

The Battle of Myeongnyang is regarded as one of the most brilliant ⓐunderline victories in the history of warfare. It ⓑwas led by Admiral Yi Sun-sin who steered Joseon to many victories against the Japanese navy. The reason why this war was so brilliant is ⓒthat Joseon only had 13 warships whereas Japan had more than 130 warships. No matter how you look at it, ㉠Joseon's fleet was too heavily outnumbered to stand a chance against Japan's fleet. However, ⓓthe impossible happened. Yi Sun-sin's fleet completely ⓔwas defeated Japan's fleet and only about 10 ships got away.

44 윗글의 ㉠과 같은 의미가 되도록 〈조건〉에 맞게 영어로 쓰세요.

보 기

chance, be, not, that, against, heavily, it, can, stand, outnumber, Japan's fleet, so, a

조 건

• 주어진 말을 모두 한 번씩만 사용하시오.
• 필요한 경우 두 단어를 축약하여 사용하시오.
• 필요한 경우 단어의 형태를 바꾸시오.

➡ Joseon's fleet ________________________

________________________________ .

45 윗글의 밑줄 친 ⓐ~ⓔ 중 어법이 <u>틀린</u> 것은?

① ⓐ
② ⓑ
③ ⓒ
④ ⓓ
⑤ ⓔ

CHAPTER 16
전치사

PSS 1 시간을 나타내는 전치사	페이지	성취도				
		100%	99~75%	74~50%	49~25%	24~0%
PSS 1-1 at, on, in Ⅰ	370					
PSS 1-2 at, on, in Ⅱ	371					
PSS 1-3 from, since	374					
PSS 1-4 by, until	375					
PSS 1-5 before, after	377					
PSS 1-6 for, during	379					

PSS 2 장소, 방향을 나타내는 전치사	페이지	성취도				
		100%	99~75%	74~50%	49~25%	24~0%
PSS 2-1 at, in, on Ⅰ	381					
PSS 2-2 at, in, on Ⅱ	384					
PSS 2-3 above, below, over, under	385					
PSS 2-4 up, down, into, out of, onto, off	386					
PSS 2-5 across, along, through, around	390					
PSS 2-6 by, in front of, behind, near	391					
PSS 2-7 between, among	392					
PSS 2-8 to, for, toward(s)	393					

PSS 3 그 밖의 전치사	페이지	성취도				
		100%	99~75%	74~50%	49~25%	24~0%
PSS 3-1 with, without, for, against	395					
PSS 3-2 like, by, in, as	396					
PSS 3-3 except, due to, according to, instead of	398					
PSS 3-4 형용사와 함께 쓰이는 전치사 Ⅰ	399					
PSS 3-5 형용사와 함께 쓰이는 전치사 Ⅱ	401					
PSS 3-6 동사와 함께 쓰이는 전치사 Ⅰ	402					
PSS 3-7 동사와 함께 쓰이는 전치사 Ⅱ	404					
중간·기말고사 대비문제	409					

PSS 1 시간을 나타내는 전치사

PSS 1-1 at, on, in Ⅰ

at		**구체적인 시각 앞에 온다.** The airplane is going to depart **at 9:10 a.m.** 비행기는 오전 9시 10분에 이륙할 것이다. His class gets started **at 10:30.** 그의 수업은 10시 30분에 시작한다. Jane and I are supposed to meet **at 2 o'clock.** Jane과 나는 두 시에 만나기로 되어 있다.
on		**날짜나 요일 앞에 온다.** I didn't do anything special **on August 17th.** 나는 8월 17일에 특별한 어떤 것을 하지 않았다. My friends and I do volunteer work **on Saturdays.** 친구들과 나는 토요일마다 자원봉사를 한다. Mom wanted us to spend time together **on Sunday.** 엄마는 일요일에 우리가 함께 시간을 보내기를 원하셨다.
in		**연도, 월, 계절과 같은 비교적 긴 시간 앞에 온다.** My family immigrated to Canada **in 2024.** 우리 가족은 2024년에 캐나다로 이민을 왔다. The fitness club is planning to move downtown **in May.** 그 헬스 클럽은 5월에 시내로 이전할 것을 계획하고 있다. I go swimming every day **in the summer.** 나는 여름에 매일 수영하러 간다.

정답 p.88

PRACTICE 1

괄호 안에 들어갈 알맞은 전치사를 골라 동그라미 하세요.

1   The Empire State Building was the world's tallest building when it was completed (at, on, in) 1931.

2   The first bus to Busan departs from the terminal (at, on, in) five in the morning.

3 Apollo 11 became the first spaceship to land on the Moon (at, on, in) July 20th, 1969.

4 Sydney is a city well-known for its various festivals and parades (at, on, in) December and January.

5 I heard that the theater is going to open (at, on, in) July 2nd.

6 The fireworks are going to start (at, on, in) 11 o'clock. Hurry up! We've only got 5 minutes.

7 Since my school is quite far away, I have to get up (at, on, in) 6 a.m. to be on time.

8 Our class will go on a field trip to the science museum (at, on, in) Friday.

9 In Britain, unlike Korea, the new school year starts (at, on, in) September.

10 Why don't we take a trip to Hokkaido (at, on, in) winter to see the snow festival?

11 I'm sorry that I can't meet you (at, on, in) Saturday. I already have an appointment.

12 When the bookstore opened (at, on, in) 10 o'clock, I rushed inside to grab a copy of the new release before it sold out.

13 Americans celebrate Thanksgiving (at, on, in) the fourth Thursday of November.

14 The Titanic sank on Sunday, April 15th, 1912 (at, on, in) 2:20 a.m.

15 (At, On, In) 1988, Korea hosted the Summer Olympic Games in Seoul.

PSS 1-2 at, on, in Ⅱ

다음은 시간을 나타내는 전치사 at, on, in과 함께 쓰이는 명사(구)이다.

1. at은 비교적 짧은 시간이나 특정 시점을 나타내는 말 앞에 쓴다.

> at noon   at night   at dawn   at lunchtime
> at present   at the moment   at sunset   at Christmas

We are going up the hill **at night** to see the stars.
우리는 별을 보기 위해 밤에 언덕 위로 올라갈 것이다.
Mr. Johnson is not in **at the moment**. Johnson 씨는 지금 안 계신다.
I didn't get any present **at Christmas**. 나는 크리스마스 때 어떤 선물도 받지 못했다.

2. on은 특정한 날이나 요일, 그날의 아침이나 저녁, 낮 시간 등을 나타내는 말 앞에 쓴다.

> on Saturday morning　　on Monday evenings　　on Friday night
> on Christmas Day　　on New Year's Eve　　on my birthday

My parents and I go to church **on Wednesday evenings**.

나의 부모님과 나는 수요일 저녁마다 교회에 간다.

My uncle's family and my family will get together **on New Year's Eve**.

작은아버지 가족과 우리 가족은 새해 전날 밤에 모일 것이다.

I didn't get anything from my best friend Jisu **on my birthday**.

나는 내 생일날 나의 가장 친한 친구 지수에게 아무것도 받지 못했다.

3. in은 비교적 긴 시간이나 불특정한 시간을 나타내는 말 앞에 쓴다.

> in the morning　　in the afternoon　　in the past
> in the future　　in the 1980s　　in the 20th century

I always feel more energetic and productive **in the morning**.

나는 항상 아침에 더 활기차고 더 생산적이라고 느낀다.

It took more than a week to get there by ship **in the past**.

과거에는 배로 그곳에 도착하는 데 1주일 이상이 걸렸다.

The population of this city expanded rapidly **in the 1990s**.

이 도시의 인구는 1990년대에 급속하게 늘어났다.

4. every, this, that, last, next 등이 붙어 시간을 나타내는 부사구를 이룰 때는 그 앞에 at, on, in을 쓰지 않는다. (학교 내신 빈출 문법사항!)

I decided to go swimming at the pool **every Saturday**.

나는 토요일마다 수영장에 수영하러 가기로 결정했다.

Yoonho's family might move to Jeju Island **this month**.

윤호의 가족은 이번 달에 제주도로 이사갈 수도 있다.

The photography club was organized **last December**.

사진 동아리는 지난 12월에 결성되었다.

정답 p.88

PRACTICE 2

다음 문장의 빈칸에 at, on, in 중 올바른 것을 쓰고, 필요하지 않은 곳에는 ×표 하세요.

1　① My friends and I are going to my favorite singer's concert _________ Saturday night.

　② My friends and I went to my favorite singer's concert _________ last night.

2 ① I have to go to piano lessons _________ Thursday nights.

  ② I have to go to piano lessons _________ every Thursday night.

3 ① We're planning to visit our grandparents in Ulleungdo _________ autumn.

  ② We're planning to visit our grandparents in Ulleungdo _________ Chuseok.

4 ① This department store is scheduled to open _________ the 1st of May.

  ② This department store is scheduled to open _________ next month.

5 ① Do you want to go see the fireworks _________ New Year's Eve with me?

  ② Do you want to go see the fireworks _________ this weekend with me?

6 ① This famous restaurant first opened _________ 2020.

  ② This famous restaurant first opened _________ last year.

7 ① My family and relatives gathered _________ my cousin's wedding day.

  ② My family and relatives gathered _________ the morning of my cousin's wedding day.

8 ① What would you like to do _________ your free time?

  ② What would you like to do _________ Monday evening?

9 ① Japanese colonial rule of Korea ended _________ August 15th, 1945.

  ② Japanese colonial rule of Korea ended _________ the summer of 1945.

10 ① The police found a dead body in the empty house _________ that night.

  ② The police found a dead body in the empty house _________ Christmas.

11 ① It is 11 o'clock now. The next bus to Haenam leaves the terminal _________ noon.

  ② It is 11 o'clock now. The bus to Haenam leaves the terminal _________ every hour.

12 ① The rescue expedition went into the forest _________ dawn to look for survivors.

  ② The rescue expedition went into the forest early _________ the morning to look for survivors.

13 ① My baby brother always starts crying late _________ night when everybody is fast asleep.

  ② My baby brother always starts crying _________ the middle of the night when everybody is fast asleep.

14 ① Charlie, why don't we meet at the gym _________ lunchtime?

  ② Charlie, why don't we meet at the gym _________ Tuesday evenings?

15 ① My mom and sister went shopping _________ half past four.

  ② My mom and sister went shopping _________ the afternoon.

PSS 1-3 from, since

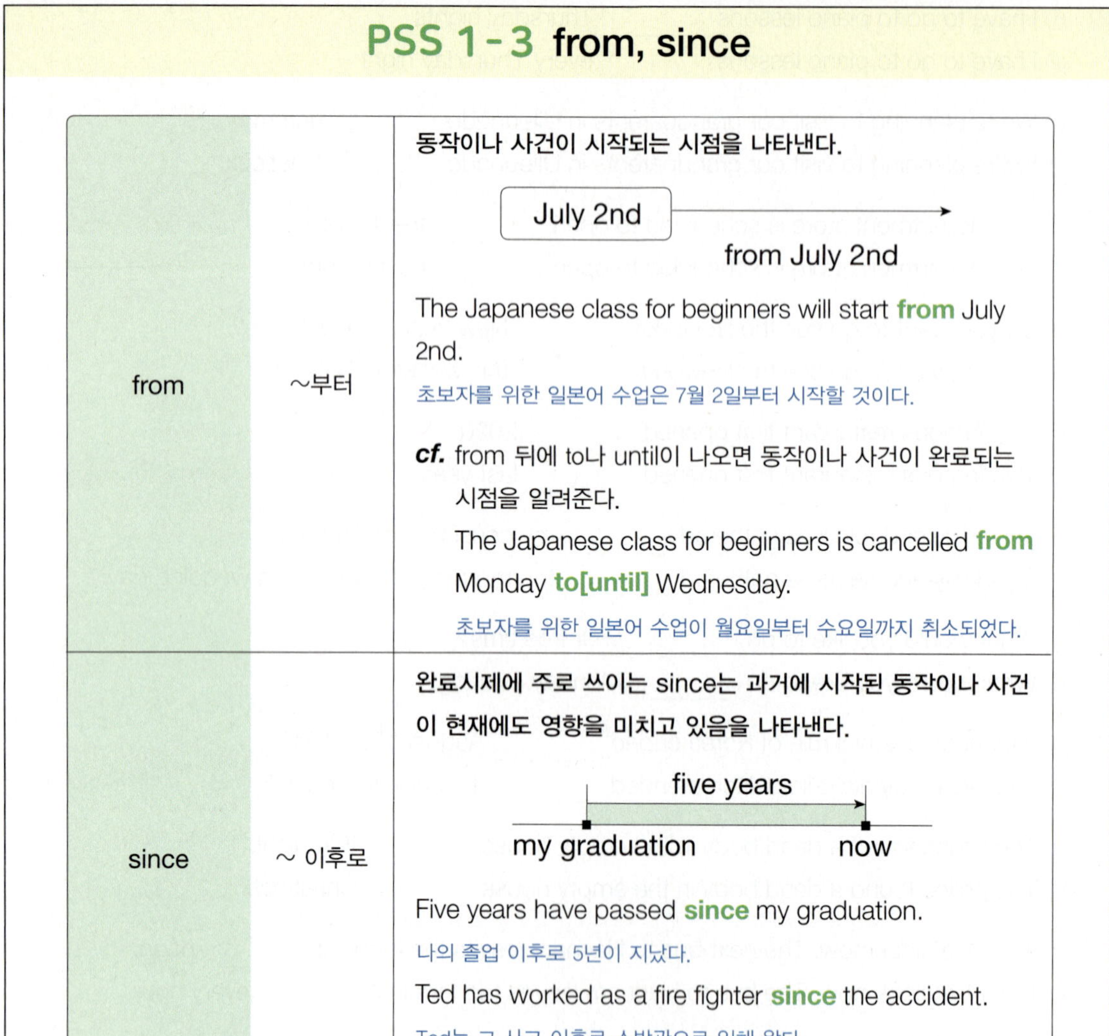

| from | ~부터 | 동작이나 사건이 시작되는 시점을 나타낸다. |

The Japanese class for beginners will start **from** July 2nd.
초보자를 위한 일본어 수업은 7월 2일부터 시작할 것이다.

cf. from 뒤에 to나 until이 나오면 동작이나 사건이 완료되는 시점을 알려준다.

The Japanese class for beginners is cancelled **from** Monday **to[until]** Wednesday.
초보자를 위한 일본어 수업이 월요일부터 수요일까지 취소되었다.

| since | ~ 이후로 | 완료시제에 주로 쓰이는 since는 과거에 시작된 동작이나 사건이 현재에도 영향을 미치고 있음을 나타낸다. |

Five years have passed **since** my graduation.
나의 졸업 이후로 5년이 지났다.
Ted has worked as a fire fighter **since** the accident.
Ted는 그 사고 이후로 소방관으로 일해 왔다.

정답 p.89

PRACTICE 3

다음 문장의 빈칸에 from과 since 중 알맞은 것을 쓰세요.

1 ① The department store across the street will be open ______________ 10:30 to 8:00.

② The department store across the street has been open ______________ last month.

2 ① I've been living in Scotland ______________ 2021.

② I started living in Scotland ______________ December last year.

3 ① Our school will accept physically and mentally disadvantaged students ______________ next March.

② Our school has accepted physically and mentally disadvantaged students ______________ last March.

4 ① Cockroaches have virtually remained the same ______________ the days of the dinosaurs.

 ② Cockroaches have virtually remained the same ______________ the time of the dinosaurs to the present day.

5 ① The museum will be closed ______________ March to May for the repairs.

 ② The museum has been closed ______________ March. It will reopen in May.

6 ① I have been studying for the final exams ______________ last week.

 ② I will start preparing for the final exams ______________ tomorrow.

7 ① I was forbidden to watch TV ______________ the day Mom saw my school report.

 ② I have been forbidden to watch TV ______________ the moment Mom saw my school report yesterday.

8 ① My brothers and I were raised on a large reindeer farm ______________ a very young age.

 ② My brothers and I have been raised on a large reindeer farm ______________ the time we were toddlers.

9 ① The generals have been in a meeting ______________ 6 o'clock.

 ② The generals held a meeting ______________ 6 o'clock to 10 o'clock.

10 ① I will start working in this office ______________ July 31st.

 ② I've been working in this office ______________ last week.

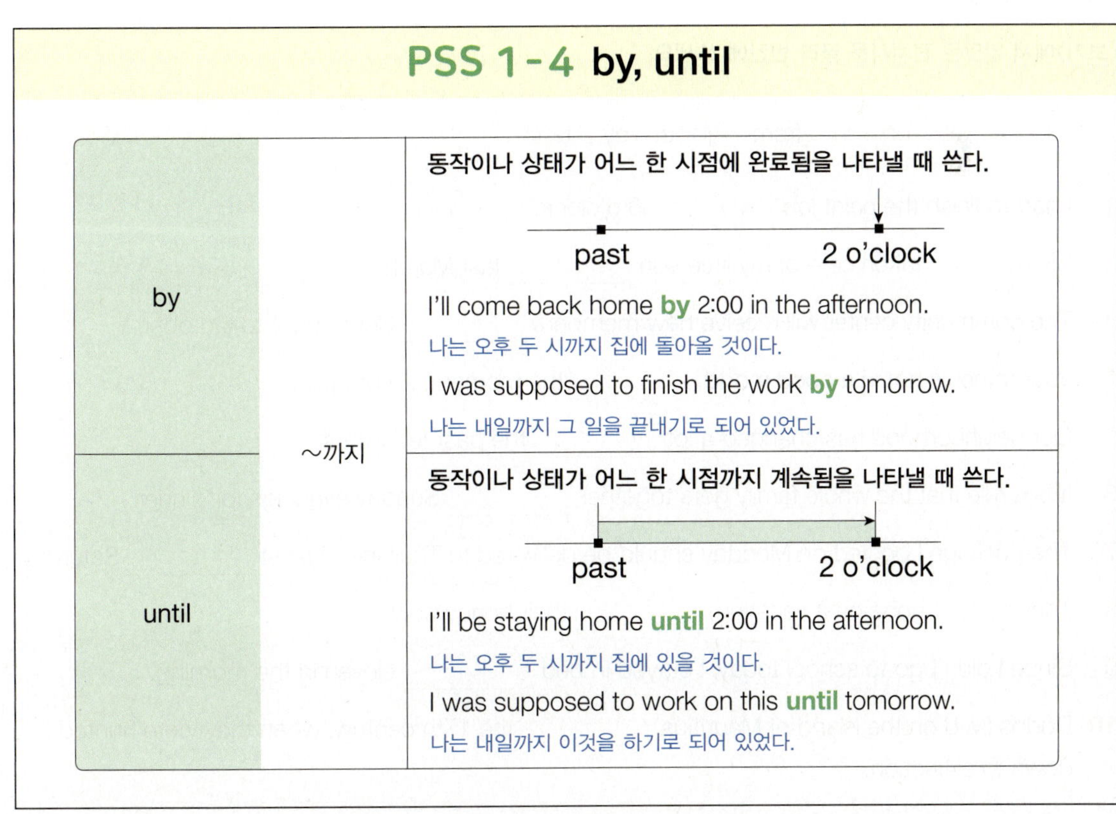

PSS 1-4 by, until

by	~까지	동작이나 상태가 어느 한 시점에 완료됨을 나타낼 때 쓴다. past　　　　　2 o'clock I'll come back home **by** 2:00 in the afternoon. 나는 오후 두 시까지 집에 돌아올 것이다. I was supposed to finish the work **by** tomorrow. 나는 내일까지 그 일을 끝내기로 되어 있었다.
until		동작이나 상태가 어느 한 시점까지 계속됨을 나타낼 때 쓴다. past　　　　　2 o'clock I'll be staying home **until** 2:00 in the afternoon. 나는 오후 두 시까지 집에 있을 것이다. I was supposed to work on this **until** tomorrow. 나는 내일까지 이것을 하기로 되어 있었다.

PRACTICE 4

괄호 안에 들어갈 알맞은 전치사를 골라 동그라미 하세요.

1 I waited for her in the lounge (by, until) 9 p.m.

2 I'll finish the laundry and the dishes (by, until) dinnertime.

3 This milk must be used (by, until) Wednesday.

4 Yesterday, my dad had to work in his office (by, until) midnight.

5 I must submit the report (by, until) 3 o'clock, but I haven't finished it yet.

6 Our flight to Toronto was delayed (by, until) the next day because of harsh weather.

7 John, tell me (by, until) tomorrow whether you'll come to the baseball game or not.

8 I'll be very glad if you can get here (by, until) noon.

9 I'll be studying (by, until) 1 a.m. to prepare for tomorrow's exam.

10 You can keep this book from the library (by, until) next week.

PRACTICE 5

〈보기〉에서 알맞은 전치사를 골라 빈칸에 쓰세요.

보 기	at on in from since by until

1 I had to finish the paint job __________ 6 o'clock.

2 My mom has taken care of my little son __________ last March.

3 The community center will receive new members __________ September to October.

4 Your father is not in a good mood __________ the moment, so be quiet.

5 Our neighborhood has changed a lot __________ the past few years.

6 It is a rule that the whole family gets together __________ Sunday evenings for dinner.

7 The package I posted on Monday should be delivered to Thailand at least __________ Saturday.

8 They haven't gone on a vacation __________ their honeymoon.

9 Since I didn't go to school today, I stayed in bed __________ eleven in the morning.

10 Dodos lived on the island of Mauritius __________ the 17th century, when they were hunted down to extinction.

11 Mr. and Mrs. Davis decided to open a one-day charity bazaar __________ Christmas Eve.

12 The World Cup football tournament was held __________ the summer of 2002, both in Korea and Japan.

13 The scouts returned to the base camp __________ dusk after hiking in the wilderness all day long.

14 Students interested in taking Intermediate French classes should register __________ February 10th to 15th.

15 The fishermen had promised to return from sea __________ the end of October.

16 The little girl has been disabled __________ birth.

17 We have to decide on a vacation spot __________ Monday.

18 My parents always go out for dinner __________ their wedding anniversary.

PSS 1-5 before, after

before 5 o'clock

after 5 o'clock

before	~ 전에	There were several kids playing basketball at the court **before** 5 o'clock. 5시 이전에 코트에는 농구를 하는 아이들이 몇 명 있었다. I had to turn off my cell phone **before** entering the room. (= before I entered the room) 나는 그 방에 들어가기 전에 휴대전화를 꺼야 했다.
after	~ 후에	There was no one at the court **after** 5 o'clock. 5시 이후에 코트에는 아무도 없었다. I turned on my cell phone **after** getting out of the room. (= after I got out of the room) 나는 그 방에서 나온 후에 휴대전화를 켰다.

PRACTICE 6

빈칸에 들어갈 말을 〈보기〉에서 골라 문장을 완성하세요.

> 보 기   after the rock festival / after classes / after getting home from work
> before entering the house   /   before coming to Australia
> before the arrival of European settlers

1 The singers gave out autographs ________________________________ .

2 In most Asian countries, you must take off your shoes first ________________________________ .

3 My friends and I stayed at school ________________________ to talk with the teacher in private.

4 I had never seen a real live kangaroo ________________________________ .

5 Native American Indians led a peaceful life ________________________________ .

6 I usually watch TV for a while ________________________________ .

PRACTICE 7

〈보기〉와 같이 주어진 문장을 before나 after를 이용한 문장으로 바꾸어 쓰세요.

> 보 기   I finished reading the last chapter of the book, and I went to bed.
> ➡ Before going to bed, I finished reading the last chapter of the book.
>
> Cathy graduated from university, and she left for London to work as an architect.
> ➡ After graduating from university, Cathy left for London to work as an architect.

1 We got up before daybreak, and we went to see the Tokyo Fishmarket.
   ➡ After ________________________________ .

2 The doctor explained the disease to me, and he gave me a prescription.
   ➡ Before ________________________________ .

3 I completed the assigned house chores, and I ran out to the street to play with my friends.
   ➡ After ________________________________ .

4 We lit a small campfire by our tent, and we cooked dinner.
   ➡ Before ________________________________ .

5 I talked to Jim over the cell phone, and I went out to meet him at the bus stop.
   ➡ After ________________________________ .

6 John gave away all his toys to his younger cousins, and he moved to Argentina.
   ➡ Before ________________________________ .

7 The typhoon landed on the coast of Taiwan, and it blew away many houses.

➡ After ____ .

8 The team went through a strict training program, and it became one of the top baseball teams.

➡ Before ____ .

9 I completed my training as a sailor, and I came back home to see my family.

➡ After ____ .

10 The submarine exploded, and it sank to the bottom of the sea.

➡ Before ____ .

PSS 1-6 for, during

for		for 다음에는 시간의 길이를 나타내는 명사(구)가 온다. I have been working with Sarah **for almost a year**. 나는 거의 1년 동안 Sarah와 함께 일해 왔다. I decided to review what I learned **for a moment**. 나는 잠시 동안 배운 것을 복습하기로 결정했다. We tried to save money **for a month**. 우리는 한 달 동안 돈을 아끼기 위해 노력했다.
during	**~동안**	during 다음에는 특정 기간을 나타내는 명사(구)가 온다. 특정 기간 중에 계속해서 일어나는 일을 강조할 때는 '~ 동안, 내내'의 뜻인 throughout과 바꾸어 쓸 수 있다. I have been working with Sarah **during[throughout] this semester**. 나는 이번 학기 동안 Sarah와 함께 일해 왔다. I decided to review what I learned **during[throughout] the lunchtime**. 나는 점심 시간 동안 배운 것을 복습하기로 결정했다. We tried to save money **during[throughout] the journey**. 우리는 여행하는 동안 돈을 아끼기 위해 노력했다. *cf.* 특정 기간 중에 계속해서 일어나는 일이 아닌 경우에는 throughout으로 바꾸어 쓸 수 없다. The project manager finished the work at home **during** his three-day vacation. 그 프로젝트 담당자는 그의 3일간의 휴가 동안 집에서 일을 끝냈다.

cf. while은 '~동안'이라는 뜻이지만, 접속사이기 때문에 뒤에 명사(구)가 아닌 「주어+동사」로 된 절이 온다.

She missed home **while** she was travelling. 그녀는 여행을 하는 동안 집이 그리웠다.

CH
16
전
치
사

PRACTICE 8

다음 문장의 빈칸에 for나 during 중 알맞은 전치사를 쓰세요.

1　① I'm planning to travel all over Europe ＿＿＿＿＿＿＿ three months.
　　② I'm planning to travel all over Europe ＿＿＿＿＿＿＿ this summer vacation.

2　① My father and I played a game of Baduk ＿＿＿＿＿＿＿ the evening.
　　② My father and I played a game of Baduk. It went on ＿＿＿＿＿＿＿ hours.

3　① England and France fought each other ＿＿＿＿＿＿＿ 116 years, from 1337 to 1453.
　　② England and France fought each other ＿＿＿＿＿＿＿ the Hundred Years' War.

4　① I'm going to stay in Fiji ＿＿＿＿＿＿＿ the summer break.
　　② I'm going to stay in Fiji ＿＿＿＿＿＿＿ a month or two.

5　① Turn off your cell phones ＿＿＿＿＿＿＿ the exams.
　　② Turn off your cell phones ＿＿＿＿＿＿＿ the time being.

6　① It's been raining ＿＿＿＿＿＿＿ almost a week. I wish the sun would come out.
　　② It's been raining ＿＿＿＿＿＿＿ the school rock festival. I wish the sun would come out.

7　① The Holy Roman Empire ruled most of Central Europe ＿＿＿＿＿＿＿ nearly 900 years.
　　② The Holy Roman Empire ruled most of Central Europe ＿＿＿＿＿＿＿ the Middle Ages and early modern period.

8　① I've been learning English ＿＿＿＿＿＿＿ many years, but it seems like there is no end to it.
　　② I learned English ＿＿＿＿＿＿＿ my middle school and high school years.

9　① The Encyclopedia Britannica was first printed ＿＿＿＿＿＿＿ the late 18th century.
　　② The Encyclopedia Britannica was in print ＿＿＿＿＿＿＿ over 200 years.

10　① The cabin seat was uncomfortable, and I couldn't get any sleep ＿＿＿＿＿＿＿ three hours until we landed.
　　② The cabin seat was uncomfortable, and I couldn't get any sleep ＿＿＿＿＿＿＿ the three-hour flight.

PRACTICE 9

〈보기〉에서 알맞은 전치사를 골라 빈칸에 쓰세요.

보 기	before　after　for　during　throughout

1　Make sure you've packed your lunchbox ＿＿＿＿＿＿＿ leaving home, Andrew.

2　The teacher caught me nodding off ＿＿＿＿＿＿＿ class.

3 On the way to downtown Bangkok, we were caught in the traffic jam _________________ two hours.

4 Where did you live _________________ moving into this neighborhood last month?

5 In Thailand, you can enjoy a variety of exotic fruit _________________ the year.

6 _________________ running 20 km, the marathon runner fell down exhausted.

7 I'm going to go to the United States _________________ two months to learn English.

8 A lot of museums were heavily bombed _________________ World War Ⅱ.

9 I realized my mistake only _________________ receiving the answer sheet.

10 My uncle served as a translator _________________ the last few months of the Vietnam War.

PSS 2 장소, 방향을 나타내는 전치사

PSS 2-1 at, in, on Ⅰ

at	~에	특정한 한 지점을 나타내거나 비교적 좁은 장소 앞에 쓰인다. The train will arrive **at** Seoul Station at 7:30 in the evening. 기차는 저녁 7시 30분에 서울역에 도착할 것이다. I saw a famous musician **at** the doctor's office. 나는 진료실에서 유명한 음악가를 보았다.
in	~ (안)에	공간 안에 속해 있는 느낌을 나타내거나 비교적 넓은 장소 앞에 쓰인다. I could feel that he was hiding something **in** his bag. 나는 그가 가방 안에 무언가를 숨기고 있다는 것을 느낄 수 있었다. There will be a third performance **in** Gwangju. 광주에서 세 번째 공연이 있을 것이다.
on	~ (위)에	표면에 접촉해 있는 것을 나타낸다. I decided to get some rest **on** the rock for a while. 나는 잠시 동안 바위 위에서 휴식을 취하기로 했다. Several ants were crawling **on** the wall. 몇 마리의 개미가 벽에 기어가고 있었다.

PRACTICE 10

그림을 보고, 빈칸에 at, in, on 중 알맞은 전치사를 쓰세요.

1 
2 
3
4 
5 
6

1 There is a tree house ____________ the big tree.
  The tree house is sitting ____________ a thick branch.

2 There are some toys ____________ the shelves in the toyshop.
  There are some kids ____________ the window of the toyshop.

3 I'm sitting ____________ the computer desk.
  I'm working with the computer ____________ my room.

4 There is a table ____________ the kitchen.
  There is a box ____________ the table.

5 The mailman is standing ____________ the door.
  He is standing ____________ the doormat.

6 Soojin is watching TV ____________ the couch.
  Soojin is watching TV ____________ the living room.

PRACTICE 11

그림을 보고, 빈칸에 at, in, on 중 알맞은 전치사를 쓰세요.

1   I put some star stickers ____________ the ceiling.

2   This airplane is now landing ____________ Sydney International Airport.

3   Some birds are perching ____________ the tree.

4   I packed my things ____________ the suitcase.

5   The student is ____________ her desk reading a book.

6   There are many students ____________ the classroom.

7   There are some people waiting for a bus ____________ the bus stop.

8   A spider is crawling ____________ the wall.

9   There are many tall buildings ____________ New York.

PSS 2-2 at, in, on Ⅱ

다음은 장소를 나타내는 전치사 at, in, on과 함께 쓰이는 명사(구)이다.

1. at

at the top	at the bottom	at the end	
at home	at school	at work	at sea
at a meeting	at a garage sale	at a contest	
at a party	at a beach	at 273 Oxford St.	

Write your name **at the top** of your answer sheet.
답안지 위쪽에 이름을 쓰세요.
It's been 17 years since I started to teach students **at school**.
내가 학교에서 학생들을 가르치기 시작한 지 17년이 되었다.
I bought these chairs **at a garage sale**.
나는 이 의자들을 차고 세일에서 샀다.

2. in

in bed	in prison	in church	in town	in a car	in a taxi
in the sky	in the world	in space	in line	in a photo	
in a mirror	in a book	in a dictionary		in a newspaper	

My parents and I went to my brother's wedding **in a taxi**.
부모님과 나는 택시를 타고 형의 결혼식에 갔다.
I stood **in line** for the school bus. 나는 스쿨버스를 타려고 줄을 섰다.
I practiced my smile **in the mirror.**
나는 거울 앞에서 미소 짓는 것을 연습했다.

3. on

on the sea	on land	on the ground	on the road
on the ship	on the subway	on the train	on the plane
on TV	on the Internet	on a farm	

There were some boats sailing **on the sea**.
바다 위에서 항해하는 몇몇 배들이 있었다.
I always listen to music **on the subway**.
나는 지하철에서 항상 음악을 듣는다.
I worked **on a farm** as a volunteer last summer.
나는 지난 여름 자원봉사자로 농장에서 일했다.

PRACTICE 12

다음 빈칸에 at, in, on 중 알맞은 전치사를 쓰세요.

1 There were nearly a thousand people ___________ the concert.

2 Life ___________ a farm may not be exciting, but it has its own simple charms.

3 Baengnokdam is a lake ___________ the top of Mount Halla.

4 I read about the accident ___________ a newspaper article.

5 I didn't notice the banana peel ___________ the floor.

6 There were a lot of coins ___________ the bottom of the fountain.

7 Jikji is the oldest movable metal print book ___________ the world.

8 If you look carefully, you might be able to find a lot of useful things ___________ a garage sale.

9 Even though the sun was already rising, I wanted to stay ___________ bed.

10 There was almost nothing to see but desert landscape ___________ the road to Alice Springs.

11 I didn't get enough sleep ___________ the plane because of the kids sitting next to me.

12 As the storm approached, all fishing boats ___________ sea had to return to the port.

13 She volunteered to teach classes ___________ prison.

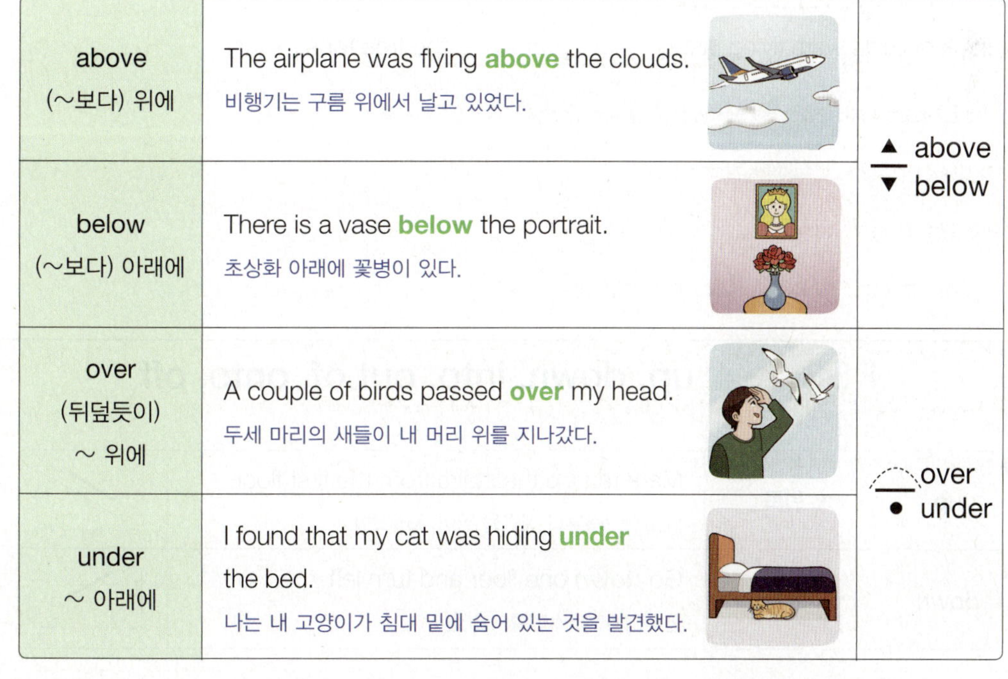

PSS 2-3 above, below, over, under

above (〜보다) 위에	The airplane was flying **above** the clouds. 비행기는 구름 위에서 날고 있었다.	▲ above ▼ below
below (〜보다) 아래에	There is a vase **below** the portrait. 초상화 아래에 꽃병이 있다.	
over (뒤덮듯이) 〜 위에	A couple of birds passed **over** my head. 두세 마리의 새들이 내 머리 위를 지나갔다.	over • under
under 〜 아래에	I found that my cat was hiding **under** the bed. 나는 내 고양이가 침대 밑에 숨어 있는 것을 발견했다.	

PRACTICE 13

그림을 보고, 빈칸에 above, below, over, under 중 알맞은 단어를 쓰세요.

1 There is a baseball _______________ the table.

2 With a powerful kick, the kangaroo leapt _______________ the fence.

3 I hurt my arm _______________ my elbow while playing basketball.

4 Freeze! Hold your hands _______________ your head!

5 The Sun is dropping _______________ the horizon.

6 The sculptor put a white sheet _______________ the sculpture.

7 The dog was _______________ the tree when it rained.

8 A flock of birds were flying just _______________ the tree tops.

PSS 2-4 up, down, into, out of, onto, off

up	~ 위로	Mark ran **up** the stairs from the first floor. Mark는 1층부터 계단을 뛰어 올라갔다.	
down	~ 아래로	Go **down** one floor and turn left. 한 층 내려가서 왼쪽으로 돌아라.	

into	~ 안으로	We went **into** the forest to find the hidden treasure. 우리는 숨겨진 보물을 찾기 위해 숲속으로 갔다.	
out of	~ 밖으로	They got **out of** the car after two hours. 그들은 두 시간 후에 차 밖으로 나왔다.	
onto	~ 위로	The cat jumped **onto** the chair. 고양이는 의자 위로 뛰어올랐다. = The cat jumped **on** the chair. ***cf.*** 한 지점으로의 움직임을 나타낼 때 onto는 on과 바꾸어 쓸 수 있다.	
off	~에서 떨어져	I once fell **off** the top of the ladder. 나는 한 번 사다리 꼭대기에서 떨어진 적이 있다.	

정답 p.90

PRACTICE 14 [1-12]

그림을 보고, 〈보기〉에서 알맞은 전치사를 골라 빈칸에 쓰세요.

보 기	up down into out of onto off

1 The little bird could finally fly ________________ the nest.

2 Suna pinned a note ________________ the bulletin board.

3 The Indians pushed the canoe ________________ the shore.

4 A thief sneaked ________________ the house through an open window.

보 기 up down into out of onto off

5

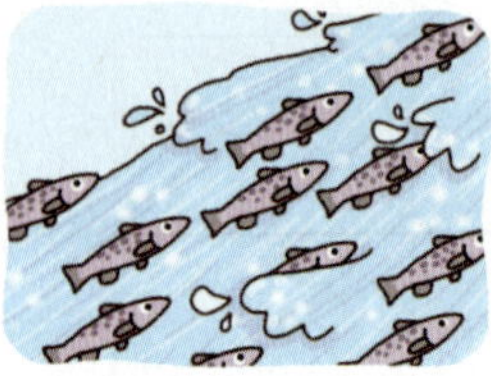

6

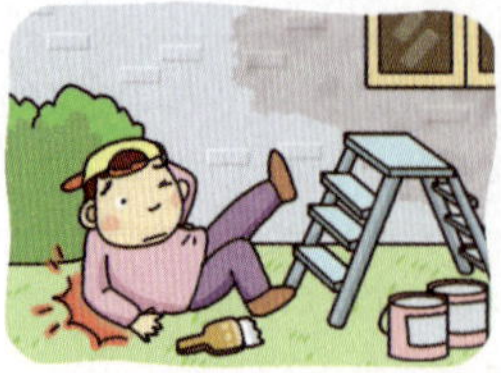

7

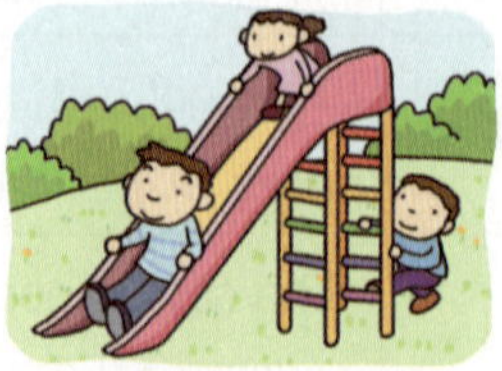

8

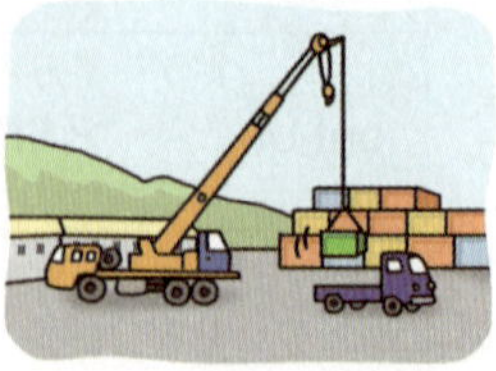

5 Salmon swim __________ the river every year to lay eggs.

6 I fell __________ the ladder while painting the wall.

7 Children are sliding __________ a slide in the playground.

8 The crane loaded the containers __________ the trucks.

9

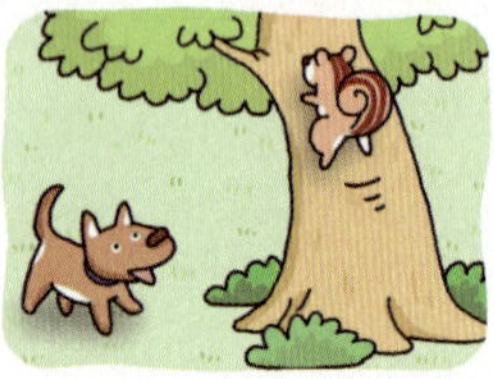

10

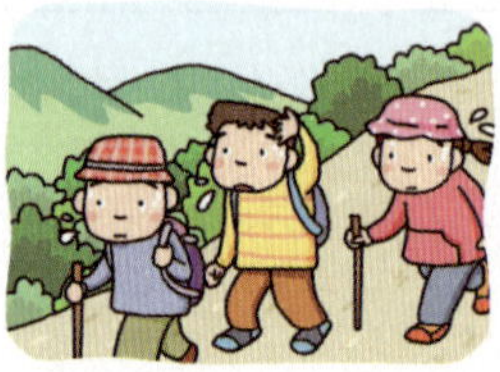

11

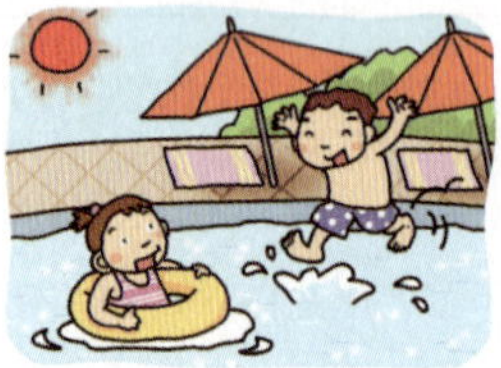

12

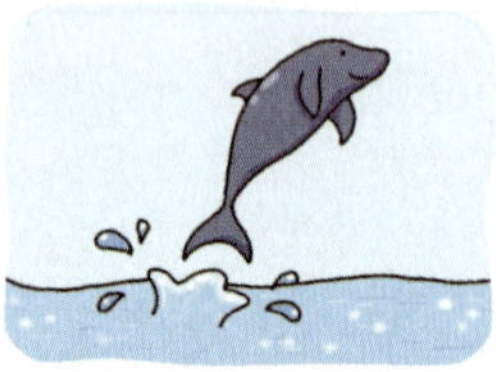

9 The squirrel quickly climbed __________ the tree to get away from the dog.

10 We climbed __________ the mountain exhausted and aching all over.

11 The weather was so hot that we jumped __________ the swimming pool.

12 With a powerful stroke of its tail, the dolphin jumped __________ the water.

정답 p.91

PRACTICE 15

그림을 보고, 괄호 안에 주어진 전치사 중 알맞은 것을 고르세요.

1

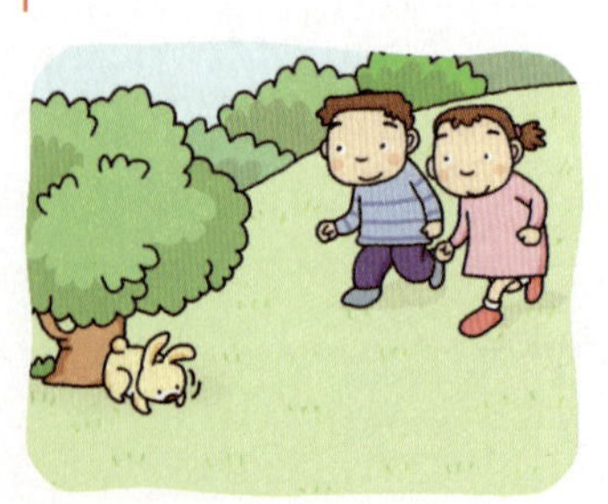

2

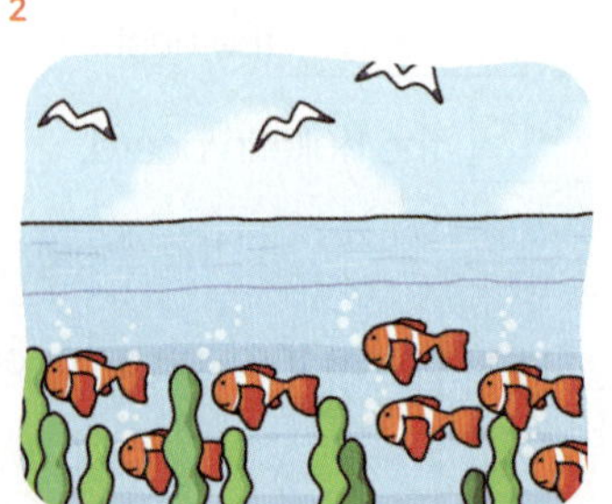

3

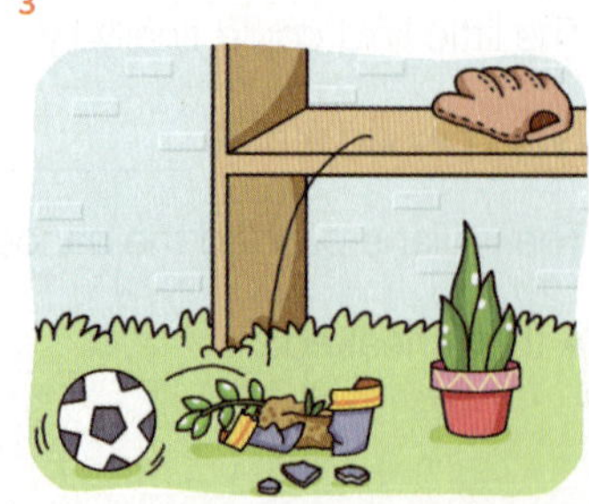

  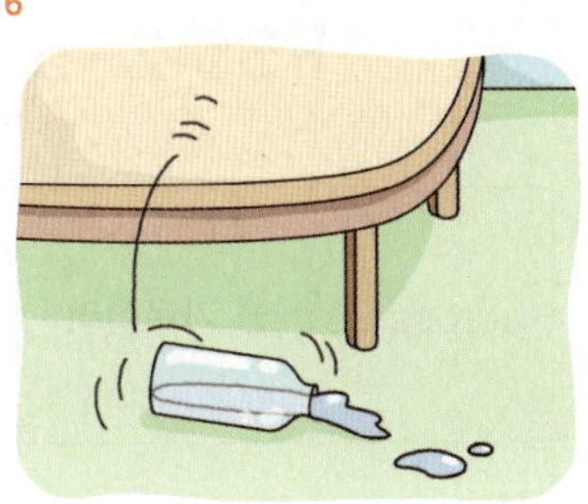

 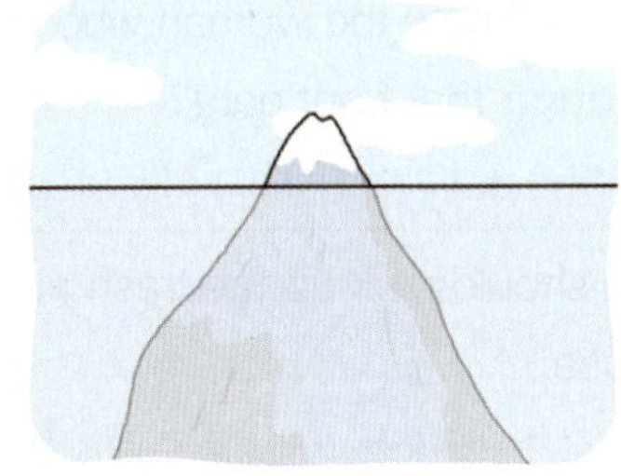 

1 ① The kids are coming (below, down) the hill.

   ② There is a rabbit eating the grass (down, under) the tree.

2 ① (Below, Under) the sea, colorful fish swim among the reefs.

   ② The seagulls are circling (over, onto) the sea.

3 ① The soccer ball rolled (off, onto) the shelf.

   ② The soccer ball broke the vase (over, below) the shelf.

4 ① The firefighter rushed (into, onto) the house on fire.

   ② He came (off, out of) the house carrying a baby in his arms.

5 ① We climbed (up, above) the hill to see the full moon.

   ② The stars were shining brightly (over, up) our heads.

6 ① The bottle fell (out of, off) the table.

   ② The water spilled (onto, into) the floor.

7 ① A girl came (into, onto) the convenience store.

   ② She had a book (down, under) her left arm.

8 ① Just a small part of an iceberg shows (over, above) the surface of the sea.

   ② Most of it lies (below, down) the surface where we cannot see it.

9 ① An astronaut is coming (out of, off) the spaceship.

   ② He climbs down a ladder (up, onto) the surface of the planet.

PSS 2-5 across, along, through, around

across	~을 가로질러	A father and a son were traveling **across** the desert. 한 아버지와 아들이 사막을 가로질러 여행을 하고 있었다.	
along	~을 따라	I saw a rabbit as I walked **along** the road. 나는 도로를 따라 걸어가다가 토끼 한 마리를 보았다.	
through	~을 통과하여	Do you know the woman who is passing **through** that front gate? 저 앞문을 통과하여 지나가고 있는 여자를 아니?	
around	~ 주위에[를]	You should pick up the trash **around** the house. 너는 집 주위에 있는 쓰레기를 주워야 한다.	

정답 p.91

PRACTICE 16

그림을 보고, 〈보기〉에서 알맞은 전치사를 골라 빈칸에 쓰세요.

보 기　　across　along　through　around

1 We drove _________________ the coast until we found the restaurant.

2 The stream is so narrow that you can swim _______________ it.

3 The police station is just _______________ the street.

4 My mother had a scarf _______________ her neck.

5 There are many natural satellites that orbit _________________ the planet, Jupiter.

6 The highway runs _________________ a tunnel in the mountains.

7 At the signal of the trainer, the seal jumped _________________ the hoop.

8 Sally and I walked _________________ the beach hand in hand, footprints trailing behind us.

PSS 2-6 by, in front of, behind, near

by	~ 옆에	You're not allowed to park your car **by** the warehouse. 창고 옆에 차를 주차시켜서는 안 됩니다. = You're not allowed to park your car **beside** the warehouse. = You're not allowed to park your car **next to** the warehouse.	
in front of	~ 앞에	I came across James **in front of** the subway station. 나는 지하철역 앞에서 James를 우연히 만났다.	
behind	~ 뒤에	We have a small field **behind** the house. 우리는 집 뒤에 작은 밭을 가지고 있다.	
near	~ 가까이에	The new bookstore is located **near** the church, just across the street. 새로운 서점은 교회 가까이에 위치해 있는데, 바로 길 건너편이다.	

정답 p.91

PRACTICE 17 [1-8]

그림을 보고, 빈칸에 들어갈 말로 알맞은 것을 고르세요.

1  2  3  4 

1 Don't go (near, behind) the dog. It might bite you.

2 The cat is sitting (by, near) Patricia.

3 There is a factory quite (near, by) our neighborhood.

4 A truck was following right (behind, in front of) our car.

5 The tourists took a photograph (in front of, behind) the statue before leaving.

6 The kids played hide-and-seek at home. One of them hid (in front of, behind) the curtain.

7 I must always have this dog (by, near) my side to help me.

8 The children couldn't take their eyes off the food (behind, in front of) them.

PSS 2-7 between, among

between	~사이에	between은 두 개의 사물 또는 두 명의 사람을 나타내는 말 앞에 오며, between A and B의 형태로도 쓴다. The conflict **between** the two towns continued for three months. 두 도시 사이의 갈등은 3달 동안 계속되었다. I placed a chair **between** Frank **and** Zack. 나는 Frank와 Zack 사이에 의자를 놓았다.	
among		among은 셋 이상의 사물 또는 사람을 나타내는 말 앞에 쓴다. I could find Jenny very easily **among** the crowd. 나는 군중들 사이에서 Jenny를 매우 쉽게 찾을 수 있었다. There is nothing I don't like **among** his novels. 그의 소설 중에서 내가 좋아하지 않는 것은 아무것도 없다.	

PRACTICE 18

빈칸에 between 또는 among 중 알맞은 것을 쓰세요.

1 I couldn't choose one _________________ Namjin and Suyoung.

2 Who is your favorite star _________________ Hollywood actors?

3 Sam and Bill are twins. I can't tell the difference _________________ them.

4 There are regular ferries that run _________________ Mokpo and Jeju Island.

5 The lion hid _________________ the tall grass, waiting for the buffalo to pass by.

6 There are many differences _________________ English dialects around the world.

7 The new office building is situated _________________ 5th Avenue and 11th Street.

8 There was a rumor _________________ my classmates that there was going to be a surprise exam.

9 The distance _________________ the two cities is about 34 km.

10 Who _________________ your friends is the most adventurous?

PSS 2-8 to, for, toward(s)

to	~로, ~까지	to는 목적지를 나타내고 주로 go, come, return, send, bring, walk 등의 동사와 함께 쓴다. I **went to** the museum to get some information for the report. 나는 보고서에 대한 정보를 얻기 위해 박물관에 갔다. He's scheduled to **return to** Rome after the conference in Paris. 그는 파리에서 있을 회의를 마친 후 로마로 돌아갈 예정이다.
for	~로, ~을 향하여	for는 운동의 방향을 나타내고 주로 start, leave 등의 동사와 함께 쓴다. She **started for** Seoul two hours ago, but hasn't reached there yet. 그녀는 두 시간 전에 서울로 떠났지만 아직 그곳에 도착하지 못했다. Mr. Carter suddenly **left for** the airport without saying anything. Carter 씨는 아무 말도 하지 않고 갑자기 공항으로 떠났다.

<table>
<tr><td>toward(s)</td><td>∼ 쪽으로,
∼을 향하여</td><td>toward(s)는 목적지 쪽으로의 방향을 나타내고 walk, come, run, drive, turn, rush 등의 동사와 함께 쓴다.

I saw a small ship **coming toward** the island last night.
나는 지난 밤에 한 작은 배가 섬을 향해 오고 있는 것을 보았다.
My dog **rushed towards** me as soon as he saw me. 나의 강아지는 나를 보자마자 내 쪽으로 달려들었다.</td></tr>
</table>

정답 p.91

PRACTICE 19

빈칸에 to, for, toward(s) 중 가장 알맞은 전치사를 써 넣으세요.

1 We went ________________ the amusement park and rode the roller coaster.

2 The dog tried to swim ________________ the shore, but the river swept him away.

3 This flight will leave ________________ Dubai shortly.

4 Jason ran ________________ the finish line, but he fell down on the way.

5 What time do you usually start ________________ school?

6 This train will leave ________________ Taebaek in five minutes.

7 The girl walked ________________ me, but just passed by without noticing me.

8 We started ________________ the mountains early in the morning.

9 I went ________________ the dentist's this afternoon.

10 Jisun went ________________ the stationery shop to pick up some supplies.

11 When is the orchestra coming ________________ town for the concert?

12 We drove the car ________________ the border to get to New Jersey.

13 In the 19th century, many Chinese left home ________________ the United States to find a better life.

14 From Melbourne, we took an express bus ________________ Brisbane.

15 William Tell's arrow flew ________________ the boy, and hit the apple on his head.

PSS 3 그 밖의 전치사

PSS 3-1 with, without, for, against

with	〈동반〉 ~와 함께	It's a good experience to work **with** foreign workers. 외국인들과 함께 일하는 것은 좋은 경험이다.
	〈조화〉 ~와, ~에 찬성하여	You should follow him this time even if you don't agree **with** his opinion. 네가 그의 의견에 동의하지 않는다 하더라도 이번에는 그를 따라야 한다.
	~에 대하여	I was upset **with** what he told me. 나는 그가 내게 한 말에 대해 화가 났다.
	~을 가지고 있는	The woman **with** long brown hair is the new science teacher. 긴 갈색 머리를 한 여자는 새로 오신 과학 선생님이다.
	~의 몸에 지니고	I don't have any money **with** me right now. 나는 지금 당장은 돈을 가지고 있지 않다.
	~을 사용하여, ~으로	Japanese people eat rice **with** chopsticks. 일본인들은 젓가락을 이용하여 밥을 먹는다.
without	~없이	I can't imagine a world **without** computers. 나는 컴퓨터가 없는 세상을 상상할 수 없다.
	~하지 않고	Will Jack be mad at me if I ride his bicycle **without** asking him? Jack은 내가 그에게 물어보지 않고 그의 자전거를 탄다면 내게 화가 날까?
for	(의견, 정책, 법안 등에) 찬성하는	I'm **for** the new policy that guarantees women's rights. 나는 여성의 권리를 보장하는 새 정책에 찬성한다.
against	(의견, 정책, 법안 등에) 반대하는	Are you **against** Mr. Smith's business plan? 당신은 Smith 씨의 사업·계획에 반대하십니까?

CH
16
전치사

PRACTICE 20

괄호 안에 들어갈 알맞은 전치사를 골라 동그라미 하세요.

1   I share the dormitory room (with, without) three other schoolmates.

2   Whatever your plan is going to be, I'm completely (for, with) you.

3   We moved to the city (against, without) any clear plan.

4   Who's that boy (with, for) the skateboard?

5   In some countries, owning a gun is (against, with) the law.

6   Although I would like to vote (without, for) the new policy, I'm still too young.

7   He was very satisfied (against, with) his brand-new car.

8   He solved the puzzle (for, without) using any hints.

9   I couldn't get his autograph since I didn't have a pen to write (with, without).

10 Many teenagers today always keep their cell phones (with, for) them wherever they go.

PSS 3-2 like, by, in, as

like	~처럼	In the movie, he ran up the wall of the building **like** a spider. 영화에서 그는 거미처럼 건물의 벽을 타고 달려 올라갔다.
	~와 같은	Eating too much fast food **like** hamburgers and pizza is harmful to your body. 햄버거와 피자와 같은 패스트푸드를 너무 많이 먹는 것은 몸에 해롭다.
by	〈수단, 방법〉 ~를 타고, ~로	This is my first time to travel **by** plane. 내가 비행기로 여행하는 것은 이번이 처음이다.
	~에 의해	My teacher recommended a book written **by** George Orwell. 나의 선생님은 George Orwell에 의해 쓰여진 책을 추천해 주셨다.
	~함으로써	Mr. William saved a lot of money **by** living a thrifty life. William 씨는 절약하는 삶을 삶으로써 많은 돈을 모았다.
	〈정도〉 ~로, ~만큼	The population of this city has decreased **by** 30% for two years. 이 도시의 인구는 2년 동안 30% 정도 감소했다.

in	~을 입고 있는	The man **in** a blue tie is the one who is in charge of customer service. 파란색 넥타이를 매고 있는 남자가 고객 서비스를 담당하는 사람이다.
	〈방법, 크기, 도구〉 ~로	I cut the hamburger **in** half to share with my brother. 나는 내 동생과 같이 먹기 위해 햄버거를 반으로 잘랐다. We can erase it because he wrote it **in** pencil. 그가 그것을 연필로 썼기 때문에 우리는 그것을 지울 수 있다.
as	~로서	Broccoli is known **as** a very nutritious vegetable. 브로콜리는 매우 영양가 있는 채소로 알려져 있다.

정답 p.92

PRACTICE 21

〈보기〉에서 알맞은 전치사를 골라 빈칸에 쓰세요.

보 기	like　by　in　as

1　The school was used ___________ a shelter during the typhoon.

2　I plan to travel in Australia ___________ bicycle after I graduate.

3　Did you know that the tune for "Twinkle Twinkle Little Star" was composed ___________ Mozart?

4　A gentleman ___________ a smart-looking suit with a briefcase walked into the room.

5　During the summer vacation, I worked ___________ a coast guard at Haeundae beach.

6　The profit of this company increased ___________ 500% this year.

7　My little brother dressed up ___________ Superman with his red underwear over his blue pants.

8　We had to use this box ___________ a table while we were camping.

9　Many refugees escaped into Hong Kong ___________ swimming across the river.

10　There are many museums in Paris ___________ the Louvre and the Center Georges Pompidou.

PSS 3-3 except, due to, according to, instead of

except	~ 외에는	Bob didn't tell anyone **except** his wife about his disease. Bob은 그의 아내를 제외하고 아무에게도 그의 병에 대해 이야기하지 않았다.
due to	~ 때문에	All of the planes are grounded **due to** the weather condition. 기후 사정으로 인해 모든 비행기들이 이륙을 못하고 있다.
according to	~에 따르면, ~에 따라	**According to** the weather forecast, there's a high chance of rain tomorrow. 일기예보에 따르면 내일 비가 올 확률이 높다.
instead of	~ 대신에	If you need exercise, use the stairs **instead of** the elevator. 운동이 필요하다면, 엘리베이터 대신 계단을 이용해라.

정답 p.92

PRACTICE 22

괄호 안에 들어갈 알맞은 말을 골라 동그라미 하세요.

1 The project was proceeding (due to, according to) the plan.

2 Some snakes can live for months (without, against) eating anything.

3 The majority of citizens were (for, like) the new constitution.

4 (Due to, According to) a school myth, our school was once a graveyard.

5 Everyone arrived on time (except, instead of) Rachel. She got up late this morning.

6 People tend to judge people (like, by) their looks.

7 I'd like to have a glass of orange juice (except, instead of) coffee, please.

8 My friend, Joongil did a fine job (as, by) the class leader this year.

9 I tried to break the lock (with, instead of) a hammer, but it didn't work.

10 My uncle was diagnosed with high blood pressure (according to, due to) his eating habits.

11 (Instead of, Except) cooking dinner, they ordered takeout from their favorite restaurant.

12 The term "Marsupial" refers to animals (as, like) kangaroos and koalas.

13 The school festival was cancelled (due to, according to) heavy rain.

14 Chimpanzees eat ants (with, by) poking ant nests with branches.

15 The construction of the laboratory was stopped (according to, due to) lack of funds.

16 We're campaigning (without, against) our school's strict regulation on hair style.

17 Nearly 90% of Koreans have access to the Internet, (due to, according to) the research.

18 We had a problem (with, without) the new exercise machine.

19 I ran as fast as my feet could go, and crossed the finish line (in, as) first place.

20 All Latin American countries speak Spanish (except, instead of) Brazil. They speak Portuguese.

PSS 3-4 형용사와 함께 쓰이는 전치사 I

1. **afraid of** '~을 두려워하는, 무서워하는'

   I'm **afraid of** needles, so I look away when getting injections.
   나는 주사를 무서워해서, 주사 맞을 때 눈을 돌린다.

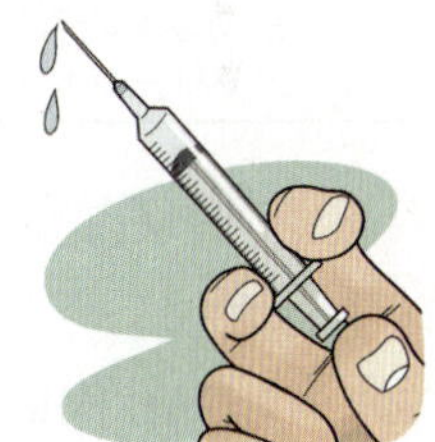

2. **ashamed of** '~을 부끄러워하는, 수치스럽게 여기는'

   Jenny felt **ashamed of** herself after she lied to her parents.
   Jenny는 그녀의 부모님에게 거짓말을 한 후에 자신에 대해 수치스러움을 느꼈다.

3. **based on** '~에 근거한'

   This movie is **based on** a true story. 이 영화는 실제 이야기에 근거한다.

4. **busy with** '~로 바쁜'

   I was **busy with** work, so I couldn't take care of the plants.
   나는 일 때문에 바빠서 식물들을 돌볼 수가 없었다.

5. **capable of** '~을 할 수 있는'

   He's not **capable of** managing the project all by himself.
   그는 전적으로 혼자서 그 프로젝트를 관리할 수 없다.

6. **crazy about** '~에 열광적인, ~를 매우 좋아하는'

   My daughter is **crazy about** movies. 내 딸은 영화를 매우 좋아한다.

7. crowded with '~로 가득한'

All the streets were **crowded with** people during the festival.
모든 거리들이 축제 동안 사람들로 가득했다.

8. familiar with '~에 익숙한, 친숙한'

Namsu isn't **familiar with** this area since he moved here last week.
남수는 지난주에 여기에 이사 왔기 때문에 이 지역에 익숙하지 않다.

9. frightened of '~에 놀란'

People were **frightened of** the unexpected accident that happened last night.
사람들은 지난밤에 일어난 예기치 못한 사건에 놀랐다.

10. full of '~로 가득한'

He was holding a basket **full of** fruit.
그는 과일로 가득한 바구니를 들고 있었다.

정답 p.92

PRACTICE 23

괄호 안에 들어갈 전치사로 알맞은 것을 골라 동그라미 하세요.

1 Andy is so crazy (about, of) Japanese animation that there's nothing else in his computer.

2 I'm not going bungee jumping because I'm afraid (about, of) heights.

3 Have you ever felt ashamed (with, of) yourself after making a mistake?

4 The rhinoceros beetle is capable (of, about) lifting 850 times its own weight.

5 I was frightened (of, with) the sudden flash of lightning.

6 This beach is crowded (with, of) people. Let's go to another beach.

7 I was so busy (with, in) the vacuum cleaner that I couldn't hear the knock on the door.

8 Younger people tend to be more familiar (about, with) smartphones and other electronics.

9 There is a room full (with, of) old books and documents on the third floor.

10 This novel is a science fiction, but most of it is based (in, on) real scientific facts.

1. **interested in** '~에 관심 있는'

   She has been **interested in** designing clothes. 그녀는 옷을 디자인하는 것에 관심 있어 했다.

2. **jealous of** '~을 질투하는'

   Vicky was **jealous of** all the attention that her sister received at her birthday party.
   Vicky는 그녀의 여동생이 생일 파티에서 받은 모든 관심을 질투했다.

3. **mad at** '~에 몹시 화난'

   Do you happen to know why Mom is **mad at** me?
   너 혹시 엄마가 내게 왜 화가 나셨는지 알고 있니?

4. **married to** '~와 결혼한'

   She has been **married to** her husband for ten years.
   그녀는 10년 동안 그녀의 남편과 결혼해 살아 왔다.

5. **similar to** '~와 비슷한'

   I was surprised to know that his voice was very **similar to** his brother's.
   나는 그의 목소리가 그의 형의 목소리와 매우 비슷한 것을 알고 놀랐다.

6. **proud of** '~을 자랑스러워 하는'

   We are **proud of** our cultural heritage. 우리는 우리의 문화 유산을 자랑스러워한다.

7. **related to** '~와 관련된'

   We have to choose a topic which is **related to** fashion.
   우리는 패션과 관련된 주제를 선택해야 한다.

8. **responsible for** '~에 책임 있는'

   You should be **responsible for** what you have done. 너는 네가 한 일에 책임을 져야 한다.

9. **sorry for** '~이 가엾은, 미안하게 생각하는'

   Yoonsoo texted her, saying "I'm **sorry for** my behavior yesterday."
   윤수는 그녀에게 "어제 내 행동에 대해 미안하게 생각해."라고 말하는 문자 메시지를 보냈다.

10. **surprised at** '~에 놀란'

   I was **surprised at** the sudden change in weather. 나는 갑작스러운 날씨 변화에 놀랐다.

CH
16
전치사

PRACTICE 24

괄호 안에 들어갈 전치사로 알맞은 것을 골라 동그라미 하세요.

1 You're beautiful in your own way. So don't be jealous (of, in) someone else's looks.

2 My uncle is proud (of, for) his daughter's career.

3 We were surprised (for, at) how much the baby girl had grown since we last saw her.

4 Yesterday, Geunho's grandmother passed away. I feel sorry (of, for) him.

5 I was mad (at, to) my little brother's impolite behavior.

6 Some people think that violent online games are related (to, about) teen crimes.

7 Please believe me! I'm not the one responsible (in, for) the broken window.

8 The actress got married (to, at) a wealthy businessman and lived happily ever after.

9 Today's weather forecast is similar (from, to) yesterday's.

10 Since Sue is interested (of, in) cooking, she might be able to help us bake the cake.

PSS 3-6 동사와 함께 쓰이는 전치사 Ⅰ

1. add … to '~에 …를 더하다'

I want to **add** some more sugar **to** my tea.
나는 내 차에 설탕을 조금 더 넣고 싶다.

2. apply for '~에 지원하다, 신청하다'

Jiho **applied for** a work visa to work in Australia.
지호는 호주에서 일하기 위해 취업 비자를 신청했다.

3. apologize for '~에 대해 사과하다'

I **apologize for** replying late to your email.
나는 당신의 이메일에 늦게 답장을 한 것에 대해 사과 드립니다.

4. believe in '~을 믿다'

My parents **believe in** the importance of education. 나의 부모님은 교육의 중요성을 믿으신다.

cf. believe는 '~이 사실이라고 여기다'라는 뜻이고, believe in은 ① '종교를 믿다' ② '~의 존재·인격을 믿다' ③ '~이 좋다고 믿다'라는 뜻을 갖는다.

5. belong to '~에 속하다'

This animal farm **belongs to** the city mayor. 이 동물 농장은 시장의 것이다.

6. care about '~에 대해 신경 쓰다'

Kevin **cares about** what others say about him.
Kevin은 다른 사람들이 그에 대해 말하는 것에 대해 신경을 쓴다.

7. care for '~을 돌보다, 좋아하다, 하고 싶어 하다'

My sister will **care for** my baby while I'm not at home.
내가 집에 없는 동안에 언니가 내 아기를 돌볼 것이다.
Would you **care for** another cup of tea? 차 한 잔 더 하시겠습니까?

8. concentrate on '~에 집중하다'

I tried to **concentrate on** writing a poem. 나는 시를 쓰는 데 집중하려고 노력했다.

9. consist of '~로 구성되어 있다'

The elementary school that I graduated from **consisted of** 300 students in six grades. 내가 졸업한 초등학교는 6개 학년에 300명으로 구성되어 있었다.

10. depend on '~에 의존하다, ~에 달려 있다'

My twin sister and I **depend on** each other. 내 쌍둥이 언니와 나는 서로에게 의존한다.
The result **depends on** how quickly he finishes the work.
결과는 그가 얼마나 빨리 그 일을 끝내느냐에 달려 있다.

정답 p.92

PRACTICE 25

다음 문장의 빈칸에 알맞은 전치사를 쓰세요.

1 Peter doesn't really care ___________ fashion trends.

2 Some people believe ___________ evolution, and others creation.

3 Some Japanese people insist that Dokdo belongs ___________ them.

4 I couldn't concentrate ___________ the book because of the noise outside.

5 The Korean economy heavily depends ___________ the Middle Eastern oil.

6 Last year, I applied ___________ the school football team, but was turned down.

7 An emperor penguin cares ___________ his chick by setting the chick on his feet.

8 Blood consists ___________ several different cells.

9 When milk is added ___________ Espresso coffee, it is called cafe au lait, which means coffee with milk.

10 Susan, I apologize ___________ yelling at you yesterday. It was wrong of me to do that.

1. die of[from] '~로 죽다'

   Mrs. Miller who lived next door **died of[from]** a heart attack yesterday.
   옆집에 살던 Miller 부인은 어제 심장마비로 사망했다.

2. dream about[of] '~를 꿈꾸다'

   I have **dreamed about[of]** becoming a news reporter.
   나는 기자가 되는 것을 꿈꿔 왔다.

3. feel like '~하고 싶다'

   I don't **feel like** going fishing now. 나는 지금 낚시하러 가고 싶지 않아.

4. focus on '~에 초점을 맞추다'

   We are currently **focusing on** making a new product.
   우리는 현재 새로운 제품을 만드는 것에 초점을 맞추고 있다.

5. laugh at '~을 보고 웃다, 비웃다'

   No one at the meeting **laughed at** my joke.
   회의 중이던 어느 누구도 내 농담에 웃지 않았다.

6. listen to '~을 듣다'

   Listen carefully **to** what the speaker is trying to say to the listener.
   화자가 청자에게 무엇을 말하려고 하는지 주의 깊게 들으세요.

7. look forward to '~를 고대하다'

   We **look forward to** your quick reply. 우리는 당신의 빠른 답장을 고대합니다.

8. prefer … to '~보다 …을 선호하다'

   Mr. Johnson **prefers** public transportation **to** his own car when he goes to work.
   Johnson 씨는 출근할 때 그의 차보다 대중교통을 선호한다.

9. succeed in '~에 성공하다'

   Did your daughter **succeed in** finding a job overseas?
   당신의 딸은 해외에서 일자리를 구하는 것에 성공했습니까?

10. wait for '~를 기다리다'

    Many people **waited for** the shop to be open on the day before Christmas.
    많은 사람들이 크리스마스 전날 그 상점이 열리기를 기다렸다.

PRACTICE 26

다음 문장의 빈칸에 알맞은 전치사를 쓰세요.

1 I am waiting ___________ the perfect moment to propose to her.

2 You hurt yourself because you didn't listen ___________ the instructor's warning.

3 This math book is mainly focused ___________ algebra.

4 My classmates laughed ___________ me because of my awkward accent.

5 When I was your age, I always dreamed ___________ becoming a pilot.

6 The doctor concluded that the man had died ___________ diabetes.

7 I feel ___________ going out for a swim in the pool.

8 We have succeeded ___________ bringing people together for a good cause.

9 My parents prefer hiking ___________ watching movies.

10 Everyone is looking forward ___________ the end of the exams and the winter vacation.

PRACTICE 27 [1-100]

괄호 안에 들어갈 알맞은 전치사를 골라 동그라미 하세요.

1 This bus will start (for, to) Daejeon as soon as all passengers have boarded.

2 I'll meet you at the clock tower (at, on) two fifteen.

3 Construction of the Berlin Wall began (in, on) August 13th, 1961.

4 This sign was printed (in, by) two different colors.

5 (Before, After) sending the text message to Betty, I waited for a reply.

6 Speeding over 100 km/h is (with, against) the traffic laws.

7 Oxford is a city located (at, on) the River Thames.

8 Most of South America had gained independence (until, by) the 19th century.

9 Feeling threatened, the snake quickly hid itself (under, down) a rock.

10 As the bus left, tears started to roll (up, down) his face.

11 When the football match ended, the crowd poured (into, onto) the field.

12 I'm going to take all courses related (to, for) Japanese culture.

13 There's a shortcut that passes (through, around) the parking lot.

14 I started living on the Solomon Islands (for, from) October last year.

15 The city of Troy was safely protected (behind, near) its fortified walls.

16 I didn't break the vase. I'm not responsible (to, for) that!

17 I saw Jinsu walking (for, toward) the park, but I don't know where he went for sure.

18 There are several pictures (above, up) the shelf.

19 I totally agree (with, for) your point of view.

20 (According to, Due to) the weather forecast, it's going to be sunny until the weekend.

21 Technology advanced at an incredible pace (during, for) the 20th century.

22 It would be better if we could go out and play (instead of, except) staying at home.

23 When he was young, my grandpa served (in, as) a civil engineer.

24 Julie has been working at a library (during, for) three months.

25 The airplane flew (across, through) the ocean, heading towards its destination.

26 This year's NBA playoffs will start (since, from) April 30th.

27 The story about a friendly bear was written (by, from) a famous writer.

28 The tomato has been cultivated in the Mediterranean (until, since) the 1540s.

29 Physical activities (like, as) cycling, jogging and swimming are good for building up your body.

30 Our class will go on a field trip to the Museum of Natural History (at, on) Friday.

31 My little brother dressed up (in, like) Spiderman and pretended to shoot webs.

32 I'm sorry, but Tiffany is not in (in, at) the moment.

33 Every summer, an ice cream vendor sets up a stall (down, in front of) my school.

34 Sharks have not changed much (since, from) the extinction of the dinosaurs.

35 My family decided to have a small party with some neighbors (on, in) Christmas Eve.

36 Walk (around, along) the street until you reach the traffic light. The bank will be on your right.

37 Make sure you've packed your textbooks (before, after) going to bed.

38 I am excited that my parents are going to be (on, in) TV.

39 The stadium was used (as, with) a temporary shelter when hurricane Katrina hit the city.

40 I felt very ashamed (in, of) the way my brother behaved in the toy store.

41 California's climate is similar (from, to) that of the Mediterranean.

42 I'm happy as long as I can travel (over, around) the world.

43 The moth that flew into the window hid itself (behind, in front of) the curtain.

44 Unemployment (between, among) the young has been a serious problem in Korea.

45 The mouse quickly crawled (into, onto) a hole in the wall to get away from the hungry cat.

46 I like winter the most (between, among) all seasons.

47 I apologize (for, in) the misunderstanding. It's all my fault.

48 I share the room (with, without) my younger brother.

49 In some countries, making graffiti is (off, against) the law.

50 A thief sneaked (onto, into) the house through an open window.

51 I couldn't read the top secret files at all as it was written (in, on) Chinese.

52 My cousin got liver cancer (according to, due to) his heavy drinking habit.

53 (Instead of, Except) finishing the book, I decided to watch TV.

54 Animals (like, as) whales and dolphins are classified as cetaceans.

55 We're planning to go to the east coast (on, in) New Year's Eve.

56 During the winter vacations, I worked (like, as) a safety guard at a ski resort.

57 People in Caribbean countries speak English (instead of, except) those who are in Haiti and Cuba.

58 There are regular commercial flights (between, among) Beijing and Pyongyang.

59 I'm really looking forward (with, to) next year's English Premier League football tournament.

60 Mr. Kim's team was very jealous (of, in) my team's success.

61 The girls were frightened (in, of) the sound of thunder and started screaming.

62 I always dreamed (for, about) becoming a racing car driver.

63 My mother was mad (at, about) me for breaking her favorite vase.

64 We were surprised (at, on) the total amount of donations.

65 Mr. Johnson prefers the bus (to, in) the subway.

66 Hundreds of people died from the terror. I feel sorry (of, for) the victims.

67 I can't get past the door, because I'm afraid (of, about) that huge dog at the doorway.

68 My classmates thought my costume was funny, so they laughed (at, for) me.

69 Last year, I applied (in, for) a job with the law firm in Seoul.

70 This history book is mainly focused (about, on) the independence of America.

71 I should have listened (at, to) what the weather forecaster said.

72 This country consists (of, in) thousands of islands.

73 The parade is going to start (at, on) 11 o'clock. Let's hurry. We've only got 2 minutes!

74 The world's economy heavily depends (on, to) China's mass production ability.

75 He died (for, of) cancer at a young age.

76 I am waiting (for, on) the perfect moment to ask him out on a date.

77 Some ants are capable (of, about) dragging an object 25 times their own weight.

78 My sister likes to care (for, about) injured or sick animals.

79 Some people believe (in, on) the existence of aliens while others do not.

80 Chinese people think that Baekdusan belongs (to, for) them.

81 My aunt is proud (of, in) her son's good school report.

82 Haitians celebrate Independence Day (on, in) the 1st of January.

83 My brother and I played a game of chess (for, during) the evening.

84 I couldn't concentrate (on, in) reading the newspaper because of the children playing in the house.

85 The bus seemed to be going (towards, for) the post office, but suddenly turned right at a junction.

86 The squirrel tried to come (off, out of) the cage.

87 The amusement park was crowded (with, of) people as we had expected.

88 Daeun is interested (at, in) learning Spanish.

89 According (to, as) the research, more and more young people like to spend time alone.

90 Scientists haven't succeeded (to, in) finding a complete cure for the common cold.

91 I was so busy (with, by) house chores that I forgot to plug off the iron.

92 Older people tend to be more familiar (of, with) Chinese characters.

93 The lungfish can survive (out of, into) water for a short period of time.

94 I don't feel (for, like) going out for a bike ride.

95 He is crazy (about, at) basketball and never misses a game.

96 We had a problem (with, without) the new laptop computer.

97 It's lunchtime (between, among) 12 and 1 o'clock.

98 Although my sister got married (to, for) a poor salesman, she is happier than ever.

99 Nature is always full (with, of) wonders unknown.

100 Marco Polo wrote a book based (in, on) his own experience in China.

1 빈칸에 들어갈 전치사로 알맞은 것을 고르세요.

> A: Is Minhee there?
> B: Sorry, she's not in ___________ the moment.

① from　　② in　　③ at
④ on　　⑤ of

2 Which is a common preposition for the blanks?

> • One sunny day ___________ spring, we were taking a walk along the street.
> • Lindsey was born ___________ California.

① on　　② in　　③ at
④ with　　⑤ of

3 다음 빈칸에 들어갈 전치사가 차례대로 짝지어진 것은?

> • I will learn how to operate the machine ___________ Monday.
> • You should sign your name ___________ pen.

① at – in　　　② in – at
③ at – since　　④ on – in
⑤ on – from

[4-5] 다음 빈칸에 들어갈 전치사로 알맞은 것을 고르세요.

4

> A: I heard you broke your arm yesterday. How did it happen?
> B: I fell ___________ my bike.
> A: That's too bad. I hope you get better soon.

① in　　② on　　③ off　　④ with　　⑤ for

5

> To protect the environment, we should use our own cups ___________ disposable paper cups, and bring reusable bags when we go shopping.

① according to　② instead　　③ due to
④ instead of　　⑤ except

6 다음 밑줄 친 ⓐ～ⓔ에 들어갈 표현이 적절하지 <u>않</u>은 것은?

> It was Paris ⓐ _____ May 10, 1998. A young player entered the stadium ⓑ _____ a midfielder for his national team. Thousands of fans welcomed him with cheers. He had worked hard every day, focusing ⓒ _____ improving his speed and control. The player devoted his life and strength ⓓ _____ soccer, determined to reach the top. ⓔ _____ effort, he finally led his team to victory.

① ⓐ on　　② ⓑ as　　③ ⓒ on
④ ⓓ in　　⑤ ⓔ With

7 Choose <u>all</u> the sentences that are grammatically <u>incorrect</u>.

① In the morning, I dressed up in my finest clothes.
② What changes do you want in the future?
③ What was the greatest invention in the 20th century?
④ You will have so many things to do in this year.
⑤ In last Monday, a messenger arrived at Sumi's home.

8 다음 글을 읽고 밑줄 친 ①~⑤ 중 의미상 잘못 쓰인 것을 찾아 번호를 쓰고 바르게 고치세요.

① On the bus, while Jane is listening to music, she is busy surfing the Internet. Even after she gets to school, she keeps looking ② at her cell phone all along. Young people like Jane ③ are called "Digital Natives" because they have been exposed ④ to this digital technology ⑤ by their childhood.

( ) ＿＿＿＿＿＿＿ ➡ ＿＿＿＿＿＿＿

9 주어진 우리말과 같은 뜻이 되도록 빈칸에 알맞은 말을 쓰세요.

• 그것들은 한 세대에서 다른 세대로 전해진다.
= They are passed on ＿＿＿＿＿ one generation ＿＿＿＿＿ another.

10 다음 빈칸에 공통으로 들어갈 전치사로 알맞은 것은?

• Maybe I'll apply ＿＿＿＿＿ the job that you mentioned yesterday.
• I apologize ＿＿＿＿＿ being late, but there was a traffic jam.

① for ② to ③ in ④ about ⑤ on

11 빈칸에 공통으로 들어갈 전치사로 알맞은 것은?

• Here I am ＿＿＿＿＿ Dokdo Island.
• I'd like to make more friends ＿＿＿＿＿ the Internet.

① in ② at ③ on
④ for ⑤ with

12 Find the grammatically <u>wrong</u> part in the following sentence and fix it correctly.

Will you be capable of teach me how to play the game?

＿＿＿＿＿＿＿ ➡ ＿＿＿＿＿＿＿

13 빈칸에 들어갈 말로 알맞은 것을 <u>모두</u> 고르세요.

We had to stay in the cabin ＿＿＿＿＿ the heavy rain.

① because of ② because that
③ because ④ as
⑤ due to

14 빈칸에 공통으로 들어갈 전치사로 알맞은 것은?

- The mother bird is sharing food __________ her babies.
- I couldn't keep up __________ the others in physical education class.

① to   ② with   ③ on
④ in   ⑤ through

15 Which is proper for the blank?

When a fire breaks out, we must use the stairs __________ the elevators.

① because of   ② in addition to
③ in case of   ④ according to
⑤ instead of

16 다음 문장에서 어법상 <u>틀린</u> 곳을 찾아 바르게 고치세요.

I usually prefer indoor activities like reading books than outdoor activities like playing soccer.

__________ ➡ __________

17 주어진 우리말을 참고하여 빈칸에 알맞은 전치사를 쓰세요.

- That bee stung him __________ his face.
  (저 벌이 그의 얼굴을 쏘았다.)
- Before you buy a new gadget, make sure to look __________ online reviews.
  (네가 새로운 도구를 구입하기 전에 꼭 온라인 리뷰들을 찾아보도록 해라.)

18 다음 대화의 빈칸에 들어갈 말이 차례대로 짝지어진 것은?

Suhee: Who do you take __________ in personality?

Inho : In my opinion, my personality is similar __________ my mother's.

① after – on   ② on   – with
③ of   – with   ④ after – to
⑤ on   – to

19 어법상 <u>어색한</u> 것 2개는?

A: Mina, do you know ① <u>that the Amazon rainforest is disappearing</u>?
B: Yes, I saw a documentary about it.
A: ② <u>It's because cutting down</u> too many trees.
B: That's terrible.
A: ③ <u>The animals are losing their homes and its future is uncertain.</u>
B: It is important for us to protect the environment for the next generation.
A: ④ <u>People should stop using so much paper.</u>
B: Right. That way, ⑤ <u>fewer trees will be cut down.</u>

20 빈칸에 들어갈 말이 차례대로 짝지어진 것은?

- The amusement park was filled __________ children.
- My school is famous __________ its long history.

① of   – for   ② with – of   ③ of   – of
④ with – with   ⑤ with – for

21 글의 흐름으로 보아, 다음 글의 빈칸 (A)와 (B)에 들어갈 말로 가장 적절한 것은?

Nowadays, many people make efforts to stay fit and be healthy. (A) research, eating whole grains such as brown rice rather than processed foods is better for your health. This is because whole grains can help decrease your cholesterol and blood pressure. Also, whole grains are (B) nutrients and vitamins.

	(A)		(B)
①	According to	–	capable of
②	Because of	–	based on
③	According to	–	full of
④	Related to	–	capable of
⑤	Because of	–	full of

22 다음 문장에서 어법상 틀린 곳을 찾아 바르게 고치세요.

The man suffered from a broken ankle for the journey.

➡ ____________________

23 빈칸에 들어갈 전치사가 차례대로 짝지어진 것은?

• The desks in the old library were covered __________ dust.
• We are crazy __________ the upcoming festival.

① with – in   ② of – about
③ with – about   ④ for – in
⑤ of – in

24 ⓐ~ⓔ에 들어갈 말로 알맞은 것을 두 개 고르면?

A: Hey, Minho, did you see the new library?
B: Yes, I went there yesterday. It ⓐ __________ really quiet and clean.
A: I know! But don't ⓑ __________ the library only by its outside.
B: What do you ⓒ __________, Jina?
A: Well, the building looks small, but inside it is very large.
B: Oh, I see. ⓓ __________ the first floor, there are many computers with free Internet.
A: That's awesome! Let's go there together ⓔ __________ school.

① ⓐ : looks like   ② ⓑ : judge
③ ⓒ : need   ④ ⓓ : Under
⑤ ⓔ : after

25 공통으로 들어갈 전치사로 알맞은 것을 쓰세요.

• We can't live __________ water.
• He went home __________ saying anything to me.

26 다음 빈칸 ①~③에 알맞은 전치사를 쓰세요.

< How to make egg salad >
• Boil the eggs ___①___ about 15 minutes.
• Put mayonnaise in the bowl and mash the boiled eggs ___②___ a fork until they become creamy.
• Cut lettuce, bell peppers, and onions ___③___ small pieces and mix them with the mashed eggs.   *mash: 으깨다

➡ ① __________ ② __________ ③ __________

27 다음 문장의 밑줄 친 like와 그 쓰임이 다른 것은?

> My friends and I hope to form an excellent dancing team like them.

① He ran like a cheetah.
② She walked like a model.
③ It looks like a mermaid.
④ She must be outgoing like you.
⑤ I hope you like what I like.

28 빈칸에 들어갈 단어가 차례대로 바르게 짝지어진 것은?

> • I was headed ___________ the library to pick up some books.
> • I have planned to study English on Wednesday ___________ 6:00 and 7:30 p.m.

① for   – of
② of – among
③ for   – between
④ of – between
⑤ from – among

29 ⓐ~ⓔ 중 밑줄 친 부분이 어법상 틀린 것을 있는 대로 고른 것은?

> ⓐ This extremely shy 10-year-old girl sings like an angel.
> ⓑ My baby sister was frightened on the sight of a big spider.
> ⓒ Success depends with hard work as well as luck.
> ⓓ I used to dream on becoming a pianist.
> ⓔ He is shooting a short film in addition a music video.

① ⓐ, ⓑ
② ⓑ, ⓒ
③ ⓑ, ⓒ, ⓓ
④ ⓐ, ⓓ, ⓔ
⑤ ⓑ, ⓒ, ⓓ, ⓔ

30 주어진 우리말과 같은 뜻이 되도록 괄호 안에서 알맞은 것을 고르세요.

> • 우리는 지구상의 모든 동물들과 식물들이 살기 위해 서로 의존한다는 것을 잊지 말아야 한다.
> = We should not forget (what / that) all animals and plants on the Earth depend (on / with) each other to live.

31 빈칸에 공통으로 들어갈 전치사로 알맞은 것은?

> • It was late winter when his grandmother died ___________ old age.
> • Is your house made ___________ wood?

① in
② of
③ on
④ to
⑤ with

32 빈칸에 들어갈 전치사가 차례대로 짝지어진 것은?

> • My dream is to travel ___________ the world.
> • I have to do a lot of work to prepare ___________ the travel.

① around – to
② around – of
③ around – for
④ over   – to
⑤ over   – of

33 빈칸에 들어갈 전치사로 알맞은 것은?

> ___________ the winter, I did not go to any mountains at all.

① Since
② Of
③ To
④ During
⑤ At

34 빈칸에 공통으로 들어갈 전치사로 알맞은 것을 쓰세요.

> Walking on a treadmill ___________ 15 minutes has almost the same effect as laughing ___________ 10 minutes.

35 주어진 우리말과 같은 뜻이 되도록 빈칸에 알맞은 전치사를 쓰세요.

> • 그 사람들은 큰 기쁨과 희망을 가지고 육지에 발을 내디뎠다.
> = The people stepped on the land ___________ great joy and hope.

36 빈칸에 공통으로 들어갈 전치사로 알맞은 말은?

> • A boy ___________ blue eyes and blond hair wants to see you.
> • The boy was very pleased ___________ the toy robot.

① from   ② of   ③ beside
④ to   ⑤ with

37 빈칸에 알맞은 전치사를 쓰세요.

> Our school offers three foreign languages in addition to English; you can choose one ___________ them.

38 다음 중 어법상 어색한 것은?

① He has a nice cabin at the top of a hill.
② She always tells him to do his best at work.
③ They learned many lessons after their adventures at sea.
④ Why don't you look it up at the dictionary by yourself?
⑤ I advised him to study hard at school.

39 밑줄 친 (A)~(C)에 들어갈 말이 알맞게 짝지어진 것은?

> *Yena*: Juho, where are you going?
> *Juho*: Hi, I'm on my way to the library. How about you?
> *Yena*: Oh, I'm going there, too. I haven't finished the book I borrowed, so I'm going to put ___(A)___ the due date.
> *Juho*: I see. I want to check ___(B)___ a book for light reading. Can you recommend one to me?
> *Yena*: Oh, do you have any genre you prefer?
> *Juho*: I prefer historical fiction ___(C)___ science fiction.

	(A)		(B)		(C)
①	off	–	out	–	than
②	out	–	out	–	than
③	off	–	in	–	than
④	out	–	in	–	to
⑤	off	–	out	–	to

40 다음 중 어법상 옳은 것은?

① She went to her uncle's house in foot.
② Frogs can live both in water and at land.
③ I guess I saw them in TV.
④ Yesterday I read the article in the newspaper.
⑤ I saw him make a noise at the subway.

41 주어진 우리말과 같은 뜻이 되도록 어법상 틀린 단어를 골라 바르게 고치세요.

> • 그는 작은 비스킷을 발견했고 새들을 위해서 그 것을 작은 조각들로 부쉈다.
> = He found a small biscuit and broke it to small pieces for the birds.

➡ ___________________

42 주어진 우리말과 같은 뜻이 되도록 빈칸에 알맞은 말을 쓰세요.

> • 위험한 가스가 오늘 배달된 상자 밖으로 나오고 있었다.
> = Dangerous gases were coming _______________ the box which was delivered today.

43 주어진 우리말과 같은 뜻이 되도록 빈칸에 들어갈 말이 차례대로 짝지어진 것은?

> • 그 달은 산 위에 있는 공처럼 보였다.
> = The moon seemed _________ a ball _________ the mountain.

① as – for
② like – above
③ as – up
④ like – beyond
⑤ like – up

44 다음 밑줄 친 As[as] 중 〈보기〉의 as와 뜻이 같은 것을 모두 고르면?

> 보 기 | He attended the meeting <u>as</u> a representative.

① As I climbed higher in the mountain, I felt the lack of oxygen.
② The actor is also known as Uncle Tom in Korea.
③ She decided to clean her room as her mother said.
④ Mr. Park was appointed as a new manager of the restaurant.
⑤ As the ship sailed into the harbor, the waves got larger.

45 다음 중 어법상 어색한 것은?

① I believe in my mother. She'll always look after me.
② I was pleased with what I heard.
③ A lot of studies on their behaviors have been done lately.
④ The library was full with many girls and boys.
⑤ I got out of my car to look at the scene closer.

46 빈칸에 공통으로 들어갈 전치사로 알맞은 것은?

> • Some people commute _________ bus or subway.
> • I think you should start _________ doing small things.

① by
② through
③ on
④ in
⑤ from

47 다음 글에서 어법상 틀린 곳을 찾아 바르게 고치세요.

His mom added, "Please be careful." Sam replied, "Don't worry. I'll come back home until 4 o'clock this afternoon."

➡ __________

48 빈칸에 들어갈 말로 알맞은 것은?

I want to get __________ with other people in the group although they are different from me.

① through ② along ③ as
④ in ⑤ from

49 다음 문장에서 어법상 틀린 곳을 찾아 바르게 고치세요.

Have you noticed any differences among New York and Seoul?

➡ __________

50 빈칸에 공통으로 들어갈 전치사로 알맞은 것은?

- The waiter became embarrassed and ran __________ the manager to ask for some help.
- This show is for the people that have negative attitudes __________ the project.

① onto ② through ③ with
④ for ⑤ toward

51 (a)～(c)에 들어갈 말로 옳은 것은?

Rose: Welcome back, Mom! How was your business trip?
Mom: It was nice. Did you take good care __________ (a) __________ our house?
Rose: Of course, Mom! I even vacuumed every floor.
Mom: Wait, Rose! What happened to our plants?
Rose: I was busy __________ (b) __________ my school work, so I couldn't water the plants.
Mom: It's okay. I'm still proud of you for doing all the chores.
Rose: I'm sorry __________ (c) __________ what happened to your favorite plants.
Mom: Don't worry about it. We can buy new plants.

	(a)		(b)		(c)
①	of	–	with	–	to
②	of	–	by	–	for
③	of	–	with	–	for
④	for	–	by	–	for
⑤	for	–	with	–	to

52 빈칸에 공통으로 들어갈 전치사로 알맞은 말은?

- As the night fog became thicker, people gathered __________ the lake.
- You should remember that it could also reduce sales __________ 25%.

① at ② through ③ by
④ round ⑤ with

53 다음 문장에서 어법상 <u>틀린</u> 곳을 찾아 바르게 고치세요.

I have been looking forward to attend the concert next week.

___________ ➡ ___________

54 주어진 우리말과 같은 뜻이 되도록 할 때, 빈칸에 들어갈 알맞은 전치사를 고르세요.

- 노래가 막 시작되었을 때 몇몇의 팬들이 무대 위로 뛰어오르려고 했다.
  = Some fans tried to jump ___________ the stage when the song just got started.

① onto ② into ③ to ④ over ⑤ off

55 빈칸에 들어갈 말로 알맞은 것은?

You must not do that! It's ___________ the law, isn't it?

① for   ② to   ③ across
④ against   ⑤ forward

56 빈칸에 들어갈 말로 알맞은 것은?

Their speed is decreasing ___________ air resistance.

① as   ② due to
③ instead of   ④ except
⑤ for

57 빈칸에 공통으로 들어갈 단어로 알맞은 것은?

(가) He is going ___________ some hard times.
(나) The police entered the building ___________ the back door.
(다) A cup of coffee helps me get ___________ the day.

① for   ② into   ③ inside
④ through   ⑤ toward

58 주어진 우리말과 같은 뜻이 되도록 빈칸에 알맞은 말을 쓰세요.

- 제복을 입는 것은 그 구성원들이 스스로를 자랑스럽게 느끼도록 만든다.
  = Wearing uniforms makes the members feel proud ___________ themselves.

① at   ② in   ③ on
④ by   ⑤ of

59 다음 문장에서 어법상 <u>틀린</u> 곳을 찾아 바르게 고치세요.

According as the weather forecast, it will rain heavily tomorrow.

___________ ➡ ___________

60 빈칸에 들어갈 말로 알맞은 것은?

She had no clothes to wear ___________ the ragged clothes. So, she put them on.

① except   ② due to   ③ according to
④ without   ⑤ of

 다음은 지하철의 안내 방송입니다. 빈칸에 알맞은 전치사를 〈보기〉에서 골라 쓰세요. (중복 가능)

보 기	in with for behind on to

____________ **the subway station**

(지하철역에서)

The train bound ____________ Suwon is now approaching. Please wait ____________ the yellow line.

____________ **the subway**

(지하철 내에서)

This stop is City Hall. You may exit ____________ the left. You can transfer ____________ the green line, line number 2. Please make sure you have all your belongings ____________ you as you leave the train. Thank you.

62 ⓐ~ⓔ의 밑줄 친 부분 중 어법상 <u>틀린</u> 것을 있는 대로 찾아 옳게 고쳐 쓰세요.

ⓐ Although they are different <u>with</u> one another, they belong to the same group.

ⓑ How much do you care <u>about</u> your health?

ⓒ Mr. Song succeeded <u>to</u> inventing a new machine.

ⓓ She doesn't laugh <u>on</u> me even when I make a funny face.

ⓔ The treasure was buried deep in the forest, waiting <u>for</u> someone to find it.

➡ ________________________________

____

63 다음 글의 빈칸 (A)~(D)에 들어갈 단어가 순서대로 짝지어진 것은?

"Mom, can I go to the United Kingdom to study English?" asked Aoi. "You know how expensive it is to study abroad. If you want to go abroad, then why don't you get a scholarship like your sister?" answered Aoi's mom. Two years ago, Aoi's sister, Tomoko, left (A) ____________ London to study after she graduated from high school. Tomoko was (B) ____________ a good student that she received all kinds of scholarships. So, Aoi was jealous (C) ____________ her sister studying abroad. Even though Aoi cannot go abroad (D) ____________ the moment, she has decided to study hard so that she can get a scholarship like her sister.

	(A)		(B)		(C)		(D)
①	for	–	such	–	of	–	at
②	for	–	so	–	of	–	in
③	for	–	such	–	at	–	for
④	to	–	so	–	at	–	at
⑤	to	–	so	–	at	–	in

CHAPTER 17
일치와 화법

PSS 1 주어와 동사의 일치	페이지	성취도				
		100%	99~75%	74~50%	49~25%	24~0%
PSS 1-1 A and B	420					
PSS 1-2 either A or B, neither A nor B, not only A but also B, not A but B	421					
PSS 1-3 every, each+단수 동사	422					
PSS 1-4 some, most, none, half+of	423					
PSS 1-5 복수 주어+단수 동사	424					

PSS 2 시제의 일치	페이지	성취도				
		100%	99~75%	74~50%	49~25%	24~0%
PSS 2-1 시제 일치의 원칙	425					
PSS 2-2 시제 일치의 예외	427					

PSS 3 화법	페이지	성취도				
		100%	99~75%	74~50%	49~25%	24~0%
PSS 3-1 평서문의 화법 전환	428					
PSS 3-2 의문문의 화법 전환	430					
PSS 3-3 명령문의 화법 전환	432					
중간·기말고사 대비문제	434					

PSS 1 주어와 동사의 일치

PSS 1-1 A and B

1. 명사가 and로 연결되어 주어 역할을 할 때는 복수 취급하여 복수 동사가 뒤따라 오는 것이 원칙이다.

   Ralph and two other candidates are sitting quietly in the waiting room.
   Ralph와 두 명의 다른 지원자들이 대기실에 조용히 앉아 있다.
   There **were interesting museums and galleries** in the city.
   그 도시에는 흥미로운 박물관들과 미술관들이 있었다.

2. and로 연결된 주어가 한 가지 사물이나 한 사람을 나타낼 때는 단수 취급하여 단수 동사가 뒤따라 온다.

   Bread and butter is going to be served for breakfast.
   버터를 바른 빵이 아침으로 제공될 것이다.
   The composer and singer is expected to release **his** new album at the end of this month.
   작곡가이자 가수인 그 사람이 이번 달 말에 그의 새 앨범을 발매할 예정이다.

   cf. **The composer and the singer are** expected to release **their** new album at the end of this month.
   그 작곡가와 그 가수는 이번 달 말에 그들의 새 앨범을 발매할 예정이다.

정답 p.97

PRACTICE 1

괄호 안에 들어갈 알맞은 말을 골라 동그라미 하세요.

1 There (be, are) plenty of candies and chocolate in the basket.

2 Pat (has, have) a black and white cat with blue eyes.

3 The two brothers, Jake and Dave, (comes, come) from California.

4 Mr. and Mrs. Newman always (greets, greet) their guests with a big hug.

5 *Snow White and the Seven Dwarves* (is, are) a well-known fairy tale.

6 Collecting autographed baseballs (is, are) his favorite hobby.

7 The businessman and the diplomat (travels, travel) together often.

8 The red and black ladybug (walks, walk) on the edge of a green leaf.

9 Jennifer and Doris (works, work) at the same office.

10 The famous singer and activist (visits, visit) Africa often to perform in charity concerts.

PSS 1-2 either A or B, neither A nor B, not only A but also B, not A but B

다음은 위치상 동사와 더 가까이에 있는 B에 동사의 수를 일치시키는 구문이다.

> either A or B 'A와 B 중 어느 하나' neither A nor B 'A도 B도 아닌'
> not only A but (also) B 'A뿐만 아니라 B도' not A but B 'A가 아니라 B'

Either you **or** Smith **has** to play the wizard. 너나 Smith 중 한 명이 마법사 역할을 맡아야 한다.

Either Smith **or** you **have** to play the wizard. Smith나 너 중 한 명이 마법사 역할을 맡아야 한다.

Neither she **nor** I **am** going to allow you to do that again.

그녀도 나도 네가 다시 그런 짓을 하도록 허락하지 않을 것이다.

Neither I **nor** she **is** going to allow you to do that again.

나도 그녀도 네가 다시 그런 짓을 하도록 허락하지 않을 것이다.

Not only the table **but (also)** the chairs **are** supposed to be sent today.

테이블뿐만 아니라 의자들도 오늘 보내지기로 되어 있다.

= The chairs **as well as** the table **are** supposed to be sent today.

cf. B as well as A 'A뿐만 아니라 B도'는 B에 동사의 수를 일치시킨다.

Not Susan **but** you **are** the one who should be responsible for the problem.

Susan이 아니라 네가 그 문제에 책임을 져야 할 사람이다.

Not you **but** Susan **is** the one who should be responsible for the problem.

네가 아니라 Susan이 그 문제에 책임을 져야 할 사람이다.

정답 p.97

PRACTICE 2 [1-10]

괄호 안에 들어갈 알맞은 말을 골라 동그라미 하세요.

1 Either Sam or you (has, have) to do the cleaning.

2 Not you but Jill (is, are) going to take this responsibility.

3 Jake and Cindy as well as Sarah (is, are) going to join the expedition.

4 Not only my brothers but also my cousin (finds, find) math very interesting.

5 The writer as well as the actors (visits, visit) us at the office every Monday.

6 Neither he nor I (has, have) the money to buy the new car.

7 Not only Spanish but also English (is, are) spoken in Belize.

8 The police and the coast guards (stops, stop) the smugglers from entering the port.

9 Neither the government nor the terrorists (appears, appear) to be willing to talk about it.

10 Either Monday or Thursday (is, are) the best day for us to get together.

PSS 1-3 every, each + 단수 동사

주어에 every와 each가 포함되어 있는 경우에는 단수 취급하여 단수 동사를 쓴다.

Every student who **takes** this class **has** to hand in the final report by this week.
이 수업을 듣는 모든 학생은 이번 주까지 마지막 보고서를 제출해야 한다.
Every doctor and nurse in this hospital **is** going to take a vacation for five days.
이 병원에 있는 모든 의사와 간호사는 5일 동안 휴가를 갈 것이다.

Each chapter of this book **contains** different information.
이 책의 각각의 장은 다른 정보를 포함하고 있다.
Each of the members **gives** 10,000 won a month to charity.
각각의 회원은 자선단체에 한 달에 만 원을 낸다.

cf. 'all[both]+셀 수 있는 명사의 복수형'은 복수 취급하여 복수 동사를 쓰고, 'all+셀 수 없는 명사의 단수형'은 단수 취급하여 단수 동사를 쓴다.
All the people in the store **were** surprised to see the famous politician.
상점에 있던 모든 사람들은 그 유명한 정치인을 보고 놀랐다.
Both of the vending machines **are** not available at the moment.
그 자판기 둘 다 지금은 이용 가능하지 않다.
You should check that **all** the information you provide **is** true.
당신은 당신이 제공하는 모든 정보가 사실인지 확인해야 한다.

정답 p.97

PRACTICE 3

괄호 안에 들어갈 알맞은 말을 골라 동그라미 하세요.

1 Each stone of the pyramid (weighs, weigh) more than 2 tons.

2 Both of my sons (sets, set) the alarm clock before they go to bed.

3 Nearly every species of penguin (lives, live) on the south side of the globe.

4 Each person (has, have) his or her own unique fingerprints.

5 Every piece of art in this gallery (shows, show) the artist's passion.

6 All the broken parts of my car (was, were) fixed.

7 Every writer I know (wants, want) to travel around the world.

8 Each can of soft drink produced in this factory (costs, cost) less than 300 won.

9 All the money I have saved (adds, add) up to two thousand dollars.

10 Every boy and girl (brings, bring) used goods to sell on the first Friday of the month.

PSS 1-4 some, most, none, half + of

주어에 「부분, 전체 등을 나타내는 표현(some, most, none, all, half, 분수, percent) + of」가 포함되어 있는 경우 of 뒤에 오는 명사의 수에 따라 동사의 단수, 복수를 결정한다.

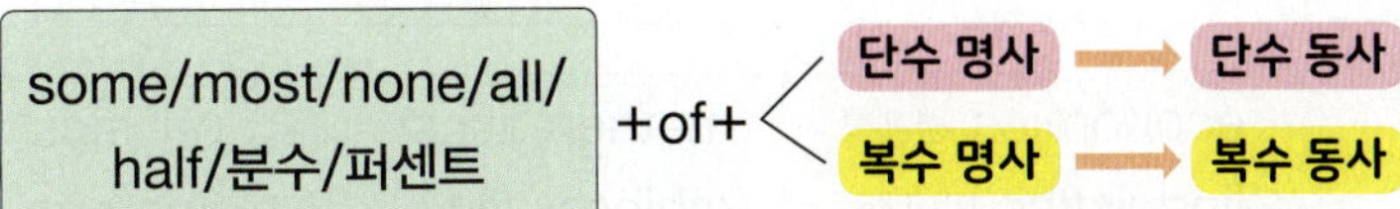

Most of the boys **like** playing baseball. 대부분의 소년들은 야구하는 것을 좋아한다.
Half of the money **was** spent on books. 그 돈의 절반은 책을 사는 데 쓰였다.
A third of the trees **were** burnt in the fire. 그 나무들의 1/3이 화재로 불탔다.
70 percent of the battery **was** used. 그 배터리의 70퍼센트가 사용되었다.
All of the lights **were** turned off after closing the store. 상점을 닫은 후에 모든 전등이 꺼졌다.

정답 p.97

PRACTICE 4

괄호 안에 들어갈 알맞은 말을 골라 동그라미 하세요.

1 90 percent of the clothes (was, were) sold out.

2 Most of the students in Korea (wear, wears) school uniforms.

3 None of the information (is, are) useful to him.

4 Some of the money (has, have) been stolen.

5 Most of the (building, buildings) need repainting.

6 All of the problems that the city had been facing (was, were) announced by the mayor last night.

7 I think half of them (has, have) never been to other countries.

8 A quarter of the students (don't, doesn't) speak Spanish.

PSS 1-5 복수 주어 + 단수 동사

시간	**Five days is** enough to complete the story. 그 이야기를 완성하는 데 5일이면 충분하다. *cf.* 시간을 나타내는 명사가 하나의 단위가 아니고 시간의 길이를 나타낼 때는 복수 동사를 수반한다. **Three years have** passed since I moved to this city. 내가 이 도시로 이사 온 지 3년이 지났다.
금액	**Thirty dollars** per month for the membership fee **is** too expensive. 회비로 한 달에 30달러는 너무 비싸다.
거리	**Two kilometers is** not that far for me to walk. 2킬로미터는 내가 걷기에 그렇게 멀지 않다.
무게	**Twelve kilograms** of luggage per person **is** permitted on the plane. 한 사람당 12킬로그램의 수하물이 기내에 반입 가능하다.
학과명	economics 경제학　mathematics 수학　physics 물리학 linguistics 언어학　ethics 윤리학　fine arts 미술 **Economics is** one of the most popular majors among my friends. 경제학은 내 친구들 사이에서 가장 인기 있는 전공 중에 하나이다. **Linguistics is** the study of human language. 언어학은 인간 언어에 대한 학문이다.
국가명	the United States 미국　the Netherlands 네덜란드 the Philippines 필리핀　the Maldives 몰디브 the United Arab Emirates 아랍에미리트연합 **The United States consists** of diverse ethnic groups. 미국은 다양한 인종 집단으로 구성되어 있다. **The Maldives is** located southwest of Sri Lanka and made up of 1,190 coral islands. 몰디브는 스리랑카의 남서쪽에 위치해 있고 1,190개의 산호섬으로 구성되어 있다.

정답 p.97

PRACTICE 5

괄호 안에 들어갈 알맞은 말을 골라 동그라미 하세요.

1 Twenty dollars (doesn't, don't) go far at the gas pump these days.

2 Mathematics really (gives, give) me a headache.

3 Two weeks (is, are) a relatively short time for a trip to Europe.

4 Ten dollars for the pears (sounds, sound) like a bargain.

5 Jerry and Julie often (visits, visit) their grandma at the nursing home.

6 Ten kilograms of coins (was, were) too heavy for you to carry alone.

7 Physics (ranks, rank) as one of my favorite subjects.

8 The Philippines (attracts, attract) millions of holidaymakers each year.

9 Eight kilometers (seems, seem) to be a reasonable distance for a short hike.

10 Sixty cents a day for taking out the garbage (looks, look) like a good deal to me.

11 The Netherlands (produces, produce) three billion tulip bulbs each year.

12 Six months (is, are) the recommended time frame to achieve your fitness goals.

13 The United Arab Emirates (has, have) built the tallest skyscraper in the world.

14 I need more money than that. Five thousand won (is, are) not enough for me.

15 Economics (was, were) so difficult that I couldn't completely understand it.

PSS 2 시제의 일치

PSS 2-1 시제 일치의 원칙

1. 주절의 동사가 현재 시제로 쓰인 경우 종속절에는 내용에 따라 어떠한 시제도 올 수 있다.

   He **says** that he **is** satisfied with the large amount of information.
   그는 많은 양의 정보에 만족한다고 말한다.
   He **says** that he **was** satisfied with the large amount of information.
   그는 많은 양의 정보에 만족했다고 말한다.
   He **says** that he **has been** satisfied with the large amount of information.
   그는 많은 양의 정보에 만족해 왔다고 말한다.

2. 주절의 동사가 과거 시제인 경우에 종속절의 시제는 과거나 과거완료가 되어야 한다.
   주절이 현재시제에서 과거시제로 바뀔 때는 종속절의 시제가 다음과 같이 바뀐다.

① 현재 → 과거

They **think** that I **am** the only proper person for the job.

그들은 내가 그 일에 유일하게 적합한 사람이라고 생각한다.

➡ They **thought** that I **was** the only proper person for the job.

그들은 내가 그 일에 유일하게 적합한 사람이라고 생각했다.

② will → would

They **think** that I **will** be the only proper person for the job.

그들은 내가 그 일에 유일하게 적합한 사람일 것이라고 생각한다.

➡ They **thought** that I **would** be the only proper person for the job.

그들은 내가 그 일에 유일하게 적합한 사람일 것이라고 생각했다.

③ 현재완료 → 과거완료

They **think** that I **have been** the only proper person for the job.

그들은 내가 그 일에 유일하게 적합한 사람이었다고 생각한다.

➡ They **thought** that I **had been** the only proper person for the job.

그들은 내가 그 일에 유일하게 적합한 사람이었다고 생각했다.

④ 과거 → 과거완료

They **think** that I **was** the only proper person for the job.

그들은 내가 그 일에 유일하게 적합한 사람이었다고 생각한다.

➡ They **thought** that I **had been** the only proper person for the job.

그들은 내가 그 일에 유일하게 적합한 사람이었다고 생각했다.

정답 p.97

PRACTICE 6

다음 문장의 시제를 과거로 바꿀 때 빈칸에 알맞은 말을 써 넣으세요.

1 She knows that I have been interested in designing shoes.

➡ She knew that I ______________ ______________ interested in designing shoes.

2 Everyone says that Herbert is an honest person.

➡ Everyone said that Herbert ______________ an honest person.

3 The wife complains that her husband is too picky about her food.

➡ The wife complained that her husband ______________ too picky about her food.

4 I am thankful that the storm did not blow away our house.

➡ I was thankful that the storm ______________ ______________ ______________ ______________ our house.

5 Jane argues that the school rules have been too strict.

➡ Jane argued that the school rules ______________ ______________ too strict.

6   The captain says that the pirates visited the mysterious island often.

➡ The captain said that the pirates _______________ _______________ the mysterious island often.

7   I promise I won't be late for the barbecue party.

➡ I promised I _______________ _______________ late for the barbecue party.

8   Many scientists believe human cloning will be achieved in a few years.

➡ Many scientists believed human cloning _______________ _______________ achieved in a few years.

PSS 2-2 시제 일치의 예외

1. **현재의 습관, 사실, 진리는 항상 현재시제로 쓴다.**

   Ted said that he **goes** to bed at 11 p.m. on weekdays.
   Ted는 주중에는 11시에 잔다고 말했다.
   I didn't know that swallows **migrate** to Korea in April.
   나는 제비들이 4월에 한국으로 이동한다는 것을 알지 못했다.
   My daughter learned that the Sun **sets** in the west.
   내 딸은 해가 서쪽으로 진다는 것을 배웠다.

2. **역사적 사실은 항상 과거시제로 쓴다.**

   Dad told me that America **was** discovered by Columbus in 1492. (O)
   Dad told me that America **had been** discovered by Columbus in 1492. (X)
   아빠는 내게 아메리카 대륙이 1492년에 Columbus에 의해 발견되었다고 말씀하셨다.

3. **비교 구문에서 than이나 as 뒤에 이어지는 구문의 시제는 내용에 따라 주절의 시제와 일치하지 않는 경우도 있다.**

   Sora **was** much healthier last month than she **is** now.
   소라는 지금보다 지난달에 훨씬 더 건강했다.
   It **was** not so cloudy yesterday as it **is** today. 어제는 오늘만큼 흐리지 않았다.

정답 p.98

PRACTICE 7 [1-15]

괄호 안에 들어갈 말로 알맞은 것을 골라 동그라미 하세요.

1   The tree is a lot taller than it (is, was) five months ago.

2   I remember that last summer wasn't as hot as it (is, was) now.

3 I can ride a skateboard much better than I (can, could) two weeks ago.

4 Charles told me that his family usually (eat, have eaten) dinner at 7 o'clock.

5 The man claimed that his wallet (had been, has been) stolen by a pickpocket.

6 The children said that Gyungsoo (went, has gone) straight home after school.

7 My grandparents always told me that time and tide (wait, waited) for no man.

8 James learned that King Sejong (has ordered, ordered) the invention of Hangul.

9 I recently found out that stag beetles (use, used) their tongues for feeding.

10 Jesse arrived late and asked me how long I (have been, had been) waiting for him.

11 In the 17th century, Galileo found evidence that the Earth (went, goes) around the Sun.

12 The guide told me that Gettysburg (has been, was) once a battlefield during the Civil War.

13 I didn't notice that I (have forgotten, had forgotten) to call Mrs. Thompson.

14 This book says that the Chinese (reached, have reached) the new world long before the Europeans.

15 I now know that the city of Machu Picchu (was, had been) constructed around 1450.

PSS 3 화법

PSS 3-1 평서문의 화법 전환

직접 화법	She **said**, "I do this to please my mom."
간접 화법	She **said** (that) she did that to please her mom.

① 전달 동사를 say[said]는 say[said]로, say[said] to는 tell[told]로 바꾼다.

② 콤마(,)와 따옴표(" ")를 빼고 두 문장을 that을 이용하여 연결시킨다. 단, that은 생략이 가능하다.

③ that절의 주어나 목적어, 보어로 쓰인 인칭대명사는 전달하는 사람의 입장으로 바꾼다.

④ 전달 동사의 시제가 현재일 때는 종속절의 시제에 변화가 없지만, 과거일 때는 시제 일치의 원칙에 따라 시제를 바꾼다.

⑤ 지시대명사나 부사(구)는 다음과 같이 전달하는 사람의 입장으로 바꾼다.

this[these] ➡ that[those] now ➡ then here ➡ there
ago ➡ before today ➡ that day tonight ➡ that night
yesterday ➡ the previous day[the day before]
tomorrow ➡ the next day[the following day]
last night ➡ the previous night[the night before]
next ~ ➡ the following ~ last ~ ➡ the previous ~

Jenny **says**, "**I'm** not going to be late for school again."

Jenny는 "나는 다시는 학교에 늦지 않을 거야."라고 말한다.

➡ Jenny **says** (that) **she's** not going to be late for school again.

Jenny는 다시는 학교에 늦지 않을 것이라고 말한다.

He **said to** me, "**You have to** prepare for the presentation **today**."

그는 내게 "네가 오늘 발표 준비를 해야 해."라고 말했다.

➡ He **told** me (that) **I had to** prepare for the presentation **that day**.

그는 내게 내가 그 날 발표 준비를 해야 한다고 말했다.

정답 p.98

PRACTICE 8 [1-10]

〈보기〉와 같이 주어진 문장을 간접 화법으로 바꿀 때, 빈칸에 알맞은 단어를 쓰세요.

보 기 Tom said, "My brother went to Canada to study three months ago."

➡ Tom _said_ that _his_ brother _had gone_ to Canada to study three months _before_.

Jina said to me, "I want to be a flight attendant."

➡ Jina _told_ me that _she wanted_ to be a flight attendant.

1 Joanne said, "I'll be home late tonight."

➡ Joanne __________ that __________ __________ be home late __________ __________.

2 Frank said, "I saw a UFO last night."

➡ Frank __________ that __________ __________ __________ a UFO __________

__________ __________.

3 Greg said, "I'm going to get up early."

➡ Greg __________ that __________ __________ __________ going to get up early.

4 Wendy said to Mom, "I don't want to eat these vegetables anymore."

➡ Wendy __________ Mom that __________ __________ want to eat __________

vegetables anymore.

5 Craig said to me, "I'll meet you here at the fountain."

➡ Craig __________ me that __________ __________ meet __________ __________ at

the fountain.

6 She said to me, "I'm so hungry and sleepy."

➡ She ___________ me that ___________ ___________ so hungry and sleepy.

7 I said to my little brother, "You should be careful of cars on the street."

➡ I ___________ my little brother that ___________ should be careful of cars on the street.

8 The weatherman said, "The typhoon is now passing Jeju Island."

➡ The weatherman ___________ that the typhoon ___________ ___________ passing Jeju Island.

9 The reporter said, "There was a terrible terrorist attack yesterday in Iraq."

➡ The reporter ___________ that there ___________ ___________ a terrible terrorist attack ___________ ___________ ___________ in Iraq.

10 Minhyuk said, "I might emigrate to New Zealand next year."

➡ Minhyuk ___________ that ___________ might emigrate to New Zealand ___________ ___________ ___________.

PSS 3-2 의문문의 화법 전환

1. 의문사가 없는 의문문의 화법 전환

① say[said]나 say[said] to를 ask[asked]로 바꾼다.
② that 대신 if나 whether로 두 문장을 연결한다.
③ 「주어+동사」의 어순으로 바꾼다.

He said, "Do you know a guy named Charles?"
그는 "너는 Charles라는 이름의 남자를 아니?"라고 말했다.
➡ He **asked if[whether] I knew** a guy named Charles.
그는 내가 Charles라는 이름의 남자를 아는지 물었다.

I said to Mary, "Did you find your passport?"
나는 Mary에게 "너의 여권을 찾았니?"라고 말했다.
➡ I **asked** Mary **if[whether] she had found** her passport.
나는 Mary에게 그녀의 여권을 찾았느냐고 물었다.

2. 의문사가 있는 의문문의 화법 전환

① say[said]나 say[said] to를 ask[asked]로 바꾼다.
② that 대신 의문사로 두 문장을 연결한다.
③ 「주어+동사」의 어순으로 바꾼다. 단, 의문사가 주어인 경우에는 「의문사+동사」의 어순을 그대로 유지한다.

The police said, "What did you see in the basement?"
경찰은 "당신은 지하실에서 무엇을 봤습니까?"라고 말했다.
➡ The police **asked what I had seen** in the basement.
경찰은 내가 지하실에서 무엇을 보았는지 물었다.

She said to Chris, "Who lent you the money?
그녀는 Chris에게 "누가 네게 돈을 빌려주었니?"라고 말했다.
➡ She **asked** Chris **who had lent him** the money.
그녀는 Chris에게 누가 그에게 돈을 빌려주었는지 물었다.

정답 p.98

PRACTICE 9

〈보기〉와 같이 주어진 문장을 간접 화법으로 바꾸세요.

보 기	Jim said, "Have you met Julie before?"

➡ Jim asked if[whether] I had met Julie before.
I said to the boy, "Where did you get this ring?"

➡ I asked the boy where he had gotten that ring.

1 Brad said to Ron, "When is your graduation ceremony?"
➡ ____

2 I said to Mom, "Do we have an electric drill at home?"
➡ ____

3 The old lady said, "Do you know the legend about this town?"
➡ ____

4 My aunt said to me, "How is your family these days?"
➡ ____

5 The gentleman said to the flight attendant, "When will dinner be served?"
➡ ____

6 Edward said, "What do Koreans do on Lunar New Year's Day?"
➡ ____

7 The doctor said to me, "Have you been bitten by a snake?"
➡ ____

8 The teacher said to the class, "Who will answer this question for me?"
➡ ____

9 I said to Mr. Gwak, "Should we come to school next Saturday?"
➡ ____

10 Sumi said to me, "Was the Russian restaurant crowded?"
➡ ____

CH
17
일치와 화법

① 전달동사는 명령문의 성격에 따라 tell, ask, advise, order 등으로 바꾼다.
② 명령문의 동사원형을 to부정사로 바꾼다.

The teacher said to us, "Finish cleaning the restroom by 5:00."
선생님은 우리에게 "5시까지 화장실 청소를 끝내라."라고 말씀하셨다.
➡ The teacher **told** us **to finish** cleaning the restroom by 5:00.
선생님은 우리에게 5시까지 화장실 청소를 끝내라고 말씀하셨다.

The doctor said to me, "Don't eat too much sugar."
의사는 내게 "설탕을 너무 많이 먹지 마세요."라고 말했다.
➡ The doctor **advised** me **not to eat** too much sugar.
의사는 내게 너무 많은 설탕을 먹지 말라고 충고했다.

정답 p.98

PRACTICE 10

〈보기〉와 같이 주어진 문장을 간접 화법으로 바꾸세요.

보 기	
He said to me, "Watch out while you are driving."	
➡ He advised me to watch out while I was driving.	
The father said to his child, "Don't go near the fire."	
➡ The father told his child not to go near the fire.	

1 I said to my dog, "Get out of the room!"

➡ ____

2 I said to Dan, "How did you climb up this cliff?"

➡ ____

3 I said to Andrea, "Why didn't you tell me the truth?"

➡ ____

4 I said to Tina, "Who did you talk with over the phone?"

➡ ____

5 I said to Mr. Carlson, "Can I go to the washroom?"

➡ ____

6 The nurse said to me, "Take your medicine 30 minutes after meals."

➡ ____

7 The secretary said to me, "Mrs. Evans has been expecting you."

➡ ____

8 The coast guard said to me, "Don't swim too far off the beach."

➡ ____

9 Mr. Wilson said to me, "Come and have tea at my home at 4 o'clock."

➡ ____

10 The judge said to the defendant, "Do 48 hours of community service."

➡ ____

11 My mother said to me, "Don't eat any junk food on your way home."

➡ ____

12 Mr. Lee said, "I'll hand out your graded exam papers tomorrow."

➡ ____

13 The sergeant said to the soldiers, "Do not shoot without my order."

➡ ____

14 The principal said, "All students must get to school before 8 o'clock."

➡ ____

15 I said to the old man, "Wait here for a minute."

➡ ____

16 The police officer said to my dad, "This road is temporarily closed today."

➡ ____

17 The mechanic said to the customer, "Change the engine oil next month."

➡ ____

18 The detective said to the woman, "Did you see any strangers last night?"

➡ ____

19 Mitch's uncle said to me, "I served in the Marine Corps twenty years ago."

➡ ____

20 The instructor said to me, "Breathe slowly and deeply before diving into the water."

➡ ____

21 My mom said to me, "Use vanilla sugar instead of honey."

➡ ____

22 The teacher said to us, "Don't use your cell phones in class."

➡ ____

1 화법 전환 과정에 오류가 <u>없는</u> 것은?

① The supervisor said to the interviewee, "Stay here and wait."
→ The supervisor told the interviewee stay there and wait.

② My husband said to me, "Are you ready?"
→ My husband asked me that I was ready.

③ Our teacher asked us whether we understood the lesson.
→ Our teacher said to us, "Do you understand the lesson?"

④ The train conductor told me that I had to change trains at Cheon-an.
→ The train conductor said to me, "You had to change trains at Cheon-an."

⑤ Tracy said to Charles, "Where did you go to school?"
→ Tracy asked Charles that where he went to school.

2 다음 문장을 간접 화법으로 바꿀 때 빈칸에 알맞은 말을 쓰세요.

> Mr. Smith said to me, "I will drive you home."

→ Mr. Smith told me that __________ __________
__________ __________ __________.

3 주어진 우리말과 같은 뜻이 되도록 빈칸에 알맞은 단어를 쓰세요. (단, make up을 사용하되, 필요시 변형할 것.)

> • 모든 진실은 광고업자들에 의해 날조되었다.
> = All of the truth __________ __________
> __________ __________ the advertisers.

4 다음 문장을 간접 화법으로 바꿀 때 빈칸에 알맞은 말은?

> • She said, "I can leave tomorrow."
> → She said that __________________________.

① she could leave the following day
② she can be leaving today
③ she can leave the next day
④ she could leave tomorrow
⑤ she would leave tomorrow

5 빈칸에 들어갈 말이 차례대로 짝지어진 것은?

> Neither bad eating habits __________ stress __________ good for the disease.

① nor – is   ② nor – are
③ or – is   ④ or – are
⑤ nor – be

6 우리말을 영어로 옮긴 것 중 옳은 것은?

> 이 농작물들 중 3/4은 실험을 위해 유전적으로 조작되었다.

① Three-quarter of these crops was genetically modified for experiments.
② Three-quarter of these crops were genetically modified for experiments.
③ Three-quarters of these crops was genetically modified for experiments.
④ Three-fourth of these crops was genetically modified for experiments.
⑤ Three-fourths of these crops were genetically modified for experiments.

7 빈칸에 들어갈 말로 알맞은 것은?

We thought we ___________ all the collected things.

① need
② will need
③ would need
④ have been needed
⑤ have needed

8 주어진 우리말과 같은 뜻이 되도록 빈칸에 알맞은 단어를 쓰세요.

• 내가 선택했던 문장들의 수는 5개가 넘는다.
= The number of sentences that I chose ___________ more than five.

9 다음 중 어법상 어색한 것은?

① Everyone likes to ride the bicycle.
② Every man and woman were shocked then.
③ No one likes a person with bad etiquette.
④ Each boy brings his own strengths to the team.
⑤ Jogging and swimming are my hobbies.

10 다음 문장을 직접 화법으로 올바르게 바꾼 것은?

My son said that he would do his best.

① My son said, "I will do his best."
② My son said, "He will do my best."
③ My son said, "I will do my best."
④ My son said to me, "I will do my best."
⑤ My son said to me, "He will do his best."

11 어법상 틀린 문장 2개는?

① Most of the information on the website is accurate.
② The Netherlands are famous for its windmills and tulips.
③ A number of problems has appeared during the project.
④ The elderly enjoy spending time with their grandchildren.
⑤ *Gulliver's Travels* describes the adventures of a traveler in strange lands.

12 다음 문장을 간접 화법으로 바꿀 때 빈칸에 알맞은 말을 쓰세요.

He said to me, "Can you make a reservation?"

➡ He ___________ me ___________ I ___________ make a reservation.

13 다음 중 화법 전환이 잘못된 것은?

① He always said to us, "Study hard."
　➡ He always told us to study hard.
② He said to me, "Where do you want to go?"
　➡ He asked me where I wanted to go.
③ His mother said to him, "I will tell you the truth."
　➡ His mother told him that she would tell him the truth.
④ Mr. Kim said to John, "Don't make a noise."
　➡ Mr. Kim told John doesn't make a noise.
⑤ I said to him, "You have to drive a car."
　➡ I told him that he had to drive a car.

14 ⓐ～ⓔ 중 틀린 것을 찾아 바르게 고친 사람은?

> ⓐ My classmates and I will play soccer tomorrow unless it rains.
> ⓑ Michael was sick for a week when I met him.
> ⓒ I was surprised by his improvement and realized that practice makes perfect.
> ⓓ In the summer of 2024, I visited New Zealand to participate in volunteer work.
> ⓔ People collected and consumed honey since prehistoric times.

① 상호: ⓐ는 내일 비가 오지 않으면 축구를 할 거라는 의미이기 때문에 unless it will rain이 되어야 해.

② 루아: ⓑ는 내가 그를 만났을 때 그가 일주일 동안 아팠다는 의미이기 때문에 was sick를 has been sick으로 고쳐야 해.

③ 민준: ⓒ는 시제 일치가 되어야 하기 때문에 practice made perfect로 수정해야 해.

④ 정윤: ⓓ는 New Zealand에 방문한 적이 있었다는 의미이기 때문에 visited를 현재완료인 have visited로 바꿔야 해.

⑤ 수진: ⓔ에서 시간을 나타내는 부사구인 since prehistoric times는 과거부터 현재까지 지속되고 있다는 의미를 나타내기 때문에 collected and consumed를 have collected and consumed로 수정해야 해.

15 빈칸에 들어갈 것이 나머지 넷과 다른 것은?

① The news on TV _____ very surprising to everyone.

② Not only my sisters but also my cousin _____ studying abroad.

③ Neither the teacher nor the students _____ ready for the trip.

④ Bread and butter _____ my favorite breakfast.

⑤ There _____ little time left before the test.

16 밑줄 친 부분을 간접 화법으로 바르게 바꾼 것은?

> This morning, I saw an old lady carrying a big bag. It looked so heavy. <u>I said to her, "Can I help you?"</u> But she said, "Thank you, but it's OK."

① I asked to her can I help you.
② I asked her can I help you.
③ I asked her if I can help her.
④ I asked her if I could help her.
⑤ I asked to her if I could help her.

17 다음 중 어법상 어색한 것은?

① Tom and Mary are good classmates.
② Either the police officers or the suspect is telling the truth.
③ The teacher and poet is my uncle.
④ I know that his family are all healthy.
⑤ Sue as well as her sisters speak perfect Chinese.

18 다음 문장을 간접 화법으로 바꿀 때 빈칸에 알맞은 말은?

> • He said to me, "Why are you looking at me?"
> = He asked me ________________________.

① whether I was looking at him
② whether I am looking at him
③ why I looked at him
④ why I had been looking at him
⑤ why I was looking at him

19 〈보기〉에서 어법상 <u>틀린</u> 문장의 개수는?

> 보 기
>
> ⓐ Both his health and money is very important to him.
> ⓑ Not you but she is the person who I want to talk with.
> ⓒ He as well as you are my good friend.
> ⓓ David studied very harder last year than he does this year.
> ⓔ The Philippines is located in Southeast Asia.

① 1개 ② 2개 ③ 3개 ④ 4개 ⑤ 5개

20 다음 각 문장의 빈칸에 들어갈 말이 바르게 짝지어진 것을 고르세요.

> • She said to him, "Be careful."
> ➡ She told him __________ careful.
> • The clerk said to the kid, "Don't run around."
> ➡ The clerk told the kid __________ around.

① is – doesn't run ② to be – didn't run
③ being – not running ④ to be – not to run
⑤ being – not to run

21 다음 중 어법상 옳은 것을 <u>모두</u> 고르세요.

① Drawing cartoon characters are my favorite pastime.
② Fifteen miles are a good distance for me to run in a day.
③ Fifty dollars are too expensive for the hat.
④ The two sisters, Jane and Sue, are from California.
⑤ Thirty kilograms is heavy for me to carry.

22 다음 중 어법상 옳은 것은?

① Every books in my room have been read.
② All of the passengers was saved from the accident.
③ Each part of the land belongs to his father.
④ Most of his paintings was about flowers and fruit.
⑤ Some of the water in the area were polluted.

23 다음 문장을 간접 화법으로 바꿀 때 빈칸에 알맞은 말은?

> • He said to me, "Are they going to announce the news?"
> ➡ He asked me __________ they were going to announce the news.

① if ② when ③ how
④ what ⑤ whenever

24 다음 문장을 간접 화법으로 바꿀 때 빈칸에 알맞은 말은?

> • The doctor said to me, "Try not to eat fast food."
> = The doctor __________________.

① asked me that to not eat fast food
② told me that not to eat fast food
③ advised me that not to eating fast food
④ advised me not to eat fast food
⑤ warned me to not eating fast food

25 다음 문장에서 어법상 <u>틀린</u> 곳을 찾아 바르게 고치세요.

Did you know that taekwondo had become Korea's national sport in 1971?

_______________ ➡ _______________

26 〈보기〉에서 어법상 옳은 문장의 개수는?

㉠ It was Sunday, so most of the shops were shut.

㉡ Each individual have a right to express their views.

㉢ A number of thin cracks has appeared in the wall.

㉣ Only a small percentage of people are interested in politics.

㉤ The number of foreign tourists have been increasing year over year.

㉥ Over half of the students will take part in the English speech contest.

㉦ All the food that the restaurant offered were fresh and delicious.

㉧ One third of the world's population consumes two third of the world's resources.

① 1개　　② 2개　　③ 3개　　④ 4개　　⑤ 5개

27 다음 문장을 간접 화법으로 바꿀 때 빈칸에 알맞은 말을 쓰세요.

• I said to a clerk, "Wrap the books, please."

➡ I asked a clerk _______________

_______________ the books.

28 빈칸에 들어갈 말로 알맞은 것은?

Either she or I _______________ made some problems.

① has　　　　② have　　　　③ have been

④ has been　　⑤ was

29 다음 문장의 밑줄 친 부분 중 어법상 <u>어색한</u> 것을 골라 그 기호를 쓰고 바르게 고치세요.

가. I knew that the Earth <u>goes</u> around the Sun.

나. He told me that he <u>goes</u> fishing on Sundays.

다. The teacher said World War II <u>broke out</u> in 1939.

라. A long time ago, people didn't believe that the Earth <u>has been</u> round.

마. He said that Columbus <u>had discovered</u> America in 1492.

기호	고친 답

30 어법상 옳은 문장을 <u>2개</u> 고르세요.

① The young usually gets used to new technologies easily.

② The number of books in the school library have increased.

③ Economics are important because it affects our everyday life.

④ Each student is required to submit their homework by Friday.

⑤ Most of the information in the textbook is essential for the final exam.

CHAPTER 18
특수구문 & 속담

Problem Solving Skill	페이지	성취도				
		100%	99~75%	74~50%	49~25%	24~0%
PSS 1 도치	440					
PSS 2 강조	페이지	성취도				
		100%	99~75%	74~50%	49~25%	24~0%
PSS 2-1 강조 어구	441					
PSS 2-2 「It ~ that …」 강조구문	443					
PSS 3 생략	페이지	성취도				
		100%	99~75%	74~50%	49~25%	24~0%
PSS 3-1 공통되는 부분의 생략	445					
PSS 3-2 「주어+be동사」의 생략	447					
PSS 4 속담	448					
중간·기말고사 대비문제	452					

PSS 1 도치

영어 문장은 일반적으로 「주어+동사」의 어순을 취한다. 하지만 「주어+동사」 앞에 다른 성분이 오면서 간혹 주어와 동사의 어순이 바뀔 수가 있는데, 이와 같은 현상을 도치라고 한다.

1. 「There / Here+동사+주어」

   There were some arguments between Mark and Liz.
   Mark와 Liz 사이에 약간의 논쟁이 있었다.
   Here are some things you should keep in mind.
   네가 명심해야 할 몇 가지 것들이 있다.

   cf. 주어가 대명사일 경우에는 주어와 동사의 위치가 바뀌지 않는다.
   Here he comes with his cane in his right hand. 그가 오른손에 지팡이를 들고 온다.

2. 「So+조동사+주어」, 「Neither+조동사+주어」

   I went to bed early last night. – **So did I.**
   나는 지난밤에 일찍 잤어. – 나도 그랬어.
   I can't agree with him about the new policy. – **Neither can I.**
   나는 새로운 정책에 대해 그에게 동의할 수 없어. – 나도 그럴 수 없어.

3. 부정어의 도치 – 「부정어(구)+조동사+주어+동사」

   He never kept his promises to me. 그는 내게 한 약속들을 한 번도 지키지 않았다.
   ➡ **Never did he keep** his promises to me.

   cf. 「not until ~ 조동사+주어+동사」 '~이 되어서야 비로소 …했다'
   Not until last night **did I know** the truth. 나는 어젯밤이 되어서야 비로소 그 진실을 알았다.

정답 p.101

PRACTICE 1

괄호 안에 주어진 말을 바르게 배열하여 문장을 완성하세요.

1 ___________________________________ why it's more expensive than the previous model.
   (some, there, are, reasons)

2 Never ___________________________ from this company.
   (John, considered, has, resigning)

3 ___________________________________ you ordered, sir.
   (are, the, pepperoni pizzas, here)

4 The girls are outside the snack bar. – ____ .

(are, the boys, so)

5 _________________________________ in the past few years.

(been, there, several, snowstorms, have)

6 Not _________________________________ the news.

(until, did, I, this morning, hear)

7 _________________________________ that is bound for Seoul.

(the last train, there, goes)

8 These oranges don't taste as good as I thought. – _________________________________ .

(bought, do, these grapes, neither, I)

9 Some birds migrating north stop by here to feed. – _________________________________ .

(so, migrating, south, do, some, birds)

10 _________________________________ standing in a long line, waiting for the tram to arrive.

(they, here, are)

PSS 2 강조

PSS 2-1 강조 어구

1. **동사의 강조 – 조동사 do**

   I **went** apple-picking at my grandfather's farm last year.

   나는 작년에 할아버지 농장에 사과 따기를 하러 갔다.

   ➡ I **did go** apple-picking at my grandfather's farm last year.

   나는 작년에 할아버지 농장에 정말 사과 따기를 하러 갔다.

   cf. 이때 조동사 do는 인칭, 시제에 따라 변하며, 그 뒤에는 동사원형이 온다.

2. **비교급의 강조 – much, far, still, a lot, even**

   This couch is **more comfortable** than I expected.

   이 소파는 내가 기대했던 것보다 더 편안하다.

   ➡ This couch is **much more comfortable** than I expected.

   이 소파는 내가 기대했던 것보다 훨씬 더 편안하다.

The kidnapper asked for **more** money than we had thought.

그 유괴범은 우리가 생각했던 것보다 더 많은 돈을 요구했다.

➡ The kidnapper asked for **a lot more** money than we had thought.

그 유괴범은 우리가 생각했던 것보다 훨씬 더 많은 돈을 요구했다.

3. 명사의 강조 – the very

That's **the book** I've been looking for all day long.

그것이 내가 하루종일 찾고 있던 책이다.

➡ That's **the very book** I've been looking for all day long.

그것이 내가 하루종일 찾고 있던 바로 그 책이다.

4. 부정어의 강조 – at all

You have**n't** changed since the last time I saw you.

마지막으로 내가 널 본 이후로 넌 변하지 않았다.

➡ You have**n't** changed **at all** since the last time I saw you.

마지막으로 내가 널 본 이후로 넌 하나도 변하지 않았다.

정답 p.101

PRACTICE 2

빈칸에 알맞은 말을 써 넣어 밑줄 친 부분을 강조하는 문장으로 바꾸세요.

1 It is <u>colder</u> today than yesterday.

➡ It is ________________________ today than yesterday.

2 The phone <u>rang</u>, but I decided not to answer it.

➡ The phone ________________________ , but I decided not to answer it.

3 Jonathan <u>didn't show up</u> for the concert.

➡ Jonathan ________________________ for the concert.

4 The doctor says that my throat got <u>better</u> than before.

➡ The doctor says that my throat got ________________________ than before.

5 This digital camera is <u>more expensive</u> than the other one.

➡ This digital camera is ________________________ than the other one.

6 This is <u>the place</u> where they hid the jewelry that they had stolen.

➡ This is ________________________ where they hid the jewelry that they had stolen.

7 Mrs. Sanders thinks that Phil is <u>more capable</u> of leading the new project than I am.

➡ Mrs. Sanders thinks that Phil is ________________________ of leading the new project than I am.

8 Some Mexican foods are <u>hotter</u> than most Korean foods.

➡ Some Mexican foods are _______________________ than most Korean foods.

9 I <u>finished</u> all my winter vacation homework before school started.

➡ I _______________________ all my winter vacation homework before school started.

10 The customer <u>was not satisfied</u> with the service at this restaurant.

➡ The customer _______________________ with the service at this restaurant _______________.

11 Macaroni and cheese tastes good, but lasagna tastes <u>better</u>.

➡ Macaroni and cheese tastes good, but lasagna tastes _______________________.

12 This is <u>the cafe</u> where I first met my wife 10 years ago.

➡ This is _______________________ where I first met my wife 10 years ago.

13 The book was <u>easier</u> to understand than the teacher's lecture.

➡ The book was _______________________ to understand than the teacher's lecture.

14 The racing car was going fast, but the driver drove the car <u>faster</u>.

➡ The racing car was going fast, but the driver drove the car _______________________.

15 Vegetables sell at a <u>cheaper</u> price at the grocery than at the department store.

➡ Vegetables sell at a _______________________ price at the grocery than at the department store.

PSS 2-2 「It ~ that …」 강조구문

1. It is / was와 that 사이에 주어, 목적어, 보어, 부사(구) 중 강조하고자 하는 말을 넣어 강조구문을 만들 수 있다. 단, 동사와 형용사는 「It ~ that …」 구문으로 강조할 수 없다.

I saw Nancy in front of the hospital an hour ago. 나는 한 시간 전에 병원 앞에서 Nancy를 보았다.

① 주어 강조

It was I that(= who) saw Nancy in front of the hospital an hour ago.

한 시간 전에 병원 앞에서 Nancy를 본 사람은 나였다.

② 목적어 강조

It was Nancy that(= whom) I saw in front of the hospital an hour ago.

내가 한 시간 전에 병원 앞에서 본 사람은 Nancy였다.

③ 장소를 나타내는 부사구 강조

It was in front of the hospital that(= where) I saw Nancy an hour ago.

내가 한 시간 전에 Nancy를 본 곳은 병원 앞이었다.

④ 때를 나타내는 부사구 강조

It was an hour ago that(= when) I saw Nancy in front of the hospital.

내가 병원 앞에서 Nancy를 본 것은 한 시간 전이었다.

He eventually became a doctor. 그는 결국 의사가 되었다.

⑤ 보어 강조

It was **a doctor** that he eventually became. 그가 결국 된 것은 의사였다.

2. 의문사를 강조하고자 할 때는 「의문사+is / was it that ~」의 형태로 쓴다.

Who saw Nancy in front of the hospital an hour ago?

누가 한 시간 전에 병원 앞에서 Nancy를 보았니?

➡ **Who** was it that saw Nancy in front of the hospital an hour ago?

한 시간 전에 병원 앞에서 Nancy를 본 사람은 누구였니?

Who did you see in front of the hospital an hour ago? 너는 한 시간 전에 병원 앞에서 누구를 보았니?

➡ **Who** was it that you saw in front of the hospital an hour ago?

한 시간 전에 병원 앞에서 네가 본 사람은 누구였니?

Where did you see Nancy an hour ago? 너는 한 시간 전에 Nancy를 어디에서 보았니?

➡ **Where** was it that you saw Nancy an hour ago? 네가 한 시간 전에 Nancy를 본 곳은 어디였니?

When did you see Nancy in front of the hospital? 너는 언제 병원 앞에서 Nancy를 보았니?

➡ **When** was it that you saw Nancy in front of the hospital? 네가 병원 앞에서 Nancy를
본 것은 언제였니?

3. 가주어/진주어 「It ~ that …」 구문과 「It ~ that …」 강조구문은 서로 형태가 비슷하여
둘의 차이점을 구별하는 문제가 시험에서 자주 출제되므로 그 차이점을 알아야 한다.

가주어/진주어 구문에서는 It is/was와 that을 생략하면 불완전한 문장이 된다.

It is a good habit **that** you wake up early. 당신이 일찍 일어나는 것은 좋은 습관이다.
　가주어　　　　　　　　　　　　진주어
➡ a good habit you wake up early (불완전한 문장)

반면, 강조구문에서는 It is/was와 that을 생략하고 강조된 내용을 that 절 뒤로 옮기면 완전한 문
장이 된다.

➡ **It was** a dog **that** I met walking home. 내가 집으로 걸어가면서 만난 것은 한 마리의 개였다.

➡ I met **a dog** walking home. 나는 집으로 걸어가면서 한 마리의 개를 만났다.

정답 p.102

PRACTICE 3

다음을 밑줄 친 부분을 강조하는 「It is / was ~ that …」 구문으로 바꾸어 쓰세요.

1　Who threw the ball out of the window?

➡ ____

2　You saw a shooting star last night.

➡ ____

3　The meeting was held in Seoul.

➡ ____

4 When did the teacher ask me to come and see him?

⇒ ______________________________________

5 The blind girl was playing the guitar in the crowd.

⇒ ______________________________________

6 Many gladiators fought and died at the Colosseum.

⇒ ______________________________________

7 Why do some animals hibernate every winter?

⇒ ______________________________________

8 Where did Wonjin's family go last December?

⇒ ______________________________________

9 The raw fish I ate last night caused my stomachache.

⇒ ______________________________________

10 Why is this restaurant so crowded every day?

⇒ ______________________________________

11 The KTX for Busan left Gwangmyeong Station two minutes ago.

⇒ ______________________________________

12 The Boy Scouts met at the park to do voluntary cleaning work.

⇒ ______________________________________

13 What are the people looking at under the bridge?

⇒ ______________________________________

PSS 3 생략

PSS 3-1 공통되는 부분의 생략

문장에서 다음과 같이 공통되는 요소가 있을 경우에는 이를 생략할 수 있다. 이때 문장의 의미에는 변화가 없다.

I went to my aunt's house and **(I)** helped her paint the house.
나는 고모 댁에 가서 집에 페인트칠 하는 것을 도왔다.
A bird in the hand is worth two **(birds)** in the bush.
손 안에 있는 새 한 마리는 수풀 속의 두 마리만큼의 가치가 있다.
Sumi tried to get out of the theater, but I didn't want to **(get out of the theater)**.
수미는 극장 밖으로 나가려고 했지만, 나는 원하지 않았다.

Some were for the manager's new system, some **(were)** against it.
몇몇은 그 지배인의 새 체제에 찬성했고, 몇몇은 그것에 반대했다.
My friend, Jimmy, found the answer easily, but I couldn't **(find the answer easily)**.
내 친구 Jimmy는 쉽게 답을 찾았지만, 나는 그럴 수 없었다.

정답 p.102

PRACTICE 4

다음 문장에서 생략된 곳을 찾아 문장을 다시 쓰세요.

1 I told him to clean his room, but he refused.

➡ ____

2 We all went to Taeho's home and had a barbecue in his backyard.

➡ ____

3 My dog is smaller than Scott's.

➡ ____

4 Grandpa says he feels much better today than yesterday.

➡ ____

5 Neil has a pair of roller skates that are much better than Mark's.

➡ ____

6 Isabel tries to get up early, but she can't.

➡ ____

7 Although most passengers survived the accident, some people didn't.

➡ ____

8 Oscar brought two fishing rods and Bob some bait for the fishing expedition.

➡ ____

9 I wanted to eat Chinese food, but Karen didn't.

➡ ____

10 He started climbing up the steep cliff at one o'clock and finally reached the top after two hours.

➡ ____

11 This cell phone is a thousand dollars, while that one is only seven hundred.

➡ ____

12 Jude is really good at math, but I'm not.

➡ ____

13 Some like their eggs scrambled, but others don't.

➡ ____

14 I went to school by bicycle, while Sharon went by bus.

➡ ____

1. 접속사가 이끄는 부사절에서의 「주어+be동사」는 주절의 주어와 같을 경우 생략할 수 있다.

   She was embarrassed when **(she was)** asked an unexpected question from the audience.

   그녀는 청중으로부터 예기치 못한 질문을 받았을 때 당황했다.

   Tony heard the phone ring while **(he was)** taking a shower.

   Tony는 샤워를 하는 동안 전화벨이 울리는 것을 들었다.

   Let me know first if **(you are)** free this weekend. 네가 이번 주말에 시간이 되면 먼저 내게 알려줘.

2. 감탄문에서의 「주어+be동사」는 생략해도 의미가 전달되는 경우에 생략할 수 있다.

   What a confusing question **(it is)**! (그것은) 정말 혼동되는 질문이구나!
   How thoughtful **(he is)**! 정말 (그는) 사려 깊구나!

3. 「관계대명사+be동사」 뒤에 분사, 형용사구, 전치사구가 나올 경우 「관계대명사+be동사」는 생략할 수 있다.

   Do you know the name of the tree **(which is)** standing near the beach?

   해변 가까이에 서 있는 나무의 이름을 너는 아니?

   The person **(who was)** hit by the motorcycle was taken to the hospital right away.

   오토바이에 치인 그 사람은 즉시 병원으로 옮겨졌다.

정답 p.102

PRACTICE 5

다음 문장에서 생략할 수 있는 부분에 괄호 표시를 하세요.

1 Larissa and Alice were best friends when they were in high school.

2 What a cute baby she is!

3 The two men who were stuck on the roof were rescued by the helicopter.

4 The science exhibition that was held last year was a great success.

5 Michael always likes to have a hotdog when he is at a baseball game.

6 What a fantastic movie it was!

7 Do you know the gentleman who is talking to your father in the living room?

8 The pizza dough will rise when it is heated.

9 What is the name of the musical instrument which was played by the musician?

10 Though she was physically disabled by the traffic accident, she never lost hope.

PRACTICE **6**

괄호 안에 들어갈 말로 알맞은 것을 골라 동그라미 하세요.

1 My friends saw a lot of famous movie stars when (they were, she was) in New York.

2 I want to live in the apartment (which is, who are) overlooking the beach.

3 I noticed a crow (whom was, that was) sitting on the telephone pole.

4 What is the name of the tower (that is, which are) in the middle of the castle?

5 The person (who was, who is) talking to me over the phone was your cousin.

6 The football match between Brazil and France is a game (that are, which is) worth watching.

7 Simon was annoyed when (he is, he was) ordered to clean up his room again.

8 The statue (that is, who is) standing in the park is of a big lion.

9 The children didn't notice that it was getting dark while (they were, they are) playing in the playground.

10 Some travelers (who is, who were) on the beach were swept away by the tsunami.

PSS 4 속담

PROBLEM
SOLVING
SKILL

---

1. **Castle in the air.**
   공중누각 (허황된 생각)

2. **What is done is done.**
   끝난 일은 끝난 일이다.

3. **He who hesitates is lost.**
   망설이는 자는 모든 것을 잃는다.

4. **Well begun is half done.**
   시작이 반이다.

5. **It is easier said than done.**
   말하기는 쉽고 행동은 어렵다.

6. **There is no place like home.**
   내 집보다 더 좋은 곳 없다.

---

7. To teach a fish how to swim.

물고기에게 수영 가르치기 (공자 앞에서 문자 쓴다.)

8. It never rains but it pours.

비가 내렸다 하면 억수로 퍼붓는다. (엎친 데 덮친 격)

9. A sound mind in a sound body.

건강한 신체에 건강한 마음이 깃든다.

10. A burnt child dreads the fire.

불에 덴 아이는 불을 무서워한다.

11. Slow and steady wins the race.

천천히 그리고 꾸준히 하면 이긴다.

12. What goes around comes around.

네가 한 일은 돌아오게 되어있다. (인과응보)

13. The pot calls the kettle black.

냄비가 주전자보고 검다고 한다. (자기 잘못은 모르고 남만 탓한다.)

14. Fine feathers make fine birds.

좋은 깃털이 좋은 새를 만든다. (옷이 날개다.)

15. It is never too late to learn.

배움에는 절대 늦음이 없다.

16. Keep something for a rainy day.

비 오는 날을 위해 무엇인가를 저축하라. (항상 만일을 대비해라.)

17. As a man sows, so he shall reap.

뿌린 대로 거둔다.

18. Birds of a feather flock together.

깃털이 같은 새들이 함께 모인다. (유유상종)

19. He that knows himself knows others.

자기를 아는 사람만이 남을 안다.

20. Put yourself in other people's shoes.

다른 사람의 입장이 되어 보아라. (역지사지)

Birds of a feather flock together.

21. A drowning man will catch at a straw.

물에 빠진 사람은 지푸라기 하나라도 잡으려 한다.

22. A man is known by the company he keeps.

사귀는 친구를 보면 그 사람을 알 수 있다.

23. One man's meat is another man's poison.

어떤 사람의 음식이 다른 사람에게는 독이 된다. (사람마다 취향이 다르다.)

24. Lock the stable after the horse is stolen.

말을 잃어버린 후 마구간을 잠근다. (소 잃고 외양간 고친다.)

25. He who would search for pearls must dive
below.

진주를 찾으려는 사람은 물 속 깊이 들어가야 한다.

(호랑이 굴에 들어가야 호랑이를 잡는다.)

26. He who runs after two hares will catch neither.

두 마리 토끼를 쫓는 사람은 한 마리도 잡지 못한다.

27. There is no rest for a family with many children.

아이 많은 집에 휴식이란 없다. (가지 많은 나무 바람 잘 날 없다.)

28. You don't know what you've got until you've lost it.

잃기 전에는 가지고 있던 것이 무엇인지 모른다. (구관이 명관이다.)

29. The grass is always greener on the other side of the fence.

담장 저편에 있는 잔디가 항상 더 푸르다. (남의 떡이 더 커 보인다.)

30. You can lead a horse to the water, but you can't make him drink.

말을 물가에 끌고 갈 수는 있지만, 물을 마시게 할 수는 없다. (남에게 어떤 행동을 억지로 강요할 수는 없다.)

He who runs after two hares
will catch neither.

정답 p.103

PRACTICE 7

다음 우리말에 맞는 속담을 보기에서 골라 그 번호를 쓰세요.

보 기
① You don't know what you've got until you've lost it.
② A man is known by the company he keeps.
③ He that knows himself knows others.
④ Birds of a feather flock together.
⑤ Keep something for a rainy day.
⑥ It is easier said than done.
⑦ What is done is done.
⑧ There is no rest for a family with many children.
⑨ One man's meat is another man's poison.
⑩ Lock the stable after the horse is stolen.

1 자기를 아는 사람만이 남을 안다. [   ]

2 말하기는 쉽고 행동은 어렵다. [   ]

3 항상 만일을 대비해라. [   ]

4 사귀는 친구를 보면 그 사람을 알 수 있다. [   ]

5 사람마다 취향이 다르다. [   ]

6 소 잃고 외양간 고친다. [   ]

7 유유상종 [   ]

8 가지 많은 나무 바람 잘 날 없다. [   ]

9 끝난 일은 끝난 일이다. [   ]

10 구관이 명관이다. [   ]

정답 p.103

PRACTICE 8

다음 우리말에 맞게 빈칸에 알맞은 말을 쓰세요.

1 내 집보다 더 좋은 곳 없다.
➡ There is ___________________________________.

2 사귀는 친구를 보면 그 사람을 알 수 있다.
➡ A man ___________________________________.

3 깃털이 같은 새들이 함께 모인다. (유유상종)
➡ ___________________________ flock together.

4 천천히 그리고 꾸준히 하면 이긴다.
➡ ___________________________ wins the race.

5 역지사지
➡ Put yourself ___________________________.

6 비가 내렸다 하면 억수로 퍼붓는다. (엎친 데 덮친 격)
➡ It never ___________________________.

7 시작이 반이다.
➡ ___________________________ is half done.

8 네가 한 일은 돌아오게 되어있다. (인과응보)
➡ ___________________________ comes around.

9 불에 덴 아이는 불을 무서워한다.
➡ ___________________________ dreads the fire.

10 두 마리 토끼를 쫓는 사람은 한 마리도 잡지 못한다.
➡ He who ___________________________.

1 다음 대화의 빈칸에 들어갈 말로 알맞은 것은?

> *Insu* : I really enjoyed the baseball game last night.
>
> *James*: Yeah! _______________ . There's no sport I like more than baseball.

① So did I
② So I did
③ Neither did I
④ Neither I did
⑤ So was I

2 두 문장이 같은 뜻이 되도록 빈칸을 채울 때 알맞은 것은?

> • She won't agree with you. I won't agree with you, either.
>
> = She won't agree with you. _____________ .

① Neither won't I
② Neither will I
③ Either I won't
④ Neither do I
⑤ Either will I

3 두 문장이 같은 뜻이 되도록 빈칸에 알맞은 말을 쓰세요.

> • When off duty, I would sometimes shop with my mom at this mall.
>
> = When _____________ _____________ off duty, I would sometimes shop with my mom at this mall.

4 다음 중 밑줄 친 부분의 쓰임이 잘못된 것은?

① The cookies do smell good today.
② I do think Bob was wrong.
③ She did put them in the refrigerator.
④ I did see him in front of City Hall.
⑤ Mr. Kim did taught Chinese two years ago.

5 우리말과 같은 뜻이 되도록 빈칸에 알맞은 말을 쓰세요.

> • 단순한 것들에 대해서 씀으로써 그는 바로 그 자연의 본질을 표현할 수 있었다.
>
> = He could express _____________ _____________ essence of nature by writing about simple things.

6 다음 중 밑줄 친 much의 의미가 나머지 넷과 다른 것은?

① They have missed you so much for 10 years.
② Things haven't changed much since I left town.
③ Eating too much is not good for your health.
④ My neighborhood is much quieter than yours.
⑤ Thank you so much for sending the letters.

7 우리말과 같은 뜻이 되도록 빈칸에 알맞은 말을 쓰세요.

> • 나는 방학 동안 운동을 전혀 하지 않아 살이 좀 쪘다.
> = I didn't exercise ___________ ___________ and gained some weight over the vacation.

8 두 문장이 같은 뜻이 되도록 빈칸을 채울 때 알맞은 말을 <u>모두</u> 고르면?

> • It is still faster to drive a car than to ride a bicycle.
> = It is ___________ faster to drive a car than to ride a bicycle.

① much ② very ③ else
④ a lot of ⑤ a lot

9 주어진 문장의 밑줄 친 부분을 강조하는 문장을 쓰세요.

(1) She <u>finished</u> her final report before the due date.

→ ___________________________________

____

(2) I saw Tom running <u>in the park</u> last night.

→ ___________________________________

____

10 다음 대화의 빈칸에 알맞은 속담을 고르세요.

> *Minji* : Do you have any special plans for New Year?
> *Jiho* : Yes, I have 35 plans!
> *Minji* : That's too much. Are you sure you can do everything?
> *Jiho* : Well, to be honest, I'm not sure.
> *Minji* : Making plans itself is not important. Keep in mind that ___________.
> *Jiho* : OK, I'll remember that and try to do as many things as possible!

① it never rains but it pours
② a sound mind in a sound body
③ it is easier said than done
④ birds of a feather flock together
⑤ you don't know what you've got until you've lost it

11 주어진 문장의 밑줄 친 부분과 쓰임이 같은 것을 있는 대로 고른 것은?

> <u>It</u> was the vase <u>that</u> I bought yesterday.

> ⓐ <u>It</u> is certain <u>that</u> the bicycle is convenient.
> ⓑ <u>It</u> was unfortunate <u>that</u> he had a traffic accident.
> ⓒ <u>It</u> was she <u>that</u> thought of the machine at first.
> ⓓ <u>It</u> is Tom <u>that</u> I will work with.
> ⓔ <u>It</u> was on the street <u>that</u> I looked for the man.

① ⓐ, ⓑ ② ⓑ, ⓒ ③ ⓐ, ⓑ, ⓒ
④ ⓒ, ⓓ, ⓔ ⑤ ⓑ, ⓒ, ⓓ, ⓔ

12 주어진 문장을 의문사를 강조하는 문장으로 바꿀 때 빈칸에 들어갈 말로 알맞은 것은?

> • Who broke the mirror on the wall?
> ➡ Who ___________ broke the mirror on the wall?

① it was that
② it that was
③ was it that
④ is it that
⑤ was that it

13 다음 강조구문이 잘못된 것은?

① It is a toy robot that he is playing with.
② It was Jamie that came through the door.
③ It was yesterday that I saw a car accident.
④ It is on the bookshelf that I put my diary.
⑤ It was me that borrowed a book from the library.

14 다음 문장에서 생략할 수 있는 부분을 쓰세요.

> The model of this picture was estimated to be in her mid-thirties when she was painted.

➡ ___________________________

15 다음 〈보기〉에서 주어진 표현의 뜻을 찾을 수 없는 것은?

> 보 기
> ⓐ to imagine or dream of impossible things
> ⓑ to point out others' faults while having the same fault oneself
> ⓒ to say something is easy but actually hard to do
> ⓓ to do two things at once with a single effort
> ⓔ to consider something good while others dislike it

① Castle in the air
② It is easier said than done.
③ Rome was not built in a day.
④ Kill two birds with one stone.
⑤ One man's meat is another man's poison.

16 ⓐ~ⓔ의 밑줄 친 부분 중, 어법상 생략 가능한 것을 있는 대로 고른 것은?

> ⓐ Those <u>who are</u> very sick need much care and concern.
> ⓑ Tony smelled the cookies baking in the oven while <u>he was</u> reading a book.
> ⓒ Do you know the boy <u>who is</u> standing by Mr. Lee?
> ⓓ Do you know <u>who is</u> playing tennis at the court?
> ⓔ He has a daughter <u>who is</u> 14 years old.

① ⓐ, ⓑ
② ⓑ, ⓒ
③ ⓐ, ⓑ, ⓒ
④ ⓐ, ⓓ, ⓔ
⑤ ⓑ, ⓒ, ⓓ, ⓔ

17 어법상 틀린 것을 있는 대로 고른 것은?

You may have heard the saying, "ⓐShow me your friends, and I'll show your future." It means that the people around you can have a profound impact on your life. ⓑIt's important that you closely surround yourself with positive, supportive people who want you to succeed. If you surround yourself with motivated and ambitious people, ⓒyou're likely to achieving your goals. The people you spend most of your time with ⓓwill determine who are you. ⓔNot only you will start thinking like them, but your thoughts and behavior will mirror theirs, as well.

① ⓐ, ⓒ 　② ⓒ, ⓓ 　③ ⓑ, ⓒ, ⓔ
④ ⓒ, ⓓ, ⓔ 　⑤ ⓑ, ⓒ, ⓓ, ⓔ

18 다음 글에 알맞은 속담을 고르세요.

Do you want to be a top student in your class? Then learn how to spend your time properly! Avoid rushing things! If you're studying for final exams, study at least a week ahead. Give yourself time and study your lessons slowly every day. By doing so, you will understand your lessons better. If you understand your lessons properly, you'll get excellent grades!

① What is done is done.
② It is never too late to learn.
③ Slow and steady wins the race.
④ To teach a fish how to swim.
⑤ He that knows himself knows others.

19 다음 문장 중 어법상 옳은 것을 모두 고르세요.

① Little did I expected to meet him.
② Not until yesterday did I hear the news.
③ Here comes the children laughing loudly.
④ Never he visits his parents on Christmas.
⑤ There lived a brave prince in the country.

20 B의 대답과 같은 뜻이 되도록 빈칸에 알맞은 말을 쓰세요.

A: I don't understand why he did such a stupid thing.
B: I don't understand it, either.

= ___________ ___________ I.

21 다음 문장에서 어법상 틀린 부분을 찾아 바르게 고치세요.

After she returned home, she wrote about her trip in her diary. Here what she wrote is.

___________ ➡ ___________

22 다음 문장의 밑줄 친 부분 중 어법상 잘못된 곳은?

① Never ② he has dreamed ③ that he would ④ marry ⑤ such a beautiful woman.

23 다음 대화에서 어법상 <u>틀린</u> 부분을 찾아 바르게 고치세요.

> *A*: Please give me something to drink.
> *B*: All right. Here is it.

_________________ ➡ _________________

24 어법상 옳지 <u>않은</u> 것을 <u>모두</u> 고른 것은?

> ⓐ It was the Japanese who first started eating sushi.
> ⓑ It was the haunted house that it scared me the most.
> ⓒ It is interesting that we are all on the same page.
> ⓓ I read the book, that was about life in the Middle Ages.
> ⓔ It was Jake that Grace met him at the art gallery yesterday.
> ⓕ I want to watch the movie, which it was directed by Chris.
> ⓖ Sam, who works at the perfume store, always recommends a scent that suits me.
> ⓗ It is thought that each animal has a different level of intelligence.

① ⓒ, ⓔ, ⓖ, ⓗ   ② ⓐ, ⓑ, ⓔ, ⓗ
③ ⓑ, ⓓ, ⓔ, ⓕ   ④ ⓑ, ⓒ, ⓔ, ⓕ, ⓗ
⑤ ⓐ, ⓑ, ⓓ, ⓕ, ⓖ

25 다음 글을 읽고 Suzy에게 해 줄 수 있는 말로 알맞은 것을 고르세요.

> At lunchtime the other day, I was sitting alone. At the table next to mine, some of my classmates were eating. One of them, Suzy, shouted at me saying, "Hey, Ray, what are you doing all alone? Don't you have a friend? You look so pitiful!" Then all the others laughed. I felt so embarrassed. She didn't need to say that loudly in front of many people. I think she didn't consider how I felt in that situation.

① Put yourself in other people's shoes.
② Keep something for a rainy day.
③ There is no rest for a family with many children.
④ A burnt child dreads the fire.
⑤ He who would search for pearls must dive below.

26 두 문장이 같은 뜻이 되도록 빈칸에 알맞은 말을 쓰세요.

> • I never told her what happened to him yesterday.
> = Never _____________ _____________
> _____________ her what happened to him yesterday.

<h1 style="text-align:center">중학영문법 3800제 3학년 교과서 활용 진도표</h1>

😊 동아 윤정미

과	교과서 문법 내용	CH	PSS
1	whether/if + 주어 + 동사~ : ~인지 아닌지	15	9-2
	명사를 꾸미는 to부정사	7	2-1
2	make/let/have + 목적어 + 동사원형~	1	2-7
	so that + 주어 + 동사~ : ~하도록	15	8
3	관계대명사의 계속적 용법	14	1-5
	명사절을 진주어로 하는 가주어 it	6	2-1
4	현재완료 진행시제	2	2-4
	의문사 + to부정사	7	1-4
5	현재분사의 한정적 용법	9	1-1
	as + 원급 + as	13	2-1
6	과거완료시제	2	2-6
	관계대명사 what	14	1-4
7	동시동작을 나타내는 분사구문	9	4-1
	접속사 as	15	6
8	부정사의 의미상의 주어	7	7
	if + 가정법 과거	12	2-1

😊 동아 이병민

과	교과서 문법 내용	CH	PSS
1	부정사의 의미상의 주어	7	7
	관계대명사 what	14	1-4
2	부분표현(분수, 퍼센트) + of + 명사의 동사 수 일치	17	1-4
	조동사가 있는 수동태	4	1
3	make/let/have + 목적어 + 동사원형~	1	2-7
	it is/was ~ that … 강조구문	18	2-2
4	the + 비교급, the + 비교급	13	3-5
	접속사 since (~때문에)	15	11
5	if + 가정법 과거	12	2-1
	의문사 + to부정사	7	1-4
6	so that + 주어 + 동사~ : ~하도록	15	8
	형용사/부사 + enough + to부정사	7	3-3
7	소유격 관계대명사 whose	14	1-1
	시간을 나타내는 접속사 while, after, until	15	10, 11
8	분사구문	9	4-1
	과거완료시제	2	2-6

😊 미래엔 최연희

과	교과서 문법 내용	CH	PSS
1	관계대명사 what	14	1-4
	접속사 although	15	12
2	it is/was ~ that … 강조구문	18	2-2
	관계대명사의 계속적 용법	14	1-5
3	분사의 한정적 용법	9	1-1
	동사의 의미를 강조하는 do	3	1
4	과거완료시제	2	2-6
	의문사 + 주어 + 동사	1	1-3
	관계대명사 what	14	1-4
5	분사구문	9	4-1
	not only A but also B	15	3
6	관계부사	14	2-1
	접속부사 however, thus	15	13
7	소유격 관계대명사 whose	14	1-1
	if + 가정법 과거	12	2-1

😊 능률 김성곤

과	교과서 문법 내용	CH	PSS
1	현재완료 진행시제	2	2-4
	관계대명사 what	14	1-4
2	관계대명사의 계속적 용법	14	1-5
	분사의 한정적 용법	9	1-1
3	과거완료시제	2	2-6
	접속사 since, after, although	15	11, 12
4	whether/if + 주어 + 동사~ : ~인지 아닌지	15	9-2
	조동사가 있는 수동태	4	1
5	부정사의 의미상의 주어	7	7
	관계부사	14	2-1
6	the + 비교급, the + 비교급	13	3-5
	분사구문	9	4-1
7	if + 가정법 과거	12	2-1
	so that + 주어 + 동사~ : ~하도록	15	8

😊 비상 김진완

과	교과서 문법 내용	CH	PSS
1	관계대명사 what	14	1-4
	관계부사	14	2-1
2	부정사의 의미상의 주어	7	7
	현재완료 진행시제	2	2-4
3	if + 주어 + 동사~ : ~인지 아닌지	15	9-2
	과거완료시제	2	2-6
4	분사의 한정적 용법	9	1-1
	가목적어 it	6	2-1
5	분사구문	9	4-1
	so that + 주어 + can	15	8
	it is/was ~ that … 강조구문	18	2-2
6	사역동사 have + 목적어 + 과거분사	9	1-2
7	접속사 as (~함에 따라, ~할수록)	15	6
	All, half of + 명사의 동사 수 일치	17	1-4
8	if + 가정법 과거	12	2-1
	with + 명사 + 분사	9	4-3

😊 YBM 박준언

과	교과서 문법 내용	CH	PSS
1	동사의 의미를 강조하는 do	3	1
	관계대명사 what	14	1-4
2	현재완료 진행시제	2	2-4
	현재분사의 한정적 용법	9	1-1
3	it is/was ~ that … 강조구문	18	2-2
	have/has/had + 목적어 + 과거분사	9	1-2
4	부정사의 의미상의 주어	7	7
	if + 가정법 과거	12	2-1
5	과거완료시제	2	2-6
	so that + 주어 + 동사~ : ~하도록	15	8
6	관계대명사의 계속적 용법	14	1-5
	to부정사의 부사적 용법 (감정의 원인)	7	3-2
7	how + 주어 + 동사~ : 어떻게 ~하는지	1	1-3
		14	2-1
	the + 비교급, the + 비교급	13	3-5
8	분사구문	9	4-1
	be worth + - ing	8	4
9	I wish + 가정법 과거	12	2-2
	whether/if + 주어 + 동사~ : ~인지 아닌지	15	9-2

중학영문법 3800제 3학년 **교과서 활용 진도표**

YBM 송미정

과	교과서 문법 내용	CH	PSS
1	too ~ to, enough to	7	3-3
1	부정사의 부정형	7	5
2	분사구문	9	4-1
2	명사절을 이끄는 접속사 if	15	9-2
3	the + 비교급, the + 비교급	13	3-5
3	it is/was ~ that … 강조구문	18	2-2
4	접속사 although	15	12
4	seem to (~인 것 같다)	6	2-2
5	관계대명사 what	14	1-4
5	현재완료 진행시제	2	2-4
6	as + 원급 + as	13	2-1
6	과거완료시제	2	2-6
7	if + 가정법 과거	12	2-1
7	so that + 주어 + can (~할 수 있도록, ~하기 위해)	15	8
8	not only A but also B	15	3
8	접속사 while (반면에)	15	10

지학사 민찬규

과	교과서 문법 내용	CH	PSS
1	관계대명사 what	14	1-4
1	지각동사 + 목적어 + 목적격 보어(현재분사)	1	2-7
2	부정사의 의미상의 주어	7	7
2	분사의 한정적 용법	9	1-1
3	not only A but also B	15	3
3	간접의문문	1	1-3
4	과거완료시제	2	2-6
4	to부정사의 부사적 용법 (감정을 나타내는 형용사 수식)	7	3-2
5	부정대명사 one	6	3-1
5	분사구문	9	4-1
6	it is/was ~ that … 강조구문	18	2-2
6	접속부사 however	15	13
7	if + 가정법 과거	12	2-1
7	목적격 보어로 명사나 형용사가 오는 동사	1	2-6
8	too + 형용사/부사 + to부정사	7	3-3
8	부정대명사 No one	6	3-1, 3-7

능률 양현권

과	교과서 문법 내용	CH	PSS
1	부정사의 의미상의 주어	7	7
1	관계대명사의 계속적 용법	14	1-5
2	it is/was ~ that … 강조구문	18	2-2
2	think + A(목적어) + B(목적보어) : A를 B라고 생각하다	1	2-1
3	관계대명사 what	14	1-4
3	사역동사 make	1	2-7
4	과거완료시제	2	2-6
4	분사구문	9	4-1
5	의문사 + to부정사	7	1-4
5	the + 비교급, the + 비교급	13	3-5
6	평서문의 화법 전환	17	3-1
6	지각동사	1	2-7
7	if + 가정법 과거	12	2-1
7	so ~ that …	15	8

금성 최인철

과	교과서 문법 내용	CH	PSS
1	사역동사 let, make, have	1	2-7
1	feel like + - ing, can't[couldn't] help + - ing, be worth + - ing	8	3, 4
2	the + 비교급, the + 비교급	13	3-5
2	부정사의 의미상의 주어	7	7
3	not only A but also B, as well as	15	3
3	I wish + 가정법 과거	12	2-2
4	과거완료시제	2	2-6
4	as + 원급 + as	13	2-1
5	so ~ that …	15	8
5	지각동사 + 목적어 + 목적격보어	1	2-7
6	it is/was ~ that … 강조구문	18	2-2
6	분사구문	9	4-1
7	to부정사의 부사적 용법 (형용사 수식)	7	3-2
7	「So + 동사 + 주어」	18	1
8	명사절을 이끄는 접속사 whether	15	9-2
8	It's (about) time ~	7	2-1

천재교육 이재영

과	교과서 문법 내용	CH	PSS
1	관계대명사 what	14	1-4
1	지각동사 + 목적어 + 동사원형	1	2-7
2	분사의 한정적 용법	9	1-1
2	접속사 Since, Though	15	11, 12
3	현재완료 진행시제	2	2-4
3	so + 형용사/부사 + that절 : 너무 …해서 ~하다	15	8
4	관계부사 when, where	14	2-1
4	if/whether	1	1-3
4		15	9-2
5	과거완료시제	2	2-6
5	it is/was ~ that … 강조구문	18	2-2
6	부정사의 의미상의 주어	7	7
6	if + 가정법 과거	12	2-1
7	분사구문	9	4-1
7	조동사가 있는 수동태	4	1
8	조동사 + have p.p.	3	10
8	관계대명사의 계속적 용법	14	1-5

천재 정사열

과	교과서 문법 내용	CH	PSS
1	간접의문문	1	1-3
1	관계대명사의 계속적 용법	14	1-5
2	과거완료시제	2	2-6
2	비교급 강조	13	3-3
3	형용사/부사 + enough + to부정사	7	3-3
3	not only A but also B	15	3
4	분사구문	9	4-1
4	관계대명사 what	14	1-4
5	if + 가정법 과거	12	2-1
5	소유격 관계대명사 whose	14	1-1
6	the + 비교급, the + 비교급	13	3-5
6	it is/was ~ that … 강조구문	18	2-2
7	평서문의 화법 전환	17	3-1
7	명사절을 이끄는 접속사 if	15	9-2
8	부정대명사	6	3-1, 3-2
8	목적격 보어로 to부정사를 취하는 동사 want, tell, ask, allow, order	1	2-6

2026 새 교과서에 맞춘 16차 개정판

중학영문법 3800제 3학년

정답과 해설

🗂 학습 추가 자료

중학영문법 3800제 학습에 필요한 추가 자료(단어장, mp3, 해석자료, 정답과 해설)를 마더텅 홈페이지 교재자료실에서 무료로 다운받을 수 있습니다.

💻 이용방법

마더텅 홈페이지 **www.toptutor.co.kr** 접속 → 상단 메뉴 중 [학습자료실] 선택

→ 자료 유형 `정답표/정오표/MP3/교재관련 자료` 선택

→ 학년 `중등` , 시리즈 `영문법` , 과목 `영어` 선택

→ 교재 선택에서 `중학영문법 3800제 3학년` 찾아 선택 → 원하는 자료 다운로드

마더텅은 1999년 창업 이래 **2025년까지 3,642만 부의 교재를 판매했습니다.** 2025년 판매량은 322만 부로 자사 교재의 품질은 학원 강의와 온/오프라인 서점 판매량으로 검증받았습니다. [마더텅 수능기출문제집 시리즈]는 친절하고 자세한 해설로 수험생님들의 전폭적인 지지를 받으며 누적 판매 950만 부, 2025년 한 해에만 95만 부가 판매된 베스트셀러입니다. 또한 [중학영문법 3800제]는 2007년부터 2025년까지 19년 동안 중학 영문법 부문 판매 1위를 지키며 명실공히 대한민국 최고의 영문법 교재로 자리매김했습니다. 그리고 2018년 출간된 [뿌리깊은 초등국어 독해력 시리즈]는 2025년까지 323만부가 판매되면서 초등 국어 부문 판매 1위를 차지하였습니다.(교보문고/YES24 판매량 기준, EBS 제외) 이처럼 마더텅은 초·중·고 학습 참고서를 대표하는 대한민국 제일의 교육 브랜드로 자리잡게 되었습니다. 이와 같은 성원에 감사드리며, 앞으로도 효율적인 학습에 보탬이 되는 교재로 보답하겠습니다.

마더텅 학습 교재 이벤트에 참여해 주세요. 참여해 주신 분께 선물을 드립니다.

이벤트 1 1분 간단 교재 사용 후기 이벤트

마더텅은 고객님의 소중한 의견을 반영하여 보다 좋은 책을 만들고자 합니다.

교재 구매 후, <교재 사용 후기 이벤트>에 **참여해 주신 모든 분께는** 감사의 마음을 담아

`네이버페이 포인트 1천 원` 을 보내 드립니다. 지금 바로 QR 코드를 스캔해 소중한 의견을 보내 주세요!

이벤트 2 중학영문법3800제 인증샷 이벤트

필수 태그 #마더텅 #중학영문법3800제

SNS에 <중학영문법3800제> 인증샷을 올려 주시면 **참여해 주신 모든 분께** 감사의 마음을 담아

`네이버페이 포인트 2천 원` 을 보내 드립니다. 지금 바로 QR 코드를 스캔해 작성한 게시물의 URL을 입력해 주세요!

이벤트 3 마더텅 우편 이벤트

본 교재의 Ch 7의 중간·기말고사 대비문제 페이지를 오려서 마더텅으로 보내 주세요!

추첨을 통해 소정의 상품을 보내 드립니다.

참여 방법 Ch 7 중간·기말고사 대비문제(p.159~166) 풀이 및 채점 완료

→ 해당 페이지를 모두 오려서 마더텅에 발송(우편, 택배 등) → QR 코드를 스캔하고 발송 인증

주소 (08501) 서울특별시 금천구 가마산로 96, 대륭테크노타운 8차 708호, 마더텅 이벤트 담당자 앞 / 010-6640-1064

※ 이벤트 기간: 2026년 12월 31일까지 (•해당 이벤트는 당사 사정에 따라 조기 종료될 수 있습니다.) ※ 자세한 사항은 해당 QR 코드를 스캔하거나 홈페이지 이벤트 공지 글을 참고해 주세요. ※ 당사 사정에 따라 이벤트의 내용이나 상품이 변경될 수 있으며 변경 시 홈페이지에 공지합니다. ※ 만 14세 미만은 부모님께서 신청해 주셔야 합니다. ※ 상품은 이벤트 참여일로부터 4~5일(영업일 기준) 내에 발송됩니다. (단, 이벤트 3은 예외) ※ 동일 교재로 세 가지 이벤트 모두 참여 가능합니다. (단, 같은 이벤트 중복 참여는 불가합니다.)

정답 및 해설
Problem Solving Skill

Chapter 1	문장의 기초 Introduction to Sentences	p.2
Chapter 2	시제 Tense	p.7
Chapter 3	조동사 Modals	p.12
Chapter 4	수동태 Passive Voice	p.17
Chapter 5	명사와 관사 Nouns and Articles	p.22
Chapter 6	대명사 Pronouns	p.27
Chapter 7	부정사 Infinitives	p.32
Chapter 8	동명사 Gerunds	p.37
Chapter 9	분사 Participles	p.42
Chapter 10	형용사 Adjectives	p.47
Chapter 11	부사 Adverbs	p.53
Chapter 12	가정법 Conditionals	p.59
Chapter 13	비교구문 Comparisons	p.66
Chapter 14	관계사 Relatives	p.74
Chapter 15	접속사 Conjunctions	p.80
Chapter 16	전치사 Prepositions	p.88
Chapter 17	일치와 화법 Agreement and Narration	p.97
Chapter 18	특수구문 & 속담 Inversion, Emphasis, Ellipsis & Proverbs	p.101

PRACTICE 1

1	isn't he	**2**	have you
3	shouldn't we	**4**	are they
5	could she	**6**	didn't they
7	weren't they	**8**	do we
9	isn't it	**10**	does he

PRACTICE 2

1	will you[won't you]	**2**	isn't it
3	shall we	**4**	am I not[aren't I]
5	can't you	**6**	shall we
7	were there	**8**	will you
9	do they	**10**	aren't there

> **1** 긍정명령문의 부가의문문은 어조에 따라 명령조일 때는 'will you?'를, 정중하게 권할 때는 'won't you?'를 쓴다.
> 어르신들께 이야기할 때는 예의 바르게 행동해라, 알겠니?
> **2, 5** 긍정문의 부가의문문은 「be/do/조동사의 부정형+인칭대명사?」 형태로 쓴다. 2번은 문장의 동사가 is이므로 isn't를, 5번은 can을 포함하므로 can't를 사용하여 부가의문문을 만들 수 있다.
> **3, 6** 'Let's~'로 시작하는 청유문의 부가의문문은 긍정 · 부정에 관계없이 'shall we?'만 사용한다.
> **4** 'I am ~'의 부가의문문은 am의 부정 축약형이 없으므로 'am I not' 혹은 구어체에서 'aren't I' 형태로 쓴다.
> **7, 10** 현재시제일 경우 'There is[are]~, isn't[aren't] there?', 과거시제일 경우 'There was[were]~, wasn't[weren't] there?' 형태로 쓴다. 7번의 경우 부정문이면서 과거시제이므로, 'were there?'가 온다. 10번의 경우 현재시제의 긍정문이므로 'aren't there'가 온다.
> **8** 부정명령문의 부가의문문은 'will you'만 사용한다.
> **9** 부정문의 부가의문문은 「be/do/조동사의 긍정형+인칭대명사?」 형태로 쓴다. 문장의 동사가 일반동사이므로 'do they' 형태로 쓴다.

PRACTICE 3

1 where the dairy products are

2 how the food tasted

3 what made her so happy

4 when the tragic accident happened

5 if[whether] he got married to the English girl

6 who will look after her while her parents are working

7 why you didn't agree with him

8 how far it is from here to the airport

9 if[whether] my dream will come true

10 if[whether] he has any brothers or sisters

> **1, 2, 4, 7, 8** 의문사가 있는 의문문을 간접의문문으로 바꿀 때, 「의문사+주어+동사」 형태로 쓴다. 의문문 구조를 만드는 데 사용되었던 do[did]동사를 없애면서 시제와 수를 일반동사에 적용하면 된다. 2, 4, 7번의 경우 주어진 문장이 과거 시제이므로 간접의문문도 과거 시제로 쓴다. 8번의 경우 how와 far을 하나의 묶음으로 간주하여 거리를 묻는 의문사로 쓸 수 있다.
> **3, 6** 의문사가 주어로 쓰인 간접의문문의 경우 주어진 문장(직접의문문)의 어순을 그대로 쓴다.
> **5, 9, 10** 의문사가 없는 의문문을 간접의문문으로 바꿀 때, 의문문의 내용은 if나 whether가 이끄는 명사절의 일부가 되어 「if[whether]+주어+동사」 형태로 쓴다. 5번은 주어진 문장의 시제가 과거, 9번은 미래, 10번은 현재이므로 간접의문문 시제도 이에 맞추어 쓴다.

PRACTICE 4

1 Why do you think she quit[quitted] school?

2 How do you guess you can discover your hidden talents?

3 Please tell me if[whether] you are an FBI agent.

4 Where do you suppose he comes from?

5 I know what you did after school yesterday.

6 When do you believe you can afford to buy the house?

7 Which do you think is the faster way to go there?

8 Where do you guess you lost your passport?

> **1, 2, 4, 6, 7, 8** 간접의문문이 포함된 문장에서 think, believe, suppose, guess와 같이 생각이나 추측을 나타내는 동사가 주절에 있을 때는 간접의문문의 의문사가 문장의 맨 앞에 위치한다.
> **3** 의문사가 없는 의문문을 간접의문문으로 바꿀 때 「if[whether]+주어+동사」 형태로 쓴다.
> **5** know, tell, hear, wonder 등의 동사가 주절에 있을 때는 간접의문문의 의문사가 문장의 앞으로 오지 않고, 일반적인 간접의문문 형식을 따른다.

PRACTICE 5

1	①, ② – 1형식	**2**	①, ②, ③ – 3형식
3	①, ②, ③, ⑦ – 5형식	**4**	①, ②, ⑥ – 2형식
5	②, ① – 1형식	**6**	①, ②, ④, ⑤ – 4형식
7	①, ②, ⑥ – 2형식	**8**	①, ②, ③, ⑦ – 5형식

> 문장 성분은 주어, 동사, 목적어(간접 목적어, 직접 목적어), 보어(주격 보어, 목적격 보어)가 있고, 그 이외에 부사(구)는 문장을 구성하는 필수 요소가 아니다.
> **1** The Sun이 주어, rises가 동사인 1형식 문장이고 주어와 동사만 있어도 완벽한 문장이 성립한다. in the east(동쪽에서)는 장소/방

향을 나타내는 부사구이다.
2 주어(Mr. Kim)와 동사(teaches)가 한 개의 목적어(English)를 가지는 3형식 문장이다. 전치사구 to us(우리에게)와 시간을 나타내는 부사구 every Thursday and Friday(매주 목요일과 금요일에)는 필수적인 문장 성분이 아니다.
3 think A B는 'A를 B라고 생각하다'라는 의미이고, him과 honest는 목적어-목적격 보어 관계이다. 따라서 이 문장은 5형식이다. At first(처음에)는 시점을 나타내는 부사구이다.
4 형용사 cold가 'colder and colder(점점 더 추운)'의 형태로 쓰여 주어를 보충하는 주격 보어 역할을 하므로 2형식 문장이다. 문장의 주어 It은 날씨를 나타내는 비인칭주어이다.
5 문장이 유도부사 there로 시작해서 동사와 주어가 도치되었다. an old castle이 주어, is가 동사인 1형식 문장이다. There과 on the hill(언덕 위에)은 부사(구)이기 때문에 필수 문장 성분이 아니다.
6 동사 give는 받는 사람(the lead male and female actors)과 주어지는 것(a big hand: 큰 박수갈채)을 모두 목적어로 가진다. 따라서 이 문장은 4형식이다.
7 unlike others(다른 사람들과 다르게)는 필수 문장 성분이 아닌 부사구이다. remain은 명사와 형용사를 보어로 가지는 동사이고, calm and patient가 주격 보어이다. 따라서 이 문장은 2형식이다.
8 '그녀가 그것을 하기'를 원한 것이므로 her과 to do it은 목적어-목적격 보어 관계이다. instead of himself(그 자신을 대신하여)는 필수 문장 성분이 아닌 부사구이다.

PRACTICE 6

1	brilliant	**2**	cloudy	**3**	tired
4	silent	**5**	popular	**6**	fluently
7	cold	**8**	late	**9**	serious
10	calmly	**11**	bad	**12**	pale
13	quickly	**14**	dry	**15**	coldly

1, 2, 4, 5, 7, 8, 9, 11, 12 주격 보어를 필요로 하는 불완전자동사 (be, keep, remain, stay, get, grow, become, go, turn)가 쓰인 2형식 문장으로 형용사가 주격 보어로 쓰일 수 있다.
　8 late: 형 늦은 /lately: 부 최근에
　11 go bad: (음식이) 상하다
　12 grow pale: 창백해지다
3 tiring(피곤하게 하는)과 tired(피곤한)는 둘 다 형용사이므로 get('~되다'라는 의미일 때 2형식 동사)의 주격 보어로 쓰일 수 있지만, 문맥상 '당신은 긴 산책 뒤에 쉽게 피곤해질 수 있다'는 뜻이므로 tired가 적절하다.
6, 13 3형식 문장으로 「주어+동사+목적어」 구조와 함께 동사를 수식하는 부사(구)(quite fluently, quickly)가 쓰였다.
10 동사(landed)를 수식하고 있으므로 부사(calmly: 차분하게)가 적절하다. calmly landed: 차분하게 착륙시켰다
14 run dry: 말라 버리다, 고갈되다
15 '차갑게 대했다'는 의미이므로 동사 treat를 수식하는 부사 coldly가 적절하다.

PRACTICE 7

1	good	**2**	strange	**3**	looks like
4	dully	**5**	fresh, energetic		
6	young	**7**	guilty	**8**	heavy
9	sweet	**10**	rich, stingy	**11**	well

12 sounds like　**13** greatly

1, 2, 7, 9 감각동사(sound, taste, feel)가 사용되어 주격 보어로 형용사가 온다.
3, 12 괄호 뒤에 명사가 오기 때문에 형용사만을 보어로 가지는 looks와 sounds는 정답이 될 수 없다.
　3 look like+명사: ~처럼 보이다
　12 sound like+명사: ~처럼 들리다
4 동사 move가 문맥상 '~이 움직이다'라는 의미의 완전자동사(보어, 목적어 필요없음)로 쓰였으므로 괄호 안에는 수식어로 부사(dully)가 들어간다.
5 feel은 형용사와 함께 쓰여 '~하게 느끼다'라는 의미를 나타내는데, 부사와 함께 쓰이는 것으로 혼동하기 쉬우므로 주의해야 한다. 또한 등위접속사 and로 연결된 요소들은 형태가 같아야 하므로 fresh and energetic이 적절하다.
6, 8, 10 '~로 보이다'라는 의미의 동사(look, seem, appear)가 사용되어 주격 보어로 형용사가 온다.
11 동사(worked)를 수식하고 있으므로 부사(well)가 적절하다.
13 과거분사(delayed)를 수식하므로 부사(greatly: 아주 많이)가 적절하다.

PRACTICE 8

1	with	**2**	after	**3**	with	**4**	to
5	for	**6**	from	**7**	with	**8**	after
9	with	**10**	to	**11**	to	**12**	for

PRACTICE 9

1 My wife's full support gave strength to me.
2 He teaches English speaking and writing to the children.
3 They didn't ask anything of me.
4 I bought an ice cream cone and a soft drink for my friend.
5 Can you tell the reason for your decision to us?
6 The machine will make different types of cookies for you.
7 Would you do a favor for me?
8 The instructor showed how to snowboard to me.
9 The gentleman found my diamond necklace for me.
10 A customer wrote a thank-you email to the manager.

PRACTICE 10

1	interesting	**2**	to come	**3**	to go
4	angry	**5**	quiet	**6**	to confess
7	to have	**8**	sour, smelly	**9**	to go
10	to get				

PRACTICE 11

1	help	**2**	to wake	**3**	decorate
4	enjoying	**5**	carry	**6**	think
7	printed	**8**	repaired	**9**	succeed
10	crossing	**11**	done	**12**	to attend
13	buy	**14**	rising	**15**	cut
16	washed	**17**	develop	**18**	moving
19	know	**20**	change	**21**	fighting
22	walk	**23**	stolen	**24**	to be
25	thinking				

📝 중간·기말고사 대비문제 정답 본문 _ p.21

1 ④ **2** ③ **3** She wants to know how long it takes to get to the airport. **4** ④ **5** ① **6** ① **7** asked[requested], to attend **8** ③,⑤ **9** ⑤ **10** ②,⑤ **11** Do you know if[whether] the birds cry like human beings? **12** ⑤ **13** What do you think we should do to get out of here? **14** ①,② **15** ③ **16** ④ **17** ③ **18** ①,⑤ **19** shall we **20** he prefers reading books at home to going out **21** ③ **22** ④ **23** ③ **24** ④ **25** ②, what he thinks about our school / ④, help him (to) find his locker **26** ③ **27** ② **28** ⓐ how challenging the experiment was ⓑ what a great result we achieved **29** (1) where the restroom is (2) what that sign means **30** ② **31** ①,⑤ **32** I wonder why they wore uncomfortable high heels. **33** ⑤ **34** ③ **35** ①

중간·기말고사 대비문제 해설

1 ④ 앞에 관사 a가 쓰였고, 형용사 quick의 수식을 받고 있으므로 명사 decision의 사용은 적절하다.
① want 뒤에 다른 동사가 목적어로 올 때는 「to+동사원형」의 형태로 쓴다. 따라서 명사 success가 아닌 동사 succeed가 올바른 형태이다. (success → succeed)
② 맥락상 '실험의 설명'이라는 의미이므로 동사 explain이 아닌 명사 explanation의 사용이 적절하다. (explain → explanation)
③ 앞에 관사 a가 쓰였으므로 명사 recommendation

이 와야 한다.
(recommend → recommendation)
⑤ 명사 translation은 '통역'이라는 의미이며, 명사 translator는 '통역가'라는 의미이다. (translation → translator)

2 ③ 부정 명령문의 부가의문문은 ', will you?'의 형태로 쓴다. for the sake of '~을 위해서'
⑤ 접속사 when이 사용된 시간의 부사절에서는 현재시제가 미래시제를 대신하므로 will eat 대신에 eat으로 쓴다.

3 의문사가 있는 간접의문문의 어순은 「의문사+주어+동사 ~」가 된다. how와 long은 하나의 묶음으로 취급한다.

4 ④ become은 주격 보어로 명사나 형용사가 온다. (richly → rich)

5 네모 안의 밑줄 친 Lies는 '거짓말'이라는 의미의 명사형으로 사용되었다. 거짓말은 단거리 달리기를 하지만, 진실은 마라톤을 한다. (거짓말은 일시적으로 빠르게 퍼질 수 있지만, 결국에는 진실이 오래 지속되고 승리한다는 의미)
① 그의 강점은 그의 결단력에 있다. (통 lie: ~에 있다)
② 그들은 거짓말로 진실을 감추려 했다.
③ 신뢰는 부서지기 쉽고 거짓말에 의해 쉽게 깨어진다.
④ 그의 거짓말은 사람들이 그를 믿는 것을 어렵게 했다.
⑤ 그녀는 거짓말에는 항상 결과가 따른다는 것을 배웠다.

6 tell은 목적격 보어로 to부정사가 오고, to부정사의 부정형은 「not+to부정사」의 형태로 쓴다.

7 ask[request]+목적어+to부정사 '~에게 …을 부탁하다'

8 prevent[keep, stop] ~ from -ing: '~가 -하는 것을 막다'
② 주어가 동명사일 경우 단수 취급하여 단수동사를 써야 한다.

9 ⓐ look 뒤에 명사가 올 때는 「look like+명사」의 형태로 쓴다.
ⓑ 동사 stay는 형용사 또는 명사를 보어로 쓴다.
ⓒ sound는 '~하게 들리다'라는 뜻의 감각동사로, 형용사를 보어로 쓴다. (beautifully → beautiful)
ⓓ smell은 '~한 냄새가 나다'라는 뜻의 감각동사로, 형용사를 보어로 쓴다. well은 good의 부사형이다. (well → good)

ⓔ 동사 grow는 형용사를 보어로 쓴다.
(palely → pale)

10 주어진 문장, ②⑤ 5형식 ① 3형식 ③④ 4형식

11 의문사 없는 의문문을 간접의문문으로 쓰면
「if[whether]+주어+동사」의 어순을 따른다.

12 [A] 준사역동사 help는 동사원형이나 to부정사를 목
적격 보어로 취한다.
[B] 지각동사 feel은 동사원형이나 현재분사를 목적
격 보어로 취한다.
[C] 사역동사 let은 동사원형을 목적격 보어로 취한다.

13 주절의 동사가 think, believe, suppose와 같이 생
각이나 추측을 나타낼 때는 간접의문문의 의문사는
문장의 가장 앞으로 나온다.

14 ① used to+동사원형: ~하곤 했다 (be used to
-ing: ~에 익숙하다)
(보는 데 익숙하다 → 보곤 했다)
② to be understood는 수동태이므로 '이해되다'로
해석해야 한다. (나는 내 상황이 더 잘 이해되기를
원한다.)

15 보기의 밑줄 친 cut은 과거분사로 목적어(her hair)
와 수동 관계임을 나타낸다.
③ washed
목적어와 목적격 보어의 관계가 수동일 때는 목적
격 보어로 과거분사가 온다.
① stand[standing]
지각동사 saw의 목적격 보어로는 동사원형 또는
현재분사가 온다.
② think
사역동사 makes의 목적격 보어로는 동사원형이
온다.
④ enjoying
동사 find는 목적격 보어로 형용사 또는 분사가 온
다. 목적어와 목적격 보어의 관계가 능동일 때는 목
적격 보어로 현재분사를 취한다.
⑤ to be
동사 ask는 목적격 보어로 to부정사가 온다.

16 ⓑ 간접의문문은 「의문사+주어+동사」의 어순으로 쓴
다.
ⓓ find out의 목적어 역할을 하는 명사절을 이끌며,
선행사를 포함하는 관계대명사 what의 사용은 적
절하다.
ⓔ since는 '~이후로'라는 뜻으로 현재완료 시제와 함
께 쓰여 사건이 시작된 시점 이래로 어떤 행위나 상

태가 지속됨을 나타낸다. 사람들이 '충격받은' 것이
므로 과거분사 shocked를 사용한 것 또한 어법상
적절하다.
ⓐ 아이들이 '흥분된' 감정을 느끼는 것이므로 과거분
사로 써야 한다. (exciting → excited)
ⓒ 간접의문문은 「의문사+주어+동사」의 어순을 따르
므로, how I can ~이 되어야 한다.
(how can I → how I can)

17 ask+직접목적어+of+간접목적어

18 help+목적어+(to)+동사원형

19 'Let's ~' 청유문은 항상 ', shall we?' 형태의 부가의
문문을 가진다.

20 prefer A to B 'B보다 A를 더 좋아하다'

21 c. 내가 당황한 감정을 느끼는 것이므로 과거분사
embarrassed를 써야 한다.
(embarrassing → embarrassed)
a. the most '가장 많이, 제일'
b. 몇몇 종류의 음료들은 따뜻하게만 제공된다는 의
미이므로 수동태(be+p.p.) 표현을 활용해 are
served로 쓰는 것이 어법상 적절하다.
d. 감탄문의 어순은 「how+형용사+주어+동사」를 따
르므로 important를 써야 한다.
e. make use of '활용하다'

22 There are로 시작하는 문장의 부가의문문은, aren't
there?의 형태로 쓴다.

23 • name ~ after … '…의 이름을 따서 ~의 이름을
짓다'
• help ~ with … '…에 대해 ~를 돕다'

24 ④의 had는 일반동사 have의 과거형이므로 hadn't
you?를 didn't you?로 고쳐야 한다.
(hadn't you → didn't you)

25 ② 의문사가 있는 의문문을 간접의문문으로 바꿀 때
의 어순은 「의문사+주어+동사」이므로 what을 간
접의문문의 주어인 he 앞으로 이동시켜야 한다.
④ help의 목적격 보어로는 동사원형 또는 to부정사
를 쓸 수 있다.

26 ③ 감각동사 sound의 주격 보어로 형용사가 온다.
(truly → true)

27 ② get은 목적어와 목적격 보어의 관계가 수동일 때
목적격 보어 자리에 과거분사가 온다.
(to finish → finished)

28 ⓐ 감탄문의 어순은 「How+형용사+주어+동사」를 따
른다. 따라서 주어 the experiment가 동사 was보다

먼저 쓰여야 한다.
ⓑ 감탄문의 어순은 「what+a+형용사+명사+주어+동사」를 따른다. 따라서 주어와 동사를 도치시키지 않고 we achieved의 형태로 써야 한다.

29 의문사가 있는 간접의문문의 어순은 「의문사+주어+동사」이다. 일반동사의 경우 3인칭 단수 현재형일 때 형태의 변화에도 유의해야 한다.

30 (b) 지각동사 heard가 쓰였고 목적어와 목적격 보어가 수동 관계이므로 목적격 보어 자리에 과거분사를 쓴다. (mention → mentioned)
(d) 동사 was breathing을 수식하고 있으므로 동사를 수식할 수 있는 부사를 써야 한다.
(heavy → heavily)
(f) 사역동사 let은 목적격 보어로 동사원형을 가질 수 있으므로 keeps가 아닌 keep을 써야 한다.
(keeps → keep)
(a) 동작이 진행 중임을 강조할 때에는 지각동사(watched)의 목적어로 현재분사(practicing)를 쓸 수 있다.
(c) 주어 The shoes는 분사구 'made in Italy'의 수식을 받고 있다. 주어가 복수이므로 복수형 동사 look을 썼고, 보어로 형용사 nice가 온 것은 적절하다.
(e) 준사역동사 help는 목적격 보어로 동사원형(feel)을 취할 수 있다.

31 의문사가 있는 간접의문문의 어순은 「의문사+주어+동사」이며, 주절의 동사가 think일 때는 간접의문문의 의문사가 문장 맨 앞에 위치한다.
② Do you think who → Who do you think
③ how can we solve → how we can solve
④ What language do you know → Do you know what language

32 의문사 why가 있으므로 I wonder 뒤에 「의문사+주어+동사」 어순의 간접의문문을 써야 한다. 시제가 과거이므로 간접의문문의 동사는 wore라고 쓴다.

33 ① 의문사가 있는 간접의문문의 어순은 「의문사+주어+동사」이다. (Where can you tell me I can → Can you tell me where I can)
② encourage+목적어+to부정사
(becoming → to become)

③ 사역동사 make+목적어+동사원형
(to laugh → laugh)
④ 지각동사 feel+목적어+동사원형[현재분사]
(to move → move[moving])

34 ⓒ stay+형용사 '~인 상태로 있다'
(to stay silently → to stay silent)
ⓓ want+목적어+to부정사 (help → to help)
ⓔ encourage+목적어+to부정사 '~가 …하도록 격려하다' (choosing → to choose)

35 ⓐ make an effort to+동사원형: ~하려고 노력하다.
ⓑ 준사역동사 help는 목적격 보어로 to부정사 또는 동사원형을 취한다.
ⓔ tell+간접목적어+직접목적어: 간접목적어에게 직접목적어를 말하다
ⓒ 사역동사 let+목적어+동사원형 (to do → do)
ⓓ 사역동사 make+목적어+동사원형
(waited → wait)
ⓕ 사역동사 have+목적어+과거분사: 목적어(new tires)와 목적격 보어가 수동 관계에 있으므로 목적격 보어로 과거분사형을 써야 한다.
(putting → put)
ⓖ 준사역동사 get은 주어가 목적어가 어떤 행동을 하도록 설득, 유도할 때 목적격 보어로 to부정사를 사용한다. 현재분사는 그 행동을 '시작'하게 함을 강조할 때 사용된다. (signing → to sign)
ⓐ Sujin은 그것을 제시간에 끝내기 위해 노력조차 하지 않는다.
ⓑ 정기적인 독서는 우리의 어휘력을 확장하는 것을 돕는다.
ⓒ Lauren은 그녀의 아이들이 좋아하는 무엇이든 하도록 허락한다.
ⓓ 그 철도 노동자들의 파업이 나를 한 시간 동안 기다리게 했다.
ⓔ 엄마는 나에게 어디에서 최고의 거래를 할 수 있는지 말해 주신다.
ⓕ 나는 그 차에 막 새 타이어를 장착했다.
ⓖ 나는 Tommy가 그 동의서에 서명하게 할 수 없었다.

PRACTICE 1

1 bowed	**2** accomplished
3 affected	**4** declared
5 chatted	**6** grabbed
7 aimed	**8** scratched
9 tied	**10** destroyed
11 soaked	**12** envied
13 appointed	**14** designed
15 tapped	**16** attempted
17 classified	**18** avoided
19 tried	**20** dispatched
21 begged	**22** carried
23 downloaded	**24** boarded
25 boiled	**26** displayed
27 disturbed	**28** dried
29 accepted	**30** dyed
31 buried	**32** buzzed
33 challenged	**34** amounted
35 defeated	**36** cherished
37 demanded	**38** applied
39 assigned	**40** clapped
41 reunified	**42** snapped
43 focused[focussed]	**44** enrolled
45 replied	**46** complained
47 performed	**48** attracted
49 connected	**50** hummed
51 established	**52** inherited
53 gasped	**54** curled
55 succeeded	**56** exported
57 coughed	**58** counted
59 crawled	**60** regarded
61 fried	**62** reviewed
63 chewed	**64** stirred
65 hugged	**66** conquered
67 controlled	**68** jogged
69 weighed	**70** pardoned
71 ripped	**72** limited
73 mixed	**74** occurred
75 perched	**76** refunded
77 permitted	**78** sniffed
79 copied	**80** published

PRACTICE 2

1 d	**2** t	**3** d
4 d	**5** t	**6** id
7 t	**8** id	**9** d
10 t	**11** d	**12** id
13 t	**14** id	**15** d
16 t	**17** id	**18** d
19 t	**20** id	**21** t
22 t	**23** id	**24** t
25 t	**26** id	**27** t
28 d	**29** d	**30** id
31 t	**32** d	**33** id
34 t	**35** d	**36** id
37 t	**38** d	**39** t
40 id	**41** id	**42** d
43 id	**44** t	**45** id

PRACTICE 3

1 began – begun	**2** drank – drunk
3 met – met	**4** dealt – dealt
5 crept – crept	**6** arose – arisen
7 paid – paid	**8** bit – bitten
9 laid – laid	**10** beat – beaten
11 wore – worn	**12** dug – dug
13 built – built	**14** cut – cut
15 sent – sent	**16** brought – brought
17 fell – fallen	**18** sold – sold
19 flew – flown	**20** sat – sat
21 bought – bought	**22** forgot – forgotten
23 came – come	**24** burst – burst
25 fought – fought	**26** bent – bent
27 shone/shined – shone/shined	
28 ate – eaten	**29** fed – fed
30 drove – driven	**31** knelt – knelt
32 slept – slept	**33** got – got(ten)
34 found – found	**35** cost – cost
36 froze – frozen	**37** ground – ground
38 kept – kept	**39** hurt – hurt
40 wove – wove(n)	**41** chose – chosen
42 forgave – forgiven	**43** spread – spread
44 hit – hit	**45** hung – hung

46 set – set   **47** rang – rung

48 knew – known   **49** led – led

50 meant – meant

PRACTICE 4

1 have already sent

2 have gone

3 has enjoyed

4 have not[haven't] visited

5 has never been

6 has won

7 has rained

8 have just arrived

9 Have, heard

10 have taught

> **4, 5** 현재완료시제 문장에서 not, never와 같은 부정어는 have[has]와 과거분사 사이에 위치한다.

PRACTICE 5

1 I have not[haven't] finished, 완료

2 Ms. Kim has lived, 계속

3 He has bought, 결과

4 My brother has been sick, 계속

5 Sally has already had, 완료

6 Have you met, 경험

PRACTICE 6

1 Jack has stayed at the hotel for two weeks.

2 I have composed songs for seven years.

3 Liz has visited the nursing home for three months.

4 My brother has had the laptop computer since 2021.

5 We have been friends since we were kids.

6 Mark has enjoyed playing tennis since 2022.

7 She has painted landscapes for five years.

8 He has enjoyed gardening since last year.

PRACTICE 7

1 did you go   **2** did you meet

3 has been   **4** came, was

5 haven't been   **6** wasn't

7 have helped, joined   **8** haven't spoken

9 haven't driven   **10** fell, met

> **1, 2, 6** 과거의 특정한 때를 나타내는 부사(last Sunday, the day before yesterday, in the summer of 2021)와 함께 쓰였기 때문에 과거시제로 쓴다.
> **3** lately는 최근 얼마간의 과거부터 현재에 이르는 기간을 가리키며 완료시제와 주로 쓰인다.
> **4, 10** '~할 때'를 의미하는 접속사 when이 이끄는 절이 과거의 특정한 때(내가 어젯밤 집에 돌아왔을 때, 우리가 파티에서 처음 만났을 때)를 나타내기 때문에 과거시제로 쓴다.
> **5** yet은 '아직'이라는 의미이고 현재완료의 완료 용법과 주로 쓰인다. There haven't been any accidents on the new highway yet.은 '(현재까지) 아직 새로운 고속도로에서 아무 사고도 없었다'는 뜻이다.
> **7, 8** since는 '~이후로'라는 뜻으로 완료시제와 함께 쓰여 사건이 시작된 시점 이래로 계속 행위나 상태가 지속됨을 나타낸다. 7번의 경우 사건이 시작된 시점이 「since+절」로 표현되었는데, 절 내에 과거의 특정한 때를 나타내는 부사구(last month)가 있으므로 since 절의 시제는 과거로 쓴다.
> **9** before은 '이전에'라는 뜻으로 구체적인 과거 시점을 가리키지 않는다. 현재완료시제와 함께 쓰여 경험을 나타낸다.

PRACTICE 8

1 haven't found   **2** ○

3 has felt   **4** baked

5 has improved   **6** ○

7 has played   **8** broke

PRACTICE 9

1 have been studying

2 have been playing

3 have been looking

4 have been knitting

5 has, been fixing

6 have been working

7 has been urging

8 have been using

9 have been receiving

10 has been suffering

PRACTICE 10

1 It has been snowing for 30 minutes.

2 Mr. Harmon has been living in Korea for six months.

3 Mom has been writing novels since she was 28 years old.

4 The boys have been planting trees and flowers since noon.

5 My dad has been building a model plane for three hours.

6 Jina has been teaching Korean in China for two years.

7 Stuart and I have been playing soccer since 2 o'clock.

PRACTICE 11

1	respects	**2**	is playing
3	was reading	**4**	know
5	admire	**6**	was sleeping
7	sounds	**8**	do you think
9	prefer	**10**	Do you have
11	don't understand	**12**	was smelling
13	am thinking	**14**	appears
15	consists	**16**	belongs
17	believed		

1, 5, 9 감정 상태를 나타내는 동사(respect, admire, prefer)는 진행형으로 쓰지 않는다.
2, 3, 6 동작이 계속되고 있음을 나타내는 진행시제를 사용한다. 2번은 now가 쓰여 현재 동작이 계속되고 있음을 나타내는 현재진행시제가 쓰였고, 3번과 6번은 문맥상 when절이 나타내는 사건과 주절의 행위가 동시에 일어났기 때문에 과거진행시제가 적절하다.
4, 8, 11, 17 인식 상태를 나타내는 동사(know, think, understand, believe)는 진행형으로 쓰지 않는다.
7 감각 상태를 나타내는 동사(sound)는 진행형으로 쓰지 않는다.
10, 16 소유 상태를 나타내는 동사(have, belong)는 진행형으로 쓰지 않는다.
　16 belong to: ~에 속하다
12, 13 smell과 think는 일반적으로 진행형으로 쓸 수 없지만 동작을 나타내는 의미로 쓰일 경우 진행형을 쓸 수 있다. 12번은 과거 시점의 부사절(when I saw him)과 함께 과거진행시제로, 13번은 right now와 함께 현재진행시제로 사용되었다.
14, 15 appear(~처럼 보이다)과 consist of(~로 구성되다)는 진행형으로 쓸 수 없다.

PRACTICE 12

1 went[had gone]

2 had given

3 met

4 spent[had spent]

5 already left[had already left]

6 became

7 had taught

8 ate[had eaten]

9 had lost

10 saw[had seen]

1, 4, 5, 8, 10 과거시제보다 이전에 일어난 동작이나 상태를 나타내므로 과거완료시제를 사용한다. before, after, last Saturday와 같이 시간의 앞뒤 순서를 분명하게 알 수 있는 접속사 또는 표현이 있을 때는 과거시제를 써서 과거완료시제를 대신할 수 있다.
2, 7, 9 과거시제보다 이전에 일어난 동작이나 상태를 나타내므로 과거완료시제를 사용한다.
3 주절에 현재시제를 사용했고, who가 이끄는 종속절이 특정한 과거 시점을 나타내는 표현(last week)을 포함하므로 과거시제가 적절하다.
6 after가 이끄는 종속절에 과거시제(started)를 썼는데, 이는 과거시제가 과거완료시제를 대신한 것으로 볼 수 있다. 따라서 주절에는 종속절의 과거완료시제보다 나중의 일을 나타낼 수 있도록 과거시제를 사용하는 것이 적절하다.

PRACTICE 13

1	had been reading	**2**	had been playing
3	had been expecting	**4**	had been snowing

PRACTICE 14

1	has played	**2**	has been watching
3	had been walking	**4**	haven't met
5	had already finished	**6**	have been trying
7	had left	**8**	had been waiting
9	did you hand	**10**	was
11	hadn't been getting	**12**	had locked
13	have stayed	**14**	has been cooking
15	had been standing	**16**	hasn't eaten
17	had been looking		

1, 4, 13, 16 과거에 시작되어 현재까지 영향을 미치는 동작이나 상태를 나타내기 위해 현재완료시제를 쓴다. 1번, 13번, 16번은 since, until now와 함께 쓰여 현재완료의 계속을, 4번은 before와 함께 쓰여 현재완료의 경험을 나타낸다.
　16 until now: 지금까지
2, 6, 14 과거에 시작한 동작이 현재에도 진행 중이므로 과거완료 진행이 아닌 현재완료 진행시제를 쓴다. 2번과 14번은 since와, 6번은 for와 함께 쓰여 현재완료의 계속의 의미를 나타낸다.
3, 8, 11, 15, 17 과거 시점을 기준으로 그 이전부터 시작하여 기준 시점까지 동작이 진행 중이었음을 강조하는 과거완료 진행시제를 사용한다.
5, 7, 12 과거 어느 시점을 기준으로 그 이전에 일어난 동작이나 상태를 나타내는 과거완료를 사용한다.
9, 10 과거의 구체적 시점을 나타내는 부사(절)가 있으므로 현재완료가 아닌 과거시제를 쓴다.

PRACTICE 15

1 will buy a necklace

2 is throwing a party

3 am going to have a piano lesson

4 will keep a diary in English

5 am eating out with my family
6 am going to do volunteer work
7 are going to have a picnic

📝 중간·기말고사 대비문제 정답   본문 _ p.46

1 ③   **2** ③   **3** ④   **4** He has been working there
5 We have been discussing the issue for an
hour.   **6** ④   **7** was late for class because his car
had broken down   **8** ②   **9** ④   **10** ③   **11** ③
12 ②,⑤   **13** ③   **14** ④   **15** ②   **16** ⑤   **17** ②
18 ⑤   **19** ③   **20** had told   **21** ⑤   **22** she
had left her pencil case   **23** ④   **24** had stolen
25 ④   **26** ②,⑤   **27** ⑤   **28** ①   **29** ④

중간·기말고사 대비문제 해설

1 현재완료의 용법 중 '결과'를 나타내는 문장이다.

2 빈칸이 포함된 문장은 현재완료의 용법 중 '계속'을 나타낸다. since(~이후로)는 사건이 시작된 과거의 시점을 나타내고 주절에는 주로 현재완료시제를 쓴다.
cf. be interested in '~에 관심이 있다'

3 a minute ago는 특정한 과거를 나타내므로 현재완료시제와 함께 쓸 수 없다. (have seen → saw)

4 현재완료 진행시제(have/has+been+~ing)는 과거에 시작된 일이 현재까지 계속되고 있음을 뜻한다.

5 「have+been+~ing」 형태의 현재완료 진행시제로 과거에 시작한 동작이 현재까지 계속되고 있음을 나타낸다.

6 <보기>의 문장은 현재완료 결과 용법의 예로, 선택지 중 결과 용법에 해당하는 문장은 ④이다. ①과 ②는 경험 용법, ③은 완료 용법, ⑤는 계속 용법의 예이다.

7 차가 고장 난 시점이 수업에 늦은 시점(과거시제)보다 더 이전이므로 과거완료시제를 쓴다.
cf. be late for: ~에 늦다

8 「had+과거분사」 형태의 과거완료시제는 과거의 어느 시점을 기준으로 그 이전에 일어난 동작이나 상태를 나타낸다. 그들이 해변에 도착했을 때쯤, 해는 (이미) 져 있었다.
② 그들은 해변에 도착한 이후 일몰을 즐겼음에 틀림없다.
cf. must have+과거분사 '~였음에 틀림없다'

① 그들이 해변에 도착하기 전에 해는 이미 져 있었다.
③ 해가 진 후에, 그들은 해변에 도착했다.
④ 그들은 해변에 도착했을 때 일몰을 즐길 수 없었다.
⑤ 그들이 해변에 도착했을 때 해는 좀 더 일찍 져 있었다.

9 <보기>의 문장은 현재완료의 경험 용법으로 쓰였다.
④ 경험 ① 결과 ②⑤ 완료 ③ 계속

10 ③ 소유를 나타내는 동사 belong은 진행형으로 사용할 수 없다. (are belonging → belong)
① 과거시점을 나타내는 when he called her보다 앞서 발생한 일이므로 현재완료 시제가 아닌 과거완료 시제를 써야 한다. 이때 for은 완료시제와 쓰여 '계속'의 의미를 나타낸다.
(has waited → had waited)
② 현재완료 시제와 같이 쓰이는 since는 '계속'의 의미를 나타낸다. 강아지가 태어났을 때부터 계속 키워왔다는 의미이므로 ⓑ는 어법상 적절하다.
④ 과거의 일을 나타내고 있으며 시간의 접속사 after를 사용해 선후관계를 분명하게 드러내고 있으므로 과거 시제를 사용해 표현한 ⓓ는 어법상 적절하다.
⑤ 가까운 미래에 있을 일이 미리 계획된 일일 경우 미래시제 대신 현재진행시제를 사용하여 미래의 일을 나타낼 수 있다. 따라서 ⓔ는 어법상 적절하다.

11 this morning은 특정한 과거를 나타내므로 첫 번째 빈칸에는 과거시제(gave)가 와야 하고, three weeks before는 this morning보다 앞선 시점이므로 두 번째 빈칸에는 과거완료시제(had bought)가 와야 한다.

12 ⓑ 5형식 문장으로 목적어(my hair)와 목적격 보어(cut)의 관계가 수동이므로 현재분사가 아닌 과거분사가 나와야 한다. (cutting → cut)
ⓔ It's 뒤 주격보어 자리에 형용사(difficult)가 나온 것으로 보아 2형식 문장임을 알 수 있다. 따라서 It's는 be동사 is가 축약된 형태이므로 부가의문문에도 be동사를 써야 한다. (hasn't → isn't)
ⓐ 감각동사 look이 나오고 주격보어 자리에 형용사(gorgeous)가 오는 것은 적절하다.
ⓒ 세 번 가 본 적이 있다는 경험을 말하고 있으므로 현재완료 시제는 적절하다.
ⓓ 미래를 나타내는 부사구 next week가 나왔으므로 조동사 will이 쓰인 것은 적절하다.

13 ③ 소유, 감정, 인식, 감각 등의 상태를 나타내는 동사

가 동작을 나타내는 의미로 쓰일 경우를 제외하고
는 진행형을 쓰지 않는다.
(have been respecting → have respected)

14 ④ '컴퓨터가 멈춘 것'보다 '그가 문서를 저장한 것'이
먼저 일어난 일이므로 주절은 대과거를 나타내는
과거완료 시제를 사용해야 한다.
(has saved → had saved)

15 현재진행형은 미래를 나타내는 부사(tonight)와 함께
쓰여 가까운 미래에 계획되어 있는 일을 나타낸다.

16 현재완료시제는 과거의 특정한 때를 나타내는 부사
(구)(When, five minutes ago, in 2022,
yesterday)와 함께 쓸 수 없다.

17 ⓒ already는 부정문에 쓰지 않으므로 already를 삭
제하고 문장의 맨 끝에 yet(아직)을 써야 한다.
ⓔ since(~이후로)는 사건이 시작된 과거의 시점을
나타내므로 시간의 길이를 나타내는 three years
와 함께 쓰지 않는다. (since → for)
ⓕ 주어 a group of tourists(관광객 단체)에서 a
group에 수를 일치시켜야 한다. (have → has)
ⓖ over 10 years는 시간의 길이를 나타내므로
since 대신 for를 써야 한다.

18 (A) last week라는 과거를 나타내는 부사구가 있으므
로 과거 시제 동사인 went가 적절하다.
(B) 두 번째 문장에는 과거시제를 나타내는 부사절
(when I was out of town)이 나왔으므로 주절
의 동사도 과거시제가 되어야 한다.

19 ①②⑤ when I was a child, 5 minutes ago, last
night은 특정한 과거를 나타내므로 현재완료시제
와 함께 쓸 수 없다.
④ 과거보다 이전 시점부터 과거(last month)까지 지
속된 일이므로 과거완료시제로 쓰거나, 과거의 습
관적인 행동을 가리키므로 과거시제로 쓸 수 있다.

20 '소년의 할머니가 특별한 약초에 대해 말씀하셨던 것'
이 '소년이 기억한' 과거보다 이전에 일어난 일이므로
과거완료시제를 쓴다.

21 ⑤ 과거 시점의 일인 경찰이 현장에 도착한 것보다 배
의 절반이 가라앉은 것이 더 이전에 일어난 사건이
므로 과거완료시제로 고쳐 쓴 것은 어법상 옳다.
① 본동사 began이 있으므로 '바다로 향하면서'라는
의미가 되도록 분사 heading을 쓰는 것이 어법상
적절하다. (headed → heading)

② 몇몇 승객들이 '깜짝 놀란' 감정을 느끼는 것이므로
과거분사로 써야 한다. (startling → startled)
③ 지각동사 hear의 목적격 보어로는 동사원형 또는
-ing 형태가 와야 한다. (to say → say(ing))
④ 자동사 disappear(사라지다)는 수동태로 쓸 수 없
다. (was disappeared → disappeared)

22 Jenny가 깨달은(realized) 시점보다 필통을 학교에
두고 온(left her pencil case at school) 일이 먼저
발생했으므로 필통을 두고 왔다는 내용은 과거완료시
제로 나타낸다.

23 ④ 여기 오는 데 다섯 시간이 걸린 것은 과거에 시작되
어 과거에 이미 종료된 사건으로, 과거시제로 나타
내야 한다. (has been taking → took)

24 '돈을 훔친 것'이 '반 친구들이 오해한' 과거보다 이전
에 일어난 일이므로 과거완료시제를 쓴다.

25 ⓐ 과거의 특정한 때를 나타내는 부사(In 1901)와 함
께 쓰였기 때문에 과거시제(invented)로 쓰는 것
이 적절하다.
ⓑ 주어가 복수(the paper and ink)이므로 동사도
복수형(were)이 오는 것이 적절하다.
ⓒ the Carrier Air Conditioning Company of
America를 설립했다는 의미이므로, '설립하다'는
뜻을 가진 동사 found의 과거형 founded가 오는
것이 적절하다.

26 상태를 나타내는 동사는 진행형으로 쓰지 않는다.
① is belonging to → belongs to
③ am wanting to → want to
④ is consisting of → consists of

27 since(~이후로)는 사건이 시작된 과거의 시점을 나타
낸다. since가 있는 문장의 주절에는 주로 현재완료시
제를 쓴다.

28 ⓐ 문장에 사건이 지속된 기간을 나타내는 부사구가
포함되어 있으므로 현재완료시제를 써야 한다.
ⓑ for(~동안)는 사건이 일어난 시간의 길이를 나타낸
다.
ⓒ 주어(The patient)가 능동적으로 고려하고 있으
므로 considering이 답이다.

29 ④ 과거보다 이전에 벌어진 동작은 과거완료시제
를 써야 하므로 they have failed를 they had
failed로 써야 한다. (have failed → had failed)

PRACTICE 1

1 Does[Did] **2** did
3 does **4** did
5 do[did] **6** did
7 does **8** does
9 didn't

> **1** 일반동사의 의문문을 만들 때 문장의 앞에 조동사 do[does, did]를 사용한다. 주어진 문장의 주어가 3인칭 단수이므로 does나 did를 사용한다.
> **2, 8** 이미 언급된 일반동사(saw, work)의 반복을 피하기 위해 did와 does를 사용한다. 이때, so나 neither과 같은 부사구가 문두로 가면서 do동사가 주어 앞에 위치한다.
> **3, 4, 6, 7, 9** 조동사 do[does, did]가 앞의 문장이나 절에 나온 동사의 반복을 피하기 위한 대동사 역할을 한다.
> **5** 일반동사의 부정문을 만들 때 동사 앞에 do[does, did]를 사용한다. 주어가 I이므로 do나 did를 사용한다.

PRACTICE 2

1 did meet **2** do think
3 does look **4** do hope
5 Do tell **6** did teach
7 does love **8** does go

PRACTICE 3

1 is able to speak
2 was able to ride
3 weren't[were not] able to play
4 will be able to drive
5 wasn't[was not] able to solve
6 won't[will not] be able to see
7 wasn't[was not] able to join
8 am able to manage
9 am not able to find
10 won't[will not] be able to change

PRACTICE 4

1 Can, be **2** Can[Could], drink
3 can't, be **4** can, tell
5 Can[Could], work[be working]
6 Can[Could], carry **7** Can[Could], see
8 can't, know **9** can[could], help
10 can[could], affect

> **1** 이게 과연 사실일까? (추측)
> **2** 나는 너무 목이 말라. 내가 이 주스를 마셔도 될까? (허락)
> **3** 그녀의 연주는 끔찍했어. 그녀는 피아니스트일 리가 없어. (추측)
> **4** 너는 이 이야기를 누구에게나 얘기해도 돼. 난 상관없어. (허락)
> **5** 이 기계가 다시 작동할까? (추측/가능성)
> **6** 이 가방은 너무 무거워. 네가 나를 위해 이것 좀 들어줄 수 있니? (요청)
> **7** 내가 너의 보고서를 잠깐 봐도 될까? (허락)
> **8** 그는 내일 있을 깜짝 파티에 대해 알 리가 없어. 아무도 그에게 얘기하지 않았어. (추측)
> **9** 이것이 네가 살을 빼는 데 성공할 수 있도록 도울 가능성이 있다. (가능성)
> **10** 수면 부족은 너의 일상 생활의 질에 영향을 미칠 가능성이 있다. (가능성)

PRACTICE 5

1 have **2** have **3** had
4 must **5** have **6** had
7 must **8** must **9** have
10 had

PRACTICE 6

1 had to return
2 has to be set
3 have to appreciate
4 will have to[have to] go
5 will have to[have to] prove
6 had to wait

> **1** 우리는 이미 2시가 되었다는 것을 알았다. 우리는 사무실로 돌아가야 했다. (과거) 과거 시제의 의무는 had to로 쓴다.
> **2** 당신이 자기 전에 알람시계가 정확한 시간에 맞추어져 있어야 한다. 그러면 당신은 제시간에 일어날 수 있다. (현재) 주어가 3인칭 단수이므로 has to로 쓴다.
> **3** 당신은 그들이 항상 당신을 돌보고 도와준다는 사실에 감사해야 한다. (현재)
> **4** White 부부는 한 달 후에 그들의 나라로 돌아가야 할 것이다. (미래) 미래의 의무는 현재형인 have to로도 쓸 수 있다.
> **5** 그 변호사는 당신에게 몇 가지 질문을 하러 여기에 올 것이다. 그때 당신은 죄가 없다는 것을 입증해야 할 것이다. (미래) 미래의 의무는 현재형인 have to로도 쓸 수 있다.
> **6** 어제, 수업이 예상했던 것보다 일찍 끝났다. Amy와 Liz는 그들의 엄마가 그들을 데리러 올 때까지 기다려야 했다. (과거) 과거 시제의 의무는 had to로 쓴다.

PRACTICE 7

1 must be **2** can't speak
3 can't be **4** must like

| 5 | must feel | 6 | can't recognize |

> **1** 이것은 유전임에 <u>틀림없다</u>. (추측)
> **2** 그는 중국어를 <u>할 리가 없다</u>. (강한 부정의 추측)
> **3** 그는 병상에 누워 <u>있을 리가 없다</u>. (강한 부정의 추측)
> *sick in bed: 병상에 누운
> **4** 그녀는 그를 많이 <u>좋아함에 틀림없다</u>. (추측)
> **5** 그는 <u>지쳤음에 틀림없다</u>. (추측)
> **6** 만약 내가 콧수염을 기르고 선글라스를 쓴다면, 그녀는 나를 <u>알아 볼 리 없다</u>. (강한 부정의 추측)

PRACTICE 8

1 must not drive

2 don't have to go

3 must not happen

4 must not tell

5 doesn't have to make

6 don't have to take

7 must not speak

8 don't have to pretend

9 must not be

10 doesn't have to climb

11 must not eat

> **1** 당신은 면허 없이 운전을 <u>해서는 안 됩니다</u>. (금지)
> **2** 나는 그곳에 일찍 갈 <u>필요가 없다</u>. (불필요)
> **3** 이러한 종류의 사고는 다시 <u>일어나서는 안 된다</u>. (금지)
> **4** 너는 너의 부모님에게 거짓말을 <u>해서는 안 된다</u>. (금지)
> **5** 그는 지금 결정을 <u>할 필요가 없다</u>. (불필요)
> **6** 나는 더 이상 이 약들을 먹을 <u>필요가 없다</u>. (불필요)
> **7** 당신은 이것에 대해 누구에게도 한 마디도 <u>해서는 안 된다</u>. (금지)
> **8** 당신은 그 음식을 좋아하는 <u>체하지 않아도 된다</u>. (불필요)
> **9** 어제 나는 제시간에 오겠다고 약속해서, 오늘 나는 <u>늦어서는 안 된다</u>. (금지)
> **10** 그 건물에 엘리베이터가 있어서, Susan은 계단을 오를 <u>필요가 없다</u>. (불필요)
> **11** 나는 너무 많이 <u>먹어서는 안 된다</u>. (금지)

PRACTICE 9

1 may[might] visit

2 may[might] ask

3 may[might] not be

4 may[might] break

5 may[might] not come

6 may[might] have

PRACTICE 10

| 1 | may | 2 | May |
| 3 | might | 4 | be able to |

5	must not	6	can't
7	have to	8	Could
9	could	10	don't have to

> **1, 2** may가 허가를 나타낸다.
> **3** might가 불확실한 추측을 나타낸다.
> **4, 7** 조동사 뒤에는 동사원형이 와야 하며, 다른 조동사가 이어서 나올 수 없다.
> **5** must not이 금지를 나타낸다.
> **6** can't가 강한 부정의 추측을 나타낸다.
> **8** could가 허가를 나타낸다.
> **9** could가 능력을 나타낸다.
> **10** don't have to가 불필요를 나타낸다.

PRACTICE 11

1	would	2	Would
3	be able to	4	Will
5	can't	6	would
7	does	8	must not
9	would	10	does
11	would	12	would
13	have to	14	would
15	did	16	be able to
17	don't have to	18	had to

> **1, 14** would rather+동사원형: 차라리 ~하는 편이 낫다
> **2, 9** would like+명사: ~을 원하다
> **3, 13, 16** 조동사 뒤에는 동사원형이 와야 하며, 다른 조동사가 이어서 나올 수 없다.
> **4, 11** Will[Would] you ~?: ~해 주시겠습니까? (요청)
> **5** can't가 강한 부정의 추측을 나타낸다.
> **6, 12** would like to+동사원형: ~을 하고 싶다
> **7, 15** 조동사 do[does/did]가 동사를 강조한다. 7번의 경우 주어가 3인칭 단수이므로 does를, 15번의 경우 문장의 시제가 과거이므로 did를 쓴다.
> **8** must not이 금지를 나타낸다.
> **10** 조동사 does가 앞의 문장이나 절에 나온 동사의 반복을 피하기 위한 대동사 역할을 한다. 주어가 3인칭 단수이므로 does를 쓴다. 이때, neither와 같은 부사가 문두로 가면서 do 동사가 주어 앞에 위치한다.
> **17** don't have to가 불필요를 나타낸다.
> **18** 의무·필요를 나타내는 had to를 써서 집에 일찍 와야 해서 수업이 끝나기 전에 떠났다는 내용을 나타낸다.

PRACTICE 12

1 should[ought to] listen

2 should[ought to] reply

3 should not[ought not to] go

4 should[ought to] cross

5 should[ought to] warn

6 should[ought to] be

7 should[ought to] apply

8 should not[ought not to] watch

9 should[ought to] apologize

10 should not[ought not to] tell

PRACTICE 13

1 'd better renew

2 'd better not be

3 'd better not lose

4 'd better not sit

5 'd better stay

6 'd better not overeat

7 'd better think

8 'd better go

PRACTICE 14

1 used to[would] jump

2 used to be

3 used to[would] wake

4 used to be

5 used to like

6 used to[would] spend

7 used to have

8 used to[would] gather

9 used to[would] hide

10 used to feel

> **1, 3, 6, 8, 9** used to[would]가 '~하곤 했다'의 뜻으로 쓰여 과거 반복적으로 일어났던 행위를 나타낸다.
> **2, 4, 5, 7, 10** used to가 행위가 아닌 과거의 상태를 나타낸다.

PRACTICE 15

1 must have rained

2 may have heard

3 should have thought

4 can't[cannot] have had

5 shouldn't[should not] have used

6 may not have gone

> **1** 「must have+p.p.」가 확신을 나타낸다. (~였음에 틀림없다)
> **2, 6** 「may have+p.p.」가 추측을 나타낸다. (~했을지도 모른다)
> **3, 5** 「should have+p.p.」가 후회를 나타낸다. (~했어야 했다)
> **4** 「can't[cannot] have+p.p.」가 부정을 나타낸다. (~였을 리가 없다)

PRACTICE 16

1 must		**2** must	
3 cannot		**4** must	
5 cannot		**6** may	
7 can		**8** should	
9 may		**10** shouldn't	
11 must		**12** should	
13 should			

> **1** '엄마와 딸은 일 년 동안 만나지 못했다. 그들은 서로가 매우 보고 싶었을 것이 틀림없다.'는 뜻으로 「must have+과거분사」가 확신을 나타낸다.
> **2** '그 고장 난 컴퓨터는 이제 잘 작동한다. 남수가 너에게 말하지 않고 고친 것이 분명하다.'는 뜻으로 「must have+과거분사」가 확신을 나타낸다.
> **3** 'Sean은 굉장히 침착하고 신중한 사람이다. 그가 그렇게 큰 실수를 했을 리 없다.'는 뜻으로 「can't[cannot] have+과거분사」가 부정을 나타낸다.
> **4** '그들은 한 시간 전에 이곳으로 오기로 했는데 그러지 않았다. 그들은 이 도시로 향하는 첫 열차를 놓쳤던 것이 틀림없다.'는 뜻으로 「must have+과거분사」가 확신을 나타낸다.
> **5** '아이들은 나와 함께 하루 종일 집에 있었다. 그들이 거기에 갔을 리가 없다.'는 뜻으로 「can't[cannot] have+과거분사」가 부정을 나타낸다.
> **6** '아빠는 민지가 오늘 돌아온다는 것을 듣고 굉장히 신이 나셨다. 그는 이미 그녀를 데리러 공항으로 출발했을지도 모른다.'는 뜻으로 「may have+과거분사」가 추측을 나타낸다.
> **7** '이 방은 너무 건조하고 빛도 들지 않았다. 그 꽃들이 이 환경에서 살아남을 수 있었을 리가 없다.'는 뜻으로 「can't[cannot] have+과거분사」가 부정을 나타낸다.
> **8** '내가 Bob을 봤을 때 그는 매우 슬프고 불행해 보였다. 너는 그를 놀리지 말았어야 했다.'는 뜻으로 「should have+과거분사」가 후회를 나타낸다.
> **9** '매니저는 오후 내내 그의 책상에 없었다. 그는 일찍 퇴근했을지도 모른다.'는 뜻으로 「may have+과거분사」가 추측을 나타낸다.
> **10** '나는 지금까지 이것을 딱 한 번 입었다. 나는 이렇게 비싼 드레스를 사지 말았어야 했다.'는 뜻으로 「should have+과거분사」가 후회를 나타낸다.
> **11** 'Susan은 Tom도 회의에 오는지 몰랐다. 그녀는 그의 갑작스러운 등장에 당황한 것이 분명하다.'는 뜻으로 「must have+과거분사」가 확신을 나타낸다.
> **12** '나는 Bill이 시험 중에 부정행위를 하는 것을 봤다. 김 선생님은 그것을 보고 그에게 경고를 했어야 했다.'는 뜻으로 「should have+과거분사」가 '~ 했어야 했다'를 나타낸다.
> **13** '나는 네가 왜 이렇게 늦었는지 궁금하다. 너는 2시간 전에 이곳에 왔어야 했다.'는 뜻으로 「should have+과거분사」가 '~ 했어야 했다'를 나타낸다.

📑 중간·기말고사 대비문제 **정답**　본문 _ p.67

1 ⑤　**2** ④　**3** must have practiced　**4** would rather eat out than　**5** ②　**6** don't have[need] to　**7** (1) ©,ⓔ (2) ⓐ,ⓑ,ⓓ,ⓕ　**8** ②　**9** ①　**10** I should have brought a jacket.　**11** ③　**12** ④　**13** ②　**14** ③　**15** ③　**16** ③　**17** ③　**18** ③　**19** had better take a taxi　**20** didn't use[used not] to like him　**21** we don't have to be rich　**22** Would you like some cheese with that wine?　**23** ④　**24** ②　**25** ③　**26** ②　**27** ⑤　**28** ④　**29** be able to　**30** ④　**31** ②　**32** Neither could I.[I couldn't either.]　**33** ④　**34** ⑤　**35** ⑤

중간·기말고사 대비문제 **해설**

1　⑤ '하다'라는 뜻의 일반동사
　　①②③④ 강조의 조동사

2　④ need not은 '~할 필요가 없다'라는 의미이며, '~하지 말아야 한다'라는 의미는 must not에 해당한다. (준비하지 말아야 한다 → 준비할 필요가 없다)
　　① have to '~해야 한다'
　　② should '~해야 한다'
　　③ must not '~해서는 안 된다'
　　⑤ don't have to '~할 필요가 없다'

3　맥락상 '~했음에 틀림없다'라는 의미가 적절하므로, 밑줄 친 부분을 「must+have+과거분사」 형태인 must have practiced로 고쳐야 한다.

4　「would rather A than B」 'B 하느니 차라리 A 하겠다'

5　ⓓⓔ 앞에 나온 동사의 반복을 피하기 위해 쓰이는 대동사 do
　　ⓐ 일반동사의 의문문을 만드는 조동사 do
　　ⓑ 일반동사의 부정문을 만드는 조동사 do
　　© 강조의 조동사 do

6　don't have[need] to '~할 필요가 없다'

7　©, ⓔ에서는 must가 '~임에 틀림없다'는 추측의 의미로 쓰였고, ⓐ, ⓑ, ⓓ, ⓕ에서는 '~해야 한다'는 의무의 의미로 쓰였다.

8　may는 '~일지도 모른다'의 뜻으로 추측을 나타낸다.

9　① 추측 ②③④⑤ 능력

10　「should have+과거분사」 '~했어야 했다'

11　③ 조동사끼리는 나란히 쓸 수 없다.
　　(Will you can → Will you be able to)

12　「would like to+동사원형」 '~을 하고 싶다'

13　영주가 개 주인에게 개와 함께 사진을 찍어도 되는지 허락을 구하는 상황이므로 조동사 May를 사용하여 질문을 한다.

14　③ '~할 필요가 없다'는 불필요의 의미는 「don't have to+동사원형」으로 쓴다. (bringing → bring)

15　had better의 부정형은 had better not으로 쓴다.

16　ⓐ need not은 조동사로 주어가 3인칭 단수라고 해서 needs not으로 쓰지 않는다.
　　(needs → need)
　　ⓑ had better의 부정은 had better not의 형태로 사용한다. (had not better → had better not)
　　© do가 동사의 의미를 강조하기 위해 사용될 때에는 뒤에 동사원형이 와야 한다.
　　(did contributed → did contribute)
　　ⓓ 「must have+과거분사」 '~였음에 틀림없다'
　　ⓔ 「used to+동사원형」 '~하곤 했다'
　　ⓕ 「should have+과거분사」 '~ 했어야 했다'

17　주어진 문장의 밑줄 친 does는 동사 help를 강조한다.
　　③ 동사의 의미를 강조하는 do
　　① 의문문을 만드는 조동사 do
　　② 대동사 do
　　④ '하다'라는 뜻의 일반동사 do
　　⑤ 부정문을 만드는 조동사 do

18　「would+동사원형」은 과거에 반복적으로 일어난 행위를 나타낸다.

19　내용상 버스가 떠나 영화를 보지 못할 것을 걱정하는 Jane에게 '택시를 타는 것이 낫다'고 조언하는 것이 적합하다. had better '~하는 편[것]이 낫다'

20　'~하곤 했다'(used to)의 부정형은 didn't use to[used not to]이다.

21　don't have to '~할 필요가 없다'

22　「would like+명사」 '~을 원하다'

23　④ 허가의 may '~해도 좋다'
　　①②③⑤ 추측의 may '~일지도 모른다, 아마 ~일 것이다'

24　② '그는 수영을 매우 잘하는 게 틀림없다'는 강한 추측의 의미가 되어야 하므로 '~임에 틀림없다'는 의미의 조동사 must가 들어가는 것이 적절하다.

25　「must have+과거분사」 '~였음에 틀림없다'

26 주어진 문장은 그가 우산을 챙기지 않았다는 것을 의미하는데 ②의 문장은 그가 우산을 챙기는 것을 기억했다고 하고 있으므로 틀린 설명이다.
그는 비를 피하기 위해 우산을 챙겼어야 했다.
② 그는 우산을 챙기는 걸 기억했기 때문에 비에 젖지 않았다.
① 그는 비에 젖어서 불편을 겪었다.
③ 과거에 다른 선택을 했더라면 더 나은 결과가 있었을 수도 있다.
④ 우산을 챙겼다면 비를 피할 수 있었을 거라는 아쉬움이 담겨 있다.
⑤ 우산을 챙기는 것이 더 나은 선택이었을 것인데, 그를 젖는 것으로부터 보호했을 것이기 때문이다.

27 「used to+동사원형」과 「would+동사원형」은 과거에 반복적으로 일어난 행위를 나타낸다. 행위가 아닌 과거의 상태를 나타낼 때는 「would+동사원형」을 쓸 수 없다.

28 「may have+과거분사」 '~했을지도 모른다'

29 「be able to」 '~할 수 있다'(= can)

30 ④ (A)와 같은 추측 ①②③⑤ 의무

31 「may have+과거분사」 '~했을지도 모른다'

32 couldn't가 포함된 부정문에 대한 동의는 「Neither could+주어」로 쓴다.

33 ④ A: Jason이 내 험담을 했다니 믿을 수 없어.
　　B: Jason은 정직하고 친절해. 그가 그런 행동을 했을 리가 없어.
① A: 나 너무 피곤해. 나는 헬스장에서 운동하느라 5시간을 보냈어.
　　B: 음. 넌 운동을 그렇게 많이 하지 말았어야 했어.
　　(should have exercised → should not have exercised)
② A: 내가 내일 피아노 경연대회에서 잘하면 좋겠어.
　　B: 너는 방과 후에 연습을 해야 해.
　　(must not have practiced → must practice)

③ A: Sally는 요즘 살을 빼려고 노력하고 있어.
　　B: 그녀는 밤늦게 간식을 먹어선 안 돼.
　　(should eat snacks → should not eat snacks)
⑤ A: 땅이 너무 건조해서 깊게 금이 가 있어.
　　B: 오랫동안 비가 오지 않은 게 틀림없어.
　　(must have rained → must not have rained)

34 「should have+과거분사」는 후회를 나타낸다. (~했어야 했다) 그는 긴 줄을 피하기 위해 공항에 더 일찍 도착했어야 했다.
⑤ 그가 공항에 일찍 왔었더라도 긴 줄을 피할 수는 없었을 것이다.
① 그것은 그에게 이미 일어난 일에 대한 유감을 표현한다.
② 그가 공항에 충분히 일찍 도착하지 않았기 때문에 그는 긴 줄을 기다렸다.
③ 만약 그가 공항에 더 일찍 도착했었다면 긴 줄을 피할 수도 있었을 것이다.
④ 공항에 일찍 도착하는 것이 그가 긴 줄을 피할 수 있었던 더 나은 방법이었을 것이다.

35 (a) 십대 팝스타가 올해 팝 콘서트에 참여한다(take part in)는 의미이므로 전치사 in이 들어가야 한다.
(b) 내가 그녀의 라이브 공연을 볼 수 있게 되어 기쁘다(I'm so excited that I can see her perform live!)는 의미가 되는 것이 자연스럽다. 따라서 조동사 can(~할 수 있다)이 적절하다.
(c) 동사(hear)가 이미 나왔으므로 강조의 do가 들어가야 한다. 'Did ~?' 의문문에 대한 대답이므로 과거시제를 써서 do는 과거형 did로 쓴다.
(d) 문맥상 우리가 공연을 위한 티켓을 사는 것이 좋겠다는 내용이 오는 것이 자연스러우므로 조동사 should(~하는 것이 좋겠다, ~해야 한다)가 오는 것이 적절하다.

PRACTICE 1

1 My proposal may be accepted by the manager.

2 An e-mail must be sent in advance by Brian.

3 They might be attracted by her natural beauty.

4 The deadline for reports should not be forgotten.

5 All the hotel rooms ought to be cleaned by the women.

6 Other people's design concepts can't be copied.

7 He will be remembered as a good leader by them.

8 Her heart could be broken by his words.

9 A piece of music will be performed by her.

10 This secret must be kept forever by the two boys.

PRACTICE 2

1 A lot of fish were being caught in the lake by James.

2 The refrigerator was being cleaned by my daughter.

3 The air and water are being polluted by people.

4 The walls of the doghouse were being painted by the kids.

5 A new business is being developed by Mr. Jones.

6 The car is being repaired in the garage by Dad.

7 The dirty plates and bowls are being washed by Kate.

8 Used books were being sold at the flea market by Bob and Paul.

9 Dinner for his wife and children was being prepared by him.

10 The shooting incident is being investigated by the police.

PRACTICE 3

1 Her family portrait has been painted by a famous artist.

2 The school has never accepted cheating.

3 Songs have been composed for five years by Paul.

4 A graduation party has been held in December by the school.

5 The government has provided a free lunch for senior citizens.

6 This app has been used since last month by me.

7 A lot of endangered animals have been preserved for several years by the park.

8 The performance has been postponed several times by the director.

9 The volunteers have helped the kindergarten teachers.

10 The master has treated the servants cruelly.

PRACTICE 4

2 I was taught English grammar by my brother.
English grammar was taught to me by my brother.

3 A new laptop was bought for my sister by Dad.

4 He wasn't[was not] asked such stupid questions by me.
Such stupid questions weren't[were not] asked of him by me.

5 Her students were told surprising news about black holes by her.
Surprising news about black holes was told to her students by her.

6 A nice hotel was found for me by her.

7 Those visitors were lent the rooms by the villa owner.
The rooms were lent to those visitors by the villa owner.

8 I was given an honest opinion by her.
An honest opinion was given to me by her.

9 He was offered a good internship program by his professor.
A good internship program was offered to him by his professor.

10 A wooden boat will be made for me by my

grandfather.

> **3** buy는 직접목적어만을 수동태의 주어로 가질 수 있는 동사로, 간접목적어인 my sister를 주어로 하는 수동태 문장을 만들면 나의 동생을 구매한다(my sister was bought)는 의미가 되기 때문에 적절하지 않다.
> **6** find는 직접목적어만을 수동태의 주어로 가질 수 있는 동사로, 간접목적어인 me를 주어로 한 수동태 문장을 만들면 내가 찾는 행위를 당한다(I was found)는 의미가 되기 때문에 적절하지 않다.
> **10** make는 직접목적어만을 수동태의 주어로 가질 수 있는 동사로, 간접목적어인 me를 주어로 한 수동태 문장을 만들면 내가 만들어진다(I was made)는 의미가 되기 때문에 적절하지 않다.

PRACTICE 5

1 The hamster was named Steve by them.

2 They are always encouraged to do their best by the coach.

3 The suspect was found guilty of fraud by the prosecutor.

4 I am called Ice Princess by my friends.

5 The kitty was helped to get out of the box by the cat.

6 She was heard speaking some foreign language on the phone by him.

7 Jina was elected chief editor by the team.

8 An airplane was seen flying under the cloud by us.

9 The singer was made popular by the talk show.

10 He was expected to arrive in time by everyone.

> 5형식 문장을 수동태로 전환할 때는 능동태의 목적어와 목적격 보어가 각각 주어, 주격 보어가 된다. 능동태의 동사는 'be동사+과거분사' 형태로 바꾸고, be동사는 바뀐 주어의 인칭과 수, 동사의 시제에 일치시킨다. 능동태의 주어는 'by+목적격' 형태로 행위자를 나타낸다.
>
> **1, 3, 5, 6, 7, 8, 9, 10** 수동태의 주어가 3인칭 단수이고, 원래 문장의 시제가 과거이므로 be동사의 형태는 was가 적절하다.
> **2** 수동태의 주어가 복수이고, 원래 문장의 시제가 현재이므로 be동사의 형태는 are가 적절하다.
> **4** 수동태의 주어가 1인칭 단수이고, 원래 문장의 시제가 현재이므로 be동사의 형태는 am이 적절하다.

PRACTICE 6

1 His daughter was heard to play the flute in her room by him.

2 I was made to water the flowers by Jim.

3 Adam was seen to hang around the house at midnight by some people.

4 His sister was allowed to take a walk with his dog last night by him.

5 He was heard to make a strange sound by me.

6 She was made to run faster for a good record by him.

7 Minho was watched to carry the bag for the elderly by Susan.

8 The tea table was felt to shake slightly by me.

9 His daughter isn't[is not] allowed to leave for New York by him.

10 A lot of people were watched to walk across the street by John.

11 She wasn't[was not] allowed to borrow anything by me.

> 지각동사나 사역동사가 목적격 보어로 동사원형을 취하는 5형식 능동태 문장을 수동태로 전환할 때, 목적격 보어로 쓰인 동사원형은 수동태 문장에서 to부정사로 바뀐다.
>
> **4, 9, 11** 사역동사 let은 수동태 문장으로 전환될 때 'be allowed to+동사원형'으로 표현됨에 유의한다.

PRACTICE 7

1 He couldn't be caught up with by the police.

2 The old people were looked after by the volunteer workers.

3 This trick is made use of by many magicians.

4 My little son was taken care of in the daytime by my sister.

5 My brother was laughed at so hard by Brian.

6 The TV was turned off at midnight by Jihye.

7 Weak and poor people are looked down on by him.

8 The meeting with that company can't be put off anymore by us.

PRACTICE 8

2 It is thought that Daniel sang better than anyone else.
Daniel is thought to have sung better than anyone else.

3 It was reported that the man had been lost in the mountain.
The man was reported to have been lost in the mountain.

4 It is expected that the book will be published soon.

The book is expected to be published soon.

5 It is known that a friend in need is a friend indeed.

A friend in need is known to be a friend indeed.

6 It is said that English examinations are always difficult.

English examinations are said to be always difficult.

7 It was believed that the man had won the lottery.

The man was believed to have won the lottery.

8 It is supposed that the movie is awesome.

The movie is supposed to be awesome.

2~8 목적어로 that 절을 취한 동사(say, think, believe, report, know, expect, consider, suppose)가 사용된 문장을 수동태로 전환할 경우 두 가지 방식이 가능하다.

첫번째는 'It is~ that절'의 형태로 주어를 it으로 하고 주절의 동사를 「be동사(is/was)+과거분사」 형태로 바꾼 뒤, that절을 그 뒤에 쓴다. It이 가주어 that절이 진주어인 문장이다.

We think that Daniel sang better than anyone else.
주어 동사　　　　　　목적어(that절)

가주어(It)　be+과거분사　　　　　진주어(that절)
It is thought that Daniel sang better than anyone else.

두번째로 that절의 주어를 문장 전체의 주어로 하여 「be동사+과거분사+to부정사」의 형태로 만든다. 이때 that절의 동사를 to부정사의 형태로 바꾸어 쓴다. that 절의 시제가 주절의 시제보다 더 과거이면 다음과 같이 「be 동사+과거분사+to have p.p.」의 형태로 나타낸다.

We think that Daniel sang better than anyone else.
주어 동사(현재) that절 주어　　　that절 동사구(과거)

주어　be(현재)+과거분사　to have p.p.(완료부정사)
Daniel is thought to have sung better than anyone else.
(by us).

PRACTICE 9

1 interested in **2** excited at[about]

3 satisfied with **4** bored with

5 pleased with **6** worried about

7 made of **8** tired of

9 filled with **10** based on

11 covered with **12** known as

13 disappointed with[in] **14** known to

15 dressed in **16** surprised at[by]

17 made from **18** supposed to

Ch
4
수
동
태

중간·기말고사 대비문제 정답　본문 _ p.86

1 ⑤ **2** ④,⑤ **3** ② **4** The scientist was considered very intelligent by his colleagues.
5 ②,③ **6** were preparing for **7** ④
8 ⓐ was awarded ⓑ pleased with
9 ③ **10** were paid, was paid to **11** ④ **12** ③
13 was elected mayor of Seoul **14** ④
15 The soccer player was called a free kick artist (by them). **16** ① **17** are not allowed to cross **18** (1) was dressed in　(2) is known to
19 Her neighbors are always spoken ill of by her. [Her neighbors are always ill spoken of by her.] **20** was looked after **21** is believed that, believed to be **22** ⑤ **23** was believed, had become, was believed, have become
24 ③ **25** ② **26** is reported to be rising
27 The decision has been put off by the committee. **28** ⑤ **29** ②,④ **30** ③
31 was called off **32** The scientists have done a lot of studies on genes since the 18th century. **33** ③

중간·기말고사 대비문제 해설

1 ⑤ 타동사 consider의 목적어가 없고 목적격 보어 (friendly)만 있으므로 수동태로 써야 한다.
(are not considering → are not considered)

2 ④ 여기서는 간접목적어가 주어 자리에 나오므로 was asked 뒤에 직접목적어를 바로 쓴다.
(asked of → asked)
⑤ 「조동사+be+과거분사」 (fix → fixed)

3 ② 전치사 until과 by는 모두 '~까지'라는 의미이나 until은 '동작이나 상태가 한 시점까지 계속되는 것'을 나타내며 by는 '동작이나 상태가 완료되는 시점'을 나타낸다. 따라서 기한의 by를 사용하여 대답을 작성해야 한다. 이때 주어가 We일 경우 능동태(We must send them by this Thursday.)로, They(the invitation letters)일 경우 수동태

4 (They must be sent by this Thursday.)로 쓰는 것이 적절하다.

5형식 능동태 문장을 수동태 문장으로 전환할 때 목적격 보어를 「be동사+과거분사」 뒤에 그대로 이어서 쓴다. 따라서 동사 consider을 주어 The scientist의 수와, 시제에 맞춰 was considered로 작성한 뒤 목적격 보어 very intelligent를 이어서 쓴다.

5 ② 목적어(you)의 상태를 설명하는 형용사(itchy)가 목적격 보어 자리에 나왔다.

③ be known for: ~로 알려져 있다

① They(모기)가 발견되는 것이므로 수동태로 고쳐야 한다. (found → are found)

④ be worried about: ~에 대해 걱정하다
(from → about)

⑤ 등위접속사 and가 by 뒤의 동명사(wearing)를 연결하고 있으므로 동명사로 고쳐야 한다.
(use → using)

6 주어진 수동태 문장의 시제가 과거진행형이므로, 능동태 문장도 과거진행형으로 써야 한다.

7 ⓐ '오늘 아침부터 현재까지 계속 장치가 사용되고 있다'는 의미이므로, 과거부터 현재까지 지속되는 사건을 나타내는 현재완료 수동태로 써야 한다. 주어 The equipment가 3인칭 단수이므로 「has+been+과거분사」로 쓰는 것이 적절하다.
(had been used → has been used)

ⓓ '코치에 의해서 선수들은 훈련받을 것이다'라는 의미가 되어야 하므로 수동태로 써야 한다. 조동사가 있는 수동태는 「조동사+be+과거분사」의 어순으로 쓴다. (trained → be trained)

ⓔ 파티가 12월 5일에 열리는 것이므로 수동태로 써야 한다. 조동사가 있는 수동태는 「조동사+be+과거분사」의 어순으로 쓴다. (hold → be held)

8 ⓐ '메달을 수여받았다'라는 의미이므로 수동태 표현인 was awarded가 알맞다.

ⓑ '~에 대해 기뻐하다'는 수동태 be pleased with로 표현한다.

9 ③ 아빠가 서류를 지니고 있다는 의미이므로 수동태가 아닌 능동태를 써야 한다. be동사의 과거형 was가 밑줄 친 단어 앞에 있으므로 과거진행 시제를 쓰는 것이 적절하다. (carried → carrying) 아빠가 그의 팔 아래에 많은 서류를 지니고 있었다.

① 좌석이 이용되고 있냐(좌석의 주인이 있냐)는 의미이므로 수동태(are taken)를 쓰는 것은 적절하다. 이 자리들은 주인이 있나요?

② 누가 음식을 제공할 것이냐는 의미이므로 능동태(be catering)를 쓰는 것은 적절하다. 누가 결혼식의 음식을 제공할 것이니?

④ 더 젊어지고 있다는 의미이므로 능동태(be getting)를 쓰는 것은 적절하다. 왜 그 배우는 점점 더 젊어지고 있는 것처럼 보이지?

⑤ 조언이 주어졌다는 의미이므로 수동태(was given)를 쓰는 것은 적절하다. 조언은 그녀가 올바른 결정을 내리는 걸 돕기 위해 주어졌다.

10 4형식 문장은 원칙적으로 직접목적어와 간접목적어를 각각 주어로 하는 2개의 수동태로 바꿀 수 있다. 동사 pay가 쓰인 4형식 문장을 수동태로 바꿀 때, 직접목적어가 수동태의 주어인 경우에는, 간접목적어 앞에 전치사 to를 쓴다.

11 ⓒ '학교 체육관을 이용하기 원하는 사람들은 특정 날짜와 시간을 우리 학교 웹사이트에서 예약해야 한다'는 의미이므로 동사는 수동이 아닌 능동이어야 한다. (may be reserved → may reserve)

12 4형식 문장을 3형식으로 전환하는 것과 마찬가지로, 4형식 문장을 수동태로 전환할 때 직접목적어가 수동태의 주어가 되는 경우에는 간접목적어 앞에 to, for, of와 같은 전치사를 써주어야 한다. write는 to를, ask는 of를 쓰는 동사이며, buy, cook, make는 for을 쓴다.

① (to → for)　　② (to → for)
④ (to → for)　　⑤ (for → to)

13 5형식 능동태 문장을 수동태 문장으로 전환할 때 목적격 보어인 명사는 「be동사+과거분사」 뒤에 그대로 이어서 쓴다.

14 동사 choose, write, buy, cook은 직접목적어만을 수동태의 주어로 쓴다.

15 5형식 능동태 문장을 수동태 문장으로 전환할 때 목적격 보어인 명사는 「be동사+과거분사」 뒤에 그대로 이어서 쓰고 주어는 목적격으로 바꿔 「by+목적격」 형태로 문장 맨 끝에 쓴다.

16 ① 지각동사(heard)의 목적격 보어가 동사원형인 능동태 문장을 수동태 문장으로 바꿀 때 동사원형은 to부정사로 바뀐다. (cry → to cry)

17 사역동사 let은 수동태 문장으로 전환될 때 「be allowed+to부정사」로 표현된다.

18 (1) be dressed in '~을 입고 있다'
(2) be known to '~에게 알려지다'

19 동사구가 있는 문장을 수동태로 전환할 때는 동사구를 하나의 단어처럼 취급하여 붙여 쓴다. speak ill of는 '~에 대해 안 좋게 말하다'라는 관용표현이다.

20 동사구가 있는 문장을 수동태로 전환할 때는 동사구를 하나의 단어처럼 취급하여 붙여 쓴다. look after은 '~을 돌보다'라는 의미로 take care of와 같은 뜻이다.

21 believe의 목적어가 that이 이끄는 절일 때는 「It is believed that …」이나 「that절의 주어+is believed to+동사원형」의 형태로 수동태를 만들 수 있다.

22 ⑤ 개집이 나의 아버지에 의해 만들어진 것이므로 행위자를 나타내는 전치사 by를 쓰는 것이 적절하다. (for my father → by my father)

23 주어진 문장의 동사 believed의 목적어가 that이 이끄는 절이므로 「It was ~ that …」이나 that절의 3인칭 단수 주어 he를 주어로 하여 「주어+was+p.p.+to부정사」의 형태로 수동태를 만들 수 있다. that절의 시제(과거완료)가 주절의 시제(과거)보다 앞서기 때문에 to부정사는 「to+have p.p.」 형태로 쓴다.

24 • be covered with '~로 덮여 있다'
• be known to '~에게 알려지다'
• be made from '~로 만들어지다' - 일련의 과정을 거쳐 재료의 성질이 변한 경우

25 ② be filled with '~로 가득 차다' (of → with)

26 report의 목적어가 that이 이끄는 절일 때는 「that절의 주어+is reported to+동사원형」의 형태로 수동태를 만들 수 있다. that절의 시제가 현재진행시제이므로 be rising을 쓰는 것이 적절하다.

27 현재완료의 수동태는 「have/has+been+과거분사」로 쓴다. 동사구가 있는 문장을 수동태로 전환할 때는 동사구를 하나의 단어처럼 취급하여 붙여 쓴다. put off는 '미루다, 연기하다'는 뜻의 동사구이다.

28 ⑤ be known as '~로 알려져 있다' (to → as)

29 ② be made from '~로 만들어지다'
④ be known to '~에게 알려지다'
① be mad at '~에게 화를 내다' (for → at)
③ be proud of '~을 자랑스러워하다' (with → of)
⑤ consist of '~로 구성되다' (with → of)

30 행위자를 나타낼 때는 「by+목적격」으로 쓴다. 전화가 회의를 방해한 행위자이므로 the call의 앞에는 by가 들어간다. 나머지는 수동태와 전치사 in을 사용한 관용표현이다.
③ by   ①②④⑤ in

31 동사구가 있는 문장을 수동태로 전환할 때는 동사구를 하나의 단어처럼 취급하여 붙여 쓴다. call off는 '취소하다'라는 뜻의 동사구이다.

32 완료형의 수동태를 능동태로 바꿀 때는 「have/has+과거분사」의 어순으로 쓴다.

33 ② 첫 번째 문장:
선행사가 없으며 뒤에 불완전한 절이 이어지므로 관계대명사 which가 아닌 선행사를 포함한 관계대명사 what을 써야 한다. (which → what)
③ 첫 번째 문장:
appear는 자동사이므로 수동태 표현이 불가능하다. (was appeared → appeared)
두 번째 문장:
책(the book)이 '출간되는' 것이므로 수동태 표현으로 고쳐야 한다. (publishes → is published)
④ 첫 번째 문장:
「let+목적어+동사원형」 구조가 되어야 한다. 불필요한 논쟁에 스스로를 끌어들이지 말라는 의미이므로 수동형을 쓰는 것이 적절하다.
(drawn → be drawn)
⑤ 첫 번째 문장:
사역동사 make가 포함된 수동태 문장이다. 「사역동사+목적어+목적격 보어(동사원형)」 형태의 5형식 문장이 수동태로 전환되면 목적격 보어가 'to+동사원형' 형태로 바뀐다. (waiting → to wait)

① • 이번 회의는 지금까지 우리가 가진 회의 중 가장 유익한 회의 중 하나였다.
• Tom은 나에게 3일 전에 전화했고, 나는 이후로 그와 얘기하지 않았다.
② • 사람들은 보통 자신이 찾고 있는 것을 보고, 자신이 들으려 하는 것을 듣는다.
• 사람이 공정한 대우를 받아야 하는 한 곳은 법정이다.
③ • 일몰 직후 산 위로 달이 나타났다.
• 책이 출간되기 전에, 그것은 정확성을 위해 몇몇 편집자들에 의해 검토된다.
④ • 스스로를 불필요한 논쟁에 휘말리게 하지 마라.
• 날씨 조건으로 인해 행사가 취소되면, 문자 메시지를 통해 공지가 전달될 것이다.
⑤ • 나는 의사에게 진료를 받기 전에 4시간 동안 기다려야 했다.
• 정부는 폭력 범죄의 증가에 대해 무엇인가를 하고 있는 것으로 보여야 한다.

PRACTICE 1

1	citizens	2	witnesses
3	dictionaries	4	journeys
5	addresses	6	straws
7	nails	8	calendars
9	therapies	10	astronauts
11	mazes	12	foxes
13	tombs	14	bottles
15	guys	16	employees
17	bunches	18	dinosaurs
19	peaks	20	copies
21	matches	22	languages
23	awards	24	dynasties
25	radishes	26	photocopiers
27	troops	28	toothbrushes
29	fairies	30	wishes
31	foreigners	32	stomachs
33	gases	34	monkeys
35	ways	36	prizes
37	souvenirs	38	principles
39	cobras	40	bushes
41	programs	42	essays
43	crabs	44	scratches
45	branches	46	babies
47	festivals	48	activities
49	eyebrows	50	opinions
51	accidents	52	professors
53	batteries	54	clients
55	factors	56	helmets
57	janitors	58	memories
59	symptoms	60	consumers
61	histories	62	magazines
63	pennies/pence	64	agents
65	bricks	66	chapters
67	sandwiches	68	columns
69	portraits	70	sketches
7	men	8	weeds
9	studios	10	cliffs
11	scarves/scarfs	12	kangaroos
13	thieves	14	sheep
15	bases	16	promises
17	teeth	18	leaves
19	volcanos/volcanoes	20	mice
21	safes	22	Japanese
23	pianos	24	reporters
25	children	26	factories
27	geese	28	feet
29	deer	30	chiefs
31	beliefs	32	keys
33	tomatoes	34	flashes
35	medicines	36	mixes
37	lives	38	calves
39	oxen	40	couches
41	aprons	42	canaries
43	characters	44	receipts
45	housewives	46	cherries
47	assistants	48	enemies
49	guests	50	instructors
51	groceries	52	proofs
53	witches	54	hobbies
55	markets	56	railways
57	architects	58	handles
59	shampoos	60	wolves
61	rumors	62	donkeys
63	ghosts	64	watches
65	methods	66	puppies
67	donuts	68	articles
69	harbors	70	zoos
71	symbols	72	designers
73	palaces	74	chimneys
75	fishermen	76	reefs
77	tailors	78	skills
79	satellites	80	instruments

PRACTICE 2

1	roofs	2	potatoes
3	heroes	4	fish/fishes
5	radios	6	Swiss

PRACTICE 3

1	girlfriends
2	brothers-in-law

3 passers-by

4 commanders in chief

5 fountain pens

6 boyfriends

7 mothers-in-law

8 mothers-to-be

9 application forms

10 merry-go-rounds

PRACTICE 4

1 apron

2 is, are

3 have

4 is

5 teams

6 was, were

7 problem

8 have

9 families

10 tricks

11 has

12 aren't

13 teams

14 was

15 activities

1, 7 a+셀 수 있는 명사의 단수형 <u>a</u> green apron / <u>a</u> serious money problem
2, 6 The class(학급)와 The audience(청중)와 같은 집합명사는 문맥에 따라 하나의 집단을 의미할 경우 단수 취급하고, 개개인의 구성원을 강조할 경우에는 복수 취급한다.
3, 8 집합 명사 The police, people은 복수 취급한다.
4, 11 family(가족), team(팀)이 하나의 집단(단위)의 의미로 쓰일 때는 단수 취급한다.
5 There are+복수 명사
9 동사(are)가 복수형이므로 주어도 복수형(families)을 써야 한다.
10 several+복수 명사
12 'either A or B: A 또는 B 중 하나'의 동사는 B의 수에 일치시킨다.
13 다섯 팀이 있으므로 명사는 복수형으로 써야 한다.
14 앞서 'a bowling class (볼링 강좌)'라고 언급하였으므로 the class는 단수이며 따라서 be동사는 was를 쓰는 것이 적절하다.
15 복수형 동사 provide가 쓰였기 때문에, 주어는 복수형 명사를 써야 한다.

PRACTICE 5

1 Japan

2 package

3 furniture

4 money

5 leaves

6 homework

7 advice

8 Thursday

9 math

10 music

11 restaurants

12 honesty

13 countries

1 국가 이름 앞에는 관사를 쓰지 않는다.
2 부정관사 a가 쓰였으므로 단수형(package)으로 써야 한다.
3 furniture(가구)는 집합명사이지만 물질명사 취급하여 복수형을 쓰지 않는다.
4 money(돈)는 물질명사이므로 복수형으로 쓰지 않는다.
5 동사가 복수형(are)이므로 주어도 복수형(leaves)으로 써야 한다.
6 homework(숙제)는 셀 수 없는 명사이므로 복수형으로 쓰지 않는다.
7, 12 추상명사인 advice(충고)와 honesty(정직)는 복수형으로 쓰거나 부정관사 a/an과 함께 쓰일 수 없다.
8 요일(Thursday) 앞에는 관사를 쓰지 않는다.
9 과목명(math) 앞에는 관사를 쓰지 않는다.
10 listen to music: 음악을 듣다
11 several+복수명사(restaurants)
13 many+복수명사(countries)

PRACTICE 6

1 pieces[slices/loaves] of bread

2 piece[sheet] of paper

3 glasses[cups] of orange juice

4 bars of soap

5 piece[slice] of cheese

6 bottles[glasses] of beer

7 cup of green tea

8 pieces of cloth

9 spoonfuls[teaspoonfuls] of sugar

10 pound of meat

11 bowl of onion soup

12 pieces of advice

13 bowls of fried rice

14 pieces of furniture

15 glass[bottle] of wine

PRACTICE 7

1 valuable

2 of no use

3 wise

4 with ease

5 punctually

6 of importance

7 courageous

8 with kindness

9 of use

10 purposely

1 of value = valuable
2 useless = of no use
3 of wisdom = wise
4 easily = with ease
5 on time = punctually
6 important = of importance
7 of courage = courageous
8 kindly = with kindness
9 useful = of use
10 on purpose = purposely

PRACTICE 8

1 his sister's smile

2 the legs of the sofa

3 The manager's office

4 the front seat of the car

5 The twins' eyes

6 thirty minutes' walk

7 next week's meeting

8 Mr. and Mrs. Wilson's house

9 the top of the page

10 other people's opinions

11 women's clothing department

12 the bottom of the fountain

13 the cost of the air conditioner

14 girls' high schools

15 yesterday's newspaper

16 Tomorrow's weather

> **1, 3** 사람을 나타내는 명사의 소유격 중 단수 명사의 소유격은 「단수명사+'s」로 표현한다.
> **2, 4, 9, 12, 13** 무생물의 소유격은 「of+명사」로 표현한다.
> **5, 14** 사람을 나타내는 명사의 소유격 중 복수 명사의 소유격은 「복수명사+'」로 표현한다.
> **6, 7, 15, 16** thirty minutes, next week, yesterday, tomorrow와 같이 시간을 나타내는 명사의 소유격은 무생물이지만 「단수명사+'s」, 「복수명사+'」로 나타낸다.
> **8** 'Mr. and Mrs.+성'은 '부부'라는 뜻으로 복수 취급하지만, -s로 끝나지 않으므로 소유격은 Mr. and Mrs. Wilson's로 쓴다.
> **10, 11** people, women처럼 명사의 복수형이 -s로 끝나지 않는 경우에 소유격은 「복수 명사+'s」로 쓴다.

PRACTICE 9

1 a friend of mine

2 no business of yours

3 This cell phone of my brother's

4 a relative of hers

5 a good idea of yours

6 some friends of my brother's

PRACTICE 10

1 an **2** a **3** a **4** an **5** a
6 an **7** a **8** a **9** an **10** an
11 a

PRACTICE 11

1 ① **2** ⑤ **3** ④ **4** ② **5** ⑥
6 ③ **7** ④ **8** ② **9** ⑤ **10** ①

> **1** for a day or two: 하루나 이틀 동안 (one: 하나의)
> **2** once a week: 일주일에 한 번 (per: ~마다, ~당)
> **3** Birds of a feather: 같은 깃털을 가진 새들 (the same: 같은, 동일한) / 같은 깃털의 새들끼리 모인다. (유유상종)
> **4** 사람의 이름 앞에 'a'가 쓰이면 '~라는 사람'이라는 뜻을 갖는다. (a certain: 어떤)
> **5** A dolphin은 돌고래 종족 전체를 나타내므로 a는 대표단수를 나타내는 역할을 하고 있다. 대표단수를 표현하는 또 다른 방법은 The dolphin(The+단수명사), Dolphins(복수형)가 있다.
> **6** after a while: 잠시 후에 (some: 약간의)
> **7** of an age: 같은 나이의, 동갑의 (the same: 같은, 동일한)
> **8** in a way: 어떤 면에서 (a certain: 어떤)
> **9** twice a year: 일 년에 두 번 (per: ~마다, ~당)
> **10** a son: 한 명의 아들 (one: 하나의)

PRACTICE 12

1 a, The **2** a **3** the **4** an
5 the **6** the **7** the **8** a
9 the **10** the

> **1** '하나'의 뜻을 나타낼 때는 a를 쓰고, 앞에 나온 명사가 다시 반복될 때는 'the+명사'를 쓴다.
> **2** '~당, ~마다'를 표현할 때는 a를 쓰는 것이 적절하다. (once a month: 한 달에 한 번)
> **3, 7** Moon, universe처럼 유일한 것을 말할 때 the를 쓴다.
> **4** '~당, ~마다'의 의미를 가지는 것이 적절하므로 an을 써야 한다. (80 kilometers an hour: 시간당 80km)
> **5, 6, 10** same, 최상급, 서수 앞에는 the를 쓴다.
> **8** a while은 '잠시, 잠깐'이라는 뜻으로, a가 some '약간의, 어느 정도'의 의미를 나타낸다.
> **9** 문맥이나 상황으로 보아 말하는 사람이 무엇을 가리키는지 알 수 있을 때 the를 쓴다.

PRACTICE 13

1 the, the **2** the **3** an **4** the
5 the **6** a **7** the **8** A
9 a **10** The

> **1** the+형용사: ~한 사람들
> (the elderly: 노인들, the pregnant: 임산부들)
> **2, 7** 동작의 대상이 되는 신체의 일부를 나타낼 때 the를 쓴다. (hit me on the head: 내 머리를 치다, look him in the eye: 그의 눈을 바라보다)
> **3** '하나의'라는 뜻을 나타낼 때는 a/an을 쓴다. (an hour: 한 시간)
> **4** the+악기명
> **5** the+특정 고유 명사 (the Philippines: 필리핀 국가)
> **6** a glass of water: 물 한 잔, 셀 수 없는 물질명사는 「수사+단위명사+of+물질명사」로 표현하여 수량을 나타낸다.
> **8** a+사람 이름: ~라는 사람
> **9** per '~당, ~마다'를 표현할 때는 a를 쓴다.
> **10** 절이 뒤에서 명사를 꾸며 줄 때, 수식을 받는 명사 앞에 the를 쓴다.

PRACTICE 14

1 X	**2** X	**3** O	**4** O	**5** O
6 X	**7** O	**8** O	**9** O	**10** X
11 X	**12** X			

PRACTICE 15

1 X	**2** the	**3** a	**4** X	**5** the
6 X	**7** a	**8** X	**9** X	**10** A
11 the	**12** the			

> **1** 식사를 나타내는 명사 앞에는 관사를 쓰지 않는다.
> **2** 말하는 사람이 무엇을 가리키는지 알 수 있는 대상을 나타낼 때는 the를 쓴다.
> **3** per '~당, ~마다'를 표현할 때는 a를 쓴다.
> **4** 「by+교통수단」으로 쓰일 때는 관사를 쓰지 않는다.
> **5, 11** only와 very 앞에는 the를 쓴다.
> **6** 장소를 나타내는 명사가 본래 목적으로 쓰일 때는 관사를 쓰지 않는다. (go to church: 교회에 예배 드리러 가다)
> **7** hold a minute: 잠깐 기다리다
> **8** 가족 구성원을 나타내는 명사 앞에는 관사를 쓰지 않는다.
> **9** 운동 경기를 나타내는 명사 앞에는 관사를 쓰지 않는다.
> **10** 소유격은 관사와 나란히 쓰일 수 없으므로 이중소유격 어순인 「a+명사+of+소유대명사」로 표현한다.
> (A friend of mine: 나의 친구 중 한 명)
> **12** the+형용사: ~한 사람들 (the old: 노인들)

중간·기말고사 대비문제 정답   본문 _ p.111

1 ②   **2** ⓑ many → much[a lot of/lots of], ⓓ few → little, ⓔ many homeworks → much[a lot of/lots of] homework   **3** of use   **4** ④
5 potato → potatoes   **6** ③,⑤   **7** with ease
8 ②   **9** of mine   **10** ④   **11** ⑤   **12** ③
13 (A) some classmates of mine study on holidays, too.   (B) I'm going to have dinner with a friend of mine.   **14** ③   **15** by   **16** ①
17 school → the school   **18** ②   **19** me, the
20 (A) my dad told me to handle it with care (B) my mom said that she would arrive home on time   **21** the young   **22** ①   **23** on purpose
24 ③   **25** ④   **26** ②   **27** ①   **28** ⑤   **29** ③
30 ③   **31** ⑤   **32** your sister's some books → some books of your sister's[some of your sister's books]   **33** ③   **34** ⑤   **35** ④

중간·기말고사 대비문제 해설

1 복합명사는 가장 중요한 의미를 가진 단어에 '-s'나 '-es'를 붙여 복수형을 만든다.

2 ⓑ many는 셀 수 있는 명사를 수식한다. information은 셀 수 없는 명사이므로, 셀 수 없는 명사를 수식하는 much나 같은 뜻의 a lot of[lots of]로 고쳐야 한다.
(many → much[a lot of/lots of])
ⓓ few는 셀 수 있는 명사를 수식한다. money는 셀 수 없는 명사이므로, 셀 수 없는 명사를 수식하는 little로 고쳐야 한다. (few → little)
ⓔ many는 셀 수 있는 명사를 수식한다. homework는 셀 수 없는 명사이므로 복수형으로 쓸 수 없다. 따라서 셀 수 없는 명사를 수식하는 much나 같은 뜻의 a lot of[lots of]로 고쳐야 한다.
(many homeworks → much[a lot of/lots of] homework)

3 of use = useful '유용한'

4 ① -ch로 끝나는 명사는 명사에 -es를 붙여 복수형을 만든다. (matchs → matches)
② way는 '방법'이라는 뜻의 셀 수 있는 명사이다. 셀 수 있는 명사는 관사와 함께 쓰거나, 관사가 없을 때는 복수형으로 써야 한다. (different way → different ways[a different way])
③ 이를 하나만 닦는 것이 아니라 여러 개를 닦으므로 복수형으로 써야 한다. tooth는 불규칙 변화하는 명사로 복수형을 teeth로 쓴다. (tooth → teeth)
⑤ -f로 끝나는 명사 leaf의 복수형은 f를 v로 바꾸고 -es를 붙여 만든다. (leafs → leaves)

5 fried potatoes(감자 튀김)는 복수형으로 쓴다.

6 ③ photo는 -o로 끝나는 명사이지만 -s를 붙여 복수형을 만든다. (photoes → photos)
⑤ -f로 끝나는 명사 thief의 복수형은 f를 v로 바꾸고 -es를 붙여 만든다. (thiefs → thieves)

7 easily = with ease '쉽게'

8 ② 시간을 나타내는 명사(today)의 소유격은 무생물이지만 's로 나타낸다. (the newspaper of today → today's newspaper)

9 소유격은 부정대명사와 나란히 쓸 수 없으므로 「of+소유대명사」의 형태로 명사 뒤에 이어서 쓴다.

10 ④ 맥주는 덩어리가 아닌 병이나 잔 단위로 세야 한다.
(a loaf of beer → a glass[bottle] of beer)

11 ⑤ '~당, 마다'
①②③④ '하나의'

12 ③ police와 같은 집합명사는 형태는 단수형이지만 복수 취급한다. (is → are)

13 소유격은 부정대명사, 관사와 나란히 쓸 수 없으므로 「of+소유대명사」의 형태로 명사 뒤에 이어서 쓴다.

14 ① hour은 h가 묵음으로 소리나지 않는다. 즉, 단어의 첫소리가 모음으로 발음되므로 부정관사 an을 쓴다. (a hour → an hour)
② 명사 앞의 형용사의 첫소리가 모음으로 발음되므로 부정관사 an을 써야 한다.
(a old woman → an old woman)
④ university는 첫소리가 [ju]로 발음되므로 자음으로 시작한다. 따라서 부정관사 a를 써야 한다.
(an university → a university)
⑤ European은 첫소리가 [ju]로 발음된다. 즉, 명사 앞의 형용사의 첫소리가 자음으로 발음되므로 부정관사 a를 써야 한다. (an European country → a European country)

15 in+부정관사+교통수단 = by+교통수단 '~을 타고'

16 서수와 악기명의 앞에는 정관사 the를 쓰며, 식사와 운동경기를 나타내는 말의 앞에는 관사를 쓰지 않는다.
② second → the second
③ the dinner → dinner
④ drums → the drums
⑤ the baseball → baseball

17 장소를 나타내는 명사 앞에 관사가 붙지 않으면 본래의 목적을 나타낸다. 따라서 'go to school'은 '공부를 하러 학교에 가다'의 의미가 된다. 여기서는 선생님을 방문하러 학교에 가는 것이므로 school 앞에 the가 붙어야 한다.

18 ② 전치사 뒤에는 명사가 나온다. 따라서 for 다음에 올 말을 '집 없는 사람들'이라는 뜻의 the homeless나 homeless people로 고쳐야 한다.
(homeless → the homeless[homeless people])

19 동작의 대상이 되는 신체의 일부 앞에는 the를 붙인다.

20 with care=carefully '조심스럽게',
on time=punctually '제시간에'

21 the+형용사 = 형용사+people '~한 사람들'

22 ② 최상급의 앞에는 정관사를 쓴다.

(a most → the most)
③ 과목을 나타내는 명사 앞에는 관사를 쓰지 않는다.
(The math → Math)
④ 가족 구성원을 나타내는 명사 앞에는 관사를 쓰지 않는다. (a father → father)
⑤ only의 앞에는 정관사를 쓴다.
(Only thing → The only thing)

23 on+추상명사 = 부사
on purpose = purposely '고의로'

24 ③ 복합명사의 복수형은 가장 중요한 의미를 가진 단어에 '-s'를 붙여 만든다.
(applications forms → application forms)

25 ① woman은 첫소리가 자음[wu]으로 발음되므로 부정관사 a를 써야 한다. (an woman → a woman)
② UFO는 첫소리가 [ju]로 발음된다. 따라서 명사의 발음이 자음으로 시작되므로 부정관사 a를 써야 한다. (an UFO → a UFO)
③ wheelchair는 첫소리가 자음[wil]로 시작하므로 부정관사 a를 써야 한다.
(an wheelchair → a wheelchair)
⑤ artist는 첫소리가 모음으로 시작하므로 부정관사 an을 써야 한다. (a artist → an artist)

26 (b) so that은 목적을 나타낼 때 쓰며, '~하기 위해서, ~하도록'을 의미한다.
(a) 사역동사 make는 목적격 보어로 원형부정사를 가진다. (to run → run)
(c) 주절이 과거 시제이므로 종속절의 시제는 과거 또는 과거완료가 되어야 한다. 이때 '실험이 성공이었다는 것'이 '선생님이 말해주신 것'보다 이전의 일이므로 과거완료 시제를 쓰는 것이 적절하다.
(is → had been)
(d) Only after를 강조하기 위해 문장의 맨 앞으로 가져올 때 주어와 동사의 도치가 일어난다.
(we realized → did we realize)
(e) equipment는 셀 수 없는 명사이므로 앞에 a(n)을 붙이거나 복수형으로 쓸 수 없다.
(a equipment → (the) equipment)

27 ① snow는 셀 수 없는 명사이므로 셀 수 없는 명사를 수식하는 little을 써야 한다. (few → little)

28 ⑤ belief는 -f로 끝나지만 -s를 붙여 복수형을 만든다. (belief → beliefs)

29 ③ 서수의 앞에는 정관사를 쓴다.
①⑤ listen to music과 watch TV는 관용적으로 관

사 없이 쓴다.
② 운동 경기명 앞에는 the를 쓰지 않는다.
④ 식사명에는 the가 붙지 않는다.

30 '~한 것 같다'는 「It seems that ~」이나 「that절의 주어+seem(s)+to부정사」로 나타낼 수 있다. 과목명은 항상 단수 취급하고 정관사 the를 필요로 하지 않는다.

31 ⑤ -s로 끝나는 명사의 복수형은 「복수명사+'」로 소유격을 만든다. (others's → others')

32 소유격은 부정대명사와 나란히 쓸 수 없으므로 「some+명사+of+소유대명사/'s」 형태로 바꾸어 쓴다.

33 ③ '하루에 사과 하나'라는 의미는 '~당, ~마다'라는 의미의 부정관사를 통해 나타낼 수 있다.
(the day → a day)

34 물질명사의 수량이 2 이상인 경우에는 단위명사에

-(e)s를 붙인다.

35 ④ 명사 economic problems를 수식하는 형용사가 오는 것이 알맞다. (persistence → persistent)
그 나라는 끊임없이 지속되는 경제 문제들로부터 고통받아 왔다.
① one of the+복수명사 '~한 것들 중의 하나'
그녀는 우리의 결혼식에서 증인들 중 하나였다.
② of no use = useless '쓸모 없는' 만약 우리가 재료들을 갖고 있지 않다면 레시피는 쓸모 없다.
③ 명사 reef의 복수형은 reefs이다.
기름 유출은 바다의 산호초에 파괴적인 영향을 미치고 있다.
⑤ 전치사(in) 뒤에 명사가 오는 것은 적절하다. in haste = hastily(서둘러) 서둘러 짐을 싸면서, 나는 내가 가장 좋아하는 책을 놓아 둔 채 잊고 왔다.

Ch 6 대명사

<table><tr><td>CHAPTER 6</td><td><h1>대명사</h1>Pronouns</td><td>본문 _ p.118</td></tr></table>

PRACTICE 1

1 myself	**2** herself	**3** himself
4 you	**5** me	**6** yourself
7 herself	**8** us	**9** yourself
10 herself	**11** them	**12** her
13 themselves	**14** herself	**15** me

> **1, 10** by oneself: 혼자
> **2** be oneself: (남의 영향을 받지 않고) 평소의 자기 모습 그대로이다
> **3** for oneself: 혼자 힘으로
> **4, 5, 8, 11, 12, 15** 주어와 목적어가 가리키는 대상이 다를 때는 동사나 전치사 다음에 재귀대명사가 아닌 인칭대명사의 목적격을 쓴다.
> **6** 주어와 목적어가 가리키는 대상이 같을 때는 목적어 자리에 재귀대명사를 쓴다. 명령문의 주어는 you가 생략된 것으로 간주하기 때문에 재귀대명사는 yourself가 적절하다.
> **7** seem oneself: 평상시와 같아 보이다
> **9** help oneself (to): ~을 마음껏 먹다
> **13** to oneself: 혼자(독차지하는)
> **14** cry oneself to sleep: 울다 잠이 들다, 잘 때까지 계속 울다

PRACTICE 2

1 생략할 수 없음	**2** (himself)
3 (themselves)	**4** 생략할 수 없음
5 생략할 수 없음	**6** (myself)
7 (herself)	**8** 생략할 수 없음
9 생략할 수 없음	**10** (himself)

> **1, 4** 재귀대명사가 전치사 to, for의 목적어로 사용되어 생략 불가능하다.
> **2, 3, 6, 7, 10** 재귀대명사가 명사나 대명사를 강조하기 위한 강조적 용법으로 쓰였고, 재귀대명사를 생략해도 문장이 완성된다.
> **5** yourself가 간접목적어로 사용되어 생략 불가능하다.
> **8** make oneself understood: 스스로를 (타인에게) 이해시키다
> **9** by oneself: 혼자, 다른 사람 없이

PRACTICE 3

1 It is necessary to participate in the debate.

2 I found it hard to tell the difference between the two paintings.

3 It was a lot of fun playing board games with friends.

4 I find it strange being here.

5 It is certain that Mr. Garcia will get promoted quickly.

6 It is interesting to learn foreign languages.

7 It was a pleasure dining with you at the new restaurant.

8 It is shocking that Tony broke the window on purpose.

9 She found it a lot of fun reading science fiction.

10 I thought it a good idea to seek others' opinions.

> **1, 6** it: 가주어, to부정사구: 진주어
> **2, 10** it: 가목적어, to부정사구: 진목적어
> **3, 7** it: 가주어, 동명사구: 진주어
> **4, 9** it: 가목적어, 동명사구: 진목적어
> **5, 8** it: 가주어, 명사절(that절): 진주어

PRACTICE 4

1 They appeared to know the truth about my family.

2 It happened that there was no one at home.

3 It seems that my brother has a plan to stay at my uncle's for a while.

4 It appears that she feels quite satisfied with the result.

5 The teacher happened to show up very late.

PRACTICE 5

1	②	**2**	⑤	**3**	③
4	①	**5**	④		

> **1** ② 문장에서 to부정사구(to join the club)와 동명사구(going on a field trip)를 대신하여 it이 가주어 역할을 한다.
> **2** ⑤ 문장에서 'It seems that ~', 'It appears that ~' (~인 것 같다) 구문이 쓰였다.
> **3** ③ 문장에서 it이 (관용적 표현에서 사용하는) 상황을 나타내는 it으로 쓰였다. 'make it'은 '(모임 등에) 참석하다'라는 뜻이며, 'it is over'은 '(상황이) 끝났다'라는 뜻이다.
> **4** ① 각각 to부정사구(to spend my holiday with Chris)와 동명사구(going there by myself)를 대신하여 it이 가목적어 역할을 한다.
> **5** ④「It ~ that …」강조 구문

PRACTICE 6

1	①	**2**	③	**3**	②
4	⑤	**5**	④	**6**	①

7	④	**8**	③	**9**	⑤
10	②				

> **1** 동명사구(crying over spilt milk)를 대신하여 it이 가주어 역할을 한다.
> **3** 동명사구(having a variety of foreign friends)를 대신하여 it이 가목적어 역할을 한다.
> **4** 주어(Ms. Lopez)를 강조하는 It ~ that 강조 구문이다.
> **5** 'take it easy'는 관용어구로 '진정해, 마음을 편하게 가져'라는 뜻으로 여기에서 it은 상황을 나타내는 it으로 쓰였다. 이때의 it은 따로 해석하지 않는다.
> **6** 길이가 긴 that절을 대신하여 it이 가주어 역할을 한다.
> **7** 'How is it going with you?'는 '(안부를 묻는 표현) 너 어떻게 지내?'라는 뜻을 갖는다. 관용어구에 쓰인 it은 상황을 나타내는 it이며 굳이 해석하지 않는다.
> **9** 직접목적어(a personal question)를 강조하는 It ~ that 강조 구문이다.
> **10** to부정사구(to read the newspaper every morning)를 대신하여 it이 가목적어 역할을 한다.

PRACTICE 7

1	it	**2**	one	**3**	one
4	ones	**5**	it	**6**	them
7	ones	**8**	one	**9**	one
10	ones	**11**	one	**12**	it
13	it	**14**	one	**15**	them
16	One	**17**	one	**18**	them

> **1, 5, 6, 12, 13, 15, 18** 앞에 언급된 특정 대상을 가리킬 때는 가리키는 대상이 단수면 it, 복수면 them을 쓴다.
> **2, 3, 4, 7, 8, 9, 10, 11, 14, 17** 앞에 나온 명사와 종류는 같지만, 대상이 다를 때 반복을 피하기 위해서 부정대명사 one(단수), ones(복수)를 쓴다.
> **16** 일반적인 사람들을 나타낼 때 부정대명사 one을 쓴다.

PRACTICE 8

1	the other	**2**	others
3	The others	**4**	another
5	other	**6**	others
7	the other	**8**	others
9	the others	**10**	another
11	other	**12**	another
13	the others	**14**	other

> **1, 7** 둘 중 하나는 one, 나머지는 the other로 지칭한다.
> **2, 6, 8** others: (불특정한) 다른 사람들
> **3, 9, 13** the others: 나머지 사람[것]들
> **4, 10, 12** another+단수명사, other는 뒤에 복수 명사가 와야 한다.
> **5, 11, 14** other+복수명사, another은 뒤에 단수 명사가 온다.

PRACTICE 9

1	The others	**2**	the other
3	the other	**4**	the others
5	another	**6**	the others
7	others		
8	One, another, the other		
9	One, the other	**10**	Some, the others
11	One, the other	**12**	the other
13	others	**14**	the others
15	another	**16**	One, the other
17	others	**18**	The others

> **1, 14** one ~ the others … : (셋 이상에서) 하나는 ~, 나머지는 …
> **2, 9, 11, 16** one ~ the other … : (둘 중에) 하나는 ~, 다른 하나는 …
> **3, 8, 12** one ~ another … the other – : (셋 중에) 하나는 ~, 다른 하나는 …, 나머지 하나는 –
> **4, 6, 10, 18** some ~ the others … : (특정한 수의 사람[것]들 중에서) 몇몇은 ~, 나머지는 …
> **5, 15** one ~ another … : (셋 이상에서) 하나는 ~, 다른 하나는 …
> **7, 13, 17** some ~ others … : (불특정한 수의 사람[것]들 중에서) 몇몇은 ~, 다른 사람[것]들은 …

PRACTICE 10

1	the emotions	**2**	was
3	have	**4**	the countries
5	They all	**6**	are
7	hotels	**8**	have
9	his friends	**10**	They both

> **1, 9** all[both] of+관사/소유격+복수명사
> **2** all+소유격+셀 수 없는 명사+단수 동사
> **3** you guys는 구어체에서 주로 사용되며 you의 2인칭 복수와 유사하게 '너희들, 당신들'이라는 의미를 가진다. both of 다음에 복수형 대명사가 사용되었으므로 동사도 복수형으로 수일치하여 have를 써야 한다.
> **4** both of+관사/소유격+셀 수 있는 명사의 복수형+복수 동사
> **5, 10** 동격을 나타내는 all, both는 동격을 나타내는 단어 뒤에 위치한다.
> **6, 7, 8** all[both]+셀 수 있는 명사의 복수형+복수 동사

PRACTICE 11

1 Every kid dreams of having a treehouse in their backyard.

2 The book club members meet every two weeks.

3 Each of these systems has its advantages and disadvantages.

4 Each member was offered dinner after the meeting.[After the meeting, each member was offered dinner.]

5 Every road is blocked because of the traffic accident.[Because of the traffic accident, every road is blocked.]

6 Each of the players was holding his national flag in his right hand.

PRACTICE 12

1	word	**2**	has
3	participants	**4**	second
5	hours	**6**	is

> **1** every가 '모든' 이라는 뜻을 갖지만 항상 단수 취급함에 유의해야 한다.
> **2, 6** each는 '각자, 각각의' 라는 뜻으로 명사를 수식하며, 단수 취급한다.
> **3** each of+관사+복수 명사+단수 동사
> **4** every+서수사+단수명사: ~ 간격으로, ~마다
> **5** every+기수사+복수명사: ~ 간격으로, ~마다

PRACTICE 13

1	anything	**2**	Somebody
3	something[anything]	**4**	anybody
5	something	**6**	anybody
7	something	**8**	somebody
9	anything	**10**	anybody

> **1, 4** 부정문에서는 anything, anybody가 쓰인다.
> **2** 긍정문에서는 somebody가 쓰인다.
> **3** 긍정문이므로 something도 가능하지만, '어떠한 ~라도'의 의미로 쓰일 수 있으므로 anything도 가능하다.
> **5, 7, 8** 긍정의 대답을 예상하는 의문문에서 something, somebody가 쓰인다.
> **6, 10** 의문문에서는 anybody가 쓰인다.
> **9** 조건을 나타내는 if 절에서 anything이 쓰인다.

PRACTICE 14

1	didn't, anything	**2**	no one
3	doesn't, anything	**4**	nobody
5	nothing	**6**	didn't, anyone

PRACTICE 15

1 Not all (of) my friends

2 Not every fruit

3 Not every piece of clothing

4   not always interesting
5   Not all TV programs
6   not always helpful

📑 중간·기말고사 대비문제 정답   본문 _ p.134

1 1) It is important how we solve the problem.
2) It was not[wasn't] clear what he really
meant.   **2** ④   **3** ③   **4** pulled himself up
5 ④   **6** Some, others   **7** ③   **8** is hard to
tame wild horses   **9** Both of us think   **10** ②
11 ③   **12** ⑤   **13** It seems, are   **14** ④
15 Air pollution makes it difficult to live in the
country.   **16** one, other   **17** ①   **18** ②
19 ①   **20** ①   **21** ②   **22** ②   **23** some
24 ⑤   **25** ④   **26** ⑤   **27** no, another, other
28 second[other]   **29** ③   **30** ④
31 It is very generous of him to make such a
big donation.   **32** ③   **33** ①   **34** ①   **35** ⑤
36 don't, any   **37** each   **38** ②   **39** ②
40 ③   **41** ⑤   **42** (1) cleans, by itself
(2) I thought to myself

중간·기말고사 대비문제 해설

1   의문사가 이끄는 절은 that절과 마찬가지로 문장 내
에서 주어, 목적어, 보어의 역할을 할 수 있으므로 가
주어 it과 함께 가주어, 진주어 구문을 이룰 수 있다.

2   ④ 비인칭 주어
①②③⑤ 「It ~ that …」 강조구문

3   ③ in itself는 '그 자체로서'의 뜻으로 itself는 전치사
in의 목적어이다.

4   '~을 끌어올리다'라는 뜻은 「타동사+부사」 형태
인 pull up으로 나타내며, 목적어인 재귀대명사
(himself)는 중간에 삽입하여 쓴다. 이때 등위접속사
and 앞의 시제가 과거이므로 답도 과거시제에 맞게
쓴다(pulled himself up).

5   a. 주어(the fan)와 목적어(가수)가 가리키는 대상이
다르므로 재귀대명사 herself가 아닌 인칭대명사의
목적격 her을 쓴다. (herself → her)
d. 「both of+소유격+셀 수 있는 명사의 복수형+복수
동사」 (cousin → cousins)

6   「Some ~, others …」 '(불특정한 수의 사람[것]들 중

에서) 몇몇은 ~, 다른 사람[것]들은 …'

7   ① 인칭대명사 it
②「It ~ that …」 강조구문
④ 비인칭 주어 it
⑤ seems[appears, happens] that ~의 주어

8   to부정사를 진주어로 하는 가주어 it

9   'both of: ~ 둘 다'가 주어에 올 경우, 복수 동사를 쓴
다.

10   ② 부정문에는 anyone을 쓴다.
(someone → anyone)

11   ③ one ~ the other …: '(둘 중에) 하나는 ~, 나머지
하나는 …'
① 부정문이므로 any가 들어간다.
② '다른, 그 밖의'라는 뜻으로 복수 명사 앞에는
other이 들어간다.
④ '또 하나의, 또 다른'이라는 뜻으로 단수 명사 앞에
는 another이 들어간다.
⑤ 특정한 수 내에서 3명을 제외한 나머지를 의미하므
로, '나머지 사람[것]들'이라는 뜻의 the others가
들어가는 것이 적절하다.

12   ⑤「each of+관사+복수명사」는 단수 취급한다.
(are → is)

13   「주어+seem(s)+to부정사」는 「It seems that ~」으
로 바꾸어 쓸 수 있다. 주어진 문장에서 to부정사구의
시제(to be interested)가 주절의 시제(seem)와 일
치하고, 주어가 복수(The kids)이므로 바뀐 문장에서
that 절의 동사는 주절과의 시제일치, 수일치를 통해
are가 된다.

14   ①②③⑤에는 it[It]이 들어갈 수 있지만 ④에는 동사
thought의 목적어 역할을 하는 명사절을 이끄는 접
속사 that이 들어가야 한다.
① 가목적어 it
②「It ~ that …」 강조구문
③ It seems that ~ 구문
⑤ 시간을 나타내는 비인칭주어 it

15   to부정사를 진목적어로 하는 가목적어 it 구문이다.

16   one '하나의, 한'
other+복수 명사 '다른 ~들'

17   ① 일반적인 사람들을 나타내는 대명사
②④ 앞에 나온 명사의 반복을 피하기 위해 쓰는 대명
사 one
③ '하나의'의 뜻으로 쓰인 형용사
⑤ '한 사람, 하나'의 뜻으로 쓰인 대명사

18   「It ~ that …」 강조용법에서 동사는 강조할 수 없다.

19 「one ~ the other …」 '(둘 중에) 하나는 ~, 다른 하나는 …'

20 주어진 문장의 밑줄 친 It은 「It ~ that…」 강조구문의 It이다.
① 「It ~ that …」 강조용법
② 가목적어   ③⑤ 가주어   ④ 상황을 나타내는 it

21 「one ~ another … the other -」 '(셋 중에) 하나는 ~, 다른 하나는 …, 나머지 하나는 -'

22 앞에 나온 명사와 종류는 같지만 대상이 다른 경우에 단수는 one, 복수는 ones로 받는다. 여기에서 ones는 habits를 받고 있다.

23 긍정문이므로 some을 쓴다.

24 앞에 나온 명사와 종류는 같지만 대상이 다른 경우에는 one으로, 대상이 같은 경우는 it으로 받는다.

25 A is one thing, B is another. 'A와 B는 별개이다.'

26 (A) 가리키는 것이 비둘기 Tom으로 단수이므로 one을 쓴다.
(B) He는 Mike를 가리킨다.
(C) 앞에 나온 명사와 대상이 같으므로 it을 쓴다.
(D) 비둘기 Tom은 앞에서처럼 it으로 받는다.
(E) 뒤에 복수 명사가 나오므로 other를 쓴다.

27 • no one '아무도 ~않다'
• another+단수 명사 '또 다른'
• other+복수 명사 '다른'

28 every+기수사+복수 명사 = every+서수사+단수 명사 '~간격으로, ~마다'
* every other day: 하루 걸러, 격일로

29 주어진 문장은 '네가 그를 다시 만나기는 어려울 것이다'라는 의미로, to부정사구를 진주어로 하는 가주어 it이 사용되었다.
③ 명사절(that 이하)을 진주어로 하는 가주어 it
① '그것'으로 해석되는 인칭대명사
② 거리를 나타내는 비인칭주어
④ 날씨를 나타내는 비인칭주어
⑤ 「It ~ that …」 강조구문

30 ④ 긍정문이므로 Anyone이 아닌 Someone이 되어야 한다. (Anyone → Someone)

31 가주어 It이 문장 맨 앞에 나오면 진주어는 문장 맨 뒤에 이어 쓰고, 의미상 주어는 진주어 앞에 쓴다. 이때, 보어 자리에 사람의 성질을 묘사하는 형용사(generous)가 나오면 의미상 주어 앞에 전치사 of를 쓴다.

32 ③ 이미 일어난 홍수로 인한 피해에 대한 글이므로, 진행형을 나타내는 flooding이 오는 것은 어색하다. (c)가 속한 문장의 주어는 Many streets이고, 홍수를 당한 것이므로 수동태로 써야 한다. (flood → flooded)

33 every, both, all 등 전체를 나타내는 말이 부정어와 함께 쓰일 때 부분부정이 된다.
① 그녀는 그들 중 누구도 초대하지 않았다.

34 ① all은 all과 동격을 나타내는 단어 뒤에 위치한다. (All we → We all)

35 other+복수 명사 '(불특정한) 다른'

36 no ~는 not ~ any로 바꾸어 쓸 수 있다.

37 each other '서로'

38 in all the world '전 세계에서'

39 ⓐ 앞에 나온 명사 my wallet과 종류와 대상이 같으므로 it을 사용한다.
ⓑ 앞에 나온 명사 wallet과 종류는 같지만 대상이 다르므로 one을 사용한다.
ⓒ '또 다른 것'이라는 의미를 가진 another의 사용이 적절하다.

40 ③ everyone과 같은 전체를 나타내는 말이 부정어와 함께 쓰이면 부분부정이 된다.
① be known for: '~로[때문에] 유명하다' / be known as: '~로서 알려져 있다'. 문장의 의미상 be known for로 쓰는 것이 적절하다. (as → for)
② 「It ~ that …」 강조구문에서 강조하고자 하는 말을 It is와 that 사이에 쓴다. 한국어 문장에서 꽃병을 강조하고 있으나 영어 문장에서는 Karl을 강조하고 있기 때문에 의미를 바르게 전달하려면 It is와 that 사이에 this vase가 들어가는 것이 적절하다. (It is Karl that broke this vase. → It is this vase that Karl broke.)
④ 감탄문의 어순은 「How+형용사/부사+주어+동사!」를 따른다. (How lovely is she! → How lovely she is!)
⑤ All 뒤에 of+관사+셀 수 없는 명사가 올 경우 단수 동사를 써야 한다. (were → was)

41 ⓐ 부정의문문에 대한 대답은 질문의 형태와 관계없이 대답의 내용이 긍정이면 Yes, 부정이면 No로 답한다.
ⓑ another+단수명사 '또 하나의, 또 다른'
ⓒ the other+복수명사 '~ 중 남아있는 전부'

42 (1) by oneself '혼자, 다른 사람 없이'
(2) think to oneself '마음속으로 생각하다, 혼자 생각하다'

PRACTICE 1

1 It is very difficult to pronounce the word correctly.

2 It was almost impossible to arrive there in time.

3 It is always exciting to play volleyball at the beach.

4 It will be nice to visit such a good place.

5 It is important to know what you can do the best.

6 It was not helpful to study for a short time just before the test.

PRACTICE 2

1 to hand out free samples on the street

2 to become a world-famous photographer

3 to take a subway

4 to send an e-mail to the teacher

5 to get to know each other better

6 to pass the exam and make my parents happy

PRACTICE 3

1 to see **2** to major

3 to join **4** to come

5 to solve **6** to forgive

7 to live **8** to preserve

9 to hurt **10** to study

PRACTICE 4

2 Cathy to fix his broken computer now

3 Brian to review the lesson

4 Brian to share her science book

5 Cathy to act more responsibly

6 Cathy to join his club

7 Brian to talk to Mr. Kim

8 Cathy to make ten copies of the report

PRACTICE 5

1 how to play **2** what to wear

3 how to cooperate **4** what[how] to prepare

5 what to do **6** how to use

7 what to say **8** how to save

9 how to get **10** what to eat

> **1** Jenny는 어떻게 골프 치는지 아니?
> **2** 나는 파티를 위해 <u>무엇을 입어야 할지</u> 결정할 수 없어. 나는 화려한 드레스가 없어.
> **3** 당신은 서로 <u>어떻게 협력할지</u> 배워야 한다.
> **4** 그가 당신에게 그 행사를 위해서 <u>무엇을[어떻게] 준비해야 할지</u> 설명해줄 것이다.
> **5** 나는 커서 <u>무엇을 할지</u>에 대해서 생각하고 있었다.
> **6** Mark가 나에게 새로운 세탁기를 <u>어떻게 사용하는지</u> 보여주었다.
> **7** 나는 그녀를 기분 좋게 하기 위해서 그녀에게 <u>무슨 말을 해야 할지</u> 모르겠다.
> **8** Park 씨는 우리에게 많은 돈을 <u>어떻게 저축할지</u> 가르쳐 줄 것이다.
> **9** 나에게 소방서로 <u>어떻게 가는지</u> 알려주실 수 있나요?
> **10** Sam과 나는 중국 식당에서 <u>무엇을 먹을지</u>에 대해 이야기하고 있었다.

PRACTICE 6

1 fun stories to tell the kids

2 nothing interesting to watch

3 true friends to talk with

4 so many places to visit

5 a house to live in

6 rules to keep the streets clean

7 anybody to help me carry the stones

8 his babies to look after

9 something to eat

10 a method to go there

> **1, 3, 4, 5, 6, 8, 10** to부정사는 '~할'의 뜻으로 명사 뒤에서 명사를 수식하는 형용사의 역할을 한다.
> **2, 7, 9** –thing, –body로 끝나는 대명사 뒤에 이들을 수식하는 형용사가 나오면 to부정사는 형용사 뒤에 위치한다.

PRACTICE 7

2 It's time to clean the living room.
[It's time I cleaned the living room.]

3 It's time to read books.
[It's time I read books.]

4 It's time to walk the dog.
[It's time I walked the dog.]

5 It's time to go swimming.
[It's time I went swimming.]

PRACTICE 8

1	are to go	**2**	are to succeed
3	was to be seen	**4**	was to die
5	are to hand	**6**	was not to be eaten
7	is to come	**8**	are to be
9	was to sleep	**10**	are not to make
11	was not to be found	**12**	is to be held

1, 7, 12 가까운 미래에 있을 이미 정해진 일을 나타내기 위해 「be+to부정사」를 쓸 수 있는데, 주어의 인칭과 수에 따라 be동사를 알맞게 써야 한다.
2, 8 의도를 나타내기 위해 「be+to부정사」를 쓸 수 있는데 주어가 you이고, 원래 문장이 현재 시제이므로 be동사를 are로 써야 한다.
3 원래 문장에 could(가능)가 쓰였으므로 과거 시제이고, 주어가 단수이므로 「was+to부정사」로 바꿔 쓸 수 있다.
4, 9 '~할 운명이다(운명)'를 나타내기 위해 「be+to부정사」를 쓸 수 있는데 주어가 단수이고, 원래 문장이 과거시제이므로 be동사를 was로 써야 한다.
5, 10 의무를 나타내는 must, have to는 「be+to부정사」로 바꿔 쓸 수 있다. 10번의 must not을 「be+to부정사」 표현으로 바꾸어 쓸 때는 부정의 not이 to부정사 앞에 위치해야 함에 유의한다.
6, 11 couldn't(~할 수 없었다)를 「be+to부정사」 표현으로 바꾸어 쓸 때는 부정의 not이 to부정사 앞에 위치해야 함에 유의한다.

PRACTICE 9

2 in order to[so as to] give him the invitation card,
so that I could give him the invitation card

3 in order to[so as to] take part in volunteer work,
so that she can take part in volunteer work

4 in order to[so as to] let him know the truth about the rumor,
so that I can let him know the truth about the rumor

5 in order to[so as to] remind me of the plans,
so that he could remind me of the plans

6 in order to[so as to] roll down the window,
so that I could roll down the window

PRACTICE 10

1	① for ② to	**2**	① for ② to
3	① to ② for	**4**	① for ② to
5	① to ② for		

PRACTICE 11

1 delighted to find the frog alive
2 glad to go there with you
3 grew up to be a great artist
4 an opera singer to sing like that
5 so hard to understand
6 disappointed not to say a word
7 excited to have a chance to talk with him
8 woke up to find himself famous

1, 2, 7 to부정사가 delighted, glad, excited와 같은 감정을 나타내는 형용사를 수식할 때는 '~해서, ~하게 되어'의 뜻으로 감정의 원인을 나타낸다.
3, 8 '~해서 (결국) …이 되다'의 뜻으로 결과를 나타낸다.
4, 6 '~하다니'의 뜻으로 판단의 근거를 나타낸다.
5 to부정사가 형용사를 뒤에서 수식할 때는 '~하기에'의 의미를 가진다.

PRACTICE 12

1	so, that, can	**2**	so, that, couldn't
3	too, to	**4**	so, that, could
5	so, that, can't	**6**	enough, to
7	so, that, couldn't	**8**	enough, to
9	so, that, could	**10**	too, for, to

PRACTICE 13

1	add	**2**	shout[shouting]
3	use	**4**	play[playing]
5	crawl[crawling]	**6**	wash[to wash]
7	get	**8**	move[moving]
9	sneak[sneaking]	**10**	rub[rubbing]
11	take[taking]	**12**	stay up

1, 3, 7, 12 사역동사(let, make, have)+목적어+동사원형
2, 4, 5, 8, 9, 10, 11 지각동사(hear, listen to, look at, watch, notice, feel, see)+목적어+동사원형[현재분사]
동작이 진행중임을 강조할 때는 지각동사의 목적격 보어로 현재분사를 쓰기도 한다.
6 준사역동사 help+목적어+동사원형[to부정사]

PRACTICE 14

1 We should try not to pollute the water.
2 She pretended not to know anything about the rumor.
3 We have to hurry up not to miss the last train.
4 She was too tired, so she chose not to drive home.
5 You'd better be more careful never to hurt yourself during practice.

6 Bob studied very hard not to fail the science test.

7 Try not to be so upset about the result.

8 He promised never to skip class but skipped it again.

PRACTICE 15

1 You can tell this to your mom if you want to.

2 I'd like to join you, but I won't be able to.

3 I will help you whenever you want me to.

4 Jason didn't want to send his puppy to his grandmother, but he decided to.

5 I don't want to go climbing with him, but I have to.

6 Mira waited for me until midnight, although I told her not to.

> 앞서 나온 말의 반복을 피하기 위해 대부정사가 사용되어 to만 남고 괄호 안의 내용은 생략되었다.
>
> **1** You can tell this to your mom if you want to (tell this to your mom).
> **2** I'd like to join you, but I won't be able to (join you).
> **3** I will help you whenever you want me to (help you).
> **4** Jason didn't want to send his puppy to his grandmother, but he decided to (send his puppy to his grandmother).
> **5** I don't want to go climbing with him, but I have to (go climbing with him).
> **6** Mira waited for me until midnight, although I told her not to (wait for me until midnight).

PRACTICE 16

1	for	**2**	for	**3**	to
4	for	**5**	of	**6**	for
7	to	**8**	of	**9**	to
10	for	**11**	of	**12**	to
13	of	**14**	for	**15**	of

> **1, 2, 4, 6, 10, 14** to부정사의 의미상의 주어를 나타내야 하는 경우에는 to부정사 앞에 「for+목적격」의 형태로 쓴다.
> **3, 9** to부정사의 의미상의 주어가 문장의 목적어와 같은 경우, 의미상의 주어를 쓰지 않는다.
> **5, 8, 11, 13, 15** to부정사 앞에 nice(좋은, 친절한), cruel(잔인한), foolish(어리석은), thoughtful(사려 깊은), wise(현명한)와 같이 사람의 성질이나 특징을 나타내는 형용사가 있으면, 의미상의 주어는 「of+목적격」으로 쓴다.
> **7** '입기에 너무 크다'라는 의미로 too ~ to 구문이 쓰였다.
> **12** to부정사의 의미상의 주어가 일반 사람일 때, 의미상의 주어를 쓰지 않으며, It(가주어) - to부정사(진주어) 구문이 쓰였다.

📑 중간·기말고사 대비문제 정답 본문 _ p.159

1 ① **2** too, to **3** to learn[learning] **4** how to use **5** ① **6** ①,③ **7** It seems that he needs some rest after all that hard work. **8** It took four hours for us to get to the valley. **9** ⑤ **10** ③ **11** ④ **12** to understand **13** ④ **14** it rewarding to complete my first marathon **15** ⑤ **16** ⑤ **17** 1) I heard my brother go[going] upstairs. 2) Would you like me to pick you up in the morning? **18** ⑤ **19** ④ **20** ① **21** ③ **22** ③ **23** ③ **24** so busy that I can't **25** ④ **26** smart enough to **27** ③ **28** ① **29** ② **30** ② **31** ① **32** It, for, to **33** seem to be **34** ⑤ **35** ②,④ **36** ④ **37** ② **38** for her to keep **39** ③ **40** ③,⑤ **41** ④ **42** ④ **43** ⑤ **44** what to say **45** ② **46** The plane ticket is too expensive for her to afford. **47** ⑤ **48** ② **49** ③ **50** ④

중간·기말고사 대비문제 해설

1 「형용사+enough+to부정사」 '~할 정도로 충분히 … 한'

2 「so+형용사+that+주어+can't」 = 「too+형용사+to부정사」

3 to부정사와 동명사는 주어에 대해 보충 설명하는 주격 보어로 쓰인다.

4 「의문사+주어+should+동사원형」 = 「의문사+to부정사」

5 ① would like는 목적격 보어로 to부정사를 쓰는 동사이다. (think → to think)

6 (A),(D) 부사적 용법 (B),(C) 형용사적 용법 (E) 명사적 용법

7 「주어+seem+to부정사」 = 「It seems that 주어+동사」 '~가 …한 것 같다'

8 「It takes ~+의미상의 주어+to부정사」 '…하는 데 ~가 걸리다'

9 주어진 문장의 밑줄 친 to send는 to부정사의 형용사적 용법으로 쓰였다.
⑤ 형용사적 용법 ①②③④ 명사적 용법

10 decide, expect, plan은 목적어로 to부정사를 쓰는

동사들이다. want는 목적격 보어로 to부정사를 쓰는 동사이다. 준사역동사 help는 목적격 보어로 to부정사와 원형부정사 모두 쓸 수 있다.

① forming → to form

② find → to find

④ see → to see

⑤ doing → to do

11 「be scared+to부정사」 '~하기를 무서워하다'

12 decide 뒤에 동사가 목적어로 올 때는 「to+동사원형」의 형태로 쓴다.

13 부정어 not은 to부정사 앞에 쓴다.

14 '가목적어(it) - 진목적어(to부정사)' 구문이 쓰였다.

15 ⑤ 「so+형용사/부사+that+주어+can/can't」 '너무~해서 …할 수 있다/없다'

①②③④ 「(in order[so as]) to+동사원형」 = 「so that+주어+can[could]+동사원형」 '~하기 위해서'

16 ⑤ 명사적 용법

17 1) 지각동사 hear은 목적격 보어로 원형부정사나 현재분사를 사용한다.

2) would like는 목적격 보어로 to부정사를 사용한다.

18 • 사역동사 let+목적어+동사원형

• ask+목적어+to부정사

19 ④ 「형용사/부사+enough+to부정사」 '~할 정도로 충분히 …한'

①②③⑤ 「too+형용사/부사+to부정사」 '~하기에는 너무 …한'

① 나는 면접 동안 좋은 인상을 만들기에는 너무 긴장했다.

② 내가 방금 걸레질한 복도는 걷기에는 너무 미끄럽다.

③ 그 아메리카노는 여전히 내가 마시기에는 너무 쓰다.

④ 그녀의 새 소설은 하루 안에 읽을 정도로 충분히 간단하다.

⑤ 카페에서 틀어진 노래는 집중하기에 너무 시끄럽다.

20 ① force는 목적격 보어로 to부정사를 사용한다. (get → to get) 오늘 아침에 나는 억지로 일어나야 했다.

② 지각동사 notice는 목적격 보어로 원형부정사나 현재분사를 사용한다. 선생님은 학생들이 어리둥절해하는 것을 알아차렸다.

③ 사역동사 have는 목적격 보어로 원형부정사를 사용한다. 나는 내 조수에게 당신을 위한 또 다른 약속을 잡게 할게요.

④ 지각동사 watch는 목적격 보어로 원형부정사나 현재분사를 사용한다. 나는 때때로 창문 옆에 앉아 사람들이 지나가는 걸 본다.

⑤ cause는 목적격 보어로 to부정사를 사용한다. 정전은 컴퓨터 시스템 전체가 종료되게 했다.

21 제시된 문장, ③ 명령·의무의 「be+to부정사」 '~해야 한다'

①② 예정의 「be+to부정사」 '~할 예정이다'

④ 가능의 「be+to부정사」 '~할 수 있다'

⑤ 운명의 「be+to부정사」 '~할 운명이다'

22 ③ both A and B 'A와 B 둘 다' 명사 an artist(예술가)와 an inventor(발명가)를 대등하게 연결한다. Leonardo da Vinci는 예술가와 발명가 둘 다로 찬양된다.

① ask는 목적격 보어로 to부정사(to+동사원형)를 사용한다. (memory → memorize) 나는 나의 선생님이 나에게 외우라고 했던 시를 암송했다.

② 맥락상 '준비하기에 빠르고 편리하다'는 의미로 to부정사구(to+동사원형)가 와야 한다. (preparation → prepare) 당신은 이 식사들이 준비하기에 빠르고 편리하다는 것을 알게 될 것이다.

④ 준사역동사 help는 목적격 보어로 원형부정사나 to부정사를 사용한다. (prevention → (to) prevent) 적절한 스트레칭은 운동 중 근육 부상을 예방하는데 도움이 된다.

⑤ '~하기 위해서'라는 목적을 나타내기 위해 to부정사(to+동사원형)를 사용한다. (representative → represent) Emily는 회의에서 회사를 대표하도록 선정되었다.

23 ⓐ 관계대명사 what은 선행사를 포함하고 불완전한 절을 이끌기 때문에 it을 삭제한다. (to do it → to do)

ⓑ 지각동사 feel은 목적격 보어로 원형부정사나 현재분사를 쓴다. (to touch → touch[touching])

ⓒ 지각동사 see는 목적격 보어로 원형부정사나 현재분사를 쓴다. (to walk → walk[walking])

24 「too+형용사+to부정사」

= 「so+형용사+that+주어+can't」

25 ④ kind는 사람의 성질을 나타내는 형용사이므로, to부정사의 의미상 주어 앞에 for 대신 of를 붙인다.

26 「so+형용사+that+주어+can」

27 = 「형용사+enough+to부정사」

27 「so+형용사+that+주어+can't/couldn't」

= 「too+형용사+to부정사」

28 사람의 성질이나 특징을 나타내는 형용사 stupid가 쓰였으므로 의미상의 주어는 「of+목적격」의 형태로 쓴다.

29 • '~하기 위해서'의 목적을 나타낼 때는 「in order to(so as to)+동사원형」을 써서 나타낼 수 있다.
나는 건강을 유지하기 위해 정기적으로 한강을 따라 달린다.
• 목적을 나타내지만 뒤에 절이 오는 경우에는 접속사 so that을 써서 '~하기 위해서'를 나타낼 수 있다.
우리는 내 남동생이 깨지 않도록 조용히 해야 한다.

30 tell은 목적격 보어로 to부정사를 취한다.

31 사역동사 make+목적어+동사원형

32 to부정사가 주어의 역할을 할 때는 가주어 it을 주어의 자리에 두고, 진주어인 to부정사구(to make their own decisions)는 문장의 뒤로 보낸다. 학생들이 결정을 내리는 것이므로 의미상의 주어는 some students이다. to부정사의 의미상의 주어는 「for+목적격」의 형태로 쓴다.

33 「It seems that ~」은 「주어+seem(s)+to부정사」로 바꾸어 쓸 수 있다.

34 사역동사 make의 목적격 보어는 원형부정사로, 전치사의 목적어는 동명사로 나타낸다.

35 ② '~에게 말하다'라는 의미는 talk to의 형태로 쓴다. (talk → talk to)
④ nothing처럼 –thing으로 끝나는 명사는 형용사가 뒤에서 수식한다. (interesting nothing → nothing interesting)

36 ④ 명사적 용법 ①②③⑤ 부사적 용법

37 to부정사가 '~하기 위해서'의 뜻으로 목적이나 의도를 나타낼 때는 in order to로 바꾸어 쓸 수 있다.
② to부정사의 부사적 용법(목적)
① to부정사의 부사적 용법(형용사 수식)
③ to부정사의 부사적 용법(감정의 원인)
④ to부정사의 부사적 용법(결과)
⑤ 「too ~ to …」 '너무 ~해서 …할 수 없다.'

38 to부정사가 주어의 역할을 할 때는 가주어 it을 주어의 자리에 두고, 진주어인 to부정사구(to keep a diary in English)는 문장의 뒤로 보낸다. 그녀가 일기를 쓰는 것이므로 의미상의 주어는 she이다. to부정사의 의미상의 주어는 「for+목적격」의 형태로 쓴다.

39 「It is time for+목적격+to부정사」 '~가 …할 시간이다'

40 ③ too ~ to 구문을 쓸 때 to부정사의 목적어가 주어와 일치하는 경우 to부정사 뒤에는 목적어를 쓰지 않는다. (it 삭제)
⑤ to부정사 앞에 사람의 성질이나 특징을 나타내는 형용사가 오면 의미상의 주어는 「of+목적격」으로 쓴다. (them → of them)

41 ④ to부정사는 의문사와 함께 「의문사+to부정사」의 형태로 쓸 수 있다. 「how to+동사원형」은 '어떻게 ~할지'라는 뜻이다. (deal → to deal)

42 (D) to부정사가 수식하는 명사(someone)가 전치사의 목적어일 경우 꼭 전치사를 써야 한다.
*talk to: ~에게 이야기하다
(A) 'What I have to do' 같은 구문이 주어로 쓰인 경우, 주격 보어로 원형부정사 혹은 to부정사가 올 수 있다.
(B) try to+동사원형: ~하려고 애쓰다
(C) 사역동사 let은 목적격 보어로 동사원형이 온다.
(E) would like to+동사원형: ~하고 싶다

43 to부정사의 의미상의 주어는 부정사 앞에 「for+목적격」의 형태로 쓴다. 부정사 앞에 사람의 성질이나 특징을 나타내는 형용사(nice, wise)가 있으면 「of+목적격」의 형태로 쓴다.
① of me → for me   ② of you → for you
③ for you → of you   ④ me → for me

44 what to+동사원형 '무엇을 ~할지'

45 「enough+to부정사」는 '~할 정도로 충분한'의 의미를 가지고, 종이 위에 쓰는 것이므로 전치사 on이 필요하다.

46 「so+형용사/부사+that+주어+can't」는 「too+형용사/부사+to부정사」로 바꿀 수 있다. 뜻은 '~하기에는 너무 …한'이다.

47 ⓔ 목적어로 to부정사구가 쓰였을 경우, to부정사를 문장의 뒤로 보내고 목적어의 자리에 가목적어 it을 쓸 수 있다. 가목적어로 this는 쓸 수 없다.
(this → it)
ⓐ 목적어 자리에 가목적어 it이 사용되고, 목적격 보어 'difficult' 뒤에 동사로 시작하는 구가 있는 것으로 보아, make는 진목적어인 to부정사로 써야 한다. (make → to make)
ⓑ 5형식 문장의 어순은 「주어+동사+목적어+목적격 보어」이다. 목적어는 to부정사구라서 문장의 뒤로 이동했으므로, 목적어의 자리에는 가목적어 it을 쓴

다. 목적격 보어인 possible은 목적어 it의 뒤에 쓴다. (possible it → it possible)

ⓒ 5형식 문장에서 목적격 보어의 자리에는 명사, 형용사, 부정사, 분사가 들어갈 수 있다. importantly는 부사이므로, 형용사인 important로 써야 한다. (importantly → important)

ⓓ 목적어 자리에 가목적어 it이 사용되고, 목적격 보어인 'a rule' 뒤에 동사 take가 쓰였다. take는 진목적어인 to부정사로 쓰여야 하므로, to부정사 형태인 to take로 고친다. (take → to take)

48 ② to부정사의 의미상의 주어는 그녀이므로, 문장의 주어와 일치하지 않는다. 따라서 「for+목적격」으로 의미상의 주어를 나타낸다.

① foolish는 사람의 성질이나 특징을 나타내는 형용사이므로, to부정사의 의미상의 주어는 「of+목적격」으로 쓴다. 인칭대명사 he의 목적격은 him이다. (he → him)

③ dangerous는 사람의 성질이나 특징을 나타내는 형용사가 아니므로, to부정사의 의미상의 주어는 「for+목적격」으로 쓴다. (of → for)

④ it을 쓰지 않아도 The dress my sister gave me를 지칭하는 것임을 알 수 있기 때문에, 의미상 중복되므로 it은 쓰지 않는다.
(to wear it → to wear)

⑤ thoughtful은 사람의 성질이나 특징을 나타내는 형용사로, to부정사의 의미상의 주어는 「of+목적격」으로 쓴다. (for → of)

49 ③ 목적을 나타내는 to부정사는, 「in order to+동사원형」, 「so as to+동사원형」으로 바꾸어 쓸 수 있

다.

① 「so+형용사/부사+that+주어+can't/couldn't」는 「too+형용사/부사+to부정사」로 바꿀 수 있다. 이때, them을 쓰지 않아도 the noodles를 먹는 것임을 알 수 있기 때문에, 의미상 중복되므로 them은 쓰지 않는다. 반면, that절에서는 완벽한 절로 써야 하기 때문에 목적어 them을 생략하지 않는다. (to eat them → to eat)

② 「so that+주어+can」 …하기 위해서
「so+형용사/부사+that+주어+can」 너무 ~해서 (그 결과) … 할 수 있다.
(첫번째 문장 해석) 나는 내 수업을 위해 준비하기 위해서 학교에 일찍 간다.
(두번째 문장 해석) 나는 학교에 매우 일찍 가기 때문에 내 수업을 위해 준비할 수 있다.

④ 사역동사 make는 목적격 보어로 원형부정사만 쓸 수 있다. (to clean → clean)

⑤ 지각동사 watch는 목적격 보어로 원형부정사와 현재분사를 쓸 수 있다. (to play → play 또는 playing)

50 ④ talk 뒤에 전치사 to가 있는 것으로 보아 '누구에게 말해야 할지'라는 의미가 되어야 하므로 빈칸에 들어갈 말은 who(m)이 적절하다.

① what to write: 무엇을 써야 할지
② how to drive: 어떻게 운전하는지
③ where to put: 어디에 둘지
⑤ when to wake up: 언제 일어나야 할지

<table>
<tr><td>CHAPTER</td><td>8</td><td>동명사
Gerunds</td><td>본문 _ p.168</td></tr>
</table>

PRACTICE 1

1 His wish is traveling around the world, 주격 보어

2 It's no use wishing for the impossible., (진)주어

3 It's worth making an appointment, (진)주어

4 Getting to know each member is the purpose, 주어

5 The last step is checking the number of guests., 주격 보어

PRACTICE 2

1 answering **2** to be **3** watching

4 reading **5** to make **6** listening

7 speaking **8** being **9** to stay

10 interrupting **11** to send **12** turning

13 planning **14** electing **15** to plant

1, 3, 4, 6, 7, 8, 12, 13, 14 avoid, enjoy, finish, give up, practice, imagine, mind, put off, consider 뒤에 다른 동사가

목적어로 오면, 목적어로 쓰이는 동사는 동명사의 형태로 쓴다.
2, 5, 9, 11, 15 pretend, agree, choose, decide, plan 뒤에 다른 동사가 목적어로 오면, 목적어로 쓰이는 동사는 to부정사의 형태로 쓴다.
10 keep ~ing: 계속해서 ~하다

'~하려고 노력하다, 애쓰다'라는 의미다. 5번은 '머리 색깔을 바꿔보다'라는 의미이므로 동명사, 12번은 '그를 설득하려고 노력했다'라는 의미이므로 to부정사가 알맞다.
8, 11 stop은 목적어로 동명사를 취한다. stop 뒤에 오는 to부정사는 stop의 목적어가 아니라 '~하기 위해서'라는 의미로 목적을 나타내는 부사적 용법의 to부정사이다. 8번은 '우는 것을 멈췄다'라는 의미이므로 동명사, 11번은 '물을 사기 위해서 멈췄다'라는 의미이므로 to부정사가 알맞다.
13 keep ~ing: 계속해서 ~하다
15 would love to+동사원형:~하고 싶다

PRACTICE 3

1	to live, living	**2**	to buy
3	to take, taking	**4**	to drive
5	to study, studying	**6**	to cause
7	making	**8**	to read, reading
9	learning	**10**	taking
11	to cut, cutting	**12**	to listen, listening
13	to wear, wearing	**14**	to take, taking
15	going	**16**	to find

1, 3, 5, 8, 11, 12, 13, 14 like, continue, start, love, begin, hate, prefer, intend는 동명사와 to부정사를 모두 목적어로 취하며, 동명사와 to부정사 중 어느 것을 목적어로 취하든지 뜻이 달라지지 않는다.
2, 4 expect, learn은 to부정사를 목적어로 취하는 동사들이다.
6, 16 mean(~을 의도하다), need(~할 필요가 있다) 뒤에는 to부정사가 오는 것이 적절하다.
(*참고로 mean과 need는 동명사를 목적어로 취하기도 하는데, mean 뒤에 동명사가 오면 '~을 의미하다'라는 뜻이 되고(예: It means leaving this city. 그것은 이 도시를 떠난다는 것을 의미한다.), need 뒤에 동명사가 오면 '~되어야 할 필요가 있다'라는 수동의 의미가 된다(예: My car needs washing.=My car needs to be washed. 내 차는 세차되어야 한다.).
7, 9, 10, 15 practice, quit, dislike, imagine은 동명사를 목적어로 취하는 동사들이다.

PRACTICE 4

1	copying	**2**	watching	**3**	to find
4	repeating	**5**	changing	**6**	writing
7	to play	**8**	crying	**9**	to take
10	to apply	**11**	to buy	**12**	to persuade
13	bothering	**14**	to send	**15**	to bring

1, 10 「forget+동명사」는 '~한 것을 잊다', 「forget+to부정사」는 '~할[하는] 것을 잊다'라는 의미다. 1번은 '전에 복사한 것을 잊었다'라는 의미이므로 동명사, 10번은 '프로그램에 신청하는 것을 잊었다'라는 의미이므로 to부정사가 알맞다.
2, 14 「remember+동명사」는 '~한 것을 기억하다', 「remember+to부정사」는 '~할[하는] 것을 기억하다'라는 의미다. 2번은 '작년에 사고를 목격한 것을 기억한다'라는 의미이므로 동명사, 14번은 '이번 목요일까지 상자를 보내는 것을 기억할 것이다'라는 의미이므로 to부정사가 알맞다.
3, 7, 9 fail, plan, choose는 to부정사를 목적어로 취하는 동사들이다.
4, 6 mind, finish는 동명사를 목적어로 취하는 동사들이다.
5, 12 「try+동명사」는 '(시험 삼아) ~해보다', 「try+to부정사」는

PRACTICE 5

1	participating	**2**	turning	**3**	using
4	breaking	**5**	inviting	**6**	hearing

1 prevent A from+-ing: A가 ~하는 것을 막다
2 instead of+-ing: ~ 대신에
3 by+-ing: ~함으로써
*use public transportation: 대중교통을 이용하다
4 apologize for+-ing: ~에 대해 사과하다
*break one's word: 약속을 어기다
5 thank A for+-ing: ~에 대해 A에게 감사하다
6 on+-ing: ~하자마자

PRACTICE 6

1 turning off the stove
2 letting the bird out
3 keeping my child's old toys
4 doing every kind of housework
5 saving 20,000 won in a week
6 having steak for dinner

1 without+-ing: ~하지 않고
2 be in favor of+-ing: ~에 찬성하다 *let ~ out: ~을 풀어주다
3 use A for+-ing: ~하는 데 A를 쓰다
4 be capable of+-ing: ~할 능력이 있다
*do housework: 집안일을 하다
5 succeed in+-ing: ~하는 데 성공하다
6 feel like+-ing: ~하고 싶다

PRACTICE 7

1 look forward to going
2 need painting, need to be painted
3 having trouble[difficulty/a hard time] speaking
4 used to skipping
5 busy making
6 spent, buying
7 worth watching[worthy of watching], worthwhile to watch
8 couldn't help feeling, couldn't but feel

9 no use telling, of no use to tell, useless to tell

10 go shopping

> **1** look forward to+-ing: ~을 고대하다
> **2** need+-ing: ~되어야 할 필요가 있다(= need to be+과거분사)
> **3** have trouble[difficulty/a hard time]+-ing: ~하는 데 어려움을 겪다
> **4** be used to+-ing: ~에 익숙하다
> **5** be busy+-ing: ~하느라고 바쁘다
> **6** spend+시간[돈]+-ing: ~하느라 (시간/돈을) 소비하다
> **7** be worth+-ing: ~할 가치가 있다(= be worthwhile+to부정사 = be worthy of+-ing)
> **8** cannot help+-ing: ~하지 않을 수 없다(= cannot but+동사원형)
> **9** It is no use+-ing: ~해도 소용없다(= It is of no use+to부정사 = It is useless+to부정사)
> **10** go+-ing: ~하러 가다

PRACTICE 8

1 not telling		**2** not being	
3 never to enter		**4** not giving	
5 not handling		**6** not taking	
7 never to see		**8** not going	
9 not to call		**10** not sending	

> **1, 2, 4, 5, 6, 8, 10** 동명사의 부정형을 만들 때는 동명사 앞에 not이나 never를 쓴다.
> **3, 7, 9** to부정사의 부정형을 만들 때는 「to+동사원형」 앞에 not이나 never를 쓴다.

PRACTICE 9

1 ①	**2** ①	**3** ③
4 ②	**5** ②	**6** ③

PRACTICE 10

1 my sister's[my sister] wearing my clothes

2 something being wrong with the engine

3 his[him] saying hello to her family

4 Minsu's[Minsu] being the chairman

5 her teacher's[her teacher] having cancer

6 the man's[the man] entering when we were having dinner

7 his[him] doing his best on the stage

8 my son's[my son] not following his directions all the time

9 my works being well-known among people

10 my[me] winning first prize in this competition

> **1, 3, 4, 5, 6, 7, 8, 10** 동명사가 나타내는 행위의 주체가 주어나 목적어와 다르므로 의미상의 주어를 소유격으로 나타내야 한다. 구어체에서는 목적격으로 쓰기도 한다.
> **2, 9** 의미상의 주어가 부정대명사(something)나 무생물(my works)일 때는 목적격으로 쓴다.

📑 중간·기말고사 대비문제 정답 본문 _ p.179

1 ② **2** ③ **3** ③ **4** ③ **5** ① **6** ④ **7** ④
8 ⑤ **9** ② **10** ① **11** ② **12** ⑤ **13** On[Upon]
14 ⑤ **15** ④ **16** to launch → in launching
17 ⑤ **18** ②,③ **19** ③ **20** Participating in sports is **21** in, of **22** I'm used to driving in Tokyo **23** ③ **24** her from going **25** ② **26** to be changed **27** ④ **28** couldn't but take
29 ③ **30** of no use, no use speaking **31** ②
32 ④ **33** ② **34** (1) to fill (2) getting **35** ④
36 (1) Sleeping eight hours a day is (2) by eating healthy food **37** ② **38** decided to stay home instead of going out **39** It's worth getting there early

중간·기말고사 대비문제 해설

1 ② 현재분사(분사구문)　①③④⑤ 동명사(주어)

2 give up은 동명사를 목적어로 취하며, decide는 to부정사를 목적어로 취한다.

3 ③ 현재분사(현재진행형) ①②④⑤ 동명사(주격 보어)

4 ③ mind는 동명사를 목적어로 쓰는 동사이다.
(to step → stepping)

5 ① continue는 to부정사와 동명사를 모두 목적어로 쓸 수 있고, 그중 어느 것을 목적어로 취하든지 뜻이 달라지지 않는 동사이다.
② remember는 동명사를 목적어로 쓰면 '~한 것을 기억하다'라는 뜻이다. 어제 그녀를 본 것을 기억하는 것이므로 동명사를 목적어로 쓰는 것이 적절하다. to부정사를 목적어로 쓰면 '~하는/할 것을 기억하다'라는 뜻이 된다. (to see → seeing)
③ consider는 동명사를 목적어로 쓰는 동사이다.
(to move → moving)
④ postpone은 동명사를 목적어로 쓰는 동사이다.
(to meet → meeting)
⑤ dislike는 동명사를 목적어로 쓰는 동사이다.
(to be → being)

6 forget은 동명사를 목적어로 쓰면 '~한 것을 잊다'라는 뜻이다. 그녀가 문을 잠근 것을 잊어버려, 확인하기 위해 되돌아가야 했다는 의미이므로 동명사를 목적어로 쓰는 것이 적절하다.

7 동사 quit은 동명사를 목적어로 쓴다. plan, pretend, agree, would like는 to부정사를 목적어로 쓰는 동사들이다.
① studying → to study ② being → to be
③ taking → to take ⑤ selling → to sell

8 ⑤ 주어로 쓰인 동명사는 단수로 취급한다. (are → is)

9 ② put off는 '(하던 것을) 미루다'라는 뜻의 동사구로 동명사를 목적어로 한다. (to buy → buying)

10 • look forward to+-ing '~을 고대하다'
• 전치사의 목적어로 동사가 올 때는 동명사의 형태로 쓴다.

11 ⓑ have trouble+-ing '~하는 데 어려움을 겪다'
(to get → getting)
ⓓ 주어로 쓰인 동명사는 단수 취급한다. (are → is)

12 주어 역할을 하는 동명사구(Learning new things)에서 마지막 단어(things)가 복수형으로 끝나서 동사도 복수형을 써야 할 것 같지만, 동명사구 주어는 무조건 단수 취급함에 유의한다. 접속사 but이 두 개의 동명사구를 대등하게 연결해야 하므로 but 다음에는 getting better at them이 와야 하고, 마찬가지로 동사도 단수형(is)을 써야 한다.

13 on[upon]+-ing '~하자마자'
= as soon as+주어+동사

14 practice, suggest, keep은 뒤에 -ing가 오는 동사들이다. agree와 promise는 to부정사를 목적어로 쓴다.
① to take → taking ② holding → to hold
③ going → to go ④ to call → calling

15 ④ Nina가 혼자서 여러 번 해외 여행을 갔고 그걸 즐긴다는 내용이므로 맥락상 혼자 하는 여행에 익숙해졌다는 내용이 들어가야 한다. 따라서 '~하는 데 익숙하다'라는 의미의 「be used to+-ing」를 사용해 작성한다. 참고로 「be used to+동사원형」은 '~하는 데 사용되다'라는 의미이며, 「used to+동사원형」은 '~하곤 했다'라는 의미이다.

16 succeed in+-ing '~하는 데 성공하다'
succeed to(to: 전치사) 뒤에는 동사원형이 오지 않고 명사 상당 어구가 온다. 'succeed to'는 '~을 물려받다'라는 뜻이다.

17 ⑤ be busy+-ing '~하느라고 바쁘다' 그녀는 어제 저녁 8시경 그녀의 숙제를 하느라고 바빴었다.
①②③ spend+목적어+(on)+-ing '~하느라 …을 소비하다'
④ stop+동사 '~하는 것을 멈추다, 그만두다'
stop+to부정사 '~하기 위해 멈추다'
'그녀는 자정 전에 TV 보는 것을 멈췄다'는 의미가 되기 위해서는 watching이 와야 한다.

18 ②「eager to+동사원형」 '~을 열망하는'
③ enjoy는 동명사를 목적어로 취한다.
① 맥락상 꽃들의 사진을 찍기 위해 멈췄다는 의미이므로 목적을 나타내는 to부정사의 부사적 용법을 활용한다. (take → to take)
④ 맥락상 '시끄러운 이웃'이라는 의미이며, 명사 neighbors를 수식하고 있으므로 형용사 noisy를 쓰는 것이 적절하다. (noise → noisy)
⑤ consider는 동명사를 목적어로 취한다.
(to buy → buying)
공원을 거닐던 중, Olivia는 꽃들의 사진을 찍기 위해 멈춰 섰다. 그녀를 둘러싼 부드러운 향기는 그녀를 강렬히 사진 찍고 싶게 만들었다. 그녀는 신선한 공기 속에서 오후를 보내는 것을 즐겼지만, 시끄러운 이웃을 만나는 걸 피하기 위해 일찍 떠나야 했다. 집에 가기 전, 그녀는 빵집에서 빵을 사는 것을 고려했고, 그날 저녁 가족을 위해 케이크를 구울 계획을 세웠다.

19 • plan+to부정사 '~을 계획하다'
• go+-ing '~하러 가다'
• look forward to+-ing '~을 고대하다'

20 동명사를 이용하여 문장의 주어를 만들고, 동명사 주어는 단수 취급한다. participate in: ~에 참여하다

21 succeed in+-ing '~하는 데 성공하다'
instead of+-ing '~대신에'

22 be used to+-ing '~에 익숙하다'

23 ③ be in favor of+-ing '~에 찬성하다' (with → of)
① without+-ing '~하지 않고'
② prevent … from+-ing '…가 ~하는 것을 막다'
④ apologize for+-ing '~에 대해 사과하다'
⑤ feel like+-ing '~하고 싶다'

24 keep … from+-ing '…가 ~하는 것을 막다'

25 (a)「forget+to부정사」는 '~할[하는] 것을 잊다'라는 의미이고,「forget+동명사」는 '~한 것을 잊다'라는 의미이다. 출발할 때 전화할 것을 잊지 말라는 뜻이므로, to부정사를 쓰는 것이 어법상 옳다. (calling → to call)
(d) dream of는 '~을 꿈꾸다'라는 의미로, 동명사를

목적어로 가진다. (travel → traveling)

(e) 「be worth+~ing」는 '~할 가치가 있다'라는 의미
이다. (to visit → visiting)

(b) admit은 동명사를 목적어로 가지는 동사이므로
어법상 적절하다.

(c) 「remember+동명사」는 '~한 것을 기억하다'라는
의미이고, 「remember+to부정사」는 '~하는/할
것을 기억하다'라는 의미이다. 따라서 지난달에 책
을 빌려준 것을 기억하냐는 뜻이므로, 동명사를 사
용한 것은 적절하다.

26 need+-ing '~되어야 할 필요가 있다'
= need to be+과거분사

27 ④ feel like+-ing '~하고 싶다'
(to taking → taking)

28 cannot help+-ing '~하지 않을 수 없다'
= cannot but+동사원형

29 ⓐ be used to+-ing '~에 익숙하다' (go → going)
ⓒ look forward to+-ing '~을 고대하다'
(see → seeing)
ⓓ be accustomed to+-ing '~에 익숙하다'
(be → being)
ⓑ cannot[could not] but+동사원형 '~하지 않을
수 없다'
ⓔ be devoted to+-ing '~에 헌신하다'

30 It is useless+to부정사 '~해도 소용없다'
= It is of no use+to부정사
= It is no use+-ing

31 ② used to+동사원형 '~하곤 했다'
(standing → stand)
cf. be used to+동사원형 '~하기 위해 사용되다'
be used to+-ing '~하는 데 익숙하다'

32 ④ prefer는 동명사와 to부정사를 모두 목적어로 쓸
수 있고, 그 중 어느 것을 목적어로 취하든지 뜻이
달라지지 않는 동사이다.
① enjoy는 동명사를 목적어로 쓰는 동사이다.
(to be → being)
② instead of는 '~대신에'라는 뜻의 전치사이다. 전
치사의 목적어로 동사가 오면 동명사의 형태로 온
다. (eat → eating)
③ imagine은 동명사를 목적어로 쓰는 동사이다.
(to meet → meeting)
⑤ 동명사의 부정형은 동명사의 바로 앞에 not이나
never를 쓴다. apologize for+-ing는 '~에 대해
사과하다'라는 뜻이다.

(not for joining → for not joining)

33 ② '~하기 위해 사용되다'라는 뜻은 「be used to+동
사원형」으로 나타낸다. (relaxing → relax)
①⑤ 「used to+동사원형」 '~하곤 했다'
③④ 「get[be] used to+-ing」 '~에 익숙해지다'

34 (1) stop by+to부정사 '~하기 위해 들르다'
(2) be used to+-ing '~에 익숙하다'

35 ⓐ It is of no use+to부정사 '~해도 소용없다'
(telling → to tell)
ⓒ 동명사의 부정형은 동명사의 바로 앞에 not이나
never를 쓴다. apologize for+-ing는 '~에 대해
사과하다'라는 뜻이다.
(doing not return → not returning)
ⓔ mind는 동명사를 목적어로 쓰는 동사이다.
(to turn → turning)
ⓕ remember+동명사는 '~한 것을 기억하다'라는 뜻
이다. 오늘 밤 식료품점에 들르는 것을 기억하라는
뜻이므로 여기서는 적절치 않다. 따라서 '~할 것을
기억하다'라는 뜻의 remember+to부정사를 사용
해야 한다. (dropping → to drop)
*drop by '~에 들르다'
ⓖ 주어로 쓰인 동명사는 항상 단수 취급한다.
(are → is)
ⓑ 동명사의 의미상의 주어는 소유격으로 쓰는 것이
원칙이다.
ⓓ have trouble+-ing '~하는 데 어려움을 겪다'

36 (1) to부정사와 동명사 모두 문장의 주어로 쓰일 수 있
지만, 빈칸에 맞추기 위하여 동명사를 활용해 주어
를 만들고 단수 취급한다. per('~마다, 당')의 의미
로 쓰이는 부정관사 a를 사용한다.
(2) 전치사 by의 목적어로 동사가 나올 때는 동명사의
형태로 쓴다. by+-ing는 '~함으로써'라는 의미이다.

37 continue와 keep 모두 '~하는 것을 계속하다'라는
의미의 동사이다. 하지만 continue는 to부정사와 동
명사를 모두 목적어로 쓸 수 있는 반면, keep의 뒤에
는 -ing 형태만 쓸 수 있다. tell은 목적격 보어로 to
부정사를 쓰는 동사이므로, '거절하지 말라고'의 의
미는 to부정사를 활용한다. to부정사의 부정형은
「not+to+동사원형」으로 쓴다. '거절하다'라는 뜻의
turn down은 타동사+부사의 형태로, 목적어가 대명
사일 때는 항상 동사와 부사 사이에 들어간다.

38 decide+to부정사 '~하기로 결심하다'
instead of+(동)명사 '~하는 대신에'

39 be worth+-ing '~하는 게 좋다(~할 가치가 있다)'

PRACTICE 1

1 painted		**2** running	
3 dancing		**4** used	
5 spoken		**6** singing	
7 founded		**8** terrifying	

> **1, 4, 5, 7** 분사와 수식 받는 명사가 '완료/수동'의 의미 관계를 이루므로 과거분사가 알맞다.
> **2, 3, 6, 8** 분사와 수식 받는 명사가 '능동/진행'의 의미 관계를 이루므로 '동사원형+-ing' 형태인 현재분사가 알맞다.

PRACTICE 2

1 sung by kids

2 fallen under the tree

3 taking a break

4 lying on the grass

5 covered with snow

6 standing in front of the gate

7 hanging on the wall

8 filled with blueberries

> **1~8** 빈칸에 올 분사와 분사의 수식을 받는 명사와의 의미 관계를 따져서 '능동/진행'의 관계이면 현재 분사를, '완료/수동'의 관계이면 과거분사를 써서 문장을 완성한다.

PRACTICE 3

1 reading		**2** screaming	
3 looking		**4** surrounded	
5 hit		**6** surprised	
7 calling		**8** fixed	
9 waiting		**10** tested	

> **1, 3, 7** 주어와 괄호 안의 동사가 능동의 관계이므로 현재분사를 쓴다.
> **2, 9** 분사가 목적어의 상태나 행위를 설명하는 목적격 보어로 쓰인 경우로, 목적어와 목적격 보어가 능동의 관계이므로 현재분사를 쓴다. '(목적어가) ~하는 것을'로 해석한다.
> **4, 6** 분사가 주어의 상태나 행위를 설명하는 주격 보어로 쓰인 경우로, 주어와 주격 보어가 수동의 관계이므로 과거분사를 쓴다. '~한, ~된, ~해진'으로 해석한다.
> **5, 8, 10** 분사가 목적어의 상태나 행위를 설명하는 목적격 보어로 쓰인 경우로, 목적어와 목적격 보어가 수동의 관계이므로 과거분사를 쓴다. '(목적어가) ~되는 것을'로 해석한다.

PRACTICE 4

1 A **2** B **3** B **4** A **5** B

6 B **7** B **8** A **9** A **10** A

> **[보기]**
> A. the dining room: 식당(식사를 하기 위한 방) → 동명사(용도, 목적)
> B. the boy smiling at you: 너에게 웃고 있는 소년→ 현재분사(행위, 상태)

> **1, 4, 9** 밑줄 친 부분이 '~하기 위한'의 의미로 명사의 용도나 목적을 나타내는 동명사로 쓰였다.
> **2, 6, 7** 밑줄 친 부분이 '~하고 있는, ~하게 하는'의 의미로 수식받는 명사의 행위나 상태를 나타내는 현재분사로 쓰였다.
> **3** 밑줄 친 부분이 '~하고 있는'의 의미로 주어의 동작이 진행 중이었다는 상태를 나타내는 현재분사로 쓰였다.
> **5** 밑줄 친 부분이 목적어의 상태나 행위를 설명하는 목적격 보어로 쓰였으므로 현재분사이다.
> **8, 10** 밑줄 친 부분이 '~하는 것'의 의미로 전치사의 목적어로 쓰였으므로 동명사이다.

PRACTICE 5

1 excited, exciting

2 disappointing, disappointed

3 boring, bored

4 surprised, surprising

5 amazed, amazing

6 confusing, confused

7 shocking, shocked

8 depressed, depressing

9 fascinating, fascinated

10 interested, interesting

11 moving, moved

12 frightened, frightening

13 satisfied, satisfying

14 embarrassed, embarrassing

> **1~14** '~한 감정을 일으키는'의 의미일 때는 현재분사를 쓰고, '~한 감정을 느끼는'의 의미일 때는 과거분사를 쓴다.

PRACTICE 6

1 Feeling tired

2 Walking along the street

3 Knowing it's her mistake

4 Not having a car anymore

5 Waiting for a taxi

6 arriving in Daejeon at 10:30

7 Opening the box

8 (Being) Given the prize

9 Not being very old

10 Turning right

11 Telling me her plans

12 serving us some tea

PRACTICE 7

1 Having just eaten pizza

2 Having read the paper

3 Because[As/Since] I lost my bag

4 Although[Though/Even though] I had not heard from her for a long time

5 (Having been) Repaired by Greg

6 Because[As/Since] she had not read the book

7 Having bought a brand-new car

8 Because[As/Since] he didn't find me

9 Not knowing what to do

10 Although[Though/Even though] I heard the truth about him

PRACTICE 8

1 with her legs crossed

2 with the light turned on

3 with his wife knitting a sweater

4 with my dog following me

5 with the door closed

6 with her daughter sitting beside her

「with+명사+분사」는 '~을 …한 채로'의 뜻으로 동시 상황을 나타낸다.

1, 2, 5 명사와 분사의 관계가 수동이거나, 이미 완료된 상황을 나타내므로 「with+명사+과거분사」 표현을 써서 문장을 완성한다.
3, 4, 6 명사와 분사의 관계가 능동이고, 상황이 진행/지속 중이므로 「with+명사+현재분사」 표현을 써서 문장을 완성한다.

PRACTICE 9

1 speaking **2** speaking **3** Compared

4 Judging **5** speaking **6** Speaking

PRACTICE 10

1 Generally speaking **2** Compared with

3 Strictly speaking **4** Considering

5 Frankly speaking

📋 중간·기말고사 대비문제 정답 본문 _ p.198

1 ③ **2** ④ **3** ①,④ **4** ② **5** no water left

6 ② **7** ⑤ **8** ① **9** (1) raised (2) blocking[block]

10 ④ **11** ④ **12** taking → taken **13** ①,④

14 Look at the baby smiling at me. **15** ③,⑤

16 (1) falling → fallen (2) slept → sleeping (3) Wanting not → Not wanting **17** ③ **18** ⑤

19 ① **20** ② **21** ⑤ **22** ② **23** ③ **24** ②

25 ④ **26** My own problems seem insignificant compared with other people's.[Compared with other people's, my own problems seem insignificant.] **27** ④ **28** ④ **29** ④ **30** ④

31 ③ **32** Watching, my mom **33** ⑤ **34** ③

35 ② **36** Not having brought **37** ③ **38** ②

39 ④ **40** Although[Though], had been **41** ③

42 ③ **43** Although[Though/Even though] he had stage fright **44** ⑤

중간·기말고사 대비문제 해설

1 • 동시동작을 나타내는 분사구문이다.
• imagine+-ing '~을 상상하다'

2 '최선을 다했지만, 그는 시험에 떨어졌다'는 해석이 적절하므로 양보를 나타내는 분사구문이다.

3 ① 지각동사 saw의 목적격 보어 자리에 현재분사 flying이 올 수 있다.
④ 시험을 '준비하는' 능동의 의미이므로 현재분사 preparing을 이용하여 주어 The students를 수식하는 것은 적절하다.
② 맥락상 내 여동생에 의해 '구워진' 케이크이므로 수동의 의미를 나타내는 과거분사 baked의 사용이 적절하다. (bake → baked)
③ 문장의 주어가 The flowers이고 planted는 주어를 수식하는 분사구이므로 본동사는 is blooming이다. 복수주어에 동사의 수를 일치시켜야 하므로 복수동사를 써야 한다. (is → are)
⑤ 문장의 주어가 She이고, 본동사가 picked up이므로 동사 lay가 또 등장할 수 없다. 맥락상 버스 정류장 근처에 '놓여 있는' 장갑이라는 의미이므로 a glove를 수식하는 현재분사 lying으로 쓰는 것이 적절하다. (lay → lying)

4 ② '나의 엄마를 돕고 있는'이라는 의미가 적절하므로

능동과 진행의 의미를 나타내는 현재분사가 알맞다.

① '사용된 차(중고차)'라는 의미가 적절하므로 수동과 완료의 의미를 나타내는 과거분사를 써야 한다. (using → used)

③ '나에게 주어진 가방'이라는 의미이므로, 수동의 의미를 나타내는 과거분사로 써야 한다. (giving → given)

④ '해변에서 놀고 있는 소년'이므로, 능동과 진행의 의미를 나타내는 현재분사로 써야 한다. (played → playing)

⑤ '일본어로 써진 책'이므로, 수동의 의미를 나타내는 과거분사로 써야 한다. (writing → written)

5 문장의 동사(had)가 이미 존재하고, 접속사 없이 동사를 두 개 쓸 수 없다. 따라서 동사 leave는 no water를 수식할 수 있는 분사의 형태로 써야 한다. '남겨진 물'이라는 의미로 써야 하므로, 수동과 완료의 의미의 과거분사로 쓴다.

6 ② '~라는 팻말'처럼 팻말의 내용을 수식하기 위해 '~하고 있는'이라는 의미의 현재분사 saying을 사용해야 한다. write는 의미상 자연스럽지 않고, signature는 '서명'을 의미한다.

7 문장의 동사(met)가 이미 존재하고, 접속사 없이 동사를 두 개 쓸 수 없다. 빈칸은 구를 이루어 명사구 an old man을 수식하는 분사의 형태로 써야 한다. '그의 고향을 방문하는 노인'이라는 의미가 되어야 하므로, 능동의 의미를 나타내는 현재분사가 들어가는 것이 알맞다.

8 '일로 지쳤으므로, 그는 집에 도착하자마자 잠자리에 들었다'라는 해석이 적절하므로, 이유를 나타내는 부사절로 바꾸어 쓸 수 있다.

9 (1) 등위 접속사(and)가 수동태의 과거분사를 연결하고 있으므로 raised로 고쳐야 한다.

(2) 지각동사(saw)가 쓰였고 목적어와 목적격 보어가 능동 관계이므로 목적격 보어 자리에는 동사원형이나 현재분사가 온다.

10 ④ 내가 감동을 느끼는 것이므로 과거분사로 쓰는 것이 알맞다.

① 그가 놀라운 감정을 느끼는 것이므로 과거분사로 써야 한다. (surprising → surprised)

② notice는 지각동사이므로 목적격 보어로 to부정사가 올 수 없다. 지각동사의 목적격 보어로는 동사원형 또는 현재분사가 올 수 있다.

(to lie → lying[lie])

③ 동사 decide는 목적어로 to부정사를 쓴다. (taking → to take)

⑤ spend+시간+-ing '~하느라 …를 소비하다' (prepared → preparing)

11 전치사 다음에 절이 나올 수 없으므로 밑줄 친 동사는 명사 many English dictionaries를 수식할 수 있는 분사의 형태로 고쳐야 한다. '출간된 사전'이라는 의미가 되어야 하므로 수동의 의미를 나타내는 과거분사로 쓰는 것이 적절하다.

12 '좋고 아름다운 것들에서 얻어진(가져온) 이름들'이라는 해석이 적절하므로 수동의 의미를 나타내는 과거분사로 써야 한다.

13 '그림을 그리는 것을 잘하기 때문에'라는 이유를 나타내는 분사구문이므로, 이유를 나타내는 접속사 Because 또는 As로 시작하는 부사절로 바꿀 수 있다.

14 「주어+동사+목적어+목적격 보어」의 어순인 5형식 문장으로 쓴다. 주어는 명령문이므로 생략한다. 목적격 보어인 smile은 '미소 짓고 있는'이라는 진행의 의미를 강조해야 하므로 현재분사의 형태로 쓴다.

15 ③ 주어인 A number of great speeches가 유명한 연설자들에 의해 전달되는 것이므로 수동태로 써야 한다. 현재완료의 수동태는 「have+been+과거분사」로 쓴다. 여기서 deliver은 '전달하다'라는 뜻으로 사용되었다. (have been delivering → have been delivered)

⑤ 목적어(your voice)가 들리는 것이므로 목적격 보어는 수동의 의미인 과거분사로 써야 한다. (hearing → heard)

16 (1) 떨어진 낙엽이므로 완료의 의미를 갖는 과거분사 fallen이 와야 한다. 'falling leaves'는 '떨어지고 있는 낙엽'이 되어 on the ground와 어울리지 않는다.

(2) 자고 있는 중이었으므로 과거진행시제가 되기 위해 sleeping이 와야 한다.

(3) 분사구문에서 분사를 부정하는 not은 분사 앞에 와야 한다.

17 주어진 문장의 밑줄 친 knowing은 주어로 쓰인 동명사이다.

③ 명사 dog를 수식하고 있는 현재분사로 '짖고 있는'이라는 능동과 진행의 의미를 더해주고 있다.

①④ 주어로 쓰인 동명사이다.

② 전치사의 목적어로 쓰인 동명사이다.

⑤ 동사 mind의 목적어로 쓰인 동명사이다.

18 ⓑ 휴대용 블루투스 스피커가 중국에서 보내진 것이므로 수동과 완료를 나타내는 과거분사를 쓰는 것이 적절하다. (sending → sent)

ⓒ 불이 꺼져야 하는 것이므로 수동태로 써야 한다. 조동사가 있는 수동태는 「조동사+be+과거분사」의 어순으로 쓴다. turn off는 동사구이므로 함께 붙여 쓴다. (turn off → be turned off)

ⓓ excited라는 감정의 원인을 나타내주는 to부정사의 부사적 용법으로 써야 한다. (hearing → hear)

ⓔ 회의가 열리는 것이므로 수동의 의미를 나타내는 과거분사를 써야 한다. (holding → held)

19 주어진 문장의 밑줄 친 sleeping은 명사 child를 수식하고 있는 현재분사이다.

① 동사 enjoy의 목적어로 쓰인 동명사이다.

② 명사 dog을 수식하고 있는 현재분사이다.

③ 주격 보어로 쓰인 현재분사이다.

④⑤ 명사 girl을 수식하고 있는 현재분사이다. 구를 이루어 수식하고 있으므로 명사의 뒤에 위치했다.

20 '~한 감정을 느끼게 하는'의 의미가 되어야 하므로 현재분사가 들어가야 한다.

21 ① 문장에서 접속사 없이 동사(know, talk)가 두 개 쓰일 수 없다. 따라서 동사 talk를 명사를 수식할 수 있는 분사로 바꿔야 하며, 소녀가 말하고 있는 것이므로 능동과 진행을 나타내는 현재분사를 쓰는 것이 적절하다. (talk → talking)

② 동사가 주어로 쓰일 때는 동명사나 to부정사의 형태로 바꾸어 주는 것이 적절하다.
(Read → Reading[To read])

③ I가 정리되는 수동의 의미가 아닌 '정리하고 있었다'는 뜻을 나타내는 문장이므로 과거분사 put을 현재분사로 바꾸어 과거진행시제를 나타내는 것이 적절하다. (put → putting)

④ 동사 finish는 동명사를 목적어로 쓰는 동사이다.
(to read → reading)

22 ② 「with+명사+분사」에서 명사와 분사의 관계가 수동이면 과거분사를 쓴다. 따라서 crossing을 crossed로 고쳐야 한다. (crossing → crossed)

23 주어진 문장은 이유를 나타내는 분사구문을 사용했다.
나이가 들어서, 그녀는 사막을 건널 수 없었다.
③ 원인, 이유   ① 양보
②⑤ 동시동작   ④ 조건

24 ⓒ 그 종이 Big Ben이라고 불리는 것이므로 수동의

의미를 나타내는 과거분사(called)가 알맞다.

ⓓ 상황이 당황스러운 감정을 느끼게 하는 것이므로 현재분사(embarrassing)가 알맞다.

ⓖ Frankly speaking은 '솔직히 말하면'이라는 의미의 관용적 표현이다.

ⓐ 불이 타고 있는 것이므로 능동과 진행의 의미를 나타내는 현재분사로 써야 한다.
(burned → burning)

ⓑ '주어진 단어를 가지고 문장을 만들어야 한다'는 해석이 되어야 하므로 수동의 의미를 나타내는 과거분사를 써야 한다. (giving → given)

ⓔ 이라크에서 말해지는 언어라는 의미가 되어야 하므로 수동의 의미를 나타내는 과거분사를 써야 한다. (speaking → spoken)

ⓕ 숨겨진 보물이므로 수동과 완료의 의미를 나타내는 과거분사로 써야 한다. (hiding → hidden)

25 ④ 진행의 의미를 나타내는 현재분사이다.

① 전치사의 목적어로 쓰인 동명사이다.

② 주격 보어로 쓰인 동명사이다.

③ 동사 stop의 목적어로 쓰인 동명사이다.

⑤ 주어로 쓰인 동명사이다.

26 seem은 형용사를 주격 보어로 취한다.
*compared with '~와 비교하면'

27 ① 소식이 충격을 주는 것이므로 현재분사로 써야 한다. (shocked → shocking)

② 영화가 흥분을 느끼게 하는 것이므로 현재분사로 써야 한다. (excited → exciting)

③ 선생님의 설명이 매력을 느끼게 하는 것이므로 현재분사로 써야 한다. (fascinated → fascinating)

⑤ 그가 의사가 되었다는 것이 놀라운 것이므로 현재분사로 써야 한다. (amazed → amazing)

28 • written in English '영어로 쓰인'
• '~한 감정을 느끼는'의 의미인 과거분사 confused가 들어가야 한다.

29 ④ carried는 과거분사로 The large bag을 뒤에서 수식하고 있다.
①②③⑤ 과거시제 동사들이다.

30 ④ 소음이 짜증나게 하는 것이므로 현재분사로 써야 한다. (annoyed → annoying)

31 ③ It은 가주어, to see 이하가 진주어인 문장이다. 너와 함께 로마에서 많은 아름다운 장소들을 보는 것이 흥미를 주는 것이므로 현재분사로 써야 한다.
(excited → exciting)

32 접속사와 부사절의 주어를 빼고 부사절의 동사를 -ing형태로 바꾸어 분사구문을 만든다. 부사절의 주어와 주절의 주어가 같은 대상을 가리키지만, 부사절의 주어가 구체적인 명사, 주절의 주어가 대명사로 쓰인 경우, 분사구문에서는 주절의 주어를 구체적인 명사로 쓴다.

33 ⑤ 동시동작 ①②③④ 양보

34 • 「with+명사+분사」에서 명사와 분사의 관계가 수동이면 과거분사를 쓴다.
• 문장의 주어로는 동명사(-ing)가 온다.

35 ② 나는 숙제를 끝내고 난 후, Michael의 파티에 갔다.
① 무엇을 말해야 할지 몰라서, 나는 조용히 있었다. (Though → Because[As/Since])
③ 공원 근처에 살지만, 나는 거기에 거의 가본 적이 없다. (As → Though[Although/Even though])
④ 나는 피곤하기 때문에, 나가는 것보다 차라리 자는 편이 낫겠다. (Though → Because[As/Since])
⑤ 내가 집에 도착했을 때, 나는 열쇠를 잃어버렸다는 것을 알아챘다. (If → When)

36 not이나 never와 같은 부정어는 분사 앞에 붙인다.

37 접속사(As)와 부사절의 주어(I)를 생략한 뒤, 부사절의 동사(was surprised)를 -ing로 바꾼다. 수동형의 분사구문에서는 being을 생략할 수 있기 때문에 빈칸에는 Surprised가 들어가는 것이 알맞다.

38 ⓑ '보람 있는'은 능동의 의미를 가지므로 현재분사로 나타낸다. (rewarded → rewarding)
ⓒ 전치사 into 뒤에는 명사가 와야 한다. (hibernate → hibernation)
ⓓ '설립하다'라는 뜻의 동사(found)의 과거분사형은 founded이다. (found → founded)

39 동시동작을 나타내는 분사구문이고, 주절의 목적어(a swallow)와 목적격 보어(fly)의 관계가 능동이므로 현재분사(flying)를 쓴다.

40 '비록 Jane이 그의 집에 여러 번 가본 적이 있지만 여전히 어떻게 가는지 기억하지 못했다'는 의미이므로 첫 번째 빈칸에는 양보의 접속사 Although[Though]를 쓴다. 주어진 분사구문은 완료형 분사구문이기 때문에 부사절의 시제가 주절의 시제보다 앞선다. 따라서 나머지 빈칸에는 주절의 과거시제보다 앞선 과거완료시제의 부사절 동사 had been을 쓴다.

41 (A) 주어(A farmer's son)가 상자를 들고 있는 것이므로 능동과 진행을 나타내는 현재분사 carrying을 쓴다.

(B) chickens와 give의 관계가 수동이므로 과거분사 given을 쓴다.
(C) '~한 감정을 느끼는'의 뜻일 때는 과거분사를 쓴다.

42 (b) 선행사가 사람이고, 관계대명사가 주어 역할을 하므로 주격 관계대명사 who를 쓴다.
(which → who)
(d) 숙제는 Jake에 의해 행해진 대상이므로, 수동의 의미를 나타내는 과거분사가 필요하다.
(doing → done)
(h) 주격 관계대명사 who 뒤에는 동사가 와야 하는데, wearing은 동사가 아니므로 be동사 is를 추가해야 한다. (wearing → is wearing)

43 부사절의 접속사는 양보를 나타내는 Although나 Though 또는 Even though를 쓴다. 분사구문에서 주어가 빠져 있기 때문에 부사절의 주어는 주절의 주어와 같은 he를 쓴다. 분사구문이 -ing로 시작하므로 부사절의 동사는 주절의 시제와 같은 과거시제로 쓴다. 목적어는 동사의 뒤에 그대로 쓴다.
무대공포증이 있음에도, 그는 관객들 앞에서 힘차게 그의 노래를 불렀다.

44 「with+명사+분사」는 '~을 …한 채로'의 의미를 갖는다. 이때 명사와 분사의 관계가 수동이면 과거분사를 사용한다.
⑤ 「with+목적어+분사」 형태에서 목적어인 his dog이 달리는 중이므로 racing을 써야 한다.
(raced → racing)
그의 개가 그의 옆에서 달리는 채로, 그는 빨리 달렸다.
① 흩어진 장난감들이므로 수동의 의미를 갖는 과거분사 scattered의 사용은 적절하다. 방 여기저기에 장난감들이 흩어진 채로 아이들은 행복하게 놀고 있는 중이었다.
② 퍼붓는 비이므로 능동의 의미를 갖는 현재분사 pouring의 사용이 적절하다. 바깥에 비가 퍼붓는 가운데 우리 가족은 집에 머물기로 결정했다.
③ 여자의 다리(her legs)와 분사가 수동 관계이므로 과거분사 crossed의 사용은 적절하다. 사진은 그녀의 다리를 꼰 채로 앉아있는 여자를 보여준다.
④ 숲이 둘러싸고 있다는 의미이므로 능동의 의미를 갖는 현재분사 surrounding의 사용은 적절하다. 그들은 그들을 둘러싸고 있는 숲을 조용히 하이킹했다.

CHAPTER 10

형용사
Adjectives

PRACTICE 1

1 Golf is an outdoor game.

2 I'm sorry that you missed an important lesson.

3 I did my best to avoid similar mistakes.

4 My sister is a famous singer in Japan.

5 They played an exciting game and the spectators enjoyed it.

6 James was the only person I talked to last night.

7 The woman standing there is the former leader.

8 No one could move the heavy rock.

9 Where did you meet the lovely kids?

10 Jenny was very shocked by her dad's sudden death.

> 형용사는 명사의 앞에서 명사를 수식한다. 첫소리가 모음으로 시작하는 형용사가 셀 수 있는 단수 명사를 수식할 경우, 명사의 발음과는 상관없이 형용사 앞에 관사 an이 온다.
>
> **1** an outdoor game: 야외 경기
>
> *outdoor는 한정적 용법으로만 쓰인다.
>
> **2** an important lesson: 중요한 수업
>
> **3** similar mistakes: 비슷한 실수들
>
> **4** a famous singer: 유명한 가수
>
> **5** an exciting game: 신나는 경기
>
> **6** the only person: 유일한 사람
>
> *only는 한정적 용법으로만 쓰인다.
>
> **7** the former leader: 전 대표
>
> *former는 한정적 용법으로만 쓰인다.
>
> **8** the heavy rock: 무거운 바위
>
> **9** the lovely kids: 사랑스러운 아이들
>
> **10** sudden death: 갑작스러운 죽음

PRACTICE 2

1 alive		**2** lone		**3** important	
4 cheerful		**5** sleeping		**6** unique	
7 afraid		**8** great		**9** alike	
10 angry					

> **1, 3, 6, 9** 주격 보어로 쓰여 주어에 대한 설명을 하는 서술적 용법의 형용사가 와야 한다. 참고로 alive와 alike는 서술적 용법으로만 사용된다.
>
> **2, 4, 5, 8, 10** 명사 앞에서 명사를 수식하는 자리이므로 한정적 용법의 형용사가 와야 한다.

> **7** 주격 보어 자리이므로 동사의 현재분사형 scaring(두렵게 하는)과 서술적 용법으로 쓰이는 afraid(두려워하는)가 모두 올 수 있으나, 주어 I가 두려움을 일으키는 주체가 아니라 두려움을 느끼는 주체이므로 의미상 afraid가 적절하다. be afraid of와 be scared of는 둘 다 '~을 두려워하다'라는 뜻으로 쓰인다.

PRACTICE 3

1 something very expensive

2 Someone famous

3 a strange thing

4 anything dangerous

5 something special

6 a meaningful party

7 anything else to say

8 a lot of nice people

9 no one humorous

10 The important thing

11 anybody attractive

12 somewhere very dangerous

13 nothing new to tell

14 somewhere quiet to talk

Ch
10
형용사

> **1, 2, 4, 5, 7, 9, 11, 12, 13, 14** –thing, -one, -body, -where로 끝나는 단어는 형용사가 뒤에서 수식한다.
>
> **1** something very expensive: 아주 비싼 어떤 것
>
> **2** someone famous: 유명한 누군가
>
> **4** anything dangerous: 위험한 무언가
>
> **5** something special: 특별한 어떤 것
>
> **7** anything else to say: 말할 다른 무언가
>
> **9** no one humorous: 재미있는 사람이 전혀 없는
>
> **11** anybody attractive: 매력적인 누군가
>
> **12** somewhere very dangerous: 아주 위험한 어떤 곳
>
> **13** nothing new to tell: 말할 새로운 것이 없는
>
> **14** somewhere quiet to talk: 말하기 위한 조용한 어떤 곳
>
> **3, 10** thing이 단독으로 쓰일 때는 형용사가 thing 앞에 온다.
>
> **3** a strange thing: 이상한 것
>
> **10** The important thing: 중요한 것
>
> **6, 8** 일반 명사일 경우는 '관사+서수+기수+형용사+명사' 순으로 쓰며, 수량 형용사는 일반 형용사 앞에 온다.
>
> **6** a meaningful party: 의미 있는 파티
>   관사　형용사　　명사
>
> **8** a lot of　nice　people: 많은 좋은 사람들
>   수량형용사 일반형용사　명사

PRACTICE 4

1 We collected some money for homeless people last year.

2 My sister went to Africa to help the doctor cure sick people.

3 We should provide some more convenient services for disabled people.

4 The city is planning to build a school for deaf people.

5 We need to find a solution for young people who don't have jobs.

6 There's a special class for blind people in this center.

7 Do you think rich people should pay more taxes to help poor people?

8 The battlefield was covered with dead people and injured people.

> 「the+형용사」는 '~한 사람들'의 뜻으로, 복수 명사처럼 쓰인다.
>
> **1** the homeless = homeless people: 노숙자들
> **2** the sick = sick people: 아픈 사람들
> **3** the disabled = disabled people: 장애인들
> *provide A for B = provide B with A: B에게 A를 제공하다
> **4** the deaf = deaf people: 청각 장애인들
> *be planning to+동사: ~할 계획이다
> **5** the young = young people: 젊은 사람들
> **6** the blind = blind people: 시각 장애인들
> **7** the rich = rich people: 부유한 사람들
> the poor = poor people: 가난한 사람들
> **8** the dead = dead people: 죽은 사람들
> the injured = injured people: 다친 사람들
> *be covered with: ~로 덮이다

PRACTICE 5

1 two purple silk

2 your favorite Italian

3 all those small

4 half these dirty plastic

5 Both my gorgeous

6 All the smart

7 double the regular

8 both his new Canadian

9 the first three

10 these two large yellow

> 명사 앞에 2개 이상의 형용사가 함께 올 때는 '서수→기수→성질→크기→신구→색깔→국적→재료' 순으로 쓰고, 형용사 앞에 다른 수식어가 올 때는 'all/both/double/half→정관사/지시형용사/소유격→형용사' 순으로 쓴다.
>
> **1** two purple silk dresses
>   기수 색깔 재료
> **2** your favorite Italian food
>   소유격 성질 국적
> **3** all those small tables
>   all 지시형용사 크기
> **4** half these dirty plastic dishes
>   half 지시형용사 성질 재료
> **5** both my gorgeous daughters
>   both 소유격 성질
> **6** all the smart students
>   all 정관사 성질
> **7** double the regular price
>   double 정관사 성질
> **8** both his new Canadian friends
>   both 소유격 신구 국적
> **9** the first three lines
>   정관사 서수 기수
> **10** these two large yellow shirts
>   지시형용사 기수 크기 색깔

PRACTICE 6

1 much	**2** many	**3** much
4 many	**5** many	**6** many
7 much	**8** much	**9** many
10 much	**11** many	**12** much

> **1, 3, 7, 8, 10, 12** 셀 수 없는 명사 앞이므로 much가 알맞다.
> **2, 4, 5, 6, 9, 11** 셀 수 있는 명사의 복수형 앞이므로 many가 알맞다.

PRACTICE 7

1 a lot of world-famous dishes

2 a lot of chances

3 a lot of salt

4 a lot of evidence

5 a lot of weight

6 a lot of workers

7 a lot of interesting stories

8 a lot of work

9 a lot of time

10 a lot of water

> **1, 2, 6, 7** a lot of가 '많은'이라는 뜻으로 셀 수 있는 명사를 수식하는 경우이므로 복수 명사 형태로 쓴다.
> **3, 4, 5, 8, 9, 10** a lot of가 '많은'이라는 뜻으로 셀 수 없는 명사를 수식하는 경우이므로 단수 명사 형태로 쓴다.

PRACTICE 8

1 a little	**2** a few	**3** few	**4** little
5 a little	**6** a few	**7** few	**8** little
9 a little	**10** a few	**11** few	**12** little

1, 5, 9 '약간의'라는 의미로 셀 수 없는 명사의 양을 나타내는 a little이 알맞다
2, 6, 10 '몇몇의, 약간의'라는 의미로 셀 수 있는 명사의 수를 나타내는 a few가 알맞다.
3, 7, 11 '거의 ~ 없는'이라는 의미로 셀 수 있는 명사의 수를 나타내는 few가 알맞다.
4, 8, 12 '거의 ~ 없는'이라는 의미로 셀 수 없는 명사의 양을 나타내는 little이 알맞다.

PRACTICE 9

1 only a few friends
2 only a little information
3 only a little practice
4 only a few hours
5 Only a few applicants
6 only a little pepper

1, 4, 5 only a few는 '극소수의'라는 뜻으로 셀 수 있는 명사의 복수형을 수식한다.
2, 3, 6 only a little은 '아주 약간의'라는 뜻으로 셀 수 없는 명사를 수식한다.

PRACTICE 10

1 any	**2** Any	**3** some	**4** some
5 any	**6** some	**7** any	**8** Some
9 any	**10** some		

1, 5 일반적으로 부정문에서는 '조금도'라는 의미로 any를 쓴다.
2 긍정문에 '어떠한 ~라도'의 뜻으로 쓰이는 any가 알맞다.
3 일반적으로 긍정문에서 '몇몇의, 약간의'라는 뜻으로 쓰이며, 셀 수 있는 명사나 셀 수 없는 명사 모두와 함께 쓸 수 있는 some이 알맞다.
4, 6 '~하시겠어요?' 또는 '~할 수 있을까요?'라는 의미로 권유나 요구를 나타내는 의문문에서 쓰이는 some이 알맞다.
7 조건을 나타내는 if절에서는 any를 쓴다.
8 some이 불특정한 일부를 나타낼 때는 부정문에 쓰일 수 있다.
9 일반적으로 의문문에서는 '얼마간의, 몇몇의'의 뜻으로 any를 쓴다.
10 긍정의 대답을 예상하는 의문문에서는 some을 쓴다.

PRACTICE 11

1 any pride	**2** some rice
3 any situation	**4** any help
5 any souvenirs	**6** some water

7 Some people	**8** any interest
9 some money	**10** some medicine

1 Don't you have <u>any</u> pride in yourself?: 너는 너 자신에게 조금도 자부심을 가지고 있지 않니? → any가 의문문/부정문에서 사용될 때
*have pride in: ~에 자부심을 가지다
2 some rice: 약간의 밥 → some이 셀 수 없는 명사를 수식할 때
3 in <u>any</u> situation: 어떤 상황에서도 → any가 '어떤 ~라도'라는 의미로 쓰일 때
4 if you don't need <u>any</u> help: 네가 어떤 도움도 필요로 하지 않으면 → any가 조건을 나타내는 if절에서 사용될 때
5 she <u>didn't</u> buy <u>any</u> souvenirs: 그녀는 기념품을 조금도 사지 않았다 → any가 부정문에서 사용될 때
6 Can I have <u>some</u> water?: 물을 좀 먹을 수 있을까요? → some이 요구를 나타내는 의문문에서 사용될 때
7 <u>Some</u> people couldn't believe ~: 몇몇 사람들은 ~을 믿을 수 없었다 → some이 부정문에서 불특정한 일부를 나타낼 때
*be elected as: ~로 선출되다
8 if you have <u>any</u> interest in baking: 네가 제빵에 관심이 좀 있으면 → any가 조건을 나타내는 if절에서 사용될 때
*have interest in: ~에 관심이 있다
9 <u>some</u> money: 약간의 돈 → some이 셀 수 없는 명사를 수식할 때
10 some medicine: 약간의 약 → some이 셀 수 없는 명사를 수식할 때

PRACTICE 12

2 two – second
3 three – third
4 five – fifth
5 nine – ninth
6 twelve – twelfth
7 fifteen – fifteenth
8 twenty – twentieth
9 twenty-two – twenty-second
10 twenty-six – twenty-sixth
11 thirty – thirtieth
12 thirty-one – thirty-first
13 forty – fortieth
14 fifty-seven – fifty-seventh
15 sixty-nine – sixty-ninth
16 seventy-three – seventy-third
17 eighty-four – eighty-fourth
18 ninety-nine – ninety-ninth
19 a[one] hundred – a[one] hundredth
20 a[one] thousand – a[one] thousandth

PRACTICE 13

1 a[one] hundred (and) ninety-five

2 three hundred (and) seventy-four

3 five hundred (and) one

4 nine hundred (and) eighteen

5 two thousand, a[one] hundred (and) sixteen

6 four thousand, (and) eighty-seven

7 five thousand, three hundred (and) two

8 nine thousand, seven hundred (and) three

9 eleven thousand, (and) ninety

10 thirty-four thousand, eight hundred (and) fifteen

11 seventy thousand, three hundred (and) two

12 eighty-six thousand, two hundred (and) forty

13 a[one] hundred (and) two thousand, three hundred (and) sixty-nine

14 two hundred (and) eighty thousand, a[one] hundred (and) sixty-six

15 six hundred (and) two thousand, eight hundred (and) one

16 nine hundred (and) eleven thousand, three hundred

17 three million, seven hundred (and) forty-four thousand

18 five million, (and) eighteen thousand, seven hundred (and) ninety-nine

19 sixteen million, nine hundred (and) fifty thousand, five hundred (and) forty-one

20 twenty-eight million, two hundred (and) twenty-seven thousand, eight hundred (and) forty-six

PRACTICE 14

1 four-sevenths

2 seven-tenths

3 five and two-fifths

4 two-thirds

5 three-fourths[three-quarters]

6 sixteen and a half[one-half]

7 twenty-five and eight-ninths

8 six and a quarter[one-quarter]

9 a seventh[one-seventh]

10 nine and three-eighths

11 two point seven six

12 thirty-one point zero four

13 zero point one two

14 three point five

15 fifty-two point nine three

16 ten point zero one

17 zero point eight nine

18 one point three nine

19 fourteen point two five one

20 two hundred (and) seventy-five point one nine

PRACTICE 15

1 two thousand (and) six

2 nineteen ninety

3 eighteen eighty-four

4 June (the) fifth[the fifth of June]

5 November (the) nineteenth[the nineteenth of November]

6 February (the) twenty-fourth[the twenty-fourth of February]

7 December (the) first, two thousand (and) twenty
the first of December, two thousand (and) twenty

8 September (the) fifteenth, two thousand (and) twenty-four
the fifteenth of September, two thousand (and) twenty-four

9 January (the) twentieth, fifteen eighty-two
the twentieth of January, fifteen eighty-two

10 April (the) ninth, seventeen thirty-five
the ninth of April, seventeen thirty-five

PRACTICE 16

1 once   **2** three times

3 half   **4** ten times

5 four times   **6** twice

7 quarters   **8** five times

9 half   **10** three times

> **1** once: 한 번
> **2, 10** 기수+times+형용사 비교급+than: ~보다 (몇) 배 …한
> **3** half+as+형용사+as: ~의 절반만큼 …한
> **4** 기수+times+as+형용사+as: ~보다 (몇) 배 …한
> **5** 기수+times: ~번, ~배
> *at least: 적어도
> **6, 8** 배수사+a+시간 단위 명사(day/week/month/year): (하루/일주일/한 달/일 년)에 ~번
> **7** a quarter: 4분의 1
> three quarters: 4분의 3
> **9** in half: 절반으로, 둘로

PRACTICE 17

1 one twenty[twenty after/past one]

2 five sixteen

3 four-o-five[five after/past four]

4 seven fifty-six

5 eight forty-five[a quarter to nine]

6 two fifteen[a quarter after/past two]

7 twelve fifty[ten to one]

8 six thirteen

9 eleven thirty-five[twenty-five to twelve]

10 nine seventeen

11 four-o-nine

12 three thirty[half past three]

13 eight twenty-three

14 nine forty-eight

15 ten forty[twenty to eleven]

📑 중간·기말고사 대비문제 정답 본문 _ p.223

1 ④ **2** ③ **3** ③ **4** ③ **5** ⑤ **6** a few
minutes to review something important **7** ④
8 ⑤ **9** ② **10** ③ **11** ④ **12** turning
something useless into something useful
13 ④ **14** ⑤ **15** ② **16** ② **17** ②,⑤
18 many, much, little, few **19** ③ **20** ③
21 ③ **22** sick, disabled, disadvantaged, sick,
disabled, disadvantaged **23** ④ **24** ①
25 ⑤ **26** brave people **27** ③ **28** ②
29 ④ **30** ③ **31** Any, relax[rest], do
32 ⓐ twelfth ⓑ fifth ⓒ three times ⓓ five
ⓔ four ⓕ a quarter[one-quarter] **33** ②

중간·기말고사 대비문제 해설

1 glad는 서술적 용법으로만 쓸 수 있는 형용사이다.

2 박쥐와 올빼미는 밤에 활동적이다.
빈칸은 주격 보어의 자리이므로, 명사 혹은 형용사가
들어간다. 보기 중 '활동적인'이라는 뜻의 형용사는
active이다.
③ active ⑱ '활동적인, 적극적인'
① act ⑧ '행동하다'
② action ⑲ '행동, 동작'

④ activity ⑲ '움직임, 활동'
⑤ actively ⑭ '활발히, 활동적으로'

3 ⓑ nothing처럼 –thing으로 끝나는 단어는 형용사가
뒤에서 수식한다.
(harmful nothing → nothing harmful)
ⓓ every는 단수 명사를 수식하고 단수 취급한다.
(people were → person was)
ⓔ 긍정문에서는 some을 쓴다. any는 '어떠한 ~라
도'의 뜻으로 긍정문에 쓰일 수 있지만 여기에서는
문맥상 적절하지 않다. (any → some)

4 worth '~의 가치가 있는'
cf. be worth '~만큼의 가치가 있다'
be worth+-ing '~할 가치가 있다'

5 ⑤ 한 단어인 thing은 형용사가 앞에서 수식한다.
(Things bad → Bad things)

6 a few는 '약간의, 몇몇의'라는 뜻으로서 셀 수 있는 명
사(minutes)와 결합한다. 부정대명사 something
은 꾸미는 말이 뒤에 나오므로, '중요한 무언가'는
'something important'라고 쓴다.

7 -thing으로 끝나는 단어는 형용사가 뒤에서 수식하
고, 부정문이므로 something이 아닌 anything을 쓴
다.

8 That was close는 '아슬아슬하다, 큰일 날 뻔하다'는
뜻으로 '근접한'의 의미로 쓰인 ⑤가 정답이다.
① 주의 깊은, 면밀한
② 친밀한
③ 문을 닫다(영업 종료)
④ (눈을) 감다

9 권유나 요구를 나타내는 의문문과 일반적인 긍정문에
쓰이는 것은 some이다.

10 ③ 명사를 수식하는 수식어구이다.
①②④⑤ '~한 사람들'의 뜻으로 복수 명사처럼 쓰인
다.

11 • 형용사 enough는 '충분한'이란 의미로 명사를 앞
에서 수식한다.
• 부사 enough '충분히', 「형용사+enough+to부정
사」 '~할 정도로 충분히 …한'
• without이 쓰여 부정의 의미가 있으며 at all은 부
정문에서 '조금도 ~아니다'의 의미로 쓰인다. 따라
서 부정문에서 쓰이는 형용사 any가 적절하다.
• get some rest는 휴식을 취하라는 권유의 표현이
다.

12 현재진행형 시제이기 때문에 동사를 -ing형태로 변형

한다. turn A into B는 'A를 B로 바꾸다'란 의미를 갖는다. something은 -thing으로 끝나는 단어기 때문에 형용사가 뒤에서 수식한다. '쓸모없는'이라는 뜻의 형용사 useless와 '유용한'이라는 뜻의 useful을 사용한다.

13 ④「소유격+성질을 나타내는 형용사+색깔을 나타내는 형용사」의 어순으로 쓴다.

14 「much+셀 수 없는 명사」 '많은~', enough '충분한'

15 ② 소유격 대명사 your는 형용사의 앞에 쓴다.
(right your hand → your right hand)
① 형용사는 「소유격+서수+기수」의 어순으로 쓴다.
③ 형용사는 「another+기수」의 어순으로 쓴다. another의 뒤에 수사가 올 때는 복수명사도 쓸 수 있다.
④ 형용사는 「all+지시형용사+성질」의 어순으로 쓴다.
⑤ 형용사는 「소유격+성질+국적」의 어순으로 쓴다.

16 ⓑ fall은 상태변화를 나타내는 동사로 주어의 상태를 설명하기 위해 형용사를 필요로 한다. sleep은 동사이고, '자는'이라는 상태를 나타내는 것은 형용사 asleep이다. (sleep → asleep)
ⓐ break / during은 특정 기간을 나타내는 명사(구)와 함께 쓰여 '~동안'의 의미를 나타낸다. break는 '쉬는 시간'이라는 뜻의 명사이다.
ⓒ actively / be engaged in '~에 참여하다'라는 뜻의 동사로 빈칸에는 동사를 수식하는 부사가 들어가야 한다.
ⓓ loyal / The dog을 보충 설명하는 형용사 dependable, adorable이 접속사 and로 동등하게 이어져 있으므로 빈칸에도 형용사 loyal을 써야 한다.
ⓔ demand / 형용사 high가 수식하는 명사가 들어갈 자리이다. demand는 '수요'라는 뜻의 명사이다.

17 (b) 과거에 대한 이야기를 하고 있고 등위접속사 and로 연결되어 앞의 동사 collected와 병렬 구조를 이루어야 하므로 planting을 과거형으로 쓴다.
(planting → planted)
(e) '우리'가 실망을 느끼는 대상이므로 수동의 의미를 드러내는 과거분사로 쓴다.
(disappointing → disappointed)

18 「many+셀 수 있는 명사의 복수형」 '많은'
「much+셀 수 없는 명사」 '많은'
「little+셀 수 없는 명사」 '거의 ~ 없는'

19 「few+셀 수 있는 명사의 복수형」 '거의 ~없는'

20 ① 'be crowded with ~' '~로 가득 차다[붐비다]'
(crowd → crowded)
② 2형식 문장에서 감각동사의 주격 보어로는 형용사가 온다. (sleep → sleepy)
④ 동사 added의 목적어로 접속사 and 앞에 명사 fried onions가 온 것과 같이 명사가 목적어로 와야 한다. (salty → salt)
⑤ 주격 보어 자리에 서술적 용법의 형용사를 넣어 주어에 대한 설명을 한다. (taste → tasty)

21 nothing '아무것도 ~없음', something '무엇인가'

22 「the+형용사」 = 「형용사+people」
= 「those who are+형용사」

23 some은 긍정문에, any는 조건절에 쓴다.

24 (A) 'spend+시간+-ing' '~하는 데 …를 소비하다'
(B) to부정사가 주어의 역할을 할 때에는 가주어 It을 주어의 자리에 두고, 진주어인 to부정사구는 문장의 맨 뒤로 보낸다. 진주어 to부정사를 보충해 주는 보어로 형용사 stressful을 사용하는 것이 적절하다.
(C) 그가 감정을 느끼는 대상이므로 과거분사 tired가 적절하다.

Carl은 최근에 그의 첫 일자리를 얻었다. 그는 그의 직업에 만족하지만, 한 가지 문제가 있다. 그의 회사가 서울 시내에 위치해 있어서, 그의 집에서부터 그곳까지 약 2시간이 걸린다. 그는 주중에 그의 차를 운전하는 데 많은 시간을 소비한다. 교통 체증에 갇혀 있는 것은 스트레스를 받는 일이다. 때때로, 그것은 그를 피곤하게 만들고 그의 업무에 영향을 미친다. 그는 그의 회사에 더 가깝게 이사하는 것에 대해 생각하는 중이다.

25 ⑤ 소수는 소수점 전까지의 숫자를 기수로 읽는다. 소수점 이하는 한 자리씩 읽는다.
(three four → thirty four)

26 「the+형용사」는 '~한 사람들'이라는 뜻으로 「형용사+people」로 바꾸어 쓸 수 있다.

27 <보기> 네 작은 여동생에게 그렇게 못되게 굴지 말렴!
(형) 못된, 심술궂은
ⓑ 너는 나에게 왜 그렇게 못되게 구니?
(형) 못된, 심술궂은
ⓕ 그녀는 영화에서 못된 새엄마를 연기했다.
(형) 못된, 심술궂은
ⓐ 나는 어떤 해를 끼치려고 의도하진 않았다.

(동 의도하다)

ⓒ 연평균 강우량은 1400mm였다. (형 평균의)

ⓓ 그녀의 아이들은 그녀에게 세상을 <u>의미한다</u>.
(동 의미하다)

ⓔ 그 구름들은 비가 올 것이라는 걸 <u>의미한다</u>.
(동 의미하다)

28 ⓐ '자고 있는 아기'라는 뜻으로 능동 진행의 의미를 가진 현재분사 sleeping을 쓰는 것이 적절하다.

ⓑ 형용사 asleep은 서술적 용법으로만 쓸 수 있다.
*fall asleep '잠들다'

29 ④ 형용사는 기수, 국적 순으로 써야 한다.
(French two → two French)

30 ③ -where로 끝나는 단어는 형용사가 뒤에서 수식한다. (quiet somewhere → somewhere quiet)

31 any가 '어떠한 ~라도'라는 뜻일 때에는 긍정문에 쓸 수 있다. do는 '적절하다, 충분하다'라는 의미를 나타낸다.

32 ⓐ 12일은 서수로 twelfth로 쓴다.

ⓑ '5번째'라는 뜻의 서수는 fifth이다.

ⓒ '3배'라는 뜻의 배수사는 three times로 쓴다.

ⓓⓔ 3시 55분은 three fifty-five 또는 five to four(4시 5분 전)로 쓴다.

ⓕ 분수 1/4은 a quarter 또는 one-quarter로 쓴다.

33 ⓑ 주어에 two-thirds와 같이 부분을 나타내는 표현이 포함되어 있을 경우, of 뒤에 오는 명사의 수에 따라 동사의 수를 결정한다. furniture은 셀 수 없는 명사이므로 단수 취급한다.

ⓒ 「the+형용사」는 '~한 사람들'이라는 뜻으로, 복수 취급한다.

ⓐ a lot of는 '많은'이라는 뜻으로 셀 수 없는 명사와 셀 수 있는 명사 앞에 모두 쓸 수 있다. 동사의 수는 a lot of 뒤에 쓰인 명사의 수에 일치시킨다. olive oil은 셀 수 없는 명사이므로 단수 취급한다.
(are → is)

ⓓ alike는 서술적 용법으로만 사용되어, 명사 앞에 쓸 수 없다. (alike → like)

ⓔ Economics와 같은 학과명은 복수형이어도 단수 취급한다. (are → is)

<table>
<tr><td>CHAPTER **11**</td><td>**부사**
Adverbs</td><td align="right">본문 _ p.230</td></tr>
</table>

PRACTICE 1

1 freely	**2** fairly	**3** creatively
4 firmly	**5** angrily	**6** wisely
7 effectively	**8** softly	**9** quickly
10 willingly	**11** fortunately	**12** heavily
13 certainly	**14** privately	**15** luckily
16 essentially	**17** similarly	**18** easily
19 seriously	**20** mainly	**21** actually
22 completely	**23** finally	**24** globally
25 naturally	**26** safely	**27** necessarily
28 colorfully	**29** formally	**30** hopefully
31 equally	**32** frequently	**33** specially
34 attentively	**35** carelessly	**36** contrarily
37 negatively	**38** originally	**39** directly
40 internationally		

PRACTICE 2

1 terribly	**2** personally	**3** definitely
4 fully	**5** happily	**6** uniquely
7 successfully	**8** gently	**9** surely
10 really	**11** currently	**12** probably
13 suddenly	**14** brightly	**15** reasonably
16 actively	**17** simply	**18** busily
19 sharply	**20** differently	**21** dully
22 politely	**23** tightly	**24** genuinely
25 proudly	**26** rarely	**27** truly
28 morally	**29** normally	**30** possibly
31 foolishly	**32** anxiously	**33** generally
34 mentally	**35** casually	**36** officially
37 cheerfully	**38** nicely	**39** perfectly
40 wholly	**41** incredibly	**42** practically

43 properly　**44** responsibly　**45** sensitively
46 pleasantly　**47** exactly　**48** severely
49 emotionally　**50** sensibly

PRACTICE 3

1 A　**2** A　**3** B　**4** A　**5** B
6 A　**7** B　**8** B　**9** A　**10** B

[보기]
(A) My mom is not well, so she's in bed.→ 주격 보어 자리이므로 형용사(건강한)로 쓰임
(B) Tony is doing well at school like his brother.→ 동사 do를 수식하는 부사(잘)로 쓰임

1, 4, 6, 9 밑줄 친 부분이 명사를 수식하는 한정적 용법의 형용사로 쓰였다.
the last performance: 마지막 공연
the most votes: 가장 많은 득표
the near distance: 가까운 거리
early morning: 이른 아침
2 his는 동명사구 being late의 의미상의 주어이다. 즉, late가 보어 역할을 하고 있으므로 형용사로 쓰였다.
I'm sick of his being late for work.: 나는 그가 늦게 출근하는 것에 진절머리가 난다.
3, 5, 7, 8, 10 밑줄 친 부분이 동사를 수식하는 부사로 쓰였다.
fly high: 높이 날다
work hard: 열심히 일하다
walk fast: 빨리 걷다
last long: 오래 지속되다
work right: 제대로 작동하다

PRACTICE 4

1 fast　**2** carefully　**3** high
4 late　**5** surely　**6** hard
7 long　**8** exactly　**9** last
10 completely

---

1 He drove the taxi는 완전한 절이므로 so 다음에는 동사 drive를 수식할 수 있는 부사가 들어가야 한다. 형용사 fast에 -ly를 붙인 fastly는 사용하지 않는 단어이다. fast의 부사형은 형용사형과 동일하게 fast임에 유의한다.
drive the taxi so fast: 아주 빠르게 택시를 운전하다
2 동사 listen을 수식하는 부사는 주어진 형용사 careful에 '-ly'를 붙여 carefully(주의 깊게)로 나타낸다.
listen carefully: 주의 깊게 듣다
3 동사 raise를 수식하는 '높이'라는 의미의 부사 high를 쓴다. '높은'을 뜻하는 형용사 high의 부사 형태는 highly(크게, 매우)가 아니라 high(높게)임에 유의한다.
raise your arms high: 네 팔을 높이 들다
4 동사 arrived를 수식하는 '늦게'라는 의미의 부사 late를 쓴다. '늦은'을 뜻하는 형용사 late의 부사 형태는 lately(최근에)가 아니라 late(늦게)임에 유의한다.
arrived late: 늦게 도착했다
5 빈칸 부분을 제외했을 때 완전한 문장이므로 빈칸에는 부사가 들어가야 함을 알 수 있다. 동사 improve를 수식하는 부사는 주어진

형용사 sure에 '-ly'를 붙여 surely로 나타낸다. 이때 surely는 '분명히'라는 뜻이다.
surely improve skills: 분명히 능력을 향상시키다
6 동사 blow를 수식하는 '세게'라는 의미의 부사 hard를 쓴다. 부사의 형태가 hardly(거의 ~않는)가 아니라 -ly가 없는 hard(세게)임에 유의한다.
blow hard: 세게 불다
7 동사 lived를 수식하는 '오래'라는 의미의 부사 long을 쓴다. '긴'을 의미하는 형용사 long의 부사형은 형용사형과 동일하게 long(길게, 오래)임에 유의한다.
lived very long: 아주 오래 살았다
8 부사구 at 9 a.m.을 수식하는 부사는 주어진 형용사 exact에 '-ly'를 붙여 exactly(정확히)로 나타낸다.
at 9 a.m. exactly: 정확히 오전 9시에
9 동사 see를 수식하는 '마지막으로'라는 의미의 부사 last를 쓴다. 형용사 last에 -ly를 붙인 lastly도 부사지만 앞서 몇 가지 단계나 대상을 나열하다가 '마지막으로,'라고 운을 뗄 때는 말로, 동사를 수식하며 '마지막으로, 가장 최근에'를 뜻하는 부사 last와는 의미가 다르다는 점에 유의한다.
see him last: 그를 마지막으로 보다
10 형용사 absorbed를 수식하는 부사는 주어진 형용사 complete에 '-ly'를 붙여 completely(완전히)로 나타낸다.
was completely absorbed: 완전히 열중했다

PRACTICE 5

1 late　**2** close　**3** mostly　**4** hardly
5 nearly　**6** friendly　**7** closely　**8** highly
9 high　**10** hard　**11** lately　**12** strange
13 near　**14** directly　**15** most

---

1 '우리 팀원들은 어제 밤 늦게까지 일해야 했다.'는 의미이므로 동사 work를 수식하는 부사 late(늦게)가 와야 한다.
*late: 늦게 / lately: 최근에
2 '그 개는 박스 가까이에 와서 먹을 것을 찾았다.'는 의미이므로 동사 came을 수식하는 부사 close(가까이)가 와야 한다.
*close: 가까이 / closely: 주의 깊게, 면밀히
3 '지은이는 여행 중에 대체로 저렴한 호텔에서 지냈다.'는 의미이므로 동사 stayed를 수식하는 부사 mostly(대체로)가 와야 한다.
*most: 가장 많이 / mostly: 대체로
4 '나는 그가 말하고 있는 것을 좀처럼 믿을 수가 없었다.'는 의미이므로 동사 could believe를 수식하는 부사 hardly(거의 ~않는)가 와야 한다.
*hard: 열심히 / hardly: 거의 ~ 않는
5 '보고서는 거의 50%의 학생들이 불행하다고 느낀다고 밝혔다.'는 의미이므로 형용사 50%를 수식하는 부사 nearly(거의)가 와야 한다.
*near: 가까이 / nearly: 거의
6 감각동사 looks의 주격 보어 자리에는 형용사 friendly(친절한)가 온다.
look friendly: 친절해 보이다
7 '이 문제들을 자세히 봐라.'라는 의미이므로 동사 look at을 수식하는 부사 closely(면밀히)가 와야 한다.
*close: 가까운 / closely: 주의 깊게, 면밀히
8 '공룡에 관한 매우 흥미로운 사실들 몇 가지에 대해 논의해 보자.'는 의미이므로 형용사 interesting을 수식하는 부사 highly(매우)가 와야 한다.
*high: 높이 / highly: 크게, 매우

9 '지구 온난화 때문에 기온이 매우 높이 올라갔다.'는 의미이므로 동사 has gone을 수식하는 부사 high(높이)가 와야 한다.
*high: 높이 / highly: 크게, 매우
10 '나는 3년 동안 매우 열심히 플루트를 연습해왔다.'는 의미이므로 동사 have practiced를 수식하는 부사 hard(열심히)가 와야 한다.
*hard: 열심히 / hardly: 거의 ~ 않는
11 '최근에 많은 외국인들이 이 도시로 이주하고 있다.'는 의미이므로 동사 are moving을 수식하는 부사 lately(최근에)가 와야 한다.
12 감각동사 sound의 주격 보어 자리에는 형용사 strange가 온다.
sound <u>strange</u>: 이상하게 들리다
13 '나는 태풍이 가까이 오고 있다는 소식을 들었다.'는 의미이므로 동사 is coming을 수식하는 부사 near(가까이)가 온다.
* near: 가까이 / nearly: 거의
14 괄호 안의 단어가 없어도 완벽한 문장이므로 부사가 들어가야 함을 알 수 있다. direct는 '직접적인'을 의미하는 형용사이므로 tell을 수식하는 부사 directly(직접적으로)가 오는 것이 적절하다.
tell him <u>directly</u>: 그에게 직접 말하다
15 '가장 많은 정답을 맞힌 사람이 이길 것이다.'라는 의미이므로 명사구 right answers를 수식하는 최상급 형용사 the most(가장 많은)가 와야 한다.
* most: 가장 많은, 가장 많이 / mostly: 대부분

PRACTICE 6

1	① hard	② hardly	
2	① regular	② regularly	
3	① logically	② logical	
4	① fast	② fast	
5	① lately	② late	
6	① effectively	② effective	
7	① high	② high	
8	① closely	② close	

1 ① 동사 work를 수식하는 부사 hard를 쓴다.
② 동사 breathe를 수식하는 부사 hardly를 쓴다.
* hard: 열심히 / hardly: 거의 ~ 않는
2 ① 명사 basis를 수식하는 형용사 regular가 온다.
* on a regular basis: 정기적으로
② 동사 exercise를 수식하는 부사 regularly를 쓴다.
3 ① 동사 think를 수식하는 부사 logically를 쓴다.
② 감각동사 sound의 보어인 형용사 logical을 쓴다.
4 ① 명사 service를 앞에서 수식하는 형용사 fast를 쓴다.
② 동사 walk를 수식하는 부사 fast를 쓴다.
5 ① 동사 have heard를 수식하는 부사 lately를 쓴다.
② 동사 read를 수식하는 부사 late를 쓴다.
* lately: 최근에 / late: 늦게
6 ① 동사 communicate를 수식하는 부사 effectively를 쓴다.
② 명사 study를 수식하는 형용사 effective를 쓴다.
7 ① 동사 held를 수식하는 부사 high를 쓴다.
② 명사 fever를 수식하는 형용사 high를 쓴다.
8 ① 동사 read를 수식하는 부사 closely를 쓴다.
② become의 보어인 형용사 close를 쓴다.

PRACTICE 7

1 You will often see movie stars in this district.

2 I sometimes feel uncomfortable with Mr. Jung.
3 Foreigners seldom learn the Korean language easily.
4 The weather is always unpredictable.
5 It rarely rained when I was staying in the town.
6 I'll never tell him what happened to you yesterday.
7 My sister is usually more impulsive than my brother and I.

1, 6 빈도부사는 조동사 뒤에 온다.
2, 3, 5 빈도부사는 일반동사 앞에 온다.
4, 7 빈도부사는 be동사 뒤에 온다.

PRACTICE 8

1 is always too loud
2 seldom rides his motorcycle
3 often got lost
4 can never win
5 Eric rarely goes
6 usually shake hands
7 is sometimes difficult
8 would often spend

1, 7 빈도부사는 be동사의 뒤에 위치한다.
2, 3, 5, 6 빈도부사는 일반동사의 앞에 위치한다.
4, 8 빈도부사는 조동사의 뒤에 위치한다.

PRACTICE 9

1	① still	② yet	③ already
2	① already	② still	③ yet
3	① already	② yet[already]	③ still
4	① yet[already]	② already	③ still
5	① already	② still	③ yet

PRACTICE 10

1 already **2** already **3** still **4** still
5 yet **6** yet **7** still **8** yet
9 still **10** already **11** yet **12** yet
13 still

1 놀람을 나타내는 의문문에서 '이미, 벌써'의 의미로 쓰이는 already가 알맞다.
2, 10 긍정문에서 '이미, 벌써'의 의미로 쓰이는 already가 알맞다.
2 make up one's mind: 결심하다
3, 4, 7, 9 긍정문에서 '여전히, 아직도'의 의미로 쓰이는 still이 알맞다.
9 keep up the good work: 계속 수고하다

5, 8, 12 부정문에서 '아직'의 의미로 쓰이는 yet이 알맞다. yet은 주로 문장 끝에 위치한다.
6, 11 의문문에서 '이미, 벌써, 이제'의 뜻으로 쓰이는 yet이 알맞다.
13 부정문에서 계속되는 행위나 상태를 강조할 때 쓰이는 still이 알맞다.

PRACTICE 11

1	either	2	too	3	too
4	Neither	5	either	6	too
7	neither	8	too	9	either
10	too	11	either	12	too

PRACTICE 12

1	more frequently	2	very
3	large	4	expensive
5	much	6	very
7	faster	8	smooth
9	much	10	easy
11	more experienced	12	very
13	much		

PRACTICE 13

1 Who else should we pick up at the airport?

2 Even his kind words couldn't calm me down.

3 Jason couldn't talk to anyone else about his problem.

4 He even resembles my father's personality.

5 I want nothing else except a bicycle for my birthday.

6 She goes jogging even when the weather is bad.

7 What else did your professor advise you to do?

8 One of my friends calls me even in the middle of the night.

1, 3, 5, 7 else는 '그 밖에'라는 뜻으로 수식하고자 하는 말 뒤에 온다.
2, 4, 6, 8 even은 '~조차(도), ~까지도'라는 뜻으로 수식하고자 하는 말 앞에 온다.

PRACTICE 14

1	else	2	even	3	else	4	even
5	Even	6	else	7	else	8	even
9	else	10	else	11	even	12	Even

PRACTICE 15

1	before	2	before	3	ago
4	before	5	before	6	before
7	before	8	ago	9	ago
10	ago	11	before	12	ago

1, 5, 6, 11 한 시점을 기준으로 하여 그 이전 시점에 일어난 일을 나타내고, 완료 시제와 함께 쓰이는 before가 알맞다. 이때 before는 시간을 나타내는 말과 함께 '~ 전에'라는 의미로 쓰일 수도 있고, 단독으로 '전에'라는 뜻으로 쓰일 수도 있다.
2, 4, 7 과거 시점에 일어난 일을 나타내고 있고, 시간을 나타내는 말이 없으므로 before가 알맞다. before가 단독으로 쓰일 때는 완료 시제는 물론 과거 시제와도 함께 쓸 수 있다.
3, 8, 9, 10, 12 현재를 기준으로 하여 과거의 한 시점에 일어난 일을 나타내고, 항상 이전의 시간을 나타내는 말과 함께 '~ 전에'라는 의미로 쓰이는 ago가 알맞다.

PRACTICE 16

1	up your sister	2	it on
3	out the gas	4	out the wrinkles
5	on the TV	6	it away
7	into your room		
8	out how to operate the machine		
9	the experiment out	10	for the keys
11	up her car	12	with him
13	up the phone	14	about it
15	it in		

1, 3, 4, 5, 8, 9, 11, 13 타동사와 부사가 함께 쓰여 동사구를 이룬 경우다. 이때 목적어가 대명사가 아닌 일반명사나 명사구라면 「동사+부사+목적어」나 「동사+목적어+부사」의 어순 둘 다 가능하다.
wake ~ up: ~을 깨우다
check ~ out: ~을 확인하다
iron ~ out: (다림질하여 옷에서) ~을 없애다
turn ~ on: ~을 켜다
figure ~ out: ~을 알아내다, 이해하다
carry ~ out: ~을 수행하다
fill ~ up: ~을 가득 채우다
pick ~ up: ~을 줍다, 찾아오다, (차에) 태우다
2, 6, 15 목적어가 대명사일 때는 「동사+목적어+부사」의 어순만 가능하다.
put ~ on: ~을 입다[신다]
throw ~ away: ~을 버리다
hand ~ in: ~을 제출하다
7, 10, 12, 14 자동사 뒤에 전치사가 온 경우로, 이때 전치사의 목적어는 반드시 전치사 뒤에 온다.
go into: ~ 안으로 들어가다
look for: ~을 찾다
agree with: ~에게 동의하다
talk about: ~에 대해 얘기하다

PRACTICE 17

1 You should care about your health.

2 Don't put it off until Friday.

3 Did he look at the memo?

4 Take it off and try this on.

5 I am waiting for my turn.

6 I checked them out at the library.

7 The cat was sitting on the chair.

8 Will you pick it up for me?

---

1 care about your health (~에 대해 신경 쓰다)
자동사+전치사
2 put it off(~을 연기하다)
　타동사　부사
3 look at the memo(~을 보다)
자동사+전치사
4 take it off(~을 벗다)
　타동사　부사
　try this on(~을 입어[신어]보다)
타동사　부사
5 wait for my turn(~를 기다리다)
자동사+전치사
6 check them out(~을 대출하다, 확인하다)
　타동사　　부사
7 sit on the chair(~에 앉다)
자동사+전치사
8 pick it up(~을 줍다)
　타동사　부사

중간·기말고사 대비문제 정답 　본문 _ p.248

1 ⑤　**2** ②　**3** ④　**4** ③　**5** ⑤　**6** ⑤　**7** ③
8 ⑤　**9** ②　**10** near → nearly　**11** ⑤　**12** ③,④
13 ①,④　**14** ③,④　**15** ②　**16** ⑤　**17** it rarely
rains　**18** ②　**19** ③　**20** usually pays a visit
to a gallery　**21** ④　**22** ⓐ either ⓑ can
23 ④　**24** ①　**25** hard → hardly　**26** ②
27 ③　**28** ③,④　**29** ⑤　**30** ③　**31** highly →
high　**32** ②　**33** ①　**34** ③

중간·기말고사 대비문제 해설

1　⑤ 명사 - 형용사　①②③④ 형용사 - 부사

2　yet은 부정문에서 '아직'의 의미를 갖는다.

3　not ~ either '~도 또한 …않다'

4　③ '~ 또한 (아니다)'라는 뜻으로 부정문에 쓰이는 것
은 either이다. neither은 「not ~ either」과 바꿔
쓸 수 있다. (neither → either)

5　① 부사 hardly는 '거의 ~ 않는'이라는 의미로 부정의
의미를 담고 있기 때문에 couldn't와 함께 사용할
경우 이중부정이 된다. (couldn't → could)
② 맥락상 동사 spread를 수식할 수 있는 부사
widely의 사용이 적절하다. (wide → widely)
③ 동사 object는 '~에 반대하다'라는 의미의 자동사
로 목적어를 가지려면 전치사 to를 함께 사용해야
한다. (objected → objected to)
④ 동사 welcomed를 수식하고 있으므로 형용사
warm이 아닌 부사 warmly의 사용이 적절하다.
(warm → warmly)

6　ⓐ 비가 세차게 오고 있다는 뜻이므로 '거의 ~ 않는'이
라는 뜻의 hardly가 아닌 '열심히, 세게'라는 뜻의
hard를 쓴다. (hardly → hard)
ⓑ 「타동사+부사」에서 목적어가 대명사일 때는 「동사
+목적어+부사」의 어순으로 쓰인다.
(throw away them → throw them away)
ⓒ much는 비교급을 수식한다.
(healthy → healthier)
ⓓ 「타동사+부사」에서 목적어가 대명사일 때는 「동사
+목적어+부사」의 어순으로 쓴다.
(hand in it → hand it in)
ⓔ 「타동사+부사」에서 목적어가 대명사일 때는 「동
사+목적어+부사」의 어순으로 쓰인다. 또한 care
about은 자동사 뒤에 전치사가 온 것이므로, 전치
사의 목적어는 반드시 전치사의 뒤에 써야 한다.

7　③ 빈도부사는 일반동사의 앞에 위치한다.
(it feels usually → it usually feels)

8　• think deeply about '~에 대해 깊이 생각하다' 그
녀는 항상 다른 사람들이 어떻게 느끼는지에 대해 깊
이 생각한다. 그녀는 매우 사려 깊다.
• under control '통제되는' 걱정하지 마세요. 모든
것은 완벽히 통제되고 있습니다.
• run out of '~이 떨어지다, 동나다' 그 작가는 아이
디어가 다 떨어져서 마지막 장을 끝낼 수 없었다.
• 맥락상 '강력하게 추천한다'는 의미이므로 동사
recommend를 수식할 수 있는 부사 strongly의
사용이 적절하다. 나는 당신이 현지 해산물 식당에
가보기를 강력하게 추천한다.
• be동사 뒤로 주격 보어 자리에 형용사 upset이 오
는 것은 어법상 옳다. 모든 사람들은 그 충격적인 뉴
스를 들은 후 화가 났다.

9　ⓑ 명사 price를 수식해야 하므로, 형용사 high를 쓰
는 것이 적절하다. highly는 '크게, 매우'라는 뜻의

부사이다. (highly → high)

ⓓ 주격 보어의 자리이므로 보어가 될 수 있는 형용사 close를 쓰는 것이 적절하다. closely는 '주의 깊게, 면밀히'라는 뜻의 부사이다. (closely → close)

10 부사 every day를 수식할 수 있는 부사 nearly를 쓰는 것이 적절하다. 형용사 near은 두 가지 부사형을 가지고 있는데, 여기에서는 '거의'라는 뜻의 nearly를 써야 한다. 부사 near은 '가까이'라는 뜻이다.

11 ⑤ 비교급을 수식하는 부사
①②③④ 명사를 수식하는 형용사

12 ③ something처럼 -thing으로 끝나는 단어는 형용사가 뒤에서 수식한다.
(strange something → something strange)
④ 타동사+부사로 구성된 동사구의 목적어가 대명사이면 목적어는 동사와 부사 사이에 위치한다.
(took out it → took it out/
carried back it → carried it back)

13 I'm not ~으로 시작하는 문장에 동의할 때는 Me, neither 또는 Neither am I로 대답한다.

14 ③ figure out은 '~을 알아내다, 이해하다'라는 의미의 「타동사+부사」로 이루어진 동사구이다. 「타동사+부사」로 이루어진 동사구의 목적어가 대명사이면, 목적어는 항상 동사와 부사 사이에 위치한다.
(figure out it → figure it out)
④ look for은 '~을 찾다'라는 뜻의 「자동사+전치사」이다. 이때 전치사의 목적어는 항상 전치사의 뒤에 위치한다. (look him for → look for him)

15 before는 ago와 달리 시간을 나타내는 말 없이 홀로 쓰일 수 있다.

16 ⑤ else는 수식하고자 하는 말 뒤에 온다.
(else anywhere → anywhere else)

17 빈도부사는 일반동사 앞에 온다.

18 ② highly '매우' → high '높이'

19 • show up '나타나다'
• pick up '태우러 가다'
• get up '일어나다'

20 빈도부사는 일반동사 앞에 온다.

21 ④ 부정문에 동의하는 표현은 「Neither+조동사+주어」이다. (Either do I. → Neither do I.)

22 부정문에 동의할 때에는 「not ~ either」, 「Neither+동사+주어」로 대답한다.

23 빈도부사는 일반동사 앞에 온다.

24 ① still은 '여전히, 아직도'의 뜻으로 보통 문장의 중간에 온다. 아직도 숙제를 끝냈다는 표현은 어색하므로 의문문에서 '이미, 벌써'라는 뜻의 already나 yet을 써야 한다. (still → already[yet])

25 '밤을 샌 후, 나는 아침 회의 동안에 거의 눈을 뜨고 있을 수 없었다.'는 의미가 되어야 하므로 '거의 ~않는'이라는 뜻의 부사 hardly를 쓰는 것이 적절하다. hard는 '열심히'라는 뜻의 부사이다.

26 ② 형용사 '가만히 있는'
①③④⑤ 부사 '아직'

27 • ever '(의문문에서) 언젠가'
• once '한 때'
• still '여전히'

28 (c) 바나나는 '수확되는' 대상이므로 수동태로 써야 한다. (harvested → are harvested)
(d) 조심스럽게 포장했다는 의미이므로 동사 pack을 수식할 수 있는 부사를 써야 한다.
(careful → carefully)

바나나는 전 세계적으로 인기 있는 과일이다. 그것들은 당신의 몸의 소화를 돕는다. 바나나는 많은 건강상의 이점을 준다. 그것들은 건강에 좋고 맛이 훌륭하다. 바나나는 따뜻한 기후에서 자라고 1년 내내 수확된다. 농부들은 신선한 바나나를 안전하게 보관하기 위해 조심스럽게 포장한다. 수확된 후, 그것들은 판매를 위해 가게로 옮겨진다. 많은 사람들이 스무디, 달콤한 요리, 다양한 아침 식사에 바나나를 넣는 것을 좋아한다.

29 ①② much는 비교급을 수식한다. 원급을 수식할 때는 very를 쓴다. (much → very)
③ 비교급을 수식할 때는 much를 쓴다. very는 원급만 수식할 수 있다. (very → much)
④ a week ago라는 특정한 과거 시점을 나타내는 부사구가 쓰였으므로 과거시제를 사용해야 한다.
(has bought → bought)

30 lately '최근에'

31 high '높은, 높게', highly '매우, 대단히'

32 ⓑ 그곳은 심지어 여름에도 추웠다. (부 심지어)
ⓓ 심지어 불이 켜져있는데도, 그것은 보기가 꽤 어려웠다. (부 심지어)
ⓐ 2, 4 그리고 6은 짝수의 숫자이다. (형 짝수의)
ⓒ 엄마는 케이크를 세 개의 동일한 양으로 나누었다. (형 동일한)
ⓔ 그녀의 첫 번째 책은 좋았지만, 이것이 훨씬 더 낫다. (부 훨씬)
ⓕ 학생 대표는 안정적이고, 차분한 목소리로 연설했다. (형 차분한)

33 형용사-명사의 관계인 ①을 제외한 나머지는 형용사-

부사의 관계이다.

① • The math problem was so ⓐdifficult that I couldn't solve it. 그 수학 문제가 너무 어려워서 나는 그것을 풀 수 없었다.
• He completed the task with great ⓑdifficulty. 그는 큰 어려움을 겪으며 일을 마무리했다.

② • His handwriting is ⓐhard to understand. 그의 글씨체는 알아보기 어렵다.
• He ⓑhardly ate anything at the party. 그는 파티에서 거의 아무것도 먹지 않았다.

③ • She has such a ⓐloud voice that I could hear her from the hall. 그녀는 매우 큰 목소리를 가지고 있어서 내가 홀에서도 그녀를 들을 수 있었다.

• The phone rang ⓑloudly in the middle of the meeting. 전화가 회의 중간에 시끄럽게 울렸다.

④ • We only invited ⓐclose friends to our wedding. 우리는 우리의 결혼식에 친한 친구들만 초대했다.
• The kids sat ⓑclose together on the bench. 아이들은 벤치에서 서로 가까이 앉았다.

⑤ • The movie was based on a ⓐtrue story. 그 영화는 실제 이야기에 기초한다.
• Dan Smith is ⓑtruly a great actor. Dan Smith는 진정으로 위대한 배우다.

34 ③ break down은 '부수다'라는 뜻의 「타동사+부사」로 구성된 동사구이다. 「타동사+부사」의 동사구의 목적어가 대명사이면 목적어는 동사와 부사 사이에 위치한다. (broke down it → broke it down)

CHAPTER 12 가정법
Conditionals

본문 _ p.254

PRACTICE 1

1	send	**2**	are	**3**	invented
4	give	**5**	breaks out	**6**	have
7	deliver	**8**	solved	**9**	let
10	become				

if는 '~한다면, ~라면'의 뜻으로 현재나 미래에 실제로 일어날 수 있는 상황에 대한 조건을 나타낸다.

1, 6, 9, 10 미래의 일을 나타낸다고 하더라도 조건을 나타내는 if절의 동사는 항상 현재형으로 쓴다.

3, 8 조건을 나타내는 if절은 과거에 실제로 일어난 사실에 대한 조건을 나타낼 수도 있다.

PRACTICE 2

1	rains	**2**	goes	**3**	don't feel
4	answer	**5**	ate	**6**	smell
7	knew				

1~4, 6 if절이 현재나 미래에 실제로 일어날 수 있는 조건을 나타내고 있다. 이때 if절은 항상 현재 시제로 쓴다.

5, 7 주절에 조동사 과거형이 쓰인 것으로 보아 가정법 과거를 나타낸다. 따라서 If절에 과거 동사를 쓴다.

1 If it rains: 비가 온다면
2 If she goes to the island: 그녀가 그 섬에 간다면

3 If you don't feel hot: 네가 덥지 않다면
4 If you answer my questions: 네가 내 질문에 답한다면
5 If she ate enough: 그녀가 충분히 먹는다면
6 If you smell gas: 네가 가스 냄새를 맡는다면
7 If we knew a country's language: 우리가 한 나라의 언어를 안다면

PRACTICE 3

1	picked	**2**	were	**3**	lose
4	played	**5**	leave	**6**	spoke
7	are	**8**	were not	**9**	get
10	use				

1, 4, 6 현재 사실에 반대되는 일에 대한 가정은 가정법 과거로 나타낸다. 가정법 과거는 「If+주어+동사의 과거형~, 주어+would/could/should/might+동사원형」의 어순으로 쓴다.

2, 8 가정법 과거 문장에서, if절의 be동사는 주어의 수나 인칭에 상관없이 were을 쓰는 것이 원칙이다.

3, 9 현재에 실제로 일어날 수 있는 상황에 대한 조건을 나타내는 if절이다.

5, 10 주절의 시제가 미래이지만, 조건을 나타내는 if절이므로 현재 시제를 쓴다.

7 주절의 시제가 미래이지만, 조건을 나타내는 if절이므로 if절의 동사는 현재시제를 쓴다. 참고로, 「형용사/부사+enough+to부정사」는 '~하기에 충분히 …한'이라는 뜻으로 「so+형용사/부사+that+주어+can」으로 바꾸어 쓸 수 있다.

PRACTICE 4

2 If I knew her email address, I could write to her.

3 If he didn't tell lies all the time, we would[could] like him.

4 If she were in the office, I could meet her.

5 If I weren't appointed as principal of this school, I would leave this city.

6 If Ms. Kim could find another apartment, she wouldn't stay here for one more month.

7 If she loved the boy, she would pay attention to him.

8 If we had a time machine, we would[could] know exactly what happened to dinosaurs.

PRACTICE 5

1 I don't spend more time with my family

2 I can't play tennis like him

3 you don't fall into a deep sleep

4 I can't meet an angel in heaven

5 I'm not the tallest among my friends

6 I'm not good at cooking

7 I know the truth about Emma

8 I am disappointed with my grade

9 it is raining right now

10 I wear these uncomfortable jeans

> **1~10** 「I wish+가정법 과거」는 '~라면 좋을 텐데'의 뜻으로, 현재의 사실과 반대되거나 이룰 수 없는 일을 소망할 때 쓰며, 「I'm sorry that+직설법」으로 나타낼 수 있다. 가정법이 긍정이면 직설법은 부정, 가정법이 부정이면 직설법은 긍정을 쓴다.

PRACTICE 6

2 I spoke Spanish fluently enough to travel alone

3 I were good at painting like my sister

4 he were strong enough to knock the boy down

5 we lived in a world free from wars

6 my parents let me ride a motorbike

7 I wouldn't[would not] need to take a math test next week

8 I were allowed to go out after 9 o'clock

9 he knew how to fix a car

10 the weather wouldn't[would not] be freezing cold tomorrow

PRACTICE 7

1 as if he were a professional dancer

2 as if she were a celebrity

3 as if he did everything by himself

4 as if he were a brave soldier at that time

5 as if she had a good relationship with her brother

6 as if she wrote the report by herself

7 as if he were not responsible for the terrible accident

8 as if his father were a successful businessman

9 as if she knew the whole story

10 as if he helped me make the bed every morning

PRACTICE 8

1	were not	**2**	would	**3**	were
4	it	**5**	couldn't	**6**	could
7	could	**8**	wouldn't		

> 「without+명사, 가정법 과거」는 '~이 없다면 …할 것이다'의 뜻으로 현재의 사실과 반대되는 일을 나타내며 without은 「if it were not for」와 바꿔 쓸 수 있다.
>
> **1** If it were not for love, life would be of no meaning.
> = Without love → 사랑이 없다면 인생은 의미가 없을 것이다.
> **2** If it were not for Jack, class would be very boring.
> = Without Jack → Jack이 없다면 수업은 지루할 것이다.
> **3** If it were not for soccer, my life would not be fun.
> = Without soccer
> → 축구가 없다면 내 인생은 재미있지 않을 것이다.
> **4** If it were not for electricity, I wouldn't be able to watch TV.
> = Without electricity
> → 전기가 없다면 나는 TV를 볼 수 없을 것이다.
> **5** Without her, I couldn't study English harder.
> = If it were not for her
> → 그녀가 없다면 나는 영어를 더 열심히 공부할 수 없을 것이다.
> **6** Without stress, she could be much healthier.
> = If it were not for stress
> → 스트레스가 없다면 그녀는 훨씬 더 건강할 것이다.
> **7** Without food, no one could live.
> = If it were not for food
> → 먹을 것이 없다면 아무도 살 수 없을 것이다.
> **8** If it were not for my smartphone, I wouldn't waste so much time.
> = Without my smartphone
> → 스마트폰이 없다면 나는 시간을 많이 낭비하지 않을 것이다.

PRACTICE 9

2 If I had known you were so busy, I would not have called on you.

3 If we tried to keep our great traditions, many of them would not disappear.

4 If I hadn't met a good English teacher, I could[would] not have become interested in English.

5 If I played the flute well enough, the symphony orchestra would accept me as a member.

6 If I hadn't been an only child in my family, I wouldn't have wanted brothers and sisters.

7 If I hadn't worked part-time after school, I couldn't have earned extra money.

8 If Mike hadn't been born and raised in such a cold area, he could have stood the hot weather here.

9 If Susan hadn't seen a scary movie at night by herself, she could have fallen asleep.

10 If he ran an anti-virus program regularly, his computer wouldn't crash frequently.

11 If my grandfather hadn't known how to send an e-mail, we couldn't have kept in touch more often.

> **2, 4, 6, 7, 8, 9, 11** 과거 사실에 반대되는 일을 가정하는 문장으로 바꾸어야 하므로 가정법 과거완료 구문으로 나타낸다. 가정법 과거완료는 「If+주어+had+과거분사 ~, 주어+would/could/should/might+have+과거분사 …」로 나타낸다.
> **3, 5, 10** 현재 사실에 반대되는 일을 가정하는 문장으로 바꾸어야 하므로 가정법 과거 구문으로 나타낸다. 가정법 과거는 「If+주어+동사의 과거형 ~, 주어+would/could/should/might+동사원형 …」으로 나타낸다.

PRACTICE 10

2 I wish my mom gave me chocolate chip cookies at night.

3 I wish I had read many good books in my school days.

4 I wish I were talented at all kinds of martial arts.

5 I wish I had not complained to my mother about everything.

6 I wish James would not[wouldn't] leave Korea after he finishes this semester.

7 I wish I had accepted my friend's sincere advice then.

8 I wish I had bought the concert ticket on the first day of selling.

9 I wish her new album sold well.

10 I wish I had prepared for the performance better.

11 I wish I had paid attention to what was going on around me.

12 I wish I hadn't[had not] made fun of one of our classmates at all times.

13 I wish there were many national museums in my city.

14 I wish I had traveled around the country when I was young and healthy.

15 I wish I had accepted the best candidate as a member of the committee.

> **2, 4, 6, 9, 13** 현재나 미래의 사실과 반대되거나 이룰 수 없는 일을 소망하는 「I wish+가정법 과거」로 바꾸어 쓰기 위해서는 「I wish+주어+동사의 과거형 ~」으로 표현하는 것이 알맞다.
> **3, 5, 7, 8, 10, 11, 12, 14, 15** 과거의 사실에 대한 후회를 나타내고 있으므로 과거의 사실과 반대되는 일을 소망하는 「I wish+가정법 과거완료」로 바꾸어 쓰기 위해서 「I wish+주어+had+과거분사 ~」로 나타낸다.

PRACTICE 11

2 as if she felt guilty about herself

3 as if he had not[hadn't] worked for the company as a sales manager

4 as if the police had not[hadn't] made much effort to find the lost child

5 as if he had studied computer science in college

6 as if she[he] had interviewed the professor regarding the issue

7 as if she could afford to buy a house near the beach at that time

8 as if he had witnessed the car accident

9 as if he[she] had sent the papers to the right place

10 as if the girl had been to Australia and had seen kangaroos

> **2, 7** as if절에 올 내용, 즉 In fact 뒤에 온 문장의 시제가 주절의 시제와 같으므로 '마치 ~인 것처럼'이라는 뜻으로 현재의 사실과 반대되는 가정을 나타내야 한다. 따라서 「as if+가정법 과거」가 적합하므로 「동사의 현재형/과거형+as if+주어+동사의 과거형 ~」으로 표현하는 것이 알맞다.
> **3, 4, 5, 6, 8, 9, 10** '마치 ~이었던 것처럼'이라는 뜻으로 과거의 사실과 반대되는 가정을 나타내야 하므로 「as if+가정법 과거완료」가 적합하다. 따라서 「동사의 현재형/과거형+as if+주어+had+과거분사 ~」로 표현하는 것이 알맞다. 이때 as if절에서 나타내는 일(In fact ~로 표현한 문장)의 시제는 주절의 시제보다 한 시제 앞선다.

Ch
12
가
정
법

PRACTICE 12

1 If it were not for you

2 If it had not been for the movie

3 If it were not for the accident

4 If it had not been for his effort

5 If it were not for this navigation app

6 if it had not been for this

> **1, 3, 5** 「without+명사, 가정법 과거」는 '~이 없다면 …할 것이다'
> 의 뜻으로 현재의 사실과 반대되는 일을 나타내며 without은 「if it
> were not for」와 바꿔 쓸 수 있다.
> **2, 4, 6** 「without+명사, 가정법 과거완료」는 '~이 없었다면 …했을
> 것이다'의 뜻으로 과거의 사실과 반대되는 일을 나타내며 without
> 은 「if it had not been for」와 바꿔 쓸 수 있다.

PRACTICE 13

1 hadn't helped		**2** had taken
3 loves		**4** hadn't set
5 invented		**6** had driven
7 know		**8** had studied
9 had been constructed			
10 won		**11** had taken
12 had exercised			

> **1, 2, 6, 8, 12** 과거 사실에 반대되는 일을 가정하고, 과거 사실이
> 현재까지 영향을 미치는 경우이므로 '~했더라면, …할 텐데'라는 의
> 미가 되도록 혼합가정법으로 나타내는 것이 알맞다. 혼합가정법은
> 「If+주어+had+과거분사 ~, 주어+would/could/should/might+
> 동사원형 …」으로 나타낸다.
> **3, 7** 현재나 미래에 실제로 일어날 수 있는 상황에 대한 조건을 나
> 타내고 있으므로 if절의 동사는 현재 시제가 되어야 한다. 미래의 일
> 을 나타낸다고 하더라도 if절의 동사는 항상 현재형으로 쓴다.
> **4, 9, 11** 과거 사실에 반대되는 일을 가정하는 문장이므로 가정법
> 과거완료 구문이다. 가정법 과거완료는 「If+주어+had+과거분사 ~,
> 주어+would/could/should/might+have+과거분사 …」로 나타
> 낸다.
> **5, 10** 현재 사실에 반대되는 일을 가정하는 문장이므로 가정법
> 과거 구문이다. 가정법 과거는 「If+주어+동사의 과거형 ~, 주어
> +would/could/should/might+동사원형 …」으로 나타낸다.

PRACTICE 14

1 I bring an umbrella

2 you prepare this presentation

3 we be respectful

4 the bag was[had been] delivered

5 we take

6 she express

7 she attend the meeting

8 he was not[wasn't] relevant

9 school uniforms be changed

> **1, 5, 7, 9** recommend, suggest, demand, request 같은 제
> 안, 주장, 명령, 요구, 권고 등을 나타내는 동사 뒤에 이어지는 that
> 절에는 「should+동사원형」이 올 수 있는데, 이때 should는 생략
> 가능하다.
> **2, 3, 6** essential, important, natural 같은 형용사 뒤에 이어지
> 는 that절에 당위성을 나타내는 내용이 온 경우 「should+동사원
> 형」 형태로 쓰며, 이때 should는 생략 가능하다.
> **4, 8** 주장을 나타내는 동사 insist 뒤에 이어지는 that절일지라
> 도 '~해야 한다'의 의미가 포함되어 있지 않고, 단지 단순한 사실만
> 을 언급할 때는 「should+동사원형」이 아니라 주절의 시제에 따라
> that절의 시제를 바꾸어 써야 한다.

PRACTICE 15

1 Were I as big as an elephant

2 Were I you

3 Had I known him better

4 Had she not been here

5 Were a satellite destroyed

6 Had he eaten breakfast

7 Had you painted the walls in your room light
green

8 Were you interested in living at the North Pole

> [보기]
> 가정법 문장의 if를 생략할 때, 가정법 과거완료 문장의 경우,
> 「Had+주어+과거분사~」의 어순으로 쓴다. 참고로, call on은 '방문
> 하다, 요청하다'의 뜻이다.
>
> **1, 2, 5, 8** 가정법 문장의 if를 생략할 때, 가정법 과거 문장의 경우,
> 「Were+주어~」의 어순으로 쓴다.
> **3, 4, 6, 7** 가정법 문장의 if를 생략할 때, 가정법 과거완료 문장의
> 경우, 「Had+주어+과거분사~」의 어순으로 쓴다.

PRACTICE 16

1 Were it not for

2 Had they been successful

3 Were he here

4 Had there been

5 Were they on the Moon

6 Had it not been raining

7 Were we in outer space

8 Had the train arrived

> **1, 3, 5, 7** 가정법 과거 문장에서 if가 생략되고, 주어와 be동사가
> 도치된 형태이다.
> Were it not for water, no one could live.
> = If it were not for water
> Were he here, I would ask for his advice on the matter.
> = If he were here
> Were they on the Moon, they would get around by

jumping, not walking.
= If they were on the Moon
<u>Were we in outer space</u>, we would experience zero gravity.
= If we were in outer space
2, 4, 6, 8 가정법 과거완료 문장에서 if가 생략되고 주어와 had가 도치된 형태이다.
<u>Had they been successful</u>, they would have been given a present.
= If they had been successful
<u>Had there been nothing to slow down the car</u>, it would have crashed.
= If there had been nothing to slow down the car
<u>Had it not been raining</u>, we would have had dinner outside.
= If it had not been raining
<u>Had the train arrived on time</u>, we would not have been late.
= If the train had arrived on time

📝 중간·기말고사 대비문제 정답   본문 _ p.271

1 shines   **2** ④   **3** ③   **4** ③   **5** ②   **6** ③   **7** ③

8 ③   **9** ④   **10** practice speaking slowly

11 ⑤   **12** ①   **13** If it were not for him[Were it not for him / But for him]   **14** ③   **15** had joined   **16** as if he had made the choice by himself   **17** had been   **18** ③,④   **19** if, as if

20 (A) Without (B) have, quit[quitted]

21 ⓐ I didn't know how to use this machine ⓑ I couldn't bake cookies easily   **22** ③

23 (1) Were it not for your support, we could not carry out this project. (2) But for your support, we could not carry out this project.

24 ③   **25** ②,④

중간·기말고사 대비문제 해설

1 조건을 나타내는 if절이 미래의 일을 나타낸다고 하더라도 if절의 동사는 항상 현재형으로 쓴다.

2 ④ 과거의 사실과 반대되는 가정을 나타내는 as if 가정법 과거완료가 쓰인 문장이다. as if절에서 나타내는 일의 시제는 주절의 시제보다 한 시제 앞선다. 가정법 문장의 주절의 시제가 현재이므로, 직설법 문장의 시제는 과거시제가 알맞다.
① 현재의 사실과 반대되는 가정을 나타내는 as if 가정법 과거가 쓰인 문장이다. as if절에서 나타내는 일의 시제는 주절의 시제와 같다. 가정법 문장의 주절의 시제가 현재시제이므로, 직설법 문장의 시제 또한 현재시제여야 한다. (was not → is not)
② 가정법 현재 명사절이 쓰인 문장이다. 가정법 현재 명사절은 suggest와 같이 제안을 나타내는 동사 뒤에 이어지는 that절에 쓰인 should+동사원형에서 should를 생략한 형태이다. 따라서 연결된 문장의 조동사 또한 '~해야 한다'라는 뜻의 should를 써야 한다. (could → should)
③ 과거의 사실과 반대되는 가정을 나타내는 if+가정법 과거완료가 쓰인 문장이다. 과거의 사실과 반대되는 내용이기 때문에 직설법 문장은 과거시제로 써야 한다. (don't → didn't, can't → couldn't)
⑤ 현재의 사실과 반대되는 가정을 나타내는 if+가정법 과거 문장에서 if가 생략되어 주어와 동사가 도치된 형태이다. 현재의 사실과 반대되는 내용이기 때문에 직설법 문장의 시제는 현재시제여야 한다. (was → am not, didn't → don't)

3 ③ '~인지 (아닌지)'의 뜻으로 간접의문문을 이끄는 if ①②④⑤ 조건을 나타내는 if

4 '비가 온다면 수확이 좋을 텐데.' 또는 '비가 왔으면 수확이 좋았을 텐데.'라는 의미가 되어야 하므로 주어진 문장은 가정법 과거 또는 가정법 과거완료 형태가 되어야 한다. 따라서 조건절이 'If+주어+과거 동사'이면 주절은 '주어+would+동사원형'이 되어 가정법 과거 구문을 이루어야 하고, 조건절이 'If+주어+had+과거분사'이면 주절은 '주어+would+have+과거분사' 형태가 되어 가정법 과거완료 구문을 이루어야 한다. 따라서 ③이 정답이다.

5 ② 만약 그의 어머니가 그가 어렸을 때 그를 지지해주지 않았다면, 그는 지금의 그가 아닐 것이다.
'지금의 그(what he is)'와 '그가 어렸을 때(when he was young)'라는 표현에서 if절과 주절이 나타내는 시제가 다름을 알 수 있다. 따라서 과거 사실에 반대되는 일을 가정하고, 과거 사실이 현재까지 영향을 미치는 경우에 쓰는 혼합가정법이 쓰인 문장이다. 혼합가정법의 if절은 「if+주어+had+과거분사~」로 쓴다. (didn't support → hadn't supported)

6 now라는 시제를 나타내는 표현과 내용상 if절과 주절이 나타내는 시제가 다름을 알 수 있다. 따라서 과거 사실에 반대되는 일을 가정하고, 과거 사실이 현재까지 영향을 미치는 경우에 쓰는 혼합가정법이 쓰인 문장이다. 혼합가정법의 주절은 「주어+would+동사원형~」으로 쓴다.

Ch
12
가정법

그가 그 비극적인 사고로 죽지 않았었다면, 그는 지금 27살일 텐데.

7 가정법 과거완료는 과거 사실에 반대되는 일을 가정할 때 쓰이므로, 직설법 문장의 시제는 과거가 되어야 한다. 따라서 ②, ④, ⑤는 적합하지 않다. 또한 가정된 내용과 반대되는 사실을 나타내야 하므로 ①도 답이 될 수 없다.

8 ⓐ 주절의 시제가 미래이더라도, 시간과 조건의 부사절에서는 미래 시제 대신 현재 시제를 사용한다. (will come → comes)
ⓑ 조건을 나타내는 if가 아닌, '~인지 아닌지'의 뜻으로 의문사가 없는 간접의문문에 쓰인 if이므로 시제에 맞게 미래시제를 쓴다. (helps → will help)
ⓒ 현재 일어날 가능성이 희박한 상황을 가정하는 가정법 과거 문장이다. 가정법 과거는 「If+주어+동사의 과거형~, 주어+would+동사원형」의 어순으로 쓴다. if절의 be동사는 주어의 수나 인칭에 상관없이 were을 쓴다. (is → were)
ⓓ now라는 시제를 나타내는 표현과 내용상 if절과 주절이 나타내는 시제가 다름을 알 수 있다. 과거 사실이 현재까지 영향을 미치는 경우에 쓰는 혼합가정법으로 적절하다.
ⓔ necessary와 같은 형용사 뒤에 이어지는 that절에서는 「should+동사원형」이 올 수 있는데, 이때 should를 생략하고 동사원형만 쓸 수 있다.

9 과거의 사실과 반대되는 일을 나타내는 가정법 과거완료가 쓰인 문장이다. 「if+가정법 과거완료」 문장에서 주절은 「주어+could+have+과거분사」로 쓴다. (could buy → could have bought)
수진이가 쇼핑몰에 있었다면, 그녀는 바지를 더 싸게 살 수 있었을 텐데.

10 제안을 나타내는 suggest 뒤에 이어지는 that절에서는 「should+동사원형」이 올 수 있다. '천천히 말하는 것을 연습해야 한다'는 뜻이 적절하므로 should practice speaking slowly로 쓴다. practice의 목적어로는 동명사를 씀에 유의한다. 이때 should는 생략이 가능하므로 빈칸에 맞추기 위해 생략한다.

11 현재 사실에 반대되는 일을 가정할 때 쓰는 가정법 과거에서 if절의 주어가 I일 때 be동사는 were를 쓴다.

12 요구를 나타내는 demand 뒤에 이어지는 that절의 동사는 「(should)+동사원형」을 쓴다.

13 가정법 과거에 쓰인 without은 but for, if it were not for와 바꿔 쓸 수 있다. If it were not for에서 if를 생략하면 be동사가 주어 앞으로 옮겨져 Were it

not for가 된다.

14 현재의 사실과 반대되는 가정을 나타내는 「as if+가정법 과거」가 쓰인 문장이다. as if절에서 나타내는 일의 시제는 주절의 시제와 같다. 가정법 문장의 주절의 시제가 현재시제이므로, 직설법 문장의 시제도 현재시제이다. 또한 주어진 문장은 그 대화에 관심이 없는 것을 가정하고 있으므로, 직설법에서는 그 대화에 관심이 있다는 내용이 되어야 한다. 따라서 문법과 문맥상 모두 알맞은 것은 ③이다.

15 과거의 사실과 반대되는 일을 소망할 때 쓰는 「I wish+가정법 과거완료」 문장으로 바꿔야 한다. I wish+가정법 과거완료는 「I wish+주어+had+과거분사 ~」로 쓴다.
cf. due to '~ 때문에' = because of, owing to
in spite of '~에도 불구하고' = despite

16 주어진 직설법 문장은 과거시제이며, as if를 이용한 가정법 문장의 주절의 시제는 현재시제이다. 따라서 주절의 시제보다 한 시제 앞선 일(과거의 사실)과 반대되는 가정을 나타내는 「as if+가정법 과거완료」를 써야 한다. 「as if+가정법 과거완료」는 「as if+주어+had+과거분사」로 쓴다. 또한 직설법과 반대되는 내용을 나타내야 하므로 가정법의 동사는 긍정형을 씀에 유의한다.

17 태어난 시점은 과거이고 대단한 미인인 것은 현재이므로, 과거의 사실과 반대되는 일을 가정하고 과거 사실이 현재까지 영향을 미치는 경우에 쓰는 혼합가정법이다. 혼합가정법에서 if절은 「if+주어+had+과거분사」로 쓴다.

18 ③ 현재 사실과 반대되는 소망을 wish를 사용해 나타내고 있으므로 뒤에 가정법 과거 표현이 와야 한다. 따라서 '부유했다면 좋았을 텐데'라는 의미를 표현하기 위해 동사의 과거형인 were을 쓰는 것이 적절하다. (becomes → were)
④ 「If+주어+동사의 과거형 ~, 주어+could+동사원형 ~」의 형태이므로 가정법 과거 표현임을 알 수 있다. 가정법 과거는 현재 사실에 반대되는 일을 가정할 때 사용되므로 직설법에서는 couldn't가 아닌 can't를 쓰는 것이 적절하다. (couldn't → can't)
① 「I wish+가정법 과거」는 현재의 사실과 반대되는 소망을 표현할 때 사용하며, 「I'm sorry (that) I+현재시제 동사 ~」로 바꿔 쓸 수 있다.
② 「의문사+to부정사」는 「의문사+주어+should+동사원형」과 같은 의미이다.
⑤ 동사 give가 사용된 4형식 문장은 전치사 to를 사

용하여 3형식으로 바꿀 수 있다.

19 첫 번째 빈칸은 '~하게 행동한다면 친구 몇몇을 잃어버릴지도 모른다'라는 뜻의 조건을 나타내고 있으므로, '~한다면, ~라면'의 뜻의 if를 쓴다.

두 번째 빈칸은 '네가 세상에서 가장 똑똑한 사람인 것처럼'이라는 뜻을 나타내고 있다. 또한 시제가 현재시제임에도 빈칸 뒤에 동사의 과거형 were를 쓴 것으로 보아 가정법임을 알 수 있다. 따라서 '마치 ~인 것처럼'이라는 뜻의 as if 가정법 과거를 써준다.

20 과거 사실의 반대를 가정하고 있으므로 가정법 과거완료 구문이다. Without을 사용한 가정법 과거완료 특수구문 「Without ~, 주어+would+have+과거분사 …」를 쓴 것이므로 (B)에 들어갈 동사는 have quit[quitted]로 쓰는 것이 적절하다.

21 가정법 과거완료가 사용된 가정법 문장이다. 가정법 과거완료는 과거의 사실과 반대되는 일을 가정할 때 쓰이므로, 직설법의 시제는 과거로 써야 한다. 또한 가정법은 사실과 반대되는 일을 나타내기 때문에, 가정법에서 긍정형으로 쓰인 부분은 직설법에서는 모두 부정형으로 고쳐야 한다.

22 ③ '그들은 내가 실종된 고양이를 찾아야 한다고 요청했다.'라는 의미이므로 that절에 '~해야 한다'는 의미가 포함되어 있다. 따라서 가정법 현재 명사절을 사용해 「should+동사원형」을 쓰거나 should를 생략하고 동사원형만 쓰는 것이 옳다.
(looked → (should) look)

① suggest와 같이 제안 등을 나타내는 동사 뒤에서 가정법 현재 명사절을 쓸 수 있다. 하지만, that절의 내용에 '~해야 한다'의 의미가 포함되어 있을 때만 should를 생략하는 것이 가능하다. 주어진 문장의 경우, '그는 내 친구를 만났었음을 암시했다.'는

뜻이므로, 시제에 맞게 과거완료로 쓰는 것이 옳다.

② '대장은 그 깃발이 올려져야 한다고 명령했다.'라는 의미이므로 that절의 내용에 '~해야 한다'는 의미가 포함되어 있다. 따라서 가정법 현재 명사절을 사용해, should를 생략하고 동사원형만 쓰는 것이 가능하다.

④ '모두에 의해 그 법이 지켜져야 하는 것은 필수적이다.'라는 의미이므로 '~해야 한다'는 의미가 포함되어 있다. 따라서 가정법 현재 명사절을 사용해, should를 생략하는 것이 가능하다.

⑤ '그녀는 우리가 지역의 사람들을 믿어야 한다고 주장했다.'라는 의미이므로 '~해야 한다'는 의미가 포함되어 있어, 가정법 현재 명사절을 사용하여 should를 생략하는 것이 가능하다.

23 (1) 「If it were not for+명사, 주어+could+동사원형 ~」의 가정법 과거 문장에서 if가 생략되고, 주어와 be동사가 도치된 형태이다.
(2) 「If it were not for+명사, 주어+could+동사원형~」의 가정법 과거 문장은 「But for+명사, 주어+could+동사원형~」의 형태로 바꿔 쓸 수 있다.

24 영화관에 가지 못한 것은 과거의 일이므로 (A)에는 과거의 사실과 반대되는 일을 가정하는 가정법 과거완료를 써야 한다. (B)에는 명령을 나타내는 동사 order 뒤에 이어지는 that절이므로 「should+동사원형」을 써야 한다. 이때 should는 생략하고 동사원형만 쓸 수 있다. (C)에는 과거의 사실과 반대되는 일을 소망해야 하므로 「wish+가정법 과거완료」를 사용해야 한다.

25 주장을 나타내는 동사 insist 뒤에 이어지는 that절에서는 「should+동사원형」을 쓸 수 있다. 이때 should는 생략이 가능하다.

Ch **12**
가정법

PRACTICE 1

1　smaller – smallest
2　weaker – weakest
3　nicer – nicest
4　deeper – deepest
5　cheaper – cheapest
6　darker – darkest
7　faster – fastest
8　wider – widest
9　cuter – cutest
10　safer – safest
11　lower – lowest
12　huger – hugest
13　larger – largest
14　shorter – shortest
15　greater – greatest
16　higher – highest
17　colder – coldest
18　closer – closest
19　sweeter – sweetest
20　warmer – warmest
21　kinder – kindest
22　ruder – rudest
23　taller – tallest
24　louder – loudest
25　stranger – strangest
26　cooler – coolest
27　softer – softest
28　longer – longest
29　thicker – thickest
30　smarter – smartest

PRACTICE 2

1　heavier – heaviest
2　funnier – funniest
3　bigger – biggest
4　curlier – curliest
5　happier – happiest
6　hotter – hottest
7　hungrier – hungriest
8　stricter – strictest

9　healthier – healthiest
10　flatter – flattest
11　easier – easiest
12　newer – newest
13　thinner – thinnest
14　tastier – tastiest
15　fresher – freshest
16　prettier – prettiest
17　fatter – fattest
18　drier – driest
19　harder – hardest
20　luckier – luckiest
21　braver – bravest
22　poorer – poorest
23　noisier – noisiest
24　earlier – earliest
25　lazier – laziest
26　uglier – ugliest
27　sunnier – sunniest
28　dirtier – dirtiest
29　crazier – craziest
30　lighter – lightest

PRACTICE 3

1　meaner – meanest
2　more easily – most easily
3　brighter – brightest
4　slimmer – slimmest
5　more shocked – most shocked
6　more effective – most effective
7　friendlier – friendliest
8　more famous – most famous
9　more curious – most curious
10　more logical – most logical
11　more quickly – most quickly
12　more surprised – most surprised
13　more pleasing – most pleasing
14　quieter – quietest
15　more formal – most formal
16　duller – dullest
17　more nervous – most nervous

18 more slowly – most slowly
19 more difficult – most difficult
20 more creative – most creative
21 more fluently – most fluently
22 more comfortable – most comfortable
23 more complicated – most complicated
24 more similar – most similar
25 richer – richest
26 more diligent – most diligent
27 more boring – most boring
28 more exactly – most exactly
29 more tired – most tired
30 more artistic – most artistic
31 more practical – most practical
32 scarier – scariest
33 more upset – most upset
34 more enjoyable – most enjoyable
35 lovelier – loveliest
36 more wonderful – most wonderful
37 more delicious – most delicious
38 more depressed – most depressed
39 more intelligent – most intelligent
40 more powerful – most powerful
41 more familiar – most familiar
42 more convenient – most convenient
43 more useless – most useless
44 more skillful – most skillful
45 more generous – most generous
46 more impressive – most impressive
47 more foolish – most foolish
48 more insistent – most insistent
49 more dangerous – most dangerous
50 more nutritious – most nutritious
51 more serious – most serious
52 more peaceful – most peaceful
53 more colorful – most colorful
54 more ambitious – most ambitious
55 more negative – most negative
56 more amazing – most amazing
57 more natural – most natural
58 more valuable – most valuable
59 more awkward – most awkward
60 more urgent – most urgent

61 more often – most often
62 more sensitive – most sensitive
63 more common – most common
64 more challenging – most challenging
65 more abstract – most abstract
66 more active – most active
67 milder – mildest
68 more helpful – most helpful
69 more attractive – most attractive
70 more awesome – most awesome
71 more cheerful – most cheerful
72 severer – severest
73 busier – busiest
74 politer[more polite] – politest[most polite]
75 more beautiful – most beautiful
76 more important – most important
77 more harmful – most harmful
78 more useful – most useful
79 more patient – most patient
80 gladder – gladdest
81 tougher – toughest
82 more fantastic – most fantastic
83 angrier – angriest
84 more crowded – most crowded
85 more recent – most recent
86 more hopeless – most hopeless
87 more loudly – most loudly
88 more positive – most positive
89 more selfish – most selfish
90 more embarrassed – most embarrassed

PRACTICE 4

1	more	**2**	better
3	worse	**4**	latest[last]
5	least	**6**	best
7	elder[older]	**8**	last
9	worse	**10**	further
11	fewer	**12**	oldest
13	more	**14**	farthest[furthest]

1 some more resources: 약간의 더 많은 자원
(many-more-most)
2 「비교급+than」은 '~보다 …한'이라는 뜻이다.
speak better than: ~보다 더 잘 말하다 (well-better-best)

3, 9 「get+비교급」은 '점점 ~해지다'라는 뜻이다.
get worse: 점점 더 나빠지다 (bad/ill-worse-worst)
4, 5, 6, 8, 12 최상급이 뒤의 명사를 수식할 때는 최상급의 앞에 정관사 the가 온다.
the latest[last] news: 최신 뉴스 (late-later/latter-latest/last)
the least amount: 가장 적은 양 (little-less-least)
the best place: 가장 좋은 장소 (good-better-best)
the last survivor of the shipwreck: 난파선의 마지막 생존자 (late-latter-last)
the oldest astronomical observatory: 가장 오래된 천문대 (old-older-oldest)
7 one elder[older] sister: 언니 한 명 (old-elder/older-eldest/oldest)
10 further education: 고등교육 (far-further-furthest)
11 fewer hours: 더 적은 시간 (few-fewer-fewest)
13 more information: 더 많은 정보 (much-more-most)
14 뒤에 비교의 대상을 한정하는 표현이 올 때는 최상급을 쓴다.
live the farthest[furthest] away from school of all of us
: 우리들 중 학교에서 가장 멀리 떨어져 살다
(far-farther[further]-farthest[furthest])

PRACTICE 5

2 five times as long as

3 as often as

4 half as long as

5 as tall as

6 as cold as

7 as many windows as

8 three times as heavy as

9 ten times as much as

10 four times as expensive as

1, 3, 5, 6, 7 비교하는 두 대상의 정도가 같으므로 「as+원급+as」 구문을 사용해서 '~만큼 …한'이라고 표현한다.
get up as early as: ~만큼 일찍 일어나다
go jogging as often as: ~만큼 자주 조깅하러 가다
as tall as: ~만큼 키가 큰
as cold as: ~만큼 추운
have as many windows as: ~만큼 많은 창문이 있다
2, 4, 8, 9, 10 비교하는 두 대상의 정도 차이가 크므로 앞에 배수사를 붙인 「배수 표현+as+원급+as」 구문을 사용해서 '~보다 …배 -한'이라고 표현한다.
study five times as long as: ~보다 다섯 배 오래 공부하다
half as long as: ~의 절반만큼 긴
three times as heavy as: ~보다 세 배 무거운
cost ten times as much as: ~보다 10배 많이 값이 나가다
four times as expensive as: ~보다 네 배 비싼

PRACTICE 6

2 isn't as[so] comfortable as

3 can't read as[so] fast as

4 doesn't write English essays as[so] well as

5 isn't as[so] long as

6 isn't as[so] fat as

7 isn't as[so] crowded as

8 don't speak French as[so] fluently as

9 don't know about their history as[so] much as

10 isn't as[so] polluted as

11 isn't as[so] complicated as

12 isn't as[so] high as

「not as[so]+원급+as」 '~만큼 …하지 않은'
2 not as[so] comfortable as: ~만큼 편안하지 않은
3 not as[so] fast as: ~만큼 빠르지 않은
4 not as[so] well as: ~만큼 잘하지 못하는
5 not as[so] long as: ~만큼 길지 않은
6 not as[so] fat as: ~만큼 살찌지 않은
7 not as[so] crowded as: ~만큼 혼잡하지 않은
8 not as[so] fluently as: ~만큼 유창하지 않은
9 not as[so] much as: ~만큼 많이는 아닌
10 not as[so] polluted as: ~만큼 오염되지 않은
11 not as[so] complicated as: ~만큼 복잡하지 않은
12 not as[so] high as: ~만큼 높지 않은

PRACTICE 7

1 as fast as possible   as fast as he could

2 as spicy as possible   as spicy as I could

3 as much as possible   as much as we can

4 as young as possible   as young as she could

5 as often as possible   as often as I can

6 as hard as possible   as hard as she can

7 as early as possible   as early as he could

8 as easy as possible   as easy as she could

「as+원급+as possible」 = 「as+원급+as+주어+can[could]」 '~가 할 수 있는 한 …하게'
1, 2, 4, 7, 8 동사가 과거 시제이므로 「as+원급+as+주어+could」 형태로 쓴다.
3, 5, 6 동사가 현재/현재진행 시제이므로 「as+원급+as+주어+can」 형태로 쓴다.

PRACTICE 8

1 as real as possible

2 enjoying their free time as long as they could

3 exercise as hard as possible

4 help other people as much as possible

5 finished her homework as fast as she could

6 talks with his children as often as he can

7 came in as quietly as possible

8 write down as many things as possible

9 spoke as loudly as I could

10 will finish my work as soon as I can

> **1** as real as possible: 할 수 있는 한 진짜처럼
> **2** as long as they could: 그들이 할 수 있는 한 오래
> **3** as hard as possible: 할 수 있는 한 열심히
> **4** as much as possible: 할 수 있는 한 많이
> **5** as fast as she could: 그녀가 할 수 있는 한 빨리
> **6** as often as he can: 그가 할 수 있는 한 자주
> **7** as quietly as possible: 할 수 있는 한 조용히
> **8** as many things as possible: 할 수 있는 한 많은 것들
> **9** as loudly as I could: 내가 할 수 있는 한 큰 소리로
> **10** as soon as I can: 내가 할 수 있는 한 빨리

PRACTICE 9

1 more difficult than	**2** bigger than
3 more popular than	**4** smarter than
5 more boring than	**6** more amazing than
7 more than	**8** more impressive than
9 more nervous than	**10** more convenient than
11 more logical than	**12** more beautiful than

PRACTICE 10

1 Mihyun's	**2** Hojung did
3 Jihoon's	**4** Kim does
5 I did	**6** diamond's
7 he does	**8** doll's
9 Heeyoung does	**10** Mike's

> **1, 3, 6, 8, 10** 비교의 대상이 같은 종류이면 소유대명사로 나타낼 수 있다.
> **2, 4, 5, 7, 9** than 다음에 나오는 비교 대상이 명사의 목적격일 때, 이를 주격으로 바꾸고 대동사 do[does, did]와 함께 「주어+동사」 구조로 쓸 수 있다.

PRACTICE 11

1 those	**2** those	**3** that	**4** those
5 that	**6** that	**7** those	**8** that
9 that	**10** those		

PRACTICE 12

1 much	**2** far	**3** a lot	**4** even
5 still	**6** far	**7** even	**8** much
9 still	**10** a lot		

> **1** much harder for me to understand: 내가 이해하기에 훨씬 더 힘든
> **2** far more comfortable than the old one: 예전 것보다 훨씬 더 편안한
> **3** a lot more skillful in fixing cars than Harry: Harry보다 차를 고치는 데 훨씬 더 능숙한
> **4** even more recent than that one: 저것보다 훨씬 더 최근의
> **5** still more peaceful than now: 지금보다 훨씬 더 평화적인
> **6** far more difficult for us to read: 우리가 읽기에 훨씬 더 어려운
> **7** even braver than I was at his age: 내가 그의 나이였을 때보다 훨씬 더 용감한
> **8** much more nutritious than those cupcakes: 저 컵케이크보다 훨씬 더 영양이 풍부한
> **9** still more tired than before when I get home from work: 퇴근해서 집에 가면 전보다 훨씬 더 피곤한
> **10** a lot farther than you imagine: 네가 상상하는 것보다 훨씬 더 먼

PRACTICE 13

1 a lot	**2** very	**3** far
4 very	**5** a lot	**6** even
7 very	**8** far	

> **1, 3, 5, 6, 8** 비교급 앞에서 '훨씬'의 뜻을 가진 비교급을 강조하는 부사가 와야 하는 자리이므로 much, still, even, far, a lot 같은 비교급 강조 부사가 알맞다.
> **2, 4, 7** 괄호 안의 말이 강조하는 대상이 원급 형용사이므로 원급을 강조하는 부사 very가 적절하다.

PRACTICE 14

2 The second series of the drama was less mysterious than the first series.

3 Your English essay was less impressive than your Korean essay.

4 He reacted less sensitively to the matter than his wife did.

5 Sujin writes a poem less creatively than other students in class.

6 The law was put into practice less effectively than we had expected.

7 Karen speaks Chinese and Japanese less fluently than Joey does.

8 Hiking is less attractive than playing online games to me.

9 His new work is less creative than his previous work.

10 My elder brother runs less quickly than my father used to.

Ch **13** 비교구문

PRACTICE 15

1 The hotter the weather gets, the more cold drinks people have.

2 The better you know the rules of the game, the more you'll enjoy it.

3 The harder you try to forget something, the more clearly you remember it.

4 The larger our society becomes, the more crime occurs.

5 The higher your energy level is, the more efficiently your body works.

6 The cheaper the price becomes, the greater the demand will be.

7 The earlier you buy the plane ticket, the bigger discount you can get.

8 The longer you expose your skin to the sun, the higher chances to get a sunburn you have.

PRACTICE 16

1 faster and faster

2 louder and louder

3 more and more interesting

4 more and more tired

5 stronger and stronger

6 darker and darker

7 less and less

8 more and more generous

9 more and more colorful

10 more and more fluently

> 「비교급+and+비교급」 표현은 '점점 더 ~한'의 뜻을 나타낸다.
>
> **1** walk faster and faster: 점점 더 빠르게 걷다
> **2** get louder and louder: 점점 더 (목소리가) 커지다
> **3** become more and more interesting: 점점 더 흥미로워지다
> **4** grow more and more tired: 점점 더 피곤해지다
> **5** get stronger and stronger: 점점 더 힘이 세지다
> **6** get darker and darker: 점점 더 어두워지다
> **7** eat less and less: 점점 덜 먹다
> **8** become more and more generous: 점점 더 관대해지다
> **9** become more and more colorful: 점점 더 색이 다채로워지다
> **10** speak more and more fluently: 점점 더 유창하게 말하다

PRACTICE 17

1 the strangest   **2** funnier

3 more easily   **4** the most familiar

5 the most diligent   **6** the most convenient

7 hotter   **8** the most valuable

9 the wealthiest   **10** the most

11 more nervous   **12** the most practical

13 earlier   **14** more fantastic

15 the most intelligent

> **1, 6, 9, 12** 비교의 대상을 한정하는 「주어+have[has]+(ever)+과거분사」절이 왔으므로 「the+최상급」의 형태로 나타내어야 한다.
> **2, 3, 7, 11, 13, 14** 빈칸 뒤에 than과 비교 대상이 있으므로 빈칸에는 비교급 형태로 써야 한다.
> **4, 8, 15** 비교의 대상을 한정하는 of가 이끄는 전치사구가 있으므로 「the+최상급」 형태로 나타내어야 한다.
> **5, 10** 비교의 대상을 한정하는 in이 이끄는 전치사구가 있으므로 「the+최상급」 형태로 나타내어야 한다.

PRACTICE 18

1 animals   **2** best

3 artists   **4** was

5 in   **6** is

7 is   **8** the most important

9 intersections

10 the most impressive novels

PRACTICE 19

1 There's nothing I worry about more than

2 There is nothing more precious than

3 There is nothing more interesting than

4 There's nothing I want more than

5 There is nothing more important than

6 There's nothing she can do better than

7 There's nothing I like more than

8 There is nothing worse than

9 There is nothing more expensive than

10 There's nothing Suji speaks more fluently than

> **1, 4, 6, 7, 10** 「There is nothing+주어+동사+비교급+than …」 구문은 '…보다 더 ~한 것은 없다'라는 뜻으로 최상급의 의미를 나타낼 수 있다.
> **2, 3, 5, 8, 9** 「There is nothing+비교급+than …」 구문은 '…보다 더 ~한 것은 없다'라는 뜻으로 최상급의 의미를 나타낼 수 있다.

PRACTICE 20

2 No (other) lake, as[so] deep as
No (other) lake, deeper than
deeper than any other lake
deeper than all the other lakes

3 No (other) dinosaur fossil, as[so] old as
No (other) dinosaur fossil, older than
older than any other dinosaur fossil
older than all the other dinosaur fossils

4 No (other) person, as[so] lucky as
No (other) person, luckier than
luckier than any other person
luckier than all the other people

5 No (other) student, as[so] artistic as
No (other) student, more artistic than
more artistic than any other student
more artistic than all the other students

6 No (other) policy, as[so] strict as
No (other) policy, stricter than
stricter than any other policy
stricter than all the other policies

📝 중간·기말고사 대비문제 정답 본문 _ p.301

1 ⑤ **2** ④ **3** ① **4** as real as possible
5 ③ **6** as much as I did **7** ② **8** ② **9** ②
10 The more comfortable you feel, the more natural you look in photos. **11** less complicated than **12** The most learned are not the wisest. **13** ③ **14** The longer she stayed in Seoul, the more she got to like the people in the city. **15** ⑤ **16** (1) is not as[so] healthy as (2) as honestly as he could **17** the more weeds you'll cultivate **18** ④ **19** ④ **20** The cooler, the better **21** possible **22** ② **23** more and more **24** ③ **25** less, than **26** ⑤ **27** ③ **28** no, more[better] than **29** ④ **30** ②,⑤ **31** ②,③ **32** ①,⑤ **33** is more intelligent than any other boy **34** I did[read] **35** ① **36** ⑤ **37** ②

중간·기말고사 대비문제 해설

1 ① fast는 형용사와 부사의 형태가 같으며 fastly는 쓰지 않는다. 여기에서는 동사 run을 수식하는 부사로 '~만큼 …하지 않은'이라는 뜻의 「not as+원급+as」로 쓰였다. (fastly → fast)
② simple은 -e로 끝나는 형용사로, 「원급+r」의 형태

로 비교급을 만든다. 비교급 앞에 more을 중복하여 쓰지 않는다. (more simpler → simpler)
③ than이 쓰인 것으로 보아 '~보다 더 …한'이라는 뜻의 「비교급+than」 비교급 표현임을 알 수 있다. bad는 불규칙으로 변화하는 형용사로 bad의 비교급은 worse이다. (very bad → worse)
④ as와 as 사이는 '유창하게'라는 뜻으로 동사 speak을 수식하는 부사의 자리이다. fluent는 -ly를 붙여 부사로 만들 수 있다. (fluent → fluently)

2 than이 있으므로 셀 수 있는 명사의 복수형을 수식하는 few의 비교급 fewer을 쓴다.

3 very는 비교급을 수식할 수 없다.

4 「as+원급+as+주어+can[could]」
=「as+원급+as possible」

5 ③ '훨씬' ① '다량, 많음' ②④⑤ '많이'

6 「as+원급+as+주어+동사」 '~만큼 …한'
문장의 시제가 과거이므로 do를 과거시제인 did로 바꾸어 써야 한다.

7 「as+원급+as+주어+can」 '~가 할 수 있는 한 …하게'

8 ② 첫 번째 문장은 비교급을 이용한 비교로 강조하는 말인 much와 함께 쓰여 '우리가 작년에 배운 책보다 훨씬 더 어려운'의 뜻을, 두 번째 문장은 원급을 이용한 비교로 '우리가 작년에 배운 책만큼 어려운'의 뜻을 나타낸다.

9 ⓐ 시골로 이사 온 후부터 지금까지 여유롭고 평화로운 삶을 즐겨왔다는 의미이므로, 현재완료 시제 have enjoyed를 사용하는 것이 적절하다. since는 과거에 시작된 사건이 현재에도 영향을 미치고 있음을 나타내며 완료시제와 함께 주로 쓰인다.
ⓑ 맥락상 동사 has changed를 수식하고 있으므로 동사를 수식할 수 있는 부사 truly의 사용이 적절하다.
ⓒ than ever before이라는 비교 표현이 사용되었으므로 비교급 표현을 사용해야 한다. 따라서 원급인 close가 아닌 비교급 closer를 쓰는 것이 적절하다.

우리 가족이 3년 전 시골로 이사 온 이후로, 우리는 더 여유롭고 평화로운 삶을 즐겨 왔다. 지난 겨울, 우리는 야채를 기르기 위해 뒷마당에 작은 온실을 지었다. 지금까지 우리는 토마토, 오이, 그리고 딸기까지도 수확해 왔다. 이곳에서 사는 것은 음식과 자연에 대해 우리가 생각하는 방식을 정말로 바꾸어 놓았다. 무엇보다도, 그것은 우리 가족을 어느 때보다 더 가깝게 만들어 주었다.

10 「the 비교급, the 비교급」'~하면 할수록 더 …하다'

11 「less+원급+than」'~보다 덜 …한'

12 'The+형용사(~한 사람들)'이란 표현과 최상급 표현이 함께 쓰였다.

13 ⓑ 화분이 두 개이므로, 하나는 one, 나머지 하나는 the other로 나타낸다. (another → the other)

ⓔ 「비교급+than any other+단수 명사」는 '다른 모든 ~보다 더 …하다'라는 뜻으로, 최상급의 다른 표현이다. (inventions → invention)

ⓐ 「one of the+최상급+복수명사」는 '가장 ~한 것 중의 하나'라는 뜻이다.

ⓒ 조건의 부사절로 주어(the water)에 맞게 현재시제(evaporates)로 쓴다.

ⓓ 'keep fruits and vegetables fresh'는 '과일과 야채를 신선하게 유지하다'라고 해석한다. 해석상 부사 freshly(신선하게)가 들어가야 하는 것으로 혼동할 수 있지만, keep의 목적격 보어 자리이므로 형용사인 fresh가 적절하다.

pot-in-pot Cooler(화분 속 화분 냉장고)는 기발한 발명품들 중 하나이다. 당신은 그것을 작동시키기 위해서 오직 두 개의 토기 화분과 젖은 모래만이 필요하다. 한 화분은 다른 화분보다 더 작다. 더 작은 화분을 더 큰 화분 안에 넣는다. 젖은 모래를 두 화분 사이에 붓는다. 그러고 나서, 음식을 더 작은 화분 안에 놓는다. 모래 안에 있던 물이 증발하면, 그것은 더 작은 화분에서 열을 빼앗아간다. 이런 식으로 당신은 과일과 야채를 신선하게 유지할 수 있다. 이 냉장고는 다른 어떤 발명품보다도 더 간단하다.

14 「the+비교급, the+비교급」'~하면 할수록 더 …한'

15 「the+비교급, the+비교급」'~하면 할수록 더 …한'

16 (1) 「not as[so]+원급+as」'~만큼 …하지 않은'

(2) 「as+원급+as possible」은 「as+원급+as+주어+can[could]」로 바꿔 쓸 수 있다.

17 「the+비교급, the+비교급」'~하면 할수록 더 …한'을 활용해 부정적인 생각을 많이 하면 할수록 정원에 잡초가 더 자란다는 의미를 표현한다.

너의 마음을 하나의 정원으로 생각해 보라. 네가 그것에게 긍정적인 생각을 더 줄수록 그것은 더 자란다[번성한다]. 매일 당신의 행동, 말, 그리고 태도가 그것을 형성하는 씨앗을 심는다. 친절, 감사, 그리고 집중의 씨앗은 행복, 생산성, 그리고 평화로 자란다. 그러나 부정과 스트레스에 더 집중할수록 너는 더 많은 잡초를 키우게 되고, 평화를 찾는 것이 더 어려워진다. 정원처럼, 너의 마음은 매일 같은 관리와 긍정적인 습관들로 번성하는데, 이는 더 큰 회복력, 명료함, 그리고 평화를 가져다준다.

18 「No ~ as[so]+원급+as」는 최상급의 의미를 나타낸다.

19 「비교급+than+any other」 다음에는 단수 명사가 와야 한다. (movies → movie)

20 「the+비교급, the+비교급」'~하면 할수록 더 …한'

21 「as+원급+as possible」'가능한 한 ~하게'

22 ① prefer A to B(B보다 A를 선호하다)는 A와 B의 형태가 일치해야 하므로 play가 아닌 동명사 playing이 적절하다. (play → playing)

③ 「one of+최상급+복수명사」(singer → singers)

④ 비교의 대상이 artwork로 같은 종류이므로 소유대명사로 나타낸다. (him → his)

⑤ '점점 더 (상태가) 나빠졌다'는 의미이므로 「비교급 and 비교급」을 사용해야 한다.

(bad and bad → worse and worse)

23 「비교급+and+비교급」'점점 더 ~한'

24 ① 우리말 해석이 '더 많이 연습할수록'이라고 되어 있음에 유의한다. 즉, more를 형용사가 아닌 부사로 써야 한다. (The more practice they were → The more they practiced)

② scared와 같은 분사 형태의 형용사는 「more+원급」의 형태로 비교급을 만든다.

(scared → more scared)

④ tired가 주격 보어로 쓰였으므로, 동사는 '~이다'라는 뜻으로 명사/형용사를 주격 보어로 사용하는 be를 쓰는 것이 적절하다. 시제는 과거이므로 was로 쓴다. (did → was)

⑤ 우리말 해석이 '책을 더 많이 읽을수록'이 아니라 '더 많은 책을 읽을수록'이라고 되어 있음에 유의한다. 형용사 more가 명사 books 앞에서 수식하도록 영작해야 한다. (The more we read books → The more books we read)

25 「not as[so]+원급+as」=「less+원급+than」

26 ⑤ 비교 대상이 the windows이므로 복수형 대명사인 those를 쓰는 것이 적절하다. (that → those)

27 ③을 제외한 나머지는 모두 large의 최상급을 나타내어 '러시아가 세계에서 가장 크다.'는 뜻이다.

28 「There is no ~ 비교급+than …」은 최상급의 의미를 나타낸다.

29 ④를 제외한 나머지는 모두 important의 최상급을 나타내어 '음악이 가장 중요하다'는 뜻이다.

30 「비교급+and+비교급」 '점점 더 ~한'
② more and more uninteresting
⑤ duller and duller

31 「No (other) ~ 비교급+than」, 「비교급+than any other+단수 명사」는 최상급의 다른 표현이다.
[보기] 김치는 우리 집에서 가장 매운 음식이다.
① 김치는 우리 집에서 매우 맵다.
② 김치는 우리 집에 있는 다른 어떤 음식보다 더 맵다.
③ 우리 집의 어떤 음식도 김치보다 더 맵지 않다.
④ 김치는 우리 집에 있는 어떤 음식보다도 덜 맵다.
⑤ 김치는 우리 집에 있는 다른 어떤 음식들만큼 맵지 않다.

32 ⓐ 명사 앞의 형용사 useful의 첫소리가 모음으로 시작되지만 자음으로 발음되므로 부정관사 a를 써야 한다. (an → a)
ⓔ 비교급 more popular를 수식할 때에는 very를 쓸 수 없다. (very → much[far/still/a lot/even])
ⓑ be in charge of '~을 담당하다, 책임지다'
ⓒ 기부된 책들이 '전달된' 것이므로 수동태로 써야 한다.
ⓓ 비교급을 수식하는 Even의 사용은 적절하다. 주어인 선행사 many children을 수식하는 주격관계대명사 who와 본동사 enjoy의 수일치, enjoy의 목적어로 쓰인 동명사 reading 또한 어법상 옳다.
지난 금요일에, 나는 이것이 얼마나 유용한 프로젝트였는지를 생각했다. 우리 동아리는 책 기부 행사를 조직하는 것을 담당했다. 기부된 책들은 우리 마을의 어린이 도서관으로 전달되었다. 더 좋은 것은, 책이 없던 많은 아이들이 이제 독서를 즐긴다는 점이다. 그 열람실은 전보다 훨씬 더 인기가 많아졌고, 부모들은 진심으로 그것을 고마워한다.

33 「비교급+than any other+단수 명사」는 최상급의 의미를 나타낸다.

34 「as+원급+as」에서 as 뒤의 목적격은 「주어+동사」로 바꾸어 쓸 수 있다.

35 ① 문맥상 '우리가 종종 인식하는 것보다 건강하지 못한 식습관이 우리의 건강에 더 위험하다'는 내용이 되어야 하므로, 전치사 to와 than의 위치를 서로 바꿔야 한다.
(more dangerous <u>than</u> our health <u>to</u> we often realize → more dangerous <u>to</u> our health <u>than</u> we often realize)
최근 우리는 영양 전문가와 이야기를 나눴다. 그녀는 우리가 종종 인식하는 것보다 건강하지 못한 식습관이 우리의 건강에 더 위험하다고 말했다. 부실한 식단 때문에 많은 사람들이 예방할 수 있는 질병으로 고통받고 있다. 건강하지 못한 식사는 운동 부족보다 우리의 웰빙에 더 큰 영향을 미칠 수 있다. 집에 돌아온 후, 우리는 균형 잡힌 식단을 유지하는 방법에 관한 교육 프로젝트를 만들었다. 또한, 우리 단체는 건강한 생활을 증진시키기 위한 다른 프로젝트도 진행하고 있다. 비록 우리는 처음에 작은 규모로 시작했지만, 큰 변화를 만들어내고 있다. 오늘 당신이 하는 일이 당신의 삶을 바꿀 수 있다. 그러니, 첫걸음을 내딛어 보아라!

36 ① 최상급 앞에는 정관사 the를 붙여야 한다.
(smartest → the smartest)
② 비교급 more이 있으므로 as가 아닌, than이 와야 한다. 「There is nothing+주어+동사+비교급+than」 '~보다 더 …한 것은 없다' (as → than)
③ as와 as 사이에는 형용사의 원급이 들어가야 하므로, more을 빼야 한다.
(more specific → specific)
④ 「비교급+than+any other」 다음에는 단수명사가 들어가야 한다. (teachers → teacher)

37 「one of+최상급+복수명사」의 순서로 배열하면 'one of the most famous painters'가 되므로 네 번째에 올 단어는 most임을 알 수 있다.

PRACTICE 1

1 who go to this school don't have to wear uniforms on Friday

2 whose office plants are not taken good care of

3 who support us when we are having a hard time

4 whose parents run a big bakery downtown

5 whom[who] I wanted to see because of an interview was not in the office

6 who was raised by wolves in the jungle

7 who have poor concentration are likely to get low grades

8 who broke into my neighbor's house last night was arrested

9 who work for the law firm are very diligent

10 whose recipes could meet our expectations

11 whose character is open and kind is welcomed by everyone

12 whom[who] I visit twice a month with some cookies lives near my house

> **1, 3, 6, 7, 8, 9** 선행사가 사람이고, 관계대명사로 연결되는 문장의 주어에 해당하므로 주격 관계대명사 who를 이용한다.
> **2, 4, 10, 11** 선행사가 관계대명사로 연결되는 문장의 맨 처음에 오는 명사와 소유의 관계를 이루므로 소유격 관계대명사 whose를 이용한다.
> **5, 12** 선행사가 사람이고, 관계대명사로 연결되는 문장의 목적어에 해당하므로 목적격 관계대명사 whom을 이용한다.

PRACTICE 2

1 The pictures which are hanging on the wall were taken in Eastern Europe.

2 Students can develop self-confidence through the program which is provided by some counselors.

3 The bicycle which had pedals was invented in the 1860s.

4 The farmer could produce a new kind of fruit which was bigger than any other fruit.

5 There was a glass of water whose temperature was under 5 degrees Celsius.

6 The bus which goes to the airport via the city hall runs every fifteen minutes.

7 People try to remember some accidents which taught them an important lesson.

8 There are many animals whose lives are in great danger.

9 The workers constructed the building which is the tallest in the city.

10 Cyberspace has given us a new kind of reality which is called a virtual reality.

> **1, 2, 3, 4, 6, 7, 9, 10** 선행사가 사물이고, 관계대명사로 연결되는 문장의 주어에 해당하므로 주격 관계대명사 which를 이용한다.
> **5, 8** 선행사가 관계대명사로 연결되는 문장의 맨 처음에 오는 명사와 소유의 관계를 이루므로 소유격 관계대명사 whose를 이용한다.

PRACTICE 3

1 have	**2** which	**3** which
4 serves	**5** whom	**6** imports
7 which	**8** don't	**9** whose
10 who	**11** was	**12** who
13 whom	**14** wants	**15** focus

> **1, 8, 15** 주격 관계대명사절의 동사는 선행사의 수에 일치시켜야 한다. 선행사가 복수 명사이므로 관계대명사절의 동사 역시 복수 동사가 알맞다.
> **2, 3, 7** 선행사가 사물이면 관계대명사는 which를 써야 한다. 이때, 관계대명사절의 목적어가 없으므로 목적격 관계대명사임을 알 수 있다.
> **4, 6, 11, 14** 주격 관계대명사절의 동사는 선행사의 수에 일치시킨다. 이때 선행사가 단수 명사이므로 관계대명사절의 동사 역시 단수 동사가 알맞다.
> **5, 13** 선행사가 사람이고 관계대명사가 이끄는 절에 목적어가 없으므로 선행사가 사람일 때 목적격 관계대명사로 쓰이는 whom이 알맞다.
> **9** 선행사 a girl과 관계대명사 바로 뒤의 명사 name이 소유의 관계(a girl's name)를 이루므로 소유격 관계대명사 whose가 알맞다.
> **10, 12** 선행사가 사람이고 관계대명사절에 주어가 없으므로 주격 관계대명사 who가 알맞다.

PRACTICE 4

1 which, that		**2** who, that
3 that		**4** which, that
5 that		**6** who, that
7 who, that		**8** that
9 whom, who, that		**10** who, that
11 that		**12** that
13 that		**14** whom, who, that

15 that

> **1** 선행사가 사물이고 빈칸 뒤 종속절에 주어가 없이 동사가 바로 이어지므로 주격 관계대명사 which가 알맞다. 이때 주격 관계대명사 which는 that으로 대체할 수 있다.
> **2, 6, 7, 10** 선행사가 사람이고 빈칸 뒤의 문장에 주어가 없이 동사가 바로 이어지므로 주격 관계대명사 who가 알맞다. 주격 관계대명사 who는 that으로 대체할 수 있다.
> **3, 11** 선행사에 anything, something이 포함되어 있을 경우는 관계대명사로 that을 쓴다.
> **4** 선행사가 동물이고 빈칸 뒤의 문장에 목적어가 없으므로 목적격 관계대명사 which가 알맞다. 목적격 관계대명사 which는 that으로 대체할 수 있다.
> **5, 13** 선행사에 형용사의 최상급이 포함되어 있을 경우에는 관계대명사 that을 쓴다.
> **8, 12** 선행사에 all, much, little, no, some이 포함되어 있을 경우에는 주로 관계대명사 that을 쓴다.
> **9, 14** 선행사가 사람이고 빈칸 뒤의 문장에 목적어가 없으므로 목적격 관계대명사 whom이 알맞다. 목적격 관계대명사 whom은 who나 that으로 대체할 수 있다.
> **15** 선행사에 서수가 포함되어 있을 경우에는 관계대명사 that을 쓴다.

PRACTICE 5

1	that	**2**	whose	**3**	that
4	that	**5**	was	**6**	who
7	that	**8**	that	**9**	is
10	that				

> **1, 4** 선행사가 사물이므로 관계대명사 who를 쓸 수 없다. that은 사람과 사물에 상관없이 who나 which를 대신하여 주격/목적격 관계대명사로 쓸 수 있다.
> **2** 선행사 Mr. Green과 괄호 뒤의 명사 shop이 소유의 관계를 이루므로 소유격 관계대명사 whose가 알맞다.
> **3, 7** 선행사가 the greatest, the last 같은 최상급 형용사의 수식을 받고 있으므로 관계대명사 that이 알맞다.
> **5, 9** 관계대명사절에 주어가 없으므로 that은 주격 관계대명사이다. 이때 관계대명사절의 동사의 수는 선행사의 수에 일치시켜야 하는데 선행사가 단수 명사이므로 단수 동사가 알맞다.
> **6** 선행사가 사람이므로 관계대명사 who가 알맞다.
> **8** 선행사가 something이므로 관계대명사로 that이 알맞다.
> **10** 괄호 뒤의 문장에 전치사 with의 목적어가 없으므로 목적격 관계대명사로 쓸 수 있는 that이 알맞다.

PRACTICE 6

1 that　　**2** who[that]
3 that produces　　**4** that
5 John had recommended to us
6 that　　**7** which[that]
8 that we wanted to have
9 you already know　　**10** that looked
11 was built 100 years ago
12 which[that]

> **1, 4** 선행사에 all, much, little, no가 포함되어 있을 경우에는 관계대명사 that을 쓴다.
> **2** 밑줄 친 부분 뒤에 동사가 바로 이어지므로 주격 관계대명사가 필요한 자리다. 선행사가 사람이므로 who나 that이 알맞다.
> **3** that은 an event를 선행사로 하는 주격 관계대명사다. 주격 관계대명사절에는 주어가 없으므로 it을 삭제한다. 또한 관계대명사절의 동사의 수는 선행사의 수에 일치시켜야 하므로 produces가 되어야 한다.
> **5** which는 a hotel을 선행사로 하는 목적격 관계대명사다. 따라서 관계대명사절 내에 목적어가 없어야 하므로 it을 삭제한다.
> **6** 선행사가 형용사의 최상급의 수식을 받고 있으므로 관계대명사 that을 쓴다.
> **7, 12** 선행사가 사람이 아니므로 who가 아닌 which나 that이 알맞다.
> **8, 9** that이 목적격 관계대명사로 쓰였으므로 관계대명사절 내에서 목적어 자리에 온 대명사 it을 삭제해야 한다.
> **10, 11** that이 주격 관계대명사로 쓰였으므로 관계대명사절 내에서 주어 자리에 온 대명사 it을 삭제해야 한다.

PRACTICE 7

1	What	**2**	which	**3**	what
4	which	**5**	What	**6**	what
7	which	**8**	which	**9**	what
10	which	**11**	what	**12**	what

> **1, 3, 5, 6, 9, 11, 12** 선행사가 따로 없으므로 선행사를 자체에 포함하는 관계대명사 what이 알맞다.
> what you believe: 네가 믿는 것
> what she must not do: 그녀가 하지 말아야 하는 것
> What I don't understand: 내가 이해하지 못하는 것
> what I meant to say: 내가 말하려던 것
> what the general ordered them to do: 장군이 그들에게 하라고 명령한 것
> what really counts: 정말 중요한 것
> what I enjoy watching: 내가 즐겨 보는 것
> **2, 4, 7, 8, 10** 선행사가 있고 괄호 뒤에 동사가 바로 이어지므로 주격 관계대명사로 쓰이는 which가 알맞다.

PRACTICE 8

1 My teacher bought me this book, which has influenced me a lot.

2 I sometimes ask my grandmother for advice, which has been very helpful.

3 An old lady, who lives next door, gave me some cookies that she had made.

4 He made a number of cartoons and movies, which have been loved by children.

5 Last Friday, I met Chris, whom[who] I hadn't seen for a long time.

6 We will fly to Busan, which means we won't have to worry about traffic jams.

Ch **14** 관계사

7 Thomas Edison, who is called the Father of Invention, was born in 1847.

8 Taekwondo, which is a kind of martial arts, requires both mental and physical training.

9 Jay, whose computer broke down yesterday, couldn't do his homework.

10 The game was shown on TV, which greatly helped it to sell well.

PRACTICE 9

1 which **2** who, that **3** who
4 who, that **5** who, that **6** who
7 whom, that **8** which **9** who, that
10 which

> **1, 3, 6, 8, 10** 관계대명사 앞에 , (콤마)가 온 것으로 보아 계속적 용법으로 쓰였음을 알 수 있는데, 관계대명사 that은 계속적 용법으로 쓰지 않는다.
> **2, 4, 5, 9** 괄호 뒤에 동사가 바로 이어지는 것으로 보아 주격 관계대명사 자리이고, 선행사는 사람이다. 선행사가 사람일 때 주격 관계대명사로 who와 that 모두 쓸 수 있다.
> **7** 괄호 뒤에 이어지는 문장에 목적어가 없는 것으로 보아 목적격 관계대명사 자리이다. 선행사가 사람(The woman)이므로 목적격 관계대명사로 whom과 that 모두 쓸 수 있다.

PRACTICE 10

2 Do you know the boy who(m)[that] Tom is talking to with a big smile?
Do you know the boy to whom Tom is talking with a big smile?

3 The bed which[that] I slept in last night was very comfortable.
The bed in which I slept last night was very comfortable.

4 These are the great inventions which[that] he is well-known for.
These are the great inventions for which he is well-known.

5 Before it is too late, we need to protect the Earth which[that] we live on.
Before it is too late, we need to protect the Earth on which we live.

6 Soccer is a sport which[that] my friends and I are very fond of.
Soccer is a sport of which my friends and I are very fond.

7 What is the title of the movie which[that] you told me about yesterday?
What is the title of the movie about which you told me yesterday?

8 We couldn't go to the birthday party which[that] we were invited to.
We couldn't go to the birthday party to which we were invited.

9 This is the port which[that] millions of immigrants from Europe entered America through.
This is the port through which millions of immigrants from Europe entered America.

10 I've never seen Susan who(m)[that] Mark fell in love with two years ago.
I've never seen Susan with whom Mark fell in love two years ago.

PRACTICE 11

1 (that) **2** (which are)
3 생략 가능한 부분 없음 **4** (who)
5 (which) **6** (who)
7 생략 가능한 부분 없음 **8** (that)
9 (whom) **10** (who is)
11 (who were) **12** (which is)

> **1, 4, 5, 6, 8, 9** 목적격 관계대명사로 쓰인 who(m), which, that은 생략할 수 있다.
> **2, 10, 11, 12** 주격 관계대명사 뒤에 be동사가 있고 그 뒤에 분사, 형용사구, 전치사구가 오면, 「관계대명사+be동사」를 생략할 수 있다.

PRACTICE 12

1 No matter what you do
2 Anyone who[that] wants some cookies
3 anything (that) she needs
4 anything (that) you choose
5 anyone (who/whom/that) you meet
6 No matter which you buy
7 No matter what I asked
8 No matter who may say so
9 anything (that) you decide
10 No matter what he hears

PRACTICE 13

1 why he missed the test

2 on which Henry and I first met / which[that] Henry and I first met on

3 where the bus picks up passengers

4 how I could repair a bicycle tire

5 for which the war broke out / which[that] the war broke out for

6 in which there live various kinds of animals / which[that] there live various kinds of animals in

7 when a man first landed on the Moon

8 in which the teacher deals with students / which[that] the teacher deals with students in

9 when people eat turkey

10 in which I had lived with my parents / which[that] I had lived with my parents in

11 where people cannot take protein easily

12 how we can relax our mind and body

13 on which we graduated / which[that] we graduated on

14 for which I'm listening to this radio show / which[that] I'm listening to this radio show for

15 How[The way in which] you talk and behave / The way which[that] you talk and behave in

> **1, 5, 14** the reason for which = the reason why: ~하는 이유
> **2, 9, 13** the day on which = the day when: ~하는 날
> **3** the place at which = the place where: ~하는 장소
> **4, 8, 12, 15** the way in which = how = the way: ~하는 방법
> **6** the country in which = the country where: ~하는 나라
> **7** the year in which = the year when: ~하는 해
> **10** the house in which = the house where: ~하는 집
> **11** the area in which = the area where: ~하는 지역

PRACTICE 14

1 where **2** when **3** how
4 when **5** where **6** why
7 where **8** when **9** why
10 how

> **1, 5, 7** 선행사가 장소와 관련한 것이므로 장소를 나타내는 관계부사 where가 알맞다.
> **2, 4, 8** 선행사가 시간과 관련한 것이므로 시간을 나타내는 관계부사 when이 알맞다.
> **3, 10** 문맥상 '가장 가까운 병원에 어떻게 갈 수 있는지', '그가 나에게 어떻게 연락했는지'의 의미가 되어야 하므로 방법을 나타내는 관계부사 how가 알맞다. the way와 how는 함께 쓸 수 없으므로 the way가 생략되었다.
> **6, 9** 선행사가 이유와 관련한 것이므로 이유를 나타내는 관계부사 why가 알맞다.

PRACTICE 15

2 when, the, time **3** why, the, reason
4 in, which, the, country **5** when, the, month
6 why, the, reason **7** where, somewhere

PRACTICE 16

1 ○ **2** ○
3 생략할 수 없음. **4** 생략할 수 없음.
5 생략할 수 없음. **6** 생략할 수 없음.
7 ○ **8** ○
9 ○ **10** ○
11 ○

> **1** 관계부사의 선행사가 the time, the day, the place, the reason과 같이 일반적일 때 선행사를 생략할 수 있다.
> **2, 10** 밑줄 친 that은 목적격 관계대명사이므로 생략할 수 있다.
> **3, 5** 소유격 관계대명사 whose는 생략할 수 없다.
> **4, 7** the way in which(~하는 방법)에서 in which 대신에 관계부사 that을 쓸 수 있다. 이때 the way만 남기고 that을 생략하는 것은 가능하지만, that을 남기고 the way를 생략하는 것은 불가능하다.
> **6** 선행사가 구체적인 장소일 때, 관계부사 where는 선행사만 남기고 생략될 수 없다.
> **8** 주격 관계대명사 뒤에 be동사가 있고 그 뒤에 분사, 형용사구, 전치사구가 오면, 「관계대명사+be동사」를 생략할 수 있다.
> **9, 11** 일반적인 선행사 다음에 오는 관계부사는 생략할 수 있다.

PRACTICE 17

1 why **2** who **3** where **4** which
5 when **6** how **7** why **8** where
9 which **10** where

> **1, 7** why는 the reason을 선행사로 받는 관계부사이다.
> **2** 괄호 뒤에 이어지는 절은 주어가 빠진 불완전한 절이다. 따라서 관계대명사가 들어가야 하며, 선행사 an old lady가 사람이므로 주격 관계대명사 who를 쓴다.
> **3** a country는 장소를 나타내는 선행사이다. 또한 괄호 뒤에 이어지는 절이 완전하므로 장소를 나타내는 관계부사 where을 쓴다.
> **4** 괄호 뒤에 이어지는 절은 직접목적어가 빠진 불완전한 절이다. 따라서 목적격 관계대명사가 들어가야 하며, 선행사 the offer이 사물이므로 목적격 관계대명사 which를 써야 한다.
> **5** 괄호 뒤에 이어지는 절이 완전하므로 관계부사가 들어가야 한다. 선행사가 a historic year로 시간을 나타내므로 관계부사 when을 쓴다.
> **6** 괄호 뒤에 이어지는 절이 완전하므로, 관계부사가 들어간다. how는 선행사 the way와 함께 쓸 수 없으므로 괄호 앞에 the way가 생략되었음을 알 수 있다.
> **8** Cambodia는 장소를 나타내는 선행사이다. 또한 괄호 뒤에 완전한 절이 이어지므로 장소를 나타내는 관계부사 where을 쓴다.
> **9** 괄호 뒤에 이어지는 절은 목적어가 빠진 불완전한 절이므로 괄호의 자리에는 관계대명사가 들어가야 한다. 이때, 선행사 Children's Day에 맞추어 which를 쓴다.
> **10** a bakery는 장소를 나타내는 선행사이다. 또한 괄호 뒤에 완전한 절이 이어지므로 장소를 나타내는 관계부사 where을 쓴다.

Ch
14
관계사

PRACTICE 18

1 wherever	**2** whenever	**3** However
4 Wherever	**5** However	**6** Whenever
7 However	**8** whenever	**9** wherever
10 whenever		

PRACTICE 19

1 Whatever	**2** whenever	**3** Wherever
4 Whoever	**5** However	**6** Whenever

> **1** whatever may happen: 무슨 일이 일어나더라도 → 복합관계대명사
> **2** whenever I see the movie: 내가 그 영화를 볼 때면 언제나 → 복합관계부사
> **3** wherever she goes: 그녀가 어디를 가든지 → 복합관계부사
> **4** whoever wins this game: 이 게임을 누가 이기든지 → 복합관계대명사
> **5** however good it is: 그것이 아무리 좋더라도 → 복합관계부사
> **6** whenever I have an exam: 내가 시험이 있을 때는 언제나 → 복합관계부사

📑 중간·기말고사 대비문제 정답 본문 _ p.328

1 who[that] is **2** ④ **3** ③ **4** ④ **5** ④ **6** ③
7 Look at the old lady whose son is a famous actor. **8** which **9** ③ **10** at which, where
11 ④,⑤ **12** Whoever breaks the law will be punished.[Anyone who breaks the law will be punished.] **13** ⑤ **14** ③ **15** ②,③ **16** ②
17 ①,④ **18** ② **19** ③ **20** need → needs
21 ⑤ **22** ③ **23** ② **24** However difficult the problem is **25** ④ **26** which[that] are
27 ①,⑤ **28** ④ **29** ② **30** ④ **31** ② **32** ④
33 ④ **34** ⑤ **35** ③ **36** ⑤ **37** ⑤
38 (1) which[that] you played last night
(2) who[that] risks his life to save others[other people]

중간·기말고사 대비문제 해설

1 선행사가 사람을 나타내는 3인칭 단수형이므로 who[that] is가 들어간다.

2 (A) 선행사(the book)가 있으므로 사물을 선행사로 하는 목적격 관계대명사 which나 that을 써야 한다. (what → which[that])
(D) 의문사가 있는 간접의문 문장이다. 이 단어가

무엇을 뜻하는지 모르겠다는 의미이므로 의문사 what을 사용한다. which는 구체적인 선택의 범위가 주어질 때 사용하는 의문사이다.
(which → what)

3 「however+형용사+주어+동사」 '아무리 ~하더라도'

4 [A] 경험을 나타내는 현재완료가 쓰였다. 현재완료는 「have+과거분사」로 쓴다.
(wonder → wondered)
[B] 'There is/are~'은 '~가 있다'라는 뜻으로 동사의 수를 뒤에 나오는 명사에 일치시킨다. 'several theories'는 셀 수 있는 명사구의 복수형이므로 복수 동사 are를 쓴다. (is → are)
[C] begin은 '(어떤 일이) 시작되다'라는 뜻의 자동사이다. 따라서 수동태로 쓰지 않는다.
(were begun → began)
[E] 선행사가 사물(the moon)이므로 관계대명사는 which를 써야 한다. (who → which)

5 ⓑ 관계대명사 that의 앞에는 전치사를 쓸 수 없다. (that → which)
ⓒ 관계대명사의 계속적 용법에서는 관계대명사 that을 쓸 수 없다. (that → which)
ⓓ 관계부사처럼 쓰이는 that은 선행사를 생략할 수 없다. 따라서 선행사의 생략이 가능한 관계부사 why나 how를 써야 한다. (that → why[how])
ⓔ the boy가 father와 소유의 관계를 이루므로 whose를 써야 한다. (that → whose)

6 ③ 선행사가 단수(the man)이므로 are를 is로 고쳐야 한다. (are → is)

7 the old lady와 son이 소유의 관계를 이루므로 소유격 관계대명사 whose를 이용한다.

8 선행사가 사물인 관계대명사의 계속적 용법이므로 which를 쓴다.

9 • 선행사가 사물인 관계대명사의 계속적 용법이므로 which를 쓴다.
• 빈칸 다음에 나오는 절이 완전하므로 관계부사가 이끄는 절임을 알 수 있는데, 빈칸 앞에 전치사 in이 있으므로 빈칸에 which를 넣어 관계부사 where를 대신할 수 있다.

10 관계부사는 「전치사+관계대명사」로 바꾸어 쓸 수 있다.

11 ④ 관계절의 동사 ran into는 구동사로 이미 전치사를 포함하고 있기 때문에 관계대명사 앞에 전치사 to를 쓰지 않는다. (to whom → whom)

⑤ 관계대명사가 전치사의 목적어로 쓰이면서 전치사가 관계대명사 바로 앞에 위치할 때는 whom 대신 who를 쓸 수 없다. (who → whom)

12 whoever+동사 = anyone who+동사 '~하는 사람은 누구나'

13 ① 선행사가 사람이므로 관계대명사 who가 알맞다.
② 관계대명사절에서 주어가 없으므로 주격관계대명사 who를 써야 한다.
③ 관계대명사의 계속적 용법을 접속사를 사용해 나타낼 때 관계대명사는 'and they'로 바꾸어 나타낸다.
④ 계속적 용법의 관계대명사 who는 that으로 바꾸어 쓸 수 없다.

14 • 선행사가 따로 없으므로 선행사를 자체에 포함하는 관계대명사 what을 쓴다.
• 선행사에 the only가 나오므로 관계대명사 that을 쓴다.
• 간접의문문의 의문사 what을 쓴다.

15 ① 'she was late for school'이 완전한 절이므로, 이 절 앞에 관계부사가 들어갈 수 있다. 선행사가 the reason으로 이유를 의미하기 때문에 관계부사 자리에 in which 가 아닌 why나 for which를 쓴다. (in which → why[for which])
④ 사람이 선행사일 때, 목적격 관계대명사는 who(m)을 쓸 수 있다. 하지만 목적격 관계대명사 앞에 전치사가 있을 경우 whom만 가능하다.
⑤ 'rely on'은 '~에 기대다, 의존하다'라는 뜻이다. 관계대명사 절에서 on이 빠져 있으므로, 관계대명사 앞에 들어갈 올바른 전치사는 on이다.

16 ② 접속사 ①③④⑤ 관계대명사

17 선행사에 형용사의 최상급이 포함되어 있으므로 관계대명사 that을 써야 한다. 혹은 목적격 관계대명사이므로 생략할 수 있다.

18 ⓐ which 뒤가 완전한 절이므로 관계대명사 which가 올 수 없다. the fact와 which 뒤의 절이 동격의 관계이므로 동격절을 이끄는 접속사 that을 써야 한다. (which → that)
ⓒ Sweet hot chocolate과 bar chocolate은 만들어지는 것이므로 수동태를 써야 한다.
(to invent → to be invented)
ⓓ hot chocolate은 전해진 것이므로 수동태를 (Being handed)를 써야 한다. 이때 앞의 Being은 생략할 수 있다. (Handing → Handed)
ⓔ 영국인들이 milk를 사용했다는 뜻이므로 능동을

의미하는 현재분사를 써야 한다. (used → using)

19 (As) the days get colder, there's nothing better than a cup of hot chocolate.
「there's nothing+비교급+than…」은 '…보다 더 ~한 것은 없다'라는 뜻으로 최상급의 의미를 나타낸다.
당신은 오늘날 우리가 즐기는 핫 초콜릿이 원래의 음료와는 다르다는 사실을 알았는가? 그것은 처음에는 뜨겁고 달콤하지 않았다. 그것의 기원은 마야 문명으로 거슬러 올라간다. 차갑게 제공되었던 초콜릿 음료를 만들기 위해, 마야인은 코코아 씨앗을 갈고 그것들을 물, 고추, 그리고 다른 재료들과 섞었다. 그 음료는 오늘날 우리가 즐기는 달콤한 핫 초콜릿과 반대로 맵고 쓴 맛이 났다. 달콤한 핫 초콜릿과 초콜릿 바는 아직 발명되지 않았다. 15세기에 아즈텍인들은 초콜릿 음료가 힘과 활력을 준다고 믿었고, 그것들을 그들의 높은 지위를 보여주기 위해 사용했다. 스페인으로 전해진 후, 핫 초콜릿은 스페인의 상류층 사이에 인기 있는 음료가 되었다. 17세기에 설탕을 이용해 만들어진 단 맛이 나는 핫 초콜릿이 발명되었다. 영국이 그것을 물 대신 우유를 이용해 만들기로 결정했을 때 그것은 유럽 귀족들 사이에서 사치품이 되었다. 지금 핫 초콜릿은 전 세계적으로 소비되고 다양한 종류로 나온다. 날이 더 추워질수록 핫 초콜릿 한 잔보다 더 좋은 것은 없다.

20 선행사(much work)가 단수형이므로 관계대명사절의 동사(need)도 단수형이 되어야 한다.

21 ⑤ 주어진 문장의 관계대명사절에서 목적어가 없으므로 관계대명사 who는 목적격이다. 그러므로 사람을 나타내는 목적격 관계대명사 who(m)을 써야 한다. 관계대명사 what은 선행사를 포함하는데 이 문장의 경우에는 선행사가 생략되어 있지 않으므로 적절하지 않다.

22 ③ 목적격 관계대명사는 생략할 수 있다.
①④ 관계대명사 앞에 전치사가 오는 경우에는 목적격 관계대명사를 생략할 수 없다.
②⑤ 주격 관계대명사는 생략할 수 없다.

23 ② 복합관계부사 however(아무리 ~하더라도)는 no matter how로 바꾸어 쓸 수 있다.

24 「however+형용사+주어+동사」 '아무리 ~하더라도'

25 목적격 관계대명사 또는 현재분사나 과거분사가 뒤따라 오는 「주격 관계대명사+be동사」는 생략할 수 있다.

26 관계대명사 what은 「the thing(s) which[that]」로 바꾸어 쓸 수 있다.

27 ② there가 가리키는 것이 선행사 a place이고, 관계

Ch
14
관
계
사

부사 where로 대체되어 관계부사절을 이루고 있기 때문에 there를 삭제하는 것이 어법상 옳다. (swim there in → swim in)

③ 관계절의 주어는 books이고 문장의 의미상 '그녀의 책들'을 가리키고 있으므로 소유격 관계대명사 whose를 쓰는 것이 적절하다. (who → whose)

④ 선행사가 the person으로 사람이고 관계절 내에 목적어가 없으며 앞에 전치사 to가 있으므로 관계대명사 whom을 쓴다. (which → whom)

① 관계대명사 which가 전치사의 목적어로 쓰이는 경우 전치사를 관계대명사 앞에 쓸 수 있다.

⑤ 관계대명사가 전치사의 목적어로 쓰이는 경우 「전치사+관계대명사」를 관계부사로 바꿔 쓸 수 있다. 장소를 나타낼 때는 관계부사 where를 쓴다.

28 (A) is (B) always (C) filled (D) with (E) freelancers (F) who (G) work

29 ② 관계부사 ①④ 의문부사 ③⑤ 접속사

30 선행사를 자체에 포함하는 관계대명사 what을 쓴다.

31 ② 밑줄 친 부분에 이어지는 절은 전치사의 목적어가 빠진 불완전한 절이므로 사물을 선행사(The hotel)로 하는 목적격 관계대명사 which나 that을 써야 한다. (where → which[that])

32 ④ 관계대명사 that 앞에는 전치사를 쓸 수 없다.

33 ④ 선행사를 자체에 포함하는 관계대명사 what은 선행사를 따로 쓰지 않으며, 이때 what은 the

thing(s) that[which]와 바꿔 쓸 수 있다. (what → that[which])

34 ⑤ 관계부사 ①②③④ 의문부사

35 세 문장 모두 빈칸 다음에 나오는 절이 완전하므로 빈칸에는 관계부사가 들어가야 한다.
- '아시아에 있는 많은 국가들이 어떻게 한국이 경제를 성장시켰는지를 배우고 있다.'는 의미이므로 빈칸에는 how가 들어가는 것이 적절하다. 선행사 the way는 생략되었다.
- 선행사 last year는 시간을 나타내는 말이므로 빈칸에는 when이 들어가야 한다.
- 선행사 the college는 장소, 공간을 나타내는 말이므로 빈칸에는 where가 들어가야 한다.

36
- 선행사가 사람이고, 명사 wife를 앞에서 꾸며줄 수 있어야 하므로 who의 소유격 whose를 쓴다.
- 선행사가 사물인 관계대명사의 계속적 용법이므로 which를 쓴다.

37 ⑤ 선행사인 the pen을 '가지고 썼다'는 뜻이 되도록 전치사 on을 with로 바꾸는 것이 적절하다.

38 (1) 선행사가 the song이므로 관계대명사 which [that]를 활용한다. 노래가 연주된 시점이 어젯밤이므로 과거시제 동사 played를 쓴다.
(2) 선행사가 the firefighter이므로 관계대명사 who[that]를 활용한다.

<table>
<tr><td>CHAPTER **15**</td><td>**접속사**
Conjunctions</td><td>본문 _ p.336</td></tr>
</table>

PRACTICE 1

1	or	**2**	but	**3**	or
4	and	**5**	but	**6**	or
7	and	**8**	but	**9**	or
10	and	**11**	but	**12**	or
13	and	**14**	and	**15**	but

1, 3, 6, 9, 12 '또는', '아니면'의 의미로 앞뒤의 구나 절이 연결되어야 문맥상 자연스럽기 때문에 or가 알맞다.
2, 5, 8, 11, 15 앞뒤가 서로 반대되는 내용이므로 '하지만, 그러나'를 의미하는 접속사 but으로 연결한다.
4, 7, 10, 13, 14 앞뒤의 내용이 대등하거나 비슷한 것, 또는 이어지는 행위를 나타내는 말을 연결할 때는 '~와, 그리고, ~하고 나서'의 의미로 쓰이는 접속사인 and를 쓴다.

PRACTICE 2

1 and **2** or **3** and **4** or **5** or
6 and **7** or **8** and **9** or **10** or

> **1, 3, 6, 8** 주어진 문장이 '~한다면, …할 수 있다[…할 것이다]'라는 의미이므로 '~해라, 그러면'의 의미인 「명령문+and」로 나타낼 수 있다.
> **2, 4, 5, 7, 9, 10** 주어진 문장이 '~하지 않는다면, …할 수 있다[…할 것이다]'라는 의미이므로 '~해라, 그렇지 않으면'의 의미인 「명령문+or」로 나타낼 수 있다.

PRACTICE 3

2 I'd like to study not only English but (also) Chinese to become a competent translator.

3 You have to consider not only your interests but (also) your talents to find a good job for yourself.

4 I do things that others don't want to do as well as work hard.

5 We need to hire not only a new salesperson but (also) a new secretary.

6 Not only I but (also) Sally wants to succeed in losing weight and being more confident.

7 You should do your best as well as set a goal.

8 It is a waste of time as well as a waste of money.

9 A clean environment is not only essential for our health but (also) good for our economy.

10 The teachers as well as the students were shocked by the principal's final decision.

11 Human genes determine what diseases people may get as well as what they look like.

12 Humans not only have researched the Earth but (also) have explored the universe.

PRACTICE 4

1 Both, and **2** Neither, nor **3** Either, or
4 Both, and **5** Neither, nor **6** either, or
7 neither, nor **8** both, and **9** either, or
10 both, and

> **1, 4, 8, 10** 'A와 B 둘 다'의 의미이므로 「both A and B」로 나타낼 수 있다.
> **2, 5, 7** 'A도 B도 ~ 아닌'의 의미이므로 「neither A nor B」로 나타낼 수 있다.
> **3, 6, 9** 'A와 B 중 어느 하나'의 의미이므로 「either A or B」로 나타낼 수 있다.

PRACTICE 5

1 have **2** are **3** are
4 use **5** are **6** like
7 want **8** takes **9** spends
10 helps

> **1, 4, 8, 10** 「either A or B」 뒤에 오는 동사는 동사에 더 가까이 있는 B의 수에 일치시킨다.
> **2, 6, 9** 「neither A nor B」 뒤에 오는 동사는 동사에 더 가까이 있는 B의 수에 일치시킨다.
> **3, 5, 7** 「both A and B」가 주어일 때는 항상 복수 동사가 뒤따라온다.

PRACTICE 6

1 유럽에서 왕족들이 골프를 쳤기 때문에 그것은 부유한 사람들 사이에서 인기를 얻기 시작했다. [결과]

2 바다에서 강한 바람이 불어오므로 제주도에 있는 집들 주위의 대부분의 벽들은 돌로 지어진다. [원인]

3 사람들은 다양한 환경에서 자라기 때문에 그들은 다른 누군가와 결코 같을 수 없다. [원인]

4 그 박물관은 독일의 침략 동안에 불타버렸기 때문에 우리는 원래의 것을 볼 수 없었다. [결과]

5 나는 낯선 학교에서 신입생이 된다는 것이 어떤 것인지 알고 있으므로 그가 적응하는 걸 돕고 싶다. [원인]

6 물이 깨끗하고 공기가 맑아서 나는 도시에 사는 것보다 시골에 사는 것을 선호한다. [결과]

7 일기를 쓰는 것은 내가 내 일상에 대해 생각하는 걸 도와주기 때문에 나는 매일 그것을 기록하려고 노력한다. [원인]

8 나는 다양한 종류의 물고기를 관찰하는 것을 좋아해서 싱가포르에 있는 그 수족관을 방문하는 걸 계획하고 있다. [원인]

9 우리는 정보 기술의 시대에 살고 있기 때문에 많은 직업들은 우리에게 컴퓨터 기술을 가질 것을 요구한다. [결과]

10 그 초콜릿 케이크가 매우 맛있어서 나는 그것을 너무 많이 먹는 걸 멈출 수 없었다. [원인]

PRACTICE 7

1 because of **2** because
3 because of **4** because of
5 because **6** because
7 because of **8** because

Ch **15** 접속사

PRACTICE 8

1	A	2	C	3	B	4	C	5	B
6	A	7	C	8	A	9	B	10	A

[보기]
(A) As Mark moved to the city, I have to visit the city to meet him. → Mark가 그 도시로 이사했기 때문에
(B) I took five pills at a time for two weeks as the doctor ordered. → 의사가 지시한 대로
(C) As time passed, my dog began to recover. → 시간이 지남에 따라

1 as it's definitely going to rain tomorrow: 내일 분명히 비가 올 것이기 때문에
2 as the show went on: 공연이 지속됨에 따라
3 as I was told: 내가 들었던 대로
4 as summer nears: 여름이 다가올수록
5 as I asked: 내가 요청한 대로
6 as Mom was not home during the weekend: 엄마가 주말 동안 집에 계시지 않았기 때문에
7 as the man walked away: 남자가 걸어가 버릴수록
8 as the bus drivers were on strike: 버스 기사들이 파업 중이었기 때문에 *on strike: 파업 중인
9 as Jenny does: Jenny가 하는 대로
10 as the electricity bill was too big last month: 지난달에 전기요금이 너무 많이 나왔기 때문에

PRACTICE 9

1 I'll just walk there unless it's far from my house.
2 The door won't open unless you know the exact password.
3 Unless you are careful with it, you might get into trouble.
4 Unless you stop spending too much money, you'll be broke soon.
5 Her heart disease will get worse unless she goes on a diet.
6 You will get soaked on the way home unless you bring your umbrella with you.
7 Unless you say anything when you need help, no one can help you.
8 You cannot build a good relationship unless you try to listen to others.
9 Unless you have much experience in that field, you won't get the job.

10 Unless you follow the directions, you will get lost in a strange city.

PRACTICE 10

1 Once he sees her
2 As long as you do your best
3 If you change your mind
4 As long as you believe in yourself
5 Once you like yourself
6 Unless you eat now
7 If you want to speak English well
8 Once he starts to read a book
9 As long as it doesn't snow
10 Once you learn the rules
11 If you don't like exercising alone
12 Unless you walk more quickly

PRACTICE 11

1 Throw the ball softly so that I can hit it well.
2 Mr. Park spoke slowly so that everyone could write down what he was saying.
3 Make your plan as specific as possible so that you can follow it step by step.
4 The fishermen start the morning by mending their nets so that they can fish with them.
5 Review your notes every day so that you don't have to study all night before the exam.
6 I had become so close to my teacher that it became easier for me to talk with him.
7 Taekwondo is so popular that thousands of its practitioners visit Korea every year.
8 I'm so terrible at drawing that I don't think I am talented in art.
9 Information is so easily accessible on the Internet that you can get anything you want.
10 My father is so busy with his work that he can't take summer holidays this year.

PRACTICE 12

1 It is interesting that sound travels much faster in steel than in water.

2 It is a pity that a lot of workers in the factory died because of the fire.

3 It was unbelievable that we survived the car crash.

4 It is very important that we must do something to help the town.

5 The young man said that his arm was badly injured.

6 I was excited to know that I could take English and other language courses.

7 I'm afraid that I may have made a lot of mistakes.

8 Mother is worried that the baby hardly eats all day long.

9 The fact is that millions of years ago there were many volcanoes in this area.

10 The difference between them is that there are no magazines that you can read in this cafe.

11 The problem was that our flight to Canada would be expensive.

12 The important thing is that you should respect other people's cultures.

PRACTICE 13

1 동격	**2** 목적어	**3** 동격
4 보어	**5** 주어	

> **1** the idea가 가리키는 것이 that이 이끄는 절의 내용이므로 the idea와 that 이하가 동격을 이룬다. → 우리가 음악으로 아침을 시작할 수 있다는 생각
> **2** that 이하가 명사절로 동사 knew의 목적어 역할을 하고 있다.
> **3** the news가 가리키는 것이 that이 이끄는 절의 내용이므로 the news와 that 이하가 동격을 이룬다. → 15살짜리 소년이 대학에 들어갔다는 뉴스
> **4** that 이하의 명사절이 주어 the worst thing의 주격 보어 역할을 하고 있다.
> **5** it은 가주어이고 that이 이끄는 명사절이 진주어 역할을 하고 있다.

PRACTICE 14

1 if she is going to study English literature or Asian history,
whether she is going to study English literature or Asian history

2 if he is going to go to graduate school or get a job,
whether he is going to go to graduate school or get a job

3 if you are going to attend the party or study for the final exam,
whether you are going to attend the party or study for the final exam

4 if she is going to face the difficult situation or run away from it,
whether she is going to face the difficult situation or run away from it

5 if you are going to keep working on the project or stop doing it,
whether you are going to keep working on the project or stop doing it

6 if he is going to take part in the competition or keep practicing a little more,
whether he is going to take part in the competition or keep practicing a little more

7 if they are going to make apologies or stay mad at each other,
whether they are going to make apologies or stay mad at each other

8 if he is going to return the shirt or keep it,
whether he is going to return the shirt or keep it

PRACTICE 15

1 As, While	**2** while, when	**3** when
4 as	**5** while, as	**6** when
7 while, as	**8** when	**9** While, As
10 while, as	**11** when	**12** while, as
13 When	**14** While, When	**15** When, As

> **1** '네가 늙어감에 따라'와 '네가 늙어가는 동안'이라는 두 가지 의미 모두 가능하므로 as와 while 모두 쓸 수 있다.
> **2, 5, 7, 9, 10, 12, 14, 15** 일반적으로 특정 기간 동안 두 가지 사건이 동시에 일어나고 있음을 나타낼 때는 when, as, while을 모두 쓸 수 있다.
> **3, 8, 11** as는 두 가지의 비교적 짧은 사건이 특정 기간 동안 동시에 또는 연속적으로 일어나는 상황에서 '~하고 있을 때'의 의미로 쓰이므로 여기서처럼 과거의 일정 기간(종이가 처음 발명되었을 때, 그가 그저 소년이었을 때)이나 불특정한 기간(자유시간이 있을 때) 동안에 일어난 일을 나타낼 때는 when이 알맞다.
> **4** 한 가지 사건에 변화가 생김에 따라 나머지 사건에도 변화가 생길 때는 '~함에 따라'의 의미로 as를 쓴다.
> **6, 13** 한 가지의 사건 직후에 일어난 다른 사건을 나타내므로 when이 알맞다.

PRACTICE 16

1	since	2	as soon as
3	while	4	until
5	Every time	6	When
7	since	8	as soon as
9	after	10	After
11	As	12	Every time
13	While	14	until
15	before		

1, 7 주절이 현재완료진행 시제인 것으로 보아 '~ 이후로 줄곧 … 해오고 있다'는 의미가 되어야 하므로 '~ 이후로'를 뜻하는 접속사 since가 알맞다.

2, 8 '~하자마자 …했다'라는 의미가 되어야 문맥에 적합하므로 '~ 하자마자'를 뜻하는 접속사 as soon as가 알맞다.

3, 13 두 가지 사건이 동시에 일어나고 있는 상황이므로 '~하는 동안'을 뜻하는 while이 알맞다.

4, 14 '(특정 시점)까지 ~않다'는 의미이므로 '~까지'를 의미하는 until이 알맞다.

5, 12 '~할 때마다'의 의미이므로 every time이 알맞다.

6 '새끼 새가 먹이를 달라고 소리치면 어미 새가 벌레를 잡으러 날아간다'는 의미이므로 한 가지의 사건 직후에 일어난 다른 사건을 나타내는 when이 알맞다.

9, 10 각각 '식사 후에 얘기하자', '각 정당의 지도자들이 만난 후에 모든 일이 제대로 진행되었다'는 의미이므로 '~ 후에'를 의미하는 after가 알맞다.

11 '날이 갈수록 점점 더 피곤해졌다'는 의미이므로 '~함에 따라'를 뜻하는 as가 알맞다.

15 '영국으로 이사오기 전에 호주에서 살았다'는 의미가 되어야 하므로 '~ 전에'를 뜻하는 before가 알맞다.

PRACTICE 17

1	even though	2	even if
3	even though	4	even if
5	Even though	6	even if
7	Even if	8	Even though
9	even if	10	even though

1, 3, 5, 8, 10 뒤에 확실한 사실 또는 실제로 일어난 일을 나타내는 내용이 오며, '비록 ~일지라도'라는 의미로 그 내용이 사실임을 강조할 때 쓰는 even though가 알맞다.

2, 4, 6, 7, 9 확실하지 않은 일을 가정하여 '가령 ~라 할지라도'라는 의미로 쓰는 even if가 알맞다.

PRACTICE 18

1	For example	2	However
3	Therefore	4	In addition
5	On the other hand	6	For example
7	However	8	Therefore
9	In addition	10	On the other hand

1, 6 앞에 진술한 내용에 대한 예시를 들고 있으므로 '예를 들면'이라는 뜻의 접속부사 for example이 알맞다.

2, 7 앞뒤 문장의 내용이 서로 반대되므로 '그러나'를 뜻하는 역접의 접속부사 however가 알맞다.

3, 8 앞뒤 문장이 각각 원인과 결과에 해당하므로 '그러므로'를 뜻하는 접속부사 therefore가 알맞다.

4, 9 앞 문장에 이어 내용을 덧붙이고 있으므로 '게다가'를 뜻하는 접속부사 in addition이 알맞다.

5, 10 앞 문장의 내용과 상반되는 내용이 이어지고 있으므로 '반면에'를 뜻하는 접속부사 on the other hand가 알맞다.

PRACTICE 19

1	Finally	2	In contrast
3	As a result	4	In other words
5	Finally	6	In contrast
7	As a result	8	In other words
9	For example	10	However
11	Therefore	12	In addition
13	On the other hand		

1, 5 앞 문장에서 서술한 상황이 이어진 끝에 '결국, 마침내' 어떤 사건이 일어난 것이므로 finally가 알맞다.

2, 6 앞 문장과 뒤 문장의 내용이 대조를 이루므로 '대조적으로'라는 뜻의 접속부사 in contrast가 알맞다.

3, 7 앞 문장은 원인, 뒤 문장은 결과에 해당하므로 '그 결과로'라는 뜻의 접속부사 as a result가 알맞다.

4, 8 앞의 내용을 다른 방식으로 추가적으로 부연 설명하거나 쉬운 말로 풀어서 말하고 있으므로 '다시 말해서'라는 뜻의 접속부사 in other words가 알맞다.

9 앞에 진술한 내용에 대한 예시를 들고 있으므로 '예를 들면'이라는 뜻의 접속부사 for example이 알맞다.

10 앞뒤 문장의 내용이 서로 반대되므로 '그러나'를 뜻하는 접속부사 however가 알맞다.

11 앞 문장에 근거하여 뒤 문장을 결론으로 내린 것이므로 '그러므로'를 뜻하는 접속부사 therefore가 알맞다.

12 앞 문장에 이어 내용을 덧붙이고 있으므로 '게다가'를 뜻하는 접속부사 in addition이 알맞다.

13 앞 문장의 내용과 상반되는 내용이 이어지고 있으므로 '반면에'를 뜻하는 접속부사 on the other hand가 알맞다.

PRACTICE 20

1	Finally[Therefore]	2	Besides
3	Therefore	4	In other words
5	For example	6	Besides
7	Finally[Therefore]	8	In contrast

1 포기하지 않고 계속 달린 끝에 마침내 마라톤에서 2등을 한 것이기도 하고, 포기하지 않고 계속 달렸기 때문에 마라톤에서 2등을 한 것이기도 하므로 Finally(마침내)와 Therefore(그러므로) 모두 알맞다.

2 비가 오기도 했고, 문학 수업을 위한 책도 다 읽어야 하기도 했어서 산책을 못 갔다는 관련 내용을 추가로 나열하고 있으므로 Besides(게다가)가 알맞다.

3 어제 결석했기 때문에 그 소식을 듣지 못한 것이므로 Therefore(그러므로)가 알맞다.

4 직장에서 심각한 실수를 하여 상사가 그만두라고 한 것을 다른 말로 표현하면 해고당한 것이므로 In other words(다시 말해서)가 알맞다.

5 일상생활에서 환경을 보호하는 방법의 예로 양치할 때 물을 잠그는 것을 제시했으므로 For example(예를 들면)이 알맞다.

6 수학 숙제 때문에 외출할 수 없고, 거기다가 집안일까지 해야 한다는 의미이므로 Besides(게다가)가 알맞다.

7 2주 동안 열심히 보고서를 작성한 끝에 마침내 성공적으로 끝냈다는 것이기도 하고, 열심히 보고서를 작성했기 때문에 성공적으로 끝낸 것이기도 하므로 Finally(마침내)와 Therefore(그러므로) 모두 알맞다.

8 도시에 살면 밤에 별을 거의 볼 수 없지만 시골에 살면 밤에 별을 많이 볼 수 있다는 말로 서로 대조적인 두 상황을 설명하고 있으므로 In contrast(대조적으로)가 알맞다.

📑 중간·기말고사 대비문제 정답   본문 _ p.361

1 ③   **2** ③   **3** ③   **4** ⑤   **5** ④   **6** ③

7 body movements as well as, verbal languages

8 ④   **9** ⑤   **10** ③   **11** rained so heavily that he drove his car slowly   **12** ④   **13** ③

14 ④   **15** ②   **16** not only, but also   **17** ②

18 ③   **19** ④   **20** I find it strange that he never uses his cellphone.   **21** ②   **22** ②   **23** while

24 Not only many citizens but also the leader of the country supports the new treaty.

25 so that   **26** ④   **27** ③   **28** ①,③   **29** ①

30 ⑤   **31** ④   **32** ②   **33** ⑤   **34** ②   **35** ③

36 ③   **37** ④   **38** ⑤   **39** ⑤   **40** ②   **41** ①

42 ④   **43** ③   **44** was so heavily outnumbered that it couldn't stand a chance against Japan's fleet   **45** ⑤

중간·기말고사 대비문제 해설

1 ③ 우리는 멋진 시간을 보냈다. 우리는 결국 하룻밤 더 머물게 되었다. → 우리는 매우 멋진 시간을 보냈기 때문에 우리는 결국 하룻밤 더 머물게 되었다.

① 네가 운동을 매일 한다면, 너는 건강을 유지할 수 있을 것이다. → 매일 운동해라, 그러면 너는 건강을 유지할 수 있을 것이다. (or → and)

② 모두가 공부하느라 너무 바쁘다. 아무도 서로에게 말을 걸지 않는다. → 모두 공부하느라 너무 바빠서 아무도 서로에게 말을 걸지 않는다. (such → so)

④ 비가 내리고 있었기 때문에, 나는 학교에 장화를 신고 갔다. → 비가 내리고 있어서, 나는 학교에 장화를 신고 갔다. (but → so)

⑤ Tom은 일을 잘 해냈다. 그의 상사는 그에게 더 하라고 북돋아 주었다. → Tom이 일을 잘 해내서 그의 상사는 그에게 더 하라고 북돋아 주었다. (so → such)

2 • 「명령문+or」 '~해라, 그렇지 않으면'
• 주어진 선택지 중 어느 것이 더 좋냐는 질문이므로 '또는'이라는 뜻의 or이 적절하다.

3 아침을 거른 것이 배가 고픈 원인이므로, 원인을 나타내는 절을 이끄는 접속사 because를 사용한다. '배가 고팠다'고 하였으므로, 주절의 시제는 과거가 적절하다. 아침을 거른 것이 배가 고픈 것보다 먼저 일어난 일(대과거)이므로, 종속절의 시제는 주절의 시제보다 앞선 과거 완료로 쓴다.

4 나쁜 자세는 당신의 등에 해로울 수 있다는 말에 근거하여 좋은 자세를 유지하라는 결론을 내리고 있으므로 Therefore(그러므로)가 적절하다.

5 젊은 사람들이 해야 하는 많은 중요한 일들이 있다는 말의 예시로 그들은 책을 읽고, 여행하고, 새로운 언어를 배우는 등의 일을 해야 한다고 제시했으므로 For example(예를 들어)이 적절하다.

6 조건을 나타내는 부사절에서는 현재시제가 미래를 대신한다.

7 not only A but also B = B as well as A
'A뿐만 아니라 B도'

8 ④ 조건을 나타내는 접속사로 '~한다면'이라는 의미로 사용되었다. 만약 오늘 밤 당신이 저녁 식사가 어렵다면 우리는 차를 같이 마셔도 된다.
①②③⑤ 명사절을 이끄는 접속사로 '~인지'라는 의미로 사용되었다.
① 내가 하고 있는 말이 말이 되는지 모르겠다.
② 경찰은 범행이 고의적인지 조사하고 있는 중이다.
③ 나는 그가 그 프로젝트에 자금을 댈 충분한 돈이 있는지 의문이다.
⑤ Sally는 버스 정류장을 찾을 수 없어서 행인에게 길을 그녀에게 안내해 줄 수 있는지 물었다.

9 ⓐ either A or B - B에 수일치 (has → have)
ⓑ not only A but also B - B에 수일치 (are → is)
ⓓ B as well as A - B에 수일치 (is → am)
ⓔ neither A nor B - B에 수일치 (is → are)

10 '대부분의 부모들은 자녀의 온라인 게임 습관에 대해 걱정한다.'는 말과 '나는 그것에 대해 그렇게 걱정되지

는 않는다.'는 말은 서로 반대되는 내용이므로 역접을 나타내는 접속부사인 However(그러나)가 적절하다.

11 보기의 단어와 주어진 해석('너무 ~해서 …하다')을 통해서 「so+형용사/부사+that」의 형태로 문장을 완성해야 하는 것을 알 수 있다.

12 (A)④ 명사절을 이끄는 접속사 that
① 명사 technology를 수식하는 지시형용사
②⑤ 주격 관계대명사
③ 앞에 나온 명사 opinion을 가리키는 지시대명사

13 ③ 우리가 피로하다는 감정을 느끼는 것이므로 과거분사 exhausted를 써야 한다.
(exhausting → exhausted)

나는 기쁨에 압도되어서 우리 주변에서 무슨 일이 일어나고 있는지조차 파악할 수 없다. 나는 주변을 둘러본다. 모든 팀원들이 우리의 첫 우승에 대한 흥분으로 울고 소리치고 있다. 결승전이 막 끝났고, 우리의 팬들은 우리를 응원하고 있다.
정말 힘든 여정이었다. 내가 경기를 준비하는 것을 포기하고 싶었던 순간들이 있었다. 조건은 열악했고, 우리는 시간이 갈수록 더 지쳐갔다. 우리는 정규 시즌 동안 잘하지 못했다. 우리가 한 경기조차 이길 거라고 결코 상상하지 못했다. 내가 할 수 있었던 유일한 것은 그 순간에 집중하고 계속 노력하는 것이었다. 한 해 동안, 우리는 종종 과소평가당했다. 어떤 사람들은 우리 팀이 일찍 탈락할 거라고까지 말했다. 매일매일이 우리를 증명할 기회였다. 하지만 마지막에는, 우리는 올해 마침내 챔피언십에서 우승했다.

14 [주어진 문장] 구름이 끼고 바람이 불었기 때문에, 그들은 소풍을 갈 수 없었다. (~ 때문에)
④ 그는 지쳤기 때문에 일찍 퇴근했다. (~ 때문에)
① 네가 춤을 출 때, 미소 지으며 박수를 치고 있는 반 전체를 상상해봐라. (~할 때)
② 여러분이 나이가 들어감에 따라, 여러분의 몸은 더 약해질 것이다. (~함에 따라)
③ 네가 건물로 들어갈 때, 너는 그것의 색깔에 감명받을 것이다. (~할 때)
⑤ 네가 답을 찾을 때, 많은 문들이 열릴 것이다(기회가 많이 올 것이다). (~할 때)

15 주어진 문장은 '그러고 나서 나는 그 물체가 비행기보다 조금 더 커 보인다는 것을 알게 되었다.'라는 뜻으로, 접속사 that이 문장의 목적어로 쓰인 명사절을 이끈다.
② Sam은 그 책이 어디 있는지 모르는 체했어. (명사절 접속사)

① 그 다음에, 우리는 컴퓨터를 가지고 작업하기 시작했다. (지시대명사)
③ 런던의 생활비는 서울의 그것보다 더 높다. (지시대명사)
④ 나는 내 남자 형제가 갖고 싶어 했던 모자를 구매했다. (관계대명사)
⑤ 이 검은 그 돌을 움직일 수 있는 사람을 위한 것이다. (관계대명사)

16 not only A but also B 'A뿐만 아니라 B도'

17 not A but B 'A가 아니라 B'

18 find out의 뒤에 오는 첫 번째 빈칸 다음에 완전한 절이 오는 것으로 보아 첫 번째 빈칸에는 명사절 접속사가 들어가야 함을 알 수 있다. or so는 '~가량'이라는 뜻으로 수나 양을 나타내는 말 다음에 오므로 두 번째 빈칸에 들어갈 수 없다. if[whether] ~ (or not) '~인지 아닌지'

19 ④ '그는 너무 어두워져 링을 볼 수 없을 때까지 농구를 연습했다.'는 의미이므로 '~까지'를 뜻하는 접속사 until을 써야 한다. (since → until)
① 그들은 그들이 이사 들어가기 전에 집을 수리했다.
② 비가 많이 왔기 때문에 거리들이 물에 잠겼다.
③ 내가 식료품을 좀 사는 동안 당신은 나를 위해 내 가방들을 봐줄래요?
⑤ 비록 그녀가 고작 1년 전에 회사에 들어갔지만, 그녀는 벌써 두 번이나 승진했다.

20 5형식 문장으로 가목적어(it)가 쓰이고 진목적어 자리에 that 명사절이 쓰인 구조이다.

21 학교가 그녀의 집과 가깝다는 사실을 강조하면서 그럼에도 불구하고 그녀의 어머니가 매일 아침 그녀를 학교에 차로 데려다 준다는 의미를 나타내기 위해서는 빈칸에 even though가 들어가는 것이 가장 적절하다.

22 주어진 문장은 '너는 네가 원하는 대로 너의 방을 꾸밀 수 있다.'는 의미이므로 여기서 접속사 as는 '~대로'를 뜻한다.
ⓑ 일기예보가 예측한 대로, 날씨가 매우 추웠다. (~대로)
ⓔ 나는 내가 너에게 말한 대로 하기를 요청했다. (~대로)
ⓐ 그는 과거에 나만큼 크지 않았다. (~만큼)
ⓒ 그것이 매우 비쌌기 때문에 예전 그때에는 TV를 사는 것이 쉽지 않았다. (~때문에)
ⓓ 그녀가 나이를 먹음에 따라, 그녀는 더 똑똑해졌다. (~함에 따라)

23 while '반면에'

24 「not only A but also B」 구조의 문장이므로 even이 아닌 only가 와야 한다. 동사의 수는 B에 일치시킨다.

25 in order to = so that ~ '~하기 위하여'

26 (B) not only A but also B – B에 수일치
　　(are → am)
　(D) both A and B – 항상 복수 취급 (was → were)

27 ③ which 뒤가 완전한 절이므로 관계대명사 which가 올 수 없다. the fact와 which 뒤의 절이 동격의 관계이므로 동격절을 이끄는 접속사 that이 들어가야 한다. (which → that)

28 ① Unless는 '~하지 않으면'이라는 뜻으로 이미 부정의 의미를 가지고 있으므로 동사를 긍정형 is로 써야 한다. (isn't → is)
　③ 조건을 나타내는 If절에서는 미래의 일을 나타내더라도 동사는 항상 현재형으로 쓴다.
　　(will come → comes)

29 빈칸 뒤의 절이 문장의 주어 자리에 있으므로, 빈칸에는 명사절을 이끌 수 있는 접속사가 와야 한다. '네가 실패할지 또는 성공할지는 너의 생각에 달렸다.'는 의미가 되는 것이 자연스러우므로 Whether이 적절하다. 명사절 접속사 If는 목적어 자리에만 사용 가능하다.

30 ⑤ 관계대명사 ①②③④ 명사절을 이끄는 접속사

31 빈칸 뒤의 절이 완전하므로 빈칸에는 접속사가 들어가야 한다. It이 가주어이므로 진주어를 이끌 수 있는 명사절 접속사 that이 적절하다.

32 • 명사절을 이끄는 접속사 if '~인지 (어떤지)'
　• 조건절을 이끄는 접속사 if '~한다면'

33 ⑤ ask 뒤의 절이 완전하므로 접속사가 들어가는 것은 맞지만, 절의 내용이 '그가 그 사실을 아는지 모르는지'이므로 that보다는 whether이나 if가 적절하다. (that → if[whether])

34 (A) 「Both A and B」가 주어일 때는 항상 복수 동사를 쓴다. (likes → like)
　(D) 「Neither A nor B」가 주어일 때는 동사에 더 가까운 B에 동사의 수를 일치시킨다. the students는 복수이므로 복수 동사 were을 써야 한다.
　　(was → were)
　(F) 「both A and B」에서 A와 B는 병렬구조로 연결된다. 따라서 Paris와 London처럼 같은 명사끼리 연결되어야 한다. to visit은 동사 want의 목적어로, want 바로 뒤에 붙여 쓰는 것이 자연스럽다.

　　(both to visit → to visit both)
　(B) 「Either A or B」가 주어일 때는 동사에 더 가까운 B에 동사의 수를 일치시킨다. your friends는 복수이므로 복수 동사를 쓴다.
　(C) 「B as well as A」 뒤에 나오는 동사는 B에 수를 일치시킨다. The manager는 단수이므로 단수 동사를 쓴다.
　(E) 「Not only A but also B」가 주어일 때는 B에 동사의 수를 일치시킨다. his parents가 복수이므로 복수 동사를 쓴다.

35 although '비록 ~일지라도'

36 while '~하는 동안', '~인 반면'

37 • 접속사 when '~할 때'
　• 관계부사 why '~하는 이유'

38 첫 번째 빈칸 뒤에는 절이 오고 두 번째 빈칸 뒤에는 명사구가 오므로 각각 접속사, 전치사가 들어가야 함을 알 수 있다. 첫 번째 빈칸에는, 밀가루가 다 떨어졌기 때문에 그녀가 케이크를 구울 수 없는 것이므로 이유를 나타내는 접속사 because가 들어가는 것이 적절하다. 두 번째 빈칸에는, 명사구 the cold weather를 받으며 이유를 나타내는 전치사 because of가 들어가는 것이 적절하다.

39 ⑤ 그가 잘생겼고 키가 크기 때문에 많은 소녀들이 그를 좋아하는 것이므로 이유를 나타내는 접속사 Because, Since, As를 써야 한다.
　(Though → Because[Since, As])

40 (A) 앞 문장과 뒤 문장이 대조/역접의 관계이므로 접속부사 However를 써야 한다.
　(B) video가 선생님에 의해 만들어진 것이므로 과거분사 made를 쓰는 것이 적절하다.
　(C) decide는 to부정사를 목적어로 쓰는 동사이다.
　작년까지만 해도 대부분의 학생들은 그냥 물보다 에너지 음료를 더 선호했다. 그러나, 한 과학 선생님이 그들에게 그 음료들에 얼마나 많은 설탕이 들어 있는지를 보여주었다. 학생들은 선생님이 만든 숨겨진 설탕에 대한 영상을 보았다. 그 수업 후, 그들은 에너지 음료를 덜 사고 대신 물을 더 마시기로 결정했다.

41 ① '매우 ~해서 …하다'는 의미의 문장을 쓸 때, '매우'가 형용사나 부사가 아닌 명사구를 강조해야 하는 경우 「such+a/an+형용사+명사+that」이라고 쓴다. (so → such)

42 빈칸 앞의 문장은 '많은 사람들이 컴퓨터를 사용할 수 있기 때문에 그들은 더 이상 타자기 치는 사람들을 필

Ch **15** 접속사

요로 하지 않는다.'는 뜻이고, 빈칸 뒤의 문장은 '체중에 대해 늘어난 관심은 과거에는 없었던 다이어트 프로그래머들을 최근에 등장하게 했다.'는 의미이다. 상반된 현상에 대한 내용을 연결해야 하므로, 빈칸에 들어갈 접속부사는 In contrast(대조적으로, 반대로)가 적절하다.

43 「in order not+to부정사」 '~하지 않기 위해서'

44 too ~ to … 구문은 '…하기에는 너무 ~한'의 부정적 의미를 포함한다. '너무 ~해서…한'의 의미를 가지는 so ~ that … 구문으로 변환하는 경우 「so+형용사/부사+that+주어+can't」로 바꾸어 쓸 수 있다.

45 ⓔ '이순신의 함대가 일본의 함대를 무찔렀다.'는 능동의 의미를 갖기 때문에 수동태가 아닌 능동태 형태의 동사를 쓰는 것이 적절하다.
(was defeated → defeated)

명량해전

명량해전은 전쟁의 역사에서 가장 대단한 승리들 중 하나로 생각된다. 그것은 일본 해군을 상대로 조선을 많은 승리로 이끈 이순신 장군에 의해 이끌려졌다. 이 전쟁이 매우 대단했던 이유는 일본이 130척보다 더 많은 군함을 가졌던 반면 조선은 단 13척의 군함을 가졌다는 것이다. 당신이 그것을 어떻게 보든지, 조선의 함대는 일본의 함대에 맞서기에 수적으로 너무 열세였다. 그러나, 불가능한 일이 일어났다. 이순신의 함대가 일본의 함대를 완전히 패배시켰고 오직 10대 정도의 배만 도망쳤다.

CHAPTER **16** 전치사
Prepositions

본문 _ p.370

PRACTICE 1

1	in	**2**	at	**3**	on	**4**	in
5	on	**6**	at	**7**	at	**8**	on
9	in	**10**	in	**11**	on	**12**	at
13	on	**14**	at	**15**	In		

1, 4, 9, 10, 15 연도, 월, 계절과 같은 비교적 긴 시간 앞에는 in이 온다.
2, 6, 7, 12, 14 구체적인 시각 앞에는 at이 온다.
3, 5, 8, 11, 13 날짜나 요일 앞에는 on이 온다.

PRACTICE 2

1 ① on ② ×		**2** ① on ② ×	
3 ① in ② on[at]		**4** ① on ② ×	
5 ① on ② ×		**6** ① in ② ×	
7 ① on ② on		**8** ① in ② on	
9 ① on ② in		**10** ① × ② on[at]	
11 ① at ② ×		**12** ① at ② in	
13 ① at ② in		**14** ① at ② on	
15 ① at ② in			

*on은 특정한 날이나 요일, 그날의 아침이나 저녁, 낮 시간 등을 나타내는 말 앞에 쓴다.

on Saturday night	on Thursday nights
on Chuseok	on the 1st of May
on New Year's Eve	on my cousin's wedding day

on the morning of my cousin's wedding day
(in the morning으로 써야 할 것 같지만 특정한 날의 아침을 가리키기 때문에 on을 써야 한다.)

on Monday evening	on August 15th, 1945
on Christmas	on Tuesday evenings

*연도, 월, 계절을 포함해서 비교적 긴 시간 앞에는 in을 쓴다.

in autumn	in 2020
in your free time	in the summer of 1945
in the morning	in the middle of the night
in the afternoon	

*at은 구체적인 시각이나 비교적 짧은 시간을 나타내는 말 앞에 쓴다.

at Chuseok	at Christmas

(추석/크리스마스 당일만이 아니라 직전과 직후 며칠까지 포함할 때)

at noon	at dawn	at night
at lunchtime	at half past four	

*every, this, that, last, next 등이 붙어 시간을 나타내는 부사구를 이룰 때는 그 앞에 at, on, in을 쓰지 않는다.

× last night	× every Thursday night
× next month	× this weekend
× last year	× that night
× every hour	

PRACTICE 3

1 ① from ② since   **2** ① since ② from
3 ① from ② since   **4** ① since ② from
5 ① from ② since   **6** ① since ② from
7 ① from ② since   **8** ① from ② since
9 ① since ② from   **10** ① from ② since

> from은 동작이나 사건이 시작되는 시점을 나타내며, 뒤에 to나 until이 나오면 동작이나 사건이 완료되는 시점을 알려준다. since는 과거에 시작된 동작이나 사건이 현재에도 영향을 미치고 있음을 나타내며, 완료시제에 주로 쓰인다.

PRACTICE 4

1 until **2** by **3** by **4** until **5** by
6 until **7** by **8** by **9** until **10** until

> **1, 4, 6, 9, 10** 어느 한 시점까지 계속되는 동작이나 상태를 나타내고 있으므로 until이 알맞다.
> **2, 3, 5, 7, 8** 어느 한 시점에 완료되는 동작이나 상태를 나타내고 있으므로 by가 알맞다.

PRACTICE 5

1 by **2** since **3** from **4** at
5 in **6** on **7** by **8** since
9 until **10** until **11** on **12** in
13 at **14** from **15** by[at] **16** since
17 by[on] **18** on

> **1, 7** 어느 한 시점에 완료되는 동작이나 상태를 나타내므로 '~까지'의 의미를 나타내는 by가 알맞다.
> **2, 8, 16** '~ 이후에'라는 의미로, 과거에 시작된 동작이나 사건이 현재에도 영향을 미치고 있음을 나타내며, 완료시제에 주로 쓰이는 since가 알맞다.
> **3, 14** '~부터'의 의미로, 동작이나 사건이 시작되는 시점을 나타내는 from이 알맞다.
> **4, 13** 구체적인 시각이나 비교적 짧은 시간을 나타내는 말 앞에 오는 at이 알맞다.
> **5, 12** 연도, 월, 계절 등 비교적 긴 시간 앞에 오는 in이 알맞다.
> **6, 11, 18** 특정한 날이나 요일, 그날의 아침이나 저녁, 낮 시간 등을 나타내는 말 앞에 오는 on이 알맞다.
> **9, 10** 어느 한 시점까지 계속되는 동작이나 상태를 나타낼 때 '~까지'의 의미를 나타내는 until이 알맞다.
> **15** '10월 말까지 돌아오기로 약속했다'와 '10월 말에 돌아오기로 약속했다' 모두 가능하므로 by(동작이나 상태가 완료되는 시점)와 at(비교적 짧은 시간) 둘 다 알맞다.
> **17** '월요일까지 결정해야 한다'와 '월요일에 결정해야 한다' 모두 가능하므로 by(동작이나 상태가 완료되는 시점)와 on(요일) 둘 다 알맞다.

PRACTICE 6

1 after the rock festival

2 before entering the house
3 after classes
4 before coming to Australia
5 before the arrival of European settlers
6 after getting home from work

PRACTICE 7

1 getting up before daybreak, we went to see the Tokyo Fishmarket
2 giving me a prescription, the doctor explained the disease to me
3 completing the assigned house chores, I ran out to the street to play with my friends
4 cooking dinner, we lit a small campfire by our tent
5 talking to Jim over the cell phone, I went out to meet him at the bus stop
6 moving to Argentina, John gave away all his toys to his younger cousins
7 landing on the coast of Taiwan, the typhoon blew away many houses
8 becoming one of the top baseball teams, the team went through a strict training program
9 completing my training as a sailor, I came back home to see my family
10 sinking to the bottom of the sea, the submarine exploded

PRACTICE 8

1 ① for ② during   **2** ① during ② for
3 ① for ② during   **4** ① during ② for
5 ① during ② for   **6** ① for ② during
7 ① for ② during   **8** ① for ② during
9 ① during ② for   **10** ① for ② during

> *for 다음에는 시간의 길이를 나타내는 명사(구)가 온다.
> for three months   for hours
> for 116 years   for a month or two
> for the time being   for almost a week
> for nearly 900 years   for many years
> for over 200 years   for three hours
> *during 다음에는 특정 기간을 나타내는 명사(구)가 온다.
> during this summer vacation
> during the evening
> during the Hundred Years' War
> during the summer break
> during the exams

Ch **16**

전
치
사

during the school rock festival
during the Middle Ages and early modern period
during my middle school and high school years
during the late 18th century
during the three-hour flight

1, 3, 8 천장, 나무, 벽 표면에 접촉해 있는 상태를 나타내므로 on이 알맞다.
2, 5, 7 공항, 책상, 버스 정류장처럼 특정한 지점이나 비교적 좁은 장소 앞에 쓰는 at이 알맞다.
4, 6, 9 가방이나 교실 같은 공간 안에 속해 있는 느낌을 나타낼 때나 도시 같은 넓은 장소 앞에 쓰는 in이 알맞다.

PRACTICE 9

1 before		**2** during	
3 for		**4** before	
5 during[throughout]		**6** After	
7 for		**8** during[throughout]	
9 after		**10** during[throughout]	

1, 4 '집을 나서기 전에 도시락을 챙겨라', '이 동네에 이사 오기 전에 어디 살았니?'라는 의미가 되어야 하므로 '~ 전에'를 의미하는 before가 알맞다.
2, 5, 8, 10 특정 기간을 나타내는 명사(구) 앞에서 '~ 동안'의 의미로 쓰이는 during이 알맞다. 5번, 8번, 10번처럼 특정 기간 중에 계속해서 일어나는 일을 강조할 때는 '~ 동안 내내'의 뜻인 throughout과 바꾸어 쓸 수 있다.
3, 7 시간의 길이를 나타내는 명사(구) 앞에서 '~ 동안'의 의미로 쓰이는 for가 알맞다.
6, 9 '20킬로미터를 달린 후에 그 마라톤 주자는 지쳐 쓰러졌다', '정답지를 받고 나서야 내 실수를 깨달았다'라는 의미가 되어야 하므로 '~ 후에'를 의미하는 after가 알맞다.

PRACTICE 10

1 in, on	**2** on, at	**3** at, in
4 in, on	**5** at, on	**6** on, in

*공간 안에 속해 있는 느낌을 나타내거나 비교적 넓은 장소 앞에는 in을 쓴다.
　a tree house in the big tree
　the computer in my room
　a table in the kitchen
　watching TV in the living room
*표면에 접촉해 있는 것을 나타낼 때는 on을 쓴다.
　sitting on a thick branch
　on the shelf in the toyshop
　a box on the table
　standing on the doormat
　watching TV on the couch
*특정한 한 지점을 나타내거나 비교적 좁은 장소 앞에는 at을 쓴다.
　at the window of the toyshop
　sitting at the computer desk
　standing at the door

PRACTICE 11

1 on	**2** at	**3** on
4 in	**5** at	**6** in
7 at	**8** on	**9** in

PRACTICE 12

1 at	**2** on	**3** at	**4** in	**5** on
6 at	**7** in	**8** at	**9** in	**10** on
11 on	**12** at	**13** in		

1 people at the concert: 콘서트에 온 사람들
2 life on a farm: 농장에서의 삶
3 a lake at the top of Mount Halla: 한라산 정상에 있는 호수
4 the accident in a newspaper article: 신문 기사 속의 사고
5 the banana peel on the floor: 바닥 위의 바나나 껍질
6 coins at the bottom of the fountain: 분수 바닥에 있는 동전들
7 the oldest book in the world: 세상에서 가장 오래된 책
8 useful things at a garage sale: 중고 물품 세일에 나온 유용한 물건들
9 stay in bed: 침대에서 머무르다
10 desert landscape on the road: 길 위의 사막 풍경
11 sleep on the plane: 비행기에서의 수면
12 fishing boats at sea: 바다 위의 낚싯배들
13 classes in prison: 교도소에서의 수업

PRACTICE 13

1 under[below]		**2** over
3 below		**4** above
5 below[under]		**6** over
7 under		**8** above[over]

1 a baseball under[below] the table: 탁자 아래의 야구공
2 leap over the fence: 담장 위로 뛰어오르다
3 my arm below my elbow: 팔꿈치 아래의 팔
4 hold your hands above your head: 머리 위로 손을 올리다
5 drop below[under] the horizon: 수평선 아래로 떨어지다
6 a white sheet over the sculpture: 조각품 위를 뒤덮은 하얀 천
7 the dog was under the tree: 나무 아래에 개가 있었다
8 fly just above[over] the tree tops: 나무 꼭대기 바로 위를 날다

PRACTICE 14

1 out of	**2** onto	**3** off
4 into	**5** up	**6** off
7 down	**8** onto	**9** up
10 down	**11** into	**12** out of

1 fly out of the nest: 둥지 밖으로 날아가다
2 pin a note onto the bulletin board: 게시판에 메모를 꽂다
3 push the canoe off the shore: 카누를 앞바다 쪽으로 밀다
4 sneak into the house: 집 안으로 몰래 들어가다
5 swim up the river: 강 상류로 헤엄치다
6 fall off the ladder: 사다리에서 떨어지다
7 slide down a slide: 미끄럼틀을 미끄러져 내려가다
8 load the containers onto the trucks: 컨테이너들을 트럭에 싣다
9 climb up the tree: 나무를 오르다
10 climb down the mountain: 산을 내려가다
11 jump into the swimming pool: 수영장으로 뛰어들다
12 jump out of the water: 물 밖으로 뛰어오르다

PRACTICE 15

1 ① down ② under
2 ① Under ② over
3 ① off ② below
4 ① into ② out of
5 ① up ② over
6 ① off ② onto
7 ① into ② under
8 ① above ② below
9 ① out of ② onto

PRACTICE 16

1 along **2** across **3** across
4 around **5** around **6** through
7 through **8** along

1 drive along the coast: 해안을 따라 운전하다
2 swim across it: 그것을 가로질러 헤엄치다
3 just across the street: 바로 길 건너에
4 have a scarf around her neck: 그녀의 목 주위에 스카프를 두르다
5 orbit around the planet: 행성 주위를 궤도를 그리며 돌다
6 run through a tunnel: 터널을 통과하여 달리다
7 jump through the hoop: 고리를 통과하여 뛰다
8 walk along the beach: 해변을 따라 걷다

PRACTICE 17

1 near **2** by **3** near
4 behind **5** in front of **6** behind
7 by **8** in front of

1 go near the dog: 개 가까이 가다
2 sit by Patricia: Patricia 옆에 앉다
3 a factory quite near our neighborhood: 우리 동네 아주 가까이 있는 공장
4 follow right behind our car: 우리 차 바로 뒤를 따라 오다
5 take a photograph in front of the statue: 조각상 앞에서 사진을 찍다
6 hide behind the curtain: 커튼 뒤에 숨다
7 have this dog by my side: 이 개를 내 곁에 두다
8 can't take their eyes off the food in front of them: 그들 앞에 있는 음식에서 눈을 떼지 못하다

PRACTICE 18

1 between **2** among **3** between
4 between **5** among **6** among
7 between **8** among **9** between
10 among

1, 3, 4, 7, 9 두 개의 사물 또는 두 명의 사람을 나타내는 말 앞에 오는 between이 알맞다. between A and B의 형태로도 많이 쓰인다.
2, 5, 6, 8, 10 셋 이상의 사물 또는 사람을 나타내는 말 앞에 오는 among이 알맞다.

PRACTICE 19

1 to **2** toward(s) **3** for
4 toward(s) **5** for **6** for
7 toward(s) **8** for **9** to
10 to **11** to **12** toward(s)
13 for **14** to[for] **15** toward(s)

1, 9, 10, 11 '~로, ~까지'라는 의미로 목적지를 나타내고, 주로 go, come, return, send, bring, walk 등의 동사와 함께 쓰는 to가 알맞다.
2, 4, 7, 12, 15 '~ 쪽으로, ~을 향하여'라는 의미로 목적지 쪽으로의 방향을 나타내고, walk, come, run, drive, turn, rush 등의 동사와 함께 쓰는 toward(s)가 알맞다.
3, 5, 6, 8, 13 '~로, ~을 향하여'라는 의미로 운동의 방향을 나타내고 주로 start, leave 등의 동사와 함께 쓰는 for가 알맞다.
14 'Brisbane까지 고속버스를 타고 갔다'는 의미와 'Brisbane으로 가는 고속버스를 탔다'는 의미 모두 가능하므로 to와 for 모두 쓸 수 있다.

PRACTICE 20

1 with **2** with **3** without
4 with **5** against **6** for
7 with **8** without **9** with
10 with

1 '~와 함께'라는 뜻으로 쓰이는 with가 알맞다.
2 '~와, ~에 찬성하여'라는 뜻으로 쓰이는 with가 알맞다. 전치사 for도 '~에 찬성하는'이라는 뜻으로 쓰이지만 for 뒤에는 사람이 아닌 의견 등이 온다.
*I am with you.: 네 의견에 찬성이야.
3, 8 '~ 없이'라는 의미로 쓰이는 without이 알맞다.
4, 10 '~을 가지고 있는, ~을 몸에 지니고 있는'이라는 의미로 쓰이는 with가 알맞다.
5 '~에 반대하는'이라는 의미로 쓰이는 against가 알맞다.
*against the law: 법에 반하는
6 '~에 찬성하는'이라는 의미로 쓰이는 for가 알맞다.
7 '~에 대하여'라는 의미로 쓰이는 with가 알맞다.
*be satisfied with: ~에 만족하다
9 '~을 사용하여, ~으로'라는 뜻으로 쓰는 with가 알맞다.

Ch
16
전치사

PRACTICE 21

1 as[like] **2** by **3** by **4** in
5 as **6** by **7** like[as] **8** as[like]
9 by **10** like

1 '학교가 피난처로서 사용되었다'와 '학교가 피난처처럼 사용되었다'는 의미가 가능하므로 '~로서'라는 의미로 자격/기능을 나타내는 as와 '~처럼, ~같이'의 의미로 쓰이는 like가 알맞다.
2 교통수단 앞에 와서 '~를 타고, ~로'라는 의미로 수단/방법을 나타내는 by가 알맞다.
3 '~에 의해'라는 의미로 행위의 주체를 밝힐 때 쓰는 by가 알맞다.
4 '~을 입고 있는'이라는 의미로 쓰이는 in이 알맞다.
5 '~로서'라는 의미로 자격이나 기능을 나타낼 때 쓰는 as가 알맞다.
6 '~로, ~만큼'이라는 의미로 정도를 나타낼 때 쓰는 by가 알맞다.
7 like와 as는 둘 다 '~처럼, ~같이'라는 의미로 쓰인다.
8 '상자를 테이블로 사용해야 했다'와 '상자를 테이블처럼 사용해야 했다'는 의미가 가능하므로 '~로서'라는 의미의 as와 '~처럼, ~같이'의 의미로 쓰이는 like가 알맞다.
9 뒤에 동명사가 와서 '~함으로써'라는 의미로 쓰는 by가 알맞다.
10 '~와 같은'이라는 의미로 예를 들 때 쓰는 like가 알맞다.

PRACTICE 22

1 according to **2** without
3 for **4** According to
5 except **6** by
7 instead of **8** as
9 with **10** due to
11 Instead of **12** like
13 due to **14** by
15 due to **16** against
17 according to **18** with
19 in **20** except

1, 4, 17 '~에 따라, ~에 따르면'이라는 의미로 쓰이는 according to가 알맞다.
2 뒤에 동명사가 와서 '~하지 않고'라는 의미로 쓰이는 without이 알맞다.
3 '~에 찬성하는'이라는 의미로 쓰이는 for가 알맞다.
5, 20 '~을 제외하고'라는 의미로 쓰이는 except가 알맞다.
6 '~로'라는 의미로 수단/방법을 나타낼 때 쓰는 by가 알맞다.
7, 11 '~ 대신에'라는 의미로 쓰이는 instead of가 알맞다.
8 '~로서'라는 의미로 자격이나 기능을 나타낼 때 쓰는 as가 알맞다.
9 '~을 사용하여, ~으로'라는 의미로 도구를 나타낼 때 쓰는 with가 알맞다.
10, 13, 15 '~ 때문에'라는 의미로 원인을 나타낼 때 쓰는 due to가 알맞다.
12 '~와 같은'이라는 의미로 예를 들 때 쓰는 like가 알맞다.
14 뒤에 동명사가 와서 '~함으로써'라는 의미로 쓰이는 by가 알맞다.
16 '~에 반대하는'이라는 의미로 쓰이는 against가 알맞다.
18 '~에 대하여'라는 의미로 쓰이는 with가 알맞다.
*have a problem with: ~에 문제가 있다
19 in first place는 '1등으로, 1위로'라는 의미이다.

PRACTICE 23

1 about **2** of **3** of **4** of **5** of
6 with **7** with **8** with **9** of **10** on

1 crazy about: ~에 열광적인, ~를 매우 좋아하는
2 afraid of: ~을 두려워하는
3 ashamed of: ~을 부끄러워하는, 수치스럽게 여기는
4 capable of: ~을 할 수 있는
5 frightened of: ~에 놀란
6 crowded with: ~로 가득한
7 busy with: ~로 바쁜
8 familiar with: ~에 익숙한, 친숙한
9 full of: ~로 가득한
10 based on: ~에 근거한

PRACTICE 24

1 of **2** of **3** at **4** for **5** at
6 to **7** for **8** to **9** to **10** in

1 jealous of: ~을 질투하는
2 proud of: ~을 자랑스러워하는
3 surprised at: ~에 놀란
4 sorry for: ~이 가엾은
5 mad at: ~에 몹시 화난
6 related to: ~와 관련된
7 responsible for: ~에 책임 있는
8 married to: ~와 결혼한
9 similar to: ~와 비슷한
10 interested in: ~에 관심 있는

PRACTICE 25

1 about **2** in **3** to **4** on **5** on
6 for **7** for **8** of **9** to **10** for

1 care about: ~에 대해 신경 쓰다
2 believe in: ~을 믿다
3 belong to: ~에 속하다
4 concentrate on: ~에 집중하다
5 depend on: ~에 의존하다, ~에 달려 있다
6 apply for: ~에 지원하다, 신청하다
7 care for: ~을 돌보다
8 consist of: ~로 구성되어 있다
9 add … to: ~에 …를 더하다
10 apologize for: ~에 대해 사과하다

PRACTICE 26

1 for **2** to **3** on
4 at **5** about[of] **6** of[from]
7 like **8** in **9** to
10 to

1 wait for: ~를 기다리다
2 listen to: ~을 듣다
3 focus on: ~에 초점을 맞추다
4 laugh at: ~을 보고 웃다, 비웃다
5 dream about[of]: ~를 꿈꾸다
6 die of[from]: ~로 죽다
7 feel like: ~하고 싶다
8 succeed in: ~에 성공하다
9 prefer … to ~: ~보다 …을 선호하다
10 look forward to: ~를 고대하다

PRACTICE 27

1	for	**2**	at	**3**	on
4	in	**5**	After	**6**	against
7	on	**8**	by	**9**	under
10	down	**11**	onto	**12**	to
13	through	**14**	from	**15**	behind
16	for	**17**	toward	**18**	above
19	with	**20**	According to		
21	during	**22**	instead of	**23**	as
24	for	**25**	across	**26**	from
27	by	**28**	since	**29**	like
30	on	**31**	like	**32**	at
33	in front of	**34**	since	**35**	on
36	along	**37**	before	**38**	on
39	as	**40**	of	**41**	to
42	around	**43**	behind	**44**	among
45	into	**46**	among	**47**	for
48	with	**49**	against	**50**	into
51	in	**52**	due to	**53**	Instead of
54	like	**55**	on	**56**	as
57	except	**58**	between	**59**	to
60	of	**61**	of	**62**	about
63	at	**64**	at	**65**	to
66	for	**67**	of	**68**	at
69	for	**70**	on	**71**	to
72	of	**73**	at	**74**	on
75	of	**76**	for	**77**	of
78	for	**79**	in	**80**	to
81	of	**82**	on	**83**	during
84	on	**85**	towards	**86**	out of
87	with	**88**	in	**89**	to
90	in	**91**	with	**92**	with
93	out of	**94**	like	**95**	about
96	with	**97**	between	**98**	to
99	of	**100**	on		

중간·기말고사 대비문제 **정답** 본문 _ p.409

1 ③　**2** ②　**3** ④　**4** ③　**5** ④　**6** ④　**7** ④,⑤
8 ⑤, by → since　**9** from, to　**10** ①　**11** ③
12 teach → teaching　**13** ①,⑤　**14** ②
15 ⑤　**16** than → to　**17** on, for　**18** ④
19 ②,③　**20** ⑤　**21** ③　**22** for → during
[throughout]　**23** ③　**24** ②,⑤　**25** without
26 ① for ② with ③ into　**27** ⑤　**28** ③　**29** ⑤
30 that, on　**31** ②　**32** ③　**33** ④　**34** for
35 with　**36** ⑤　**37** among[of]　**38** ④　**39** ⑤
40 ④　**41** to → into　**42** out of　**43** ②
44 ②,④　**45** ④　**46** ①　**47** until → by　**48** ②
49 among → between　**50** ⑤　**51** ③　**52** ③
53 attend → attending　**54** ①　**55** ④　**56** ②
57 ④　**58** ⑤　**59** as → to　**60** ①　**61** In, for,
behind, On, on, to, with　**62** ⓐ with → from,
ⓒ to → in, ⓓ on → at　**63** ①

중간·기말고사 대비문제 **해설**

1 at은 비교적 짧은 시간을 나타내는 말 앞에 쓴다.
2 · 시간을 나타내는 전치사 in은 계절과 같은 비교적
　긴 시간을 나타내는 말 앞에 쓴다.
　· 장소를 나타내는 전치사 in은 비교적 넓은 장소 앞
　에 쓰인다.
3 · 요일 앞에는 on을 쓴다.
　· in '<도구> ~로'
4 fall off '~에서 떨어지다'
5 환경을 보호하기 위해서 일회용 종이컵 대신에 개
　인컵을 사용해야 한다는 해석이 자연스러우므로 '~
　대신에'라는 뜻의 전치사 instead of를 사용한다.
　instead는 '대신에'라는 뜻의 부사이다.
6 ⓓ devote A to B 'A를 B에 바치다[헌신하다]'
　　(in → to)
　ⓐ 5월 10일 같은 날짜 앞에는 전치사 on을 쓴다.
　ⓑ as는 '~로서'라는 뜻으로 자격을 나타낼 때 쓰는 전
　　치사이다.
　ⓒ focus on '~에 초점을 맞추다'
　ⓔ With+명사 '~와 함께, ~으로 인해'
　1998년 5월 10일, 파리였다. 한 젊은 선수가 그의 국가
　대표 팀의 미드필더로 경기장에 들어왔다. 수천 명의
　팬들이 응원하며 그를 맞이했다. 그는 그의 속도와 컨

Ch
16
전
치
사

트롤을 향상시키는 데 집중하며 매일 열심히 훈련했다. 그 선수는 정상에 오르겠다는 결심을 하며 그의 삶과 힘을 축구에 바쳤다. 그 노력으로, 그는 마침내 그의 팀을 승리로 이끌었다.

7 this, last 등이 붙어 시간을 나타내는 부사구를 이룰 때는 그 앞에 전치사를 쓰지 않는다.

④ in this year → this year

⑤ In last Monday → Last Monday

8 ⑤ 문맥상 현재완료 시제와 쓰여 '~부터, 이래로'의 의미를 갖는 전치사 since가 와야 한다.

① on the bus '버스에서'

② look at '~을 보다'

③ 문장의 주어는 전치사구(like Jane)의 수식을 받는 Young people

④ be exposed to '~에 노출되다'

버스에서, Jane이 음악을 듣는 동안, 그녀는 인터넷을 서핑하느라 바쁘다. 심지어 그녀가 학교에 도착한 다음에도, 그녀는 내내 휴대폰을 본다. Jane같은 젊은 사람들은 "디지털 원주민"이라고 불리는데 그들은 이런 디지털 기술에 어린 시절부터 계속 노출되었기 때문이다.

9 from A to B 'A에서 B로'

10 apply for '~에 지원하다, 신청하다'
apologize for '~에 대해 사과하다'

11 • 섬을 나타내는 명사 앞에는 on을 쓴다.
• on the Internet '인터넷으로'

12 전치사의 목적어로 동사가 올 때는 동명사의 형태로 쓴다.

13 because of와 due to 뒤에는 명사(구)가 온다. because와 as는 '~ 때문에'라는 뜻이지만 접속사이므로 뒤에 절이 온다.

14 • share A with B 'A를 B와 나누다'
• keep up with '~에 뒤지지 않다, 따라가다'

15 화재가 발생하면, 엘리베이터 대신에 계단을 이용해야 한다는 뜻이 되어야 하므로 '~대신에'라는 뜻의 instead of를 사용한다.

16 prefer A to B 'B보다 A를 더 좋아하다'

17 • sting ~ on ⋯ '~의 ⋯를 쏘다'
• look for '~을 찾다'

18 • take after '~를 닮다'
• similar to '~와 유사한'

19 ② cutting으로 시작하는 동명사구가 따라오고 있으므로 접속사 because가 아닌 전치사 because of를 써야 한다. (because → because of)

③ 가리키는 대상이 The animals이므로 복수 인칭대명사 their을 쓰는 것이 적절하다. (its → their)

① 동사 know의 목적어로 쓰인 명사절을 이끄는 접속사 that의 쓰임은 적절하다.

④ 「stop+-ing」 '~하는 것을 멈추다'

⑤ trees는 셀 수 있는 명사이므로 fewer의 사용은 적절하다. 미래의 일을 예상하고 있고, 나무는 베어지는 것이므로 미래시제 수동태를 쓴 것은 적절하다.

A: 미나야, 너는 아마존 열대우림이 사라지고 있다는 걸 아니?

B: 응, 나는 그것에 관한 다큐멘터리를 봤어.

A: 그것은 너무 많은 나무를 베어내기 때문이야.

B: 그거 끔찍하다.

A: 동물들은 그들의 집을 잃고 있고 그들의 미래는 불확실해.

B: 우리가 다음 세대를 위해 환경을 보호하는 것이 중요해.

A: 사람들은 너무 많은 종이를 사용하는 것을 멈춰야 해.

B: 맞아. 그렇게 하면 더 적은 나무가 베어질 거야.

20 • be filled with '~로 가득차다'
• be famous for '~로 유명하다'

21 (A) '연구에 따르면, 가공 식품보다 현미와 같은 통곡물을 먹는 것이 건강에 더 좋다.'는 뜻이 되어야 하므로 '~에 따르면'이라는 뜻의 According to를 쓰는 것이 적절하다. Because of는 '~ 때문에'라는 뜻이며, Related to는 '~와 관련된'이라는 뜻이므로 여기에서는 적절하지 않다.

(B) '또한, 통곡물은 영양소와 비타민으로 가득하다.'는 뜻이 되어야 하므로 '~로 가득한'이라는 뜻의 full of가 적절하다. based on은 '~에 근거한', capable of는 '~을 할 수 있는'이라는 뜻이다.

22 during[throughout] 다음에는 특정 기간을 나타내는 명사(구)가 온다. for의 다음에는 구체적인 시간이 온다.

23 • be covered with '~로 덮여있다'
• be crazy about '~에 열광적이다, ~를 매우 좋아하다'

24 ⓐ 빈칸 뒤에 형용사 quiet와 clean이 있으므로 be동사나 look 같은 상태를 묘사하는 말이 와야 한다. (looks like → is[looks])

ⓒ 문맥상 Jina가 앞에 한 말이 무슨 의미인지 묻고 있으므로 동사 mean을 쓰는 것이 적절하다.

(need → mean)

ⓓ 어느 층에 있다는 것을 나타낼 때는 전치사 On을 쓴다. (Under → On)

ⓑ 문맥상 '판단하다'라는 뜻이 와야 한다. 부정형 명령문이므로 빈칸에는 동사원형 judge를 쓰는 것이 적절하다.

ⓔ after school '방과 후'

A: 민호야, 너 새 도서관을 봤니?

B: 응, 나는 어제 거기 갔었어. 그것은 아주 조용하고 깨끗해 보여.

A: 맞아! 하지만 도서관을 그것의 겉모습만으로 판단하지 마.

B: 무슨 뜻이야, 지나야?

A: 음, 그 건물은 작아 보이지만 그 안은 아주 넓어.

B: 아, 그렇구나. 1층에는 무료 인터넷이 되는 컴퓨터들이 많이 있어.

A: 그거 멋지다! 방과 후에 같이 거기에 가자.

25 without '~없이, ~하지 않고'

26 ① 시간의 길이를 나타내는 명사구 앞에는 '~동안'의 의미를 갖는 전치사 for를 쓴다.
② 도구를 나타내는 경우 '~을 사용하여'의 의미를 갖는 전치사 with를 쓴다.
③ 기존의 것을 다른 형태로 변화시킬 때는 전치사 into를 쓴다.

27 ⑤ 동사 - '좋아하다'
①②③④ 전치사 - '~처럼'

28 • be headed for '~로 향하다'
• between A and B 'A와 B 사이에'

29 ⓑ frightened of '~에 놀란' (on → of)
ⓒ depend on '~에 달려 있다' (with → on)
ⓓ dream of[about] '~를 꿈꾸다' (on → of[about])
ⓔ in addition은 '게다가'라는 뜻으로 두 문장 간의 논리 관계를 나타내는 접속부사이다. 밑줄 친 부분 뒤에 명사구(a music video)가 오므로, 명사구를 목적어로 할 수 있는 전치사 in addition to를 써야 한다. in addition to는 '~에 더하여'라는 뜻이다. (in addition → in addition to)

30 • forget의 목적어로 완전한 구조의 명사절이 나오므로 접속사 that이 적절하다. what은 불완전한 구조의 절을 이끈다.
• depend on '~에 의존하다'

31 • die of '~로 죽다'
• be made of '~로 만들어지다' (재료의 성질이 변하지 않은 경우)

32 • travel around the world '세계 일주를 하다'
• prepare for '~를 준비하다'

33 '겨울 동안에, 나는 어떤 산에도 전혀 가지 않았다.'는 해석이 적절하므로 '~동안'이라는 뜻으로 특정 기간을 나타내는 명사(구) 앞에서 쓰이는 전치사 During을 쓰는 것이 적절하다.

34 for 다음에는 시간의 길이를 나타내는 명사(구)가 온다.

35 with '~와 함께, ~을 가지고'

36 • with '~을 가지고 있는'
• be pleased with '~에 기뻐하다'

37 among은 셋 이상의 사물 또는 사람을 나타내는 말 앞에 쓴다. 의미상 전치사 of도 가능하다.

38 ④ the dictionary는 주로 전치사 in과 함께 쓰이는 명사구이다. (at → in)

39 (A) put off '미루다, 연기하다'
(B) check out '(책을) 대출받다'
(C) prefer A to B 'B보다 A를 선호하다'
예나: 주호야, 너는 어디 가는 중이야?
주호: 안녕, 난 도서관에 가는 길이야. 너는?
예나: 오, 나도 그곳에 가는 중이야. 난 내가 빌렸던 책을 끝내지 못해서 반납일을 연기하려고 해.
주호: 그렇구나. 난 가볍게 읽을 책을 대출하고 싶어. 너는 내게 하나 추천해줄 수 있니?
예나: 오, 너는 선호하는 어떤 장르가 있니?
주호: 나는 과학 소설보다 역사 소설을 선호해.

40 ① '걸어서'라는 뜻은 전치사 on을 사용하여 나타낸다. (in → on)
② land와 같은 명사 앞에는 '~ (위)에'라는 뜻으로 표면에 접촉해 있는 것을 나타내는 전치사 on을 사용한다. (at → on)
③ TV와 같은 통신수단을 나타내는 말 앞에는 전치사 on을 사용한다. (in → on)
⑤ [관사+교통수단]의 앞에는 전치사 on을 사용한다. 참고로, 교통수단을 나타내는 말의 앞에 관사가 없을 경우 전치사 by를 사용한다. (at → on)

41 into pieces '조각들로'
cf. break A into B 'A를 부수어 B를 만들다'

42 out of '~밖으로'

43 • 동사 seem은 뒤에 명사가 나올 때 전치사 like와 같이 쓴다. as도 '~처럼'이라는 뜻이지만 동사 seem과 함께 쓰지 않는다.

Ch **16** 전치사

	• 산 위에 있다고 하였으므로 '(~보다) 위에'라는 뜻의 전치사 above를 쓰는 것이 적절하다. up은 방향성을 나타내는 전치사로 '~ 위로'라는 뜻이며 beyond는 '~ 저편에, 너머'라는 의미이므로 여기에서는 적절하지 않다.

44 [보기] 문장의 as는 전치사로 '~로서'로 해석한다.
①⑤ 접속사 as '~함에 따라'
③ 접속사 as '~대로'

45 ④ be full of = be filled with
(full → filled/with → of)

46 • 「by+교통수단」 '~를 타고'
• 「by+-ing」 '~함으로써'

47 동작이나 상태가 어느 한 시점에 완료됨을 나타낼 때는 by를 쓴다.

48 get along with '~와 잘 지내다'

49 두 개의 사물 또는 두 명의 사람을 나타내는 말 앞에는 between을 쓴다.

50 • toward는 '~을 향하여'라는 뜻으로 목적지 쪽으로의 방향을 나타내고 run 등의 동사와 함께 쓴다.
• toward는 태도나 관계를 나타낼 때 '~에 대하여, 관하여'라는 의미로도 쓰인다.

51 (a) take care of '~을 돌보다'
(b) busy with '~로 바쁜'
(c) sorry for '~에 대해 미안하게 생각하는'

52 • 사람들이 호수 옆에 모였다는 해석이 적절하므로 '~ 옆에'라는 뜻의 전치사 by를 쓰는 것이 적절하다. 특정한 한 지점을 나타내는 전치사 at이나 '~를 둘러'라는 뜻의 round를 쓰는 것도 가능하다.
• 25%로 감소했다는 해석이 적절하므로 '~로, ~만큼'이라는 뜻으로 정도를 나타내는 전치사 by를 쓰는 것이 적절하다.

53 look forward to+-ing '~을 고대하다'

54 onto '~ 위로'

55 against '~에 반대하는'

56 due to '~때문에'

57 (가) 그는 힘든 시간을 겪고 있는 중이다.
go through '(힘든 일·시간 등을) 겪다'
(나) 경찰들은 뒷문을 통해 건물로 들어갔다.
enter through ~ '~를 통해 들어가다'
(다) 한 잔의 커피는 내가 하루를 버티는 데 도움을 준다.
get through the day '하루를 버티다[견디게 하다]'

58 proud of '~을 자랑스러워하는'

59 according to '~에 따르면'

60 except '~을 제외하고'

61 • 역과 같은 장소 안에 속해 있는 느낌을 나타낼 때 전치사 in을 사용한다.
• for은 '~로, ~을 향하여'라는 뜻으로 bound 등의 형용사와 함께 운동의 방향을 나타낸다.
• 노란선 뒤에서 기다려달라는 해석이 자연스러우므로 '~ 뒤에'라는 뜻의 전치사 behind를 사용한다.
• 지하철과 같은 교통수단을 나타내는 말이 관사와 함께 쓰였을 경우 전치사 on을 사용한다.
• '왼쪽으로'라는 표현은 전치사 on을 사용하여 나타낸다.
• to는 '~로'라는 뜻으로 transfer와 같은 동사와 함께 쓴다.
• 소지품을 가지고 내리라는 해석이 자연스러우므로, '~의 몸에 지닌'이라는 뜻의 with를 사용한다.

62 ⓐ be different from '~와 다르다' (with → from)
ⓒ succeed in '~에 성공하다' (to → in)
ⓓ laugh at '~을 비웃다' (on → at)

63 (A) leave for '~을 향해 떠나다'
(B) 「(a/an)+형용사+명사」가 원인, that절이 결과가 되는 경우에는 so 대신 such를 쓴다.
(C) jealous of '~을 질투하는'
(D) at the moment '지금'

CHAPTER 17 일치와 화법
Agreement and Narration

본문 _ p.420

PRACTICE 1

1	are	**2**	has	**3**	come	**4**	greet
5	is	**6**	is	**7**	travel	**8**	walks
9	work	**10**	visits				

1 유도부사 There로 시작하여 「주어+동사」가 도치된 「There+동사+주어」 형태의 문장이다. 이때 동사의 수는 동사의 뒤에 따라오는 주어의 수에 맞춘다.
2 주어가 단수이므로 단수 동사가 와야 한다.
3 주어(The two brothers)가 복수이므로 복수 동사가 와야 한다.
4, 7, 9 명사가 and로 연결되어 주어 역할을 할 때는 복수 취급하므로 복수 동사가 온다.
5 '백설공주와 일곱 난쟁이' 작품을 가리키므로 단수 취급하여 단수 동사로 받는다.
6 주어(Collecting autographed baseballs)가 복수형으로 끝나서 동사를 복수 취급해야 할 것 같지만 동명사(구) 주어는 단수 취급하므로 단수 동사를 써야 한다.
8 빨간색과 검정색의 무늬를 가진 무당벌레를 가리키므로 단수 취급한다.
10 정관사 the가 한번 쓰인 것으로 보아 주어는 유명한 가수이자 활동가인 한 사람을 가리키는 것을 알 수 있다. 그러므로 단수 동사를 써야 한다.

PRACTICE 2

1	have	**2**	is	**3**	are	**4**	finds
5	visits	**6**	have	**7**	is	**8**	stop
9	appear	**10**	is				

1, 2, 4, 6, 7, 9, 10 either A or B(A와 B 중 어느 하나), neither A nor B(A도 B도 아닌), not only A but (also) B(A뿐만 아니라 B도), not A but B(A가 아니라 B)는 동사와 더 가까이에 있는 B에 동사의 수를 일치시킨다.
3, 5 B as well as A(A뿐만 아니라 B도)는 B에 동사의 수를 일치시킨다.
8 명사가 and로 연결되어 주어 역할을 할 때는 복수 취급하므로 복수 동사가 온다. 참고로 The police는 항상 복수 취급한다.

PRACTICE 3

1	weighs	**2**	set	**3**	lives
4	has	**5**	shows	**6**	were
7	wants	**8**	costs	**9**	adds
10	brings				

1, 3, 4, 5, 7, 8, 10 주어에 every와 each가 포함되어 있는 경우에는 단수 취급하여 단수 동사를 쓴다.
2, 6 셀 수 있는 명사를 수식하는 all이나 both가 주어이거나 주어에 포함되어 있는 경우에는 복수 취급하여 복수 동사를 쓴다.
9 셀 수 없는 명사를 수식하는 all이 주어에 포함된 경우 단수 취급하여 단수 동사를 쓴다.

PRACTICE 4

1	were	**2**	wear	**3**	is
4	has	**5**	buildings	**6**	were
7	have	**8**	don't		

주어에 「부분, 전체 등을 나타내는 표현(some, most, none, all, half, 분수, percent)+of」가 포함되어 있는 경우에는 of 뒤에 오는 명사의 수에 동사의 수를 일치시킨다.

1, 2, 6, 7, 8 of 뒤에 오는 명사가 복수이므로 복수 동사가 온다.
3, 4 of 뒤에 오는 명사가 단수이므로 단수 동사가 온다
5 복수 동사가 왔으므로 of 뒤의 명사도 복수가 되어야 한다.

PRACTICE 5

1	doesn't	**2**	gives	**3**	is
4	sounds	**5**	visit	**6**	was
7	ranks	**8**	attracts	**9**	seems
10	looks	**11**	produces	**12**	is
13	has	**14**	is	**15**	was

1, 4, 10, 14 금액이 주어일 경우에는 복수 형태이더라도 단수 취급하므로 단수 동사가 온다.
2, 7, 15 학과명이 주어일 경우에는 복수 형태이더라도 단수 취급하므로 단수 동사가 온다.
3, 12 시간이 주어일 경우에는 복수 형태이더라도 단수 취급하므로 단수 동사가 온다.
5 명사가 and로 연결되어 주어 역할을 할 때는 복수 취급하므로 복수 동사가 온다.
6 무게가 주어일 경우에는 복수 형태이더라도 단수 취급하므로 단수 동사가 온다.
8, 11, 13 국가명이 주어일 경우에는 복수 형태이더라도 단수 취급하므로 단수 동사가 온다.
9 거리가 주어일 경우에는 복수 형태이더라도 단수 취급하므로 단수 동사가 온다.

PRACTICE 6

1	had been	**2**	was
3	was	**4**	had not blown away
5	had been	**6**	had visited
7	wouldn't be	**8**	would be

1, 5 주절이 현재시제에서 과거시제로 바뀌었으므로 종속절의 시제를 현재완료에서 과거완료로 바꾼다.
2, 3 주절이 현재시제에서 과거시제로 바뀌었으므로 종속절의 시제를 현재에서 과거로 바꾼다.
4, 6 주절이 현재시제에서 과거시제로 바뀌었으므로 종속절의 시제를 과거에서 과거완료로 바꾼다.
7, 8 주절이 현재시제에서 과거시제로 바뀌었으므로 종속절의 will을 would로 바꾼다.

PRACTICE 7

1 was	**2** is	**3** could
4 eat	**5** had been	**6** went
7 wait	**8** ordered	**9** use
10 had been	**11** goes	**12** was
13 had forgotten		**14** reached
15 was		

> **1, 3** 과거 시점 부사구 five months ago, two weeks ago가 있으므로 과거 동사가 알맞다. 이처럼 비교 구문에서 than이나 as 뒤에 이어지는 구문의 시제는 내용에 따라 주절의 시제와 일치하지 않는 경우도 있다.
> **2** 현재 시점 부사 now가 있으므로 현재 시제가 알맞다.
> **4, 7, 9, 11** 현재의 습관, 사실, 진리는 항상 현재시제로 쓴다.
> **5, 6, 10, 13** 주절의 동사가 과거 시제인 경우에 종속절의 시제는 과거나 과거완료가 되어야 한다.
> **8, 12, 14, 15** 역사적 사실은 항상 과거시제로 쓴다.

PRACTICE 8

1 said, she would, that night

2 said, he had seen, the night before[the previous night]

3 said, he was

4 told, she didn't, those

5 told, he would, me there

6 told, she was

7 told, he

8 said, was then

9 said, had been, the day before[the previous day]

10 said, he, the following year

PRACTICE 9

1 Brad asked Ron when his graduation ceremony was.

2 I asked mom if[whether] we had an electric drill at home.

3 The old lady asked if[whether] I knew the legend about that town.

4 My aunt asked me how my family was those days.

5 The gentleman asked the flight attendant when dinner would be served.

6 Edward asked what Koreans do on Lunar New Year's Day.

7 The doctor asked me if[whether] I had been bitten by a snake.

8 The teacher asked the class who would answer that question for him[her].

9 I asked Mr. Gwak if[whether] we should come to school the following Saturday.

10 Sumi asked me if[whether] the Russian restaurant had been crowded.

> **1, 4, 5, 8** 의문사가 있는 의문문을 간접 화법으로 전환할 때는
> ① say[said]나 say[said] to를 ask[asked]로 바꾼다.
> ② that 대신 의문사로 두 문장을 연결한다.
> ③「주어+동사」의 어순으로 바꾼다. (의문사가 주어인 경우에는 「의문사+동사」의 어순 유지)
> **2, 3, 7, 9, 10** 의문사가 없는 의문문을 간접 화법으로 전환할 때는
> ① say[said]나 say[said] to를 ask[asked]로 바꾼다.
> ② that 대신 if나 whether로 두 문장을 연결한다.
> ③「주어+동사」의 어순으로 바꾼다.
> **6** 한국인들이 설날에 무엇을 하는지 묻는 것은 현재의 습관을 묻는 것으로 시제 일치의 예외에 따라 현재시제를 쓴다.

PRACTICE 10

1 I ordered my dog to get out of the room.

2 I asked Dan how he had climbed up that cliff.

3 I asked Andrea why she hadn't[had not] told me the truth.

4 I asked Tina who she had talked with over the phone. / I asked Tina with whom she had talked over the phone.

5 I asked Mr. Carlson if[whether] I could go to the washroom.

6 The nurse told[advised] me to take my medicine 30 minutes after meals.

7 The secretary told me (that) Mrs. Evans had been expecting me.

8 The coast guard told[advised] me not to swim too far off the beach.

9 Mr. Wilson asked me to come and have tea at his home at 4 o'clock.

10 The judge ordered the defendant to do 48 hours of community service.

11 My mother told me not to eat any junk food on my way home.

12 Mr. Lee said (that) he would hand out our[my] graded exam papers the next[following] day.

13 The sergeant ordered[told] the soldiers not to shoot without his order.

14 The principal said (that) all students must[had

to] get to school before 8 o'clock.

15 I asked the old man to wait there for a minute.

16 The police officer told my dad (that) that road was temporarily closed that day.

17 The mechanic told[advised] the customer to change the engine oil the following month.

18 The detective asked the woman if[whether] she had seen any strangers the previous night[the night before].

19 Mitch's uncle told me (that) he had served in the Marine Corps twenty years before.

20 The instructor told[advised] me to breathe slowly and deeply before diving into the water.

21 My mom told[advised] me to use vanilla sugar instead of honey.

22 The teacher told[ordered] us not to use our cell phones in class.

1, 6, 8, 9, 10, 11, 13, 15, 17, 20, 21, 22 명령문을 간접 화법으로 전환할 때는 ① 명령문의 성격에 따라 전달 동사를 tell, ask, advise, order 등으로 바꾸고, ② 명령문의 동사원형을 to부정사로 바꾼다.
2, 3, 4 의문사가 있는 의문문의 화법을 전환하는 경우이므로 의문사로 두 문장을 연결하고 「주어+동사」의 어순으로 바꾼다.
5, 18 의문사가 없는 의문문의 화법을 전환하는 경우이므로 if나 whether로 두 문장을 연결하고 「주어+동사」의 어순으로 바꾼다.
7, 12, 14, 16, 19 평서문의 화법을 전환하는 경우이므로 that으로 두 문장을 연결하는데, 이때의 that은 생략이 가능하다.

📝 중간·기말고사 대비문제 **정답**   본문 _ p.434

1 ③　**2** he would drive me home　**3** was made up by　**4** ①　**5** ①　**6** ⑤　**7** ③　**8** is
9 ②　**10** ③　**11** ②,③　**12** asked, if[whether], could　**13** ④　**14** ⑤　**15** ③　**16** ④　**17** ⑤
18 ⑤　**19** ③　**20** ④　**21** ④,⑤　**22** ③　**23** ①
24 ④　**25** had become → became　**26** ③
27 to wrap　**28** ②　**29** 라, is/마, discovered
30 ④,⑤

중간·기말고사 대비문제 **해설**

1　③ 우리 선생님이 우리에게 우리가 이 수업을 이해했는지 물었다. → 우리 선생님이 "너희들은 이 수업을 이해하니?"라고 우리에게 말했다.
　① 명령문을 간접 화법으로 전환할 때는 명령문의 동

사원형을 to부정사로 바꾸어 쓴다. (stay → to stay) 그 감독관은 면접자에게 "여기서 기다리세요."라고 말했다. → 그 감독관은 면접자에게 여기서 기다리라고 말했다.
② 의문사가 없는 의문문을 간접 화법으로 전환할 때는 that 대신 if나 whether로 두 문장을 연결한다. (that → if[whether]) 나의 남편은 나에게 "준비 됐어?"라고 말했다. → 나의 남편은 나에게 준비 됐는지를 물어봤다.
④ 평서문을 직접 화법으로 전환할 때는 종속절의 시제를 현재시제로 바꾸어 쓴다. (had to → have to) 그 열차 차장이 나에게 내가 천안에서 기차를 갈아타야 한다고 말했다. → 그 열차 차장이 나에게 "당신은 천안에서 기차를 갈아타야 합니다."라고 말했다.
⑤ 의문사가 있는 의문문을 간접 화법으로 전환할 때는 that 대신 의문사로 두 문장을 연결한다. 또한 시제 일치의 원칙에 따라 과거시제를 과거완료시제로 바꾸어 쓴다. (that 삭제, went → had gone) Tracy는 Charles에게 "너는 어디서 학교를 다녔니?"라고 말했다. → Tracy는 Charles에게 그가 어디서 학교를 다녔는지를 물어봤다.

2　주절의 시제가 과거이므로 종속절의 will은 would로 바뀐다.

3　주어진 우리말과 같은 뜻이 되려면 빈칸에는 수동태가 들어가야 한다. 한편, 「all of+셀 수 없는 명사+단수동사」이고, 시제가 과거이므로 수동태의 be동사 자리에는 was가 들어간다.

4　주절의 시제가 과거이므로 종속절의 시제도 과거로 바뀌고, tomorrow는 the following day 또는 the next day로 바뀐다.

5　neither A nor B는 위치상 동사와 더 가까이에 있는 B에 동사의 수를 일치시킨다.

6　분수는 분자는 기수로, 분모는 서수로 읽는다. 분자가 2 이상이면 분모에 '-s'를 붙이며, 3/4는 three-quarters 또는 three-fourths로 쓸 수 있다. 분수+of가 포함된 주어는 of 뒤에 오는 명사의 수에 따라 동사의 수를 일치시킨다. 따라서 동사는 these crops(복수 명사)에 맞추어 복수형 동사(were)를 써야 한다.

7　주절의 시제가 과거이므로 종속절의 시제는 과거, 과거완료만 가능하기 때문에 빈칸에 적절한 것은 ③ would need뿐이다.

8 the number of(~의 수)는 단수 취급한다.
cf. a number of '다수의, 많은' (복수)

9 ② every가 포함된 주어는 단수 취급한다.
(were → was)

10 간접 화법을 직접 화법으로 바꿀 때 that절의 주어와 목적어는 주절의 주어의 입장으로 바꾼다.

11 ② 국가명이 주어일 때는 복수형으로 쓰여 있어도 단수 취급한다. (are → is)
③ A number of는 '많은'이라는 뜻으로 복수 명사와 함께 쓰여 복수 취급한다. (has → have)
① information은 셀 수 없는 명사로 단수 취급한다.
④ 「The+형용사」는 '~한 사람들'이라는 뜻으로 복수 명사처럼 쓰인다.
⑤ 책 제목이 주어일 때는 복수형으로 쓰여 있어도 단수 취급한다.

12 의문사가 없는 의문문의 화법 전환이므로 said to를 asked로 바꾸고, if나 whether로 두 문장을 연결하고 「주어+동사」의 어순으로 바꾼다.

13 ④ 부정 명령문을 간접 화법으로 전환할 때는 don't를 [not+to부정사]로 바꾼다. (doesn't → not to)

14 ⑤ 과거에 시작되어 현재까지 영향을 미치는 동작이나 상태를 나타내기 위해 사용되는 현재완료 시제는 since와 함께 쓰여 '계속'의 상태를 드러낸다.
① 조건의 부사절에서는 미래의 일을 나타낸다고 하더라도 현재 시제를 사용한다. ⓐ는 어법상 옳다.
② Michael이 일주일 동안 아팠던 일은 과거 시점 (when I met him)보다 이전에 일어난 것이므로 과거완료 시제를 활용하여 표현한다. 따라서 had been sick으로 수정하는 것이 적절하다. (was → had been)
③ 격언을 나타낼 때에는 현재시제를 사용하므로 ⓒ는 어법상 옳다.
④ In the summer of 2024라는 과거 시점 부사구가 있으므로 현재완료 시제가 아닌 과거 시제 visited가 어법상 적절하다. 따라서 ⓓ는 어법상 옳다.

15 ③ 「Neither A nor B」 구조에서는 B에 동사의 수를 일치시킨다. the students가 복수이므로 복수 동사를 쓴다. (are)
①⑤ news와 time은 셀 수 없는 명사로 단수 취급한다. (is)
② 「Not only A but also B」 구조에서는 B에 동사의 수를 일치시킨다. my cousin이 단수이므로 단수 동사를 쓴다. (is)

16 ④ Bread and butter처럼 and로 연결된 주어가 한 가지 사물을 나타낼 때는 단수 취급한다. (is)

16 의문사가 없는 의문문의 화법 전환이므로 said to를 asked로 바꾸고, if나 whether로 두 문장을 연결하고 「주어+동사」의 어순으로 바꾼다. 주절의 시제에 맞게 종속절의 시제도 과거로 바꾼다.

17 ⑤ B as well as A는 B에 동사의 수를 일치시킨다. (speak → speaks)
④ family가 가족 구성원 각각을 의미할 때 복수 취급하며 복수 동사를 쓴다.

18 의문사가 있는 의문문의 화법 전환이므로 said to를 asked로 바꾸고, 의문사로 두 문장을 연결하고 「주어+동사」의 어순으로 바꾼다. 주절의 시제가 과거이므로 종속절의 시제도 과거로 바꾼다.

19 ⓐ Both A and B 형태의 주어는 복수 취급하여 복수 동사를 쓴다. (is → are)
ⓒ B as well as A는 B에 동사의 수를 일치시킨다. He가 3인칭 단수이므로 be동사도 3인칭 단수형인 is로 쓴다. (are → is)
ⓓ very는 형용사나 부사의 원급을 수식한다. 비교급을 수식할 수 있는 much/even/still/far/a lot를 써야 한다. (very → much/even/still/far/a lot)

20 명령문의 화법 전환이므로 said to를 told로 바꾸고, 명령문의 동사원형을 to부정사로 바꾼다. 이때 부정 명령문은 don't를 없애고 not[never]+to부정사의 형태로 바꾼다.

21 ① 동사 바로 앞이 복수형 명사(characters)여서 복수형 동사를 써야 할 것 같지만, 주어가 동명사구 (Drawing cartoon characters)이므로 단수 취급한다. (are → is)
②③ 주어가 거리, 금액일 경우 단수 취급한다. (are → is)

22 ① Every는 단수 명사를 수식하며, Every가 포함된 주어도 단수 취급한다. (books → book, have → has)
② 셀 수 있는 명사를 수식하는 all이 포함된 주어는 복수 취급하여 복수 동사를 쓴다. (was → were)
④ most of가 주어에 포함되어 있는 경우 of 뒤에 오는 명사의 수에 동사의 수를 일치시킨다. his paintings는 복수이므로 동사도 복수 동사를 쓴다. (was → were)
⑤ some of가 주어에 포함되어 있는 경우 of 뒤에 오는 명사의 수에 동사의 수를 일치시킨다. water는

셀 수 없는 명사이므로 동사도 단수 동사를 쓴다.
(were → was)

23 의문사가 없는 의문문의 화법 전환이므로 said to를 asked로 바꾸고, if나 whether로 두 문장을 연결하고 「주어+동사」의 어순으로 바꾼다.

24 직접 화법의 전달동사를 advised로 바꾸고 명령문의 Try not to ~는 not to ~로 바꾼다.

25 역사적 사실은 항상 과거시제로 쓴다.

26 ㉡ 주어에 each가 포함되어 있는 경우 단수 취급하여 단수 동사를 쓰는 것이 적절하다. (have → has)
ⓒ 문장의 주어 cracks가 복수이므로 복수 동사를 쓰는 것이 적절하다. a number of는 '다수의'라는 뜻으로 복수 명사와 함께 쓰이며 many로 바꾸어 쓸 수 있다. (has → have)
ⓔ the number of는 '~의 수'라는 뜻으로 뒤에 따라오는 명사에 상관없이 the number에 맞춰 단수 취급을 한다. (have → has)
ⓢ All은 단수 명사와 사용될 경우 단수 동사를 쓴다. (were → was)
ⓞ 분수를 쓸 때는 분자를 기수로, 분모를 서수로 쓰되 분자가 1보다 큰 숫자라면 분모에 s를 붙여 쓴다. (two third → two thirds)
㉠ 일요일이었어서, 대부분의 가게들이 문을 닫았다.
㉡ 각각의 개인은 그들의 관점을 표현할 권리를 가진다.

ⓒ 다수의 얇은 금이 벽에 나타났다.
ⓔ 그저 적은 비율의(소수의) 사람들만이 정치에 관심 있다.
ⓜ 외국인 관광객의 수가 해를 거듭하여 늘어나고 있다.
ⓗ 절반 이상의 학생들이 영어 말하기 대회에 참여할 것이다.
ⓢ 그 레스토랑이 제공한 모든 음식은 신선하고 맛있었다.
ⓞ 세계 인구의 3분의 1이 세계 자원의 3분의 2를 소비한다.

27 명령문의 화법 전환에서 명령문의 동사원형은 to부정사로 바꾼다.

28 either A or B는 위치상 동사와 더 가까이에 있는 B에 동사의 수를 일치시킨다.

29 라. 현재의 습관, 사실, 진리는 항상 현재시제로 쓴다.
마. 역사적 사실은 항상 과거시제로 쓴다.

30 ④ each가 포함된 주어는 단수 취급한다.
⑤ most of가 포함된 주어는 of 뒤에 오는 명사의 수에 동사의 수를 일치시킨다. information은 셀 수 없는 명사이므로 단수 취급한다.
① the+형용사는 '~한 사람들'의 뜻으로 복수 취급한다. (gets → get)
② the number of는 '~의 수'라는 뜻으로 단수 취급한다. (have → has)
③ 학과명(Economics)은 단수 취급한다. (are → is)

CHAPTER 18 특수구문 & 속담
Inversion, Emphasis, Ellipsis & Proverbs

본문 _ p.440

PRACTICE 1

1 There are some reasons
2 has John considered resigning
3 Here are the pepperoni pizzas
4 So are the boys
5 There have been several snowstorms
6 until this morning did I hear
7 There goes the last train
8 Neither do these grapes I bought
9 So do some birds migrating south
10 Here they are

1, 3, 5, 7, 10 「주어+동사」 앞에 there이나 here이 오면 「There/Here+동사+주어」 어순으로 쓴다. 단, 10번처럼 주어가 대명사일 경우에는 주어와 동사의 위치가 바뀌지 않는다.
2, 6 부정어(구)가 문장 맨 앞에 올 때는 「부정어(구)+조동사+주어+동사」 어순으로 쓴다.
4, 8, 9 「So+조동사+주어」, 「Neither+조동사+주어」 어순으로 쓴다.

PRACTICE 2

1 much[far, still, a lot, even] colder
2 did ring
3 didn't show up at all
4 much[far, still, a lot, even] better
5 much[far, still, a lot, even] more expensive

6 the very place

7 much[far, still, a lot, even] more capable

8 much[far, still, a lot, even] hotter

9 did finish

10 was not satisfied, at all

11 much[far, still, a lot, even] better

12 the very cafe

13 much[far, still, a lot, even] easier

14 much[far, still, a lot, even] faster

15 much[far, still, a lot, even] cheaper

> **1, 4, 5, 7, 8, 11, 13, 14, 15** 비교급을 강조할 때는 앞에 much, far, still, a lot, even을 쓰고 '훨씬 더 ~하다'라는 의미가 된다.
> **2, 9** 동사를 강조할 때는 동사 앞에 조동사 do을 쓴다. 이때 동사의 시제가 과거시제이므로 did를 쓴다.
> **3, 10** 부정어를 강조할 때는 at all을 붙이고 '전혀 ~하지 않다'라는 의미가 된다.
> **6, 12** 명사를 강조할 때는 명사 앞에 the very를 쓰고 '바로 그 ~'이라는 의미가 된다.

PRACTICE 3

1 Who was it that threw the ball out of the window?

2 It was a shooting star that you saw last night.

3 It was in Seoul that the meeting was held.

4 When was it that the teacher asked me to come and see him?

5 It was the blind girl that was playing the guitar in the crowd.

6 It was at the Colosseum that many gladiators fought and died.

7 Why is it that some animals hibernate every winter?

8 Where was it that Wonjin's family went last December?

9 It was the raw fish I ate last night that caused my stomachache.

10 Why is it that this restaurant is so crowded every day?

11 It was two minutes ago that the KTX for Busan left Gwangmyeong Station.

12 It was at the park that the Boy Scouts met to do voluntary cleaning work.

13 What is it that the people are looking at under the bridge?

> **1, 4, 7, 8, 10, 13** 의문사를 강조하고자 할 때는 「의문사+is/was it that ~」의 형태로 쓴다.
> *It is/was와 that 사이에 주어, 목적어, 보어, 부사(구) 중 강조하고자 하는 말을 넣어 강조 구문을 만든다
> **2** 목적어(a shooting star)를 It was와 that 사이에 넣어 강조한다.
> **3, 6, 12** 장소를 나타내는 부사구를 It was와 that 사이에 넣어 강조한다.
> **5, 9** 주어를 It was와 that 사이에 넣어 강조한다.
> **11** 때를 나타내는 부사구(two minutes ago)를 It was와 that 사이에 넣어 강조한다.

PRACTICE 4

1 I told him to clean his room, but he refused to clean his room.

2 We all went to Taeho's home and we all had a barbecue in his backyard.

3 My dog is smaller than Scott's dog.

4 Grandpa says he feels much better today than he felt yesterday.

5 Neil has a pair of roller skates that are much better than Mark's roller skates.

6 Isabel tries to get up early, but she can't get up early.

7 Although most passengers survived the accident, some people didn't survive the accident.

8 Oscar brought two fishing rods and Bob brought some bait for the fishing expedition.

9 I wanted to eat Chinese food, but Karen didn't want to eat Chinese food.

10 He started climbing up the steep cliff at one o'clock and he finally reached the top after two hours.

11 This cell phone is a thousand dollars, while that one is only seven hundred dollars.

12 Jude is really good at math, but I'm not really good at math.

13 Some like their eggs scrambled, but others don't like their eggs scrambled.

14 I went to school by bicycle, while Sharon went to school by bus.

PRACTICE 5

1 (they were) **2** (she is) **3** (who were)

4 (that was) **5** (he is) **6** (it was)

7 (who is)　**8** (it is)　**9** (which was)
10 (she was)

> **1, 5, 8, 10** 접속사가 이끄는 부사절에서의 「주어+be동사」는 주절의 주어와 같을 경우 생략할 수 있다.
> **2, 6** 감탄문에서의 「주어+be동사」는 생략해도 의미가 전달되는 경우에 생략할 수 있다.
> **3, 4, 7, 9** 「관계대명사+be동사」 뒤에 분사가 나올 경우 「관계대명사+be동사」는 생략할 수 있다.

PRACTICE 6

1　they were　**2**　which is　**3**　that was
4　that is　**5**　who was　**6**　which is
7　he was　**8**　that is　**9**　they were
10　who were

> **1, 7, 9** 접속사가 이끄는 부사절이 「대명사 주어+be동사」 형태인 경우, 대명사와 be동사의 시제는 주절의 주어와 시제에 일치시켜야 한다.
> **2, 3, 4, 6, 8** 사물 선행사 뒤에 「관계대명사+be동사」가 올 때는 관계대명사로 which나 that을 쓰고, be동사의 수를 선행사의 수에 일치시켜야 한다.
> **5** 사람 선행사 뒤에 「관계대명사+be동사」가 올 때는 관계대명사로 who나 that을 쓰고, be동사의 시제는 주절의 시제에 따라 달라진다. 주절의 동사가 was로 과거시제이므로, 관계대명사절의 동사로 현재형(is)을 사용할 수 없다.
> **10** 사람 선행사 뒤에 「관계대명사+be동사」가 올 때는 관계대명사로 who나 that을 쓰고, be동사의 수를 선행사의 수에 일치시켜야 한다.

PRACTICE 7

1　③　**2**　⑥　**3**　⑤　**4**　②　**5**　⑨
6　⑩　**7**　④　**8**　⑧　**9**　⑦　**10**　①

PRACTICE 8

1　no place like home
2　is known by the company he keeps
3　Birds of a feather　**4**　Slow and steady
5　in other people's shoes
6　rains but it pours　**7**　Well begun
8　What goes around
9　A burnt child
10　runs after two hares will catch neither

📋 중간·기말고사 대비문제 정답　본문 _ p.452

1 ①　**2** ②　**3** I was　**4** ⑤　**5** the very　**6** ④
7 at all　**8** ①,⑤　**9** (1) She did finish her final

report before the due date. (2) It was in the park that[where] I saw Tom running last night.
10 ③　**11** ④　**12** ③　**13** ⑤　**14** she was
15 ③　**16** ②　**17** ④　**18** ③　**19** ②,⑤
20 Neither do　**21** what she wrote is → is what she wrote　**22** ②　**23** is it → it is　**24** ③
25 ①　**26** did I tell

중간·기말고사 대비문제 해설

1　「So+조동사+주어」를 써서 앞에 나온 긍정문의 내용에 동의할 수 있다.

2　「Neither+조동사+주어」를 써서 앞에 나온 부정문의 내용에 동의할 수 있다.

3　접속사가 이끄는 부사절에서의 「주어+be동사」는 주절의 주어와 같을 경우 생략할 수 있다. 주어는 주절의 주어와 같은 I로 쓰고, be동사는 주절의 시제가 과거이므로 과거형 단수 동사로 쓴다.

4　⑤ 동사를 강조할 때는 「조동사 do+동사원형」을 사용한다. 과거를 나타내는 부사구(two years ago)가 있으므로 과거형인 「did+동사원형」으로 써야 한다. (did taught → did teach)

5　the very를 써서 명사를 강조한다.

6　④ '훨씬' (비교급 강조)　①②③⑤ '많이'

7　at all을 써서 부정어를 강조한다.

8　비교급 강조 - much, far, still, a lot, even

9　(1) 동사의 강조는 조동사 do로 한다. 시제가 과거이므로 did로 쓴다. 뒤에는 동사원형을 쓴다.
　　(2) 부사구의 강조는 「It is/was ~ that…」으로 한다. 강조하는 것이 장소일 때 that 대신에 where을 쓸 수 있다.

10　새해 계획을 지나치게 많이 세워놓은 지호에게 민지가 해 줄 수 있는 말로는 '말하기는 쉽고 행동은 어렵다.'는 뜻의 It is easier said than done.이 적절하다.

11　ⓒⓓⓔ 「It is/was ~ that…」 강조구문
　　ⓐⓑ 가주어-진주어

12　의문사를 강조하고자 할 때는 「의문사+is/was it that ~」의 형태로 쓴다.

13　「It ~ that…」 강조구문은 It is/was와 that을 생략하고 강조된 내용을 that절 뒤로 옮기면 완전한 문장이 되는 특성이 있다. ⑤번의 경우 강조된 내용인 me를 that절 뒤로 옮기면 'Me borrowed a book from the library.'가 되고, 주어 자리에 목적격 대명사가 들

어가게 되므로 틀린 문장이다. (me → I)

14 접속사가 이끄는 부사절에서의 「주어+be동사」는 주절의 주어와 같을 경우 생략할 수 있다.

15 ⓐ 불가능한 것들을 상상하거나 꿈꾸다
ⓑ 스스로 같은 잘못을 가지고 있으면서 다른 사람들의 잘못을 지적하다 (The pot calls the kettle black.)
ⓒ 어떤 것이 쉽다고 말하지만 실제로는 하기 어렵다
ⓓ 한 번의 노력으로 동시에 두 가지 일을 하다
ⓔ 다른 사람들은 그것을 싫어하는 반면 그것을 좋다고 여기다
① 공중누각(허황된 생각)
② 말하기는 쉽고 행동은 어렵다
③ 로마는 하루 아침에 지어지지 않았다.
④ 한 개의 돌멩이로 두 마리의 새를 죽인다. (일석이조)
⑤ 어떤 사람의 음식이 다른 사람에게는 독이 된다.

16 ⓑ 접속사가 이끄는 부사절에서 「주어+be동사」는 주절의 주어와 같을 경우 생략할 수 있다.
ⓒ 「관계대명사+be동사」 뒤에 분사가 나올 경우 「관계대명사+be동사」는 생략할 수 있다.

17 ⓒ be likely to + 동사원형 '~할 가능성이 높다'
(achieving → achieve)
ⓓ 간접의문문은 '의문사+주어+동사'의 어순으로 쓴다. (who are you → who you are)
ⓔ Not only가 문장 앞으로 온 도치 문장이므로 '부정어+조동사+주어+동사'의 어순이 되어야 한다.
(Not only you will start ~ → Not only will you start ~)

"당신의 친구들을 나에게 보여줘라, 그러면 내가 당신의 미래를 보여주겠다.(친구를 보면 그 사람을 알 수 있다)"라는 속담을 들어 본 적이 있을 것이다. 그것은 당신의 주변에 있는 사람들이 당신의 인생에 깊은 영향을 줄 수 있다는 것을 의미한다. 당신 스스로를 당신이 성공하기를 바라는 긍정적이고, (당신을) 지지하는 사람들로 단단히 둘러싸는 것이 중요하다. 만약 당신이 스스로를 의욕이 넘치고 야망 있는 사람들로 둘러싼다면, 당신은 당신의 목표를 이룰 가능성이 높다. 당신이 대부분의 시간을 함께 보내는 사람들이 당신이 누구인지를 결정할 것이다. 당신은 그들처럼 생각하기 시작할 뿐만 아니라, 당신의 생각과 행동 또한 그들의 것을 비출 것이다.

18 서두르지 말고 천천히 매일매일 공부하면 좋은 성적을 얻을 수 있다는 내용이므로 '천천히 그리고 꾸준히 하면 이긴다.'라는 뜻의 Slow and steady wins the race.가 적절하다.
① 끝난 일은 끝난 일이다.
② 배움에는 절대 늦음이 없다.
④ 물고기에게 수영 가르치기 (공자 앞에서 문자 쓴다.)
⑤ 자기를 아는 사람만이 남을 안다.

19 ① 부정어의 도치는 「부정어+조동사+주어+동사」의 어순으로 써준다. 이때의 동사는 동사원형이다. (expected → expect)
③ 주어 the children이 복수이므로 동사도 복수형으로 수일치시킨다. (comes → come)
④ 부정어의 도치는 「부정어+조동사+주어+동사」의 어순으로 써준다.
(Never he visits → Never does he visit)

20 부정적인 내용에 동의하는 표현은 부정문의 끝에 either를 붙여서 표현하거나, 「Neither+조동사+주어」의 어순으로 나타낼 수 있다.

21 「Here+동사+주어」

22 ② 부정어가 문장의 앞으로 나오면 조동사가 주어의 앞으로 온다. (he has → has he)

23 주어가 대명사일 경우에는 도치되지 않고 「Here+주어+동사」의 어순으로 쓴다.

24 ⓑ It ~ that… 강조구문에서 강조하는 대상인 the haunted house는 원래 문장에서 주어 역할을 하므로 that절의 it은 삭제한다. (that절의 it 삭제)
ⓓ 계속적 용법의 관계대명사 which는 that으로 바꾸어 쓸 수 없다. (that → which)
ⓔ It ~ that… 강조구문에서 강조하는 대상인 Jake가 이미 that 앞에 나타나 있으므로 that 이후의 절에서 him은 불필요하다. (him 삭제)
ⓕ 계속적 용법으로 쓰인 주격 관계대명사 which가 이끄는 절은 불완전해야 한다. (it 삭제)

25 Suzy는 I의 기분을 생각하지 않고 큰 소리로 많은 사람들 앞에서 I를 당황하게 만들었으므로 '다른 사람의 입장이 되어 보아라.'는 뜻의 Put yourself in other people's shoes.가 적절하다.
② 비 오는 날을 위해 무엇인가를 저축하라.
③ 아이 많은 집에 휴식이란 없다.
④ 불에 덴 아이는 불을 무서워한다.
⑤ 진주를 찾으려는 사람은 물 속 깊이 들어가야 한다.

26 부정어가 문장 앞으로 나오면 「부정어+조동사+주어+동사」의 어순으로 써준다.

2026 새 교과서에 맞춘 16차 개정판

중학영문법 3800제 3학년

단어·표현 암기장

MOTHERTONGUE
마더텅출판사
since 1999.4.1.

중학영문법 3800제 단어·표현 암기장 활용법

1 중학영문법 3800제 단어·표현 암기장은 한 달 학습 계획(총 31일)으로 구성되어 있습니다.

2 오늘 외울 단어를 원어민 녹음 MP3파일을 활용하여 암기합니다.

3 세트로 구성된 Word Test를 스스로 또는 선생님과 함께 풀어 본 후 단어·표현 암기장을 확인하며 채점합니다. (정답표가 필요하신 경우 마더텅 홈페이지를 통해 다운로드 받으실 수 있습니다. www.toptutor.co.kr)

4 [오늘 외울 단어]로 제공되는 단어들은 3800제 본문에서 선정된 중학 필수 영단어입니다. 빈출 단어의 경우 반복적으로 제시하여 복습이 가능하도록 하였습니다.

5 교재와 함께 시작하여 매일의 학습 단어를 암기해 나가면, 한 달(31일)이면 3800제 주요 단어를 모두 학습할 수 있습니다.

중학영문법 3800제 3학년

단어·표현 암기장

Problem Solving Skill

MOTHERTONGUE
마더텅출판사
since1999.4.1.

Chapter 1 문장의 기초

👤 PSS & PRACTICE

001 **understanding** [ʌ̀ndərstǽndiŋ]	형 이해심 있는 명 이해	
002 **symphony** [símfəni]	명 교향곡	
003 **principal** [prínsəpəl]	명 우두머리, 장, 교장	
004 **environment** [inváirənmənt]	명 환경	
005 **biology** [baiálədʒi]	명 생물학	
006 **tragic** [trǽdʒik]	형 비극적인	
007 **suppose** [səpóuz]	동 가정하다, 〜이라고 하다	
008 **agent** [éidʒənt]	명 대리인, 요원	
009 **can afford to**	〜할 여유가 있다	
010 **cartoon** [kɑːrtúːn]	명 시사 풍자 만화	
011 **audience** [ɔ́ːdiəns]	명 청중, 관객	
012 **make a reservation**	예약하다	
013 **remain** [riméin]	동 〜인 채로 있다, 남다	
014 **patient** [péiʃənt]	형 참을성이 있는	
015 **instead of**	〜대신에	
016 **fit** [fit]	형 몸 상태가 좋은, 적합한	

017 **absolutely** [ǽbsəlúːtli]	부 절대적으로	
018 **brilliant** [bríliənt]	형 명석한, 빛나는	
019 **performance** [pərfɔ́ːrməns]	명 공연	
020 **language** [lǽŋgwidʒ]	명 언어	
021 **thigh** [θai]	명 넓적다리	
022 **refrigerator** [rifrídʒərèitər]	명 냉장고	
023 **pale** [peil]	형 창백한	
024 **tremble** [trémbl]	동 떨다	
025 **run away**	도망가다	
026 **smooth** [smuːð]	형 부드러운	
027 **puzzled** [pʌ́zld]	형 당혹스러운	
028 **fence** [fens]	명 울타리, 담	
029 **energetic** [ènərdʒétik]	형 활기 있는	
030 **guilty** [gílti]	형 유죄의, 양심의 가책을 느끼는	
031 **appear** [əpíər]	동 〜처럼 보이다	
032 **stingy** [stíndʒi]	형 인색한	
033 **prevent** [privént]	동 막다, 방해하다	
034 **newborn** [njúːbɔ́ːrn]	형 갓 태어난	

☐ 035 **supply** [səplái] 통 공급하다

☐ 036 **victim** [víktim] 명 희생자

☐ 037 **costume** [kástjuːm] 명 복장, 의상

☐ 038 **injury** [índʒəri] 명 부상

☐ 039 **statue** [stǽtʃuː] 명 조각상

☐ 040 **suitcase** [súːtkèis] 명 여행 가방

☐ 041 **dishwasher** [díʃwàʃər] 명 식기세척기

☐ 042 **strength** [streŋθ] 명 힘

☐ 043 **instructor** [instrʌ́ktər] 명 강사

☐ 044 **snowboard** [snóubɔ̀ːrd] 통 스노보드를 타다 / 명 스노보드

☐ 045 **elect** [ilékt] 통 선출하다

☐ 046 **encourage** [inkə́ːridʒ] 통 용기를 북돋워주다, 격려하다

☐ 047 **participate** [paːrtísəpèit] 통 참가하다

☐ 048 **confess** [kənfés] 통 자백하다, 고백하다

☐ 049 **temperature** [témpərətʃər] 명 온도

☐ 050 **haunted** [hɔ́ːntid] 형 유령이 나오는

☐ 051 **stain** [stein] 명 얼룩, 때

☐ 052 **chore** [tʃɔːr] 명 허드렛일

☐ 053 **punish** [pʌ́niʃ] 통 벌주다

🚶 중간기말대비

☐ 054 **conversation** [kànvərséiʃən] 명 회화, 대화

☐ 055 **complete** [kəmplíːt] 통 완료하다, 끝마치다

☐ 056 **project** [prádʒekt] 명 계획, 기획

☐ 057 **training** [tréiniŋ] 명 훈련, 현장 교육

☐ 058 **symptom** [símptəm] 명 징후, 증상

☐ 059 **designer** [dizáinər] 명 디자이너, 설계자

☐ 060 **existence** [igzístəns] 명 존재, 생활

☐ 061 **concentrate** [kánsəntrèit] 통 집중시키다, 집중하다

☐ 062 **recover** [rikʌ́vər] 통 되찾다, 회복하다

☐ 063 **disease** [dizíːz] 명 병, 질환

☐ 064 **human being** [hjúːmən bíːiŋ] 명 인간, 사람

☐ 065 **flight attendant** [fláit ətèndənt] 명 비행기 승무원

☐ 066 **appeal** [əpíːl] 통 간청하다, 호소하다

☐ 067 **miracle** [mírəkl] 명 기적

☐ 068 **stream** [striːm] 명 시내, 개울

☐ 069 **diskette** [dísket] 명 디스켓, 플로피 디스크

□ 070 **lava** [láːvə]	명 용암	□ 086 **arrange** [əréindʒ]	통 정돈하다, 마련하다
□ 071 **volcano** [vɑlkéinou]	명 화산	□ 087 **breathe** [briːð]	통 숨을 쉬다
□ 072 **allow** [əláu]	통 허용하다, 허락하다	□ 088 **classify** [klǽsəfài]	통 분류하다
□ 073 **get out of**	벗어나다	□ 089 **spray** [sprei]	통 뿌리다
□ 074 **provide ~ with …**	~에게 …을 제공하다	□ 090 **survey** [sərvéi]	통 조사하다
□ 075 **gesture** [dʒéstʃər]	명 제스처, 몸짓	□ 091 **grab** [græb]	통 움켜쥐다, 잡아채다
□ 076 **correctly** [kəréktli]	부 올바르게, 정확하게	□ 092 **clap** [klæp]	통 손뼉을 치다
□ 077 **find out**	발견하다, 생각해 내다	□ 093 **commit** [kəmít]	통 범하다, 위탁하다
□ 078 **improve** [imprúːv]	통 향상시키다, 개선하다	□ 094 **refer** [rifə́ːr]	통 ~의 탓으로 하다, 언급하다
□ 079 **alarming** [əláːrmiŋ]	형 놀라운, 걱정스러운	□ 095 **bow** [bau]	통 머리를 숙이다, 절하다
□ 080 **beggar** [bégər]	명 거지, 걸인	□ 096 **accomplish** [əkámpliʃ]	통 성취하다
□ 081 **conduct** [kándʌkt]	통 실시하다, 수행하다	□ 097 **affect** [əfékt]	통 영향을 미치다
□ 082 **clone** [kloun]	통 복제하다	□ 098 **declare** [diklέər]	통 선언하다, 공표하다
□ 083 **Belgium** [béldʒəm]	명 벨기에 (나라 이름)	□ 099 **aim** [eim]	통 겨누다, 목표로 삼다
□ 084 **be in trouble**	곤경에 처하다	□ 100 **scratch** [skrætʃ]	통 긁다
		□ 101 **destroy** [distrɔ́i]	통 파괴하다
		□ 102 **soak** [souk]	통 담그다, 흠뻑 적시다

Chapter 2 시제

👤 **PSS & PRACTICE**

| □ 085 **maintain** [meintéin] | 통 유지하다 | □ 103 **appoint** [əpɔ́int] | 통 임명하다 |

Day 04

- ☐ 104 **tap** [tæp] 〔통〕 가볍게 두드리다
- ☐ 105 **attempt** [ətémpt] 〔통〕 시도하다
- ☐ 106 **dispatch** [dispǽtʃ] 〔통〕 발송하다
- ☐ 107 **display** [displéi] 〔통〕 보여주다, 전시하다
- ☐ 108 **disturb** [distə́:rb] 〔통〕 방해하다
- ☐ 109 **accept** [əksépt] 〔통〕 받아들이다
- ☐ 110 **dye** [dai] 〔통〕 물들이다, 염색하다
- ☐ 111 **buzz** [bʌz] 〔통〕 윙윙거리다
- ☐ 112 **challenge** [tʃǽlindʒ] 〔통〕 도전하다 〔명〕 도전
- ☐ 113 **amount** [əmáunt] 〔통〕 ~에 달하다[이르다] 〔명〕 양
- ☐ 114 **defeat** [difí:t] 〔통〕 패배시키다 〔명〕 패배
- ☐ 115 **cherish** [tʃériʃ] 〔통〕 소중히 여기다
- ☐ 116 **demand** [dimǽnd] 〔통〕 요구하다
- ☐ 117 **assign** [əsáin] 〔통〕 할당하다, 배정하다
- ☐ 118 **reunify** [ri:júːnəfài] 〔통〕 재통합하다
- ☐ 119 **snap** [snæp] 〔통〕 낚아채다
- ☐ 120 **focus** [fóukəs] 〔통〕 초점을 맞추다 〔명〕 초점
- ☐ 121 **enroll** [inróul] 〔통〕 등록하다
- ☐ 122 **complain** [kəmpléin] 〔통〕 불평하다
- ☐ 123 **attract** [ətrǽkt] 〔통〕 끌다, 유인하다
- ☐ 124 **connect** [kənékt] 〔통〕 결합시키다, 연결시키다
- ☐ 125 **hum** [hʌm] 〔통〕 콧노래를 부르다, 흥얼거리다
- ☐ 126 **establish** [istǽbliʃ] 〔통〕 설립하다
- ☐ 127 **inherit** [inhérit] 〔통〕 상속하다, 물려받다
- ☐ 128 **gasp** [gæsp] 〔통〕 헐떡거리다, 숨이 막히다
- ☐ 129 **curl** [kə:rl] 〔통〕 곱슬곱슬하게 하다 〔명〕 (머리의) 컬
- ☐ 130 **crawl** [krɔ:l] 〔통〕 기다, 기어가다
- ☐ 131 **regard** [rigá:rd] 〔통〕 ~로 평가하다[여기다]
- ☐ 132 **stir** [stə:r] 〔통〕 휘젓다, 뒤섞다
- ☐ 133 **conquer** [káŋkər] 〔통〕 정복하다
- ☐ 134 **rip** [rip] 〔통〕 찢다
- ☐ 135 **perch** [pə:rtʃ] 〔통〕 앉다, 자리잡다
- ☐ 136 **refund** [ri:fʌ́nd] 〔통〕 환불하다
- ☐ 137 **permit** [pərmít] 〔통〕 허락하다, 허가하다
- ☐ 138 **sniff** [snif] 〔통〕 코를 훌쩍이다
- ☐ 139 **publish** [pʌ́bliʃ] 〔통〕 발행하다, 출판하다

☐ 140 **wound** [wu:nd]	통 상처 입히다 명 상처, 부상	
☐ 141 **regret** [rigrét]	통 후회하다	
☐ 142 **convert** [kənvə́:rt]	통 전환시키다	
☐ 143 **reward** [riwɔ́:rd]	통 보답하다, 상을 주다 명 보수, 보상	
☐ 144 **embarrass** [imbǽrəs]	통 난처하게 하다	
☐ 145 **approve** [əprú:v]	통 찬성하다, 승인하다	
☐ 146 **survive** [sərváiv]	통 살아남다	
☐ 147 **stretch** [stretʃ]	통 펴다, 뻗다	
☐ 148 **fulfill** [fulfíl]	통 이행하다, 완수하다	
☐ 149 **refill** [ri:fíl]	통 다시 채우다, 보충하다	
☐ 150 **object** [ɔ́bdʒekt]	통 반대하다 명 물체, 대상	
☐ 151 **nod** [nɑd]	통 끄덕이다	
☐ 152 **scrape** [skreip]	통 긁다	
☐ 153 **furnish** [fə́:rniʃ]	통 공급하다, 제공하다	
☐ 154 **intend** [inténd]	통 의도하다	
☐ 155 **contact** [kɔ́ntækt]	통 접촉시키다 명 접촉, 교제	
☐ 156 **leap** [li:p]	통 뛰어오르다, 도약하다	
☐ 157 **polish** [pɔ́liʃ]	통 닦다, 광을 내다	

☐ 158 **enable** [inéibl]	통 (사람에게) ~을 가능하게 하다
☐ 159 **pronounce** [prənáuns]	통 발음하다
☐ 160 **explode** [iksplóud]	통 폭발하다, 파열하다
☐ 161 **arise** [əráiz]	통 발생하다, 일어나다
☐ 162 **bet** [bet]	통 돈을 걸다, 내기를 하다
☐ 163 **burst** [bə:rst]	통 폭발하다, 파열하다
☐ 164 **creep** [kri:p]	통 기어가다
☐ 165 **deal** [di:l]	통 다루다, 처리하다
☐ 166 **forgive** [fərgív]	통 용서하다
☐ 167 **freeze** [fri:z]	통 얼다, 얼어붙다
☐ 168 **grind** [graind]	통 갈다
☐ 169 **kneel** [ni:l]	통 무릎을 꿇다
☐ 170 **overcome** [òuvərkʌ́m]	통 극복하다
☐ 171 **sew** [sou]	통 꿰매다
☐ 172 **shrink** [ʃriŋk]	통 줄다, 수축하다
☐ 173 **sweep** [swi:p]	통 쓸다, 털다
☐ 174 **swing** [swiŋ]	통 흔들어 움직이다, 휘두르다
☐ 175 **weave** [wi:v]	통 짜다, 엮다

Day 06

- ☐ 176 **psychology** [saikálədʒi] — 명 심리학
- ☐ 177 **compose** [kəmpóuz] — 동 작곡하다, 구성하다
- ☐ 178 **nursing home** [nə́:rsiŋ hòum] — 명 요양원
- ☐ 179 **diplomat** [dípləmæ̀t] — 명 외교관
- ☐ 180 **temple** [témpl] — 명 사원
- ☐ 181 **lately** [léitli] — 부 최근에
- ☐ 182 **knit** [nit] — 동 짜다, 뜨다
- ☐ 183 **emigrate** [émigrèit] — 동 이주하다, 이민가다
- ☐ 184 **stadium** [stéidiəm] — 명 경기장
- ☐ 185 **suddenly** [sʌ́dnli] — 부 갑자기
- ☐ 186 **chef** [ʃef] — 명 주방장, 요리사
- ☐ 187 **show up** — 나타나다
- ☐ 188 **fairy tale** [fɛ́əri teil] — 명 동화
- ☐ 189 **pile up** — 쌓다, 축적하다

👤 중간기말대비

- ☐ 190 **dig** [dig] — 동 파다, 파내다
- ☐ 191 **major** [méidʒər] — 동 전공하다 명 전공
- ☐ 192 **issue** [íʃu:] — 명 주제, 문제

- ☐ 193 **cigarette** [sìgərét] — 명 담배
- ☐ 194 **authority** [əθɔ́:rəti] — 명 당국, 권한, 권위
- ☐ 195 **forbid** [fərbíd] — 동 금지하다, 금하다
- ☐ 196 **gambling** [gǽmbliŋ] — 명 도박, 노름
- ☐ 197 **take care of** — ～을 돌보다, ～을 맡다
- ☐ 198 **orphanage** [ɔ́:rfənidʒ] — 명 고아원
- ☐ 199 **frozen** [fróuzən] — 형 동결된, 냉담한
- ☐ 200 **misunderstand** [mìsʌndərstǽnd] — 동 오해하다
- ☐ 201 **rotten** [rátn] — 형 썩은, 부패한
- ☐ 202 **admire** [ədmáiər] — 동 존경하다, 감탄하다
- ☐ 203 **manufacture** [mæ̀njufǽktʃər] — 동 제조하다, 생산하다 명 제조, 생산
- ☐ 204 **automobile** [ɔ̀:təməbí:l] — 명 자동차
- ☐ 205 **diabetes** [dàiəbí:ti:z] — 명 당뇨병
- ☐ 206 **consider** [kənsídər] — 동 고려하다, 생각하다
- ☐ 207 **retirement** [ritáiərmənt] — 명 은퇴

Chapter 3 조동사

👤 PSS & PRACTICE

- ☐ 208 **warm-hearted** [wɔ́:rmhá:rtid] — 형 마음씨가 따뜻한

Day 07

☐ 209 **fluently** [flú:əntli] 　부 유창하게

☐ 210 **disappear** [dìsəpíər] 　동 사라지다

☐ 211 **handkerchief** [hǽŋkərtʃif] 　명 손수건

☐ 212 **quality** [kwɔ́ləti] 　명 질, 품질

☐ 213 **presentation** [prèzəntéiʃən] 　명 발표

☐ 214 **appreciate** [əpríːʃièit] 　동 고맙게 생각하다, ～의 진가를 알다

☐ 215 **innocent** [ínəsnt] 　형 결백한, 순결한

☐ 216 **genetic** [dʒənétik] 　형 유전의

☐ 217 **exhausted** [igzɔ́:stid] 　형 지친

☐ 218 **illegal** [ilíːgəl] 　형 불법의

☐ 219 **decision** [disíʒən] 　명 결정

☐ 220 **separately** [sépərətli] 　부 따로따로, 떨어져서

☐ 221 **exchange** [ikstʃéindʒ] 　동 교환하다

☐ 222 **embassy** [émbəsi] 　명 대사관(저)

☐ 223 **bake** [beik] 　동 (빵 등을) 굽다

☐ 224 **cut down on** 　～을 줄이다

☐ 225 **cancel** [kǽnsl] 　동 취소하다

☐ 226 **overeat** [òuvərí:t] 　동 과식하다

☐ 227 **flow** [flou] 　동 흐르다

☐ 228 **experiment** [ikspérəmənt] 　동 실험하다　명 실험

☐ 229 **lab** [læb] 　명 실험실

☐ 230 **hide-and-seek** [háidænsíːk] 　명 숨바꼭질

☐ 231 **defend** [difénd] 　동 방어하다

☐ 232 **scold** [skould] 　동 꾸짖다

☐ 233 **stay up** 　깨어 있다

☐ 234 **appointment** [əpɔ́intmənt] 　명 약속

☐ 235 **cautious** [kɔ́:ʃəs] 　형 조심성 있는, 주의 깊은

👤 중간기말대비

☐ 236 **silly** [síli] 　형 어리석은, 바보같은

☐ 237 **crop** [krap] 　명 농작물

☐ 238 **uncertain** [ʌnsə́:rtn] 　형 불확실한

☐ 239 **musical instrument** [mjúːzikəl ínstrəmənt] 　명 악기

☐ 240 **shelter** [ʃéltər] 　명 보호, 대피소

☐ 241 **survive** [sərváiv] 　동 살아남다

☐ 242 **especially** [ispéʃəli] 　부 특히, 더욱

☐ 243 **destination** [dèstənéiʃən] 　명 목적지

☐ 244 **lifetime**
[láiftàim]
명 일생, 생애

☐ 245 **favor**
[féivər]
명 호의

☐ 246 **delay**
[diléi]
동 지연시키다, 연기하다

☐ 247 **increase**
[inkríːs]
동 늘리다

☐ 248 **concentration**
[kànsəntréiʃən]
명 집중, 전념

☐ 249 **nutrition**
[njuːtríʃən]
명 영양물, 영양

☐ 250 **rescue**
[réskjuː]
동 구조하다

☐ 251 **achievement**
[ətʃíːvmənt]
명 성취, 업적

☐ 252 **rude**
[ruːd]
형 무례한

☐ 253 **be in good shape**
(신체적으로) 건강하다

Chapter 4 수동태

👤 **PSS & PRACTICE**

☐ 254 **spring**
[spriŋ]
명 샘

☐ 255 **proposal**
[prəpóuzəl]
명 제안

☐ 256 **in advance**
미리

☐ 257 **deadline**
[dédlàin]
명 최종 기한, 마감 시간

☐ 258 **concept**
[kánsept]
명 개념, 발상

☐ 259 **perform**
[pərfɔ́ːrm]
동 공연하다, 수행하다

☐ 260 **cottage**
[kátidʒ]
명 오두막집

☐ 261 **incident**
[ínsidənt]
명 사건

☐ 262 **politician**
[pàlətíʃən]
명 정치인

☐ 263 **portrait**
[pɔ́ːrtrit]
명 초상화

☐ 264 **cheat**
[tʃiːt]
동 속이다, (시험에서) 부정행위를 하다

☐ 265 **graduation**
[grædʒuéiʃən]
명 졸업

☐ 266 **preserve**
[prizə́ːrv]
동 보호하다, 보존하다

☐ 267 **endanger**
[indéindʒər]
동 위험에 빠뜨리다

☐ 268 **kindergarten**
[kíndərgàːrtn]
명 유치원

☐ 269 **volunteer**
[vàləntíər]
명 자원 봉사자
동 자진해서 하다

☐ 270 **servant**
[sə́ːrvənt]
명 하인

☐ 271 **cruelly**
[krúəli]
부 잔인하게

☐ 272 **life vest**
[láif vèst]
명 구명조끼

☐ 273 **internship**
[íntəːrnʃip]
명 인턴쉽, 실무수습

☐ 274 **announcement**
[ənáunsmənt]
명 발표, 공고

☐ 275 **prosecutor**
[prásikjùːtər]
명 (법조계) 검사

☐ 276 **suspect**
[sʌ́spekt]
명 용의자

☐ 277 **fraud**
[frɔːd]
명 사기, 속임

Day 09

☐ 278 **editor** [éditər] 몡 편집자

☐ 279 **slightly** [sláitli] 튀 약간, 조금

☐ 280 **folk dance** [fóuk dǽns] 몡 민속 무용

☐ 281 **catch up with** ~을 따라잡다

☐ 282 **make use of** ~을 이용하다

☐ 283 **look down on** ~을 깔보다, 경멸하다

☐ 284 **indeed** [indí:d] 튀 실로, 정말로

☐ 285 **examination** [igzæmənéiʃən] 몡 시험, 검사

☐ 286 **honeymoon** [hʌ́nimù:n] 몡 신혼 여행

☐ 287 **awesome** [ɔ́:səm] 혱 멋있는, 최고의

☐ 288 **routine** [ru:tí:n] 몡 판에 박힌 일, 일과

☐ 289 **religion** [rilídʒən] 몡 종교

☐ 290 **violence** [váiələns] 몡 폭력

☐ 291 **hand in** 제출하다

☐ 292 **behavior** [bihéivjər] 몡 행동, 행위

☐ 293 **lengthy** [léŋθi] 혱 장황한, 지루하게 긴

☐ 294 **salesman** [séilzmən] 몡 판매원

☐ 295 **rate** [reit] 몡 비율

☐ 296 **sigh** [sai] 몡 한숨 통 한숨 쉬다

☐ 297 **throughout** [θru:áut] 전 ~동안 내내

☐ 298 **ceremony** [sérəmòuni] 몡 의식, 예식

☐ 299 **expense** [ikspéns] 몡 비용

중간기말대비

☐ 300 **melt** [melt] 통 녹이다, 녹다

☐ 301 **polar** [póulər] 혱 극지방의

☐ 302 **region** [rí:dʒən] 몡 지대, 지방, 지역

☐ 303 **smoke** [smouk] 통 담배를 피우다

☐ 304 **tourism** [túərizəm] 몡 관광, 관광 여행

☐ 305 **record** [rikɔ́:rd] 통 녹음하다, 기록하다

☐ 306 **post** [poust] 통 게시하다, 올리다

☐ 307 **software** [sɔ́:ftwὲər] 몡 소프트웨어, 프로그램

☐ 308 **prepare** [pripέər] 통 준비하다, 대비하다

☐ 309 **award** [əwɔ́:rd] 통 수여하다

☐ 310 **coach** [koutʃ] 몡 (스포츠 팀의) 코치

☐ 311 **offer** [ɔ́:fər] 통 제공하다, 제안하다

☐ 312 **scholarship** [skɑ́lərʃip] 몡 장학금

Day 10

□ ³¹³ **semester** [siméstər] 명 학기

□ ³¹⁴ **employee** [implɔiíː] 명 종업원, 피고용인

□ ³¹⁵ **present** [prizént] 통 선사하다, 증정하다

□ ³¹⁶ **direction** [dirékʃən] 명 방향

□ ³¹⁷ **enormous** [inɔ́ːrməs] 형 거대한

□ ³¹⁸ **wage** [weidʒ] 명 임금, 급료

□ ³¹⁹ **witness** [wítnis] 명 목격자

□ ³²⁰ **demonstrator** [démənstrèitər] 명 시위 참가자, 논증자

□ ³²¹ **essential** [isénʃəl] 형 본질적인, 필수적인

□ ³²² **human rights** [hjúːmən ráits] 명 인권

□ ³²³ **committee** [kəmíti] 명 위원회

□ ³²⁴ **sightseeing** [sáitsìːiŋ] 명 관광, 유람

□ ³²⁵ **interrupt** [ìntərʌ́pt] 통 가로막다, 중단시키다

□ ³²⁶ **flour** [flauər] 명 밀가루

Chapter 5 명사와 관사

PSS & PRACTICE

□ ³²⁷ **peak** [piːk] 명 산꼭대기, 절정, 최고점

□ ³²⁸ **souvenir** [sùːvəníər] 명 기념품

□ ³²⁹ **dinosaur** [dáinəsɔ̀ːr] 명 공룡

□ ³³⁰ **astronaut** [ǽstrənɔ̀ːt] 명 우주비행사

□ ³³¹ **crab** [kræb] 명 게

□ ³³² **branch** [bræntʃ] 명 가지, 지점, 지사

□ ³³³ **dynasty** [dáinəsti] 명 왕조

□ ³³⁴ **therapy** [θérəpi] 명 치료

□ ³³⁵ **straw** [strɔː] 명 짚, 밀짚, 빨대

□ ³³⁶ **calendar** [kǽləndər] 명 달력

□ ³³⁷ **maze** [meiz] 명 미궁, 미로

□ ³³⁸ **tomb** [tuːm] 명 무덤, 묘비

□ ³³⁹ **bunch** [bʌntʃ] 명 다발, 무리

□ ³⁴⁰ **radish** [rǽdiʃ] 명 무

□ ³⁴¹ **troop** [truːp] 명 무리, 떼

□ ³⁴² **principle** [prínsəpl] 명 원리, 원칙

□ ³⁴³ **bush** [buʃ] 명 관목, 덤불

□ ³⁴⁴ **client** [klaiənt] 명 고객

□ ³⁴⁵ **factor** [fǽktər] 명 요인, 요소

□ ³⁴⁶ **janitor** [dʒǽnətər] 명 수위, 관리인

☐ 347 **column** [káləm]	명 기둥, 칼럼	
☐ 348 **echo** [ékou]	명 메아리	
☐ 349 **mosquito** [məskí:tou]	명 모기	
☐ 350 **calf** [kæf]	명 송아지	
☐ 351 **belief** [bilí:f]	명 믿음, 신념	
☐ 352 **cliff** [klif]	명 벼랑, 절벽	
☐ 353 **basis** [béisis]	명 기초, 토대	
☐ 354 **weed** [wi:d]	명 잡초	
☐ 355 **apron** [éiprən]	명 앞치마	
☐ 356 **canary** [kənéri]	명 (조류) 카나리아	
☐ 357 **character** [kǽriktər]	명 성격, 특징	
☐ 358 **receipt** [risí:t]	명 영수증	
☐ 359 **assistant** [əsístənt]	명 조수, 보조원	
☐ 360 **enemy** [énəmi]	명 적	
☐ 361 **witch** [witʃ]	명 마녀	
☐ 362 **railway** [réilwèi]	명 철도	
☐ 363 **architect** [á:rkitèkt]	명 건축가	
☐ 364 **method** [méθəd]	명 방법	

☐ 365 **harbor** [há:rbər]	명 항구, 항만	
☐ 366 **chimney** [tʃímni]	명 굴뚝	
☐ 367 **reef** [ri:f]	명 암초	
☐ 368 **tailor** [téilər]	명 재봉사, 재단사	
☐ 369 **satellite** [sǽtəlàit]	명 위성	
☐ 370 **instrument** [ínstrəmənt]	명 기구, 도구	
☐ 371 **passer-by** [pǽsərbái]	명 통행인	
☐ 372 **mother-to-be** [mʌðərtəbì:]	명 임부	
☐ 373 **commander in chief** [kəmǽndər in tʃí:f]	명 최고 사령관	
☐ 374 **bystander** [báistændər]	명 구경꾼, 방관자	
☐ 375 **fountain pen** [fáuntn pèn]	명 만년필	
☐ 376 **application form** [æplikéiʃən fɔ:rm]	명 신청서, 지원서	
☐ 377 **merry-go-round** [mérigouràund]	명 회전 목마	
☐ 378 **forget-me-not** [fərgétminàt]	명 물망초	
☐ 379 **square** [skwɛər]	명 광장	
☐ 380 **mayor** [méiər]	명 시장(市長)	
☐ 381 **arrest** [ərést]	동 체포하다	
☐ 382 **trick** [trik]	명 계략, 속임수, 비법	

☐ 383 **register** [rédʒistər] 통 등록하다

☐ 384 **intercultural** [ìntərkʌ́ltʃərəl] 형 이(종)문화간의

☐ 385 **background** [bǽkgràund] 형 배경의, 배경이 되는 명 배경

☐ 386 **float** [flout] 통 (물에) 뜨다, 떠오르다

☐ 387 **piece** [pi:s] 명 조각, 작품, 소곡

☐ 388 **courage** [kə́:ridʒ] 명 용기

☐ 389 **hastily** [héistili] 부 서둘러서, 급히

☐ 390 **purposely** [pə́:rpəsli] 부 고의로

☐ 391 **punctually** [pʌ́ŋktʃuəli] 부 정각에, 시간대로

☐ 392 **gradually** [grǽdʒuəli] 부 점차로

☐ 393 **industry** [índəstri] 명 산업

☐ 394 **relative** [rélətiv] 명 친척, 일가

☐ 395 **heritage** [héritidʒ] 명 유산

☐ 396 **aggressive** [əgrésiv] 형 공격적인

☐ 397 **flock** [flɑk] 통 떼를 짓다 명 떼, 무리

☐ 398 **pregnant** [prégnənt] 형 임신한

중간기말대비

☐ 399 **furniture** [fə́:rnitʃər] 명 가구, 비품

☐ 400 **knowledge** [nɑ́lidʒ] 명 지식

☐ 401 **seaport** [sí:pɔ̀:rt] 명 항구 (도시), 해항

☐ 402 **pat** [pæt] 통 가볍게 두드리다

☐ 403 **application** [æ̀plikéiʃən] 명 신청, 지원(서)

☐ 404 **chase** [tʃeis] 통 쫓다, 추격하다

☐ 405 **historical** [histɔ́:rikl] 형 역사적인, 역사의

☐ 406 **politics** [pɑ́litiks] 명 정치, 정치학

☐ 407 **diligent** [dílədʒənt] 형 부지런한, 근면한

☐ 408 **faithful** [féiθfəl] 형 충실한, 독실한

Chapter 6 대명사

PSS & PRACTICE

☐ 409 **assignment** [əsáinmənt] 명 숙제, 할당된 일

☐ 410 **community center** [kəmjú:nəti sèntər] 명 지역 문화 회관

☐ 411 **gorgeous** [gɔ́:rdʒəs] 형 화려한, 매우 멋진

☐ 412 **deserve** [dizə́:rv] 통 ~을 받을 자격이 있다

☐ 413 **certain** [sə́:rtn] 형 확신하는, 확실한

☐ 414 **promote** [prəmóut] 통 승진시키다, 촉진하다

☐ 415 **magician** [mədʒíʃən] 명 마술사

Day 13

오늘 외울 단어 **35개**

☐ 416 **variety** [vəráiəti]	명 다양성, 변화	☐ 434 **alive** [əláiv]	형 살아 있는
☐ 417 **watermelon** [wɔ́:tərmèlən]	명 수박	☐ 435 **interesting** [íntərəstiŋ]	형 흥미로운
☐ 418 **recommend** [rèkəménd]	동 추천하다	☐ 436 **harmful** [há:rmfəl]	형 해로운

중간기말대비

☐ 419 **cuckoo** [kú:ku:]	명 뻐꾸기	☐ 437 **clear** [kliər]	형 명확한, 분명한
☐ 420 **mop** [mɑp]	동 (걸레로) 닦다, 청소하다 명 걸레질	☐ 438 **as well as**	~뿐만 아니라
☐ 421 **ancient** [éinʃənt]	형 고대의	☐ 439 **earn** [ə:rn]	동 (돈을) 벌다, 얻다
☐ 422 **modern** [mɑ́dərn]	형 현대의	☐ 440 **aim** [eim]	동 겨누다, 목표로 하다
☐ 423 **backbone** [bǽkbòun]	명 등뼈, 척추	☐ 441 **suppose** [səpóuz]	동 가정하다, ~이라고 하다
☐ 424 **misbehavior** [mìsbihéivjər]	명 나쁜 행실, 무례한 짓	☐ 442 **dry up**	바싹 마르다, 말리다
☐ 425 **express** [iksprés]	동 표현하다	☐ 443 **impress** [imprés]	동 감동시키다
☐ 426 **reputation** [rèpjutéiʃən]	명 명성, 평판	☐ 444 **blanket** [blǽŋkit]	명 담요, 모포
☐ 427 **claim** [kleim]	명 요구, 주장 동 요구하다, 주장하다	☐ 445 **desert** [dézərt]	명 사막
☐ 428 **achieve** [ətʃí:v]	동 이루다, 성취하다	☐ 446 **native** [néitiv]	형 원주민의, 모국의
☐ 429 **overseas** [òuvərsí:z]	형 해외에 있는	☐ 447 **humid** [hjú:mid]	형 습기 찬, 눅눅한
☐ 430 **exhibition** [èksəbíʃən]	명 전시회	☐ 448 **seem** [si:m]	동 ~인 것 같다, ~인 것처럼 보이다
☐ 431 **security** [sikjúərəti]	명 보안, 안전	☐ 449 **tame** [teim]	동 길들이다
☐ 432 **permission** [pərmíʃən]	명 허락, 허가	☐ 450 **maybe** [méibi]	부 아마, 어쩌면
☐ 433 **request** [rikwést]	명 요구, 요청 동 요청하다		

- ☐ [451] **eager** [í:gər] — 형 열망하는, 열심인
- ☐ [452] **foggy** [fɔ́:gi] — 형 안개가 낀
- ☐ [453] **come up with** — 생각해내다, 떠올리다
- ☐ [454] **quit** [kwit] — 동 그만두다, 끊다
- ☐ [455] **struggle** [strʌ́gl] — 명 노력, 고투
- ☐ [456] **plastic surgery** [plǽstik sə́:rdʒəri] — 명 성형외과, 성형수술
- ☐ [457] **brilliant** [bríliənt] — 형 빛나는, 훌륭한
- ☐ [458] **ecosystem** [ékousìstəm] — 명 생태계
- ☐ [459] **damage** [dǽmidʒ] — 동 손해[상해]를 입히다
- ☐ [460] **affect** [əfékt] — 동 영향을 주다, (병에) 걸리다
- ☐ [461] **appearance** [əpí:ərəns] — 명 외모, 출연
- ☐ [462] **official** [əfíʃəl] — 형 공식의, 공공의
- ☐ [463] **mortal** [mɔ́:rtl] — 형 죽을 운명의
- ☐ [464] **disappoint** [dìsəpɔ́int] — 동 실망시키다, 낙담시키다
- ☐ [465] **cheat** [tʃi:t] — 동 속이다, 바람 피우다
- ☐ [466] **lemonade** [lèmənéid] — 명 레모네이드
- ☐ [467] **vaccine** [væksí:n] — 명 백신
- ☐ [468] **scale** [skeil] — 명 규모

- ☐ [469] **fingernail** [fíŋgərnèil] — 명 손톱
- ☐ [470] **defeat** [difí:t] — 동 패배시키다, 이기다
- ☐ [471] **fierce** [fiərs] — 형 난폭한, 사나운
- ☐ [472] **unique** [ju:ní:k] — 형 독특한, 유일한

Chapter 7 부정사

🚹 **PSS & PRACTICE**

- ☐ [473] **correctly** [kəréktli] — 부 올바르게, 정확히
- ☐ [474] **impossible** [impásəbl] — 형 불가능한
- ☐ [475] **helpful** [hélpfəl] — 형 도움이 되는
- ☐ [476] **pretend** [priténd] — 동 ~인 체하다
- ☐ [477] **manage** [mǽnidʒ] — 동 ~을 잘 해내다, 관리하다
- ☐ [478] **quarrel** [kwɔ́:rəl] — 명 싸움 / 동 싸우다, 다투다
- ☐ [479] **share** [ʃɛər] — 동 나누다, 공유하다 / 명 몫, 할당량
- ☐ [480] **responsibly** [rispánsəbli] — 부 책임감 있게
- ☐ [481] **cooperate** [kouápərèit] — 동 협동하다
- ☐ [482] **fancy** [fǽnsi] — 형 화려한, 고급의 / 명 공상, 상상
- ☐ [483] **destined** [déstind] — 형 ~할 운명인, 예정된
- ☐ [484] **autograph** [ɔ́:təgræ̀f] — 명 서명, (유명인의) 사인

☐ 485 **counselor** [káunsələr]	명 상담 교사, 고문	
☐ 486 **grow up**	자라다	
☐ 487 **nervous** [nə́ːrvəs]	형 신경 과민인, 긴장한	
☐ 488 **license** [láisəns]	명 면허증, 허가증	
☐ 489 **distance** [dístəns]	명 거리	
☐ 490 **skillful** [skílfəl]	형 숙련된	
☐ 491 **track** [træk]	명 발자국, 흔적	
☐ 492 **notice** [nóutis]	동 알아차리다	
☐ 493 **sneak** [sniːk]	동 몰래 움직이다, 살금살금 들어가다	
☐ 494 **skip** [skip]	동 건너뛰다, 빼먹다, 결석하다	
☐ 495 **pollute** [pəlúːt]	동 오염시키다	
☐ 496 **literature** [lítərətʃər]	명 문학	
☐ 497 **careless** [kɛ́ərlis]	형 부주의한	
☐ 498 **thoughtful** [θɔ́ːtfəl]	형 생각이 깊은, 사려 깊은	

👥 중간기말대비

☐ 499 **transportation** [trænspərtéiʃən]	명 운송, 수송
☐ 500 **anywhere** [éniwɛ̀ər]	부 어디에도, 아무데나
☐ 501 **suggestion** [səʤéstʃən]	명 암시, 제안

☐ 502 **figure out**	이해하다, 알아내다
☐ 503 **imagine** [imǽʤin]	동 상상하다, 생각하다
☐ 504 **valley** [vǽli]	명 계곡, 골짜기
☐ 505 **engineer** [ènʤiníər]	명 기술자, 기사
☐ 506 **article** [áːrtikl]	명 기사, 조항
☐ 507 **miniature** [míniətʃər]	형 소형의, 축소 모형의
☐ 508 **literal** [lítərəl]	형 문자 그대로인, 문자의
☐ 509 **enable** [inéibl]	동 가능하게 하다
☐ 510 **completely** [kəmplíːtli]	부 완전히, 전적으로
☐ 511 **partly** [páːrtli]	부 부분적으로, 어느 정도
☐ 512 **in advance**	미리, 사전에
☐ 513 **embarrassed** [imbǽrəst]	형 난처한, 당황스러운
☐ 514 **mention** [ménʃən]	동 언급하다
☐ 515 **explore** [iksplɔ́ːr]	동 탐험하다
☐ 516 **automation** [ɔ̀ːtəméiʃən]	명 자동조작, 자동제어
☐ 517 **productivity** [pròudəktívəti]	명 생산력, 생산성
☐ 518 **rapidly** [rǽpidli]	부 급속히, 빠르게
☐ 519 **to be honest**	솔직히 말하자면

☐ 520 **rumor**
[rúːmər]
명 소문

☐ 521 **volunteer**
[vàləntíər]
명 지원자, 자원 봉사자

Chapter **8** 동명사

👤 PSS & PRACTICE

☐ 522 **countryside**
[kʌ́ntrisàid]
명 시골, 지방

☐ 523 **purpose**
[pə́ːrpəs]
명 목적

☐ 524 **put off**
연기하다, 미루다

☐ 525 **avoid**
[əvɔ́id]
동 피하다

☐ 526 **postpone**
[poustpóun]
동 연기하다, 미루다

☐ 527 **detective**
[ditéktiv]
명 탐정, 형사

☐ 528 **spacecraft**
[spéiskræ̀ft]
명 우주선

☐ 529 **interrupt**
[ìntərʌ́pt]
동 방해하다, 훼방놓다

☐ 530 **cabbage**
[kǽbidʒ]
명 양배추

☐ 531 **congress**
[kɑ́ŋgrəs]
명 국회, 의회

☐ 532 **cause**
[kɔːz]
동 ～의 원인이 되다
명 원인

☐ 533 **persuade**
[pərswéid]
동 설득하다

☐ 534 **bother**
[bɑ́ðər]
동 괴롭히다

☐ 535 **opportunity**
[àpərtjúːnəti]
명 기회

☐ 536 **author**
[ɔ́ːθər]
명 저자

☐ 537 **measure**
[méʒər]
동 재다, 측정하다

☐ 538 **length**
[leŋθ]
명 길이

☐ 539 **apologize**
[əpálədʒàiz]
동 사과하다

☐ 540 **public transportation**
[pʌ́blik trænspərtéiʃən] 명 대중교통

☐ 541 **reduce**
[ridjúːs]
동 줄이다

☐ 542 **capable**
[kéipəbl]
형 ～할 능력이 있는

☐ 543 **format**
[fɔ́ːrmæt]
명 형태, 포맷,
동 서식을 만들다

☐ 544 **worthwhile**
[wə́ːrθwáil]
형 가치가 있는, 훌륭한

☐ 545 **praise**
[preiz]
동 칭찬하다
명 칭찬

☐ 546 **beforehand**
[bifɔ́ːrhæ̀nd]
부 미리, 사전에

☐ 547 **competition**
[kàmpətíʃən]
명 대회, 시합, 경쟁

👤 중간기말대비

☐ 548 **judge**
[dʒʌdʒ]
동 재판하다, 판단하다

☐ 549 **dizzy**
[dízi]
형 현기증이 나는

☐ 550 **valuable**
[vǽljuəbl]
형 귀중한

☐ 551 **asset**
[ǽset]
명 재산, 자산

☐ 552 **energetic**
[ènərdʒétik]
형 힘이 넘치는, 활기찬

☐ 553 **funeral**
[fjú:nərəl]
명 장례식

☐ 554 **aside**
[əsáid]
부 곁에, 조금 떨어져

☐ 555 **apply**
[əplái]
동 지원하다, 신청하다

☐ 556 **journalist**
[dʒə́:rnəlist]
명 저널리스트, 언론인

☐ 557 **regard**
[rigá:rd]
동 ~로 여기다, 평가하다

☐ 558 **hostage**
[hástidʒ]
명 인질, 볼모

☐ 559 **lung**
[lʌŋ]
명 폐

☐ 560 **surgery**
[sə́:rdʒəri]
명 수술, 외과

☐ 561 **treaty**
[trí:ti]
명 조약, 협정

☐ 562 **attempt**
[ətémpt]
동 시도하다

☐ 563 **conference**
[kánfərəns]
명 회의, 협의회

☐ 564 **participate**
[pɑːrtísəpèit]
동 참가하다

☐ 565 **mutual**
[mjú:tʃuəl]
형 서로의, 상호간의

☐ 566 **cooperation**
[kouàpəréiʃən]
명 협력, 협조

☐ 567 **kidnapper**
[kídnæpər]
명 납치범, 유괴범

☐ 568 **locate**
[lóukeit]
동 위치시키다, 위치를 알아내다

☐ 569 **portrait**
[pɔ́:rtrit]
명 초상화

☐ 570 **worth**
[wə:rθ]
형 ~할(의) 가치가 있는
명 가치, 진가

☐ 571 **thoroughly**
[θə́:rouli]
부 완전히, 철저하게

☐ 572 **access**
[ǽkses]
동 접근하다 명 접근

☐ 573 **detail**
[ditéil]
명 세부, 상세

☐ 574 **due to**
~ 때문에, ~ 이유로

☐ 575 **be accustomed to**
~에 익숙하다

☐ 576 **tone**
[toun]
명 어조, 음색

☐ 577 **appliance**
[əpláiəns]
명 기구, 장치

Chapter 9 분사

🚶 PSS & PRACTICE

☐ 578 **escape**
[iskéip]
동 도망가다, 탈출하다

☐ 579 **through**
[θru:]
전 ~을 통과하여, 지나서

☐ 580 **terrify**
[térəfài]
동 겁나게 하다

☐ 581 **thunderstorm**
[θʌ́ndərstɔ̀:rm]
명 뇌우

☐ 582 **scream**
[skri:m]
동 비명을 지르다
명 비명

☐ 583 **surround**
[səráund]
동 둘러싸다

☐ 584 **sudden**
[sʌ́dn]
형 갑작스러운

☐ 585 **walking stick**
[wɔ́:kiŋ stìk]
명 지팡이

☐ 586 **toward**
[təwɔ́:rd]
전 ~을 향하여

587 **monster** [mɔ́nstər]	명 괴물	604 **presentation** [prìːzəntéiʃən]	명 발표, 설명
588 **attack** [ətǽk]	동 공격하다	605 **publish** [pʌ́bliʃ]	동 출판하다, 발표하다
589 **amaze** [əméiz]	동 놀라게 하다	606 **deliver** [dilívər]	동 전달하다, 배달하다
590 **fascinate** [fǽsənèit]	동 황홀하게 하다, 매혹하다	607 **proverb** [prɑ́vəːrb]	명 속담, 격언
591 **frighten** [fráitn]	동 흠칫 놀라게 하다	608 **confidence** [kɑ́nfidəns]	명 자신감, 신뢰
592 **move** [muːv]	동 감동시키다	609 **entertain** [èntərtéin]	동 즐겁게 하다
593 **satisfy** [sǽtisfài]	동 만족시키다	610 **adventure** [ədvéntʃər]	명 모험, 도전
594 **get rid of**	제거하다	611 **confusing** [kənfjúːziŋ]	형 혼란시키는
595 **brand-new** [brændnjúː]	형 아주 새로운	612 **satisfying** [sǽtisfàiiŋ]	형 만족시키는
596 **fold** [fould]	동 접다	613 **annoy** [ənɔ́i]	동 짜증나게 하다, 성가시게 하다

🏃 중간기말대비

597 **direct** [dirékt]	동 감독하다, 연출하다	614 **talented** [tǽləntid]	형 재능이 있는, 우수한
598 **forefather** [fɔ́ːrfàːðər]	명 조상, 선조	615 **relax** [rilǽks]	동 늦추다, 긴장을 풀다
599 **control** [kəntróul]	동 통제하다, 관리하다	616 **remain** [riméin]	동 ~인 채로 있다
600 **miner** [máinər]	명 광부	617 **seldom** [séldəm]	부 좀처럼 ~ 않는
601 **absence** [ǽbsəns]	명 없음, 결석	618 **swallow** [swɑ́lou]	명 제비 동 삼키다
602 **left-handed** [lefthǽndid]	형 왼손잡이의	619 **unsure** [ʌnʃúər]	형 자신 없는, 확신이 없는
603 **trailer** [tréilər]	명 트레일러	620 **stage fright** [stéidʒ fràit]	명 무대 공포증

Chapter 10 형용사

👤 **PSS & PRACTICE**

□ 621 **inner**
[ínər]
형 내부의, 안쪽의

□ 622 **outer**
[áutər]
형 외부의, 외면의

□ 623 **former**
[fɔ́:rmər]
형 앞의, 전자의

□ 624 **mere**
[miər]
형 겨우 ~의, ~에 불과한

□ 625 **upper**
[ʌ́pər]
형 위쪽의, 상부의

□ 626 **ashamed**
[əʃéimd]
형 부끄러워하는

□ 627 **spectator**
[spékteitər]
명 구경꾼, 관람객

□ 628 **sole**
[soul]
형 하나뿐인, 유일한

□ 629 **cheerful**
[tʃíərfəl]
형 명랑한, 쾌활한

□ 630 **personality**
[pə̀:rsənǽləti]
명 성격, 인품

□ 631 **orphan**
[ɔ́:rfən]
명 고아

□ 632 **meaningful**
[mí:niŋfəl]
형 의미심장한, 의미 있는

□ 633 **attractive**
[ətrǽktiv]
형 매력 있는, 사람을 끌어당기는

□ 634 **take a risk**
위험을 무릅쓰다

□ 635 **collect**
[kəlékt]
동 모으다, 수집하다

□ 636 **convenient**
[kənví:njənt]
형 편리한

□ 637 **disabled**
[diséibld]
형 지체 부자유한, 신체 장애의

□ 638 **deaf**
[def]
형 청각 장애가 있는

□ 639 **solution**
[səlú:ʃən]
명 해결, 해답

□ 640 **regular**
[régjulər]
형 통상의, 규칙적인

□ 641 **dormitory**
[dɔ́:rmətɔ̀:ri]
명 기숙사

□ 642 **law firm**
[lɔ́: fə:rm]
명 법률 회사

□ 643 **evidence**
[évidəns]
명 증거

□ 644 **construction**
[kənstrʌ́kʃən]
명 건축, 건설

□ 645 **gallery**
[gǽləri]
명 미술관, 화랑

□ 646 **education**
[èdʒukéiʃən]
명 교육

□ 647 **rainstorm**
[réinstɔ̀:rm]
명 폭풍우, 호우

□ 648 **applicant**
[ǽplikənt]
명 신청자, 지원자

□ 649 **position**
[pəzíʃən]
명 위치, 입장, 지위

□ 650 **receive**
[risí:v]
동 받다, 수령하다

□ 651 **salary**
[sǽləri]
명 봉급, 급료

□ 652 **donate**
[dóuneit]
동 기부하다

□ 653 **orphanage**
[ɔ́:rfənidʒ]
명 고아원

👤 **중간기말대비**

□ 654 **alike**
[əláik]
형 비슷한 부 비슷하게

☐ 655 **perfume** [pə́:rfjuːm]	명 향수	☐ 671 **actual** [ǽktʃuəl]	형 실제의
☐ 656 **innocent** [ínəsənt]	형 순결한, 무죄인	☐ 672 **attentive** [əténtiv]	형 주의를 기울이는
☐ 657 **military** [míliteri]	형 군사의, 군대의	☐ 673 **constant** [kánstənt]	형 끊임없는
☐ 658 **operation** [àpəréiʃən]	명 작전, 운영	☐ 674 **effective** [iféktiv]	형 효과적인
☐ 659 **comparable** [kámpərəbl]	형 비교할 수 있는	☐ 675 **immediate** [imí:diət]	형 즉시의
☐ 660 **precious** [préʃəs]	형 소중한, 귀중한	☐ 676 **moral** [mɔ́:rəl]	형 도덕적인
☐ 661 **imaginable** [imǽdʒənəbl]	형 상상할 수 있는	☐ 677 **fair** [fɛər]	형 공정한, 공평한
☐ 662 **mushroom** [mʌ́ʃruːm]	명 버섯	☐ 678 **firm** [fə:rm]	형 견고한, 단단한
☐ 663 **roar** [rɔːr]	명 포효, 으르렁거리는 소리	☐ 679 **willing** [wíliŋ]	형 기꺼이 ~하는, 자발적인
☐ 664 **disable** [diséibl]	동 무능하게 하다, 쓸모없게 하다	☐ 680 **fortunate** [fɔ́:rtʃənət]	형 운이 좋은
☐ 665 **idealistic** [aidì:əlístik]	형 이상주의적인	☐ 681 **contrary** [kántreri]	형 반대의, 상반되는
☐ 666 **jobless** [dʒáblis]	형 일이 없는, 실직 중인	☐ 682 **original** [ərídʒənl]	형 최초의, 독자적인, 원작의
☐ 667 **greedy** [grí:di]	형 욕심 많은, 탐욕스러운	☐ 683 **international** [ìntərnǽʃənl]	형 국제적인
☐ 668 **ignorance** [ígnərəns]	명 무지, 무식	☐ 684 **probable** [prábəbl]	형 있을 법한
☐ 669 **professional** [prəféʃənl]	형 전문의, 직업의	☐ 685 **reasonable** [rí:znəbl]	형 합리적인
☐ 670 **handicapped** [hǽndikæpt]	형 장애가 있는	☐ 686 **definite** [défənit]	형 명확한, 한정된
		☐ 687 **current** [kə́:rənt]	형 현재의, 지금의, 통용되는
		☐ 688 **genuine** [dʒénjuin]	형 진짜의

Chapter 11 부사

👤 PSS & PRACTICE

□ 689 **rare** [rɛər]	혱 드문, 진기한	□ 707 **impress** [imprés]	통 감동시키다, 깊은 인상을 주다
□ 690 **normal** [nɔ́:rməl]	혱 표준적인, 정상적인	□ 708 **communicate** [kəmjú:nikèit]	통 연락을 주고 받다, 의사 소통을 하다
□ 691 **anxious** [ǽŋʃəs]	혱 불안해 하는, 염려하는	□ 709 **district** [dístrikt]	몡 구역, 지역
□ 692 **general** [dʒénərəl]	혱 일반적인	□ 710 **unpredictable** [ʌ̀npridíktəbl]	혱 예측할 수 없는
□ 693 **mental** [méntl]	혱 정신적인	□ 711 **impulsive** [impʌ́lsiv]	혱 충동적인
□ 694 **casual** [kǽʒuəl]	혱 우연한, 격식 없는, 평상의	□ 712 **annual** [ǽnjuəl]	혱 1년의, 해마다의
□ 695 **whole** [houl]	혱 전부의, 전체의	□ 713 **flu** [flu:]	몡 독감
□ 696 **incredible** [inkrédəbl]	혱 믿을 수 없는	□ 714 **vaccination** [væ̀ksənéiʃən]	몡 예방접종
□ 697 **practical** [prǽktikəl]	혱 실제적인, 실용적인	□ 715 **complex** [ká:mpleks]	몡 단지, 복합 빌딩
□ 698 **proper** [prápər]	혱 적합한	□ 716 **mammal** [mǽməl]	몡 포유동물
□ 699 **sensitive** [sénsətiv]	혱 민감한, 예민한	□ 717 **realistic** [rìəlístik]	혱 현실적인
□ 700 **exact** [igzǽkt]	혱 정확한	□ 718 **resemble** [rizémbl]	통 닮다
□ 701 **severe** [sivíər]	혱 엄한, 엄격한	□ 719 **suffer** [sʌ́fər]	통 고통을 받다, 괴로워하다
□ 702 **emotional** [imóuʃənəl]	혱 감정적인	□ 720 **stroke** [strouk]	몡 뇌졸중
□ 703 **sensible** [sénsəbl]	혱 분별이 있는, 현명한	□ 721 **be fed up with**	∼에 싫증나다
□ 704 **vote** [vout]	몡 투표, 득표 통 투표하다	□ 722 **criticize** [krítisàiz]	통 비평하다, 비판하다
□ 705 **directly** [diréktli]	븟 직접적으로	□ 723 **recognize** [rékəgnàiz]	통 알아보다, 인지하다
□ 706 **logical** [ládʒikəl]	혱 논리적인	□ 724 **break up**	헤어지다, 관계를 끊다

□ 725 **government** 명 정부
[ɡʌ́vər(n)mənt]

□ 726 **expressway** 명 고속도로
[ikspréswèi]

□ 727 **iron** 동 다림질하다
[aiərn] 명 철, 다리미

□ 728 **wrinkle** 명 주름
[ríŋkl]

□ 729 **experiment** 명 실험, 시험
[ikspérəmənt] 동 실험하다

중간기말대비

□ 730 **similar** 형 유사한, 비슷한, 닮은
[símələr]

□ 731 **slippery** 형 미끄러운, 미끌거리는
[slípəri]

□ 732 **downtown** 명 상업 지구, 도심 지구
[dauntáun]

□ 733 **imagination** 명 상상력, 상상
[imædʒənéiʃən]

□ 734 **relationship** 명 관계, 친척 관계
[riléiʃənʃip]

□ 735 **even** 형 짝수의, 동일한
[í:vən] 부 훨씬

□ 736 **tasty** 형 맛있는
[téisti]

□ 737 **effectively** 부 효과적으로
[iféktivli]

□ 738 **rarely** 부 드물게, 좀처럼 ~ 않다
[réərli]

□ 739 **unfortunately**
[ʌnfɔ́:rtʃənətli] 부 불행하게도

□ 740 **afford** 동 ~할 여유가 있다
[əfɔ́:rd]

□ 741 **material** 명 재료, 소재, 물질
[mətíəriəl]

□ 742 **variable** 형 변화하기 쉬운
[veriəbl]

□ 743 **predict** 동 예측하다, 전망하다
[pridíkt]

□ 744 **package** 명 패키지, 소포
[pǽkidʒ]

□ 745 **make a living**
생계를 꾸리다

Chapter 12 가정법

PSS & PRACTICE

□ 746 **idiot** 명 바보
[ídiət]

□ 747 **heart attack** 명 심장마비
[há:rt ətæk]

□ 748 **reputation** 명 명성, 평판
[rèpjutéiʃən]

□ 749 **sue** 동 고소하다, 소송을
[su:] 제기하다

□ 750 **genius** 명 천재
[dʒí:njəs]

□ 751 **break out** 일어나다, 발발하다

□ 752 **spread** 동 퍼지다, 펼쳐지다
[spred]

□ 753 **fortune** 명 부, 재산, 운명
[fɔ́:rtʃən]

□ 754 **luxurious** 형 사치스러운, 호화로운
[lʌgʒúriəs]

□ 755 **freezing** 형 몹시 추운
[frí:ziŋ]

□ 756 **celebrity** 명 유명 인사
[səlébrəti]

□ 757 **meaning** 명 의미
[mí:niŋ]

☐ 758 **electricity** [ilektrísəti] 몡 전기

☐ 759 **mysterious** [mistíriəs] 혱 신비로운, 불가사의한

☐ 760 **squid** [skwid] 몡 오징어

☐ 761 **scary** [skɛ́əri] 혱 무서운

☐ 762 **crash** [kræʃ] 동 충돌하다, 추락하다

☐ 763 **martial art** [má:rʃəl à:rt] 몡 무도, 무술

☐ 764 **sincere** [sinsíər] 혱 진심에서 우러난, 진실의

☐ 765 **candidate** [kǽndidèit] 몡 지원자, 후보자

☐ 766 **committee** [kəmíti] 몡 위원회

☐ 767 **construct** [kənstrʌ́kt] 동 건설하다

☐ 768 **require** [rikwáiər] 동 요구하다

☐ 769 **occur** [əkə́:r] 동 일어나다, 생기다

☐ 770 **global warming** [glóubəl wɔ́:rmiŋ] 몡 지구 온난화

☐ 771 **evolve** [ivάlv] 동 진화하다, 발달하다

☐ 772 **ape** [eip] 몡 유인원

👨 중간기말대비

☐ 773 **hang** [hæŋ] 동 걸다, 매달다

☐ 774 **clothes line** 몡 빨랫줄

☐ 775 **take part in** ～에 참여하다

☐ 776 **accept** [əksépt] 동 받아들이다

☐ 777 **grave** [greiv] 몡 무덤

☐ 778 **fiance** [fì:ɑ:nséi] 몡 약혼자

☐ 779 **eyesight** [áisàit] 몡 시력, 시각

☐ 780 **attention** [əténʃʌn] 몡 관심, 주목

☐ 781 **forecast** [fɔ́:rkæ̀st] 몡 예상, 예보

☐ 782 **support** [səpɔ́:rt] 동 지지하다, 부양하다

☐ 783 **decision** [disíȝn] 몡 결정, 판결

☐ 784 **in spite of** ～에도 불구하고

☐ 785 **qualify** [kwάləfài] 동 자격을 얻다, 자격을 주다

☐ 786 **recruit** [rikrú:t] 동 채용하다, 모집하다

☐ 787 **goddess** [gάdis] 몡 여신

☐ 788 **keep one's word** 약속을 지키다

☐ 789 **suggest** [səgdȝést] 동 제안하다

☐ 790 **demand** [dimǽnd] 동 요구하다

☐ 791 **local** [lóukl] 혱 지역의, 지방의

☐ 792 **desert** [dézərt] 동 버리다, 유기하다 / 몡 사막

☐ 793 **desire** [dizáiər]	통 원하다, 바라다 명 욕망	☐ 809 **vow** [vau]	통 맹세하다, 단언하다 명 맹세, 서약

Chapter 13 비교구문

👤 PSS & PRACTICE

☐ 794 **complicated** [kámpləkèitid]	형 복잡한	☐ 810 **previous** [prí:viəs]	형 이전의, 사전의
☐ 795 **enjoyable** [indʒɔ́iəbl]	형 즐거운, 유쾌한	☐ 811 **condition** [kəndíʃən]	명 상태
☐ 796 **impressive** [imprésiv]	형 인상적인, 감명 깊은	☐ 812 **starve** [sta:rv]	통 굶주리다, 몹시 배고프다
☐ 797 **insistent** [insístənt]	형 강요하는, 집요한	☐ 813 **emergency** [imə́:rdʒənsi]	명 비상사태, 응급 상황
☐ 798 **ambitious** [æmbíʃəs]	형 야심적인, 열망하는	☐ 814 **distinguish** [distíŋgwiʃ]	통 구별하다
☐ 799 **awkward** [ɔ́:kwərd]	형 미숙한, 불편한	☐ 815 **newcomer** [njú:kʌmər]	명 새로 온 사람
☐ 800 **urgent** [ə́:rdʒənt]	형 긴박한, 긴급한	☐ 816 **efficiently** [ifíʃəntli]	부 능률적으로, 효율적으로
☐ 801 **challenging** [tʃælindʒiŋ]	형 도전적인	☐ 817 **expose** [ikspóuz]	통 드러내다, 노출시키다
☐ 802 **abstract** [æbstrǽkt]	형 추상적인	☐ 818 **sunburn** [sʌ́nbə̀:rn]	명 햇볕에 탐
☐ 803 **recent** [rí:snt]	형 최근의	☐ 819 **theory** [θí:əri]	명 이론
☐ 804 **emperor** [émpərər]	명 황제	☐ 820 **jewelry** [dʒú:əlri]	명 보석류
☐ 805 **technology** [teknálədʒi]	명 기술	☐ 821 **destination** [dèstənéiʃən]	명 목적지, 도착지
☐ 806 **astronomical** [æ̀strənámikl]	형 천문학의, 천문학적인	☐ 822 **director** [diréktər]	명 감독
☐ 807 **observatory** [əbzə́:rvətɔ̀:ri]	명 관측소, 전망대	☐ 823 **figure** [fígjər]	명 인물, 숫자
☐ 808 **specifically** [spəsífikli]	부 명확하게, 특별히	☐ 824 **fossil** [fá:sl]	명 화석

🏃 중간기말대비

☐ 825 **flexible** [fléksəbl]	형 유연한, 탄력적인

□ 826 **calorie** [kǽləri] 명 칼로리, 열량

□ 827 **contrary** [káːntreri] 형 반대의, 정반대의

□ 828 **technician** [tekníʃən] 명 기술자, 전문가

□ 829 **complicate** [kámplikeit] 통 복잡하게 하다

□ 830 **obey** [oubéi] 통 복종하다, 준수하다

□ 831 **with effort** 애써, 공들여

□ 832 **prefer** [prifə́ːr] 통 더 좋아하다, 선호하다

□ 833 **policy** [páləsi] 명 정책, 제도, 방침

□ 834 **global** [glóubl] 형 세계적인, 전체적인

□ 835 **communication** [kəmjùːnəkéiʃən] 명 통신, 소통

Chapter **14** 관계사

👤 **PSS & PRACTICE**

□ 836 **burglar** [bə́ːrglər] 명 강도, 도둑

□ 837 **expectation** [èkspektéiʃən] 명 기대, 예상

□ 838 **self-confidence** [selfkáːnfidəns] 명 자신감

□ 839 **pedal** [pédl] 명 페달, 발판

□ 840 **via** [víːə] 전 ~을 거쳐, 경유해서

□ 841 **cyberspace** [sáibərspèis] 명 사이버 공간, 가상 현실

□ 842 **virtual reality** [və́ːrtʃuəl riǽləti] 명 가상 현실

□ 843 **break down** 고장 나다

□ 844 **chemistry** [kémistri] 명 화학

□ 845 **vacant** [véikənt] 형 빈, 사용되지 않는

□ 846 **riverside** [rívərsàid] 명 강가 형 강가의

□ 847 **laughter** [lǽftər] 명 웃음

□ 848 **remodel** [riːmádl] 통 개조하다

□ 849 **documentary** [dàkjuméntri] 명 다큐멘터리, 기록물

□ 850 **force** [fɔːrs] 통 강요하다, 억지로 시키다

□ 851 **rectangular** [rektǽŋgjulər] 형 직사각형의

□ 852 **influence** [ínfluəns] 통 영향을 주다 명 영향

□ 853 **constitution** [kànstətjúːʃən] 명 헌법, 구조, 관행

□ 854 **immigrant** [ímigrənt] 명 이주민, 이민

□ 855 **treetop** [tríːtàp] 명 나무 꼭대기

□ 856 **indicate** [índikèit] 통 나타내다, 암시하다, 가리키다

👤 **중간기말대비**

□ 857 **found** [faund] 통 설립하다

□ 858 **facility** [fəsíləti] 명 설비, 시설

☐ 859 **out-of-date** [autʌvdéit] 형 시대에 뒤떨어진, 구식의

☐ 860 **microscope** [máikrəskòup] 명 현미경

☐ 861 **purchase** [pə́ːrtʃəs] 동 구입하다, 구매하다

☐ 862 **glitter** [glítər] 동 반짝반짝 빛나다

☐ 863 **serve** [səːrv] 동 제공하다, 복무하다

☐ 864 **moisture** [mɔ́istʃər] 명 습기, 수분

☐ 865 **separate** [sépəréit] 동 분리하다

☐ 866 **opinion** [əpínjən] 명 의견, 생각, 견해

☐ 867 **graduate** [grǽdʒueit] 동 졸업하다

☐ 868 **archaeologist** [àːrkiáːlədʒist] 명 고고학자

☐ 869 **primitive** [prímətiv] 형 원시의, 태고의

Chapter 15 접속사

PSS & PRACTICE

☐ 870 **detail** [ditéil] 명 세부, 상세

☐ 871 **competent** [kámpitənt] 형 유능한, 충분한

☐ 872 **translator** [trænsléitər] 명 번역가

☐ 873 **confident** [kánfidənt] 형 확신하는, 자신이 있는

☐ 874 **economy** [ikánəmi] 명 경제

☐ 875 **gene** [dʒiːn] 명 유전자

☐ 876 **aquarium** [əkwɛ́əriəm] 명 수족관

☐ 877 **footstep** [fútstèp] 명 발자국

☐ 878 **on strike** 파업 중인

☐ 879 **for free** 공짜로, 무료로

☐ 880 **regret** [rigrét] 동 후회하다

☐ 881 **mend** [mend] 동 수선하다, 고치다

☐ 882 **practitioner** [præktíʃənər] 명 실천하는 사람, 전문가

☐ 883 **well-mannered** [wélmǽnərd] 형 정중한, 예의 바른

☐ 884 **astronomy** [əstránəmi] 명 천문학

☐ 885 **clay** [klei] 명 흙, 점토

☐ 886 **battlefield** [bǽtlfiːld] 명 전쟁터

☐ 887 **globalization** [glòubəlaizéiʃən] 명 세계화, 국제화

☐ 888 **extend** [iksténd] 동 연장하다, 뻗다, 늘리다

☐ 889 **wag** [wæg] 동 (꼬리를) 흔들다, 흔들리다

☐ 890 **impression** [impréʃən] 명 인상, 감동

☐ 891 **edge** [edʒ] 명 가장자리, 모서리

☐ 892 **expression** [ikspréʃən] 명 표현

- ☐ 893 **outgoing** [áutgòuiŋ] 형 외향적인, 사교적인
- ☐ 894 **typhoon** [taifúːn] 명 태풍
- ☐ 895 **mess** [mes] 명 혼잡, 혼란
- ☐ 896 **vacuum** [vǽkjuːm] 동 진공청소기로 청소하다

중간기말대비

- ☐ 897 **besides** [bisáidz] 부 게다가, 그리고 / 전 ~ 외에
- ☐ 898 **posture** [pástʃər] 명 자세, 형세
- ☐ 899 **harmful** [háːrmfəl] 형 해로운, 유해한
- ☐ 900 **verbal** [vɔ́ːrbl] 형 구두의, 언어의
- ☐ 901 **movement** [múːvmənt] 명 운동, 움직임
- ☐ 902 **clap** [klæp] 동 손뼉을 치다, 박수갈채하다
- ☐ 903 **sword** [sɔːrd] 명 검, 칼, 무력
- ☐ 904 **negative** [négətiv] 형 부정적인, 부정의
- ☐ 905 **last** [læst] 동 지속되다, 계속되다
- ☐ 906 **decorate** [dékərèit] 동 장식하다, 꾸미다
- ☐ 907 **depend** [dipénd] 동 ~에 달려 있다, 의존하다
- ☐ 908 **store** [stɔːr] 동 비축하다, 저장하다
- ☐ 909 **appear** [əpíər] 동 나타나다, 발생하다

- ☐ 910 **exist** [igzíst] 동 존재하다, 살다
- ☐ 911 **attitude** [ǽtitjùːd] 명 태도, 자세

Chapter 16 전치사

PSS & PRACTICE

- ☐ 912 **fitness club** [fítnis klʌ́b] 명 헬스 클럽
- ☐ 913 **fireworks** [fáiərwɔ̀ːrks] 명 불꽃놀이
- ☐ 914 **host** [houst] 동 주최하다, 개최하다
- ☐ 915 **expand** [ikspǽnd] 동 확장되다, 팽창하다
- ☐ 916 **rapidly** [rǽpidli] 부 급속히
- ☐ 917 **photography** [fətágrəfi] 명 사진술, 사진촬영
- ☐ 918 **organize** [ɔ́ːrgənàiz] 동 조직하다
- ☐ 919 **colonial** [kəlóuniəl] 형 식민지의
- ☐ 920 **expedition** [èkspədíʃən] 명 원정, 탐험, 탐험대
- ☐ 921 **survivor** [sərváivər] 명 생존자
- ☐ 922 **disadvantaged** [dìsədvǽntidʒd] 형 불리한
- ☐ 923 **cockroach** [kákròutʃ] 명 바퀴벌레
- ☐ 924 **forbid** [fərbíd] 동 금지하다
- ☐ 925 **reindeer** [réindìər] 명 순록

□ 926 **general** [dʒénrəl]	몡 장군, 대장
□ 927 **uprising** [ʌ́pràiziŋ]	몡 반란, 모반
□ 928 **extinction** [ikstíŋkʃn]	몡 소멸, 멸종, 소등
□ 929 **charity** [tʃǽrəti]	몡 자선, 자선 기금
□ 930 **tournament** [tə́ːrnəmənt]	몡 토너먼트, 승자 진출전
□ 931 **prescription** [priskrípʃən]	몡 처방전, 규정, 지시
□ 932 **submarine** [sʌ̀bməríːn]	몡 잠수함
□ 933 **in print**	인쇄되어, 출판되어
□ 934 **bomb** [bɑm]	툉 폭격하다, 폭탄을 투하하다 몡 폭탄
□ 935 **charm** [tʃɑːrm]	몡 매력
□ 936 **peel** [piːl]	몡 껍질 툉 껍질을 벗기다
□ 937 **fountain** [fáuntn]	몡 분수대
□ 938 **approach** [əpróutʃ]	툉 다가가다, 접근하다
□ 939 **protest** [prətést]	툉 항의하다
□ 940 **racial** [réiʃəl]	톙 인종의
□ 941 **discrimination** [diskrìminéiʃən]	몡 차별 대우, 구별
□ 942 **horizon** [həráizn]	몡 지평선, 수평선
□ 943 **sculptor** [skʌ́lptər]	몡 조각가

□ 944 **sculpture** [skʌ́lptʃər]	몡 조각품, 조각
□ 945 **pin** [pin]	툉 핀으로 고정시키다
□ 946 **bulletin board** [búlətən bɔ́ːrd]	몡 게시판
□ 947 **canoe** [kənúː]	몡 카누, 통나무 배
□ 948 **container** [kəntéinər]	몡 (화물용) 컨테이너, 용기, 그릇
□ 949 **squirrel** [skwə́ːrəl]	몡 다람쥐
□ 950 **convenience store** [kənvíːnjəns stɔ́ːr]	몡 편의점
□ 951 **iceberg** [áisbəːrg]	몡 빙산
□ 952 **surface** [sə́ːrfis]	몡 표면
□ 953 **seal** [siːl]	몡 바다표범, 물개
□ 954 **hoop** [huːp]	몡 훌라후프, 굴렁쇠
□ 955 **trail** [treil]	툉 뒤를 쫓다, 추적하다
□ 956 **warehouse** [wérhàus]	몡 창고
□ 957 **hide-and-seek** [háidənsíːk]	몡 숨바꼭질
□ 958 **conflict** [kánflikt]	몡 투쟁, 논쟁, 갈등
□ 959 **buffalo** [bʌ́fəlòu]	몡 (아메리카) 들소
□ 960 **dialect** [dáiəlèkt]	몡 방언, 지방 사투리
□ 961 **conference** [kánfərəns]	몡 회의, 회담

- 962 **thrifty** [θrífti] 형 알뜰한, 검소한
- 963 **nutritious** [njuːtríʃəs] 형 영양분이 풍부한
- 964 **briefcase** [bríːfkèis] 명 서류 가방
- 965 **profit** [práfit] 명 이익, 수익
- 966 **refugee** [rèfjudʒíː] 명 피난민, 난민
- 967 **kidnap** [kídnæp] 동 유괴하다, 납치하다
- 968 **proceed** [prəsíːd] 동 나아가다, 진척되다
- 969 **majority** [mədʒɔ́ːrəti] 명 대부분, 대다수
- 970 **myth** [miθ] 명 신화
- 971 **graveyard** [gréivjàːrd] 명 묘지
- 972 **diagnose** [dáiəgnòus] 동 진단하다
- 973 **poke** [pouk] 동 쿡쿡 찌르다, 쑤시다
- 974 **regulation** [règjuléiʃən] 명 규정, 규제
- 975 **attention** [əténʃən] 명 주의, 배려
- 976 **pass away** 죽다
- 977 **evolution** [èvəlúːʃən] 명 발전, 진화
- 978 **conclude** [kənklúːd] 동 결론을 내리다
- 979 **shortcut** [ʃɔ́ːrtkλt] 명 지름길

- 980 **fortify** [fɔ́ːrtəfài] 동 요새화하다, 강화하다
- 981 **play-off** [pleiɔ̀ːf] 명 결승전
- 982 **vendor** [véndər] 명 노점 상인, 행상인
- 983 **stall** [stɔːl] 명 상품 진열대, 노점
- 984 **temporary** [témpərèri] 형 일시적인
- 985 **vertical** [və́ːrtikl] 형 수직의 명 수직선
- 986 **unemployment** [λnimplɔ́imənt] 명 실업, 실업률
- 987 **commercial** [kəmə́ːrʃəl] 형 상업의, 무역의, 영업용인
- 988 **donation** [dounéiʃən] 명 기부(금)
- 989 **independence** [ìndipéndəns] 명 독립
- 990 **drag** [dræg] 동 끌다
- 991 **alien** [éiliən] 명 이방인, 외국인, 외계인

중간기말대비

- 992 **operate** [ápərèit] 동 움직이다, 작동시키다
- 993 **invention** [invénʃən] 명 발명, 발명품
- 994 **messenger** [mésindʒər] 명 메신저, 심부름꾼
- 995 **generation** [dʒènəréiʃən] 명 세대, 동시대의 사람들
- 996 **sting** [stiŋ] 동 (침으로) 쏘다

□ 997 **personality** [pɛ́:rsənǽləti] 명 성격, 성질, 인격

□ 998 **upcoming** [ʌ́pkʌ̀miŋ] 형 다가오는, 머지않아 일어나는

□ 999 **consist** [kənsíst] 동 구성되다, 이루어져 있다

□ 1000 **excellent** [éksələnt] 형 훌륭한, 뛰어난

□ 1001 **cheetah** [tʃíːtə] 명 치타

□ 1002 **mermaid** [mə́:rmèid] 명 인어

□ 1003 **ankle** [ǽŋkl] 명 발목

□ 1004 **concentrate** [kánsəntrèit] 동 집중시키다, 전념하다

□ 1005 **representative** [rèprizéntətiv] 명 대표자

□ 1006 **commute** [kəmjúːt] 동 통근하다

□ 1007 **gather** [gǽðər] 동 모이다, 집합하다

□ 1008 **reduce** [ridʒúːs] 동 줄이다, 감소시키다

□ 1009 **transfer** [trænsfə́:r] 동 갈아타다

□ 1010 **resistance** [rizístəns] 명 저항, 저항력

□ 1011 **ragged** [rǽgid] 형 너덜너덜한, 누더기의

Chapter 17 일치와 화법

👤 **PSS & PRACTICE**

□ 1012 **composer** [kəmpóuzər] 명 작곡가

□ 1013 **wizard** [wízərd] 명 마법사

□ 1014 **responsibility** [rispànsəbíləti] 명 책임

□ 1015 **smuggler** [smʌ́glər] 명 밀수업자

□ 1016 **port** [pɔːrt] 명 항구

□ 1017 **contain** [kəntéin] 동 포함하다

□ 1018 **fingerprint** [fíŋgərprìnt] 명 지문

□ 1019 **passion** [pǽʃən] 명 열정

□ 1020 **participant** [pɑːrtísipənt] 명 참가자, 관계자

□ 1021 **soft drink** [sɔ́:ft dríŋk] 명 무알콜 음료, 청량음료

□ 1022 **announce** [ənáuns] 동 발표하다, 알리다

□ 1023 **diverse** [daivə́:rs] 형 다양한

□ 1024 **ethnic** [éθnik] 형 민족의, 인종의

□ 1025 **relatively** [rélətivli] 부 비교적

□ 1026 **rank** [ræŋk] 동 등급을 매기다

□ 1027 **bulb** [bʌlb] 명 구근, 전구

□ 1028 **picky** [píki] 형 까다롭게 구는

□ 1029 **pirate** [páirət] 명 해적, 약탈자

□ 1030 **emigrate** [émigrèit] 동 이주하다, 이민가다

Day 31

오늘 외울 단어 33개

☐ 1031 **drill** [dril]	명 송곳, 드릴	
☐ 1032 **defendant** [diféndənt]	명 피고인	

👤 중간기말대비

☐ 1033 **advertiser** [ǽdvərtàizər]	명 광고자
☐ 1034 **sentence** [séntəns]	명 문장, 판결
☐ 1035 **etiquette** [étiket]	명 예의, 에티켓
☐ 1036 **nutrient** [njú:triənt]	명 영양물, 영양제
☐ 1037 **belong to**	～에 속하다
☐ 1038 **wrap** [ræp]	동 포장하다
☐ 1039 **discover** [diskʌ́vər]	동 발견하다, 알다

Chapter 18 특수구문 & 속담

👤 PSS & PRACTICE

☐ 1040 **resign** [rizáin]	동 사임하다, 퇴직하다
☐ 1041 **grocery** [gróusəri]	명 식료품점, 식료품
☐ 1042 **gladiator** [glǽdièitər]	명 검투사
☐ 1043 **hibernate** [háibərnèit]	동 동면하다
☐ 1044 **rod** [rɑd]	명 낚싯대, 막대
☐ 1045 **bait** [beit]	명 미끼, 먹이
☐ 1046 **scramble** [skrǽmbl]	동 휘저어 섞다

☐ 1047 **dough** [dou]	명 빵 반죽
☐ 1048 **hesitate** [hézitèit]	동 망설이다
☐ 1049 **pour** [pɔːr]	동 (비가) 마구 쏟아지다
☐ 1050 **sound** [saund]	형 건전한, 건강한
☐ 1051 **dread** [dred]	동 두려워하다
☐ 1052 **sow** [sou]	동 (씨를) 뿌리다
☐ 1053 **reap** [riːp]	동 거두다, 수확하다
☐ 1054 **stable** [stéibl]	명 마구간
☐ 1055 **hare** [hɛər]	명 토끼

👤 중간기말대비

☐ 1056 **agree with**	～에 동의하다
☐ 1057 **essence** [ésns]	명 본질, 정수
☐ 1058 **convenient** [kənvíːnjənt]	형 편리한, 간편한
☐ 1059 **estimate** [éstəmeit]	동 추정하다, 예상하다
☐ 1060 **concern** [kənsə́ːrn]	명 우려, 관심
☐ 1061 **properly** [prɑ́pərli]	부 제대로, 적절히
☐ 1062 **pitiful** [pítifəl]	형 비참한, 불쌍한
☐ 1063 **pearl** [pəːrl]	명 진주

중학영문법 3800제 3학년

Word Test

Problem Solving Skill

MOTHERTONGUE
마더텅출판사
since 1999.4.1.

날짜:　　　　　학급:　　　　　이름:　　　　　점수　　/34

●영어를 우리말로 쓰세요.

01 | refrigerator

02 | make a reservation

03 | fit

04 | appear

05 | puzzled

06 | suppose

07 | tremble

08 | newborn

09 | patient

10 | smooth

11 | stingy

12 | agent

13 | prevent

14 | brilliant

15 | can afford to

16 | remain

17 | energetic

●우리말을 영어로 쓰세요.

18 | ～대신에

19 | 울타리, 담

20 | 넓적다리

21 | 생물학

22 | 창백한

23 | 유죄의, 양심의 가책을 느끼는

24 | 시사 풍자 만화

25 | 환경

26 | 절대적으로

27 | 우두머리, 장, 교장

28 | 청중, 관객

29 | 도망가다

30 | 언어

31 | 이해심 있는, 이해

32 | 비극적인

33 | 공연

34 | 교향곡

날짜:　　　　학급:　　　　이름:　　　　점수　　 / 35

●영어를 우리말로 쓰세요.

01 | stream

02 | costume

03 | recover

04 | encourage

05 | stain

06 | conversation

07 | complete

08 | suitcase

09 | instructor

10 | supply

11 | concentrate

12 | disease

13 | flight attendant

14 | participate

15 | human being

16 | strength

17 | project

●우리말을 영어로 쓰세요.

18 | 벌주다

19 | 디스켓, 플로피 디스크

20 | 허드렛일

21 | 온도

22 | 존재, 생활

23 | 스노보드를 타다, 스노보드

24 | 훈련, 현장 교육

25 | 디자이너, 설계자

26 | 자백하다, 고백하다

27 | 조각상

28 | 부상

29 | 유령이 나오는

30 | 선출하다

31 | 희생자

32 | 간청하다, 호소하다

33 | 기적

34 | 징후, 증상

35 | 식기세척기

날짜:　　　　　학급:　　　　　이름:　　　　　점수　　/34

●영어를 우리말로 쓰세요.

01 | survey

02 | find out

03 | maintain

04 | arrange

05 | improve

06 | accomplish

07 | conduct

08 | be in trouble

09 | allow

10 | breathe

11 | alarming

12 | correctly

13 | clap

14 | affect

15 | get out of

16 | provide ~ with …

17 | destroy

●우리말을 영어로 쓰세요.

18 | ～의 탓으로 하다, 언급하다

19 | 벨기에 (나라 이름)

20 | 제스처, 몸짓

21 | 움켜쥐다, 잡아채다

22 | 화산

23 | 머리를 숙이다, 절하다

24 | 분류하다

25 | 담그다, 흠뻑 적시다

26 | 선언하다, 공표하다

27 | 복제하다

28 | 겨누다, 목표로 삼다

29 | 뿌리다

30 | 범하다, 위탁하다

31 | 긁다

32 | 임명하다

33 | 거지, 걸인

34 | 용암

날짜:　　　　　학급:　　　　　이름:　　　　　점수　　/36

●영어를 우리말로 쓰세요.

01 | cherish

02 | attract

03 | inherit

04 | crawl

05 | rip

06 | display

07 | attempt

08 | gasp

09 | regard

10 | perch

11 | connect

12 | disturb

13 | demand

14 | enroll

15 | snap

16 | permit

17 | establish

18 | dispatch

●우리말을 영어로 쓰세요.

19 | 물들이다, 염색하다

20 | 할당하다, 배정하다

21 | 발행하다, 출판하다

22 | 휘젓다, 뒤섞다

23 | 정복하다

24 | ~에 달하다[이르다], 양

25 | 가볍게 두드리다

26 | 초점을 맞추다, 초점

27 | 재통합하다

28 | 불평하다

29 | 윙윙거리다

30 | 환불하다

31 | 패배시키다, 패배

32 | 코를 훌쩍이다

33 | 받아들이다

34 | 도전하다, 도전

35 | 콧노래를 부르다, 흥얼거리다

36 | 곱슬곱슬하게 하다, (머리의) 컬

날짜:　　　　학급:　　　　이름:　　　　점수　　/ 36

●영어를 우리말로 쓰세요.

01	shrink	10	fulfill
02	furnish	11	pronounce
03	approve	12	deal
04	arise	13	creep
05	burst	14	scrape
06	reward	15	convert
07	overcome	16	weave
08	swing	17	leap
09	intend	18	wound

●우리말을 영어로 쓰세요.

19	갈다	28	폭발하다, 파열하다
20	끄덕이다	29	다시 채우다, 보충하다
21	무릎을 꿇다	30	(사람에게) ～을 가능하게 하다
22	접촉시키다, 접촉, 교제	31	닦다, 광을 내다
23	용서하다	32	살아남다
24	난처하게 하다	33	쓸다, 털다
25	반대하다, 물체, 대상	34	돈을 걸다, 내기를 하다
26	꿰매다	35	후회하다
27	얼다, 얼어붙다	36	펴다, 뻗다

Word Test 176-208   Day 06

날짜: 학급: 이름: 점수   /33

●영어를 우리말로 쓰세요.

01	forbid	09	admire
02	suddenly	10	chef
03	show up	11	rotten
04	consider	12	issue
05	take care of	13	warm-hearted
06	lately	14	cigarette
07	emigrate	15	compose
08	automobile	16	manufacture

●우리말을 영어로 쓰세요.

17	동결된, 냉담한	26	당국, 권한, 권위
18	동화	27	심리학
19	외교관	28	고아원
20	경기장	29	당뇨병
21	은퇴	30	짜다, 뜨다
22	파다, 파내다	31	오해하다
23	사원	32	요양원
24	쌓다, 축적하다	33	도박, 노름
25	전공하다, 전공		

날짜:　　　　　학급:　　　　　이름:　　　　　점수　　/ 35

●영어를 우리말로 쓰세요.

01	appointment	10	separately
02	cut down on	11	overeat
03	innocent	12	defend
04	fluently	13	musical instrument
05	cancel	14	appreciate
06	uncertain	15	handkerchief
07	hide-and-seek	16	exhausted
08	silly	17	stay up
09	cautious	18	especially

●우리말을 영어로 쓰세요.

19	실험하다, 실험	28	목적지
20	농작물	29	질, 품질
21	(빵 등을) 굽다	30	결정
22	대사관(저)	31	흐르다
23	불법의	32	보호, 대피소
24	꾸짖다	33	발표
25	유전의	34	사라지다
26	실험실	35	교환하다
27	살아남다		

Word Test 244 - 277

Day 08

날짜:　　　　학급:　　　　이름:　　　　점수　　 / 34

●영어를 우리말로 쓰세요.

01 | preserve

02 | be in good shape

03 | concept

04 | announcement

05 | incident

06 | delay

07 | concentration

08 | spring

09 | fraud

10 | endanger

11 | cruelly

12 | rude

13 | rescue

14 | perform

15 | in advance

16 | life vest

17 | kindergarten

●우리말을 영어로 쓰세요.

18 | 초상화

19 | 용의자

20 | 영양물, 영양

21 | 제안

22 | 호의

23 | 하인

24 | 인턴쉽

25 | 오두막집

26 | 최종 기한, 마감 시간

27 | 자원 봉사자, 자진해서 하다

28 | 일생, 생애

29 | 정치인

30 | (법조계) 검사

31 | 졸업

32 | 성취, 업적

33 | 속이다

34 | 늘리다

Word Test 278-312   **Day 09**

날짜: 학급: 이름: 점수   /35

●영어를 우리말로 쓰세요.

01	region		10	offer
02	awesome		11	indeed
03	behavior		12	routine
04	throughout		13	prepare
05	make use of		14	catch up with
06	post		15	lengthy
07	coach		16	scholarship
08	hand in		17	salesman
09	record		18	slightly

●우리말을 영어로 쓰세요.

19	비용		28	관광, 관광 여행
20	종교		29	수여하다
21	비율		30	신혼 여행
22	～을 깔보다, 경멸하다		31	담배를 피우다
23	녹이다, 녹다		32	극지방의
24	소프트웨어, 프로그램		33	민속 무용
25	폭력		34	시험, 검사
26	한숨, 한숨 쉬다		35	의식, 예식
27	편집자			

날짜:　　　　학급:　　　　이름:　　　　점수　　　/ 34

●영어를 우리말로 쓰세요.

01 | therapy

02 | demonstrator

03 | direction

04 | wage

05 | principle

06 | janitor

07 | interrupt

08 | essential

09 | tomb

10 | enormous

11 | factor

12 | bunch

13 | client

14 | present

15 | sightseeing

16 | employee

17 | peak

●우리말을 영어로 쓰세요.

18 | 위원회

19 | 게

20 | 달력

21 | 무리, 떼

22 | 밀가루

23 | 목격자

24 | 인권

25 | 가지, 지점, 지사

26 | 학기

27 | 우주비행사

28 | 기념품

29 | 관목, 덤불

30 | 왕조

31 | 공룡

32 | 무

33 | 짚, 밀짚, 빨대

34 | 미궁, 미로

● 영어를 우리말로 쓰세요.

01	passer-by	10	bystander
02	assistant	11	arrest
03	instrument	12	basis
04	forget-me-not	13	mother-to-be
05	square	14	column
06	character	15	trick
07	calf	16	weed
08	application form	17	belief
09	method	18	fountain pen

● 우리말을 영어로 쓰세요.

19	시장(市長)	28	영수증
20	적	29	마녀
21	위성	30	최고 사령관
22	앞치마	31	항구, 항만
23	(조류) 카나리아	32	모기
24	암초	33	철도
25	굴뚝	34	메아리
26	재봉사, 재단사	35	회전 목마
27	벼랑, 절벽	36	건축가

날짜: 학급: 이름: 점수   / 33

●영어를 우리말로 쓰세요.

01 | seaport

02 | certain

03 | intercultural

04 | gorgeous

05 | purposely

06 | assignment

07 | gradually

08 | application

09 | magician

10 | register

11 | deserve

12 | hastily

13 | community center

14 | punctually

15 | diligent

16 | aggressive

●우리말을 영어로 쓰세요.

17 | 지식

18 | 정치, 정치학

19 | 가볍게 두드리다

20 | 충실한, 독실한

21 | 승진시키다, 촉진하다

22 | 가구, 비품

23 | 쫓다, 추격하다

24 | 역사적인, 역사의

25 | 산업

26 | (물에) 뜨다, 떠오르다

27 | 용기

28 | 조각, 작품, 소곡

29 | 친척, 일가

30 | 유산

31 | 떼를 짓다, 떼, 무리

32 | 임신한

33 | 배경의, 배경이 되는, 배경

Word Test 416-450   Day 13

날짜: 학급: 이름: 점수   / 35

●영어를 우리말로 쓰세요.

01	clear	10	interesting
02	earn	11	achieve
03	suppose	12	overseas
04	impress	13	harmful
05	recommend	14	permission
06	mop	15	request
07	misbehavior	16	express
08	alive	17	claim
09	reputation	18	exhibition

●우리말을 영어로 쓰세요.

19	~뿐만 아니라	28	아마, 어쩌면
20	수박	29	~인 것 같다, ~인 것처럼 보이다
21	다양성, 변화	30	습기 찬, 눅눅한
22	겨누다, 목표로 하다	31	길들이다
23	고대의	32	등뼈, 척추
24	뻐꾸기	33	현대의
25	보안, 안전	34	담요, 모포
26	사막	35	바싹 마르다, 말리다
27	원주민의, 모국의		

날짜:　　　　학급:　　　　이름:　　　　점수　　 / 34

● 영어를 우리말로 쓰세요.

01 | autograph
02 | come up with
03 | fancy
04 | struggle
05 | quarrel
06 | mortal
07 | pretend
08 | impossible
09 | correctly
10 | defeat
11 | scale
12 | manage
13 | plastic surgery
14 | cooperate
15 | quit
16 | destined
17 | eager

● 우리말을 영어로 쓰세요.

18 | 책임감 있게
19 | 안개가 낀
20 | 생태계
21 | 손해[상해]를 입히다
22 | 외모, 출연
23 | 공식의, 공공의
24 | 속이다, 바람 피우다
25 | 백신
26 | 나누다, 공유하다, 몫, 할당량
27 | 도움이 되는
28 | 독특한, 유일한
29 | 손톱
30 | 난폭한, 사나운
31 | 실망시키다, 낙담시키다
32 | 영향을 주다, (병에) 걸리다
33 | 레모네이드
34 | 빛나는, 훌륭한

날짜: 학급: 이름: 점수   / 35

●영어를 우리말로 쓰세요.

01 | to be honest

02 | track

03 | mention

04 | sneak

05 | completely

06 | careless

07 | miniature

08 | anywhere

09 | figure out

10 | suggestion

11 | article

12 | thoughtful

13 | enable

14 | pollute

15 | embarrassed

16 | notice

17 | automation

18 | skillful

●우리말을 영어로 쓰세요.

19 | 상상하다, 생각하다

20 | 계곡, 골짜기

21 | 거리

22 | 미리, 사전에

23 | 신경 과민인, 긴장한

24 | 생산력, 생산성

25 | 자라다

26 | 건너뛰다, 빼먹다, 결석하다

27 | 탐험하다

28 | 운송, 수송

29 | 기술자, 기사

30 | 문자 그대로인, 문자의

31 | 부분적으로, 어느 정도

32 | 면허증, 허가증

33 | 문학

34 | 상담 교사, 고문

35 | 급속히, 빠르게

날짜:　　　　학급:　　　　이름:　　　　점수　　/33

●영어를 우리말로 쓰세요.

01 | asset

02 | put off

03 | beforehand

04 | volunteer

05 | capable

06 | congress

07 | measure

08 | persuade

09 | bother

10 | reduce

11 | cause

12 | opportunity

13 | interrupt

14 | worthwhile

15 | avoid

16 | competition

17 | countryside

●우리말을 영어로 쓰세요.

18 | 대중교통

19 | 연기하다, 미루다

20 | 현기증이 나는

21 | 사과하다

22 | 양배추

23 | 저자

24 | 길이

25 | 탐정, 형사

26 | 소문

27 | 형태, 포맷, 서식을 만들다

28 | 목적

29 | 재판하다, 판단하다

30 | 귀중한

31 | 칭찬하다, 칭찬

32 | 힘이 넘치는, 활기찬

33 | 우주선

날짜: 학급: 이름: 점수   / 34

● 영어를 우리말로 쓰세요.

01	due to	10	surround
02	attempt	11	cooperation
03	terrify	12	mutual
04	scream	13	aside
05	kidnapper	14	walking stick
06	sudden	15	treaty
07	regard	16	escape
08	toward	17	conference
09	worth		

● 우리말을 영어로 쓰세요.

18	기구, 장치	27	참가하다
19	지원하다, 신청하다	28	~을 통과하여, 지나서
20	저널리스트, 언론인	29	수술, 외과
21	뇌우	30	완전히, 철저하게
22	위치시키다, 위치를 알아내다	31	인질, 볼모
23	세부, 상세	32	~에 익숙하다
24	접근하다, 접근	33	폐
25	초상화	34	장례식
26	어조, 음색		

날짜:　　　　　학급:　　　　　이름:　　　　　점수　　/ 34

●영어를 우리말로 쓰세요.

01 | seldom

02 | fascinate

03 | annoy

04 | entertain

05 | get rid of

06 | brand-new

07 | remain

08 | unsure

09 | amaze

10 | forefather

11 | relax

12 | talented

13 | frighten

14 | satisfying

15 | move

16 | proverb

17 | confusing

●우리말을 영어로 쓰세요.

18 | 왼손잡이의

19 | 만족시키다

20 | 광부

21 | 없음, 결석

22 | 괴물

23 | 트레일러

24 | 출판하다, 발표하다

25 | 통제하다, 관리하다

26 | 모험, 도전

27 | 접다

28 | 제비, 삼키다

29 | 무대 공포증

30 | 발표, 설명

31 | 자신감, 신뢰

32 | 공격하다

33 | 감독하다, 연출하다

34 | 전달하다, 배달하다

●영어를 우리말로 쓰세요.

01 | alike

02 | receive

03 | ashamed

04 | gallery

05 | cheerful

06 | donate

07 | take a risk

08 | disabled

09 | evidence

10 | construction

11 | sole

12 | position

13 | upper

14 | salary

15 | attractive

16 | orphanage

17 | mere

●우리말을 영어로 쓰세요.

18 | 청각 장애가 있는

19 | 고아

20 | 통상의, 규칙적인

21 | 편리한

22 | 법률 회사

23 | 성격, 인품

24 | 폭풍우, 호우

25 | 신청자, 지원자

26 | 앞의, 전자의

27 | 외부의, 외면의

28 | 모으다, 수집하다

29 | 구경꾼, 관람객

30 | 해결, 해답

31 | 의미심장한, 의미 있는

32 | 기숙사

33 | 내부의, 안쪽의

34 | 교육

Word Test 655 - 688

Day 20

날짜: 학급: 이름: 점수   / 34

● 영어를 우리말로 쓰세요.

01 | genuine

02 | operation

03 | actual

04 | imaginable

05 | original

06 | greedy

07 | immediate

08 | precious

09 | attentive

10 | constant

11 | handicapped

12 | firm

13 | fortunate

14 | mushroom

15 | jobless

16 | probable

17 | innocent

● 우리말을 영어로 쓰세요.

18 | 군사의, 군대의

19 | 비교할 수 있는

20 | 반대의, 상반되는

21 | 포효, 으르렁거리는 소리

22 | 국제적인

23 | 무지, 무식

24 | 전문의, 직업의

25 | 도덕적인

26 | 효과적인

27 | 기꺼이 ~하는, 자발적인

28 | 이상주의적인

29 | 합리적인

30 | 현재의, 지금의, 통용되는

31 | 공정한, 공평한

32 | 명확한, 한정된

33 | 향수

34 | 무능하게 하다, 쓸모없게 하다

●영어를 우리말로 쓰세요.

01	anxious	10	impress
02	break up	11	communicate
03	mental	12	sensible
04	be fed up with	13	unpredictable
05	incredible	14	proper
06	impulsive	15	realistic
07	severe	16	whole
08	district	17	recognize
09	directly	18	general

●우리말을 영어로 쓰세요.

19	닮다	28	독감
20	표준적인, 정상적인	29	민감한, 예민한
21	투표, 득표, 투표하다	30	포유동물
22	실제적인, 실용적인	31	단지, 복합 빌딩
23	1년의, 해마다의	32	뇌졸중
24	정확한	33	드문, 진기한
25	예방접종	34	고통을 받다, 괴로워하다
26	우연한, 격식 없는, 평상의	35	감정적인
27	논리적인	36	비평하다, 비판하다

Word Test 725 - 757　　Day 22

날짜:　　　학급:　　　이름:　　　점수　　/33

●영어를 우리말로 쓰세요.

01 | predict

02 | fortune

03 | tasty

04 | sue

05 | rarely

06 | idiot

07 | material

08 | variable

09 | downtown

10 | make a living

11 | unfortunately

12 | reputation

13 | effectively

14 | break out

15 | even

16 | freezing

17 | spread

●우리말을 영어로 쓰세요.

18 | 실험, 시험, 실험하다

19 | 유사한, 비슷한, 닮은

20 | 천재

21 | 다림질하다, 철, 다리미

22 | 상상력, 상상

23 | 고속도로

24 | ~할 여유가 있다

25 | 패키지, 소포

26 | 미끄러운, 미끌거리는

27 | 관계, 친척 관계

28 | 정부

29 | 심장마비

30 | 주름

31 | 유명 인사

32 | 의미

33 | 사치스러운, 호화로운

●영어를 우리말로 쓰세요.

01 | scary

02 | desert

03 | require

04 | keep one's word

05 | ape

06 | accept

07 | clothes line

08 | take part in

09 | hang

10 | qualify

11 | eyesight

12 | attention

13 | recruit

14 | in spite of

15 | grave

16 | occur

17 | squid

18 | committee

●우리말을 영어로 쓰세요.

19 | 전기

20 | 진화하다, 발달하다

21 | 요구하다

22 | 지원자, 후보자

23 | 약혼자

24 | 여신

25 | 지역의, 지방의

26 | 예상, 예보

27 | 건설하다

28 | 신비로운, 불가사의한

29 | 지구 온난화

30 | 제안하다

31 | 무도, 무술

32 | 충돌하다, 추락하다

33 | 지지하다, 부양하다

34 | 결정, 판결

35 | 진심에서 우러난, 진실의

날짜:　　　학급:　　　이름:　　　점수　　/ 33

●영어를 우리말로 쓰세요.

01 | desire

02 | expose

03 | enjoyable

04 | newcomer

05 | insistent

06 | condition

07 | challenging

08 | specifically

09 | theory

10 | previous

11 | awkward

12 | distinguish

13 | impressive

14 | efficiently

15 | complicated

16 | vow

●우리말을 영어로 쓰세요.

17 | 비상사태, 응급 상황

18 | 굶주리다, 몹시 배고프다

19 | 긴박한, 긴급한

20 | 유연한, 탄력적인

21 | 야심적인, 열망하는

22 | 목적지, 도착지

23 | 기술

24 | 인물, 숫자

25 | 관측소, 전망대

26 | 천문학의, 천문학적인

27 | 화석

28 | 황제

29 | 감독

30 | 최근의

31 | 보석류

32 | 추상적인

33 | 햇볕에 탐

날짜:　　　　　학급:　　　　　이름:　　　　　점수　　　/ 33

●영어를 우리말로 쓰세요.

01 | technician

02 | immigrant

03 | complicate

04 | force

05 | with effort

06 | laughter

07 | burglar

08 | break down

09 | virtual reality

10 | expectation

11 | vacant

12 | prefer

13 | remodel

14 | obey

15 | influence

16 | contrary

17 | indicate

●우리말을 영어로 쓰세요.

18 | 칼로리, 열량

19 | 직사각형의

20 | 세계적인, 전체적인

21 | 설비, 시설

22 | 페달, 발판

23 | 통신, 소통

24 | 헌법, 구조, 관행

25 | 사이버 공간, 가상 현실

26 | 화학

27 | 다큐멘터리, 기록물

28 | ~을 거쳐, 경유해서

29 | 설립하다

30 | 자신감

31 | 나무 꼭대기

32 | 정책, 제도, 방침

33 | 강가, 강가의

날짜:　　　　　　학급:　　　　　　이름:　　　　　　점수　　　/ 34

●영어를 우리말로 쓰세요.

01 | out-of-date

02 | expression

03 | glitter

04 | wag

05 | opinion

06 | battlefield

07 | competent

08 | practitioner

09 | regret

10 | mend

11 | for free

12 | well-mannered

13 | detail

14 | extend

15 | serve

16 | impression

17 | purchase

●우리말을 영어로 쓰세요.

18 | 파업 중인

19 | 경제

20 | 유전자

21 | 고고학자

22 | 천문학

23 | 분리하다

24 | 세계화, 국제화

25 | 가장자리, 모서리

26 | 현미경

27 | 습기, 수분

28 | 흙, 점토

29 | 졸업하다

30 | 수족관

31 | 원시의, 태고의

32 | 번역가

33 | 발자국

34 | 확신하는, 자신이 있는

날짜:　　　학급:　　　이름:　　　점수　　/ 33

●영어를 우리말로 쓰세요.

01	outgoing	10	survivor
02	forbid	11	depend
03	besides	12	movement
04	organize	13	rapidly
05	harmful	14	posture
06	expand	15	exist
07	clap	16	disadvantaged
08	host	17	mess
09	expedition		

●우리말을 영어로 쓰세요.

18	순록	26	불꽃놀이
19	장식하다, 꾸미다	27	헬스 클럽
20	구두의, 언어의	28	나타나다, 발생하다
21	식민지의	29	사진술, 사진촬영
22	부정적인, 부정의	30	검, 칼, 무력
23	지속되다, 계속되다	31	태도, 자세
24	진공청소기로 청소하다	32	바퀴벌레
25	비축하다, 저장하다	33	태풍

날짜: 학급: 이름: 점수   / 36

●영어를 우리말로 쓰세요.

01	general		10	protest
02	conflict		11	peel
03	extinction		12	pin
04	trail		13	bomb
05	in print		14	surface
06	bulletin board		15	charity
07	charm		16	warehouse
08	sculpture		17	uprising
09	conference		18	approach

●우리말을 영어로 쓰세요.

19	지평선, 수평선		28	방언, 지방 사투리
20	인종의		29	카누, 통나무 배
21	(화물용) 컨테이너, 용기, 그릇		30	차별 대우, 구별
22	바다표범, 물개		31	빙산
23	조각가		32	토너먼트, 승자 진출전
24	편의점		33	훌라후프, 굴렁쇠
25	잠수함		34	분수대
26	숨바꼭질		35	다람쥐
27	(아메리카) 들소		36	처방전, 규정, 지시

●영어를 우리말로 쓰세요.

01	evolution	10	conclude
02	donation	11	pass away
03	proceed	12	play-off
04	temporary	13	regulation
05	poke	14	stall
06	vendor	15	graveyard
07	attention	16	unemployment
08	fortify	17	kidnap
09	profit	18	operate

●우리말을 영어로 쓰세요.

19	독립	28	대부분, 대다수
20	신화	29	끌다
21	이방인, 외국인, 외계인	30	상업의, 무역의, 영업용인
22	진단하다	31	지름길
23	수직의, 수직선	32	(침으로) 쏘다
24	서류 가방	33	세대, 동시대의 사람들
25	메신저, 심부름꾼	34	영양분이 풍부한
26	알뜰한, 검소한	35	피난민, 난민
27	발명, 발명품		

날짜: 학급: 이름: 점수   /34

●영어를 우리말로 쓰세요.

01 | transfer

02 | picky

03 | concentrate

04 | ethnic

05 | gather

06 | contain

07 | consist

08 | resistance

09 | wizard

10 | responsibility

11 | port

12 | reduce

13 | diverse

14 | representative

15 | rank

16 | excellent

17 | emigrate

●우리말을 영어로 쓰세요.

18 | 무알콜 음료, 청량음료

19 | 너덜너덜한, 누더기의

20 | 비교적

21 | 발목

22 | 열정

23 | 작곡가

24 | 발표하다, 알리다

25 | 밀수업자

26 | 성격, 성질, 인격

27 | 인어

28 | 참가자, 관계자

29 | 치타

30 | 구근, 전구

31 | 해적, 약탈자

32 | 통근하다

33 | 지문

34 | 다가오는, 머지않아 일어나는

●영어를 우리말로 쓰세요.

01 | sound

02 | properly

03 | wrap

04 | estimate

05 | resign

06 | grocery

07 | hare

08 | hesitate

09 | defendant

10 | dread

11 | reap

12 | scramble

13 | agree with

14 | discover

15 | concern

16 | nutrient

17 | pitiful

●우리말을 영어로 쓰세요.

18 | 검투사

19 | 마구간

20 | 예의, 에티켓

21 | 편리한, 간편한

22 | ~에 속하다

23 | 빵 반죽

24 | (비가) 마구 쏟아지다

25 | (씨를) 뿌리다

26 | 광고자

27 | 본질, 정수

28 | 문장, 판결

29 | 진주

30 | 미끼, 먹이

31 | 낚싯대, 막대

32 | 동면하다

33 | 송곳, 드릴

16차 개정판 **중학영문법 3800제** 3학년 **학습계획표**

DAY	Ch	학습내용	학습날짜		DAY	Ch	학습내용	학습날짜
DAY 1		PSS 1-1 ~ 1-4	월 일		DAY 31		PSS 1-1 ~ 1-4	월 일
DAY 2	1	PSS 2-1 ~ 2-7	월 일		DAY 32	11	PSS 2-1 ~ 2-7	월 일
DAY 3		중간·기말고사 대비문제	월 일		DAY 33		중간·기말고사 대비문제	월 일
DAY 4		PSS 1-1 ~ 2-2	월 일		DAY 34		PSS 1 ~ 2-4	월 일
DAY 5	2	PSS 2-3 ~ 3	월 일		DAY 35	12	PSS 3-1 ~ 3-4	월 일
DAY 6		중간·기말고사 대비문제	월 일		DAY 36		PSS 4 ~ 6	월 일
DAY 7		PSS 1 ~ 5	월 일		DAY 37		중간·기말고사 대비문제	월 일
DAY 8	3	PSS 6 ~ 10	월 일		DAY 38		PSS 1-1 ~ 2-2	월 일
DAY 9		중간·기말고사 대비문제	월 일		DAY 39	13	PSS 3-1 ~ 3-6	월 일
DAY 10		PSS 1 ~ 5	월 일		DAY 40		PSS 4-1 ~ 4-4	월 일
DAY 11	4	PSS 6 ~ 9	월 일		DAY 41		중간·기말고사 대비문제	월 일
DAY 12		중간·기말고사 대비문제	월 일		DAY 42		PSS 1-1 ~ 1-4	월 일
DAY 13		PSS 1-1 ~ 2-4	월 일		DAY 43	14	PSS 1-5 ~ 1-8	월 일
DAY 14	5	PSS 3-1 ~ 6	월 일		DAY 44		PSS 2-1 ~ 2-3	월 일
DAY 15		중간·기말고사 대비문제	월 일		DAY 45		중간·기말고사 대비문제	월 일
DAY 16		PSS 1 ~ 3-3	월 일		DAY 46		PSS 1 ~ 4	월 일
DAY 17	6	PSS 3-4 ~ 3-8	월 일		DAY 47	15	PSS 5 ~ 9-2	월 일
DAY 18		중간·기말고사 대비문제	월 일		DAY 48		PSS 10 ~ 14	월 일
DAY 19		PSS 1-1 ~ 2-2	월 일		DAY 49		중간·기말고사 대비문제	월 일
DAY 20	7	PSS 3-1 ~ 7	월 일		DAY 50		PSS 1-1 ~ 1-6	월 일
DAY 21		중간·기말고사 대비문제	월 일		DAY 51	16	PSS 2-1 ~ 2-8	월 일
DAY 22		PSS 1 ~ 2-3	월 일		DAY 52		PSS 3-1 ~ 3-7	월 일
DAY 23	8	PSS 3 ~ 6	월 일		DAY 53		중간·기말고사 대비문제	월 일
DAY 24		중간·기말고사 대비문제	월 일		DAY 54		PSS 1-1 ~ 1-5	월 일
DAY 25		PSS 1-1 ~ 3	월 일		DAY 55	17	PSS 2-1 ~2-2	월 일
DAY 26	9	PSS 4-1 ~ 4-4	월 일		DAY 56		PSS 3-1 ~3-3	월 일
DAY 27		중간·기말고사 대비문제	월 일		DAY 57		중간·기말고사 대비문제	월 일
DAY 28		PSS 1 ~ 5-3	월 일		DAY 58		PSS 1 ~ 2-2	월 일
DAY 29	10	PSS 6-1 ~ 6-6	월 일		DAY 59	18	PSS 3-1 ~ 4	월 일
DAY 30		중간·기말고사 대비문제	월 일		DAY 60		중간·기말고사 대비문제	월 일

2026 제6기 마더텅 중학교 학습수기 공모전 안내

대상 100 만 원

금상 20 만 원

은상 10 만 원

 지원 자격 및 장학금

중1·중2·중3

지원 과목 국어 / 영어 중 1과목 이상 지원 가능

※여러 과목 지원 시 가산점이 부여됩니다.

성적 기준 아래 2가지 항목 중 1개 이상의 조건에 해당하면 지원 가능

① 2025년 2학기 중간·기말고사 또는 2026년 1학기 중간·기말고사 성적표

② 2025년 7월~ 2026년 6월 시행 중학생 대상 국어/영어 해당 인증시험 성적표

　책과함께 KBS한국어능력시험, J-ToKL, 전국 영어 학력경시대회, TOEIC, TOEFL, G-TELP, TOSEL

위 조건에 해당한다면

마더텅 중학 교재로 공부하면서 **느낀 점**과 **공부 방법**, **학업 성취**, **성적 변화** 등에 관한 자신만의 수기를 작성해서 마더텅으로 보내 주세요. 우수한 글을 보내 주신 분들께 **학습수기 공모 장학금**을 드립니다!

응모 대상 마더텅 중학 교재로 공부한 중1·중2·중3

뿌리깊은 중학국어 독해력, 중학영문법 3800제, 중학영문법 3800제 스타터, 중학영문법 3800제 중간·기말고사 대비편, 중학영문법 3800제 워크북, 중학영문법 3800제 쓰기 WRITING, 마더텅 100% 실전대비 MP3 중학영어듣기 24회 모의고사, 중학영단어 9000, 문법별/주제별로 정리한 중학 영어 독해 101 및 기타 교재 중 1권 이상 신청 가능

응모 방법

① 마더텅 홈페이지 커뮤니티 - 이벤트 게시판에 접속

② [2026 마더텅 중학교 학습수기 공모전 게시글] 클릭 후 [2026 마더텅 중학교 학습수기 공모전 첨부 파일]을 다운

③ [2026 마더텅 중학교 학습수기 공모전 지원서] 작성 후 메일(mothert.marketing@gmail.com)로 발송

접수 기한 2026년 7월 31일　**수상자 발표일** 2026년 8월 17일　**장학금 수여일** 2026년 9월 17일

※세부 일정은 당사 사정에 따라 변경될 수 있습니다.

영어의 8품사

		예문
명사	**사람, 사물, 동물의 이름**을 나타내는 말 → 주어, 목적어, 보어 예 Jane, Mr. Brown, desk, chair, computer, bag, dog, bird	This computer looks new. 이 컴퓨터는 새것처럼 보인다. I have a dog. 나는 개가 한 마리 있다.
대명사	명사를 **대신**하는 말 → 주어, 목적어, 보어 예 I, my, you, he, she, it, them, we, myself, yourself, ourselves	Look at the dog! It is cute. 개 좀 봐! 그것은 귀여워. I'm proud of myself. 나는 내 자신이 자랑스럽다.
동사	**행위, 동작, 상태를 묘사**하며 '~다'로 해석되는 말 → 서술어 - 일반동사: 주로 움직임을 나타내며 '~하다'라고 해석 예 walk, run, eat, study, play, make, buy, love, like - be동사: 상태나 위치를 주로 묘사하며 '~이다'라고 해석 예 am, are, is, was, were	We eat dinner at 7. 우리는 7시에 저녁을 먹는다. She loves her daughter. 그녀는 그녀의 딸을 사랑한다. I am an artist. 나는 예술가이다.
형용사	**명사**를 꾸미거나 보충 설명하는 말 → 수식어, 보어 **생김새, 색깔, 크기, 성격, 특징**을 묘사하는 말 예 pretty, beautiful, red, tall, big, small, nice, kind, easy, difficult	She has big eyes. 그녀는 큰 눈을 가지고 있다. He is a kind boy. 그는 친절한 소년이다. The book is easy. 그 책은 쉽다.
부사	**형용사, 동사, 다른 부사, 문장 전체**를 자세히 설명하여 문장의 의미를 더욱 풍부하게 하는 말 → 수식어 **시간, 장소, 정도, 빈도**를 묘사하는 말 예 now, here, very, well, always, early, really, happily, sadly	What are you doing now? 지금 뭐 하고 있어? Your sister is very pretty. 네 언니는 무척 예쁘다. We really enjoyed the party. 우리는 정말 그 파티를 즐겼다.
접속사	**단어와 단어, 구와 구, 절과 절**을 이어주는 말 - 등위접속사: **같은 종류**의 말을 연결 예 and, but, or, so - 종속접속사: **명사절, 부사절, 형용사절**을 **주절**에 연결 예 because, when, as, if	She is old and wise. 그녀는 나이가 있고 지혜롭다. I slept early, because I was tired. 나는 피곤했기 때문에 일찍 잤다.
전치사	명사 앞에서 **시간, 장소, 방향, 위치**를 나타내는 말 예 at, on, in, before, after, under, from, to, for, with, between, in front of	I sleep at 11 p.m. 나는 밤 11시에 잔다. Your pen is under the chair. 네 펜은 의자 밑에 있다. Let's meet in front of the building. 건물 앞에서 만나자.
감탄사	**감정**을 표현하는 말 예 Oh, Wow, Well	Wow, you got a new phone! 와, 너 새로운 전화기를 샀구나!

<table>
<tr><td colspan="2"></td><td>예문</td></tr>
<tr>
<td>단어</td>
<td>의미를 지니는 **말의 최소 단위**
명사, 대명사, 동사, 형용사, 부사, 전치사, 접속사, 감탄사로 나눌 수 있음</td>
<td>He lied to all of us.
그는 우리 모두에게 거짓말을 했다.</td>
</tr>
<tr>
<td>구</td>
<td>완결된 의미를 가지고 있는 두 단어 이상의 모음으로 **주어와 동사를 포함하지 않음**
- 명사구 → 주어, 목적어, 보어
- 형용사구 → 명사 수식
- 부사구 → 동사, 형용사, 다른 부사, 문장 전체 수식</td>
<td>There is a pencil on the desk.
책상 위에 연필이 있다.
Thank you for helping me.
나를 도와주어서 고마워.</td>
</tr>
<tr>
<td>절</td>
<td>완결된 의미를 가지고 있는 두 단어 이상의 모음으로 **주어와 동사를 반드시 포함**
- 대등절: 등위접속사로 연결된 대등한 절
- 종속절: 주절에 종속접속사로 연결되어 명사, 형용사, 부사의 역할을 함</td>
<td>She got very angry, but she tried not to show it.
그녀는 매우 화가 났지만, 그것을 보이려고 하지 않았다.
Please let me know if he is kind.
그가 친절한지 아닌지 내게 알려 줘.</td>
</tr>
<tr>
<td>주어</td>
<td>동작이나 상태의 **주체**를 가리키는 말</td>
<td>She arrived at her office.
그녀는 그녀의 사무실에 도착했다.</td>
</tr>
<tr>
<td>동사</td>
<td>주어의 **동작이나 상태**를 나타내는 말</td>
<td>He is a nurse.
그는 간호사이다.
They call her an angel.
그들은 그녀를 천사라 부른다.</td>
</tr>
<tr>
<td>목적어</td>
<td>동작이나 상태의 **대상**을 가리키는 말</td>
<td>I put this rabbit in the hat.
나는 모자에 이 토끼를 넣는다.</td>
</tr>
<tr>
<td>보어</td>
<td>주어나 목적어를 **보충 설명**해 주는 말</td>
<td>I want to become a teacher.
나는 선생님이 되고 싶다.
He forced me to hurry.
그는 내가 서두르도록 강요했다.</td>
</tr>
<tr>
<td>수식어</td>
<td>문장의 주요 성분을 **부연 설명**하는 역할
생략해도 문법적인 오류를 일으키지 않음</td>
<td>You look pretty tired.
너 꽤 피곤해 보여.</td>
</tr>
</table>

필수문법용어 : 문장의 구성 단위와 성분